F. C. Gray

Drawn and engraved by [illegible], after a photograph.

CATALOGUE

OF THE

GRAY COLLECTION OF ENGRAVINGS.

CATALOGUE

OF THE

COLLECTION OF ENGRAVINGS

BEQUEATHED TO

HARVARD COLLEGE

BY

FRANCIS CALLEY GRAY.

BY LOUIS THIES.

CAMBRIDGE:
WELCH, BIGELOW, AND COMPANY,
PRINTERS TO THE UNIVERSITY.
1869.

PREFACE.

The engravings described in the following Catalogue were collected by the late Hon. Francis Calley Gray, LL. D., a graduate of Harvard College of the class of 1809. To those who knew him it is hardly necessary to say that he had a mind of uncommon natural vigor, disciplined and enriched by a wide and thorough course of cultivation. In variety and accuracy of knowledge, he was admitted, by common consent, to have no superior in the community in which he lived.

Frequent visits to Europe, begun early in life, developed in Mr. Gray a strong love of art, the result of which was the gradual and careful acquisition of a large and precious collection of engravings. His purchases were made with judgment and taste. His object was to secure the best representations in engraving of the best works of the great masters in art. He sought not merely to gratify his love of beauty, but also to satisfy his love of knowledge. In his engravings he studied the history of art in all periods, and in every country; and they were regarded by him as a part of and complement to his admirable library. Thus many of the engravings in this collection are valuable as beautiful and accurate transcripts of paintings, while others were acquired on account of some peculiar merit of their own, irrespective of that of their subject, or because they were of essential importance in the history of art.

Mr. Gray's attention being early drawn to engraving as an art by itself, he was led to take a peculiar interest in the works of those artists who are known as *peintres-graveurs*, that is, painters who have engraved their own works, either with the burin or with aqua-fortis. The most distinguished of the former, Albrecht Dürer and his precursors, and of the latter, Rembrandt, are well represented here. The collection also contains fine impressions of all the most important works of Marc-Antonio Raimondi, who transferred to copper the drawings of Raphael, under the supervision of the latter; so that the engraver has preserved for us true fac-similes of the great master's first conceptions. In painting these subjects, Raphael departed more or less from his original designs. Engravings were not made directly from paintings till about a century later.

The collection has a specimen of the work of the earliest known German engraver, "The Master E. S. 1466," and also a very early Italian engraving,— one of the celebrated prints of the Otto collection, formerly attributed to Maso Finiguerra, but now believed to be the work of his pupil Baccio Baldini. This print is unique, and is the choicest of the series, the rest of which are now in the British Museum.

Mr. Gray devised this fine collection of engravings to Harvard College, together with a choice library of works on art, and several valuable illustrated books, among them Rosellini's *Monumenti dell' Egitto* and Audubon's *Birds* and *Quadrupeds of America*. He also provided for the publication of a catalogue of the engravings, and left the College a sum of money, the income of which was to be expended for the increase of the collection, and for keeping it in order. The whole bequest was subject, however, to the approval of his nephew, the Hon. William Gray, himself a liberal benefactor of the College, who, emulating his uncle's generous spirit, caused the books and prints to be at once transferred to that institution.

As I was thoroughly acquainted with Mr. Gray's plans and wishes touching his collection, he expressed in his will a desire that I should be consulted in regard to it, and at his request I undertook the preparation of a catalogue.

The task was not an easy one. We have, indeed, the excellent works of Bartsch, Robert-Dumesnil, and others, to aid us in identifying and classifying engravings of early date. But no existing treatise contains full and correct information as to the different states of modern engravings. The best general manual for the collector's use is Heller's *Praktisches Handbuch für Kupferstichsammler*, but this is very incomplete and often incorrect. Even such a monograph as Palmerini's *Opere d' intaglio del Cav. Raffaello Morghen* fails to distinguish the different states of the principal works of that artist, as, for instance, his engraving of Raphael's Transfiguration. Mr. Gray wished that the catalogue of his collection should supply these deficiencies as far as possible, and mention all the different states of each important plate, as well as that of his own impression. He also desired that under the head of each engraving should be found all the information that could be obtained as to the original which it represents.

In determining the states of the earlier engravings I have relied mainly upon the works of Bartsch and Robert-Dumesnil. Some excellent monographs, also, have been recently issued,— such, for instance, as that by Andresen on the two Müllers, and that by William Smith on Cornelius Visscher. Of all these helps I have gladly availed myself. But much of the information which the present Catalogue contains is the result of personal observation and long-continued research; and it is to be hoped that the pains which have been taken to determine the states of the prints, and to make references to the original pictures, will prove of use to other collectors, as well as to future compilers of manuals of engraving.

The prices of some of the most interesting and important engravings have been given. It is hardly necessary to add that the value of an engraving depends upon the earliness of the impression, as well as upon its general condition. The prices mentioned have reference to good impressions in good condition.

The arrangement of the prints in the portfolios, as originally made by Mr. Gray, has been retained. It is not strictly systematic, but it was found by him the most convenient for reference and study. Engraved portraits from originals by the great masters, such as Raphael, Titian, Rubens, and Van Dyck, have been placed with their other works. Portraits from artists of lesser note have been arranged under the engravers of the same, or by schools. Collectors will understand the propriety of keeping together the works of such engravers as Nanteuil and Edelinck.

Landscapes have also been put by themselves, and a special portfolio is devoted to those by Woollett. The works of Strange and Wille are also in separate portfolios, as each is distinguished by marked and peculiar characteristics, wholly independent of the originals which they have reproduced.

The future practical use of this collection might be facilitated by an alphabetical catalogue, in manuscript, of all the painters and designers whose works are found in it, with a very brief designation of the subjects. With the same object, it might be well to have an alphabetical catalogue of the portraits, indicating the names of the painter and engraver in each case. But all the portraits are made conspicuous in this Catalogue by having prefixed to them a capital 𝔓.

I must not conclude without expressing my grateful acknowledgments to my friend Mr. Ezra Abbot, for his kind assistance in the revision of the manuscript and proof-sheets.

L. T.

Cambridge, Mass., June 4th, 1869.

LIST

OF THE

PRINCIPAL WORKS ON ART

CONSULTED OR REFERRED TO.

I. ENCYCLOPÆDIAS, DICTIONARIES, AND OTHER GENERAL WORKS.

BRYAN, Michael. A Biographical and Critical Dictionary of Painters and Engravers. 2 vol. London, 1816. 4to.

"This book includes the whole of Strutt's Dictionary of Engravers, and Pilkington's Dictionary of Painters." — Maberly, *The Print Collector*, p. 198.

——— A Biographical and Critical Dictionary of Painters and Engravers. A new edition, by George Stanley. London, 1849. Large 8vo.

OTTLEY, Henry. A Biographical and Critical Dictionary of Recent and Living Painters and Engravers, forming a Supplement to Bryan's Dictionary of Painters and Engravers, as edited by George Stanley. London, 1866. Large 8vo.

This latter work is got up with unpardonable carelessness.

BRULLIOT, François. Dictionnaire des monogrammes, marques figurées, lettres initiales, noms abrégés, etc., avec lesquels les peintres, dessinateurs, graveurs et sculpteurs ont designé leurs noms. Nouvelle édition, corrigée et augmentée. 3 vol. Munich, 1832 – 34. 4to.

FINE ARTS Quarterly Review. London, 1863 *et seqq.* Large 8vo.

GAILHABAUD, Jules. L'Art dans ses diverses branches, ou l'architecture, la sculpture, la peinture, la fonte, la ferronnerie, etc., chez tous les peuples et à toutes les époques jusqu'en 1789, d'après les travaux des principaux architectes et artistes, reproduits par les plus habiles graveurs et chromo-lithographes. 1re partie. Livraisons 1 – 36. Paris, 1863 – 65. 4to.

The work will comprise from 500 to 750 livraisons, published at 1 *fr.* 75 *c.* on common paper, and 3 *fr.* on China paper.

[HEINEKEN, Carl Heinrich VON.] Nachrichten von Künstlern und Kunstsachen. 2 Theile. Leipzig, 1768 – 69. 8vo.

[———] Neue Nachrichten von Künstlern und Kunstsachen. Erster Theil. Leipzig, 1804. 8vo.

No more was published.

JAMESON, *Mrs.* A. M. Visits and Sketches. 2 vol. New York. 1834. 8vo.

LÜBKE, Wilhelm. Grundriss der Kunstgeschichte. 4e Aufl. Mit 403 Holzschnitt-Illustrationen. Stuttgart, 1868. Large 8vo.

——— The History of Art. With 415 Illustrations. Translated by F. E. Bunnètt. 2 vol. London, 1869. Large 8vo.

NAGLER, G. K. Neues allgemeines Künstler-Lexicon. 22 Bde. München, 1835–52. 8vo.

Though this work contains many errors, contradictions, and repetitions, it is incomparably the best of its kind, the result of indefatigable labor and research. The plan was modified as the author advanced, and the earlier volumes are far less complete than the later.

——— Die Monogrammisten. München, 1858 *et seqq.*

NAUMANN, R. *and* WEIGEL, R. Archiv für die zeichnenden Künste, mit besonderer Beziehung auf Kupferstecher und Holzschneider. Ier–XIVer Jahrg. Leipzig. 1855–68. 8vo.

SCHNAASE, Carl. Geschichte der bildenden Künste. 7 Bde. Düsseldorf, 1843–64. 8vo.

I., II. Geschichte der bildenden Künste bei den Alten.
III.–VII. Geschichte der bildenden Künste im Mittelalter.
A new edition of Vols. I. and II. was published in 1866–67.

SEROUX D'AGINCOURT, J. B. L. G. Histoire de l'art. See p. 458.

ZANI, Pietro. Enciclopedia metodica critico-ragionata delle belle arti. Parte prima. 19 vol. Parma, 1819–24. 8vo.

——— *The same.* Parte seconda. 9 vol. Parma, 1817–22. 8vo.

II. CATALOGUES OF GALLERIES AND COLLECTIONS OF PICTURES; ENUMERATIONS OF PICTURES IN PARTICULAR PLACES.

Antwerp. CATALOGUE du Musée d'Anvers. 2e édition. Publié par le Conseil d'administration de l'Académie royale des beaux-arts. Anvers, 1857. 12mo.

"A pattern of a catalogue."

Berlin. WAAGEN, G. F. Verzeichniss der Gemälde-Sammlung [in Berlin]. 10e Aufl. Berlin, 1850. 8vo.

A very carefully prepared catalogue, full of information.

Dresden. [MATTHÄI.] Neues Sach- und Ortsverzeichniss der Königlich Sächsischen Gallerie zu Dresden. In zwei Abtheilungen. Dresden, 1833. 8vo.

HÜBNER, Julius. Verzeichniss der Königlichen Gemälde-Gallerie zu Dresden. Mit einer historischen Einleitung und Notizen über die Erwerbung der einzelnen Bilder. Auf hohe Veranlassung verfasst. Dresden, 1856. 8vo.

England. BÜRGER, W. Trésors d'art en Angleterre. 3e édit. Paris, 1865. 8vo.

Treats of the works of art in the exhibition at Manchester.

PASSAVANT, J. D. Tour of a German Artist in England. 2 vol. London, 1836. 8vo.

WAAGEN, G. F. Treasures of Art in Great Britain; being an Account of the Chief Collections of Paintings, Drawings, Sculptures, Illuminated MSS., &c. 3 vol. London, 1854. 8vo.

——— Galleries and Cabinets of Art in Great Britain, etc., now for the first time described. Forming a Supplemental Volume to the Treasures of Art in Great Britain. London, 1857. 8vo.

The author may, in some instances, have been mistaken in his judgment, or have not had sufficient time for close examination, and he may also have occasionally modified his expressions out of politeness; yet, on the whole, this is a work of very great value.

WORNUM, R. N. Descriptive and Historical Catalogue of the Pictures in the National Gallery; with Biographical Notices of the Painters. Foreign Schools. 44th Edition. London, 1866.

A very carefully prepared catalogue.

WALPOLE, Horace. Anecdotes of Painting in England. With some Account of the Principal Artists; and Incidental Notes on other Arts, collected by the late Mr. George Vertue; and now digested and published from his Original MSS. 3 vol. Strawberry-Hill. 1762–63. 4to.

——— A Catalogue of Engravers who have been born, or resided in England; digested by Mr. Horace Walpole, from the MSS. of Mr. George Vertue. Strawberry-Hill. 1763. 4to.

——— Anecdotes of Painting in England. Also a Catalogue of Engravers who have been born or resided in England. Collected by the late George Vertue. With Additions by the Rev. James Dallaway. A New Edition, with Additional Notes. By R. N. Wornum. 3 vol. London, 1849. 8vo.

Though the new edition contains many additions, the original quarto edition is much sought after, on account of the well-engraved portraits.

RICHARDSON, Jonathan. Works. Containing: I. The Theory of Painting. II. Essay on the Art of Criticism (so far as it relates to Painting). III. The Science of a Connoisseur. A New Edition, with an Essay on the Knowledge

Richardson, Jonathan, *continued.* of Prints, and Cautions to Collectors. The whole intended as a Supplement to the Anecdotes of Painters and Engravers. Printed at Strawberry-Hill. [London.] 1792. 4to.

France. Waagen, G. F. Kunstwerke und Künstler in Paris. Berlin, 1839. 8vo.

Villot, Frédéric. Notice des tableaux exposés dans les galeries du Musée impérial du Louvre. 3 parties. Paris, 1855–57. 12mo.

I. Écoles d'Italie et d'Espagne. 13e édit. 1857.—II. Écoles allemande, flamande et hollandaise. 7e édit. 1855.—III. École française. 3e édit. 1857. The catalogue identifies the pictures well, and mentions engravings after them.

Standish. Catalogue des tableaux, dessins et gravures de la collection Standish, légués au Roi Louis Philippe, par Frank Hall Standish. Paris, 1842. 8vo.

——— Catalogue des tableaux formant la célèbre collection Standish, léguée à S. M. feu le Roi Louis Philippe, par Frank Hall Standish. Vente à Londres, le 27, 28 mai 1853. Londres, 1853. 8vo.

Louis Philippe. Catalogue des tableaux formant la célèbre galerie espagnole de S. M. feu le Roi Louis Philippe. Vente à Londres le 6, 7, 13, 14, 20, 21 mai 1853. Londres, 1853. 8vo.

Munich. Dillis, Georges de. Catalogue des tableaux de la Pinacothèque royale à Munich. Munich, 1845. 12mo.

Italy. Lavice, A. Revue des Musées d'Italie. Paris, 1862. 12mo.

Rome. Beschreibung der Stadt Rom, von Ernst Platner, Carl Bunsen, Eduard Gerhard, Wilhelm Röstell, und Ludwig Urlichs. Mit Plänen, Umrissen, und Ansichten. 3 Bde. in 6 Abth. Stuttgart und Tübingen, 1830–42. 8vo, and Atlas, 4to.

A very important work.

Spain. Ford, Richard. Handbook for Travellers in Spain. London, John Murray, 1855. 12mo.

Madrazo, Pedro de. Catálogo de los cuadros del real Museo de pintura [Madrid]. Madrid, 1845. 12mo.

Passavant, J. D. Die Christliche Kunst in Spanien. Leipzig, 1853. 8vo.

St. Petersburg. Waagen, G. F. Die Gemäldesammlung in der Kaiserlichen Ermitage zu St. Petersburg. München, 1864. 8vo.

The first good and reliable catalogue of this Gallery.

Vienna. Kraft, A. Verzeichniss der Kais. Königl. Gemälde-Gallerie im Belvedere zu Wien. Wien, 1845. 12mo.

Vence. Catalogue des livres, tableaux, dessins, et estampes de feu le comte de Vence, lieutenant-général des armées du Roy. Vente le 25 Juin 1760. Paris, 1760. 8vo.

WILLIAM II., *King of Holland.* Catalogue de tableaux anciens et modernes de diverses écoles, dessins et statues, formant la galerie de feu Sa Majesté Guillaume II. Par les experts Jérôme de Vries, Corneille François Roos et Jean Albert Brondgeest. Vente le 12 Août. Amsterdam, 1850. 8vo.

Brought 1,221,873 florins.

III. WORKS ON PAINTING AND PAINTERS.

BIE, Cornelis DE. Het Gulden-Cabinet van de edel vry schilderconst. 3 delen. Antwerpen, 1661 – 62. 4to.

The numerous portraits are after the painters' own pictures, engraved by H. Snyers, W. Hollar, P. de Jode, L. Vorsterman, P. Pontius, etc.

CEAN BERMUDEZ, J. A. Diccionario historico de los mas ilustres profesores de las bellas artes en España. 6 vol. Madrid, 1800. Small 8vo.

CROWE, J. A., *and* CAVALCASELLE, G. B. A New History of Painting in Italy, from the Second to the Sixteenth Century. 3 vol. London, 1864 – 66. 8vo.

DESCAMPS, J.-B. La vie des peintres flamands, allemands et hollandois, avec des portraits gravés en taille-douce. 4 vol. Paris, 1753 – 64.

All that is valuable in this work is taken from Carel van Mander's *Schilderboeck* and De Bie's *Gulden-Cabinet.*

Besides these, however, Descamps also copied from Houbraken's *Groote schouburgh der Nederlandsche kunstschilders*, Campo Weyerman's *Levensbeschryvingen der Nederlandsche kunstschilders*, and Johan van Gool's *Nieuwe schouburgh der Nederlandsche kunstschilders*, — works which are entirely unreliable.

The book is valued chiefly for the really finely engraved portraits, principally by Ficquet, and therefore only the original edition is esteemed.

DEZALLIER D'ARGENVILLE, A. J. Abrégé de la vie des plus fameux peintres avec leurs portraits gravés en taille-douce. 2 part. Paris, 1745. 4to.

——— Supplément. Paris, 1752. 4to.

There is a later edition, Paris, 1762, 4 vols. in 8vo, but the original edition is preferred on account of the plates, which constitute, at present, the principal interest of the work.

FÖRSTER, Ernst. Geschichte der deutschen Kunst. 5 Bde. Leipzig, 1851 – 60. 12mo.

A popular work.

HOTHO. Die Malerschule Hubert's van Eyck nebst deutschen Vorgängern und Zeitgenossen. Ier Theil. Geschichte der deutschen Malerei bis 1450.

HOTHO, *continued.*

II[er] Theil. Die flandrische Malerei des 15. Jahrhunderts. Erste Lieferung. Berlin, 1855 – 58. 8vo.

KUGLER, Franz. Handbuch der Geschichte der Malerei seit Constantin dem Grossen. Zweite Auflage von Dr. Jacob Burckhardt. 2 Bde. Berlin, 1847. 8vo.

A new edition is now in course of publication in Germany.

KUGLER, Franz. Handbook of Painting. The Italian Schools. Translated from the German of Kugler, by a Lady. Edited with Notes by Sir Charles L. Eastlake. 3d Edit. 2 vol. London, 1855. 8vo.

——— Handbook of Painting. The German, Flemish, Dutch, Spanish, and French Schools. Partly translated from the German of Kugler, by a Lady. Edited with Notes by Sir Edmund Head. 2 vol. London, 1854. 8vo.

LASTRI, Marco. L'Etruria pittrice. See p. 458.

MANDER, Carel VAN. Het Schilderboeck waerin voor eerst de leerlustighe Jueght den grondt der edel vry schilderconst . . . . wort voorghedraghen . . . . daernae . . . . t' leven der . . . . schilders des ouden ende nieuwen tydts. Haerlem, 1604. 4to. — 2d edit., Amsterdam, 1618. 4to.

Contains the earliest collected information respecting Flemish art, but goes no farther than to Hubert van Eyck, the beginning of the fifteenth century.

RACZYNSKI, *Comte* Athanase. Histoire de l'art moderne en Allemagne. 3 vol. Paris, 1836 – 41. Imp. 4to.

With 240 woodcuts and folio Atlas of 30 engravings.

ROSINI, Giovanni. Storia della pittura italiana. See p. 458.

RUMOHR, C. F. L. VON. Italienische Forschungen. 3 Bde. Berlin, 1826 – 27. 8vo.

A work of great research.

SANDRART, Joachim VON. L'Academia Tedesca della architettura, scultura e pittura, oder Deutsche Academie der Bau- Bildhauer- und Mahler-Kunst. 4 Theile in 2 Bdn. Nürnberg, 1675 – 79. fol.

With numerous plates. What is valuable in this work is mostly extracted from Carel van Mander, but it contains interesting original accounts of some contemporary artists. In 1683 there appeared an edition with Latin text. The later edition in octavo is not esteemed, on account of the inferior engravings.

SMITH, John. A *Catalogue raisonné* of the works of the most eminent Dutch, Flemish, and French Painters. 8 vol. and Supplement. London, 1829 – 42. Roy. 8vo.

A very useful work, the result of immense labor and research.

STIRLING, William. Annals of the Artists in Spain. 3 vol. London, 1848. 8vo.

VASARI, Giorgio. Le vite de' più eccellenti architetti, pittori, et scultori italiani, da Cimabue insino a' tempi nostri : descritte in lingua toscana. 3 parti in 2 vol. Firenze, 1550. 4to.

Editio princeps.

——— Le vite de più eccellenti pittori, scultori, ed architetti. Publicata per cura di una società di amatori delle arti belli. 14 vol. Firenze, 1846 – 57. 12mo.

WAAGEN, G. F. Handbook of Painting. The German, Flemish, and Dutch Schools. Based on the Handbook of Kugler, enlarged, and for the most part rewritten. 2 vol. London, 1860. 8vo.

IV. ON ENGRAVING.

ANDRESEN, Andreas. Der deutsche Peintre-Graveur oder die deutschen Maler als Kupferstecher, nach ihrem Leben und ihren Werken, von dem letzten Drittel des 16. Jahrhunderts bis zum Schluss des 18. Jahrhunderts. 3 Bde. Leipzig, 1864 – 66. 8vo.

BALDINUCCI, Filippo. Cominciamento e progresso dell' arte dell' intagliare in rame, colle vite di molti de' più eccellenti maestri della stessa professione. Firenze, 1686. 4to.

A new edition with notes by D. M. Manni, Florence, 1767, 4to.

——— Notizie de' professori del disegno da Cimabue in qua. 6 tom. in 3 vol. Firenze, 1681 – 1728. 4to.

A new edition with notes by D. M. Manni was published at Florence in 1767 – 74, 21 tom. in 7 vol., small 4to.

BARTSCH, Adam. Anleitung zur Kupferstichkunde. 2 Bde. Wien, 1821. 8vo. *Plates.*

A standard work, of which a new edition is desirable.

——— Notice de quelques copies trompeuses d'estampes anciennes, extraite et traduite de l'ouvrage intitulé Anleitung zur Kupferstichkunde, par Bartsch, avec additions par M. Charles Le Blanc. Paris, 1849. 12mo.

The "additions" do not amount to much. But the book contains the original plates of this part of Bartsch's work, and the text in a French translation.

——— Le peintre graveur. 21 tom. Vienne, 1803 – 21. 8vo.

With 80 plates accompanying the text, and 16 in 2 cahiers, 4to. The important text-book continually referred to.

Bartsch, Adam. Suppléments au Peintre-graveur de Adam Bartsch, par R. Weigel. Tome premier. Leipzig, 1843. 12mo.

No more was published.

——— Zusätze zu Adam Bartsch's Le Peintre Graveur. Von Joseph Heller. Bamberg, 1844. 12mo.

Bartsch, Friedrich von. Die Kupferstichsammlung der K. K. Hofbibliothek in Wien. Wien, 1854. 8vo.

Basan, François. Dictionnaire des graveurs anciennes et modernes, avec une notice des principales estampes qu'ils ont gravées. Suivi des catalogues des œuvres de J. Jordaens, et de Corn. Visscher. 3 vol. Paris, 1767. 12mo.

The third volume, containing "Catalogue des estampes gravées d'après P. P. Rubens," is the only part of the work which is now of any use.

Baudicour, Prosper de. Le peintre-graveur français continué, ou Catalogue raisonné des estampes gravées par les peintres et les dessinateurs de l'école française, nés dans le XVIIIe siècle. 2 vol. Paris, 1859 – 61. 8vo.

Cicognara, Leopoldo, *Count.* Memorie spettanti alla storia della calcografia. Prato, 1831. 8vo, with Atlas, fol.

Duchesne, Jean, *aîné.* Essai sur les Nielles, gravures des orfèvres florentins du XVe siècle. Paris, 1826. 8vo.

——— Voyage d'un iconophile. Revue des principaux cabinets d'estampes, bibliothèques et musées d'Allemagne, de Hollande et d'Angleterre. Paris, 1834. 8vo.

Duplessis, Georges. Essai de bibliographie, contenant l'indication des ouvrages relatifs à l'histoire de la gravure et des graveurs. Paris, 1862. 8vo, pp. 48.

An excellent first attempt.

——— Histoire de la gravure en France. Paris, 1861. 8vo.

"Ouvrage couronné par l'Institut de France."

Ferrario, Giulio. Le classiche stampe dal cominciamento della calcografia fino al presente, compresi gli artisti viventi. Milano, 1836. 8vo.

Füsslin, H. R. Kritisches Verzeichniss der besten, nach den berühmtesten Malern aller Schulen vorhandenen Kupferstichen. 4 Bde. Zürich, 1798 – 1806. 8vo.

A very good book for the time.

[Haake.] Practisches Handbuch zur Kupferstichkunde. Magdeburg, 1840. 8vo.

Treats almost exclusively of such prints as are fit to be framed as ornaments for the wall.

[Heineken, Carl Heinrich von.] Idée générale d'une collection complette d'estampes. Avec une dissertation sur l'origine de la gravure et sur les premiers livres d'images. Leipzig et Vienne, 1771. 8vo.

[Heineken, Carl Heinrich von.] Dictionnaire des artistes dont nous avons des estampes, avec une notice détaillée de leurs ouvrages gravés. 4 vol. Leipsig, 1778 - 90. 8vo.

A — Diz. All that was published.

The work was complete in manuscript, and deposited in the Royal Library at Dresden, where Mr. Nagler had access to it, and incorporated what was of use to him into his *Künstler-Lexicon.*

Heller, Joseph. Praktisches Handbuch für Kupferstichsammler. Leipzig, 1850. 8vo.

Of all the manuals of engraving this has been hitherto the best; it is, however, not sufficient for the present time; a more extensive work is wanted, that gives the different states of the plates more correctly. The notices of prices for which the prints have been sold are also a guide no longer.

Huber, Michel. Notices générales des graveurs divisés par nations, et des peintres rangés par écoles. Par M. Huber. 2 part. Dresde et Leipzig, 1787. 8vo.

This is the first edition of the following work:

Huber, Michel, *and* Rost, C. C. H. Manuel des curieux et des amateurs de l'art, contenant une notice abrégée des principaux graveurs, et un catalogue raisonné de leurs meilleurs ouvrages; depuis le commencement de la gravure jusques à nos jours: les artistes rangés par ordre chronologique, et divisés par école. 9 tom. Zurich, 1797 - 1808. 8vo.

At the time of its publication this was a work of great importance. A German translation, by C. C. H. Rost and C. G. Martini was published at Zurich in 1796 - 1808, with the title, *Handbuch für Kunstliebhaber und Sammler*, etc.

Jackson, John. A Treatise on Wood Engraving, Historical and Practical. With upwards of Three Hundred Illustrations, engraved on Wood, by John Jackson. London, 1839. Large 8vo. — 2d edition, enlarged, London, 1861.

The historical portion of this work is chiefly by William A. Chatto.

Joubert, F. E., *père.* Manuel de l'amateur d'estampes, dans lequel on trouvera, depuis l'origine de la gravure, les remarques qui déterminent le mérite et la priorité des épreuves, etc. 3 vol. Paris, 1821. 8vo.

Laborde, Léon de. Histoire de la gravure en manière noire. Paris, 1839. 8vo.

The book is out of print and has become very rare.

Le Blanc, Charles. Manuel de l'amateur d'estampes, ouvrage destiné à faire suite au Manuel du Libraire par Brunet. Livraisons 1 - 9. Paris, 1850. 8vo.

The work was to have been completed in 16 livraisons, but no more has been published. It is very carelessly compiled.

Longhi, Giuseppe. La calcografia. Vol. I. concernente la teorica dell' arte. Milano, 1830. 8vo.

No more was published. The volume concludes with "Notizie biografiche di Giuseppe Longhi, raccolte da Francesco Longhena."

LONGHI, Giuseppe. Die Kupferstecherei oder die Kunst in Kupfer zu stechen und zu äzen. I. Theoretischer Theil, von J. Longhi. Aus dem Italiänischen übersetzt von C. Barth. II. Praktischer Theil, von C. Barth. 2 Theile. Hildburghausen u. Meiningen, 1837. 8vo.

[MABERLY, Joseph.] The Print Collector, an Introduction to the Knowledge Necessary for forming a Collection of Ancient Prints. London, 1844. Small 4to.

An experienced collector here gives in a pleasant way instruction to beginners.

MALASPINA DI SANNAZARO. Catalogo di una raccolta di stampe antiche compilato dallo stesso possessore. 5 vol. Milano, 1824. 8vo.

OTTLEY, William Young. An Inquiry into the Origin and Early History of Engraving upon Copper and in Wood, with an Account of Engravers and their Works, from the Invention of Chalcography by Maso Finiguerra, to the Time of Marc-Antonio Raimondi. 2 vol. London, 1816. Large 4to. *Plates.*

A very important work.

PALGRAVE, Francis Turner. Essay on the First Century of Italian Engraving. (Appended to KUGLER'S *Handbook of Painting, The Italian Schools,* 3d Ed., London, 1855, Vol. II.)

PASSAVANT, J. D. Le peintre-graveur. 6 tom. Leipsic, 1860-66. 8vo.

QUANDT, Johann Gottlob VON. Entwurf einer Geschichte der Kupferstecherkunst. Leipzig, 1826. Small 8vo.

RENOUVIER, Jules. Histoire de l'origine et des progrès de la gravure dans les Pays-Bas et en Allemagne jusqu'à la fin du XVe siècle. Bruxelles, 1860. 8vo.

"Ouvrage couronné par l'Académie royale de Belgique."

RENOUVIER, Jules. Des types et des manières des maîtres graveurs, pour servir à l'histoire de la gravure en Italie, en Allemagne, dans les Pays-Bas et en France. 4 part. Montpellier, 1853-56. 4to.

ROBERT-DUMESNIL, A. P. F. Le peintre-graveur français, ou Catalogue raisonné des estampes gravées par les peintres et les dessinateurs de l'école française. Ouvrage faisant suite au Peintre-graveur de M. Bartsch. — Tome IXe, X[e], publié par M. Georges Duplessis. 10 tom. Paris, 1835-69. 8vo.

The important text-book continually referred to.

STRUTT, Joseph. A Biographical Dictionary; containing an Historical Account of all the Engravers, from the Earliest Period of the Art of Engraving to the Present Time; and a Short List of their most esteemed Works. 2 vol. London, 1785. 4to.

The work itself is superseded, but the Introduction, "On the Origin and Progress of Engraving," is worthy of perusal.

VALLARDI, F. S. Manuale del raccoglitore e del negoziante di stampe. Milano, 1843. 8vo.

The author is a printseller, and the book is partly calculated to inform the public at what prices they can obtain the prints mentioned by him. At the same time he attacks Ferrario. But neither he nor Ferrario gives sufficient information about the different states of the prints.

VALLARDI, G. Catalogo dei più celebri intagliatori in legno ed in rame e capiscuola di diverse età e nazioni. Milano, 1821. 8vo.

V. GALLERIES AND COLLECTIONS OF PAINTINGS REPRODUCED BY ENGRAVING OR LITHOGRAPHY.

GALERIE AGUADO, Choix des principaux tableaux de la Galerie de M. le Marquis de las Marismas del Guadalquivir, dédiée à Mad. la Marquise de las Marismas par Ch. Gavard. Notices sur les peintres par Louis Viardot. Paris, 1837–39. Roy. fol. 38 *plates.*

BETTONI, Nicolò. Le Panthéon des nations : 100 portraits d'hommes illustres de tous les temps et de toutes les nations, gravés en taille-douce par cent artistes les plus distingués etc. Paris, 1833, *et seqq.* Small fol.

This work does not appear to have been completed.

BIRCH, Thomas. The Heads of the most Illustrious Persons of Great Britain, engraved by Houbraken and Vertue. With their Lives, etc. 2 parts in 1 vol. London, *Knapton.* 1743–52. fol.

BOISSERÉE, S. *and* M., *and* BERTRAM, J. Sammlung Alt- Nieder- und Ober-Deutscher Gemälde. Stuttgart und München. 1822–36. Roy. fol.

Containing 120 plates, including the Supplement.

BOYER D'AIGUILLES. Recueil d'estampes d'après les tableaux des peintres les plus célèbres d'Italie, des Pays-Bas et de France, qui sont dans le Cabinet de M. Boyer d'Aiguilles, Procureur-général du Roi au Parlement de Provence. Gravées par Jacques Coelemans d'Anvers, etc., avec une description de chaque tableau par Pierre Jean Mariette. Paris, 1744. Large fol.

BRÜHL. Recueil d'estampes gravées d'après les tableaux de la Galerie et du Cabinet de S. E. M. le Comte de Brühl, premier ministre de S. M. le Roi de Pologne, Électeur de Saxe. Ière partie, contenant 50 pieces. Dresde, 1754. Roy. fol.

The work was not continued, and the Gallery was sold to the Empress Catherine II. of Russia, for 75,000 thalers.

BUCHANAN, William. Gallery of Pictures, published under the Direction of Mr. Buchanan. 11 *plates.*

CROZAT. Recueil d'estampes d'après les plus beaux tableaux et d'après les plus beaux dessins qui sont en France dans le Cabinet du Roy, dans celuy de Mgr. le Duc d'Orléans et dans d'autres Cabinets. Divisé suivant les différentes écoles; avec un abrégé de la vie des peintres et une description historique de chaque tableau. Tome I. II. L'école romaine et vénitienne. Paris, 1729–42. fol.

The second volume was published after Crozat's death in 1740, by Mariette.

In 1764 Basan acquired the plates, and separated those after the best Italian pictures in the Palais of the Duke of Orleans, which he published in one volume, with explanatory text for each subject, under the title *Recueil d'après la Galerie du Palais Royal.*

Crozat's own collection of paintings was purchased by the Empress Catherine II. of Russia, and formed, with the Houghton and Brühl Galleries, the basis of the Gallery of the Hermitage.

DESNOYERS, Auguste BOUCHER. Recueil d'estampes, gravées d'après des peintres antiques italiennes. Paris, 1821. 34 *plates.*

DRESDEN. Recueil d'estampes d'après les plus célèbres tableaux de la Galerie Royale de Dresde. 2 vol. Dresde, 1753–57. Roy. fol. 102 *plates.*

Of a third volume there appeared 38 plates, when the work was discontinued; but its publication has been recently resumed.

——— Die vorzüglichsten Gemälde der Königlich Sächsischen Gallerie in Dresden, nach den Originalen auf Stein gezeichnet. Herausgegeben von Franz Hanfstängl. Dresden, 1836, *et seqq.* Roy. fol.

Complete in 60 numbers, containing 193 lithographs. The lithographs are distinguished for their correctness in drawing, especially those of the Netherland schools, and, among the Italian schools, the Venetian.

FLORENCE. Raccolta de' quadri dei granduchi di Toscana. Serie de' quadri più celebri esistenti nel Real Palazzo de' Pitti e nella R. Galleria di Firenze. [The old Florentine Gallery.] Firenze, 1690–1710. fol.

A later issue: "Serie de' quadri più celebri esistenti nel Real Palazzo de' Pitti e nella R. Galleria di Firenze. Firenze, *presso N. Pagni e G. Bardi,* 1789." Large fol. 104 *plates. See* R. Weigel, *Kunst-Catalog,* XXXIII. No. 24,267.

Heineken, *Idée générale,* 1771, p. 56, remarks: "Ce grand ouvrage, qui n'a point de discours, commence par un titre historié, où l'on voit le portrait du Grand Duc Cosme II. suivi de cent cinquante cinq estampes, dont quelques unes sont de trois planches, et d'autres de deux; mais la plus grande partie d'une seule planche."

——— Galerie de Florence et du Palais Pitti, dessinée par M. Wicar et gravée sous la direction de Lacombe et Masquelier, avec les explications par Mongez l'ainé. 50 livraisons in 4 vols., containing 200 plates.

1st edition, Paris, chez Lacombe et Masquelier. 1789, 1792, 1802, 1807.

FLORENCE, *continued.*

2d edition, Paris, chez Lacombe et Masquelier. 1789, 1804, 1814. (The two last numbers appeared in 1821.)

3d edition, Paris, chez Froment et Fenet. 1827.

Since then Messrs. Didot purchased the plates, and had them retouched.

4th edition, of the ugly retouched plates, Paris, chez F. Didot. 1853.

GIUSTINIANI. Galleria Giustiniana, del marchese Vincenzo Giustiniani. 2 vol. Roma, 1640. Roy. fol. 322 *plates.*

The earliest impressions are before the numbers. The latest recent impressions are of very little value.

HAMILTON, Gavin. Schola Italica Picturae, sive selectae quaedam summorum e Schola Italica Pictorum Tabulae Aere incisae. Romae, 1773. Large fol. 41 *plates, including the title.*

Only the early impressions on stout paper, especially of bluish tint, are desirable. There is a new edition of most execrable impressions, which has been added to Piranesi's works. There appeared a continuation of this work:

——— Schola Italica Artis Pictoriae, sive Tabulae insigniores in Romanis Pinacothecis adservatae, Tabulis Aere incisis nunc primum editae, sumptibus Pet. Pauli Montagnani-Mirabili. Romae, 1806. fol. 40 *plates.*

HOUGHTON Gallery, formerly in the possession of Lord Orford, now in the collection of the Empress of Russia. 2 vol. London, *Boydell,* 1788. Imp. fol. 133 *plates.*

LUXEMBOURG. La Gallerie du Luxembourg, peinte par Rubens, dessinée par les sieurs Nattier, et gravée par les plus illustres graveurs du temps. Paris, *Duchange,* 1710. Large fol.

27 plates, by Edelinck, J.-B. Massé, etc.

MADRID. Coleccion de las estampas grabados á buril de los cuadros pertenecientes al Rey de España. Madrid, 1792, *et seqq.* Roy. fol.

There appeared but 48 plates, in numbers, of 6 plates each, engraved by R. Morghen, F. Muntaner, B. Ametllér, J. Vasquez, J. Volpato, M. S. Carmona, F. Selma, and others.

——— Coleccion de cuadros del Rey de España que se conservan en sus Reales Palacios Museo y Academia de San Fernando con inclusion de los del Real Monasterio del Escorial: obra litografiada por habiles artistas baxo la direccion de D. Jose de MADRAZO. Con el texto por D. Juan Augustin Cean Bermudez. Madrid, 1826–36. Roy. fol.

48 numbers, each of 4 plates.

ODIEUVRE. L'Europe illustre, contenant l'histoire abrégée des souverains et de divers personnages illustres, etc. du XVe siècle compris, jusqu'au milieu du XVIIIe, par Dreux du Radier. 6 vol. Paris, *Odieuvre.* 4to. 592 *plates.*

PARIS. Musée Français, ou collection complète des tableaux statues et bas-reliefs qui composent la collection nationale; avec l'explication des sujets, et des discours sur la peinture [par S.-C. Croze Magnan, Visconti et Éméric David]. Publié par Robillard Péronville et Pierre Laurent. 4 vol. Paris, 1803 – 11. Large fol.

These 4 volumes are also called *Musée Napoléon.* They were followed, after the restoration in France, by 2 more volumes, namely:—

——— Musée Royale, publié par Henri Laurent [avec des descriptions par MM. Visconti, Guizot et le comte de Clarac]. 2 vol. Paris, 1816 – 22. Large fol.

PATIN. Tabellæ selectæ ac explicatæ a Carola Catharina Patina, Parisina, Academica. Patavii, 1691. fol.

PERRAULT, Charles. Les hommes illustres qui ont paru en France pendant ce siècle. 2 vol. Paris, 1696 – 1700. fol.

Containing 101 portraits by Edelinck and other good engravers.

REYNST. Variarum Imaginum a celeberrimis Artificibus pictarum Caelaturae, elegantissimis Tabulis representatae. Ipsae Picturae partim extant apud Viduam Gerardi Reynst, quondam hujus Urbis Senatoris ac Scabini, partim Carolo II. Britanniarum Regi a Potentissimis Hollandiae Westfrisiaeque Ordinibus dono missae sunt. Amstelodami. *Sine anno.* Large fol.

TURIN. La Reale Galleria di Torino illustrata da Roberto d'Azeglio, direttore della medesima. Torino, 1836, *et seqq.* fol.

Up to 1859, 39 fascicoli had been published, containing 156 plates; the work was to have been completed in 41 numbers.

VIENNA. See under PRENNER, p. 293, and STEEN, p. 353.

VITE e Ritratti di illustri Italiani. 2 vol. royal 4to, containing 60 plates and text. Padova, 1812, and Milano, 1820, tipografia Bettoni.

WOUVERMANS. Œuvres de Philippe Wouvermans, hollandais, gravées d'après ses meilleurs tableaux qui sont dans les plus beaux cabinets de Paris, et ailleurs, par J. Moyreau. Paris, Moyreau. 1737. Royal fol.

The work contains 78 plates by J. Moyreau, of which the last bears the date 1754. But Le Bas, Beaumont, Cochin, A. Laurent, and others engraved numerous pieces after Wouvermans, more or less of which are added to Moyreau's plates, and there occur copies of the work of more or less numbers, up to 202 plates.

The new edition, Paris, Treuttel et Würtz, is not desirable.

VI. WORKS ON PARTICULAR ARTISTS. MONOGRAPHS.

BAUSE. Catalog des Kupferstichwerkes von Johann Friedrich Bause, mit einigen biographischen Notizen von Dr. Georg KEIL. Leipzig, 1849. 8vo.

CALLOT. Recherches sur la vie et les ouvrages de J. Callot, par E. MEAUME. 2 vol. Paris, 1860. 8vo.

CHODOWIECKI. Daniel Chodowiecki's sämmtliche Kupferstiche. Von Wilhelm ENGELMANN. Leipzig, 1857. 8vo.

——— Nachträge und Berichtigungen zu Daniel Chodowiecki's sämmtliche Kupferstiche. Leipzig, 1860. 8vo.

CORREGGIO. Memorie istoriche di Antonio Allegri detto Il Correggio. [By Luigi PUNGILEONE.] 3 vol. Parma, 1817-21. 8vo.

——— Sketches of the Lives of Correggio and Parmegiano. [By William COXE.] With Portrait. London, 1823. 8vo.

CRANACH. Lucas Cranach des Aeltern Leben und Werke. Von Christian SCHUCHARDT. 2 Bde. Leipzig, 1851. 8vo.

DELLA BELLA. Essai d'un catalogue de l'œuvre d'Étienne de la Belle, peintre et graveur florentin. Avec la vie de cet artiste, traduit de l'italien [de Baldinucci] et enrichie de notes. Par C. A. JOMBERT. Paris, *chez l'auteur*, 1772. 8vo.

DIETRICH. Monographie der von C. W. E. Dietrich radirten, geschabten und in Holz geschnittenen malerischen Vorstellungen. Von J. F. LINCK. Berlin, 1846. 8vo.

DÜRER. Das Leben und die Werke Albrecht Dürer's. Von Joseph HELLER. In drei Bänden. 2ter Band, in drei Theilen. [Beschreibung seiner Werke.] Leipzig, 1831. 8vo.

All that appeared. A work of great care and labor, still the standard authority on this master.

——— Reliquien von Albrecht Dürer, seinen Verehrern geweiht. [Von Friedrich CAMPE.] Nürnberg, 1828. 16mo.

A very interesting collection of letters by Albrecht Dürer, with his diary.

——— Leben und Wirken Albrecht Dürer's. Von Dr. A. von EYE. Nördlingen, 1860. 8vo.

——— Albrecht Dürer's Kupferstiche, Radirungen, Holzschnitte und Zeichnungen, unter besonderer Berücksichtigung der dazu verwandten Papiere und deren Wasserzeichen. Vom Oberbaurath B. Hausmann. Hannover, 1861. Large 4to.

Van Dyck. Pictorial Notices: consisting of a Memoir of Sir Anthony van Dyck, with a Descriptive Catalogue of the Etchings executed by him. By William Hookham Carpenter. London, 1844. 4to.

Only 250 copies of this work were printed.

——— Catalogue raisonné d'une collection de portraits gravés par et d'après Antoine van Dyck. Par Hermann Weber. Bonn, 1852. 8vo.

This catalogue describes the different states of the plates composing Van Dyck's *Iconographia*. See also the additions and corrections by H. Wolff, in the *Archiv für die zeichnenden Künste*, X. 1864.

——— Anton van Dyck's Bildnisse bekannter Personen. Von Ignaz von Szwykowski. Leipzig, 1859. 8vo.

Compiled with great care.

Van Dyck's *Iconographia.*

Under this designation are comprised those engraved portraits of this master, of which Martin van den Enden's publications, 84 in number, form the basis. It appears that the latter, though issued twice by that editor, were never published with a collective title, but were issued singly, as each plate was finished. 80 of them became the property of Gillis Hendricx, the next publisher, who had the name of Martin van den Enden erased from the plates, and his own initials placed in the middle below, and had the inscription, names, and titles changed, an additional line added, etc. This publisher also acquired 15 of the 21 plates of portraits etched by Van Dyck himself, which had likewise appeared in single sheets, without a collective title, probably first issued by Van Dyck himself. 11 of these remained in the state in which Van Dyck left them; the rest were now more or less finished, in the drapery, with the burin. To these two sets he added six plates of which he was the original publisher, and then published the whole with a title-piece, the portrait of Van Dyck, as a bust, etched by the painter himself, and finished with the burin by J. Neeffs; on the pedestal which supports the bust is the title:

Icones principum virorum doctorum, pictorum, chalcographorum, statuariorum, nec non amatorum pictoriae artis numero centum: ab Antonio van Dyck pictore ad vivum expressae ejusq. sumptibus aeri incisae. Antverpiae: Gillis Hendricx excudit A° 1645.

101 plates, title included.

This edition, with the year on the title-page, is followed by a second edition with the same title-page, in which only the year, after "Antverpiae Gillis Hendricx," is wanting. It is not known who owned the plates at that time; they may have been owned by his heirs: they are often called a second issue by G. Hendricx himself. The impressions do not differ from the preceding ones, except by the absence of the address, — the initials "G. H.," which have been erased from the plates. The inscriptions are otherwise exactly the same, nor have the plates any retouch. The edition is also printed on the same kinds of paper as the preceding, that is, such as have the watermark of the *Cross of Lorraine*, a kind of *Beehive*, sometimes a *Double Eagle*, an *Agnus Dei*, or a *Foolscap of the larger size.*

The date of this edition is supposed to be before 1665.

VAN DYCK, *continued.*

This first edition *without the* "G. H." was followed by many others, with the addition of more or less plates; there is no other mark of difference, except the inferiority of the impressions.

One edition on paper with the watermark of the *Smaller Foolscap* is still tolerably good. It is followed by another much inferior one on paper with the *Arms of the City of Amsterdam.* Both, however, precede the edition of Verdussen.

About the same time that G. Hendricx published his collection, another publisher at Antwerp, Jan Meyssens, began to form a similar collection, the plates of which corresponded in size and arrangement with those of Martin van den Enden, so that they are well suited to complete that series. The exact number of Meyssens's plates is not known; their publication commenced about 1645, and was not finished till 1650.

There are but two states of these pieces to be distinguished, the 1st with the address of the editor in full, the 2d with the address erased.

At the beginning of the eighteenth century the plates of the two collections — that originally of Martin van den Enden and that of Jan Meyssens — were in the hands of H. and C. Verdussen in Antwerp, who published an edition in 2 volumes, containing 124 pieces, besides the bust of Van Dyck, which served as title. The inscription of the title is not changed, except that after *Numero centum* the words *et viginti quatuor* have been added, the address of Gillis Hendricx is erased and replaced by the following address: *Antverpiae, Henricus et Cornelius Verdussen excud.* Besides the engraved title there is a printed title, as follows: *Le Cabinet des plus beaux portraits* etc. *peints par Van Dyck, gravés en taille-douce par les meilleurs graveurs. Anvers, Verdussen.* Without year. The impressions are on thick paper, with the watermark of a *fleur-de-lis.* "They are very bad, and can at best only give an idea of the composition." (Weber.)

Still this edition is by no means the last; the plates have often changed hands, they have been re-etched, and impressions still worse have been issued. Quite recently, however, the Calcographie Impériale at Paris has purchased the plates and issues impressions, which, of course, are inferior to any preceding impressions.

See Weber, *Catalogue raisonné,* and Szwykowski, *Anton van Dyck's Bildnisse.*

HANS HOLBEIN. Some Account of the Life and Works of Hans Holbein, painter of Augsburg. With numerous illustrations. By Ralph Nicholson WORNUM. London, 1867. Large 8vo.

——— Hans Holbein und seine Zeit. Von Dr. Alfred WOLTMANN. 2 Bde. Leipzig, 1866 – 68. 8vo.

——— Supplement, enthaltend Verzeichniss der Werke Holbein's, nebst Namen- und Sachregister. Leipzig, 1868. 8vo.

WENZEL HOLLAR. Beschreibendes Verzeichniss seiner Kupferstiche. Von Gustav PARTHEY. Berlin, 1853. 8vo.

——— Nachträge und Verbesserungen. Berlin, 1858. 8vo.
Prepared with great care.

LE CLERC. Catalogue raisonné de l'œuvre de Sébastien Leclerc, par Charles Antoine JOMBERT. 2 vol. Paris, 1774. 8vo.

LEONARDO DA VINCI. Catalogue de l'œuvre de Léonard de Vinci. Par le Dr. RIGOLLOT. Paris, 1849. 8vo. pp. xxxiv., 112.

Not a work of original research, but the best which has yet appeared.

LONGHI. Della vita, delle opere ed opinioni del cav. Giuseppe Longhi. Commentario dell' allievo Giuseppe BERETTA. Milano, 1837. 8vo.

——— Notizie biografiche di Giuseppe Longhi, raccolte da Francesco LONGHENA. (Appended to Longhi's *Calcografia*, pp. 395 – 436.)

MELLAN. Catalogue raisonné de l'œuvre de Claude Mellan d'Abbeville par M. Anatole de MONTAIGLON. Précédé d'une notice sur la vie et les ouvrages de Mellan par P. J. Mariette. Abbeville, 1856. 8vo.

MICHEL-ANGELO. The Life of Michael Angelo Buonarroti. By John S. HARFORD. 2 vol. London, 1857. 8vo.

——— Illustrations, Architectural and Pictorial, of the Genius of Michael Angelo Buonarroti, with descriptions of the Plates by the Commendatore Canina, C. R. Cockerell, and John S. Harford. London, 1857. fol. 18 *plates*.

——— Leben Michelangelo's. Von Herman GRIMM. 3e Aufl. 3 Bde. Hannover, 1868. 8vo.

A charming book, which has deservedly been translated into French, English, and Italian.

MORGHEN. Opere d' intaglio del cav. Raffaello Morghen raccolte ed illustrate da Niccolò PALMERINI. 3a ediz. Firenze, 1824. 8vo.

MÜLLER. Johann Gotthard von Müller und [sein Sohn] Johann Friedrich Wilhelm Müller. Beschreibendes Verzeichniss ihrer Kupferstiche. Von Dr. A. ANDRESEN. Leipzig, 1865. 8vo.

RAPHAEL. Rafael von Urbino und sein Vater Giovanni Santi. Von J. D. PASSAVANT. 3 Bde. Leipzig, 1839 – 58. 8vo, and Atlas, folio, with 14 plates.

For the references in this Catalogue this original edition has been used. It has been translated into French: "Raphael d'Urbin et son père Giovanni Santi par J.-D. Passavant. Édition française refaite, corrigée et augmentée par l'auteur sur la traduction de M. Jules Lunteschutz, revue et annotée par M. Paul Lacroix." 2 vol. (without the Atlas). Paris, 1860.

A most important work, the result of life-long researches.

——— Beschreibendes Verzeichniss einer Privat-Sammlung von Kupferstichen. I. Raphael. [Von Wilhelm ENGELMANN.] Leipzig, 1866. 8vo.

Printed for private distribution.

REMBRANDT. Catalogue raisonné de toutes les estampes qui forment l'œuvre de Rembrandt, et ceux de ses principaux imitateurs. Composé par les Sieurs Gersaint, Helle, Glomy et P. Yver. Nouvelle édition entièrement refondue, corrigée et considérablement augmentée par Adam BARTSCH. 2 part. Vienne, 1797. 8vo. *Plates.*

Bartsch's catalogue of the etchings of Rembrandt is in Germany still preferred to the others.

——— Catalogue raisonné de toutes les estampes qui forment l'œuvre de Rembrandt, et des principales pièces de ses élèves. Par M. le chev. de CLAUSSIN. Paris, 1824. 8vo.

——— Supplément au catalogue de Rembrandt, suivi d'une description des estampes de ses élèves, etc. Paris, 1828. 8vo.

The Appendix includes an account of the works of G. F. Schmidt.

——— A Descriptive Catalogue of the Prints of Rembrandt. By an Amateur [Thomas WILSON]. London, 1836. 8vo.

In general follows Claussin, and distinguishes more "states" than Bartsch.

——— L'œuvre complet de Rembrandt, décrit et commenté par M. Charles BLANC. 2 tom. Paris, 1859–61. 8vo.

The most copious work on the subject.

RUBENS. Rubens et l'école d'Anvers. Par Alfred MICHIELS. Paris, 1854. 8vo.

——— Catalogue des tableaux et dessins de Rubens, avec l'indication des endroits où ils se trouvent. Paris, 1854. 8vo.

SARTO, Andrea DEL. Andrea del Sarto. Von Alfred REUMONT. Leipzig, 1835. 8vo.

SCHEFFER, Ary. Memoir of the Life of Ary Scheffer. By Mrs. GROTE. London, 1860. 8vo.

G. F. SCHMIDT. Schmidt's Werke, oder beschreibendes Verzeichniss sämmtlicher Kupferstiche und Radirungen, etc. Von L. D. JACOBI. Berlin, 1815. 8vo.

STRANGE. Le graveur en taille-douce. Catalogue de l'œuvre de Robert Strange. Par Charles LE BLANC. Leipzig, 1848. 8vo.

SUYDERHOEF. Jonas Suyderhoef. Beschreibendes Verzeichniss seiner Kupferstiche. Von Johann WUSSIN. Leipzig, 1863. 8vo.

VELAZQUEZ. Velazquez and his Works. By William STIRLING. London, 1855. 12mo.

VISSCHER, CORNELIS. A Catalogue of the Works of Cornelius Visscher. By William SMITH. Reprinted from the Fine Arts Quarterly Review [Vol. I. 1863, *et seqq.*] for Private Circulation only, by John Childs and Son, Bungay. 1864. 4to.

WILLE. Le graveur en taille-douce. Catalogue de l'œuvre de Jean Georges Wille. Par Charles LE BLANC. Leipzig, 1847. 8vo.

VII. CATALOGUES OF COLLECTIONS OF PRINTS.

MAROLLES. Catalogue de livres d'estampes et de figures en taille-douce, avec un dénombrement des pièces qui y sont contenues, par M. de Marolles, abbé de Villeloin. Paris, 1666. 8vo.

This first collection was purchased entire for King Louis XIV., and formed the foundation of the Cabinet of Engravings in the Imperial Library. — A copy of this catalogue was offered in 1868 by A. Claudin, Paris, catalogue No. 35,802, for 28 *fr.*

——— Catalogue de livres d'estampes et de figures en taille-douce par M. de Marolles, abbé de Villeloin. Paris, 1672. 12mo.

This second collection was dispersed, and it is not known where the prints went. This catalogue and the preceding were sold in the Bruzard sale for 50 *fr.*

Under the reign of Henry III., about 1576, Maugis, abbot of St. Ambrose, took it into his head to collect engravings, and, since he had no competitor in this pursuit, he succeeded, in the course of forty years, in acquiring a great number, and among them many that afterwards became very rare. A selection from his collection came, after his death, into the possession of M. de Lorme, and of him Michel de Marolles bought again the finest and rarest prints for 1,000 louis-d'or. To these he made so many other additions, that his collection, without doubt, was the most important in Europe. It contained, in 440 volumes, about 125,000 plates, 17,300 of which were portraits. This was the collection of the catalogue of 1666, which Colbert caused to be bought in 1667. *See* Waagen, *Kunstwerke und Künstler in Paris*, p. 40.

MARIETTE. Catalogue raisonné des différens objets de curiosités [*sic*] dans les sciences et arts, qui composoient le Cabinet de feu Mr Mariette, Contrôleur général de la grande Chancellerie de France. Par F. BASAN. Paris, *chez l'Auteur.* 1775. 8vo.

There are also two supplements to this catalogue, according to G. Duplessis, *Essai de bibliographie*, Nos. 598, 599, namely: "Catalogue d'estampes des plus grands maîtres italiens, flamands et français . . . dépendant de la succession de M. Mariette . . . dont la vente commencera le 1er février 1775. . . . Par F. Basan, graveur, [Paris,] Basan et Me Chariot," 8vo, and "Supplément au catalogue des estampes de la succession de feu M. Mariette, dont la vente a commencé le premier février dernier et

MARIETTE, *continued.*

laquelle continuera en mai prochain, après la vente de la bibliothèque, qui finira le 13." [1775.]

"Pierre Mariette . . . an eminent collector and dealer about the middle of the seventeenth century. He was accustomed, whenever he happened to become possessed of an impression of more than ordinary beauty, to write his name in full, and a date, on the face of the print [as well as on the back], and although this is certainly a disfigurement, yet such is Pierre Mariette's reputation for judgment, that to be thus disfigured, is no disparagement to a print, but the contrary." Maberly, *The Print Collector*, p. 81.

This was the grandfather of Pierre Jean Mariette, the writer on art, and father of Jean Mariette. The collection, continued and enlarged through three generations, was dispersed in 1775.

Pierre Jean Mariette, born at Paris, 1694, died at the same place, 1774, a son of Jean Mariette. Waagen speaks of him as follows (*Kunstwerke und Künstler in Paris*, p. 63): "At the head of all the collectors of engravings, as well as of the connoisseurs of his time, stood the celebrated Mariette. . . . His collection contained, in the choicest impressions and with rare completeness, all the principal works which the art of engraving had till then produced, comprising the works of more than 1,500 artists, without any doubt the most exquisite ever possessed by a private individual."

ACKERMANN. Catalog der . . . Sammlung von . . . Kupferstichen, Radirungen, etc., vereinigt [und beschrieben] von Dr. W. A. Ackermann. Versteigert in Leipzig den 29ten März, 1853. Dresden, 1853. 8vo.

This is the catalogue of Ackermann's principal collection, which was rich in Alb. Dürers, Rembrandts, etc. There is another of a previous sale.

——— Verzeichniss vorzüglicher . . . Kupferstiche, etc., gesammelt [und beschrieben] von Dr. W. A. Ackermann. Versteigert in Leipzig 25. Juni, 1844. Leipzig, 1844. 8vo.

ALIBERT. Catalogue d'une nombreuse collection d'estampes et de dessins de grands maîtres, après le décès de madame Alibert. Par REGNAULT. Vente le 5 floréal an XI (1803). Paris, 1803. 8vo.

The richest collection of portraits after Van Dyck ever sold. It contained the 522 portraits by and after Van Dyck, from the collection of Mariette, which M. Guillaume Alibert increased to 908. — Szwykowski, p. 141.

AMANN. Sammlung von Kupferstichen, Radirungen, etc., aus dem Nachlasse Herrn J. J. Amann's, vormaligen Rathsherrn in Schaffhausen. 3 Abth. Leipzig, 1840-41. 8vo.

Sold at Leipzig in 1840-41.

AMSLER AND RUTHARDT. Lager-Catalog I. Verzeichniss von Kupferstichen der berühmtesten neueren Meister . . . . in trefflichen Abdrücken vor der Schrift, aus dem Lager von Amsler und Ruthardt, Kunsthandlung in Berlin. Mit beigesetzer Preisen. Berlin, 1864. 8vo.

APELL. Verzeichniss der von Herrn Aloys Apell in Dresden gesammelten Kupferstiche von Wenzel Hollar. Dresden, Mai, 1857. Versteigert in Leipzig 26. October, 1857, mit Kupferstichsammlung des Herrn Moritz Steinla, etc. Leipzig, 1857. 8vo.

Describes some "states" of prints by Hollar, not mentioned by Parthey.

ARCHINTO. Catalogue de la magnifique collection d'estampes anciennes et modernes, provenant du cabinet de M. le Comte Arch[into], de Milan. [Par M. CLÉMENT.] Vente 17, 18, et 19 mars, 1862. Paris, 1862. 8vo.

Contained fine proofs of modern engravings, an artist's proof of R. Morghen's Last Supper, Müller's Sistine Madonna in the same state, Nanteuil's portrait of Pomponne in the 1st state, etc.

[ARNDT.] Catalog einer . . . Sammlung von Kupferstichen und Radirungen der Deutschen und Italienischen Schule. Versteigert in Leipzig am 20ten October, 1847. [Abth. I.] Berlin, 1847. 8vo.

——— Catalog einer . . . Sammlung von Kupferstichen, Radirungen und Schwarzkunstblättern der Niederländischen, Französischen und Englischen Schule, etc. [Verfasst von Rud. WEIGEL.] Versteigert in Leipzig am 1sten Mai, 1848. [Abth. II.] Leipzig, 1848. 8vo.

[AROZARENA.] Catalogue de la très-belle collection d'estampes anciennes provenant du cabinet de M. D. G. de A. Par M. CLÉMENT. Vente le 11 mars. Paris, 1861. 8vo.

ARTARIA ET FONTAINE. Catalogue d'une collection d'estampes. Vente Août 1856. Leipzig, 1856. 8vo.

BAMMEVILLE. Catalogue of the very Important and Interesting Collection of Engravings by Ancient Masters, the Property of M. de Bammeville. Sold by S. Leigh Sotheby and John Wilkinson, the 8th of May, 1854. London, 1854. 8vo.

BARNARD, John. Catalogue of the Superb and Entire Collection of Prints, and Books of Prints of John Barnard, Esq. Sold by Mr. Th. Philipe. London, April, 1798. 8vo.

The catalogue of this fine collection is, unfortunately, too summary.

BAUSE. Catalog der . . . von . . . Joh. Friedr. Bause und dessen Enkel Georg Keil hinterlassenen . . . Sammlung von Kupferstichen, etc. . . . Versteigert in Leipzig [unter der Aufsicht von R. Weigel]. 1e Abth. Deutsche Schule, 5. Dec. 1859. — 2e Abth. Niederländische und Englische Schule, 24. Sept. 1860. — 3e Abth. Italienische und Französische Schule, 9. Sept., 1861. 3 Abth. Leipzig, 1859–61. 8vo.

BÖRNER. Catalog der von Johann Andreas Börner zu Nürnberg hinterlassenen Kupferstiche, Radirungen, etc. Versteigert in Leipzig [unter der Aufsicht von R. Weigel]. 1e Abth. Niederländische Schule, 22. Jan. 1863.—2e Abth.

BÖRNER, *continued.*
Französische und Englische Schule, 15. Juni, 1863. — 3e Abth. Italienische Schule, 20. Aug. 1863. — 4e Abth. Erste Hälfte. Deutsche Schule, Kupferstiche, 11. Jan. 1864. — 4e Abth. Zweite Hälfte. Deutsche Schule, Radirungen, Lithographien. 17. Oct. 1864. — 5e Abth. Originalzeichnungen . . . Bücher . . . 28. Nov. 1864. 6 Abth. Leipzig, 1862 – 64. 8vo.

BRANDES. Catalogue raisonné du Cabinet d'estampes de feu Monsieur Brandes, secrétaire intime de la Chancellerie royale d'Hannovre. Rédigé et publié par M. HUBER. 2 tom. Leipzig, 1793 – 94. Large 8vo.

The first, larger catalogue, with the measurements of the plates. . . . The sale of this collection took place at Leipzig April 18th and Oct. 3d, 1796, and there appeared a smaller catalogue of this collection, Leipzig, 1795, 2 vol. small 8vo.

BRISART. Catalogue de la magnifique et précieuse collection de livres, manuscrits dessins et estampes, formant le cabinet de M. Brisart. Vente à Gand le 10 décembre, 1849. Gand, 1849. 8vo.

[BUCKINGHAM, Duke of.] A Catalogue of a Valuable and Extensive Collection of Ancient and Modern Prints, the Property of a Nobleman of High Rank. Sold by Auction by Mr. Phillips, May, June, and July, 1834. 3 parts. London, 1834.

A magnificent collection; a great part of the collection Paignon-Dijonval went into it. It is a pity, that the careful and instructive description of the prints by M. Bénard was not reproduced in the catalogue, which is, like most English catalogues, too summary.

CAMESINA. Catalogue de l'intéressante collection d'estampes et de dessins du cabinet de feu M. Joseph de Camesina. 4 parties. Vente à Vienne en 1831 – 33. Small 4to.

CICOGNARA. Le premier siècle de la chalcographie, ou catalogue raisonné des estampes du cabinet du comte Léopold Cicognara. Par Alexandre ZANETTI. Venise, 1837. 8vo.

The collection was sold by auction, and the following is the catalogue of the sale: —

——— Catalogue de la riche collection d'estampes du comte Cicognara, par A. ZANETTI. Vente à Vienne le 4 novembre, 1839. 8vo.

[COLNAGHI.] Catalogue of a very Valuable Collection of Ancient and Modern Engravings, Fine Ancient Drawings, etc., the Property of an Eminent Firm. Sold by Sotheby, Wilkinson, and Hodge, May 15th, 1865. London, 1865. 8vo.

DEBOIS. Catalogue raisonné de la rare et précieuse collection d'estampes, réunie par le soin de M. F[rançois] Debois. Rédigé par P. DEFER. Paris, 1843. 8vo.

A well-prepared catalogue of a most important collection.

"Il faut joindre à ce catalogue, pour avoir la description complète des estampes

DEBOIS, *continued.*

possédées par M. Debois, trois ordres de vacation dans lesquels se trouvent mentionnées plusieurs planches omises dans le catalogue raisonné. — " Duplessis, *Essai de bibliographie*, Paris, 1862, No. 583.

——— Ordre de vacation de la première partie de la vente aux enchères de la rare et précieuse collection d'estampes de M. F. Debois, le 23 avril 1844. — Deuxième partie, le 26 nov., 1844. — Troisième et dernière partie, le 21 avril, 1845. 8vo.

DEFER, P. Catalogue général des ventes publiques de tableaux et estampes depuis 1737 jusqu'à nos jours. Paris, 1863, *et seqq.*

Appears in numbers.

DELBECQ. Alliance des arts. Catalogue des estampes anciennes formant la collection de M. Delbecq, de Gand, rédigé par DELANDE et THORÉ. Vente à Paris, les 18 février, 11 mars et 1 avril, 1845. 3 parties. Paris, 1845. 8vo.

The collection contained, among others, very rare old Netherlandish prints.

DELESSERT. Catalogue raisonné d'une belle collection d'estampes d'anciens graveurs italiens, allemands, flamands et hollandais, aux XVe, XVIe, et XVIIe siècles, qui composaient le cabinet de M. B[enjamin] D[elessert]. Par P. DEFER. Vente 29 mars, 1852. Paris, 1852. 8vo.

DENON. Description des objets d'art qui composent le cabinet de M. le baron V. Denon. Estampes et ouvrages à figures, par DUCHESNE ainé. Paris, 1826. 8vo.

DREUX, Henri. Catalogue de belles estampes anciennes et modernes de célèbres graveurs, la plupart avant la lettre ou de remarque, provenant du cabinet de M. H. D. Vente le 15 mars. Paris, 1858. 8vo.

——— Catalogue d'une belle collection d'estampes anciennes, provenant du cabinet de M. H. D. Vente le 8 avril. Paris, 1861. 8vo.

DRUGULIN. Catalogue of the Entire Collection of Engravings, the Property of Mr. William Drugulin [of Leipzig]. Sold at London, 11th June, 1866, by Messrs. Sotheby, Wilkinson, and Hodge. London, 1866. 8vo.

——— Allgemeiner Portrait-Katalog. Leipzig, 1860. 8vo.

DURAND, Edme. Catalogue des estampes du cabinet de M. E. Durand. Paris, 1819. 8vo.

——— Catalogue de la précieuse collection d'estampes, recueillie par M. E. D. Rédigé par N. BÉNARD, fils. Vente à Paris le 19 mars, 1821. Paris, 1821. 8vo.

The sale of this very important collection, which contained a Pax by Maso Finiguerra, was discontinued, because the prices obtained were not satisfactory. The rest was otherwise disposed of. The impression of the Pax by Finiguerra is now

DURAND, *continued.*
in Vienna, in the collection of Prince Albert of Saxe-Teschen.—Defer, *Catalogue général.*

——— Catalogue d'une collection d'estampes anciennes, de livres sur les arts, de gouaches et dessins, provenant du cabinet de feu M. E. Durand. Par PIERRI-BÉNARD. Vente le 25 janvier. Paris, 1836, 8vo.

DURRANT. Catalogue of the very Choice Collection of Engravings by Hollar and Faithorne, formed by the Late Colonel Durrant. Sold by Messrs. S. Leigh Sotheby & John Wilkinson, May 29th. London, 1856. 8vo.

EINSIEDEL. Catalogue raisonné des estampes du cabinet de feu Mad. la Comtesse d'Einsiedel de Reibersdorf. Par J. G. A. FRENZEL. 2 tom. Dresde, 1833-34. 8vo.

ESDAILE. A Catalogue of Engravings, Books of Prints, &c., of William Esdaile. Sold at London, 19th March, 1838. London, 1838. 8vo.

EVANS. The Fine Art Circular and Print Collector's Manual. A. E. Evans & Sons. London, 1854-56. 8vo.

A sale catalogue.

FRANCK. Catalogue de la très-belle et précieuse collection de portraits anciens et modernes de M. le chevalier Jacq. de Franck. Vente à Vienne en février, avril et juin, 1836. 3 parties. Vienne. 1836. 8vo.

FRIES. Catalogus der uitmuntende en beroemde verzameling van prenten, boeken en prentwerken . . . des Heeren Moritz grave von Fries te Weenen. 2 delen. Amsterdam, 1824. 8vo.

——— Catalogue du reste de la collection d'estampes de M. le comte Maurice de Fries, appartenant à la masse de Fries et Co. Vente en 1828. 3 parties. Vienne, 1827. 4to.

FRIESEN. Verzeichniss der Kunstsammlung des verstorbenen Freiherrn H. A. von Friesen [angefertigt von J. G. A. FRENZEL]. Versteigert in Dresden, den 12. Juli, 1847. Dresden, 1847. 8vo.

GAWET. Catalogue raisonné des estampes du cabinet de feu M. le Duc d'Ursel [acheté par M. Gawet a Vienne]. Par P. M. BÉNARD. Paris, 1806. 8vo.

GERSTÄCKER. Catalog der von Herrn Theodor Gerstäcker, Inhaber der Kunsthandlung Schenk und Gerstäcker zu Berlin, hinterlassenen Kupferstichen, Radirungen, etc. Versteigert in Leipzig [unter R. Weigel's Aufsicht] den 12. Januar und 2. März, 1857. 2 Abth. Leipzig, 1856. 8vo.

GODDARD. Catalogue of the very Important and exceedingly Choice Collection of Ancient and Modern Engravings of the Rev. Edward H. Æ. Goddard, sold March, 1867, by Messrs. Sotheby, Wilkinson, and Hodge. London, 1867. 8vo.

A small collection, but containing some fine prints.

[HARRACH.] Catalogue d'une magnifique collection d'estampes . . . provenant du cabinet de M. le comte ***, de Vienne. [Par M. CLÉMENT.] Vente le 24 février, 1867. Paris. 8vo.

HILLIG. Verzeichniss der Kupferstichsammlung des Dr. C. H. Hillig. [Verfasst von Rudolph WEIGEL.] Versteigert in Leipzig 28. April, 1845. Leipzig, 1845. 8vo.

[HIPPISLEY.] Catalogue of a very Valuable Collection of Engravings, all in the Finest Condition, the Modern Portion of the Collection of a Distinguished Amateur [Sir Joseph Hippisley]. Sold by Auction by Messrs. Christie and Manson, June 3, 1857. London, 1857. 8vo.

A very small collection, only 238 numbers, but of fine prints, among others a set of artist's proofs of Toschi's engravings of Correggio's frescos.

HOHWIESNER. Catalogue raisonné de la rare et précieuse collection d'estampes anciennes et modernes de toutes les écoles etc. de feu Mr Clémence Aloys Hohwiesner, banquier. Par C. E. G. PRESTEL. Vente à Francfort s. M. au mois de Septembre, 1819. 2 vol. Francfort s. M. 1819. 12mo.

HOLLOWAY AND SON. A Catalogue of Choice Engravings and Etchings, on Sale by Holloway and Son. I. London, 1865. 8vo.

HÖSEL. Verzeichniss der kleinen aber vortrefflichen Sammlung von Kupferstichen, Radirungen etc. des verstorbenen Herrn Heinr. Aug. Hösel. [Von Rudolph WEIGEL.] Versteigert in Leipzig den 23. September, 1844. Leipzig, 1844. 8vo.

JOHNSON. Catalogue of the Small but most Valuable Collection of Engravings, collected by the Late M. J. J. Johnson, Esq., Radcliffe Observer, Oxford. Sold by S. Leigh Sotheby and John Wilkinson, 18th April, 1860. London, 1860. 8vo.

A very small collection of uncommonly fine prints in artist's proofs, etc.

JOSI. Catalogus van prenten teekeningen prent- en boekwerken van het gerenomeerd kunstmagazyn van den Heere C. Josi. Verkocht . . . den 20sten April, 1818, te Amsterdam. Amsterdam, 1818. 8vo.

——— A Catalogue of the Collection of Engravings, Etchings, and Original Drawings, and Books of Prints, of Christian Josi, Esq., deceased. Sold by Auction [March 18, 30, 1829]. 2 parts. London, 1829. 8vo.

LA MOTTE FOUQUET. Catalogue raisonné de la rare et précieuse collection d'estampes, composant le cabinet de M. H. F. de La Motte Fouquet. [Par Hermann WEBER.] Vente à Cologne le 21 Oct. 1847. Cologne, 1847. 8vo.

Interesting, among other things, for some states of Wille's engravings not described by Le Blanc.

LASALLE. Catalogue de la collection d'estampes anciennes provenant du cabinet de M. H[is] de L[asalle]. Par M. DEFER. Vente à Paris le 21 avril, 1856. Paris, 1856. 8vo.

LEHRS. Verzeichniss der von Herrn Philipp Lehrs in Berlin hinterlassenen ausgezeichneten Sammlung von Kupferstichen, meist in Remarque- und avant-la-lettre-Drücken. Versteigert [unter der Verantwortlichkeit von Amsler und Ruthardt] in Berlin den 7ten Mai 1866. Berlin, 1866. 8vo.

LOGETTE. Catalogue raisonné de la rare et précieuse collection d'estampes de feu M. Logette. Par REGNAULT-DELALANDE. Vente à Paris le 6 mai 1817. Paris, 1817. 8vo.

A small collection of highly interesting prints.

LLOYD. A Catalogue of a Collection of Prints, Paintings, Manuscripts, Books, etc. of Thomas Lloyd, Esq., comprising British Portraits, etc., with the Chef-d'œuvres and Rarest Specimens of Engraving from the Earliest Period of Chalcography. Sold by Auction by Mr. Sotheby 6th of December, 1820. London, 1820. 8vo.

——— A Catalogue of the Extensive, Valuable, and highly Interesting Collection of Prints, the Property of Thomas Lloyd, Esq., containing Numerous Specimens of Great Rarity in the Italian, German, Flemish, French, and English Schools, from the Earliest Period of the Art of Engraving; many of them unknown to Bartsch, and probably Unique. Sold by Auction by Mr. George Jones, 1st July, 1825. [London,] 1825. 4to.

The second is the more important collection.

MABERLY. Catalogue of the Entire and very Choice Collection of Engravings, the Property of Joseph Maberly, Esq. Sold by S. Leigh Sotheby and John Wilkinson, 26th of May, 1851. London, 1851. 8vo.

Joseph Maberly was the author of the *Print Collector*, and his collection was exceedingly choice.

MACREADY. Catalogue of a Valuable Collection of Engravings . . . collected by the Tragedian William Charles Macready, Esq. Sold March, 1868, by Sotheby, Wilkinson, & Hodge. London, 1868. 8vo.

A very small collection of fine modern prints.

MALASPINA DI SANNAZARO. Catalogo di una raccolta di stampe antiche compilato dallo stesso possessore, marchese Malaspina di Sannazaro. 5 vol. Milano, 1824. 8vo.

MARMOL. Catalogue de la plus précieuse collection d'estampes de P. P. Rubens et d'A. van Dyck qui ait jamais existé, recueillie par messire del Marmol [de Bruxelles]. Bruxelles, 1794. 8vo.

Compare with this the catalogue of Alibert.

MARSHALL. Catalogue of the Entire and very Choice Collection of Engravings, the Property of Julian Marshall, Esq. Sold at Auction by Sotheby, Wilkinson, and Hodge on the 30th of June, 1864, and eleven following days. London, 1864. Roy. 8vo.

This was a very important collection, and the catalogue is prepared with great care.

[MEYER, *in Hildburghausen.*] Catalog der Kupferstichsammlung eines der grössten Kunstsammlers Deutschlands. Versteigert Januar bis Juni 1858, bei R. Weigel in Leipzig. 4 Abth. Leipzig, 1858. 8vo.

OTTLEY. The Ottley Collection of Prints. Catalogue of the very Valuable and Extensive Collection of Engravings the Property of the late William Young Ottley Esq., F. A. S., comprising most Interesting Specimens of the Works of the Early Italian and German Masters, etc. Sold by Auction by Mr. Leigh Sotheby, 17th of May, 1837. — Part II., sold 10th of July, 1837. London, 1837. 8vo.

A very important collection.

OTTO. Catalog der Otto'schen Kupferstichsammlung [verfasst] von Rudolph WEIGEL. 1e Abth. Deutsche und Englische Schulen. Versteigert 29. Sept. 1851. — 2e Abth. Italienische und Französische Schulen. Versteigert 1. März 1852. — 3e Abth. Holländische und Flamländische Schulen. Versteigert 17. Mai 1852. 3 Bde. Leipzig, 1851–52. 8vo.

A renowned collection, described by Duchesne and others.

DE PAAR. Catalogue of the Celebrated Collection of Valuable Engravings formed during the Last Century by the Prince de Paar of Vienna, — a Series of the Italian, German, Flemish, Dutch, French, and English Schools of the XVth, XVIth, XVIIth, and XVIIIth Centuries. Sold in London 13th July, 1854. London, 1854. 8vo.

PAIGNON-DIJONVAL. Cabinet de M. Paignon-Dijonval. État détaillé et raisonné des dessins et estampes dont il est composé. Rédigé par M. BÉNARD. Paris, 1810. 4to.

A large and important collection.

In 1816 it was bought by Samuel Woodburn, and a great part of the engravings passed into the collection of the Duke of Buckingham, the drawings into that of Sir Thomas Lawrence. The catalogue is so well prepared that it is a valuable book of reference.

PETZOLD. Verzeichniss einer Sammlung von Kupferstichen, Radirungen, etc. [des Dr. Benj. Petzold in Wien. Angefertigt von J. G. A. FRENZEL.] Versteigert zu Dresden den 20. Nov. 1848, und den 21. Mai 1849. Dresden, 1848–49. 8vo.

Earlier catalogues, arranged by Sigism. Beermann, of 9 different sales of prints, the

Petzold, *continued.*
property of Dr. Petzold, and sold at Vienna, appeared at the latter place from 1835 to 1845.

Poggi. Catalogue raisonné des estampes anciennes, qui composaient la collection de M. de Poggi. Par P. Defer. Paris, 1836. 8vo.

Albrecht Dürer, Rembrandt, etc.

Potocki. Catalogue d'une collection nombreuse d'estampes anciennes, provenant du cabinet de M. le comte V[incent] P[otocki]. Par Regnault-Delalande. Vente à Paris le 9 févr. 1820. Paris, 1820. 8vo.

Important engravings after Rubens.

Quandt, Johann Gottlob von. Verzeichniss meiner Kupferstichsammlung, als Leitfaden zur Geschichte der Kupferstecherkunst und Malerei. Leipzig, 1853. Large 8vo.

Only 220 copies were printed.

——— Catalog der vortrefflichen Kupferstichsammlung und Kunst-Bibliothek des verstorbenen Herrn Johann Gottlob von Quandt. [Von Rudolph Weigel.] Versteigert in Leipzig, 12. Juni, 1860. Leipzig, 1860. 8vo.

Révil. Catalogue d'une belle et rare collection d'objets d'art, antiquités, tableaux et dessins, estampes anciennes et modernes, et livres sur les arts, composant le cabinet de feu M. N. Révil. Vente 24 févr. 1845. Paris, 1845. 8vo.

Besides this catalogue of Révil's, to which reference is made in our catalogue, there appeared:—

——— Catalogue de la collection d'estampes anciennes et modernes recueillies par M. Révil. Rédigé par Pierri-Bénard. Paris, 1830. 8vo.

——— Catalogue raisonné de la rare et précieuse collection d'estampes, chefs-d'œuvre de la gravure du 15e au 19e siècle, provenant du cabinet de M. R[évil]. Par P. Defer. Vente 26 mars 1838. Paris, 1838. 8vo.

Another catalogue of an auction sale of engravings of M. Révil, also by P. Defer, is of the year 1839.

Rigal. Catalogue raisonné des estampes du cabinet de M. le comte Rigal. Par Regnault-Delalande. Paris, 1817. 8vo.

An important collection, and so well described that the catalogue continues to be a work of reference.

Robert-Dumesnil, A. P. F. Catalogue des estampes de Rembrandt, F. Bol, J. Livens, J. G. van Vliet, Rodermont et leurs imitateurs, colligées par M. A. P. F. Robert-Dumesnil. Vente à Londres le 12 avril 1386. [Paris, 1835.] 8vo.

Only 120 copies issued.

——— Catalogue des estampes des écoles allemande, flamande, hollandaise et

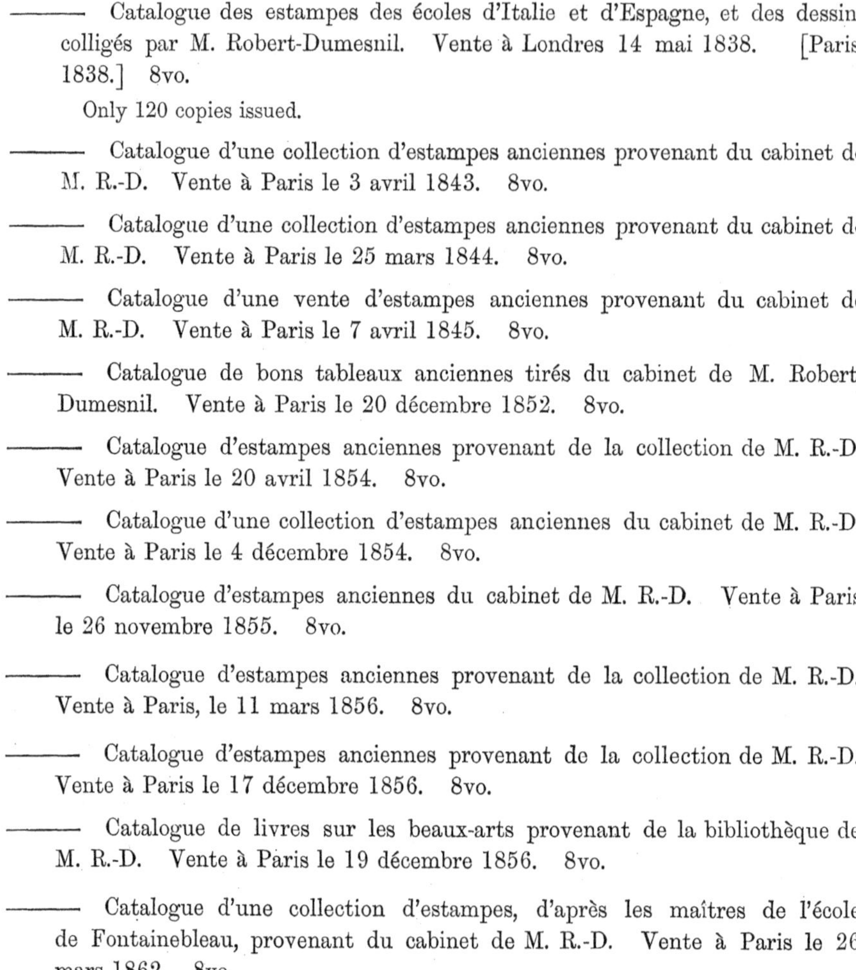

ROBERT-DUMESNIL, *continued.*
anglaise colligées par M. Robert-Dumesnil. Vente à Londres le 1er mai, 1837. 8vo. [Paris, 1837.] 8vo.

Only 120 copies issued.

——— Catalogue des estampes des écoles d'Italie et d'Espagne, et des dessins colligés par M. Robert-Dumesnil. Vente à Londres 14 mai 1838. [Paris, 1838.] 8vo.

Only 120 copies issued.

——— Catalogue d'une collection d'estampes anciennes provenant du cabinet de M. R.-D. Vente à Paris le 3 avril 1843. 8vo.

——— Catalogue d'une collection d'estampes anciennes provenant du cabinet de M. R.-D. Vente à Paris le 25 mars 1844. 8vo.

——— Catalogue d'une vente d'estampes anciennes provenant du cabinet de M. R.-D. Vente à Paris le 7 avril 1845. 8vo.

——— Catalogue de bons tableaux anciennes tirés du cabinet de M. Robert-Dumesnil. Vente à Paris le 20 décembre 1852. 8vo.

——— Catalogue d'estampes anciennes provenant de la collection de M. R.-D. Vente à Paris le 20 avril 1854. 8vo.

——— Catalogue d'une collection d'estampes anciennes du cabinet de M. R.-D. Vente à Paris le 4 décembre 1854. 8vo.

——— Catalogue d'estampes anciennes du cabinet de M. R.-D. Vente à Paris le 26 novembre 1855. 8vo.

——— Catalogue d'estampes anciennes provenant de la collection de M. R.-D. Vente à Paris, le 11 mars 1856. 8vo.

——— Catalogue d'estampes anciennes provenant de la collection de M. R.-D. Vente à Paris le 17 décembre 1856. 8vo.

——— Catalogue de livres sur les beaux-arts provenant de la bibliothèque de M. R.-D. Vente à Paris le 19 décembre 1856. 8vo.

——— Catalogue d'une collection d'estampes, d'après les maîtres de l'école de Fontainebleau, provenant du cabinet de M. R.-D. Vente à Paris le 26 mars 1862. 8vo.

ROST. Kupferstich-Kabinet des verstorbenen C. Chr. H. Rost, berühmten Kunsthändler in Leipzig. Leipzig, 1800. 8vo.

The 20th of Rost's sales.

RUMOHR. Die Kunstsammlung des Freiherrn C. F. L. von Rumohr, beschrieben von J. G. A. FRENZEL. Versteigerung zu Dresden den 19. October. Lübeck, 1846. 8vo.

SCHLETTER. Catalog der von Herrn Heinrich Schletter hinterlassenen Sammlung von Prachtblättern der neueren Kupferstichkunst, versteigert in Leipzig den 26. März 1855. 8vo.

A very small collection containing some fine proofs.

SCHWARZENBERG. Kunstsammlung des Fürsten Karl von Schwarzenberg. [Kupferstiche, Zeichnungen, etc. Verfasst von Rudolph WEIGEL.] Leipzig, 1826. 8vo.

SCITIVAUX, Charles. Catalogue d'un beau choix d'estampes anciennes et modernes, recueils sur la peinture, l'antique, etc., du cabinet de M. Ch. Scitivaux. REGNAULT-DELALANDE, expert. Vente le 11 mai. Paris, 1819. 8vo.

After the death of M. Scitivaux there was a very choice collection of rare prints left, which his heirs sold, about 1843, to M. Villedieu, a print-dealer, for 36,000*fr.*, part of which went into the celebrated collection of F. Debois.

SILVESTRE. Catalogue raisonné d'objets d'art du cabinet de feu M. de Silvestre. Par F. L. REGNAULT-DELALANDE. Vente 28 février, 1811. Paris, 1810. 8vo.

——— Catalogue d'une collection de tableaux, dessins anciens, estampes etc., qui composaient le cabinet de M. le baron Silvestre. Vente à Paris, le 4 décembre 1851. Paris, 1851. 8vo.

SMITH, George. Catalogue of a most Superb and Valuable Collection of Engravings and Etchings, in the Finest possible Condition, mostly Proofs, etc., formed by George Smith, Esq. Sold by Auction by S. Leigh Sotheby and John Wilkinson, 4th March, 1861, and seven following days. London, 1861. 8vo.

A very rich collection containing a great many proofs, and not so insufficiently described as many others.

STERNBERG. Sammlung der Kupferstiche und Handzeichnungen des weiland Grafen Franz von Sternberg-Manderscheid, verfasst von J. G. A. FRENZEL. I. Italienische Schulen, versteigert in Dresden den 5. Sept. 1836.— II. Deutsche Schulen, versteigert in Dresden den 1. Oct. 1838.— III. Niederländische Schulen, versteigert in Dresden den 4. Mai 1840.— IV. Französische und Englische Schule; und Portraits, versteigert in Dresden den 24. Oct. 1842. V. Handzeichnungen, und Supplemente zu den Stichen aller Schulen, versteigert in Dresden den 10. Nov. 1845. 5 Bde. Dresden, 1836–45. 8vo.

SYKES. A Catalogue of the highly Valuable Collection of Prints, the Property of the Late Sir Mark Masterman Sykes, Bart. [By S. WOODBURN and W. Y. OTTLEY.] 5 parts. London, 1824. 4to.

One of the most important sales of engravings that ever occurred.

THIEME. Catalog der sehr vorzüglichen Kupferstich-Sammlung des Herrn H.

THIEME, *continued.*

Thieme. Versteigert im R. Weigel'schen Kunst-Auctions-Lokal in Leipzig den 28. Januar 1867. Leipzig, 1866. 8vo.

Interesting as containing a very rare impression of an artist's proof of Müller's Sistine Madonna. See p. 258 of the Catalogue of Engravers.

[THOREL.] Catalogue raisonné d'estampes du cabinet de M. Th. . . . Par DEFER. Vente à Paris le 5 décembre 1853. 8vo.

Contained some very fine prints from the Debois and other collections.

VALOIS. Catalogue raisonné d'une précieuse collection d'estampes, du cabinet de feu M. Charles de Valois. Par F. L. REGNAULT. Vente le 14 déc. 1801. Paris, 1801. 8vo.

VANDEN ZANDE. Catalogue d'une riche collection d'estampes et de dessins, composant le cabinet de feu M. Vanden Zande. Rédigé par F. GUICHARDOT. Vente à Paris le 30 avril 1855. Paris, 1855. Large 8vo.

A very carefully digested catalogue.

VERSTOLK. Catalogue du célèbre cabinet des gravures de feu S. E. M. J. Gisbert baron Verstolk de Soelen. Vente à Amsterdam les 28 juin et 26 octobre 1847, et 31 mars 1851. 3 parties. Amsterdam, 1847 – 51. 8vo.

A very rich and very important collection, the catalogue of which is highly prized. The collection of Drawings of Baron Verstolk was sold at Amsterdam the 22d of March, 1847.

VISCHER. Catalogue des livres d'heures, dessins et estampes, formant le cabinet de feu M. Pierre Vischer de Bâle. Rédigé par Ch. LE BLANC. Vente à Paris 19 avril 1852. Paris, 1852. 8vo.

A very rich collection. It contained some fine specimens of the earliest prints — but, above all, a very extensive collection of Holbein's woodcuts in the earliest state, and fine impressions. It is to be regretted that the catalogue does not specify them sufficiently. Under No. 979, "Holbein, Son Œuvre," it gives only eight lines of description, saying at the end, "272 pièces."

WEBER. Catalogue de la superbe collection d'estampes laissée par feu M. Hermann Weber à Bonn. 1re partie, École allemande, italienne, francaise et néerlandaise. Vente le 17 sept. 1855. — 2e partie, Œuvre de Rembrandt, et de son école. Vente le 28 avril 1856. 2 parties. Leipzig, 1855 – 56, chez Rud. Weigel. 8vo.

WEIGEL, Rudolph. Kunst-Catalog. 1ste bis 35ste Abtheilung. 5 Bände, mit General-Register. Leipzig, 1838 – 67. 8vo.

WELLESLEY. Catalogue of the Choice and Valuable Collection of Engravings the Property of the Rev. H. Wellesley, D. D., Principal of New Inn Hall, Oxford. Sold by Auction by S. Leigh Sotheby and John Wilkinson. Part First – Third. 29th June, 1858; 2d June, 1860; 9th July, 1861. London, 1858 – 61. 8vo.

A really choice collection of rare early Italian prints.

[Wilcox.] Catalogue of a Magnificent Assemblage of Ancient and Modern Engravings, — the Property of a well-known Collector. Sold by S. Leigh Sotheby and John Wilkinson, the 27th of May, 1856. London, 1856. 8vo.

A small collection of only 333 numbers, but containing some very fine proofs, among others a set of Toschi's engravings of Correggio's frescos in artist's proofs.

[Wilson, Thomas.] A *Catalogue raisonné* of the Select Collection of Engravings of an Amateur [described by the owner]. London, 1828. 4to.

Winckler. Catalogue raisonné du cabinet d'estampes de M. Winckler, banquier à Leipzig. Par M. Huber. 5 tomes en 8 parties. Leipzig, 1805 – 10. 8vo.

One of the catalogues that serve as standard works of reference.

CATALOGUE

OF

THE ENGRAVERS.

CATALOGUE

OF

THE ENGRAVERS.

A.

ACQUA, CRISTOFANO DELL', designer and engraver, born at Vicenza about 1750.

MAGNARONI *del.* The Amphitheatre of Verona.

AGOSTINO VENEZIANO (*family name* DE' MUSI), designer and engraver, was born at Florence about 1490, and died about 1540, probably at Rome, where he went from Florence in 1516, and became, together with Marco da Ravenna, Marc-Antonio's principal pupil and assistant. Bartsch, XIV.

RAPHAEL *del.* The Israelites gathering the Manna. B. 8.
1st state, before address.

RAPHAEL *del.* The Death of Ananias. B. 42.
1st state, before address.

FRANCESCO FRANCIA *del.?* Holy Family, with two Angels. B. 50.
The design is attributed to Francesco Francia; according to Passavant (*Rafael von Urbino,* I. p. 586), however, it is by a pupil of Raphael.
Late impression, with Antonio Salamanca's address.

RAPHAEL *del.* Hercules and Antæus. B. 347.
Very early and powerful impression.

MICHEL-ANGELO *del.* Les Grimpeurs, Soldiers bathing in the Arno. B. 423.
The principal part of the Cartoon of Pisa.
2d state, with the year MDXXIIII. (*instead of* MDXXIII.), *which, in fine impressions like this, is, according to Bartsch, not inferior to the 1st state.*
Purchased for £7 7*s.*

RAPHAEL *del.* Lo Stregozzo.* A Witch riding on a Skeleton. B. 426.
2d state, with A. V. *on the horn.*
The first impressions are before these or any letters. A copy in God-

* According to Prof. Andreas Müller (*Kunstblatt,* 1858), after Timoteo delle Vite.

AGOSTINO VENEZIANO, *continued.*

dard's collection, No. 447, "in the most perfect condition, and the finest impression known," sold for £66.

A picture by Spagnoletto, taken from this engraving and of the same size, is in the collection of the Duke of Wellington, at Apsley House. Waagen, *Treasures*, II. p. 276.

RAPHAEL *del.?* Woman with a Vase. B. 474.

The drawing for this piece is attributed to Raphael.

Fine early impression.

RAPHAEL *del.* Man with the Base of a Column. B. 477.

Very early impression.

From Otto's collection.

AGRICOLA, CARL, miniature painter, etcher, and engraver, was born at Sickingen in Baden, in 1779. After 1796 he resided at Vienna.

RAPHAEL *pinx.* Madonna called The Virgin in the Meadow, "Die Jungfrau im Grünen."

See Passavant, II. No. 37, and III. p. 91. The picture is in the Vienna Gallery. — Engraved in 1812.

The 1st proof is before letters, with only the artists' names; 2d proof, *lettres grises.*

PARMEGIANO *pinx.* Holy Family.

Engraved in 1817, while in the collection of Count Fries. Afterwards in the collections of Baron Sternberg and Sir Thomas Lawrence.

2d state, with Sprenger's address.

The 1st state is before address.

HOLBEIN *pinx.* Virgin and Child.

In 8vo. The plate has only the names of the artists; no title was ever engraved.

DOMENICHINO *pinx.* Diana and Callisto.

Engraved in 1811.

Proof before letters, with only the names of the artists.

DOMENICHINO *pinx.* The same.

First etching of the plate, which has likewise the artists' names.

ALDEGREVER, HEINRICH, painter and engraver, born at Paderborn in 1502, died at Soest in 1562. Pupil of Albrecht Dürer. Bartsch, VIII.

The Judgment of Solomon. B. 29.

Susanna Surprised. B. 30.

The Two Elders Accused. B. 31.

The Crucifixion. B. 49.

ALDEGREVER, HEINRICH, *continued.*

Sophonisba. B. 62.

Fortuna. B. 106.

P. Aldegrever's own Portrait, when 28 years of age. B. 188.

ALIAMET, JEAN JACQUES, engraver, born at Abbeville in 1728, died at Paris in 1788. A pupil of Philippe Le Bas.

TENIERS *pinx.* Arrivée au Sabat.

A witch scene. Engraved from the collection of Count de Vence.

AERT VAN DER NEER *pinx.* Vue de Boom sur le Rupel.

A landscape with moonlight. Engraved from the collection of Count de Vence.

BERGHEM *pinx.* Shepherds and Cattle fording a Stream.

See Smith, *Catalogue raisonné*, No. 318. The picture is in the Dresden Gallery. Engraved for *Recueil d'estampes de la Galerie de Dresde*, II. No. 50.

ALIAMET, FRANÇOIS, engraver, younger brother of Jacques and an inferior artist, born at Abbeville in 1734, died in 1787. He studied in Paris under Garet and Lisle, and in London under Sir Robert Strange.

ANNIBALE CARACCI *pinx.* The Adoration of the Shepherds (one blowing a tin trumpet).

"From the original picture in New College Chapel, Oxford, published by J. Boydell."

ALLAIS, ALEXANDRE, engraver, born at Paris in 1792, a pupil of R. U. Massard and Fosseyeux.

RIOULT *pinx.* Phrosine et Mélidore.

Open letter proof.

ALTDORFER, ALBRECHT, painter and engraver, born at Altdorf in Bavaria in 1488, died at Ratisbon in 1538. A pupil of Albrecht Dürer. Bartsch, VIII.

Christ driving the Money-changers from the Temple. B. 6.

With the name C. Meister on the back of the print.

The Virgin and Child on a Throne, surrounded by Angels. B. 13.

From the collection of F. Geissler, and with his name on the back.

The Virgin and Child, with St. Anne preparing the Cradle. B. 14.

With the stamp of Ackermann's collection.

St. Christopher. B. 19.

A Nun in the colonnaded Court of a Cloister. B. 24.

From Otto's collection.

AMETLLÉR, BLAS, pupil of Carmona, engraved at Madrid at the close of the last and the beginning of the present century.

SPAGNOLETTO *pinx.* St. Gregory performing a Miracle, probably that of the Brandeum.

Very incorrectly called "The Mass of St. Gregory," in which miracle the Saviour appeared with the instruments of his torture. The picture is in the Madrid Gallery. Engraved for the *Coleccion de las estampas de los cuadros ... pertenecientes al Rey de España.*

Proofs are before letters, with only the names of the artists.

VELAZQUEZ *pinx.* The Water-carrier of Seville.

The picture is now in the collection of the Duke of Wellington at Apsley House, to whom it was presented by King Ferdinand VII. of Spain.

Proof, with only the names of the artists.

Engraved for the *Coleccion de las estampas de los cuadros ... pertenecientes al Rey de España.*

AMLING, CARL GUSTAV VON, designer and engraver, born at Nuremberg in 1651, died at Munich in 1701. A pupil of François de Poilly.

P. Maximilian Emanuel, Duke of Bavaria, in his younger years.

Medallion, held by two angels, who support also a ducal crown. A label above has the inscription: *Date Caesari quae sunt Caesaris, et Deo quae sunt Dei.* The following inscription is below: *Justitia et Pax osculatae sunt.* Not mentioned by Le Blanc.

From Otto's collection, I. No. 1041.

P. Henrietta Maria Adelaide, Duchess of Bavaria.

Le Blanc, No. 17.

P. CANDIDO (Pieter de Witte) *pinx.* The Four Seasons.

Four plates: "Ver," "Aestas," "Autumnus," "Hiems." Designs of tapestry in the palace of Munich. Defer, *Catalogue générale.*

AMSLER, SAMUEL, engraver, born at Schinznach in Switzerland in 1793, died at Munich in 1856. He was a pupil of Oberkogler and H. Lips, and of C. E. C. Hess; but formed his style by the study of Dürer and Marc-Antonio.

RAPHAEL *pinx.* The Entombment.

Engraved in 1832, with the predella. Passavant, II. 54. The picture is in the Borghese Gallery in Rome, but without the predella representing the three Christian Virtues, Faith, Hope, and Charity, which is now in the gallery of the Vatican. The predella is separately engraved by Desnoyers. *See* DESNOYERS.

Impression with the engraver's address, and before the cross on the host over the chalice held by Faith, also with the white stamp of the engraver's initials.

AMSLER, SAMUEL, *continued.*

Artist's proofs are before the name of the engraver, with merely the monogram of his initials and the year 1831, and the name Felsing as printer, in the middle below. No inscription was ever put on the plate.

There exist also a very few, probably not more than six, impressions of the plate, which were taken before the predella was added by the artist to fill the lower margin of the plate, because the engraving appeared too square. They are otherwise entirely finished.

The plate became the property of the Bibliographic Institution in Hildburghausen, and the later impressions have its address as well as the cross on the host.

RAPHAEL *pinx.* The Holy Family of the House of Canigiani.

See Passavant, II. 52. The picture is in the Munich Gallery. Engraved in 1836.

Proof, with open letters.

This is the earliest state of the plate. We have found mention of one artist's proof before letters, but Mr. Hermann Amsler, the son of the artist, states that this must have been an impression from the unfinished plate.

RAPHAEL *pinx.* Madonna Staffa.

See Passavant, II. 18. The picture is in the possession of the Count Connestabile della Staffa in Perugia. Engraved in 1821.

Proof, with the coat of arms, and the dedication in traced open uncial letters, with the white stamp of the engraver's initials.

OVERBECK *pinx.* The Triumph of Religion in the Arts.

The original is in Städel's Museum in Frankfort. Engraved in outline.

BEGAS *pinx.* **P.** Thorwaldsen.

With the engraver's autograph dedication to Baron Rumohr.

ANDERLONI, FAUSTINO, engraver, born in the province of Brescia about 1766. He lived in Pavia, and his last work appeared about 1830.

RAPHAEL *pinx.* The Virgin and Child, in the Gallery of Naples.

Repetition, or rather old copy, of the Bridgewater Madonna. Passavant, II. 97. a.

Open letter proof.

RAPHAEL *pinx.* The same.

Rare artist's proof, before any letters.

The state between this and the preceding is before letters, with merely the names of the artists.

CORREGGIO *pinx.* Magdalen, sleeping, with a Cross.

Artist's proof, before any letters, and before the border.

There are four kinds of proofs of this plate, viz. : — I. Before any letters

ANDERLONI, FAUSTINO, *continued.*

and before the border, like ours. II. Before letters (*Dilexit multum*), but with the artists' names. III. Open letter proof, before the dedication. IV. Open letter, with dedication. *See* Messrs. Holloway and Son's sale *Catalogue*, London, 1865, I. Nos. 25 – 28.

SASSOFERRATO *pinx.* Mater Amabilis.

The picture is in the Gallery of the Uffizj in Florence.

Artist's proof. In the middle, below, only slightly traced with the needle: " F. Anderloni incise."

The proofs have the name of the painter and of the engraver.

NIC. POUSSIN *pinx.* Holy Family.

The infant St. John presenting a scroll to the Virgin, who is seated with the infant Saviour at the base of a column, St. Joseph standing behind, reading. Engraved in 1827, from a picture owned by the publisher of the plate, Sign. Zanetti, in Manchester.

Proofs are before letters, with the names of the artists, and the arms. Artist's proofs are before any letters, and before the coat of arms.

SEBASTIANO DEL PIOMBO *pinx.* **P.** Andrea Doria, bust.

The original full length portrait is in the Doria palace in Rome, formerly in Genoa. Platner and Bunsen, III. iii. p. 545. Engraved for *Vite e Ritratti di illustri Italiani*, Milano, Tipografia Bettoni, 1820.

Proofs are with open letters. Artist's proofs have merely the artists' names; and still earlier impressions are without any letters.

KÜGELGEN *pinx.* **P.** Schiller.

Artist's proof, without any letters.

GUIDO *pinx.* The Assumption of the Virgin.

Engraved by Garavaglia, finished by F. Anderloni. *See* GARAVAGLIA.

ANDERLONI, PIETRO, engraver, born in 1784 at St. Eufemia in the Brescian Territory, died in 1849. He was a pupil of his brother Faustino and of Longhi.

NIC. POUSSIN *pinx.* Moses at the Well, defending the Daughters of Jethro.

See Smith, *Cat. rais.* No. 23. The picture is in the collection of the Countess Pino at Milan. Engraved in 1818.

Proof, with but one line of inscription in open letters.

Artist's proofs are before any letters, with merely " P. A. f." traced with the needle, and with the white lacing of the sandal. Geo. Smith, No. 503, £6 15*s.*; Archinto, No. 2, 280*fr.*; Lehrs, No. 11, 72*th.*

RAPHAEL *pinx.* The Judgment of Solomon.

From the ceiling of the Camera della Segnatura. Passavant, II. 78. Engraved in 1845.

ANDERLONI, PIETRO, *continued.*

Proof; one line of open letters and arms only traced, before the dedication.

The artist's proofs are without the names of the artists, without the inscription of the title, and without the coat of arms and dedication. They have, however, in the shaded socle below, in open letters, the inscription: *Date illis infantem vivum et nolite interficere eum.* Reg. III. — *Raphael Santius pinx. in aedibus Vaticanis.*

An earlier state of the artist's proof is before the finished border of the plate, formed of lines. The socle is shaded.

The *earliest* state of the artist's proofs of the finished plate have the *socle* below *white*, unshaded, but have likewise in it the inscription, in open letters, which are formed of two lines. Johnson, No. 24, £ 8 10*s.*; Archinto, No. 4, 200 *fr.*

RAPHAEL *pinx.* The Vision of Ezekiel.

The plate was *finished by Longhi.* The picture, of the same size as the engraving, is in the Gallery of the Pitti palace. Passavant, II. 118.

Proof, with merely the names of the artists.

RAPHAEL *pinx.* Heliodorus driven out of the Temple.

Fresco in the Stanza of Heliodorus in the Vatican. Passavant, II. 105. Engraved in 1830.

Proof; one line of open letters, with the coat of arms, and before dedication.

RAPHAEL *pinx.* The same.

Artist's proof, "*avec remarque*" (i. e. the white ring on the hand of the man in the group at the left), *before any letters, and before the coat of arms, also before the corners on the two sides of the arch were finished.*

The finished artist's proofs have also the letters "P. A. f." below, traced with the needle.

TITIAN *pinx.* The Woman taken in Adultery.

Engraved in 1821, from a picture then in the collection of the Countess Pino in Milan, now in England.

With the address of Tanner (the later address is Lissant) followed by two dots, indicating it to be an impression of the second hundred.

TITIAN *pinx.* The same.

Artist's proof, before any inscription, and with merely the letters "P. A. f." *traced with the needle; — further* (avec remarque), *before the flowers on the ground were finished.*

A similar copy, Debois, No. 22, 300 *fr.*; Johnson, No. 25, £ 11; Archinto, No. 1, 301 *fr.*; Lehrs, No. 9, 85 *th.*

The proofs have one line of inscription, like "Moses at the Well."

CALISTO DA LODI *pinx.* Christ bearing the Cross.

Proofs are before letters.

ANDERLONI, PIETRO, *continued.*

RAPHAEL *pinx.* Madonna called The Virgin in the Meadow, "Die Jungfrau im Grünen."

See Passavant, II. 37, and III. p. 91. The picture is in the Vienna Gallery. Engraved in 1810.

Proof before letters, with merely the artists' names, traced with the needle in small letters.

The rare artist's proofs are before any letters.

RAPHAEL *pinx.* Madonna del Passeggio.

See Passavant, II. 263. The original is in the Bridgewater Gallery, and there are several repetitions.

Proof before letters.

Quandt, No. 2194, 27 *th.*

Artist's proofs are before any letters, and have only the initials of the engraver in the middle below, traced with the needle. Wilcox, No. 16 (London, May, 1856), £ 8; Debois, No. 21, 290 *fr.* In Evans's sale catalogue, £ 12 12 *s.*

TITIAN *pinx.* Virgin and Child, adored by two Angels.

Engraved from the picture in the collection of the Countess Pino in Milan.

Proof before letters, with only the artists' names and the address.

Artist's proofs have merely the initials of the engraver cut with the needle.

RAPHAEL *pinx.* The Defeat of Attila.

Fresco in the Stanza of Heliodorus in the Vatican. Engraved in 1837. Passavant, II. 107.

Proof, with one line of inscription in open letters, with the coat of arms, and before dedication.

The artist's proofs are before any letters, i. e. before the names of the artists, and before the inscription in open letters.

The artist's proofs *avec remarque* are before the upper corners were shaded, but with an inscription in them in open letters: *Raphael Santius pinx.*, etc. They have also the *remarque* of the *white reins* of the horse of the last horseman on the right side of the plate.

ANDREWS, JOSEPH, engraver, residing in Boston, U. S., where he was born in 1806. A pupil of Goodyear.

HEALY *pinx.* **P.** Adams, John Quincy.

Proof.

HEALY *pinx.* **P.** Grahame, James.

STUART *pinx.* **P.** Washington.

From the original, in the Athenæum Gallery, Boston, U. S.

Proof.

ANDREWS, JOSEPH, *continued.*

ALLSTON *pinx.* The Witch of Endor.

Engraved in conjunction with Wagstaff. *See* WAGSTAFF.

ANGUS, WILLIAM, an English engraver who flourished from about 1786 to 1820.

ELSHEIMER *pinx.* Tobit and the Fish.

"From the original picture in the collection of the Right Honorable Earl Grosvenor, 1790." Not mentioned by Waagen.

AQUILA, FRANCESCO FARAONE, designer, painter, and engraver, born at Palermo in 1676. He worked at Rome about 1700, in the style of Santi Bartoli.

CORREGGIO *pinx.* La Vierge au Panier.

Madonna, with the child, at her side a basket with a large pair of shears, in the background Joseph, working at his trade. The picture is in the National Gallery. There is another in the Bridgewater collection, and there are numerous repetitions.

AQUILA, PIETRO, painter, etcher, and engraver, brother of Francesco, born at Marzella near Palermo in 1677. He also went to Rome, where he became a monk, but still pursued his art. No work of his has a later date than 1700.

ANNIBALE CARACCI *pinx.* The Dead Christ on the Lap of his Mother, St. Mary Magdalen, St. Francis, and two Angels.

Etched. The picture is in the Gallery of the Louvre. Villot, No. 140.

ARDELL, JAMES Mc. *See* MCARDELL.

AUBIN, SAINT. *See* SAINT-AUBIN.

AUBRY-LECOMTE, HYACINTHE LOUIS VICTOR JEAN-BAPTISTE, historical painter and lithographer at Paris, born at Nizza in 1797, a pupil of Girodet-Trioson.

RAPHAEL *pinx.* Madonna di San Sisto.

A lithograph after the repetition, or rather copy, of the picture in Dresden, formerly in the Abbey of Saint-Amand, now in the City Hall of Rouen, Normandy. This differs from the original in that St. Sixtus has, besides the crosier, a bishop's mitre at his feet, instead of the papal tiara. Passavant, II. No. 240, p. 341, considers the picture a work of the 17th century.

It is stated that M. Aubry-Lecomte received from the publisher M. Gaugain 12,000*fr.* for this work. Impressions were sold for 40 – 80*fr.*

The print is of uncommonly large size, and our impression is without any letters.

AUDENAERDE, ROBERT VAN, painter and engraver, born at Ghent in 1663, where he died in 1743. A pupil of Jan van Cleef and Carlo Maratti.

CARLO MARATTI *pinx.* Dead Christ, and Mourners.

2d state, with Frey's address.

CARLO MARATTI *pinx.* Madonna of the Rosaries.

2d state, with Frey's address.

GUIDO RENI *pinx.* Aurora with Apollo and the Hours.

Fresco in the casino of the garden of the Palace Rospigliosi in Rome. Compare the same subject under MORGHEN, RAFFAELLO.

Impression with the address of Westerhout.

AUDOUIN, PIERRE, designer and engraver, born at Paris in 1768, died there in 1822. A pupil of Beauvarlet.

CARAVAGGIO *pinx.* The Entombment.

The picture is in the Gallery of the Vatican. Platner and Bunsen, II. ii. p. 431. Engraved for the *Musée Français.*

ANDREA DEL SARTO *pinx.* Charity.

See Alfred Reumont, p. 106; Crowe and Cavalcaselle, III. p. 563. The picture is in the Gallery of the Louvre. Villot, No. 437. Engraved in 1812 for the *Musée Français.*

RAPHAEL *pinx.* Venus extracting a Thorn from her Foot, the dripping blood coloring the white rose.

From the fresco painting in the Bathing Room of the Cardinal Bibbiena (over the Loggie) in the Vatican. Passavant, II. 218.

Artist's proof, with coat of arms, before letters, and before the names of the artists.

CORREGGIO *pinx.* Jupiter and Antiope.

In the collections of Charles I., Cardinal Mazarin, and Louis XIV.; now in the Gallery of the Louvre. Villot, No. 28. Not mentioned by Coxe.

BOUILLON *pinx.* Girl with an Arrow: *Il n'est plus tems.*

RAPHAEL *pinx.* **P.** Raphael and his *maître d'armes.*

See Passavant, II. 278, and III. p. 176. The picture is in the Gallery of the Louvre. Villot, No. 386. Engraved for the *Musée Français.*

VELAZQUEZ *pinx.* **P.** Velazquez painting the Infanta Margarita Maria; called "Las Meniñas," "The Maids of Honor."

Stirling, *Velazquez,* p. 171. The picture is in the Madrid Gallery. Engraved for the *Coleccion de las estampas de los cuadros . . . pertenecientes al Rey de España.*

Proofs are before letters, with only the artists' names.

AUDOUIN, PIERRE, *continued.*

SALVATOR ROSA *pinx.* **P.** Salvator Rosa.

In the Florence Gallery of the Uffizj. Engraved for Wicar's *Tableaux ... de la Galerie de Florence et du Palais Pitti.*

CHATILLON *pinx.* **P.** Napoleon.

AUDRAN, BENOÎT, THE ELDER, designer, etcher, and engraver, born at Lyons in 1661, died in 1721. A pupil of Gérard Audran, his uncle, whose works he approached nearer than the second Benoît. Le Blanc, *Manuel de l'amateur d'estampes.*

LE BRUN *pinx.* Moses at the Well, defending the Daughters of Jethro. Le Bl. 9.

"A Paris Chez Audran ruë St. Jacques aux deux Piliers d'Or avec privilege du Roy."

DANIELE DA VOLTERRA *pinx.* David cutting off Goliath's Head. Le Bl. 26.

DANIELE DA VOLTERRA *pinx.* The same subject, different view. Le Bl. 27.

One composition, painted under two aspects. In the Gallery of the Louvre. Villot, No. 347. Engraved with the name of Michel-Angelo as the painter, the first in 1716, the second in 1717.

J. VIVIEN *pinx.* **P.** Fénelon. Le Bl. 258.

Impression of the 1st state, before address.

The 2d state has the inscription: *Se vend à Paris chez B. Audran ... Luxembourg.*

LE BRUN *pinx.* The Presentation of the Virgin in the Temple.

With dedication to the Archbishop Harlay by Le Brun.

Otto's *Catalogue,* No. 2729.

LE BRUN *pinx.* The Presentation of the Infant Christ in the Temple.

"*C. le Brun pinxit. Audran fecit et excud. Cū. priuil. Regis. Se vend a Paris rue St. Iacques aux* 2 *Piliers d'or.* Oblatus est quia ipse voluit. *Is.* LIII. 7. *Il a êtê offert parcequ'il a bien voulu l'être.*" Le Blanc has only one "Presentation in the Temple" after Le Brun, under No. 32.

From Otto's collection.

"*Ein Hauptblatt im erstem Druck mit des Meisters Adresse, spätere Drücke haben die von Buldet.*" Weigel, in Otto's *Catalogue,* No. 2731.

ALBANO *pinx.* The Baptism of Christ.

The picture was in the old Royal collection, but is not now in the Louvre. Waagen, *Kunstwerke in Paris,* p. 777, No. 4. Le Bl. 37.

R. NANTEUIL *del.* **P.** Behringen, Henri de. Le Bl. 242.

AUDRAN, BENOÎT, the younger, designer, etcher, and engraver, born at Paris in 1700, died there in 1772. Son and pupil of Jean Audran. Le Blanc, *Manuel.*

AUDRAN, BENOÎT, *continued.*

PAOLO VERONESE *pinx.* Pélerins d'Emmaüs. Le Bl. 5.

Arched plate; engraved while in the Gallery of Count Brühl in Dresden.

WATTEAU *pinx.* Danse paysanne. Le Bl. 47.

AUDRAN, GÉRARD, designer, etcher, and engraver, born at Lyons in 1640, died at Paris in 1703. A pupil of his father, Claude, and his uncle, Charles, whom he left, to study under Carlo Maratti in Rome. In 1681 he was called to Paris as engraver to Louis XIV. Le Blanc, *Manuel.*

RAPHAEL *pinx.* The Lord speaking to Moses from the Burning Bush. Le Bl. 2.

From the ceiling of the Stanza of Heliodorus in the Vatican. Passavant, II. 104.

Proof before letters in the margin; the artists' names are engraved at the right hand in the foreground.

An impression of the same state, Debois, No. 28, 101*fr.*

RAPHAEL *del.* The Death of Ananias. Le Bl. 40.

See Passavant, II. 196. Engraved after a copy by Jervas of Raphael's cartoon at Hampton Court.

RAPHAEL *del.* Paul and Barnabas at Lystra. Le Bl. 59.

See Passavant, II. 199. Engraved after a copy by Jervas of Raphael's cartoon at Hampton Court.

DOMENICHINO *pinx.* The Temptation of St. Jerome. Le Bl. 54.

Fresco in San Onofrio in Rome. Platner and Bunsen, III. iii. p. 583. With the address of Audran: *A Paris rüe St. Jacques au* [sic] *deux pilliers d'Or.*

From Gawet's collection.

DOMENICHINO *pinx.* The Martyrdom of St. Agnes. Le Bl. 64.

Bologna Gallery. Address: *A Paris Chez Audran, rue St. Iacques, aux 2 pilliers d'Or.*

DOMENICHINO *pinx.* The Mystery of the Rosary. Le Bl. 67.

Bologna Gallery.

Before letters; without inscription, except the names of the painter and engraver, and the engraver's address, "rue St. Jacques aux 2 Piliers d'or."

P. MIGNARD *pinx.* The Felicity of the Blessed. Le Bl. 68.

Ceiling of the church Val de Grace. Six plates joined, forming a large circle.

From Otto's collection.

DOMENICHINO *pinx.* Æneas saving Anchises. Le Bl. 225.

In the Gallery of the Louvre. Villot, No. 409. The picture is now ascribed to Spada.

AUDRAN, GÉRARD, *continued.*

LE BRUN *pinx.* The Battles of Alexander. Le Bl. 228 – 231.

In the Gallery of the Louvre. Villot, No. 70, et seqq. Four representations, engraved on 13 plates, to be joined, so as to form 4 pieces : —

1. The Passage of the Granicus.
2. The Defeat of Darius at Arbela.
3. Porus brought before Alexander.
4. The Triumphal Entry of Alexander into Babylon.

The 5th piece, "Alexander entering the Tent of Darius," also belonging to this set, is engraved by Edelinck. *See* EDELINCK.

Impressions with the name of Goyton (the letters in dots) as printer, followed by four points, indicating them as from the 4th hundred.

From the collection and with the stamp of Ackermann.

LE BRUN *pinx.* The Battle of Constantine and Maxentius. Le Bl. 236.

Engraved on 3 plates, to be joined.

LE BRUN *pinx.* Triumphal Entry of Constantine into Rome. Le Bl. 237.

Engraved on 4 plates, to be joined.

NIC. POUSSIN *pinx.* Time bearing Truth above the reach of Envy and Slander. Le Bl. 101.

See Smith, *Cat. rais.* No. 280. In the Gallery of the Louvre, Villot, No. 446.

2d state, with letters and coat of arms, before the drapery, and with the address, "aux gobellins."

From the collection and with the name of P. Mariette.

The 1st state is before the letters and arms as well as before the drapery. Such an impression occurred at Debois's sale, No. 35 ; it came from the collections Valois, 200 *fr.*, Logette, 33 *fr.*, and Scitivaux, and sold for 660 *fr.*

NIC. POUSSIN *pinx.* The same. Le Bl. 101.

4th state, with the drapery, but still with the address of the 3d state, "aux deux piliers d'or," *before the address of Buldet (5th state).*

RAPHAEL *pinx.* Allegorical Figures, Caryatides, and Termini, from the Stanza of Heliodorus. Le Bl. 295 – 307.

See Passavant, II. 109. Thirteen plates, as follows : —

1. La Noblesse.
2. La Religion.
3. La Paix.
4. La Loi.
5. L'Abondance.
6. Vignoble.
7. La Navigation.
8. La Marine.

AUDRAN, GÉRARD, *continued.*

9. Commerce.
10. Colonie.
11. Protection.
12. Two halves of Termini, one male, one female.
13. Two ditto.

AUDRAN, JEAN, engraver, born at Lyons in 1667, died at Paris in 1756. He was inferior to Gérard and the two Benoîts, and a pupil of his uncle Gérard. Le Blanc, *Manuel.*

NOEL COYPEL *pinx.* **P.** Noel Coypel. Le Bl. 355.

The plate was engraved for Audran's admission into the Academy.

AVELINE, PIERRE, designer and engraver, was born at Paris in 1710, and died there in 1760. He studied after Jean Baptiste Poilly.

GIORGIONE *pinx.* The Finding of Moses.

The picture is in the Brera Gallery of Milan, formerly in the archiepiscopal palace of the same place. Engraved for the *Cabinet Crozat.*

B.

BACHELEY, JACQUES, designer and engraver, born at Pont-L'Evêque in 1712, died at Rouen in 1781. A pupil of Philippe Le Bas.

JAC. RUYSDAEL *pinx.* Château de Ryswick.

Not mentioned by Smith (*Cat. rais.*), but by Nagler (*Künstler-Lexicon*). "Tirée du Cabinet de M. Ribard, à Rouen," to whom the plate is dedicated.

BAHMANN, FERDINAND, steel engraver of the present day.

DOMENICHINO *pinx.* St. John the Evangelist.

Copy of Fr. Müller's engraving, from the picture now in the Imperial Gallery in St. Petersburg, which is a repetition of the one in Castle Howard.

DOMENICHINO *pinx.* The same.

Proof.

BAILLIE, CAPTAIN WILLIAM, amateur designer, etcher and engraver with the needle and the burin and in mezzotinto, was born in Ireland in 1736, and died after 1777.

REMBRANDT *del.* The Gold-weigher.

Copy after Rembrandt's etching. Wilson, No. 283.

REMBRANDT *del.* An aged Rabbi with large beard, represented in front view, half length.

He wears a broad and flat velvet cap and a large fur-lined cloak; his

BAILLIE, CAPTAIN WILLIAM, *continued.*

hands are joined in front over his caftan. On the left, "Rembrandt 1646"; on the right, "W. Baillie f." Inscription: *Agli Dilitanti che anno il Sapere senza pregiudizio Questa e dedicata.* Mezzotinto, in brown. Folio.

BALDINI, BACCIO, goldsmith and engraver, born at Florence about 1436. *See* BOTTICELLI.

BALLIU (*sometimes* **BAILLU**), **PIETER DE,** designer and engraver, born at Antwerp about 1614. One of his pieces has the date 1649.

MARTIN PEPYN *pinx.* Susanna and the Elders.

G. Hendricx *exc.*

BALECHOU, JEAN JOSEPH, engraver, born at Arles in 1715, died at Avignon in 1764. A pupil of Michel and Lépicié.

CARLE VANLOO *pinx.* Ste. Geneviève.

"De la galerie de M. Stiffredi Mornas à Avignon."

Artist's proof, not only with the riband round the neck unshaded, but before letters and arms, and in some of the shades, though nearly, yet not entirely finished.

An impression of the same state, Logette, No. 4, 160*fr.*; Debois, No. 47, 190*fr.*

HYAÇINTHE RIGAUD *pinx.* **P.** Auguste III., Roi de Pologne.

Engraved as frontispiece for Vol. I. of *Rec. d'est. de la Galerie de Dresde.*

Cat. Archinto, No. 11, "Épreuve avant l'année 1750, placée au-dessous du nom du graveur, et avant les mots: *Chevalier de l'ordre de Saint-Michel,* placés sous le nom de pointre," sold for 155 *fr.*

LOUIS SILVESTRE *pinx.* **P.** Brühl, Count Heinrich.

Impression before any letters, before the face was altered, and before the alteration in the coat of arms. (*Like the copy in the Duke of Buckingham's Catalogue, No.* 1664.)

The print of this plate forms the frontispiece of *Rec. d'estampes de la Galerie Brühl,* Dresde, 1754.

J. M. NATTIER *pinx.* **P.** "La Force," portrait of the Duchesse de Châteauroux.

JACQUES ANTREAU *pinx.* **P.** Grillot, Jacques Gabriel.

FRANÇOIS DE TROY *pinx.* **P.** Julien, Jean de.

JACQUES ANDRÉ JOSEPH AVED *pinx.* **P.** Taschereau de Linyères, Bertrand Claude, Confesseur du Roi.

J. VERNET *pinx.* The Storm.

The picture, at the time of the engraving, was owned by M. Poulharies at Marseille.

BALECHOU, *continued.*

3d state, before the horizontal lines over the inscription.

The 1st state is before any letters or arms. Debois, No. 49, 295 *fr.* 2d state, before any address, and with the misspelling in the inscription "compagine" instead of "compagnie." Debois, No. 50, 210 *fr.*; Lehrs, No. 25, 45 *th.* 3d state, with the spelling corrected, and the address, *Se vend a Auignon Chez l'auteur et a Paris Chez Buldet rue de Geure.* In the 4th state the inscription is covered with horizontal lines.

J. VERNET *pinx.* The Calm.

"Tiré du cabinet de M. Renaud chanoine de St. Didier d'Avignon."

3d state, before the horizontal lines over the inscription.

The 1st state is before address. 2d state, with the address, *Se vend à Avignon chez l'auteur.* 3d state, *à Auignon Chez P. Arnavon pres St. Eutrope.* The 4th state has the inscription covered with horizontal lines.

J. VERNET *pinx.* The Bathers.

"Du cabinet de M. Poulharies à Marseille."

2d state, "épreuve au mollet blanc"; *the inscription is covered with horizontal lines.*

The 1st state is before any letters. 3d state, inscription again on white ground, without the lines.

BALESTRA, GIOVANNI, engraver in Rome, pupil of Giovanni Folo.

SPAGNOLETTO *pinx.* Archimedes.

Vienna Gallery.

BALLAGNY.

𝔓. Carlo Botta.

Lithograph.

BANZO, ANTONIO, engraved in Rome in 1810.

RAPHAEL *pinx.* The Adoration of the Kings.

See Passavant, II. 17. b. p. 23. Engraved from the picture in the Vatican of the size of the engraving, for the Calcografia Camerale in Rome.

BARON, BERNARD, engraver, born at Paris about 1700, died at London in 1762. A pupil of Nicolas Tardieu.

TITIAN *pinx.* Jupiter and Antiope.

The picture is in the Gallery of the Louvre (Villot, No. 468); formerly in the collection of Charles I., who received it from Philip IV. Engraved for the *Cabinet Crozat.*

TITIAN *pinx.* The Cornaro Family kneeling before an Altar.

Collection of the Duke of Northumberland, Northumberland House. Waagen, *Treasures,* I. p. 393.

BARON, BERNARD, *continued.*

VAN DYCK *pinx.* **P.** Charles I. of England on horseback, accompanied by his Master of the Horse, who carries his helmet.

See Smith, *Cat. rais.* No. 207. The picture is in Windsor Castle. Waagen, *Treasures,* II. p. 429.

HOGARTH *pinx.* **P.** Hoadly, Bishop Benjamin.

BARTH, CARL, designer and engraver, born in 1787 at Hildburghausen, where he resided. A pupil of Johann Gotthard von Müller.

GRAFF *del.* **P.** Goethe.

In 8vo.

Proof, before letters.

"H." *del.* **P.** Savonarola.

BARTOLI, PIETRO SANTI: PIETRO SANTI, OF BARTOLA, where he was born in 1635. Died at Rome in 1700. He was a pupil of Le Maire and Nic. Poussin.

RAPHAEL *inv.* The Adoration of the Kings.

See Passavant, II. 205. After an arras-hanging in the Vatican, from the second series, representations from the Life of Christ. Engraved on 3 plates, to be joined. Mariette attributes the third plate to A. Corneille.

ALBANO *pinx.* The Birth of the Virgin.

The picture, now in the Gallery of the Capitol, was formerly in the Gallery of the Vatican; and originally in Bologna, in the Oratorio Sta. Maria del Piombo. Platner and Bunsen, III. i. p. 132.

RAPHAEL *inv.* Socle-pictures and Borders of Fresco Paintings and Arras-hangings in the Vatican.

I. 15 plates. New impressions of the Stamperia Camerale in Rome.

1. Device of the Medici family, with Dedication to Nicolò Simonelli, by Giov. Giac. Rossi (Jo. Jac. de Rubeis).
2. St. Paul reading the Scriptures. Pass. II. p. 247.
   Arras-hangings under "Paul and Barnabas at Lystra."
3. Christ and the Apostles: "Feed my Sheep." Pass. II. p. 200. b.
   Fresco, Room of Torre Borgia.
4. Christ appearing to St. Peter near Rome: "Domine quo vadis." Pass. II. p. 200. d.
   Fresco, Room of Torre Borgia.
5. St. Mark's Departure for Antioch. Pass. II. p. 247.
   Arras-hanging, under "Paul and Barnabas at Lystra."
6. Donation of Rome by Constantine. Pass. II. p. 163.
   Fresco, Stanza of Heliodorus.

BARTOLI, PIETRO SANTI, *continued.*

Judgment of Seleucus. Pass. II. p. 116.
Fresco, Camera della Segnatura.

7. Paul before Festus (Paul before Gallio). Pass. II. p. 249. d.
Paul blessing Converts at Corinth. Pass. II. p. 249. c.
Arras-hanging, under "Paul preaching at Athens."

8. Joseph before Pharaoh. Pass. II. p. 162. a.
Fresco, Stanza of Heliodorus.

9. St. Paul at Ephesus; according to others, at Corinth. Pass. II. p. 249. b.
St. Paul working as Tentmaker; according to Bartoli, before the Tabernacle.
Arras-hanging, under "Paul preaching at Athens."

10. Christ appearing to the Disciples fishing. Pass. II. p. 199. a.
Fresco in the Room of Torre Borgia.

11. Egyptians drowned in the Red Sea. Pass. II. p. 162. b.

12. Moses receiving the Tablets of the Law. Pass. II. p. 163. c.
Fresco, Stanza of Heliodorus.

13. Simon Magus and St. Peter before Nero. Pass. II. p. 200. c.
Room of Torre Borgia.

14. The Annunciation. Pass. II. p. 163. d.
Stanza of Heliodorus.

15. Christ and the Apostles: "Here are two Swords." Pass. II. p. 116.
Camera della Segnatura.
A Pope celebrating Mass. Pass. II. p. 163. e.
Stanza of Heliodorus.

RAPHAEL *inv.* Socle-pictures of Arras-hangings in the Vatican.

II. 15 plates. New impressions of the Stamperia Camerale. Inscription: *Leonis X admirandæ uirtutis Imagines,* etc.

1. Arms of the Medici, and Dedication to Prince Leopoldo de' Medici, by Rossi (Jo. Jac. de Rubeis).

2. Cardinal Giovanni de' Medici going as Legate to Florence. Pass. II. p. 240.
Under "The Stoning of St. Stephen."

3. The Cardinal's Reception at Florence. Pass. II. p. 240.
Under the same.

4. The Cardinal flying from Florence, disguised as a Monk. Pass. II. p. 239.
Under "Feed my Sheep."

5. Plundering of the Medici Palace. Pass. II. p. 239.
Under the same.

6. The same. Pass. II. p. 239.

BARTOLI, PIETRO SANTI, *continued.*

Under the same.

7. Capture of the Cardinal at the Battle of Ravenna. Pass. II. p. 242.

Under "The Healing of the Cripple."

8. Escape of the Cardinal. Pass. II. p. 242.

Under the same.

9. Punishment of the Conspirators. Pass. II. p. 245.
10. Massacre of the Inhabitants of Prato. Pass. II. p. 245.
11. Scene after the Capture of Prato. Pass. II. p. 245.

Nos. 9 – 11 are under "The Conversion of St. Paul." Passavant describes them as representing the persecution of the Christians by Saul.

12. Reception of the Cardinal, on his returning to Florence. Pass. II. p. 243.

Under "The Death of Ananias."

13. The Gonfalonier Rudolfi's Address to the People. Pass. II. p. 243.

Under the same.

14. The Cardinal going to Rome, after the Death of Julius I. Pass. II. p. 237.

Under "Miraculous Draft of Fishes."

15. The Cardinal receiving as Leo X. the Homage of the Cardinals. Pass. II. p. 237.

Under the same.

For these socle-pictures compare also Waagen, *Treasures of Art in England,* II. p. 395 et seq.

BARTOLI *del.* et *sc.* after the antique, "Veteres Arcus Augustorum Triumphis insignes ex Reliquiis quae Romae adhuc supersunt."

New impression by the Stamperia Camerale, 1824, with 50 plates and 12 pages text, besides 4 pages preface by Carlo Fea.

The original edition was published in 1690 with 40 plates and 12 pages text by G. G. de Rossi (de Rubeis).

BARTOLOZZI, FRANCESCO, painter, etcher, and engraver, born at Florence in 1730, died at Lisbon in 1813. He studied drawing with Ferretti in Florence, and engraving with Joseph Wagner in Venice; in 1764 he went to London, where he remained 40 years, till in 1807 he went to Lisbon. Le Blanc, *Manuel.*

PAOLO VERONESE *del.* The Judgment of Solomon. Le Bl. 11.

After a drawing.

GUERCINO *pinx.* The Circumcision. Le Bl. 40.

The picture is in Bologna, in the church of Giesù e Maria.

AG. CARACCI *pinx.* The Woman taken in Adultery. Le Bl. 47.

From the Zampieri palace in Bologna, now in the "Royal English collection."

BARTOLOZZI, FRANCESCO, *continued.*

B. West *pinx.* St. Paul at Malta.

The picture is in the Chapel of the Hospital at Greenwich. Not mentioned by Le Blanc.

Ann. Caracci *pinx.* Le Silence, Virgin with the Sleeping Child and St. John. Le Bl. 28.

The engraving has the inscription: *From a painting of Annibale Carracci, in His Majesty's collection.* The composition differs from the picture in the Louvre only by the absence of the flowers on the couch, and the absence of the cross and of the halo of St. John.

Raphael *pinx.* Madonna with the Fish. Le Bl. 45.

The picture is in the Madrid Gallery. Passavant, II. 100.

Correggio *pinx.* Madonna of St. Jerome, Il Giorno, The Day of Correggio. Le Bl. 38.

Virgin and Child with St. Jerome, St. Magdalen, and two Angels.

The picture is in the Gallery of Parma. Coxe, p. 86. Le Blanc calls it erroneously "The Night, in Dresden." Bartolozzi engraved this plate for Laurent's *Musée de Louvre,* when he was 85 years old, and died before he finished it. It was completed by Heinrich Carl Müller, in 1822. The latter was an engraver in Paris, born at Strassburg in 1784, and a pupil of Guérin. Nagler, *Künstler-Lex.* IX. p. 564, No. 7.

Nic. Poussin *pinx.* Holy Family with Angels offering Flowers and Fruit.

Smith, *Cat. rais.* 83. In the Grosvenor Gallery. Waagen, *Treasures,* II. p. 172. Not mentioned by Le Blanc.

Proof, before letters, only the names of the artists traced with the needle.

Carlo Dolce *pinx.* Mater Dolorosa, with the inscription "Madonna." Le Bl. 24.

From a picture of the size of the engraving, owned by Clothworthy Upton, Esq. Small 4to.

Open letters.

Van Dyck *pinx.* **P.** "Van Dyck's Wife, Daughter of Earl Gowry," as Madonna and Child.

Smith, *Cat. rais.* 427. At the time of the engraving, in the collection of Sir Richard Lyttelton. Not mentioned by Le Blanc.

Copley *pinx.* The Death of Lord Chatham. Le Bl. 447.

The picture is in the Vernon Gallery.

Impression with shaded letters, but with the sword-sheath white, between the regular 2d and 3d state.

The 1st state of the plate is before letters, and with the sword-sheath white.

BARTOLOZZI, FRANCESCO, *continued.*

The 2d state is with open letters, and with the sheath still white. In the 3d state the letters and the sheath are shaded.

MICHEL-ANGELO *del.* Atlas.

After a drawing; engraved in the dotted manner. Not mentioned by Le Blanc.

ANN. CARACCI *pinx.* Clytie. Le Bl. 122.

The picture was, while engraved, in the collection of Mr. John Strange.

Proof, before letters.

CIPRIANI *del.* Venus sailing on a Shell, surrounded by Amorini. Le Bl. 296.

Ticket for a Concert of Giardini.

CIPRIANI *del.* Apollo and Daphne; in the right corner a River-god and two Nymphs. Le Bl. 293.

Ticket for a Concert of Giardini.

ANN. CARACCI *pinx.* Orlando rescuing Olimpia. Le Bl. 312.

The picture is in the collection of the Earl of Scarsdale at Keddelstone. Waagen, *Treasures*, III. p. 393.

FRANCESCHINI *del.* Satyr, Children, and Goat.

After a drawing. Not mentioned by Le Blanc.

ELISABETTA SIRANI *del.* A Sleeping Child. Le. Bl. 644.

After a drawing.

SIR JOSHUA REYNOLDS *pinx.* **P.** Burghersh, Lord, a child. Le Bl. 483.

Open letter proof.

P. Gozzi, Gasparo. Le Bl. 531.

From *Vite e Ritratti di illustri Italiani*, 2 vol. 4to, containing 60 portraits and text; Milano, Tipografia Bettoni, 1820. Originally engraved, according to Le Blanc, as frontispiece to *Rime piacevole del Sign. Conte Gaspare Gozzi*, Venezia, 1758, 8vo.

GUERCINO *pinx.* **P.** Guercino. Le Bl. 260.

The picture is in Windsor Castle. Waagen, *Treasures*, II. p. 433.

HAMILTON *pinx.* **P.** Kilwarden, Chief Justice.

Not mentioned by Le Blanc.

Proof, with open and traced letters.

SIR JOSHUA REYNOLDS *pinx.* **P.** Mansfield, Lord. Le Bl. 570.

Proof, before letters, with merely the names of the artists; and in the middle of the lower margin of the plate, cut with the needle, the inscription: "Published as the Act directs, 24 Aug. 1786, by F. Bartolozzi, London."

ZUCCARO *pinx.* **P.** Mary, Queen of Scots, with her little son, James I. Le Bl. 515.

BARTOLOZZI, FRANCESCO, *continued.*

"The lovely picture by Zuccaro is at Chiswick." Mrs. Jameson, *Visits and Sketches,* New York, 1834, I. p. 252.

Proof, before letters; it has merely the names of the artists and the year 1777, *with traced letters.*

ROSALBA *pinx.* **P.** Rosalba. Le Bl. 597.

After her own painting, in the possession of the publisher, J. Walker. Engraved in the dotted manner.

SIR JOSHUA REYNOLDS *pinx.* **P.** Thurlow, Lord. Le Bl. 612.

Artist's proof, before letters and address; the artists' names are cut with the needle in very small letters. Of the coat of arms, held by two birds, there is only the white empty shield.

SIR JOSHUA REYNOLDS *pinx.* **P.** Yorke, Philip, a child. Le Bl. 622.

Open letter proof.

CIPRIANI and BARRETT *pinx.* Shakespeare's Tempest.

CIPRIANI and BARRETT *pinx.* Shakespeare's As You Like It.

Landscapes in oval, engraved in conjunction with Middiman. *See* MIDDIMAN.

BARTSCH, ADAM VON, designer, etcher, and engraver, born at Vienna in 1757, where he died in 1821. A pupil of Schmutzer. He was Principal Keeper of the Imperial Cabinet of Engravings in Vienna, and author of *Le Peintre-Graveur.*

DIETRICH *del.* Philip baptizing the Eunuch.

From a drawing owned by the Duke of Saxe-Teschen.

2*d proof, with open letters.*

FÜGER *del.* **P.** Boy with a palette and brushes. Portrait of Füger's Son.

Etched.

F. BOL *pinx.* **P.** Ferdinand Bol's portrait, etched after his own picture.

BARY, HENDRIK, designer and engraver, born at Antwerp, about 1625, follower of Corn. Visscher.

FRANS VAN MIERIS *pinx.* "De wyn is een spotter." A Young Woman gone to Sleep over her Wine.

2*d state.* "Peter Schenck jun. exc."

The 1st state is before address.

A. BAKKER *del.* **P.** Barth. Prevost.

BASAN, PIERRE FRANÇOIS, etcher and engraver, born at Paris in 1723, died there in 1797. A pupil of Fessard and Daullé.

BASAN, PIERRE FRANÇOIS, *continued.*

𝔓. Coppenol.

The larger portrait; copy after Rembrandt's etching. Wilson, No. 285. There is a painting by Rembrandt, corresponding with this print (Smith, *Cat. rais.* 307), in the collection of Lord Ashburton, formerly in Prince Lucien Bonaparte's collection.

TITIAN *pinx.* Portrait of a Blooming Matron in Widow's Attire.

Dresden Gallery. Engraved for *Rec. d'est. de la Gal. de Dresde,* I. No. 11.

TITIAN *pinx.* Portrait of a Young Woman with a Fan in the Form of a Small Flag.

Dresden Gallery. Engraved for *Rec. d'est. de la Gal. de Dresde,* I. No. 12.

BAUDET, ÉTIENNE, designer and engraver, born at Blois in 1643, died at Paris in 1716. A pupil of Sébastien Bourdon and Cornelis Bloemaert.

ALBANO *pinx.* The Four Elements.

Four plates. The pictures are in the Gallery of Turin.

BAUSE, JOHANN FRIEDRICH, designer and engraver, born at Halle in 1738, died at Weimar in 1814. He studied after Wille. Keil, *Catalog des Kupferstichwerkes von J. F. Bause,* Leipzig, 1849.

MENGS *pinx.* The Little Cupid. K. 13.

Dresden Gallery. Engraved for *Rec. d'est. de la Gal. de Dresde,* III. No. 14.

Proof.

FRANS MIERIS *pinx.* The Persian. K. 33.

CASPAR NETSCHER *pinx.* Rosetta. K. 36.

SIR JOSHUA REYNOLDS *pinx.* La petite Rusée. K. 39.

SIR JOSHUA REYNOLDS *pinx.* The same. K. 39.

Proof.

A. GRAFF *pinx.* 𝔓. Bodmer, J. J. K. 212.

A. GRAFF *pinx.* 𝔓. Böhme, J. G. K. 207.

A. GRAFF *pinx.* 𝔓. Böhme, Chr. Regina, wife of the preceding. K. 208.

A. GRAFF *pinx.* 𝔓. Ernesti, J. A. K. 162.

A. GRAFF *pinx.* 𝔓. Forster, J. R. K. 206.

A. GRAFF *pinx.* 𝔓. Frederick Augustus of Saxony. K. 136.

A. GRAFF *pinx.* 𝔓. Frederick II. of Prussia. K. 128.

A. GRAFF *pinx.* 𝔓. Gellert, Chr. F. K. 180.

8vo. Engraved as frontispiece to Gellert's *Schriften,* Leipzig, 1775.

BAUSE, JOHANN FRIEDRICH, *continued.*

A. Graff *pinx.* **P.** Gessner, Salomon. K. 190.

Fittler *pinx.* **P.** Gustavus Adolphus of Sweden. K. 132.

Œser *pinx.* **P.** Jerusalem, J. F. W. K. 163.

V. H. Schnorr *pinx.* **P.** Kant. K. 217.

A. Scheits *pinx.* **P.** Leibnitz. K. 204.

A. Graff *pinx.* **P.** Spalding, J. J. K. 165.

P. Utenbogaert, the Dutch minister. K. 246.

Copy of Rembrandt's print (Wilson, 281), not in an octagon border, but square and arched.

May *pinx.* **P.** Wieland. (1782.) K. 209.

A. Graff *pinx.* **P.** Wieland. (1797.) K. 210.

A. Maron *pinx.* **P.** Winckelmann, J. J. K. 205.

A. Graff *pinx.* **P.** Winckler, Gottfried. K. 225.

BAZIN, NICOLAS, designer and engraver, born at Troyes in Champagne about 1636. A pupil of Claude Mellan. He worked in Paris, and his plates bear date from 1681 to 1707.

Correggio *pinx.* Madonna and Child, St. John bringing Fruit.

The picture is in the Imperial Gallery of St. Petersburg.

Bazin *del.* (?) **P.** Madame Helyot.

With the address : *Mariette excud.*

BEATRIZET (*Lat.* **BEATRICIUS**), **NICOLAS,** the elder, "the Master of the Die" [B]. His name very likely was Dado, or Daddo, and he used the die as an emblem of his name. He appears to have been a pupil of the school of Marc-Antonio. He is supposed to be a native of Venice, and flourished in Rome 1532 – 1550. Bartsch, xv.

Raphael *pinx.* The Transfiguration. B. 6.

After Raphael's first design, before the two deacons were introduced on Mount Tabor. Passavant, ii. 244.

Giulio Romano *inv.* Triumph of Cybele. B. 18.

Retouched impression, with the 1*st address of Salamanca.*

Raphael *inv.* Æneas saving Anchises. B. 72.

Retouched impression, with the address of Thomassin, which is erased on the print.

Raphael *inv.* Scipio's Victory over Syphax. B. 73.

Without the inscription : "Summum," *etc., and without Lafreri's address.*

BEATRIZET, NICOLAS, le Lorrain, or the younger, born in Lorraine about 1507. He studied after the works of Marc-Antonio, engraved in Rome from 1540 to 1562, and died there about 1570. Bartsch, xv.

MICHEL-ANGELO *inv.* Fall of Phaëthon. B. 38.

With the original address A(ntonii) L(afreri) F(ormis).

From Geissler's collection.

MICHEL-ANGELO *inv.* Tityus gnawed by the Vulture. B. 39.

With the original address of Ant. Salamanca.

From Otto's collection.

PERINO DEL VAGA *inv.* The Sacrifice of Iphigenia. B. 43.

1st state, before the coat of arms, but mended.

The Battle of the Romans with the Dacians. B. 94.

After the antique; bas-relief from the Arch of Constantine in Rome.

Fine impression, with the original address of Lafreri.

BEAUVAIS, NICOLAS DAUPHIN DE, designer and engraver, born at Paris in 1687, died there in 1763. A pupil of G. Audran.

CORREGGIO *pinx.* St. George, with other Saints, before the Virgin and Child.

See Coxe, p. 32. The picture is in the Dresden Gallery. Engraved with N. Dupuis, for *Rec. d'est. de la Gal. de Dresde,* I. No. 2.

VAN DYCK *pinx.* St. Jerome Penitent.

Dresden Gallery. Engraved for *Rec. d'est. de la Gal. de Dresde,* II. No. 49.

BEAUVARLET, JACQUES FIRMIN, designer and engraver, born at Abbeville in 1731, died at Paris in 1797. A pupil of Ch. Dupuis and of L. Cars.

GUIDO *pinx.* Les Couseuses.

The Virgin, surrounded by eight other Maidens, sewing.

The picture is in the Imperial Gallery of St. Petersburg.

Proof, before any letters.

ALESSANDRO TURCHI *pinx.* Venus lamenting Adonis.

Dresden Gallery. Engraved for *Rec. d'est. de la Gal. de Dresde,* II. No. 15.

Proof, before any letters.

VIEN *pinx.* L'Offrande à Vénus.

VIEN *pinx.* La Marchande d'Amours.

Engraved from a picture in the collection of the Duke de Cossé.

A. VAN OSTADE *pinx.* Le Café Hollandais.

See Smith, *Cat. rais.* 11. Engraved when in the collection of Count de Vence.

OUDRY *pinx.* La Surprise du Rénard.

"À Paris chez l'auteur."

BEAUVARLET, JACQUES FIRMIN, *continued.*

DROUAIS *pinx.* **P.** Charles Philippe, Count of Artois, afterwards Charles X., 6 years old, and his Sister, Mme. Clotilde, afterwards Queen of Sardinia, 4 years old, mounting a Goat.

The picture is in the Gallery of the Louvre. Villot, No. 187.

DROUAIS *pinx.* **P.** Bouchardon.

Engraved for his admission into the Academy.

BECK, lithographer.

LE BLANC *pinx.* Die Kirchgängerin.

BEGA, CORNELIS, painter and etcher, pupil of Ostade, born at Haarlem in 1620, where he died in 1664. Bartsch, v.

Bust of an Old Woman, in oval. B. 7.

1st state, before the border, and before the plate was cleaned.

Woman Smoking. B. 11.

1st state, before the plate was cut, and before the cleaning.

BEHAM, BARTHEL, painter and engraver, born at Nuremberg in 1502, or, according to some, in 1490, died in Italy in 1540. A pupil of Albrecht Dürer, and, later, of Marc-Antonio. Bartsch, VIII.

Woman seated on a Cuirass. B. 20.

Apollo and Daphne. B. 25.

Cupid as Postilion. B. 32.

The Miser. B. 38.

P. Ferdinand I., Emperor of Germany. B. 61.

1st impression, before address of J. ab Heyden.

BEHAM, HANS SEBALD, painter and engraver, born at Nuremberg in 1500, died at Frankfort in 1550. He studied with his uncle, and then entered the school of Albrecht Dürer. Bartsch, VIII.

The Marriage-feast at Cana. B. 23.

From Ackermann's collection.

Christ Triumphant. B. 30.

The Prodigal Son wasting his Fortune. B. 32.

St. Sebaldus. B. 65.

2d state, plate made smaller.

Dido. B. 80.

From the collection, and with the name of Gawet, 1795.

The Magnanimity of Trajan. B. 82.

The same. B. 82.

1st state, before the year, 1537.

BEHAM, HANS SEBALD, *continued.*

Patience. B. 138.

Fortune. B. 140.

1st state, before retouch.

From Otto's collection, No. 367.

Misfortune. B. 141.

Melancholy. B. 144.

The earliest impressions are before the date, 1539.

A Young Woman accompanied by Death. B. 149.

1st state, before the additional blade of grass near the vase.

Three Soldiers with a Dog. B. 196.

1st state, with the tablet bordered with strokes of different length.

The Sentinel over the Powder Cask. B. 197.

The Ensign with Drummer and Fifer. B. 198.

1st state, before tablet or inscription.

From Ackermann's collection.

The Ensign and the Drummer. B. 199.

A Woman's Head. "Eines Weibes Havpt." B. 220.

The Little Buffoon with a Scroll. B. 230.

BELLA, STEFANO DELLA, painter, designer, and etcher, born at Florence in 1610, died there in 1664. He studied drawing with Cesare Dandini, and engraving with Canta-Gallina, becoming acquainted with Callot, and imitating, for a while, his manner. Jombert, *Essai d'un Catalogue de l'Œuvre d'Étienne de la Belle*, Paris, 1772.

Landscape. Jombert 79. Le Bl. 1068.

Two horsemen, near an old tree, preceded by a dog; on the right side of the road 7 sheep and a goat; on the left, 3 sheep, a goat, and a cow, with a shepherd, and a shepherdess with a distaff in her hand. "*Bella in. & f. cum Pri. Reg. christ.*" Folio.

View of the Pont Neuf in Paris. Jomb. 112. Le Bl. 1047.

2d state, with the weathercock.

Livre des Paysages. Jomb. 127. Le Bl. 1082–1094.

Dedicated to Ant. Le Charron, Baron de Dormelles. 1646. Suite of 13 pieces, round. "*F. L. D. Ciartres ex. cum Privil. Regis Christ.*"

1st state, with the above address, and before the inscription on the stone, which is the dedication.

2d address, *N. Langlois fils;* 3d address, *P. Mariette.*

A Polish stable-groom on horseback, leading another horse through water. Le Bl. 985.

Without the name.

BELLA, STEFANO DELLA, *continued.*

A Negro in Eastern Costume, half-size. Jomb. 205. Le Bl. 995.

Represented as holding a horse, eating, whose head is adorned with ostrich-feathers; on the right hand, farther back, a Turk on horseback. In the right upper corner, *S. D. B. fec.*

Four Turks, half length figures. Jomb. 207. Le Bl. 993.

Two of them are looking to the right, the other two to the left.

Without the name.

Five half length figures. Jomb. 208. Le Bl. 991.

Three Turks and a negro looking to the right; another Oriental with a kerchief tied round his head, looking to the left.

Without the name.

BENAGLIA, GIUSEPPE, an engraver of our own time; born at Monza, died at Milan. He was a pupil of Vangelisti.

LEONARDO DA VINCI *inventò*, SALAINO *dipinse.* Madonna and Child with a Lamb and St. Anne.

The picture is in the Leuchtenberg Gallery in Munich; a repetition is in the Gallery of the Louvre. The composition is different from the celebrated Cartoon of the Royal Academy in London. Rigollot, No. 20, p. 31; compare also No. 21.

Impression with open letters.

P. Beccaria.

Engraved for *Vite e Ritratti di illustri Italiani.*

BERGER, DANIEL, engraver and etcher, born at Berlin in 1744, where he died in 1824. A pupil of his father, Friedrich Gottlieb Berger, and of G. F. Schmidt.

REMBRANDT *pinx.* The Duke Adolphus of Gueldres threatening his Imprisoned Father.

In the Berlin Gallery. Smith, *Cat. rais.* 166, incorrectly states that there is a duplicate of this picture in Dresden. He also misunderstands the meaning of the picture. The two black servants behind the prince, which this engraving represents, are in the picture, though G. F. Schmidt, in his etching, left them out.

BERGHEM, NICOLAAS, painter and etcher. His family name was Klaasze, and he was born at Haarlem in 1624, where he died in 1683. His first instruction he received from his father, Pieter Klaasze of Haarlem, a very inferior painter; and he studied afterwards with Van Goyen, with Grebber, and with Weeninx. Bartsch, v., and Weigel, *Suppléments.*

Shepherd with Flock, fording a Stream. B. 9.

BERGHEM, NICOLAAS, *continued.*

3d state, with the Number.

Three Goats under a Tree. B. 50.

3d state, with the Number.

BERNARDI, JACOPO, engraver, born at Verona, pupil of Raphael Morghen; worked in Venice, Paris, etc.

LEONARDO DA VINCI *pinx.* The Virgin nursing the Child, who holds a Pigeon in one hand.

See Rigollot, No. 34. Engraved from the picture then in the collection of Count Litta in Milan, but since 1865 in the Gallery of the Hermitage of St. Petersburg. There are several repetitions of this picture.

LEONARDI DA VINCI *pinx.* The same.

Artist's proof, with merely the words, "J. Bernardi dis. ed. inc. 1828," *cut with the needle.*

ARY SCHEFFER *pinx.* St. Cecilia, half length figure.

Artist's proof No. 39, *on India paper. With the inscription, in very small needle writing:* "Gravé par Jacopo Bernardi d'après Ary Scheffer."

RAPHAEL *pinx.* **P.** "Raphaelis Amicitia Celeberrima."

The picture is in the Marlborough collection in Blenheim.

The repetition, from which this engraving was made in 1830, was owned by Signora Cavallini-Brenzoni in Verona. Pass. II. No. 281, p. 429.

P. Washington.

Engraved from Greenough's statue.

BERNARD, J., mezzotinto engraver in Vienna, at the beginning of this century.

FRANCESCO FRANCIA *pinx.* The Virgin adoring the Child amid Flowers.

Inscribed erroneously with the name of Raphael as painter. Passavant, II. p. 412. kk. The picture is in the Munich Gallery. Engraved in mezzotinto.

BERNINGEROTH, JOHANN MARTIN, designer and engraver, born at Leipzig in 1713, died there in 1767. A pupil of his father, Martin.

P. Lebrecht Behrisch, jurisconsult. (*See* Goethe's Autobiography.)

BERTAUD, MARIE ROSALIE, engraver, born at Paris in 1738. She was a pupil of Saint-Aubin and Choffard.

JOS. VERNET *pinx.* La Barque mise à flot.

BERVIC, CHARLES CLÉMENT, designer and engraver, born at Paris in 1756, died there in 1822. His real name was Jean Guillaume Barvez. A pupil of Wille.

BERVIC, CHARLES CLÉMENT, *continued.*

RAPHAEL *pinx.* St. John the Baptist.

See Passavant, II. 243. The picture is in the Tribune of the Florence Gallery.

Engraved in 1791 for J. B. Wicar's *Tableaux ... de la Galerie de Florence et du Palais Pitti.*

1st proof before letters; the open uncial letters of the artists' names are merely traced with the needle.

A similar copy, Hösel, No. 53. George Smith, No. 527, £5 10*s.*

Laocoön.

Engraved, after the antique, for the *Musée Français.*

Impression of the finished plate with letters, on India paper, with the name of Ramboz as printer; 1st state.

The same.

2d artist's proof. Merely the name "Bervic," *traced in the centre under the plate, and before the additional name:* "Ramboz, imprimeur."

1st artist's proof, before any letters, Lamotte-Fouquet, No. 168, 82 *th.*; Debois, No. 80, 700 *fr.*; (Wilcox,) London, May, 1856, No. 23, £7 10*s.* — 2d artist's proof, like ours, Debois, No. 80 *bis*, 275 *fr.* — 3d state, proof before letters, with Bervic's name, and that of Ramboz as printer. — 4th state, print, with the inscription. The first impressions were made by Ramboz.

GUIDO *pinx.* L'Enlèvement de Déjanire.

The picture, formerly in Jabach's collection, is in the Gallery of the Louvre. Villot, No. 337. Engraved in 1798.

Artist's proof, before any letters, G. Smith, March, 1861, No. 528, £11 15*s.* — 1st proof, with only the names of the artists, Debois, No. 81.

REGNAULT *pinx.* L'Éducation d'Achille.

The picture is in the Gallery of the Louvre. Villot, No. 466. Engraved in 1803.

3d proof, before letters, i. e. before the inscription of the title, but with the names of the artists, the registration, and the engraver's address.

Artist's proof, before any letters, Debois, No. 82, 180 *fr.*

The states of the last two plates are alike, and there are five, viz.: I. Before any letters, *artist's proof.* — II. With merely the names of the artists: before the registration, and before the address; *1st proof.* — III. With the artists' names, and the registration, but before the address; *2d proof.* — IV. Still before letters, i. e. before the inscription of the title, the lower margin of the plate being all blank, except (*a*) above, close under the print: *Peint par Guide, gravée par Bervic* (or *Peint par Regnault, — gravée par Bervic*). *Enregistrée le* XV *Prairial de l'an* VI, on the first plate, Guido's picture, — and *Enregistrée le* XIX *Germinal* VI, on the second; and (*b*) at the bottom of the margin of the plate: *Se vend*

BERVIC, CHARLES CLÉMENT, *continued.*

chez Bervic. Galerie du Muséum, No. 12. 3d proof, like ours. — V. With the title and full inscription. There is, however, a great difference in the impressions of this state, and the plates are still in existence.

LÉPICIÉ *pinx.* La Demande acceptée.

Engraved in 1784.

Proof, with the names of the artists and the coat of arms, and one line of inscription, the title, but before the dedication.

First proofs are before letters and arms, and have only the name "Bervic."

LÉPICIÉ *pinx.* Le Repos.

Engraved in 1783.

2d state of the plate, and 1st state of the print, with letters, and the address of the two artists, but before the address of Martin.

The 1st state is before letters, but with the names of the artists. The 3d state has the inscription and the address.

CALLET *pinx.* **P.** Louis XVI. of France.

Engraved in 1790. The picture is in the Historical Museum at Versailles.

Impression from the plate before it had been cut in the middle (during the French Revolution) and with the signature of the engraver's name in pencil.

The 1st state is before any letters, and before the border was finished at the top and bottom. Logette, No. 14, 601 *fr.* — The 2d state, before any letters, with the border finished, Rigal, No. 88, 259 *fr.* — The 3d state, with only the names of the artists and the address of the engraver, also his signature in pencil, Debois, No. 83, 191 *fr.* In the sale catalogue of Amsler and Ruthardt, Berlin, 1865, I. No. 46, priced at 70 thalers. — The 4th state, like our copy, with the inscription, i. e. with letters, but before the plate was cut, and with the engraver's signature. — To the 5th state belong the impressions made after the restoration from the rejoined plate.

BERVIC *del.* **P.** Charles Gravier, Comte de Vergennes.

Engraved in 1780.

BETTAZZI, R., engraved for V. Marchese's "San Marco in Firenze." *See* MARCHESE.

BETTELINI, PIETRO, designer and engraver, born at Lugano in 1763, died at Rome in 1828. A pupil of Gandolfi and Bartolozzi; in his later works approaching the style of R. Morghen.

RAPHAEL *pinx.* The Transfiguration.

See Passavant, II. under 244, p. 362. m. The composition differs somewhat from the picture in the Vatican. Christ is represented in a glory

BETTELINI, PIETRO, *continued.*

of elliptical form, and the two deacons on Mount Tabor are absent. Compare also Luigi Pizzi and Francesco Pozzi in this catalogue.

Proof, open traced letters.

Andrea del Sarto *pinx.* The Entombment, or Pietà.

The picture is in the Gallery of the Pitti palace in Florence. Alfred Reumont, p. 174; for this engraving see p. 179. See also Crowe and Cavalcaselle, III. p. 571.

Proof: "Andrea del Sarto dipinse, Pietro Bettelini inc. in Roma nel 1811." *One line of inscription in open letters:* "Et vidimus eum despectum, et novissimum virorum, virum dolorum Is. C. 53." *An open space, and below:* "Luigi Bardi impresse — In Firenze presso Nicolo Pagni."

Artist's proofs have *A. del Sarto pinx. — P. Bettelini sc.* slightly traced with the needle. There are still earlier impressions, before any letters.

Titian *pinx.* Virgin with the Child and a Book in her Hand.

Proof, with the inscription "Mater Sapientiae" *in open letters, and the artists' names written with the needle.*

Artist's proofs have only the names of the artists traced with the needle.

Raphael *pinx.* Madonna dei Candelabri.

See Passavant, II. 264, and III. p. 168. The picture is in the collection of H. A. J. Munro, Esq., in London. Formerly in the Gallery of the Duke of Lucca.

Proofs have open letters. Artist's proofs are before any letters (Marshall's *Cat.*), others have merely the artists' names, written with the needle.

Correggio *pinx.* Madonna col Divoto.

The Madonna appearing to the donor in a Glory, St. James and St. Jerome seated below. In the Munich Gallery. Not mentioned by Coxe.

Proofs have open letters.

Domenichino *pinx.* St. John the Evangelist in Ecstasy, supported by two Angels.

The picture, formerly in the Giustiniani Gallery, is now in the collection of John P. Miles, Esq., at Leigh Court. Waagen, *Treasures,* III. p. 182.

Artist's proof, before any letters, with only the coat of arms.

Schidone *pinx.* St. Magdalen.

There is a corresponding picture in the Munich Gallery, only in that composition one of the angels holds a skull, whereas here he holds a book in his hand. Engraved in 1810.

Proof before letters; with only the artists' names traced, very small, with the needle, and with the coat of arms.

Artist's proofs are like the preceding.

Guido *pinx.* Virgin and Child in a Glory, below St. Thomas and St. Jerome.

BETTELINI, PIETRO, *continued.*

The picture is in the Gallery of the Vatican. Platner and Bunsen, II. ii. p. 432.

GUIDO *pinx.* The Assumption of the Virgin.

The picture is now in the Munich Gallery. It was formerly in the church Santa Croce in Rome, afterwards in the Düsseldorf Gallery.

Proof, open and traced letters.

BETTONI, a celebrated printer, born at Porto-Guaro in Lombardy in the latter part of the last century. He established presses in Brescia, Padova, Milan, and other cities of Italy, and published several collections of portraits.

𝔓. Volta, Alessandro.

With merely the inscription, *Per Nicolò Bettoni.* Engraved for his *Vite e Ritratti di illustri Italiani.*

BEZZI, an Italian engraver of the present day.

Alexander's Entry into Babylon.

18 plates. Thorwaldsen's bas-reliefs.

Before any letters.

BINK, JACOB, painter and engraver, born at Cologne about 1490, died at Königsberg in 1568. A follower of the school of Albrecht Dürer.

Combat of eleven Naked Men on foot.

See Bartsch, VIII. art. "I B.," No. 21.

BIONDI, VINCENZO, an engraver of the present day, born in Florence.

RAPHAEL *pinx.* St. John the Baptist.

The picture is in the Tribune of the Florence Gallery. Passavant, II. 243.

Proofs have only the names of the artists. Artist's proofs are before any letters. Lehrs, Nos. 30 and 31.

BISI, ERNESTA, painter and engraver. She was born at Lugano, and belongs to the school of Longhi.

𝔓. Agnesi, Gaetana.

𝔓. Colonna, Vittoria.

These two portraits were engraved for *Vite e Ritratti di illustri Italiani.*

BISI, MICHELE, engraver, born at Genoa about 1788, a pupil of Rosaspina and afterwards of Longhi.

LUINI *pinx.* Virgin and Child with St. Anthony and St. Barbara.

Fresco painting cut out of the wall and removed to the Brera Gallery in Milan.

BISI, MICHELE, *continued.*

LUINI *pinx.* The same.

Artist's proof, before any letters. In the middle of the lower margin a large white stamp, representing an owl holding a palette, and around it the inscription: "I. R. Academia di belle arti di Milano."

Amsler and Ruthardt's sale catalogue, Berlin, 1865, I. No. 62, 45 *th.*

Proofs have the inscription, *Bernardo Luini Dipinse a fresco — Michele Bisi disegnò ed incise,* delicately written with the needle; a white space, and below, in open letters, *Premiata dalla Reale Academia di Milano nell' Agosto del* 1815 *e nello stesso tempo publicata.*

Arndt, I. No. 1782, 49⅔ *th.*

APPIANI *pinx.* Venus embracing Cupid.

Engraved from a picture in the possession of Count Sommariva.

P. Amerigo Vespucci.

Engraved for *Vite e Ritratti di illustri Italiani.*

P. Franklin.

Engraved in 1818 for Nicolò Bettoni's collection of portraits entitled *Panteon delle Nazioni.*

BITTHEUSER, JOHANN PLEIKARD, engraver, pupil of J. G. von Müller, born at Butthard in 1774, lived in Würzburg.

TISCHBEIN *pinx.* **P.** August von Kotzebue.

Proof, open letters.

Artist's proofs are before any letters.

BLAKE, WILLIAM, a very eccentric English artist. Born in 1757. His instruction in engraving he received from Basire.

HOGARTH *pinx.* The Beggar's Opera.

With the key of the portraits. The picture is owned by John Murray, Esq.

BLANCHARD, the father, born at Paris in 1766.

MURILLO *pinx.* Ste. Juste.

See Stirling, *Annals,* III. p. 1439. In the collection of the Duke of Sutherland in Stafford House, No. 54. Not mentioned in Waagen's *Treasures.*

1*st proof, No.* 19, *before letters, with only the names of the artists, the printer, and the publisher. On India paper.*

COUDER *del.* **P.** Washington.

"Dessiné par Couder. Gravé par A. Blanchard."

Open letter, India paper.

The print is dedicated to General Jackson by the publisher, N. Bettoni.

BLANCHARD, AUGUSTE JEAN BAPTISTE MARIE, the son, born at Paris in 1792, a pupil of his father.

ARY SCHEFFER *pinx.* Christus Remunerator.

Proof before letters, with the tablet below white. On India paper.

MURILLO *pinx.* **P.** The painter's own portrait.

See Stirling, *Annals,* II. 898 and III. 1445. The picture was owned by King Louis Philippe of France.

Proof, with only the names of the artist, the printer, and the publisher.

The artist's proof is before any letters, except the inscription in the picture, *Vera effigies,* etc.

BIENNOURRY *del.* **P.** Pope Pio Nono.

Proof, with only the names of the artists. In the background of the picture is the coat of arms of the Pope.

BLASCHKE, J., engraver at Vienna, at the beginning of this century.

MURILLO *pinx.* St. John the Baptist, as a Child.

The picture is in the Vienna Gallery.

BLOEMAERT, CORNELIS, etcher and engraver, born at Utrecht in 1603, died at Rome in 1680. A pupil of his father, Abraham, and of Crispin de Passe.

"RAPHAEL *pinx.*" The Adoration of the Shepherds.

The composition is not Raphael's, but, as Mariette has observed, by Andrea Meldolla, called Schiavone, painter and etcher, who was born in Dalmatia, 1522, and died at Venice in 1582. *See* R. Weigel, in Otto's *Catalogue,* II. p. 63, No. 842; also Sternberg's *Cat.* I. No. 2469, and Einsiedel's, I. No. 898. J. B. Franceschi of Venice, the publisher of the plate, states, in the dedication to the Emperor Ferdinand III., that he owns the original, which he calls a Raphael. Bloemaert's name is not on the plate. The medallion, suspended on a column in the picture, contains the portrait of Franceschi.

2*d impression, with the address of Rossi (de Rubeis).*

ANN. CARACCI *pinx.* Christ on the Cross.

1*st state, before address.*

TITIAN *pinx.* The Virgin and Child in a Glory with St. John.

The picture was in the Giustiniani collection; it is not in the Berlin Gallery.

1*st state, with the engraver's address.*

With P. Mariette's name on the back of the print.

RAPHAEL *pinx.* St. Luke painting the Virgin.

See Passavant, II. 272. The picture is in the Academy of St. Luke in Rome.

BLOEMAERT, CORNELIS, *continued.*

2d state, with the address of Rossi (de Rubeis).

The 1st state is without address.

GUERCINO *pinx.* St. Peter raising Tabitha.

The picture is in the Gallery of the Pitti palace in Florence. Kugler's *Handbook*, 3d edit. II. p. 495.

Impression before address.

St. Yves, 273*fr.*; Logette, 100*fr.*; Révil, 60*fr.*; Debois, 39*fr.*

ANDREA DEL SARTO *pinx.* The Marriage of St. Catherine with St. John.

Engraved when in the Giustiniani Gallery in Rome. Not mentioned by Alfred Reumont. The picture is not in Berlin. Winckler's *Cat.* II. ii. No. 4502; Nagler's *K.-L.* XIX. p. 419.

ANN. CARACCI *pinx.* St. Margaret.

After the picture in Santa Caterina de' Funari in Rome, which is a repetition of a figure from a picture in the Dome of Reggio. Platner and Bunsen, III. iii. p. 517.

2d state, with Rossi's address.

ABRAHAM BLOEMAERT *pinx.* Christ appearing to St. Ignatius Loyola.

The picture is in the Jesuit church at Bois-le-Duc.

1st state, with the engraver's address.

PIETRO DA CORTONA *pinx.* Apollo.

PIETRO DA CORTONA *pinx.* Diana.

Frescos in the Room of Apollo in the Pitti palace in Florence.

2d state, with Rossi's address.

RUBENS *pinx.* Meleager and Atalanta with the Boar's Head.

See Smith, *Cat. rais.* 841. The picture is in the Marlborough collection in Blenheim.

Impression with the engraver's address.

BLOOTELING, ABRAHAM, designer and engraver with the burin and with aqua-fortis and in mezzotinto, born at Amsterdam in 1634, died in 1690 or 1695. Believed to be a pupil of the Visschers.

P. "Michael-Angelus Bonarotus nobilis Florentinus."

"A. Blooteling Fecit et Excudit." Mezzotint, in 8vo.

PALAMEDES *pinx.* **P.** Cocceius, Johannes.

VAN DYCK *pinx.* **P.** The Marquis of Mirabella.

"Marquis de Mirabelle. A. van Dyck pinxit. A. Bloteling sculp. et excud." The watermark of the paper is the coat of arms of Amsterdam.

There is a corresponding portrait in the collection of Warwick Castle. Smith, *Cat. rais.* 727. Waagen, *Treasures*, III. p. 214.

BLOOTELING, ABRAHAM, *continued.*

The plate, though corresponding in size, was never added to the collection of Van Dyck's portraits (the *Iconographia*).

P. Ruyter, Admiral Michiel Adriensz.

"A. Blotelingh fecit aqua forti et Exc."

With the engraver's address.

BLOT, MAURICE, designer and engraver, born at Paris in 1754, died in 1818. A pupil of Saint-Aubin.

RAPHAEL *pinx.* La Vierge aux Candelabres.

See Passavant, II. 264, and III. p. 168. From the Gallery Borghese and of Lucien Bonaparte in Rome the painting came into the collection of the Duke of Lucca, in which it was sold in London; it is now in the collection of H. A. J. Munro, Esq., in London. Engraved for the *Galerie Lucien Bonaparte,* No. 134.

Proof. The artists' names below the socle — which has the title, "La Vierge aux Candelabres," *in finished shaded letters — are in large cursive letters, but delicately cut with the needle.*

VAN DER WERFF *pinx.* The Judgment of Paris.

See Smith, *Cat. rais.* 83. The picture was in the Orleans Gallery. The Dresden picture differs a little in the composition from this.

LEONARDI DA VINCI *pinx.* La Vanité.

From the picture "Vanity and Modesty" in the Gallery of the Sciara palace in Rome, of which there are several repetitions. Rigollot, No. 56.

BOISSIEU, JEAN JACQUES DE, painter and etcher, born at Lyons in 1736, died there in 1810. His first lessons in drawing were received from Lombard and Frontier, and he perfected himself by the study of the great masters of the Netherlands, but especially after Nature. The references are to Rigal's *Catalogue,* and Le Blanc's *Manuel.*

The impressions are nearly all modern.

P. Boissieu's own portrait. R. 1. Le Bl. 20.

He holds a design of a landscape with cattle in his hands, and before him stands a cast of the head of one of the sons of Laocoön.

Folio.

St. Jerome writing; in a Landscape, by a Tree. R. 2. Le Bl. 1.

Large folio, upright.

The two Fathers of the Desert. R. 3. Le Bl. 2.

Large folio, upright.

Pope Pius VII. blessing the Children. R. 4. Le Bl. 23.

Folio, upright.

BOISSIEU, JEAN JACQUES DE, *continued.*

"Transeundo Benefaciebat." Pius VII. with his Train, in Boats on the Saône. R. 5. Le Bl. 19.
Folio, oblong.

Friars, chanting. R. 6. Le Bl. 25.
4to, oblong.

"La Soirée Villageoise." R. 7. Le Bl. 26.
A rustic family round the fireplace. Folio, oblong.

"Écrivain public." R. 8. Le Bl. 27.
Folio, oblong.

Four Coopers in a Cellar. R. 9. Le Bl. 28.
The larger plate of this subject. Folio, oblong.

"Ancienne Porte de Vaize à Lion." People bowling in the foreground. R. 10. Le Bl. 63.
Folio, oblong.

An open Wine Vault; on the right an Old Man fondling a Child on the Lap of his Mother. R. 12. Le Bl. 29.
Folio, oblong.

An open vaulted Cow-house, with two Cows; on the right an Old Man surrounded by five Children. R. 13. Le Bl. 30.
Folio, oblong.

The Schoolmaster, reprimanding a Boy. R. 14. Le Bl. 31.
Folio, oblong.

Alms given by an Old Man to a Woman who has a Child with her. R. 16. Le Bl. 33.
4to, oblong.

An Old Beggar; with his Hat on his Knee, to receive Alms. R. 17. Le Bl. 34.
Folio.

An Old Man, making a Boy read. R. 18. Le Bl. 35.
4to, upright.

Two Coopers in a Cellar. R. 23. Le Bl. 40.
4to, oblong.

Two Boys blowing Soap-bubbles. R. 25. Le Bl. 42.
Large folio, oblong.

A Painter, painting a long-bearded Old Man. R. 26. Le Bl. 43.
Folio, oblong.

A Man playing the Oboe to two young Shepherd Boys. R. 27. Le Bl. 44.
Folio, oblong.

BOISSIEU, JEAN JACQUES DE, *continued.*

View of the Ferry of Garillano. R. 31. Le Bl. 61.
Folio, oblong.

" Entrée du Village de Lantilly." R. 38. Le Bl. 62.
Large folio, oblong.

View of the Lake and Château of Sainte-Colombe. R. 39. Le Bl. 76.
Folio, oblong.

View of Saint-Andéol. R. 41. Le Bl. 75.
Large folio, oblong.

" Vue de Saint-Romain-sur-Gier." R. 45. Le Bl. 77.
Small 4to, oblong.

" Entrée de la forêt de Fontainebleau sur la route de Lyon." R. 47. Lo Bl. 60.
4to, oblong.

View of the Fountain of Choulan, near Lyons. R. 48. Le Bl. 66.
Small 4to, upright.

Mountainous Rocks, with Cascades. R. 49. Le Bl. 82.
Small 4to, upright.

Cascade falling from a very elevated building, reminding one of Tivoli. R. 50. Le Bl. 83.
Small 4to, upright.

Men on the Bank of a River, carrying a Drowned Man; on the left a Tower, like Cæcilia Metella's. R. 57. Le Bl. 86.
Large folio, oblong.

Villagers reposing on the Border of a Wood; with them a Woman feeding her Child. R. 59. Le Bl. 88.
4to, oblong.

A Man on Horseback and one on Foot, fording a Stream, with two Cows. R. 61. Le Bl. 90.
Folio, oblong.

An Old Chapel bordered by Trees; in the foreground a peasant girl near a young man who makes a dog dance, on the right a river with a cascade. R. 65. Le Bl. 94.
Folio, oblong.

A Boat in Repair, in a Dock at Savigny. R. 69. Le Bl. 78.
Large 4to, oblong.

A Shepherd on foot and a Shepherdess on horseback, driving four Cows. R. 70. Le Bl. 98.
Folio, oblong.

BOISSIEU, JEAN JACQUES DE, *continued.*

Entrance of a Forest; on the left two peasants and a little girl, before a thatched old hut; on the right a man on horseback inquiring his way. R. 72. Le Bl. 100.
Folio, oblong.

Winter Landscape. On the left are six persons round a fire, on the right the barren old trunk of a tree. R. 73. Le Bl. 101.
4to, upright.

A Landscape in Spring. A shepherd and two shepherdesses sitting on the ground; on the right, near them, are cattle; on the left, the trunk of an old cherry-tree, sprouting. R. 74. Le Bl. 102.
4to, upright.

Landscape. On the left an old open thatched shed, in the foreground a little girl gathering wood, preceded by a man with an infant, driving a cow. In the style of Wynants. R. 75. Le Bl. 103.
Small 4to, oblong.

An Ass with her Foal crouched behind her. R. 77. Le Bl. 105.
4to, oblong.

Study of a Grove; on the right a Huntsman. R. 78. Le Bl. 106.
4to, oblong.

A Marine Piece. On the left a bark sailing, on the right a round tower backed by steep rocks. R. 80. Le Bl. 108.
4to, oblong.

A Mill in Italy, near a rock, from which three cascades are streaming down. R. 81. Le Bl. 109.
4to, oblong.

P. De Boissieu, M. D., brother of the Artist. R. 101. Le Bl. 21.
Small 4to.

P. The Servant-woman of the Artist. R. 102. Le Bl. 24.
4to.

Bust of an Old Man, with Bald Head; nearly full profile view to the right. R. 103. Le Bl. 47.
4to.

Bust of an Old Man with Cap, nearly a full face view; looking to the right. R. 104. Le Bl. 48.
4to.

Bust of an Old Man with Long Hair, almost a full face view, looking toward the left. R. 105. Le Bl. 49.
4to.

BOISSIEU, JEAN JACQUES DE, *continued.*

"La Boudeuse." Bust of a cross old woman, looking downwards with a kerchief tied over her cap; nearly profile, to the right. R. 106. Le Bl. 50.

Large 4to.

The Hurdy-gurdy Player. Le Bl. 45.

The first representation of this subject; he grinds with his left hand, and has his right hand on the keys. 4to.

In the 2d plate (Le Bl. 46), the man is represented as using his right hand in turning.

Eight studies: a man playing the guitar, a dog's head, five heads of old men; a sixth, a faint outline of the head of an old man, has disappeared in this impression. R. 110. Le Bl. 8.

Large 4to.

Thirteen studies: a long-bearded man with a muff, a barber lathering a beard, and other heads. R. 112. Le Bl. 10.

Large 4to.

A Cat sitting with a Kitten crouched before her. R. 113. Le Bl. 4.

12mo.

Eight studies: among which is a woman seated, and leaning on her elbows, with a book in her hand, her hair gathered at the top of her head. R. 120. Le Bl. 17.

8vo, oblong.

Two studies: a woman with a large, round hat, holding a distaff, and an old man with beard and bare head. R. 121. Le Bl. 18.

16mo, oblong.

Five studies, occupying the upper half of the plate; the lower half is blank. Three heads in profile from the left looking to the right: the first slightly traced, looking down; the second head the form of Michel-Angelo's portrait; the third a monk with a cowl. The fourth head is a profile, and the fifth a three-quarters profile to the left, of a child.

8vo, oblong. Ackermann's collection, 2d catalogue, No. 1010.

After other masters.

VAN DYCK *pinx.* Bust of a man with a short beard, wearing a square linen collar, nearly full face looking to the right. R. 126. Le Bl. 53.

Smith, *Cat. rais.* Van Dyck, No. 665. 4to.

An old impression, with burr, and on old paper.

TENIERS *pinx.* A man with crossed hands and short hair, half figure; in a black cloak and muslin collar. R. 127. Le Bl. 54.

4to.

BOISSIEU, JEAN JACQUES DE, *continued.*

Fouquières *del.* Landscape; a young man leading a donkey, on which a girl is seated, through a stream, and driving two cows before him. R. 128. Le Bl. 128.

Folio, oblong.

Berghem *pinx.* A Shepherd with a Dog, driving three Beeves through a Stream. R. 131. Le Bl. 131.

Folio, oblong.

Asselyn *pinx.* The Breach of a Dike. B. 133. Le Bl. 133.

"Gravé à l'eau forte d'après un tableau d'Asselin Craesbéke. Tiré du Cabinet de Monsieur Tronchin de La Bossière." Folio, oblong.

The painter of this landscape is Jan Asselyn, born at Antwerp in 1610, who studied with Jan van de Velde and then went to Rome, where he had much intercourse with Pieter van Laer, whose influence is perceptible in this composition. He was nicknamed Krabbetje, on account of his contorted, crab-like hand, with crooked fingers. Josse van Craesbeke is a different painter, born in 1608; originally a baker and a boon companion of Adriaen Brouwer in his carousals, he became his pupil and imitator.

Jac. Ruysdael *pinx.* A Mill; on the right two Draftsmen. R. 135. Le Bl. 135.

Large folio, oblong.

Jac. Ruysdael *pinx.* A Mill; on the left a Ferry-boat crossing the River. R. 136. Le Bl. 136.

Folio, oblong.

Jac. Ruysdael *pinx.* Landscape divided by a Road; on the left two thatched huts, near them a traveller reposing with a dog; in the background two houses with two men near them. R. 137. Le Bl. 137.

Folio, oblong.

Jac. Ruysdael *pinx.* A Hut near Water, through which a Boy is driving an Ox. R. 138. Le Bl. 138.

4to.

Dujardin *pinx.* The Quack Doctor with his booth on a stage, and a Merry-Andrew (the larger representation); in the background Roman ruins. A composition of 14 figures. R. 140. Le Bl. 55.

Folio, oblong. The original is in the Gallery of the Louvre. Villot, No. 243.

BOL, FERDINAND, painter and etcher, born at Dordrecht about 1610, died at Amsterdam in 1681. One of the best pupils of Rembrandt, and coming nearest to him in his style. Bartsch, *Cat. rais. de . . . Rembrandt,* II.

BOL, FERDINAND, *continued.*

The Officer. B. 11.

With the stamp of Ackermann's collection.

A Man with two Plumes in his Cap. B. 13.

With Ackermann's stamp.

A Woman with a Pear. B. 14.

BOLDRINI, NICOLÒ, painter, and engraver on wood. It is supposed that he was born in Vicenza about 1510, and worked in Venice till about 1560.

TITIAN *inv.* Group of Monkeys in the attitude of Laocoön.

See Baseggio, *Intorno tre celebri intagliatori*, ec., Boldrini, No. 7. A satire on the work in marble of Baccio Bandinelli, who boasted that he had surpassed the antique.

BOLOGNONI, GIOVANNI BATTISTA, painter and etcher, born at Bologna in 1612, died in 1689. A pupil of Guido Reni. Bartsch, XIX.

GUIDO *pinx.* Massacre of the Innocents. B. 1.

In the Bologna Gallery.

Impression without the letter-press plate below.

BOLSWERT, BOÉTIUS À, (*family name* ADAM,) born at Bolswert in Friesland about 1580, died at Antwerp in 1634. He is supposed to have been a pupil of Corn. Bloemaert.

RUBENS *pinx.* The Raising of Lazarus.

See Smith, *Cat. rais.* 357. The picture is in the Berlin Gallery. Waagen's catalogue, No. 783. Formerly in the Gallery of Potsdam. Basan, 61.

1*st state, with the engraver's own address.*

Nagler (*K.-L.*) states that the picture from which this engraving was taken was painted for an altar of the Abbey of Audenaerde, and that it is now in the Gallery of Turin. We do not find such a picture mentioned there; comp. Lavice, *Revue des Musées d'Italie.*

RUBENS *pinx.* Christ crucified between the two Thieves, and pierced in the side.

Altar-piece formerly in the church of the Recollets, now in the hall of the Academy of Antwerp. Smith, *Cat. rais.* 27; Basan, 87.

1*st state, before the name of the engraver, the year and address.*

The 2d state has the inscription: *à Bolswert sculp. C. P. R. C. S. I. et O. C.* — The 3d state has the addition of the year, 1631.

BAROCCIO *pinx.* "Pardon of St. Franciscus."

A copy of Baroccio's own etching. Bartsch, No. 4. "Le tableau est dans l'Église des Anges à Assise." — Heineken, *Diction.* II. p. 149.

BOLSWERT, BOETIUS À, *continued.*

VINCKBOONS *pinx.* Time and Death slaying Men of all conditions, and also Beasts.

Nagler, *K.-L.* II. p. 22, and XX. p. 351. The original picture is owned by the writer of this catalogue.

1st state, with the address: "B. a Bolsuerd excudit."

VINCKBOONS *pinx.* The same.

2d state, with the address: "Hugo Allardt excudit."

BOLSWERT, SCHELTE À, (*family name* ADAM,) a brother of the preceding, designer and engraver. He was born at Bolswert about 1586, and lived at Antwerp, where he died at an advanced age. He was one of the most prominent members of that school of engravers of which Rubens was the head. It is said that the latter often retouched Schelte's proofs of the plates after his pictures.

THEODOR ROMBOUTS *pinx.* Abraham offering up Isaac.

2d plate, or rather repetition, or copy in reverse, of Scheltius's plate, by a contemporary engraver of the same school.

Nagler (*K.-L.* XIII. p. 339, art. *Rombouts*) speaks of this print. After mentioning Schelte à Bolswert's engraving, dedicated to the bishop Antoni Triest, he goes on to say: "The composition is also engraved in reverse, the ram caught in the thorns appearing at the left. It has the inscription: *Poscit Abrahamus* etc. *Gaspar ex.* . . . " The description is taken from Count Sternberg-Manderscheid's catalogue, III. p. 256, No. 2086 (2085 being Schelte's engraving). Through an error the catalogue has "Abrahamus" instead of "Abram," and the extreme lower right corner was wanting, so that of the address there was only "Gaspar" ("Huberti exc." being torn off). Our print is the identical one from the Count's collection, and as we do not find it described except from this collection, we give the inscription in full. It is in two rows, each of two lines:—

Poscit Abram poscit vitam Deus, annuit Isac
Et patris primus gaudet ab ense mori.
Disce puer legesq. patris matrisq. tenere
Vt videas longos et sine labe dies.

RUBENS *pinx.* The Raising of the Brazen Serpent.

Smith, *Cat. rais.* 769, and *Suppl.* 260; Basan, 16. The picture is in the National Gallery, from T. B. Owen, Esq.; formerly in the Marana palace at Genoa. Waagen, *Treasures*, I. p. 316, and p. 349. A duplicate is in the Royal Gallery at Potsdam, according to Michiels. There is a school copy in the Madrid Gallery. Smith, *ibid.*

Before any address.

BOLSWERT, SCHELTE À, *continued.*

From the collection of the Duke of Buckingham. (Catal. No. 58.) Purchased for £5 5 *s.*

1st address, Gil. Hendricx; 2d address, Van Merlen.

SEGHERS *pinx.* The Annunciation.

Without any address.

RUBENS *pinx.* The Marriage of the Virgin.

Smith, *Cat. rais.* 1000. Basan, 1.

Before (Hendricx's) *address.*

RUBENS *pinx.* The Nativity.

Mary, in adoration, on one side of the crib; Joseph, with a cane, on the other; overhead three angels, holding a scroll. Smith, *Cat. rais.* 934; Basan, 7.

1*st address, Martin van den Enden.*

2d address, Gil. Hendricx.

RUBENS *pinx.* The Adoration of the Shepherds.

The figures cast long shadows on the wall. Smith, *Cat. rais.* 117. Painted for the church of the Capuchins at Lille. Basan, 11.

3*d state, with Bolswert's name as engraver, who retouched the plate, which was originally engraved by Witdoeck.*

For earlier states of the plate see WITDOECK.

RUBENS *pinx.* The Feast of Herodias; with the Head of St. John presented at the Table.

Smith, *Cat. rais.* 603; comp. also *Suppl.* p. 307, No. 229; Basan, 41.

With the address of Gillis Hendricx.

RUBENS *pinx.* The Daughter of Herodias receiving the Head of St. John.

Smith, *Cat. rais.* 1010, and *Suppl.* p. 308, No. 230. Basan, 39. A corresponding picture is in the Dresden Gallery, and there is a similar one in the collection of the Earl of Carlisle.

1*st state, with engraver's address.*

The 2d state has Bonenfant's address.

RUBENS *pinx.* The Miraculous Draught of Fishes.

Engraved on three plates. Smith, *Cat. rais.* 130. The picture, in the church of Notre Dame at Malines, was originally painted for the Chapel of the Fishmonger's Company in this church. Basan, 48.

1*st state, with the engraver's address.*

Purchased for £4 4 *s.*

VAN DYCK *pinx.* Christ crowned with Thorns.

The picture is in the Berlin Gallery. Waagen, *Handb.* II. p. 285.

2*d state, still with the address of Martin van den Enden. It has the cross-hatching on the garment and the cheek of the second soldier on the right.*

BOLSWERT, SCHELTE À, *continued.*

The 1st state is before this crosshatching. Logette, No. 25, 244*fr.*; Rigal, No. 150, 340*fr.*; Archinto, No. 26, 200*fr.*; Marshall, No. 214, £12.

VAN DYCK *pinx.* The Elevation of the Cross.

Smith, *Cat. rais.* 33. Painted for the church of Notre Dame at Courtray, and still there.

Without any address.

VAN DYCK *pinx.* The Crucifixion; "Christ à l'Éponge."

Altar-piece in the church of St. Michael at Ghent, for which it was originally painted. Smith, *Cat. rais.* 31.

3*d state. With the shading of four lines in front of the great toe of the man with the sponge; with the shadow of the bone in the foreground extending its entire length; and with the name of Van Dyck transferred from the left to the right. These three changes were made in the preceding* 2*d state. In addition to these, in this* 3*d state, the hand of St. John — which in the* 2*d state rested on the shoulder of the Virgin Mary — has been erased, to make it appear like the* 1*st state. The single line of inscription of the* 2*d state (the first line of the inscription of the* 1*st and* 3*d)* — "Cum vidisset Jesus matrem," *etc. — has been erased, and the inscription of the* 1*st state, which has the addition of a dedication to Franc. de Moncada, has been re-engraved. The letters however are thicker and less graceful than those of the* 1*st state. The address of this* 3*d state, as of the* 2*d and* 1*st, is Martin van den Enden.*

See Rigal, No. 151; also the description in Bartsch's *Anleitung*, II. p. 92.

1st *finished* state, Marshall, No. 215, £12 12*s.*

JORDAENS *pinx.* The Crucifixion.

Basan, 10.

2*d state, with* "cum privilegio regis" *before the coat of arms of the* 3*d state.*

RUBENS *pinx.* Maria Mater Dei, Regina Coeli.

Virgin with crown and globe, Child with sceptre. Smith, *Cat. rais.* 953; Basan, 36.

1*st state, before any address.*

1st address, the engraver's; 2d address, Martin van den Enden's.

RUBENS *pinx.* Holy Family with a Lamb.

The picture is in the collection of the Earl of Lonsdale at Lowther Castle. A repetition was in the Houghton Gallery, and is now in the Imperial Gallery of St. Petersburg. Smith, *Cat. rais.* 546, and *App.* p. 329, No. 313; Basan, 44.

1*st state, with the address of Martin van den Enden.*

The 2d state has Hendricx's address.

RUBENS *pinx.* Saint Anne teaching the Virgin to read.

BOLSWERT, SCHELTE À, *continued.*

Painted for the church of the Minor Carmelites at Antwerp, and now in the hall of the Academy there. Smith, *Cat. rais.* 77.

2d state, with 4 lines of inscription and Gillis Hendricx's address.

The 1st state is before the dedication, and has but 2 lines inscription and Martin van den Enden's address.

RUBENS *pinx.* The Assumption of the Virgin.

Engraving with a square top (not arched).

1st state, with the dedication: "R. P. Gvardiano FF. Minorvm . . . Martinvs vanden Enden D. C. Q." *Before any further address.*

The addresses are, (1.) *Martinus vanden Enden excud.* (2.) *G. Hendricx excud.* (3.) Retouched, *Corn. van Merlen.*

M. Huber states, in Brandes's *Cat.* I. p. 454, that the picture is "à l'Église Cathédrale d'Anvers." In that painting the composition is different, and the picture is arched at the top; comp. Smith, *Cat. rais.* 148. This engraving differs more or less from any composition of this subject described by Smith. It is perhaps after the picture (or from a drawing corresponding with the picture) which was destroyed by fire in the Jesuits' church at Antwerp.

RUBENS *pinx.* St. Teresa interceding for the Souls in Purgatory.

Smith, *Cat. rais.* 75. In the Gallery of Antwerp, painted for the church of the Minor Carmelites in Antwerp. Waagen, *Handb.* II. p. 268; Basan, 33. A picture corresponding with this was sold in the collection of Patureau in Paris, in 1857, and purchased by the Marquis de Blézié for 16,000*fr.* Charles Blanc, *Le Trésor,* II. p. 529.

1st state, with the address of Martin van den Enden.

RUBENS *pinx.* St. Francis Xavier, standing in Prayer before a Crucifix.

Smith, *Cat. rais.* 144. The picture was formerly in the Jesuits' church at Brussels. Basan, 18.

JORDAENS *pinx.* The Family Concert.

Waagen, *Handb.* II. p. 293. The engraving differs a little in composition from the picture of this subject in the Gallery of Berlin (Waagen's catal. No. 879), and also from that in the Gallery of the Louvre (Villot, No. 256). Basan, 24.

2d state, with Blooteling's address, but before the retouch.

The 1st state is before address.

RUBENS *pinx.* The Great Lion Hunt.

In the Munich Gallery. Smith, *Cat. rais.* 247; Waagen, *Handb.* II. p. 272.

With the engraver's address.

RUBENS *pinx.* Le Retour de Chasse.

BOLSWERT, SCHELTE À, *continued.*

Basan, 26. Diana with three Dogs, followed by three Nymphs; before her, two Satyrs, with fruit, and a third person. "Sic vobis lassae sint ... bene." In the Dresden Gallery, according to Smith, *Cat. rais.* 252; but the picture there does not entirely correspond with this engraving.

With G. Hendricx's address.

JORDAENS *pinx.* Mercury and Argus.

1st state, before Blooteling's address.

RUBENS *pinx.* Philemon and Baucis.

Vienna Gallery. Smith, *Cat. rais.* 297. The first of the series of six engravings, — "The Great Landscapes" (the sixth engraved by Clouet).

With Gillis Hendricx's address.

RUBENS *pinx.* Dance of Peasants.

The 20th of the set of 21 small Landscapes.

2d state, address of Gillis Hendricx.

The 1st state has the address of Martin van den Enden.

There is a similar picture in the Madrid Gallery that has been lithographed by F. de Craene in the *Coleccion litografica* of Madrazo.

VAN DYCK *pinx.* **P.** Brouwer, Adriaan, painter.

"*Adrianus Brauwer* [sic], *gryllorum pictor Antverpiae.*" Engraved for M. van den Enden, Van Dyck's *Iconographia*, No. 4. Weber, *Cat. rais.* p. 52.

4th state, after the address of M. van den Enden, but before the letters "G. H.," *Gillis Hendricx's address, and before the 3d line of inscription,* "Natione Flander." "*État intermédiaire et extrêmement rare.*" (Weber.) *Paper with the watermark of the Smaller Foolscap and the letter* H *with a* P *joined, above in the middle.*

The 5th state is with the 3d line, with the spelling of the name corrected ("Brouwer"), and with the letters "G. H." "Beau et rare." — In the 6th state these letters are effaced.

VAN DYCK *pinx.* **P.** Ertvelt, Andreas van, painter.

Engraved for G. Hendricx. Weber, p. 101.

2d state, without "G. H." *Brilliant impression on paper with the watermark of the Cross of Lorraine. Weber remarks, however, that though such impressions pass for proofs before the address, they are after the same.*

VAN DYCK *pinx.* **P.** Lipsius, Justus, historiographer.

Engraved for M. van den Enden, Van Dyck's *Iconographia*, No. 5. Weber, p. 53.

4th state, after the erasure of "G. H." *on the plate. Paper with the watermark of the Smaller Foolscap.*

VAN DYCK *pinx.* **P.** Pepyn, Martin, painter.

Engraved for M. van den Enden's *Iconographia*, No. 6. Weber, p. 53.

BOLSWERT, SCHELTE À, *continued.*

4th state, after the address " G. H." *Paper with the watermark of the coat of arms of Amsterdam.*

VAN DYCK *pinx.* 𝔓. Vos, Willem de, painter.

Van Dyck etched the head and doublet. Carpenter, p. 117, No. 20; Weber, p. 34.

4th state, after " G. H." *Fine impression, on paper with the watermark of a kind of beehive.*

VAN DYCK *pinx.* 𝔓. Vos, Paul de, painter.

Van Dyck etched the head, doublet, and part of the background.

Smith, *Cat. rais.* 355. The picture is in the collection of the Prince of Saxe-Coburg. Carpenter, p. 119, No. 21; Weber, p. 35.

5th state. (" S. à Bolswert sculpsit " *has been erased from the print.*) *The watermark has the letters* " C. A.," *etc.*

See further under VAN DYCK. Van Dyck etched merely the head and coat, and part of the background; pure aqua-fortis, before letters; *1st state.* — The plate was then finished, in an unsatisfactory manner, by J. Meyssens, who published two states of the plate, the second with cross-hatchings on the cloak over the right shoulder; they have the inscription *Pavlvs de Vos pictor*, and below, on the left, *Anton Van Dyck fecit*, on the right, *Joan Meyssens excudit; 2d and 3d states.* — The plate was then well retouched by S. à Bolswert, with the title in two lines, *Pavlvs de Vos pictor venationum Antverpiae*, and below, on the left: *Anton van Dyck pinxit et fecit aqua forti*, on the right, *S. à Bolswert sculpsit.* First with the address " G. H."; *4th state.* — In the *5th state*, the address is effaced.

BOLT, JOHANN FRIEDRICH, designer, engraver, and etcher, born at Berlin in 1769, where he died in 1836. A pupil of D. Berger.

F. LIEDER *del.* 𝔓. Friedrich Schleiermacher, Doctor der Theologie.

Engraved in 1817, in the dotted manner.

BONAINI.

FRA ANGELICO *pinx.* Adoration of the Magi. Wound with the Spear.

See MARCHESE, V. San Marco in Firenze, etc. Nos. 13, 25.

BONASONE, GIULIO, designer and engraver, born at Bologna about 1500, died at Rome about 1580. He studied painting with Sabbatini, but took, in engraving, Marc-Antonio for his model. Bartsch, XV.

POLIDORO DA CARAVAGGIO *pinx.* The Flight of Clelia. B. 83.

2d state, with the address of Lafreri.

Jason and Medea. B. 98.

From the collections and with the signatures of P. Mariette and W. Esdaile, and with Ackermann's stamp.

BONASONE, GIULIO, *continued.*

P. Michel-Angelo Buonarroti. B. 345.

The plate was used, in a later state, for the frontispiece of Condivi's Life of Michel-Angelo. Harrach, No. 435, 76*fr.*

BONATO, PIETRO, engraver, born at Bassano in 1765, died at Rome in 1820. He was a pupil of Volpato.

"RAPHAEL *pinx.*" Apollo and Diana and the Five Planets.

Frescos on the ceiling of the Sala Borgia in the Vatican, falsely ascribed to Raphael. They were really painted by Giovanni da Udine and Perino del Vaga. Passavant, II. p. 422, b. and 423. Engraved in conjunction with Bettelini, Bortignoni, and Fontana. Seven plates, viz. : —

Apollo,	Pietro Bonato.
Diana,	Fontana.
Mars,	Bettelini.
Mercury,	Pietro Bonato.
Jupiter,	Pietro Bonato.
Venus,	Giuseppe Bortignoni.
Saturn,	Pietro Bonato.

BOND, WILLIAM.

P. Sir Joshua Reynolds.

"From a picture in the Council-chamber of the Royal Academy."

BOSSI, BENIGNO, designer and engraver, born in the Milanese territory in 1727, died at Parma in 1800.

12 plates, heads, etched.

BOSSI, GIACOMO, engraver, worked at Rome from 1782 to 1798.

RAPHAEL *pinx.* GIOV. CAPPELLI *del.* The Coronation of the Virgin.

See Passavant, II. 251. From the convent of Monte Luce. Now in the Gallery of the Vatican.

For other works, see MONTAGNANI, *Raphael's Bible.*

BOTH, JAN, painter and etcher, born at Utrecht in 1610, died there in 1650. A pupil of his father and A. Bloemaert. Bartsch, v.

Woman on a Mule. B. 1.
Ox-cart. B. 2.
The Muleteer. B. 6.
The Ferry-boat. B. 7.

All of these are in the 5th and last state. Weigel, *Suppl.*

BOTTICELLI, SANDRO (ALESSANDRO), painter, goldsmith, and engraver, born at Florence in 1437, where he died in 1515. His own name

BOTTICELLI, SANDRO, *continued.*

was Filipepi, but he assumed the name Botticelli from a goldsmith, who instructed him in his art; painting he studied afterwards with Filippo Lippi.

BALDINI, BACCIO, goldsmith and engraver, born at Florence about 1436. All we know of this artist is contained in a passage of Vasari, in the life of Marc-Antonio, where, after relating Finiguerra's discovery, he says that this artist was followed by Baldini, who, being himself deficient in drawing, engraved only after designs of Sandro Botticelli. He produced likewise many plates in copartnership with the latter, whom he followed so closely that it is very difficult to identify their individual works. But Sandro, though not so skilful in handling the graver, was far superior in design, and his works have a more artistic effect.

FINIGUERRA, MASO (TOMASO), goldsmith and niellist, "the Italian discoverer of the art of engraving," was born at Florence according to Zani in 1418, according to Ottley in 1410, and is considered a scholar of Masaccio.

Unique impression of a silver plate of circular form, 4 inches 5 lines in diameter, old French measure, or 120 millimetres new measure.

A young woman in classical costume and a young man dressed in a tabard, which has the figure of an eagle on the breast, each holding a ball in one hand, and standing as supporters to a circular shield with six balls (the arms of the Medici family), which are sketched in with pen and ink, as is also the inscription at the top: *ò amore te* q^a *piglia* q^a. The shield rests on a flower-basket, and is surmounted by a basket, full of balls, in the form of a crown. The woman holds in her other hand a wreath, the left hand of the young man rests on his hip. Bartsch, XIII. No. 2; Ottley, No. 2.

Carving, chiselling, and engraving in metal had always been a practice with goldsmiths. Works of this kind were executed in the middle ages, and even among the antique bronzes we find specimens with ornamental engraving on them; but it seems that no impressions from them were made on paper till the middle of the fifteenth century. At this time some of the finest designs were executed on silver in "niello," so called (from the Latin *nigellum, niellum*) on account of the black color of the drawing, which was produced by filling up the hatches with a mixture of oxide of silver, sulphur, etc., which was burned in. Of these plates the artists were in the habit of making a cast in sulphur before they filled up the hatches, and it is recorded of Maso Finiguerra, that he was the first who added to this process that of making an imprint on paper by filling up the lines and tracings of the plate with a mixture of lamp-black and oil, and pressing

BOTTICELLI, SANDRO, *continued.*

damped paper upon it, by rubbing it with the hand or with a common roller. These impressions are extremely rare, as seldom more than one or two were made.

Some of the engraved silver plates of which impressions have come down to us seem not to have been destined to have the design on them filled up with a niello or enamel substance, because they are more delicately or slightly worked, rather traced or scratched.

Our print is one of this latter class. It is the 2d in number of a set of 24 as described by Huber, Bartsch, and Ottley, which Baron von Stosch bought a hundred years ago in Florence, and which, after his death and that of his heir, Mr. Muzel, were for half a century the ornament of the Otto collection in Leipzig. They are unique with the exception of one (Huber, Bartsch, and Ottley, No. 13), of which, according to Zani, there is a duplicate in the Durazzo collection in Genoa.

Heineken, *Neue Nachrichten von Künstlern und Kunstsachen*, is the first who has described them, attributing them to Maso Finiguerra. He gives a fac-simile of our print, No. 2 (as also of No. 1 of the set). Huber, in his *Manuel des curieux et des amateurs de l'art*, also ascribes them to Maso Finiguerra, and gives a full description of the prints. The same account will be found in Huber and Rost's *Handbuch für Kunstliebhaber*, III. p. 34, et seqq. They were further described by Baldinucci, who attributes them to an unknown Italian master. Bartsch, who speaks of them under Maso Finiguerra, is inclined to ascribe them to the unknown Italian master who engraved the playing cards usually called *Gioco di Mantegna*. Ottley, in his *Inquiry into the Origin and Early History of Engraving*, gives (Vol. I.) a description of this set of prints, which he ascribes to Baccio Baldini, and also (p. 354) a fac-simile of the two first, like Heineken. Duchesne ainé, in his *Voyage d'un Iconophile*, attributes them to Baccio Baldini, and says, "Though not by Maso Finiguerra (under whose name they were in the Otto collection) they are not the less '*excessivement précieuses.*'" Rudolph Weigel, in his *Catalog der Otto'schen Kupferstichsammlung*, ascribes the engraving of the plates as well as the design to Sandro Botticelli.

The prints are further spoken of in Huber, *Notices générales des graveurs;* Zani, *Enciclopedia metodica*, Parte I. Vol. I. p. 18; Parte II. Vol. IV. pp. 19, 39; Bryan's *Dictionary of Painters and Engravers*, under *Finiguerra;* and Nagler's *Künstler-Lexicon*, IV. p. 336. Waagen, *Treasures of Art in Great Britain*, I. p. 253, and *Supplement*, p. 42, describes 16 of them, which are now in the British Museum.

When the Otto collection was broken up in 1852 there were but 18 of the original set of 24 left, so that the British Museum now possesses all that were then sold, with the exception of two. One of these, No. 11 of Huber, Bartsch, and Ottley, did not go to the British Museum, though bought by

BOTTICELLI, SANDRO, *continued.*

Mr. Evans, who bid in others that went there. The other, H. B. and O. No. 2, is ours, the above described. It was bought by the compiler of this catalogue as the most desirable of the number, the most pleasing, and for a higher price than any of the rest. Nagler, *Die Monogrammisten*, I. p. 716, gives an account of this set of engravings, and also states the prices for which they were sold, and the names of the purchasers.

Mr. Otto, who died in 1799, had parted before with the other 6 pieces: with 3 to the engraver Bause, who died in 1814, and at the auction of whose collection in Leipzig, 1861, they were sold at the following prices:— H. B. and O. No. 13, for 182 *th.*; No. 17, for 208 *th.*; No. 23, for 182 *th.*; Mr. Weigel must know to whom. No. 4 of H. B. and O. Count Fries received from Mr. Otto, and it is now in the collection of the Archduke Albert, in Vienna; No. 18 came into Rost's collection, in which it was sold in Leipzig in 1800; No. 20 Mr. Otto presented to the Abbate Zani. This print has also been recently acquired by the British Museum.

BOULANGER, JEAN, designer and engraver, was born at Troyes in 1613, and died in Paris at an advanced age. He was a pupil of Guido Reni.

RAPHAEL *pinx.* Madonna with the Pink; both Mother and Child holding stems of Carnation in their hands.

See Passavant, II. 55. There are numerous repetitions of this picture, the original of which is not known; the most familiar one was that in the Camuccini collection in Rome, now in the collection of the Duke of Northumberland, in Alnwick Castle. Waagen, *Galleries and Cabinets*, or *Treasures*, IV. p. 466.

BOULONOIS, EDME or **ESME DE,** designer and engraver, worked at Paris towards the end of the 17th century.

VAN DYCK *pinx.* **P.** Callot.

Engraved for the *Académie des Sciences et des Arts*, published by Is. Bullard, Bruxelles, 1682, 2 vols. fol., containing 94 pieces.

BOUVIER, CHARLES, engraver of the present day in Paris, a pupil of N. Schenker.

TITIAN *pinx.* **P.** Ariosto.

"D'après le tableau original du cabinet de M. F. Duval à Geneve."

VELAZQUEZ *pinx.* **P.** Cervantes.

"D'après le tableau original du cabinet de M. Briere à Geneve."

Proof, open and traced letters.

BOYDELL, JOHN, designer and engraver, the eminent publisher. He was born at Dorington in 1719, and died at London in 1804. A pupil of Toms.

BOYDELL, JOHN, *continued.*

REYNOLDS *pinx.* The Window in New College Chapel, Oxford, representing the Nativity, and the Cardinal Virtues.

Designed by Jervaise, after Sir J. Reynolds. "Boydell exc."

BOYDELL, JOSHUA, son of John, painter and mezzotinto engraver, was born at London in 1750, and died there in 1817.

REMBRANDT *pinx.* **P.** "Renier Ansloo, and his Wife," more correctly his mother.

The picture is in the collection of the Earl of Ashburnham. Waagen, *Treasures,* III. p. 27.

BREBIETTE, PIERRE, painter and etcher, was born at Mantes-sur-Seine in 1598, and died about 1650.

RAPHAEL *pinx.* Holy Family under the Oak.

Passavant, II. 230, and III. p. 136. The picture is in the Gallery of Madrid.

BRIDOUX, FRANÇOIS EUGÈNE AUGUSTIN, engraver, was born at Abbeville in 1813, and lives in Paris. A pupil of Forster.

MURILLO *pinx.* The Conception.

Engraved in 1845. The picture, of the size of the engraving, was in Louis Philippe's collection. Stirling, *Annals,* III. p. 1419.

Artist's proof, before any letters, with the white flower.

A similar proof, Colnaghi, May, 1865, No. 154, £13 5*s.*; Wilcox, 1856, No. 35, £11.

MURILLO *pinx.* "Holy Family."

The Christ-child standing between the Virgin and Joseph, who holds the Sprouting Stick in his hand; over him the Dove, and, above, the First Person of the Trinity. The picture is in the National Gallery. Stirling, *Annals,* III. p. 1424.

Artist's proof, before any letters.

RAPHAEL *pinx.* Madonna dei Candelabri.

See Passavant, II. No. 264, and III. p. 168. Engraved in 1841, with but one candelabre of the two in the picture, and without the two angels' heads (which are a later addition in the picture, and not by Raphael). From the Gallery Borghese and Lucien Bonaparte in Rome the painting came into the collection of the Duke of Lucca, in which it was sold in London and bought by the present owner, H. A. J. Munro, Esq.

Proof, before letters, artists' names in small open uncial letters, and names of printer and publishers. India paper.

Artist's proofs have only the letters "A. B." below, in the middle of the margin, traced with the needle.

BRIDOUX, F. E. A., *continued.*

RAPHAEL *pinx.* Madonna Aldobrandini.

Engraved in 1858. Passavant, II. No. 90. The picture, of the size of the engraving, is in the National Gallery. Purchased in 1865 from Lord Garvagh for £ 9,000. See *Fine Arts Quarterly Review,* June, 1866.

Proof before letters, with the names of the artists.

Artist's proofs are before any letters.

SIMONE MEMMI *pinx.* **P.** Petrarch's Laura.

After a miniature in a MS. in the Laurentian Library at Florence.

Proof, with merely the artists' names, and before the inscription on the tablet, which is shaded gray.

Artist's proofs are before any letters. The tablet is entirely blank.

LEONARDO DA VINCI *pinx.* **P.** "La Belle Ferronière."

The portrait of Lucrezia Crivelli of Milan. The picture is in the Gallery of the Louvre. Rigollot, No. 61; Villot, 483.

Open letter proof.

LEONARDO DA VINCI *pinx.* The same.

Artist's proof, before any letters; on the right hand, close under the plate, stands only "A. Bridoux," *slightly cut with the needle. It has the number* 18 *stamped on it. On India paper.*

WINTERHALTER *pinx.* **P.** Louis Philippe, King of the French.

With open letters.

BROMLEY, WILLIAM, engraver, born in 1773.

SIR THOMAS LAWRENCE *pinx.* **P.** Wellington.

SIR THOMAS LAWRENCE *del.* **P.** Mrs. Wolff.

Fac-simile of the drawing.

Proof before letters.

BROSAMER, HANS, painter and engraver, born at Fulda in 1506, died at Erfurt in 1552. Bartsch, VIII.

Solomon's Idolatry. B. 2.

From Otto's collection, with the name Clauss (the heir of the collector) on the back of the print.

Bathsheba. B. 3.

With the name C. Meister on the back.

A Man ridden by his Wife. B. 18.

With Ackermann's stamp on the back.

BROWN, M. D.

WELCH *pinx.* **P.** David B. Ogden.

Lithograph.

BROWNE, JOHN, designer and engraver, born at Oxford in 1719, died at London in 1790.

BOTH, J. et A. *pinx.* Philip baptizing the Eunuch.

Smith, *Cat. rais.* 48. The picture is in Mr. Holford's collection, London (Waagen, *Treasures*, II. p. 203); formerly at Corsham Court.

SALVATOR ROSA *pinx.* Apollo and the Sibyl.

The picture is in the collection of the Marquis of Hertford; lately in Lord Ashburnham's. Waagen, *Treasures*, II. p. 155.

CLAUDE LORRAIN *pinx.* Cephalus and Procris.

Smith, *Cat. rais.* 163. When engraved, 1779, in the collection of Lord Clive.

BOTH, J. et A. *pinx.* Banditti Prisoners.

Smith, *Cat. rais.* 26. When engraved, 1795, in the collection of Sir Thomas Dundas.

RUBENS *pinx.* The Watering-Place.

Smith, *Cat. rais.* 630. The picture is in the collection of the Duke of Buccleugh.

For landscapes engraved by Browne in conjunction with Woollett, see WOOLLETT.

BRUDER, landscape designer and engraver in Dresden, worked about 1830. A pupil of J. P. Veith.

J. RUYSDAEL *pinx.* The Cemetery.

Dresden Gallery. Hübner's *Cat.* No. 1366. Etching, finished with the graver, after a drawing by Veith. Small folio, oblong.

J. RUYSDAEL *pinx.* The Cloister.

Dresden Gallery. Hübner's *Cat.* No. 1375. Etching, finished with the graver, after a drawing by Veith. Small folio, oblong.

J. RUYSDAEL *pinx.* A Cascade.

On the right in the distance is a hill, in the foreground a solitary fir, on the left a low cottage. Dresden Gallery. Matthäi's *Cat.* 186;* Hübner's *Cat.* 1372. Etched, and finished with the graver, after a drawing by Veith. Small folio, upright.

J. RUYSDAEL *pinx.* A Bridge.

On the right, over the tree-tops, rises the steeple of a church; in the middle of the background is a square tower, on the left a windmill. Dresden Gallery. Etched, and finished with the graver. Small folio, oblong. Matthäi's *Cat.* 146; Hübner's *Cat.* 1368.

* We have had recourse to the old catalogue of Matthäi, since the new official catalogues, unlike Villot's of the Louvre, Madrazo's of the Gallery of Madrid, and others, do not identify the pictures in the Dresden Gallery.

BRUDER, *continued.*

J. Ruysdael *pinx.* A Cart driven through a Swamp.

Dresden Gallery. Etched, and finished with the graver, after a drawing by Veith. Small folio, oblong. Matthäi's *Cat.* 147; Hübner's, 1370.

J. Ruysdael *pinx.* A Forest with a Road through the middle; through the opening shines the horizon.

Dresden Gallery. Etched, and finished with the graver, after a drawing by Veith. Small folio, upright. Matthäi's *Cat.* 596; Hübner's, 1371.

BRUNA, VINCENZO DELLA, engraver of the present day in Florence.

Correggio *pinx.* Virgin adoring the Child.

The picture is in the Tribune of the Uffizj Gallery in Florence.

Proof before letters.

BRUNI, FRANCESCO, painter and etcher, born at Porto Maurizio in 1648, died at Genoa in 1726.

Guido *pinx.* The Assumption of the Virgin.

The picture is in the church of San Ambrogio at Genoa.

BRUYN, NICOLAS DE, designer and engraver, born at Antwerp in 1570, died, it is supposed at Amsterdam, in 1656. He was a pupil of his father, Abraham.

Abr. Bloemaert *pinx.* The Golden Age.

BRY, THEODOR DE, the father, goldsmith, designer and engraver, and publisher, born at Liege in 1528, died at Frankfort in 1598.

Pride and Folly, round design for a saucer.

BRY, JOHANN THEODOR DE, the son, born at Liege in 1561, died at Frankfort in 1623.

Giulio Romano *pinx.* Triumphal Procession of Bacchus.

From Ackermann's collection.

The two preceding De Bry, with the assistance of the second son, Johann Israel (died 1611), engraved the following 20 plates belonging to the work "Virginia." The impressions are early and on thicker paper, viz.:—

Pl. 3. Princes and Lords of Virginia.
4. Noble matron of Sacota.
5. Priest of Sacota.
6. Noble maiden of Sacota.
7. Gentry of Roanoak.
8. Noble lady of Pomeiooc.

BRY, JOHANN THEODOR DE, *continued.*

Pl. 9. Old man of Pomeiooc.
10. Mode in which the women of Dasamonquepeuc carry their infants.
11. A Magician.
12. Making of a canoo.
13. Fishing of the Virginians.
14. Broiling of Fishes on a wooden grate.
15. Cooking in an earthen pot.
16. Mode of eating.
17. Feast at the fire.
18. Festival Dance of the Virginians.
19. The city Pomeiooc.
20. The city Sacota.
21. The idol Kiwasa.
22. A toomb of the great in Virginia.

BUCKER, enamel painter, designer and lithographer of the present time in Dresden.

TITIAN *pinx.* Venus in the Dresden Gallery.

A lithograph. The Dresden picture is a repetition of the one in the Fitzwilliam collection of Cambridge in England, which comes from the Orleans Gallery. — That the figure of Venus represents the princess Eboli is as false as that the youth at her side, playing the mandoline, represents Philip II.

BUONAFEDE, GIOVANNI, an engraver of the present day.

GUIDO RENI *pinx.* La Speranza.

The picture is in Rome.

Proof, before letters, with merely the names of the artists and the address in traced, open letters.

BURNET, JOHN, engraver, born about 1785, worked in London.

WILKIE *pinx.* The Reading of the Will.

The picture is in the Gallery of Modern Painters in Munich.

NEWTON *pinx.* The Vicar of Wakefield.

NEWTON *pinx.* The same.

Artist's proof, before letters, with only the names of the artists, and address of publishers.

LANDSEER *pinx.* "The Lassie herding Sheep."

Proof before letters, with only the inscription just mentioned, on the right-hand lower margin, cut with the needle.

BYRNE, WILLIAM, engraver, born at Cambridge in 1746, died in 1805. A pupil of Wille.

BOTH *pinx.* Morning.

Smith, *Cat. rais.* 69. The picture is in the National Gallery. The figures were engraved by Schumann.

Proof, open letters.

BOTH *pinx.* Evening.

Smith, *Cat. rais.* 74. Engraved in 1778 from a picture then in the possession of Edmund Antrobus, Esq. The figures are by Bartolozzi.

Proof before letters.

FILIPPO LAURI *pinx.* Apollo as herdsman to King Admetus.

When engraved, 1768, in the collection of Robert Bragg, M. D.

C.

CADUCÉE, LE MAÎTRE AU, also called **JACOPO DA BARBARI,** born about 1460 – 1470, worked principally in Venice. It is now generally believed that his real name was Walch, and that he was a native of Nuremberg.* Bartsch, VII.

Victory. B. 23.

CALAMATTA, LOUIS, designer and engraver in Paris, born at Cività Vecchia in 1802. A pupil of Marchetti.

ARY SCHEFFER *pinx.* Francesca da Rimini.

The original, first owned by the Duke of Orleans, is now in the collection of Prince Demidoff in Florence. Lord Ellesmere owns a replica of smaller size. Another repetition, said to surpass the first picture, being likewise by Scheffer himself, is (or was in 1859) in the possession of his daughter Mme. Marjolin in Paris. *See* Mrs. Grote's *Memoir of Ary Scheffer*, London, 1860, pp. 50, 51.

A painting owned by John Dillon, Esq., was in the Manchester Exhibition in 1857; No. 643.

CALAMATTA *dis. e inc.* **P.** Masaccio.

Proof; the inscription Masaccio, *the artist's name, and the date, are in very delicately cut open letters.*

CALLOT, JACQUES, painter and engraver, was born at Nancy in 1592, and died there in 1635.

A pupil of Canta-Gallina, Ph. Thomassin, and Parigi.

Heineken, *Diction.*; Le Blanc, *Manuel.* Compare also E. Meaume, *Recherches sur la vie et les ouvrages de J. Callot*, Paris, 1860, 2 vols. 8vo.

* Comp. Harzen, in Naumann's *Archiv für die zeichnenden Künste*, Jahrg. I. p. 210 et seq.

CALLOT, JACQUES, *continued.*

POCCETTI *inv.* The Inferno, according to Dante. Le Bl. 44.

Large composition, on two plates. Comp. Nagler, XI. p. 429.

The Great Fair of the Madonna del Imprunetta. H. p. 515, No. 41. Le Bl. 1251.

Inscription beginning with Dedication to Cosmo, and terminating with: "An. sal. 1620 . . . fe. Florentiae et excudit Nancy." *Engraved, the second time, on two plates.*

From the collection and with the name of W. Esdaile.

The Temptation of St. Anthony. H. p. 509, No. 21. Le Bl. 28.

2d state, with 21 *rosettes and Israel's address.*

Assumption of the Virgin: *Non est hic.*

Square 16mo.

Martyrdom of St. Sebastian. H. p. 510, No. 24. Le Bl. 40.

1st state, before the address of Israel.

16 plates, the series of Martyrium Apostolorum. H. p. 498, No. 10. Le Bl. 162–177.

32mo.

3d state, with Israel's address and the numbers.

The Crucifixion of 23 Martyrs in Japan. H. p. 510, No. 27. Le Bl. 41.

2d state, with Sylvestre's address.

The Virgin receiving Martyrs at the Gate of Heaven.

View of Pont Neuf and Tour de Nesle. H. p. 515, No. 32. Le Bl. 1365.

1st state, before Sylvestre's address.

View of the Louvre and Tour de Nesle. H. p. 515, No. 33. Le Bl. 1366.

1st state, before Sylvestre's address.

La Chasse au Cerf. H. p. 516, No. 44. Le Bl. 1162.

2d state, with Israel's address.

Les Supplices. H. p. 512, No. 7. Le Bl. 1277.

1st state, before Sylvestre's address.

Les grandes Misères de la Guerre. Le Bl. 1252–1270.

2 plates, Nos. 14 and 17 of the set of 18. H. p. 500, No. 20.

Departure of the Troops against the Turks. Le Bl. 1217.

From "Les Batailles des Médicis," the 7th plate of the set.

Before any letters.

The Storming of the City of Bone in Africa by the Troops of Ferdinand I. and the Knights of St. Stephen. Le Bl. 1222.

From "Les Batailles des Médicis," the 12th plate and the second composition of this subject in the set. "*Matteo Roselli inv. Jac. Callot inc.*"

CALLOT, JACQUES, *continued.*

Capitano di Baroni. H. p. 502, No. 29. Le Bl. 977 - 1001.

8 plates of the set of 25. They are copies.

P. Louis de Lorraine. H. p. 505, No. 7. Le Bl. 1241.

CAMERATA, GIUSEPPE, designer and engraver, born at Frascati, or at Venice, in 1718, died at Dresden in 1803. A pupil of his father and of Cattini.

GUIDO *pinx.* The Infant Bacchus.

Dresden Gallery. Engraved for *Rec. d'estampes de la Gal. de Dresde,* I. No. 24.

THOMAS WYCK *pinx.* "Le Chimiste."

"Commencé à l'eau forte par P. Hutin. Terminé par J. Camerata."

1*st impression, with the inscription* "d'après le Tableau d'Eckhout," *which was afterwards corrected.*

The original picture of this plate is *not* in the Dresden Gallery.

CAMPAGNOLA, GIULIO, painter and engraver, born at Padua, about 1481. Bartsch, XIII.

The Old Shepherd. B. 7.

CAMPANELLA, ANGELO, painter and engraver, born at Rome in 1748, died about 1815. A pupil of Volpato.

RAPHAEL *inv.* The Massacre of the Innocents.

After an arras-hanging in the Vatican, from the second series, representations from the Life of Christ. Passavant, II. 203. B.

RAPHAEL *inv.* Christ at Emmaus.

After an arras-hanging in the Vatican, from the second series, representations from the Life of Christ. Passavant, II. 210.

The border, and some other additions, are by a foreign hand.

RAPHAEL *pinx.* Jupiter and Antiope, or Pan and Syrinx.

A Nymph risen from the bath sits under the shade of trees, combing her hair; a Satyr is watching her. Fresco in the Bathing-room of the Cardinal Bibbiena, over the Loggie, in the Vatican. Passavant, II. p. 281, No. 217. Engraved for Hamilton's *Schola Italiana.*

The same subject, but freer, was engraved by Marc-Antonio: "Pan and Syrinx." B. 325.

LEONARDO DA VINCI *pinx.* Vanity and Modesty.

Rigollot, No. 56. The picture is in the Sciara palace in Rome.

Proof, that is, with open letters.

RAPHAEL *pinx.* The Nuptials of Psyche with Cupid.

Fresco in the Farnesina. *See* RICCIANI.

CANALE, ANTONIO, often called CANALETTO, prospetto painter and etcher, born at Venice in 1697, died there in 1768. A pupil of his father, Bernardo Canale.

View of Pietra della Valle.

CANALE, GIUSEPPE, designer and engraver, born at Rome in 1725, died at Dresden in 1802. A pupil of J. Frey.

DOMENICHINO *pinx.* Glory rewarding Merit.

Engraved for *Rec. d'estampes de la Gal. de Dresde,* III. No. 29.

REMBRANDT *pinx.* A Flemish Gentleman.

CANALETTO, ANTONIO CANALE. *See* CANALE.

CANALETTO, whose real name was **BERNARDO BELLOTTI,** prospetto painter and etcher, born at Venice in 1724, died at Warsaw in 1780. He was a nephew and pupil of Antonio Canale, whom he closely resembles in his works, and after whom he was called Canaletto.

View of Dresden: The Bridge over the Elbe with the Catholic Church.

View of Dresden: New Market with the (old) Picture Gallery and the Church of Our Lady.

CANOT, PETER CHARLES, designer and engraver, born in France in 1710, died in Kentish Town in 1777.

BRAMER *pinx.* Pyramus and Thisbe.

HOLBEIN *pinx.* Ship Great Henry.

The picture is at Hampton Court.

CLAUDE LORRAIN *pinx.* Sunrise.

A marine piece. In oval. Smith, *Cat. rais.* 309. Engraved in 1771, from a picture then in the possession of Sir Richard Lyttleton.

Proof before letters, artists' names and address traced with the needle, and coat of arms.

W. VAN DE VELDE *pinx.* "Vent frais," A fresh Breeze.

Smith, *Cat. rais.* 34. In the collection of the Dowager Lady Stuart.

Proof before letters; only artists' names traced, and coat of arms, with Boydell's address.

BACKHUYSEN *pinx.* "Vent doux," A light Breeze.

Smith, *Cat. rais.* 86. In the collection of the Dowager Lady Stuart.

Proof before letters; only artists' names traced, and coat of arms, with Boydell's address.

PILLEMENT *pinx.* La Chaumière Hollandaise.

Landscape, with skaters.

CANTARINI, SIMONE, called PESARESE, painter and etcher, born at Oropezza near Pesaro in 1612, died at Verona in 1648. A pupil of Guido Reni. Bartsch, XIX.

Rest in Egypt. B. 3.

1st state, before the name of Guido. Contre-épreuve.

Holy Family with Elizabeth and St. John. B. 10.

2d state, with the inscription: "G. Renus in. et fec."

The Rape of Europa. B. 30.

2d state, in Guido's name.

CANTINI, GIOVACCHINO, an engraver of the early part of this century.

VASARI *pinx.* **P.** Michel-Angelo.

Engraved in 1815. The plate was used for the frontispiece of Condivi's *Vita di Michelangelo Buonarroti*, Pisa, 1823, 8vo.

CAPEZZUOLI, follower of R. Morghen.

CARLO DOLCE *pinx.* Salvator Mundi: *Sic Deus dilexit mundum.*

Copy of R. Morghen's engraving.

Artist's proof, before any letters.

CARACCI, AGOSTINO, painter and engraver, born at Bologna in 1557, died at Parma in 1602. He was the cousin of Lodovico and the elder brother of Annibale Caracci. He studied painting with Prospero Fontana and Bartolomeo Passerotti, and engraving with Cornelis Cort. Bartsch, XVIII.

CORREGGIO *pinx.* Ecce Homo. B. 20.

The picture is in the National Gallery, from the Marquis of Londonderry's collection; formerly in the Colonna palace in Rome. Waagen, *Treasures*, I. p. 327.

PAOLO VERONESE *pinx.* The Crucifixion. B. 21.

With the signature of P. Mariette's name.

TINTORETTO *pinx.* The Great Crucifixion. B. 23.

Engraved in 1589 on three plates. The picture is in St. Roch in Venice. With the address: *Venetijs Donati Rascichotti formis.*

FR. VANNI *pinx.* "The great" St. Francis, in Ecstasy. B. 67.

FR. VANNI *pinx.* "The small" St. Jerome. B. 74.

AG. CARACCI *dis.* "The great" St. Jerome. B. 75.

2d state, finished by Fr. Brizio. With Steffanoni's address.

TINTORETTO *pinx.* St. Jerome in the Desert, to whom appears the Virgin. B. 76.

1st state, before "c. priv.," *and before address.*

PAOLO VERONESE *pinx.* The Marriage of St. Catherine. B. 97.

2d state.

CARACCI, AGOSTINO, *continued.*

PAOLO VERONESE *pinx.* Christ's Body supported by the Virgin and an Angel. B. 102.

1st address.

BAROCCIO *pinx.* The Flight of Æneas. B. 110.

The original picture, painted for the Emperor Rudolph II., is in the Gallery of the Borghese palace in Rome. Platner and Bunsen, III. iii. p. 278.

AG. CARACCI *dis.* Love conquering Nature, Pan subdued by Cupid. B. 116.

A picture of this subject is in the collection of Lord Feversham. The subject is also introduced into one of the compositions, painted by Agostino, of the frescos in the Farnese palace in Rome.

TINTORETTO *pinx.* Mercury and the Graces. B. 117.

Tintoretto's picture is, according to Bartsch, in the palace of San Marco in Venice.

TINTORETTO *pinx.* Mars and Minerva. B. 118.

This picture is likewise, according to Bartsch, in the palace of San Marco in Venice.

2d state, with "A. C." *instead of* "1589."

CARACCI, ANNIBALE, painter and etcher, born at Bologna in 1560, died at Rome in 1609. A pupil of Lodovico Caracci. Bartsch, XVIII.

Christ Crowned with Thorns. B. 3.

2d state, with the name of the artist (which is wanting in the 1st state), and before the address of Van Aelst of the 3d state, which was removed again in the 4th state.

Pietà. Christ of Caprarola. B. 4.

3d state, with Van Aelst's address.

1st state, *Caprarolae* 1597. 2d state, *Annibal Caracius fe. Caprarolae* 1597. The 3d state has the addition of the above address.

The Madonna with the Porringer. B. 9.

1st state, before address.

The Holy Family of 1590. B. 11.

1st state, with the letter C in "Car." *going below the line.*

From Camesina's collection, with his name, and with Ackermann's stamp.

CARACCI, LODOVICO, painter and etcher, born at Bologna in 1555, died in 1619. A pupil of P. Fontana and Passignano. Bartsch, XVIII.

La Vierge aux Anges. B. 2.

3d state, with Steffanoni's address, and that of Van Aelst in addition.

The 4th state has Orlandi's address. The 1st state is before address.

CARAGLIO, GIOVANNI JACOPO, designer and engraver, born at Parma in 1500, died on his estate near Parma in 1570. A pupil of Marc-Antonio. Bartsch, xv.

RAPHAEL *inv.* Holy Family with the Cradle. B. 5.

See Passavant, II. 235.

1*st state, with the face of the cradle white.*

CARATTONI, GIROLAMO, engraver in Rome, in the 18th century. *See* CUNEGO, D., Frescos of Michel-Angelo in the Sistine Chapel, and MONTAGNANI, Raphael's Bible.

CARDON, ANTOINE, the younger, born at Brussels in 1773, died in London in 1813. A son and pupil of Antoine Cardon the elder.

GIORGIONE *pinx.* **P.** "Portrait of Gaston de Foix."

A warrior, apparently wounded, with a youth unbuckling his armor.

The picture is in the Earl of Carlisle's town residence, London. Waagen, *Treasures*, II. p. 278.

CARMONA, MANUEL SALVADOR, engraver, born at Madrid in 1730, died there in 1807. A pupil of Dupuis.

RUBENS *pinx.* **P.** Rubens' Son, an infant in a chair.

Smith, *Cat. rais.* 780. The picture is in Städel's Museum in Frankfort. Nagler, *K.-L.*

ROSLIN *pinx.* **P.** François Boucher.

Engraved for his admission into the Academy.

ROSLIN *pinx.* **P.** Hyacinthe Collin de Vermont.

Engraved for his admission into the Academy.

CARONNI, PAOLO, engraver, born at Monza, about 1779, died at Milan in 1842. A pupil of Longhi.

PARMEGIANO *pinx.* Venus and Cupid.

Proof, before letters, with only the artists' names. With the white stamp of the engraver's initials.

P. Filangieri.

Engraved for *Vite e Ritratti di illustri Italiani.*

G. STEINER *pinx.* **P.** Metastasio.

Engraved for *Vite e Ritratti di illustri Italiani.*

P. Raphael Morghen.

P. Palladio.

Engraved for *Vite e Ritratti di illustri Italiani.*

REMBRANDT *pinx.* **P.** Rembrandt.

Engraved in conjunction with Longhi.

CARS, LAURENT, designer and engraver, born at Lyons in 1702, died at Paris in 1771. Son and pupil of Jean François Cars.

WATTEAU *pinx.* "Fêtes Vénitiennes."

"Du Cabinet de Mr de Jullienne."

CASPAR, JOSEPH, an engraver of the present day in Berlin. A pupil of Longhi and Anderloni.

RAPHAEL *pinx.* Madonna di Casa Colonna.

See Passavant, II. 59. In the Berlin Gallery. Engraved in 1830, for the Berlin Art Union.

Has open letters.

TITIAN *pinx.* **P.** Titian's Daughter, bearing a dish of fruit.

In the Berlin Gallery. Engraved in 1835.

Proof: "Titian's Tochter," *and dedication to King Frederick III. of Prussia, in delicately traced open letters. With the white stamp of the engraver's initials.*

Artist's proofs are before any letters, with merely: *Gemalt v. Titian, Gezeichnet v. E. Eichens, Gestochen v. Joseph Caspar* 1835, in very small letters, traced with the needle.

HENSEL *pinx.* **P.** Felix Mendelssohn Bartholdi.

CASTIGLIONE, GIOVANNI BENEDETTO, painter, etcher, and engraver, born at Genoa in 1616, died at Mantua in 1670. A pupil of G. B. Paggi and Andrea Ferrari. Bartsch, XXI.

Magdalen Penitent. B. 26.

CAUKERKEN, CORNELIS VAN, engraver, born at Antwerp about 1625.

VAN DYCK *pinx.* Charity.

A woman with three children. Smith, *Cat. rais.* 425.

The picture is in the collection of Paul Methuen, Esq., another in the collection of Thomas Hope, Esq., a third in the collection of Earl Lonsdale.

2d state, with address of Abr. a Diepenbeke.

CECCHINI, FRANCESCO, an engraver in Rome, towards the close of the last century.

PERUGINO *pinx.* Prophets and Sibyls.

Fresco in the Hall of the Collegio del Cambio in Perugia. Passavant, I. p. 494.

Artist's proof, before any letters.

Cecchini engraved also, for Montagnani, Raphael's Bible. *See* MONTAGNANI.

CHALON, JAN, designer and engraver, born at Amsterdam in 1738, worked in London, where he died in 1795.

REMBRANDT *inv.* An Old Woman.

Etched in Rembrandt's style.

CHAMBERS, THOMAS, engraver, born at London about 1724.

RUBENS *pinx.* St. Martin dividing his Cloak with a Beggar.

The picture is in Windsor Castle. Smith, *Cat. rais.* 822. It is the prototype of the famous altar-piece by Van Dyck in the parish church of the village of Savelthem, which is precisely the same in composition, except that the woman and two children are omitted. Waagen, *Handbook,* II. p. 285; Smith, *Cat. rais.* Van Dyck, No. 34. See also Carpenter's *Pictorial Notices, consisting of a Memoir of Van Dyck,* &c. p. 11.

VAN DYCK *pinx.* **P.** Helena Forman, Rubens's second wife.

Engraved for the Houghton Gallery; now in the Imperial Gallery of St. Petersburg. Smith, *Cat. rais.* 646.

RAPHAEL *pinx.* "Raphael's Mistress."

See Passavant, II. 281. In the Marlborough collection at Blenheim. Waagen, *Treasures,* III. p. 125. Engraved in 1765.

CHASTEAU, GUILLAUME, engraver, born at Orleans in 1631, died in 1683. A pupil of Greuter and C. Bloemaert.

ANN. CARACCI *pinx.* The Assumption of the Virgin.

The smaller plate — reverse of the larger one — engraved for the *Cabinet Crozat.* The picture was in the old Royal French collection, but is not now in the Gallery of the Louvre. Compare Waagen, *Kunstwerke und Künstler in Paris,* pp. 66, 776.

CHATILLON, HENRI GUILLAUME, painter and engraver, born at Paris in 1780. A pupil of Girodet and Girardet.

GIULIO ROMANO *pinx.* Holy Family.

Engraved for the *Musée Français.*

RAPHAEL *pinx.* The Archangel Michael vanquishing the Dragon.

The larger picture of this subject in the Louvre, painted for Francis I. as Grand Master of the Order of St. Michael. Passavant, II. 232.

Proof before letters, with only the artists' names engraved, and with the stamp of the engraver's initials.

The artist's proofs have the names of the artists in larger letters, etched in dots.

CHENEY and DOBSON, American engravers of our day.

STAIGG *pinx.* **P.** Daniel Webster.

CHÉREAU, FRANÇOIS, designer and engraver, born at Blois in 1680, died at Paris in 1729. A pupil of Gérard Audran.

L. DE BOULLONGNE *pinx.* **P.** Boullongne, Louis de.

HYAC. RIGAUD *pinx.* **P.** Dehn, Detlev à.

LARGILLIÈRE *pinx.* **P.** Geoffroy, Math. François.

HYAC. RIGAUD *pinx.* **P.** Launay, Nicolas de.

TOURNIÈRE *pinx.* **P.** Pécour, Louis.

CHÉREAU, JACQUES, *le jeune,* designer and engraver, born at Blois in 1694, died at Paris in 1776. A pupil of his brother François.

RAPHAEL *pinx.* Holy Family : La Belle Jardinière.

See Passavant, II. 60. The picture is in the Gallery of the Louvre. Engraved for *Cab. Crozat,* No. 6.

Le Blanc has this engraving by mistake under François Chéreau, and then again under Jacques.

RAPHAEL *pinx.* Holy Family: with Joseph beardless.

See Passavant, II. 44. The picture is in the Imperial Gallery of St. Petersburg. Engraved for *Cab. Crozat,* No. 30.

CHIOSSONE, D., engraved for Vincenzo Marchese's San Marco in Firenze. *See* MARCHESE.

CHODOWIECKI, DANIEL NICOLAUS, painter, designer, and engraver, born at Dantzig in 1726, died at Berlin in 1801. *See* W. Engelmann, *D. Chodowiecki's sämmtliche Kupferstiche,* Leipzig, 1857, and Appendices.

P. Erasmus, with the Terminus. E. 377. A.

After Holbein's woodcut.

Proof, before the inscription below.

P. The same. E. 377. B.

Print, with the inscription : "La Philosophie," *and* 5 *lines of verse :* "Plus legère — la Folie"; *and the name* "J. B. Rousseau" *below.*

Engraved as frontispiece for Erasmus's *Lob der Narrheit,* Berlin, 1781.

EICH *pinx.* **P.** Pascha-Weitsch, painter. E. 181.

Wilhelm Tell before Gessler. E. 384.

CIPRIANI, GALGANO, engraver, a native of Sienna, and pupil of Raphael Morghen.

P. Guido Reni's portrait, after his own picture.

"Cipriani sculps. R. Morghen direxit." The painting is in the Artists' Portrait Gallery of the Uffizj in Florence.

FABRE *pinx.* **P.** Vittorio Alfieri.

CIPRIANI, GALGANO, *continued.*

"Galgano Cipriani incise dalla pittura, Raffaello Morghen dires."

The engraving is of the size of Raphael Morghen's portraits of the great Italian poets. It was published in 1806, and dedicated to "La Sig. Principessa Luisa di Stolberg, Contessa d'Albany." The coat of arms has the arms of Great Britain joined to those of the Counts of Stolberg.

CLAESSENS, LAMBERTUS ANTONIUS, painter and engraver, born at Antwerp in 1764, died at Paris in 1834. A pupil of Bartolozzi.

REMBRANDT *pinx.* Jacob blessing the Sons of Joseph.

The picture is in the Gallery of Cassel. Waagen, *Handbook*, II. p. 344. Engraved for the *Musée Français.*

Proof, with only the artists' names.

RUBENS *pinx.* The Descent from the Cross.

The great altar-piece in the Cathedral of Antwerp. Smith, *Cat. rais.* 5, and App. p. 244. Engraved in 1808.

*Artist's proof, with the artists' names only slightly etched in dots.**

Debois, No. 159, 500*fr.*

RUBENS *pinx.* The same.

Proof, with open letters.

Amsler & Ruthardt, Berlin, sale cat. I. No. 96, 100*th.*

REMBRANDT *pinx.* "The Night-watch."

The Archers' guild of Amsterdam going out to shoot at a mark. Composition of 20 portrait figures. Smith, *Cat. rais.* 139. In the Gallery of Amsterdam, formerly in the City Hall (*Stadhuis*). Waagen, *Handbook*, II. p. 342. Engraved in 1797.

First, or artist's proof, before letters, with only the artists' names traced.

The second proofs have the full inscription, with the names of the persons represented in open and traced letters.

GER. DOW *pinx.* La Femme hydropique.

In the Gallery of the Louvre. Villot, No. 121. Smith, *Cat. rais.* 95. Engraved in 1823.

Proof, with open letters.

Artist's proofs are before letters, with only the artists' names traced with the needle. La Motte-Fouquet, No. 192, 46*th.*; Debois, No. 160, 195*fr.*†

* A deceptive copy of this plate sometimes occurs *without any letters*, which may, however, be distinguished from the artist's proof of Claessens's plate by the absence of the artist's name, and by the inferiority of the engraving, especially of the design. Guichardot in his *Catalogue Van den Zande* gives a fuller account of it.

† There occur spurious proofs without any letters, made by covering up the inscription of the plate while under the press.

CLAESSENS, LAMBERTUS ANTONIUS, *continued.*

ADR. VAN OSTADE *pinx.* The Fishmonger.

Smith, *Cat. rais.* 110. In the Gallery of the Louvre. Villot, No. 371. Engraved for the *Musée Français.*

ADR. VAN OSTADE *pinx.* The Smoker.

Smith, *Cat. rais.* 99. In the Gallery of the Louvre. Villot, No. 374.

Proof before any letters.

DE LELIE *pinx.* Musiciens de Village.

Open letter proof.

J. ASSELYN *pinx.* Le Cavalier.

The plate is marked "No. 14."

Open letter proof.

J. STEEN *pinx.* Le Villageois en belle Humeur.

Open letter proof.

RUBENS *pinx.* Rubens's own portrait.

Smith, *Cat. rais.* 880, and Appendix, p. 330, No. 316. The picture is in the Duke of Aremberg's collection in Brussels.

REMBRANDT *pinx.* **P.** "Portrait de Rembrandt."

Portrait, nearly front view of a youth of about 15 years, with bushy hair and ear-rings. He has on a black velvet cap, and wears a mantle lined with fur and a white plaited shirt, with bare neck, which gives him the appearance of a girl. Smith, *Cat. rais.* 232.

The plate has the No. 4.

LE NAIN *pinx.* Le Maréchal dans sa Forge.

The picture is in the Gallery of the Louvre. Villot, No. 375. Engraved by Claessens, in conjunction with Levasseur, for the *Musée Français.*

Proof before letters, with merely the artists' names.

CLAUDE GELLÉE, called LE LORRAIN, painter and etcher, born at the chateau Chamagne near Charmes, département des Vosges, in 1600, died at Rome in 1682, — according to others in 1678. A pupil of Agostino Tassi and Gottfried Wals. Robert-Dumesnil, I.

Shepherds and Cattle crossing a Brook. R.-D. 3.

1st state (of 3), "rare."

From Geissler's collection.

The Cowherd. R.-D. 8.

Represented as blowing his horn while the herd is crossing a rivulet.

2d state (of 3), "rare."

The Dance under the Trees. R.-D. 10.

4th and last state, "very common."

CLAUDE GELLÉE, *continued.*

The Robbers. R.-D. 12.

4th and last state, "common."

Seaport, with a large Tower. R.-D. 13.

2d state (of 4), "rare."

The Wooden Bridge. R.-D. 14.

Good impression of the 2d and last state.

The Goatherd. R.-D. 19.

3d and last state, "common."

CLAUSSIN, JOSEPH DE, amateur designer and etcher, born in France about 1795, died at Batignolles in 1844.

REMBRANDT *inv.* Head of "the Princess of Orange."

A copy in reverse of Schmidt's etching. Jacobi, 147.

CLOUWET, or **CLOUET, PIETER,** engraver, born at Antwerp in 1606, where he died in 1677.

VAN DYCK *pinx.* **P.** Lamen, Christoffel van der, painter.

Van Dyck's portraits, Weber, p. 117.

Watermark of the paper, the coat of arms of Amsterdam.

VAN DYCK *pinx.* **P.** Rogiers, Theodor, chaser in silver.

Van Dyck's portraits, Weber, p. 117.

2d state, with "Jacobus de Man exc."

VAN DYCK *pinx.* Scribanus, Carolus, e Societate Jesu.

The picture is in the Vienna Gallery. Smith, *Cat. rais.* 93. Van Dyck's portraits, Weber, p. 117.

Watermark of the paper, the Smaller Foolscap.

COCHIN, CHARLES NICOLAS, *fils,* designer and engraver, born at Paris in 1715, died there in 1788. A pupil of his father of the same name.

WATTEAU *pinx.* La Mariée de Village.

"Du Cabinet de M. de la Faye."

COCK, HIERONYMUS, painter, engraver, and publisher, born at Antwerp in 1510, died in 1570.

RAPHAEL *del.* The Adoration of the Kings.

See Passavant, II. 205. Engraved after the drawing for an arras-hanging in the Vatican, second series, representations from the Life of Christ. 4to.

COELEMANS, JACOB, engraver, born at Antwerp about 1670, died at Aix in 1735. A pupil of Vermeulen.

COELEMANS, JACOB, *continued.*

PAOLO VERONESE *pinx.* The Poet, conjuring up Fortune.

Inscribed *Que La Fortune est bizarre*, etc.

Engraved for the *Recueil d'estampes . . . dans le Cabinet de Boyer d'Aiguilles. See* Sternberg-Manderscheid's catalogue, I. p. 432, No. 4189, where it is called "Virtue and Fortune."

PAOLO VERONESE *pinx.* **P.** Paolo Veronese.

Engraved for the *Cabinet de Boyer d'Aiguilles.*

TITIAN *pinx.* Portrait of a Venetian Nobleman.

Engraved for the *Cabinet de Boyer d'Aiguilles.* Winckler, *Cat.* II. ii. p. 1033, No. 4863.

COLLAS, ACHILLE, born at Paris in 1795, died there in 1859. He invented in 1830 the process and apparatus named after him for copying and reproducing the effect of subjects in relief, as medals, etc.

P. Goethe.

After a medal.

COLLYER, JOSEPH, designer and engraver, born at London about 1748, died about 1790.

TENIERS *pinx.* Dutch Pastime.

Smith, *Cat. rais.* 347, and *Suppl.* p. 436, No. 94. Now in the collection of the Earl of Ashburnham, Battle. When engraved, owned by Sir Thomas Dundas.

Open letter proof.

COLOMBO, AURELIO, engraver of the present century at Milan.

RAPHAEL *del.* The Massacre of the Innocents.

A copy of Marc-Antonio's engraving. Bartsch, XX.

COOPER, RICHARD, designer and engraver in line and in mezzotinto, was born about 1736, probably in Edinburgh. A pupil of Le Bas.

VAN DYCK *pinx.* **P.** Portraits of the Children of Charles I.

Charles, Prince of Wales, with his hand on the head of a very large dog, the Princesses, Mary and Elizabeth, and the Princess Anne with her infant brother James, Duke of York, at whose feet is a spaniel. Smith, *Cat. rais.* No. 208.* The picture, formerly owned by the Earl of Portmore, is in Windsor Castle. Engraved in line.

* "Here, by mistake, he states that the picture was also engraved by Strange. The latter engraved only the picture described by Smith under No. 211, and more fully in Appendix, p. 374, No. 25. For Strange's engraving see Le Blanc, *Catalogue de l'Œuvre de Rob. Strange.* Both pictures are in Windsor Castle.

CORNILLET, mezzotinto engraver of our own day.

RUBENS *pinx.* **P.** "Le Chapeau de Paille."

The famous picture in the collection of Sir Robert Peel.

Portrait of a young lady, said to be Mademoiselle Lundens, wearing a black Spanish beaver hat with feathers. Smith, *Cat. rais.* No. 811.

Open letter proof.

COROT, engraver in Paris at the commencement of this century.

GIULIO ROMANO *pinx.* Holy Family "with the Lizard."

The picture is in the Gallery of the Pitti palace in Florence. Passavant, *Rafael,* II. No. 230, Copy a. A repetition of Raphael's Holy Family "under the Oak Tree," in the Madrid Gallery. Passavant, II. 230.

Impression with the engraver's address.

CORT, CORNELIS, painter and engraver, born at Horn in Holland in 1536, died at Rome in 1578. He was a pupil of Hieronymus Cock, but on his arrival in Italy he spent a considerable time in Venice, where he lived with Titian.

GIULIO CLOVIO *pinx.* The Adoration of the Kings.

BAROCCIO *pinx.* Rest in Egypt.

The picture, formerly in the Orleans Gallery, was bought by Lady Lucas, since Countess De Grey. Waagen, *Treasures,* II. p. 486. There are also repetitions elsewhere.

Late impression, with the address of C. Losi.

RAPHAEL *pinx.* The Transfiguration.

See Passavant, II. 244. In the Gallery of the Vatican.

2d state, with "Cornelis Cort fe.," *Lafreri's address, and the year* 1573.

1st state, before the engraver's name. — 3d state, with Orlandi's address, and the year 1602.

LIVIO AGRESTI *pinx.* The Last Supper.

TITIAN *pinx.* St. Jerome in the Desert, reading in a book.

There is a picture of this subject in Santa Maria Nuova in Venice. Engraved in 1565.

1st state, before Cort's name, with burr on the plate, on thin paper with the watermark of three circles, one within another, and with the signature of P. Mariette.

From Otto's collection.

TITIAN *pinx.* The Martyrdom of St. Lawrence.

The picture is in the church of the Jesuits at Venice.

From Otto's collection.

TITIAN *pinx.* La Gloria di Tiziano, or La Toussaint.

All Saints before the Trinity. Passavant, *Christliche Kunst in Spanien,*

CORT, CORNELIS, *continued.*

p. 166. The picture is now in the Madrid Gallery. Madrazo, No. 752. Engraved in 1566.

Amidst the saints the coffin of Charles V. is carried to heaven. It owes its origin to a dream of the Emperor, and was designed for the Convent of St. Justus. The picture was held up before the king on his death-bed. There was an original sketch of this picture in the collection of the poet Rogers.

1st state, before Cort's name.

TITIAN *pinx.* Diana and Callisto.

Engraved in 1566. The picture is in the Madrid Gallery. Passavant, *Tour of a German Artist*, I. p. 129, and *Christliche Kunst in Spanien*, p. 165. Another picture, on a larger scale, is in the Bridgewater Gallery, formerly in the Orleans collection. A picture of the same subject is also in the Vienna Gallery of the Belvedere. Krafft, *Verzeichniss*, Wien, 1845, p. 17, No. 17.

1st state, before Cort's name. On thin paper, with the watermark of three circles, one within another.

TITIAN *pinx.* Perseus and Andromeda.

A painting of this subject was in the Orleans Gallery, bought by Mr. Bryan. Waagen, *Treasures*, II. p. 497, No. 23.

The same has been engraved by Delignon. *See* DELIGNON.

2d state, with the address of Scolari.

MICHEL-ANGELO *inv.* Tomb of Giulio de' Medici, with the figures of Night and Morning.

After the sculpture in the Sacristy of the Lorenzo Chapel in Florence. Harford, II. pp. 27 – 30.

COSSIN, LOUIS, painter and engraver, born at Troyes in 1633.

RAPHAEL *pinx.* The School of Athens.

See Passavant, II. 67. Stanze in the Vatican, Camera della Segnatura. The representation corresponds very nearly with Ghisi's engraving; both are without the second, higher arch, which Volpato's has. On the left, the head of the old man with a child in his arm is but half given, and of the child only the fore-arm appears. The tablet at the base of the column is without inscription, but shaded with horizontal lines. On the right are wanting half the figure of the king, and Raphael and Perugino, together with the two figures which are above them, and behind the man with a staff; the latter is represented without a beard, and in front view, not in profile, as in Ghisi's plate. On the floor in the print stands, on the left: *Raphael pinx. — Parisiis.* On the right: *A Paris chez Cars rue St. Iacques au nom de Iesus. — L. Cossin sculp.* The impression is in bad condition.

RAPHAEL *pinx.* The same.

COSSIN, LOUIS, *continued.*

Proof, before any letters on the floor. The tablet at the base of the column is white, without any lines. Our copy is cut close at the top.

COUCHÉ, JACQUES, *père*, engraver, born at Gournai in 1750 (Le Blanc erroneously says "at Gournay, or at Abbeville, in 1769"). A pupil of Levasseur.

PONTE BASSANO *pinx.* "The Circumcision." More correctly, The Presentation in the Temple.

In the collection of Lord Gower; formerly in the Orleans Gallery. Waagen, *Treasures*, II. p. 61. Engraved for the Orleans Gallery.

COUCHÉ, FRANÇOIS LOUIS, *fils*, engraver, born at Paris in 1782. A pupil of Lafitte in drawing, and of his father, Jacques, in engraving.

GÉRARD *pinx.* The Battle of Austerlitz.

Artist's proof.

COUSINS, HENRY, a London engraver of our own day, in mezzotinto and aquatinta in the modern style, — needle, graver, and roulette combined.

MIDDLETON *pinx.* **P.** Lady Cust.

Proof, before letters.

HOR. VERNET *pinx.* **P.** Vittoria of Albano.

Artist's proof, on India paper.

COUSINS, SAMUEL, a London engraver of our day in mezzotinto and aquatinta in the modern style, — needle, graver, and roulette combined.

E. LANDSEER *pinx.* Bolton Abbey in the Olden Time.

The original is in the collection of the Duke of Devonshire, Chatsworth. Waagen, *Treasures*, III. p. 351.

Proof, open and traced letters.

E. LANDSEER *pinx.* **P.** Return from Hawking.

Portraits of the family of Lord Egerton.

Proof; title with unshaded letters, formed of three lines, and the dedication in traced, slender letters.

W. ALLSTON *pinx.* **P.** S. T. Coleridge.

Open letter proof, India paper.

SIR THOMAS LAWRENCE *pinx.* **P.** Master Lambton.

Proof, traced letters.

SIR THOMAS LAWRENCE *pinx.* **P.** Sir Thomas Lawrence.

SIR THOMAS LAWRENCE *pinx.* **P.** Miss McDonald.

Proof before any letters, with only the engraver's name slightly cut in.

COUSINS, SAMUEL, *continued.*

SIR THOMAS LAWRENCE *pinx.* 𝔓. Pope Pius VII.

Open letter proof.

𝔓. Shakespeare.

The Chandos portrait, in the Bridgewater Gallery. "Engraved for the Shakespeare Society, June, 1849."

Open letters.

LANDSEER *pinx.* 𝔓. Sutherland Children with a Fawn.

"The Lady Evelyn Gower and the Marquis of Stafford" slightly cut with the needle, on the right below.

Proof, before letters.

SIR THOMAS LAWRENCE *pinx.* 𝔓. The Duchess of Sutherland, with her little daughter on her knee, one of whose shoes is on the table.

The picture is in the Stafford House. Waagen, *Treasures,* II. p. 72.

Proof, before letters, with only the artists' and the publisher's names.

COUVAY, JEAN, designer and engraver, born at Arles in 1622.

RAPHAEL *pinx.* The Madonna with the Pink.

See Passavant, II. 55. There are numerous repetitions of this picture, the original of which is not known; the most familiar one is that in the Camuccini collection in Rome, now in the collection of the Duke of Northumberland in Alnwick Castle. Waagen, *Galleries and Cabinets,* or *Treasures,* IV. p. 466.

CRANACH, LUCAS, the elder, painter, engraved seven plates in copper, and published woodcuts under his name, for which he drew the blocks. He was born at Kronach in Franconia in 1472, and died at Weimar in 1553. His real name was Sunder, but by mistake he has been called Muller, because he signed himself Lucas Maller (instead of Maler, i. e. painter). Bartsch, VII.

𝔓. Duke Albert of Saxony and his son Henry. B. 2.

Engraved for the *Wittenberger Heiligthum,* 1509. 4to.

The Baptism of Christ, woodcut from the Evangelion.

On the back of the print in Black Letter: "Das Fyerdt teyl dißer Postill Von den Heyligen. Diße nachfolgenden zwölf Euangelia," etc.

CROUTELLE, L., engraver, pupil of Delaunay, worked at Paris at the commencement of the nineteenth century, and died there in 1824.

VELAZQUEZ *pinx.* 𝔓. Portrait of the great Pirate Barbarossa.

"Ritrato de Barba Rosa, Real Palacio de Madrid." In the Madrid Gallery. Madrazo, No. 127; Stirling, *Velazquez,* p. 244. Engraved for *Coleccion de las estampas . . . pertenecientes al Rey de España.*

CROUTELLE, L., *continued.*

Croutelle engraved also, in conjunction with Fosseyeux and others, Raphael's *Hours of the Night.* *See* FOSSEYEUX.

CRUYS, VER, whose real name was Theodor Krüger, engraver; he was born about 1646, and worked in Italy.

TITIAN *pinx.* Hippolyte d' Este, Cardinal de' Medici, in Hungarian costume.

The picture is in the Gallery of the Pitti palace. Engraved for *Raccolta de' quadri dei Granduchi di Toscana.* Without the name of the person represented.

CUNEGO, DOMENICO, designer and engraver, born at Verona in 1727, died at Rome in 1794. A pupil in drawing of Francesco Ferrari.

DOMENICHINO *pinx.* Scenes from the Life of the Virgin.

Frescos in the Capella Nolfi of the Cathedral of Fano; comp. Kugler, Berlin edit. 1847, II. p. 362; Eastlake's edit., London, 1851, p. 485; Nagler, *Künstler-Lex.*; Zampieri, XXII. p. 189.

16 plates, as follows:—

1. The Almighty. "Te æternum Patrem."
2. Birth of the Virgin. "Egredietur virga."
3. Virgin ascending the Steps of the Temple. "In domo Dei."
4. Betrothment of the Virgin. "Desponsatio gloriosæ V. Mariæ."
5. Annunciation. "Ne timeas."
6. Visitation. "Et unde hoc mihi."
7. Adoration of the Shepherds. "Et peperit filium."
8. Adoration of the Kings. "Reges Tarsis."
9. Presentation in the Temple. "Viderunt oculi mei."
10. Circumcision. "Et postquam consummati sunt."
11. Flight to Egypt. "Qui consurgens."
12. Virgin and Angels mourning over Christ. "O vos omnes."
13. Death of the Virgin. "Cum divina gloria."
14. Mary Queen of Angels. "Ave Domina."
15. Assumption of the Virgin. "Maria Virgo."
16. Coronation of the Virgin. "Veni de Libano."

MICHEL-ANGELO *pinx.* The Frescos of Michel-Angelo in the Sistine Chapel.

Engraved by D. Cunego with the assistance of, and completed by, his eldest son and pupil Aloisio Cunego, born at Verona in 1750 or 1757; Girolamo Carattoni, an engraver, who worked at Rome about the middle of the last century; Alois or Luigi Fabri, engraver, who was born at Rome in 1778 and died there in 1835; and Pietro Savorelli, born at Rome in 1765.

CUNEGO, DOMENICO, *continued.*

40 plates, as follows: —

1. Outline of the whole ceiling, including outlines of all the frescos, excepting those in the soffits over the arches above the windows and at the four corners, which are left blank and numbered, and the blank for the Last Judgment, from 1 to 13. D. Cunego.
2. Outlines of the frescos in No. 1, from 1 to 13, except 7. D. Cunego.
3. Outline of the Last Judgment, 7. D. Cunego.

In the flat of the ceiling.

4. God dividing Light from Darkness. D. Cunego.
5. Vegetation, and Sun and Moon. D. Cunego.
6. Creation of Animals. D. Cunego.
7. Creation of Man. D. Cunego.
8. Creation of Woman. D. Cunego.
9. Temptation and Expulsion. D. Cunego.
10. Noah's Sacrifice. Carattoni.
11. The Deluge. Fabri.
12. Noah Drunken. Carattoni.

Prophets and Sibyls.

13. Jeremiah. D. Cunego.
14. Ezekiel. D. Cunego.
15. Joel. D. Cunego.
16. Zechariah. Fabri.
17. Isaiah. Fabri.
18. Daniel. Fabri.
19. Jonah. Fabri.
20. Sibylla Persica. Fabri.
21. Sibylla Erythræa. D. Cunego.
22. Sibylla Delphica. Fabri.
23. Sibylla Cumæa. Fabri.
24. Sibylla Libica. Fabri.

Each engraving of a Prophet or Sibyl includes the genius supporting and two figures in the arches beneath, as well as the medallion and figures above to the flat of the ceiling.

25. 2 external figures not beneath any prophet, — Achim and Amminadab. D. Cunego.
26. 2 similar figures, — Azor and Nahshon. Fabri.
27. 2 figures at one end, — Jacob and Joseph. Al. Cunego.
28. 2 figures at the other end, — Eleazar and Matthan. Al. Cunego.
29. David and Goliath. Fabri. Blank No. 1.
30. Zerubbabel. Pietro Savorelli. Blank No. 2.
31. Uzziah. D. Cunego. Blank No. 3.

CUNEGO, DOMENICO, *continued.*

32. Rehoboam. D. Cunego. Blank No. 4.
33. Salmon. D. Cunego. Blank No. 5.
34. Haman Hanged. D. Cunego. Blank No. 6.
The Last Judgment, by L. Gaultier. *See* GAULTIER. Blank No. 7.
35. The Brazen Serpent. Fabri. Blank No. 8.
36. Jesse. Pietro Savorelli. Blank No. 9.
37. Asa. Pietro Savorelli. Blank No. 10.
38. Hezekiah. Pietro Savorelli. Blank No. 11.
39. Josiah. D. Cunego. Blank No. 12.
40. Judith with the head of Holofernes. Blank No. 13.

RAPHAEL *pinx.* P. The Fornarina in the Barberini palace.
See Passavant, II. No. 87. Engraved for Hamilton's *Schola Italiana.*

TITIAN *pinx.* Filia Roberti Strozzi, nobilis Florentini.
Engraved for Hamilton's *Schola Italiana.*

RAPH. MENGS *pinx.* P. Raphael Mengs's own portrait.
Artist's proof, before any letters.

. Brulliot, *Dict.* I. No. 1291.
Christ teaching the Doctors.

D.

DADO, or **DADDO,** was probably the name of the "Master of the Die," also called Beatrizet or Beatricius the Elder. *See* BEATRIZET.

DALCO, engraver in Parma, a pupil of Toschi.

ANDREA DEL SARTO *pinx.* Salvator Mundi.
The picture is on the altar of the Chapel of the Annunciation of the Church of the Servites in Florence. Alfred Reumont, pp. 93, 94. Engraved in 1833.
Artist's proofs are before any letters.

DALEN, CORNELIS VAN, engraver, son of the publisher of the same name, born at Antwerp about 1630. A pupil of Corn. Visscher.

RUBENS *pinx.* The Four Fathers of the Church.
Figures $\frac{3}{4}$ length, standing. *See* Smith, *Cat. rais.* 658 ; Basan, 3.
2d state, with the address of Blooteling.

TITIAN *pinx.* P. Aretino ,Pietro.
Engraved for the *Cabinet Reynst.*
Proof, before any letters.

TITIAN *pinx.* P. Boccaccio.
Engraved for the *Cabinet Reynst.*

DALEN, CORNELIS VAN, *continued.*

With Blooteling's address.

J. VAN TEYLINGEN *pinx.* **P.** Triglandius, Jacobus.

With the address of J. du Pré.

DAMELE, E.

FRA FIESOLE *pinx.* Noli me tangere.

See MARCHESE, V. "San Marco," No. 31.

DANFORTH, M. J., an English engraver of the present day.

C. R. LESLIE *pinx.* The Sisters of Bethany.

Open letter proof.

C. R. LESLIE *pinx.* Uncle Toby and the Widow Wadman, in the Sentry-box.

The picture formerly belonged to John Sheepshanks, Esq. It is now in the Vernon Gallery. Waagen, *Treasures,* I. p. 378.

Proof, on India paper.

DARET, PIERRE, designer and engraver, born at Paris in 1610, died at Aix in 1675.

SIMON VOUET *pinx.* Holy Family.

DARNSTEDT, JOHANN ADOLPH, engraver, born at Auma, 1769, died at Dresden, after he had become blind. A pupil of Schulz and Zingg.

ANGELO QUAGLIO *dis.* The Cathedral of Cologne.

Engraved for Boisserée's *Geschichte und Beschreibung des Doms zu Köln.*

Artist's proof, having the artists' names only, slightly traced with the needle.

DIETRICH *pinx.* "Le Mage."

Landscape in the style of Salvator Rosa.

Impression with the artist's retouch in pencil, though with letters.

In the proofs the inscription was covered up.

DIETRICH *pinx.* "Le Mage parmi les Pasteurs."

Companion piece to the one above.

Impression the same.

The original pictures from which these two plates were engraved were owned by Count Marcolini in Dresden.

DASORI, GIOVANNI BATTISTA. *See* MONTAGNANI, *Raphaelis Picturae Peristyli Vaticani.*

DAUDET, ROBERT, the son, engraver, born at Lyons in 1737, died at Paris in 1824. A pupil of his father, of Balechou, and of Wille.

BACKHUYSEN *pinx.* Le Coup de Vent.

In the Gallery of the Louvre. Villot, No. 7; Smith, *Cat. rais.* 15.

DAUDET, ROBERT, *continued.*

Engraved for the *Musée Français.*

Van der Heyden *pinx.* Village on a Canal.

In the Gallery of the Louvre. Villot, No. 204; Smith, *Cat. rais.* 121. Engraved for the *Musée Français.*

DAULLÉ, JEAN, engraver, born at Abbeville in 1703, died at Paris in 1763. A pupil of Hecquet.

Carlo Maratti *pinx.* Virgin and Child.

The picture is in the Dresden Gallery. Engraved for *Rec. d'est. de la Gal. de Dresde,* I. No. 45.

Correggio *pinx.* Magdalen reading.

In the Dresden Gallery. Coxe, p. 125. Engraved for *Rec. d'est. de la Gal. de Dresde,* I. No. 4.

Correggio *pinx.* The same.

Impression before the Number.

Correggio *pinx.* The same.

Proof before letters, with the artists' names in smaller letters than those of the prints, and with the addition of the date 1758, *which the prints have not.*

Albano *pinx.* La Charité humaine.

The original painting was in the old Royal Collection at Paris, but is not now in the Louvre. Waagen, *Kunstwerke und Künstler in Paris,* p. 777, No. 6.

Nic. Poussin *pinx.* Jupiter as Diana, with Callisto.

See Smith, *Cat. rais.* 183. The picture was sold in 1789, in the collection of Baron d'Holbach.

Van Dyck *pinx.* Child playing with Love.

See Smith, *Cat. rais.* 395. Engraved from a picture owned by "M. Prousteaux, capitaine des Gardes de la Ville."

Rubens *pinx.* "Quos ego."

Painted to celebrate the prosperous voyage to Belgium of the Cardinal Ferdinand of Austria. It formed one of the embellishments of the triumphal arches after the battle of Nördlingen, and is now in the Dresden Gallery. Smith, *Cat. rais.* 268. Engraved for the *Rec. d'est. de la Gal. de Dresde,* I. 48.

Rubens *pinx.* The same.

Proof before any letters.

Spagnoletto *pinx.* Diogenes with the Lantern.

The picture is in the Dresden Gallery. Engraved for *Rec. d'est. de la Gal. de Dresde,* I. No. 31.

DAULLÉ, JEAN, *continued.*

Teniers *pinx.* The Village Surgeon. "Chirurgeon Flamand."

"Tiré du Cabinet de M. Peilhon." Not mentioned by Smith. Engraved in 1760.

Rubens *pinx.* Portrait of a Spanish gentleman with short hair and bushy beard, wearing a full ruffle.

See Smith, *Cat. rais.* 272. The picture is in the Dresden Gallery.

Rubens *pinx.* **P.** Two sons of Rubens.

In the Dresden Gallery. A duplicate is in the Lichtenstein Gallery in Vienna. Engraved for the *Rec. d'est de la Gal. de Dresde,* I. No. 50.

Proof, before letters.

J. L. Tocqué *pinx.* **P.** Marie, Princess of Poland, Queen of Louis XV. of France.

Full length portrait in the costume of coronation.

In the Duke of Buckingham's collection, No. 1430, there was a proof before letters.

Robert Tournière *pinx.* **P.** Maupertuis, in the dress of a Laplander.

See Le Blanc, *Wille,* 132.

Tournière *pinx.* **P.** The same.

Artist's proof, with the names written in ink.

Tournière *pinx.* **P.** Puységur, Jacques François de Chastenet de, Maréchal de France.

Proof, before letters.

H. Rigaud *pinx.* **P.** Hyacinthe Rigaud painting the Portrait of his Wife.

Engraved by Daullé for admission into the Academy. The statement in the catalogue of Marshall's engravings, London, 1864, that the original of this engraving is in the Dresden Gallery, is erroneous.

DAVID, JÉRÔME, engraver, worked at Paris and at Rome in the middle of the seventeenth century.

Paolo Farinati *pinx.* The Martyrdom of St. Erasmus.

From Otto's collection.

DELAULNE, ÉTIENNE, called Stephanus, goldsmith, designer, and engraver, born at Orléans in 1520.

Raphael *inv.* The Martyrdom of St. Felicitas, or rather Cecilia.

After a drawing for the fresco in the chapel of the Villa Magliana. Passavant, II. 242, and III. p. 151. A copy of Marc-Antonio's engraving (B. 117), but in reverse and smaller.

Raphael *inv.* The Rape of Helena.

DELAULNE, ÉTIENNE, *continued.*

See Passavant, II. p. 662, No. 79. A copy of Marc-Antonio's engraving (B. 209), but in reverse and smaller.

DELAUNAY, NICOLAS, engraver, born at Paris in 1739, died there in 1792. A pupil of Lempereur.

J. RAOUX *pinx.* Angelica and Medoro.

"Tiré du cabinet de M. le President du Plaa."

DELEGORGUE-CORDIER, JEAN, designer and engraver, born at Abbeville in 1781.

DOMENICHINO *pinx.* Æneas saving Anchises.

The original is in the Gallery of the Louvre, where it is now attributed to Spada. Villot, No. 409.

Proof, with the names of the artists cut in the margin, and the inscription ENEE *in uncial open letters in the border.*

DELFF, WILLEM JAKOBSZ. (i. e. Jacob's son), usually called W. DELPHIUS, painter and engraver, born at Delft in 1580, died in 1638. A pupil of his father Jacob Willemsz., and father of Jacob Willemsz., called Delphius the younger. He was a son-in-law of Mich. Mierevelt of Delft.

MIEREVELT *pinx.* **P.** Buckingham, George Villiers, Duke of.

Proof before any letters.

Purchased from Messrs. Evans, *Fine Art Circular*, No. 1207, for £ 21.

MIEREVELT *pinx.* **P.** Hugo Grotius.

The picture is in the Hôtel de Ville at Delft. Waagen, *Handbook*, I. p. 239.

VAN DYCK *pinx.* **P.** Mierevelt, Michel, painter.

Engraved for M. van den Enden, Van Dyck's *Iconographia*, No. 9. Weber, *Cat. rais.* p. 55.

1st state, with the name of H. Hondius as engraver.

"Extrêmement rare."

VAN DYCK *pinx.* **P.** The same.

3d state, with "W. J. Delff sculps." *and after the letters of Hendricx's address,* "G. H.," *were effaced from the plate.*

DELFINI, J., an engraver of the present day, a pupil of Toschi.

RAPHAEL *pinx.* **P.** Pope Julius II.

From the repetition or copy of the picture in the Gallery of the palace at Turin (Passavant, III. p. 110), of which the original is in the Gallery of the Pitti palace at Florence. Passavant, II. No. 83.

DELIGNON, JEAN LOUIS, engraver, worked at Paris in the latter half of the eighteenth century. A pupil of Nic. Delaunay.

TITIAN *pinx.* Perseus and Andromeda.

Engraved for the Orleans Gallery. When that Gallery was sold in England, the picture was bought by Mr. Bryan.

Compare remark under CORT.

DELLA ROCCA, CARLO. *See* ROCCA.

DENZLER and **HESSLÖHL,** *sc.*

LÉOP. ROBERT *pinx.* Les Moissonneurs.

The picture is in the Gallery of the Louvre.

Proof, before any letters, except the names of the artists and printer. On India paper.

DESCLAUX, VICTOR, engraver in the modern mixed style, with much etching, and the atmosphere produced by aquatinta.

LÉOP. ROBERT *pinx.* Les Moissonneurs.

The picture is in the Gallery of the Louvre.

Proof before any letters, except the names of the artists, the printers, and the publishers. On India paper.

LÉOP. ROBERT *pinx.* Les Pêcheurs de l'Adriatique.

Proof like the preceding.

DESNOYERS, LOUIS AUGUSTIN BOUCHER, designer and engraver, born at Paris in 1779, died there in 1857. A pupil of Alexandre Tardieu.

NIC. POUSSIN *pinx.* Eliezer and Rebecca at the Well.

See Smith, *Cat. rais.* 6. In the Gallery of the Louvre. Villot, No. 415.

Impression with the title in shaded letters and two lines of description. With the stamp of the engraver's initials "A. D."

NIC. POUSSIN *pinx.* The same.

Proof, with one line of open letters. Engraver's stamp the same as the preceding.

RAPHAEL *pinx.* The Visitation.

See Passavant, II. 229, and III. p. 135. In the Madrid Gallery.

See also Passavant's *Christliche Kunst in Spanien*, p. 156.

Proof, with open and traced letters, and with the smaller stamp of the engraver's initials, and these in the middle *below, close under the engraving.*

The prints have the date 1824 in the middle below; they have further the *larger*, the common stamp of the initials, and this is placed on the

DESNOYERS, LOUIS AUGUSTIN BOUCHER, *continued.*

left side below, opposite the inscription, which in this state is in shaded letters.

RAPHAEL *pinx.* The Transfiguration.

See Passavant, II. 244, and III. p. 152. In the Gallery of the Vatican. Engraved in 1839 on two plates, of which the impressions are carefully joined.

Proof, with the words "La Transfiguration" *and the artists' names in open letters.*

With the Key.

LEONARDO DA VINCI *pinx.* La Vierge aux Rochers.

See Rigollot, No. 22. Painted for the Chapel of the Conception of the Franciscan church in Milan; now owned by the Earl of Suffolk, Charlton Park. Waagen, *Treasures*, III. p. 168. Engraved from the repetition of this picture in the Gallery of the Louvre. Villot, No. 482.

The lower margin of this impression is artificial.

LEONARDO DA VINCI *pinx.* The same.

*Artist's proof, with merely the artists' names.**

Purchased from Messrs. Evans for £ 26 5 *s.* Impressions of the same state, Johnson, No. 48, £ 29; Marshall, No. 375, £ 30 10 *s.*

The proofs have the inscription, *Léonard de Vinci Pinxit. Aug. Desnoyers Delt. & Sculpt. Tableau du Musée Napoléon;* the title, *La Vierge aux Rochers,* in open uncial letters; the coat of arms; the dedication to the Duc de Bassano, in open traced cursive letters; the address of Ramboz; and on the left below, the stamp of two antique heads. Amsler & Ruthardt's sale cat. I. No. 136, 100 *th.*; Quandt, No. 2281, 96 *th.*; Lehrs, No. 56, 101 *th.*; Macready, No. 22, £ 23. — The 1st impressions of the prints have the stamp of the two antique heads. — The 2d have the stamp of the engraver's initials. — Later ones have no stamp.

RAPHAEL *pinx.* La Belle Jardinière.

The Virgin and Child with the infant St. John.

See Passavant, II. 60. The picture is in the Gallery of the Louvre. Engraved in 1805.

The engravings of this plate have no stamp of the engraver.

From the collection of William Esdaile. The dedication is cut off.

RAPHAEL *pinx.* The same.

* According to Desnoyers' own emphatic declaration, there are genuine *épreuves d'artiste,* i. e. impressions with merely the artists' names, of only two of his plates, namely, of the above La Vierge aux Rochers and of La Belle Jardinière. Impressions of the other plates, without further inscription, are either spurious proofs, made by covering the letters while printing, or impressions of the unfinished plate, obtained without the sanction of the engraver, with the exception of the Sistine Madonna, which he engraved afterwards.

DESNOYERS, LOUIS AUGUSTIN BOUCHER, *continued.*

Artist's proof, with merely the words, "Aug. Desnoyers Delt. & Sculpt. an. 11." *With the white stamp:* "Calcographie du Louvre, Musées Nationaux."

Purchased from Messrs. Evans for £35. Same state, Johnson, No. 47. £29. Hippisley, No. 24, £32 11 *s.* Lehrs, No. 54, 260 *th.*

The proofs have *La Vierge dite La Belle Jardinière* in open uncial letters, a Dedication to M. D. V. Denon in open traced cursive letters, and *Se vend à la Calcographie du Musée Napoléon.—Imprimée par Ramboz,* in small letters below.

George Smith, No. 610, £11 11 *s.*

RAPHAEL *pinx.* "La Vierge au Linge."

See Passavant, II. 91, "La Vierge au Diadème." The picture is in the Gallery of the Louvre.

At the left a stamp with the letters "A. D."

RAPHAEL *pinx.* The same.

Proof, before the inscription of the title; the space for it is left blank, and below it is traced with the needle, "Dessiné et gravé d'après le tableau original de Raphael, par Aug. Boucher Desnoyers, Membre des Académies de Vienne et de Genève." *With the white stamp* "A. D." *on the left.*

Purchased for £14. Some proofs are without the stamp.

RAPHAEL *pinx.* La Vierge au Poisson.

See Passavant, II. 100. The picture is in the Gallery of Madrid.

1*st impression, with the date* 1822 *in the middle below, and without stamp.*

The date has been taken out in later impressions.

RAPHAEL *pinx.* The same.

1*st impression, with the date, on India paper, with the stamp* "A. D." on *the left below.*

The proof has open letters. G. Smith, No. 608, £11 11 *s.*; Lehrs, No. 60, 65 *th.*

RAPHAEL *pinx.* La Vierge au Berceau.

See Passavant, II. 235. In the Gallery of the Louvre.

Proof, before the inscription, "La Vierge au Berceau," *the space for which is left blank; below it are the words, traced only:* Déssiné et gravé d'après le tableau de Raphael par le B[ar]on* Boucher Desnoyers, P[remi]er graveur du roi. *Stamp* "A. D." *on the left.*

RAPHAEL *pinx.* La Vierge à la Chaise.

See Passavant, II. 226. In the Gallery of the Pitti palace in Florence.

With the common (the larger) stamp of the initials "A. D." *in the lower margin on the left.*

* The engraver was made a Baron in 1828.

DESNOYERS, LOUIS AUGUSTIN BOUCHER, *continued.*

Besides the inscription *La Vierge à la chaise,* in lightly shaded uncial letters, in the socle of the picture, the proofs have below in the margin: *Dessiné et gravé d'après le Tableau Original de Raphael par Aug. Boucher Desnoyers, Membre des Acadêmies de Vienne et de Genève,* in very thin slightly traced letters, and the same larger stamp of the engraver's initials as the prints. Lehrs, No. 65, 40 *th.*

RAPHAEL *pinx.* La Vierge de la Maison d'Albe.

See Passavant, II. 89. In the Imperial Gallery of St. Petersburg.

With the extended drapery on the child, with 1827 *in the middle under the print, and with the common, the* larger *stamp* "A. D." *in the lower margin on the left below.*

RAPHAEL *pinx.* The same.

Proof, before the extended drapery on the nude parts of the child, with the smaller *stamp of the initials, and this in the middle under the engraving, where the prints have the date. The inscription in the lower margin,* "Le Tableau," *etc., is in very thin slightly traced letters; the title,* "La Vierge de la maison d'Albe," *is shaded in the proofs as well as in the print impressions.*

Purchased from Messrs. Evans for £14 14*s.* Lehrs, No. 58, 61 *th.*; No. 59, 80 *th.*

RAPHAEL *pinx.* Madonna di San Sisto.

See Passavant, II. 240. Engraved in 1841.

Without any stamp of the engraver.

For a proof, before the inscription, *La Vierge de Dresde dite de St. Sixte,* see Engelmann, *Raphael* (1866), p. 20.

RAPHAEL *pinx.* La Vierge au Donataire, dite de Foligno.

See Passavant, II. 92. The picture is in the Gallery of the Vatican. Engraved in 1810.

Impression of the 1*st state, with the stamp of the two antique heads.*

RAPHAEL *pinx.* The same.

Proof, "La Vierge au Donataire, dite de Foligno," *in open letters. Stamp of the two heads.*

Purchased from Messrs. Evans for £16 16*s.* Lehrs, No. 61, 97 *th.*

RAPHAEL *pinx.* La belle Jardinière de Florence.

See Passavant, III. p. 170. "Under this name Desnoyers engraved a picture as Raphael's which, however, bears indications of an Italico-Belgic origin." Engraved in 1841.

Proof, with open letters.

RAPHAEL *pinx.* St. Catherine of Alexandria.

See Passavant, II. 53. The picture is in the National Gallery. Engraved in 1824.

DESNOYERS, LOUIS AUGUSTIN BOUCHER, *continued.*

With the larger *stamp of the engraver's initials, on the left.*

RAPHAEL *pinx.* The same.

Proof, with open letters, and the smaller *stamp of initials in the middle.*

RAPHAEL *pinx.* St. Margaret.

See Passavant, II. 234. Gallery of the Louvre. Engraved in 1832.

Proof, with the inscription "Ste. Marguerite" *in open letters in the engraved border of the plate, and in the margin,* "Marguerite nacquit à Crémone dans le 3ème Siècle ... et périt ... à Antioche ou elle eut la tête tranchée," *in letters delicately traced. With the* smaller *stamp of initials, in the middle.*

RAPHAEL *pinx.* The same.

Print, title the same; open letters in the border. Inscription the same, but with strengthened letters, and an additional inscription beginning near the middle of the last line of the first, "Ce tableau qui fait partie ... Dessiné et gravé en 1832 ... par le Baron Boucher Desnoyers." *With the* larger *stamp of initials, on the left.*

CORREGGIO *del.* Magdalen.

A bust. No. 13 of Desnoyers' *Recueil d'estampes gravées d'après des peintures antiques italiennes par lui, ou exécutées sous sa direction.* This is one of the best of the 34 plates.

RAPHAEL *pinx.* The Three Christian Virtues.

Originally the predella of the Entombment (the altar-piece of San Francesco in Perugia, now in the Borghese Gallery in Rome). This predella, painted in chiaroscuro, is now in the Gallery of the Vatican. Passavant, II. 54, p. 78.

Three plates, — Faith, Love, Hope.

1*st impressions, with the engraver's stamp of the two antique heads on the first and third plate. The second plate was not stamped; it has a medallion engraved in the middle of the lower margin.*

The proofs have only the artist's names, and the medallion in the middle plate. Johnson, No. 45, £13 13 *s.*

A. CARAFFE *inv.* Hope supporting the Unfortunate unto the Grave.

INGRES *del.* L'Amour.

After the antique. Engraved for the *Musée Français.*

PERINO DEL VAGA *pinx.* Les Muses et les Piérides.

The original painting, now ascribed to Rosso de Rossi, "Le maître Roux," is in the Gallery of the Louvre. Villot, No. 639. Engraved in 1829.

Proof with open letters. This engraving has the smaller *stamp of the engraver's initials.*

RICHARD *pinx.* **P.** François I. et Marguerite de Navarre.

DESNOYERS, LOUIS AUGUSTIN BOUCHER, *continued.*

Proof, with open letters. With the larger *stamp in white of the engraver's initials on the left side below. With the autograph of the engraver.*

DESNOYERS *del.* **P.** Jefferson, Thomas.

GÉRARD *pinx.* **P.** Napoleon I.

Whole length figure in his coronation robes.

1*st impression, before the eagle was added below in the middle under the plate; and with the stamp of the two heads.*

GÉRARD *pinx.* **P.** The same.

Proof, before the artists' names. Without any stamp.

These proof impressions were taken for the Emperor.

GÉRARD *pinx.* **P.** Le Roi de Rome. "Napoléon II."

Infant in a chemise with the great Napoleonic star across his shoulders, sitting on a couch, in one hand a sceptre, the other upon a globe.

In the left corner, below the stamp, N.

GÉRARD *pinx.* **P.** Talleyrand.

Proof, with open letters. With the stamp of the two heads.

DESPLACES, LOUIS, designer and engraver, born at Paris in 1682, died there in 1739.

C. MARATTI *pinx.* Danaë.

"Tableau du cabinet de M. de la Faye, Secrét. du Cabinet du roi."

PAOLO VERONESE *pinx.* La Sagesse compagne d'Hercule. Wisdom leading Strength.

Engraved for the *Cabinet Crozat,* while in the Orleans Gallery.

Now in the collection of H. T. Hope, Esq. Waagen, *Treasures,* II. p. 113.

DICKINSON, WILLIAM, designer and engraver in mezzotinto, born at London about 1740, died about the end of the eighteenth century.

SIR JOSHUA REYNOLDS *pinx.* **P.** Mrs. Sheridan as Cecilia.

DIE, MASTER OF THE. *See* BEATRIZET, *the elder.*

DIEN, C. M. F., engraver, born about 1782, worked in Paris.

RAPHAEL *pinx.* The Sibyls.

A fresco painting in Santa Maria della Pace in Rome. Passavant, II. 112.

Proof before letters, with only the artists' names traced, the date 1838, *and with the stamp of a pallet bearing the name Raphael.*

A similar proof, Quandt, No. 2164, 23*th.*

The artist's proofs are before any letters.

RAPHAEL *pinx.* Holy Family of Francis I.

DIEN, C. M. F., *continued.*

Dien finished the second, the larger plate of Richomme's engraving of this picture. *See* Richomme.

DIES, CHRISTOPH ALBERT, painter and etcher, born at Hannover in 1755; from 1775 to 1796 in Rome; etched, with Reinhart, *Collection de vues pittoresques d'Italie.* He died at Vienna in 1822. *See* Reinhart.

DIETRICH, CHRISTIAN WILHELM ERNST, painter and etcher, born at Weimar in 1712, died at Dresden in 1774. A pupil of Thiele. Linck, *Monographie der von ... Dietrich radirten ... Vorstellungen,* Berlin, 1848.

The Prodigal Son. L. 27.

The Mountebank. L. 74.

Nymphs bathing near a Cave. L. 136.

DIXON, JOHN, engraver in mezzotinto, born about 1740, died at London about 1780.

Sir Joshua Reynolds *pinx.* Ugolino and his Sons.

The picture is in Earl Amherst's collection at Knole Park. Waagen, *Galleries and Cabinets,* or *Treasures,* iv. p. 338.

DOO, GEORGE T., an English engraver of the present day.

G. S. Newton *pinx.* Bassanio and Portia.

Engraved in 1839, from the original picture in the possession of John Sheepshanks, Esq.

Proof, with open and traced letters.

G. S. Newton *pinx.* Dutch Girl.

The original picture is in the possession of William Wells, of Redleaf, near Tonbridge.

Open letter proof.

G. S. Newton *pinx.* Shylock and Jessica.

The original picture is in the possession of Henry Labouchère, Esq.

Lettre grise proof.

G. S. Newton *pinx.* The Bride.

Engraved in 1831.

Proof before letters, with only the artists' names, and address of the publishers.

G. S. Newton *pinx.* Yorick and the Grisette.

Vernon Gallery. Waagen, *Treasures,* i. p. 378.

Lettre grise proof.

Sir Charles Eastlake *pinx.* Pilgrims coming in sight of Rome.

DOO, GEORGE T., *continued.*

The original is owned by the Duke of Bedford at Woburn Abbey. Waagen, *Treasures,* III. p. 466. Engraved in 1842.

Artist's proof, the artists' names and address very slightly traced. With autograph in pencil of Sir Charles Eastlake. On India paper.

PICKERSGILL *pinx.* **P.** Cuvier.

Open letters.

DORIGNY, SIR NICOLAS, designer and engraver, born at Paris in 1657, where he died in 1746. In 1711 he was invited to England to engrave Raphael's Cartoons. They were finished in 1719, and dedicated to George I., whereupon Dorigny was knighted.

RAPHAEL *pinx.* The Transfiguration.

The picture is in the Gallery of the Vatican. Passavant, II. 244.

2d state with Eq(ues) *before the name of the engraver, but before Strange's retouch.*

RAPHAEL *pinx.* The Transfiguration.

1st state, before Eques *was added to the name of the engraver, and before any retouch.*

RAPHAEL *pinx.* "Pinacotheca Hamptoniana."

See Passavant, II. p. 250, and p. 256. a. Compare also Waagen, *Treasures,* II. p. 369 *et seqq.*

8 plates, namely :—

1. Title and Dedication.
2. St. Paul preaching at Athens. P. II. p. 255.
3. The Miraculous Draught of Fishes. P. II. p. 253.
4. Feed my Sheep. P. II. p. 253.
5. Peter and John healing the Cripple. P. II. p. 254.
6. The Death of Ananias. P. II. p. 254.
7. Elymas struck with Blindness. P. II. p. 254.
8. Paul and Barnabas at Lystra. P. II. p. 255.

Impressions before the retouch, but with the word Eq(ues) *before* Nicolaus Dorigny, *therefore made after he had received knighthood.*

Very few impressions were issued before the "Eques."

From Professor Vogel von Vogelstein's collection.

GUERCINO *pinx.* The Burial of Saint Petronella.

Gallery of the Capitol. Platner and Bunsen, III. i. p. 132.

DOMENICHINO *pinx.* The Martyrdom of St. Sebastian.

The original in Santa Maria degli Angeli is a fresco, originally painted on the wall of St. Peter's, where it is replaced by a copy in mosaic. Platner and Bunsen, III. ii. p. 356.

DORIGNY, SIR NICOLAS, *continued.*

RAPHAEL *pinx.* Psyches et Amoris Nuptiae, *etc.*

After the frescos in the Loggia of the Villa Farnesina in Rome. Engraved in 1693. Passavant, II. No. 241, and p. 344, a.

12 plates, namely : —

1. Title.
2. Venus points out Psyche to Cupid.
3. Cupid points out Psyche to the Graces.
4. Venus, Juno, and Ceres. }
Venus going to Olympus. }
5. Venus before Jupiter.
6. Mercury with a Trumpet.
7. Psyche with a Vase.
8. Psyche giving the Vase to Venus. }
Jupiter and Cupid. }
9. Mercury carrying Psyche to Olympus.
10. The Assembly of the Gods.
11. The Nuptial Feast;
to which is added as
12. The Triumph of Galatea, a fresco in the same house.

RAPHAEL *pinx.* Mosaics in the Cupola of the Chigi Chapel, in the Church Santa Maria del Popolo, in Rome.

6 plates only of the 9, contained in "Raphaelis . . . Planetarium . . . delineatum . . . a Nicolao Dorigny . . . ," 1695, sm. fol., dedicated "Ludov. Duci Burgundiae." Passavant, II. p. 448.

Namely : —

The Creator, centre piece of the ceiling. *Wanting.*
The Angel pointing to the firmament. *Wanting.*
The Sun (Apollo).
The Moon (Diana).
Saturn. *Wanting.*
Jupiter.
Mars.
Venus.
Mercury.

See GRUNER, *Mosaics in the Cappella Chigiana*, in which the whole is represented.

DREVET, CLAUDE, engraver, born at Lyons in 1710, died at Paris in 1782.

A pupil and nephew of Pierre, and cousin of Pierre Imbert Drevet.

HYAC. RIGAUD *pinx.* **P.** D'Auvergne, Cardinal H. Oswald.

HYAC. RIGAUD *pinx.* **P.** Sinzendorf, Philippe Louis, Comte de.

DREVET, CLAUDE, *continued.*

JOH. RUD. HUBER *pinx.* 𝔓. Steigerus, Christophorus, Consul Reipubl. Bernensis.

HYAC. RIGAUD *pinx.* 𝔓. Vintimille, Charles Gaspard Guillaume de, Archevêque de Paris.

DREVET, PIERRE, the father, engraver, born at Lyons in 1664, died at Paris in 1739. A pupil of Gérard Audran.

PIERRE MIGNARD *pinx.* The Family of Darius in the Tent, at the Feet of Alexander.

G. Edelinck coepit, P. Drevet perfecit. On 2 plates. *See* EDELINCK.

HYAC. RIGAUD *pinx.* 𝔓. Beauveau, René de, Archevêque de Narbonne.

HYAC. RIGAUD *pinx.* 𝔓. Colbert, Jac. Nic., Archiepiscopus Rothomagensis.

1*st state, before the inscription on the pedestal,* "Offerebant obsequentissimi servi monachi de charitate." Like Paignon-Dijonval, No. 7397.

HYAC. RIGAUD *pinx.* 𝔓. Conti, François Louis de Bourbon, Prince de.

DE TROY *pinx.* 𝔓. Dombes, Louis Auguste de Bourbon, Prince de.

Bust in armor, oval.

NIC. DE LARGILLIÈRE *pinx.* 𝔓. Forest, Jean, peintre.

JOS. VIVIEN *pinx.* 𝔓. Girardon, François, sculpteur.

HYAC. RIGAUD *pinx.* 𝔓. Keller, Jean Balthasar, Cmiss. des fonds de l'artillerie de France.

NIC. DE LARGILLIÈRE *pinx.* 𝔓. Lambert, Nicolas, Seigneur de Thorigny.

NIC. DE LARGILLIÈRE *pinx.* 𝔓. Lambert, Marie de Laubespine, femme de.

PEZEY *pinx.* Lesdiguières, La Duchesse Douarière de.

She holds with one hand a kitten on her lap, and in the other a small book; behind her chair stands a negro boy with a garland of flowers, and there are flowers on the table before her.

The plate has no inscription of the name of the person represented, but it has the following dedication: "Dédié à Madame la Duchesse Douarière de Lesdiguières, par Son très humble et très obéissant seruiteur Pezey."

HYAC. RIGAUD *pinx.* 𝔓. Louis XIV., King of France.

Whole length figure in coronation robes. The picture is in the Gallery of the Louvre. Villot, No. 475.

2*d state* (*according to Nagler, Heller,* etc., 1*st state*), *before the lengthened shadow on the right thigh.*

NIC. DE LARGILLIÈRE *pinx.* 𝔓. Mitantier, J. M. de, Greffier.

Without the name of the person represented, but with the following address: "A Paris chez Dreuet, rue du Foin deuant les Mathurins."

DREVET, PIERRE, *continued.*

Hyac. Rigaud *pinx.* **P.** Marie Souveraine de Neufchâtel, Duchesse de Nemours.

G. Revel *pinx.* **P.** Palliot, Pierre, Historiographe.

Hyac. Rigaud *pinx.* **P.** Rigaud, Hyacinthe, holding a port-crayon.

4th state, with the date 1721.

Drevet *del.* **P.** Christine Caroline, Margrave de Brandenbourg, née Duchesse de Würtemberg.

Without the name of the painter or designer.

DREVET, PIERRE IMBERT, engraver, born at Paris 1697, where he died in 1739. He was a son and pupil of Pierre Drevet.

Ant. Coypel *pinx.* Rebecca at the Well, receiving the Presents from Eliezer the servant of Abraham.

"Tableau au Cabinet du Roy." Not now in the Louvre.

Louis de Boullongne *pinx.* The Presentation in the Temple.

The picture is in the Church of Notre Dame in Paris.

J. Restout *pinx.* Christ praying in the Garden.

2d state, with Surugue's address. On the right below after the name of the engraver is inscribed, "Priez Dieu pour lui."

The 3d state has the address of Buldet.

J. Andray *pinx.* The Resurrection.

Engraved at the age of 19.

Hyacinthe Rigaud *pinx.* **P.** Bernard, Samuel.

1st state, before the words "Conseiller d'État."

Hyacinthe Rigaud *pinx.* **P.** Bossuet.

The picture is in the Louvre. Villot, No. 477.

Before any dot after the name of the painter, but with the corrected spelling in the inscription, and the finished back of the arm-chair.

After every hundred impressions one dot was added.

A proof in Jos. Maberly's collection (No. 129) was sold at London, March 26, 1851,—"a superb impression of the first state, with the spelling 'Constorianus' instead of 'Consistorianus,' and 'Trecens*es*' instead of 'Trecens*is*,' and before the top of the chair was finished, called *épreuve au fauteuil blanc.*" The same state occurs in the catalogue of the Duke of Buckingham's collection, 1834, No. 202; and in Debois' catalogue, Paris, 1843, No. 205. In the collection of Count Archinto (No. 46), it sold at Paris, March, 1862, for 900*fr.*; and the same copy sold again, in the Marshall collection, London, June, 1864, No. 441, for £35.

DREVET, PIERRE IMBERT, *continued.*

HYAC. RIGAUD *pinx.* **P.** Cisternay du Fay, Charles Jérome de, Capitaine aux gardes françaises.

In 8vo.

2d state, with the coat of arms.

HYAC. RIGAUD *pinx.* **P.** Cotte, Robert de.

2d state, with the word "architecte."

ROBERT TOURNIÈRE *pinx.* **P.** Couvay, Petrus Nolascus.

HYAC. RIGAUD *pinx.* **P.** Dubois, Guillaume, Cardinal.

HYAC. RIGAUD *pinx.* **P.** Herbault, Charles Gasp. Dodun, Marquis d'.

ADRIEN LE PRIEUR *pinx.* **P.** Le Blanc, Claude, Ministre et Secrétaire d'État.

CHARLES COYPEL *pinx.* **P.** Le Couvreur, Adrienne, as Cornelia.

1st state of the print, with the spelling "model" *instead of* "modèle."

CHARLES COYPEL *pinx.* The same.

2d state, with the correction "modèle."

The proofs are before any letters, i. e. before the name in the oval border surrounding the portrait, and before the four verses in the pedestal. Debois, No. 207; Johnson, No. 53, £11 11*s.*; Marshall, No. 445, £10 15*s.*; Lehrs, No. 87, 70*th.*

DUCHANGE, GASPARD, engraver, born at Paris in 1666, died there in 1757. A pupil of Jean Audran.

CORREGGIO *pinx.* Jupiter and Leda.

See Coxe, p. 111. In the Berlin Gallery.

1st state, before the name of Sornique.

CORREGGIO *pinx.* Jupiter and Danaë.

See Coxe, p. 111. In the Borghess Gallery in Rome. Platner and Bunsen, III. iii. p. 297.

1st state, before the name of Sornique.

CORREGGIO *pinx.* Jupiter and Io.

See Coxe, p. 112. The picture is in the Berlin Gallery.

1st state, before the name of Sornique.

HYAC. RIGAUD *pinx.* **P.** Girardon, François.

Engraved for his admission into the Academy.

HYAC. RIGAUD *pinx.* **P.** La Fosse, Charles de, peintre.

DUFLOS, CLAUDE, the father, engraver, born at Coucy about 1665, died at Paris about 1727.

DUFLOS, CLAUDE, *continued.*

DOMENICHINO *pinx.* The Annunciation.

1st state, with but one line of inscription and Audran's address.

The 2d state has Buldet's address.

PAOLO VERONESE *pinx.* The Supper at Emmaus.

The picture is in the collection of the Duke of Sutherland at Strafford House; it was formerly in the Orleans Gallery. Waagen, *Treasures,* II. p. 60. Engraved for the *Cabinet Crozat.*

PERUGINO *pinx.* The Entombment.

From the Orleans Gallery. Engraved for the *Cabinet Crozat,* No. 3.

RAPHAEL *pinx.* The Entombment, or, more correctly, Pietà, The Dead Christ mourned over by his Friends.

The third picture of the predella of the altar-piece for the cloister San Antonio di Padova in Perugia. (Madonna in trono with St. John, St. Catharine, St. Peter, and St. Paul.) Passavant, II. p. 42, under 31. c. Now owned by Mrs. H. Dawson. *Manchester Exhibition,* 1857, No. 138. Engraved for the *Cabinet Crozat,* No. 27, of the size of the original picture.

RAPHAEL *pinx.* The Archangel Michael vanquishing the Dragon.

From the smaller picture in the Gallery of the Louvre, painted on the back of a chess-board. Passavant, II. 26. Engraved, of the size of the original, for the *Cabinet Crozat,* No. 15.

DUJARDIN, KAREL, painter and etcher, born at Amsterdam in 1635, died at Venice in 1678. A pupil of Berghem and Potter. Bartsch, I. and Weigel, *Supplêments.*

The Fountain with Water-Trough. B. 1.

A title-piece.

Three Pigs lying before a Sty. B. 8.

A Sheep lying before a Fence. B. 39.

Savoyard Boy with dancing Dog. B. 51.

*** *These pieces are all in the 4th and last state.*

DUNKARTON, ROBERT, painter and engraver in mezzotinto; born about 1744.

BENJ. WEST *pinx.* The Martyrdom of St. Stephen.

The picture is in St. Stephen's Church in London. Nagler, *Künstler-Lexicon,* XXI. p. 321.

Proof before any letters.

HOGARTH *pinx.* Sigismunda.

DUNKARTON, ROBERT, *continued.*

"The original picture ... is in the collection of Mr. Sam. Ireland of Norfolk Street."

Proof, with open and traced letters.

DUNKER, BALTHASAR ANTON, painter and engraver, born at Saal, near Stralsund, in 1746, died at Bern in 1807. A pupil of Philipp Hackert.

PH. HACKERT *pinx.* View of St. Peter's from Ponte Molle.

Engraved in conjunction with Volpato.

DUPLESSI-BERTAUX, JOSEPH, designer and etcher, born at Paris in 1747, died there in 1813.

After STEFANO DELLA BELLA. **P.** Masaniello.

Engraved as a bas-relief.

DUPONT, HENRIQUEL, designer and engraver, born at Paris in 1797. A pupil of Bervic and P. Delaroche.

ARY SCHEFFER *pinx.* Christus Consolator.

In the Fodor Museum in Amsterdam, from the collection of the Duchess of Orleans.

Impression before the retouch, with open letters.

DELAROCHE *pinx.* Lord Strafford on his Way to Execution, receiving the Blessing of Archbishop Laud.

In the collection of the Duke of Sutherland at Stafford House. Waagen, *Treasures*, II. p. 66.

With open letters.

H. DUPONT *del.* **P.** Madame Pasta, as Anne Boleyn.

Proof before the inscription of the name of the represented person. "Dessiné et gravé par Henriquez Dupont," *and with the address of the publishers.*

DELAROCHE *pinx.* **P.** Pope Gregory XVI.

Proof with only the artists' names etched, and the date 1845. *In the background of the picture the coat of arms of the Pope.*

H. LEHMANN *pinx.* **P.** Mademoiselle Rachel.

Proof, with only "H. Lehmann 20 mars 1851. Henriquel 1852," *and in the right upper corner of the picture, in open letters,* "Rachel."

DELAROCHE *pinx.* **P.** Peter the Great of Russia.

Proof No. 21. *India paper.*

DUPUIS, NICOLAS GABRIEL, designer and engraver, born at Paris in 1696, died there in 1770. A pupil of Duchange.

GIORGIONE *pinx.* Pastorale, Concert champêtre.

DUPUIS, NICOLAS GABRIEL, *continued.*

Two young men sitting in a landscape, one playing the lute, accompanied by a young woman with a fife; a second female bringing a pitcher of water. The picture, now in the Gallery of the Louvre (Villot, No. 44), was formerly in the collections of Charles I., E. Jabach, and Louis XIV. Engraved for the *Cabinet Crozat.*

C. DE VISSCHER *del.* **P.** Philip Wouwermans.

DÜRER, ALBRECHT, painter, etcher, and engraver on metal and on wood, born at Nuremberg, May 20, 1471, died there April 18, 1528. He was an apprentice of Michael Wohlgemuth, of whom, however, he could learn very little beyond the technicalities of his trade. Bartsch, *Peintre-graveur,* VII. Heller, *Leben und Werke A. Dürer's.* Hausmann, *Albrecht Dürer's Kupferstiche, Radirungen, Holzschnitte, und Zeichnungen,* Hannover, 1861. Compare also A. von Eye, *Leben und Wirken Albrecht Dürer's,* Nördlingen, 1860.

Engravings.

Adam and Eve. B. 1.

Brilliant early impression of deep black color, and with the strong shading on the neck of Eve. Paper with the watermark of the Great Bull's Head.

Purchased from Messrs. Evans in London for £21. Lasalle, No. 415, 760 *fr.*; Johnson, No. 57, £46; Marshall, No. 451, £41 10 *s.*; Harrach, No. 644, 1050 *fr.*

The Nativity. B. 2.

Most delicate and powerful impression, of perfect harmony.

From the collection of the Prince de Paar, No. 1633. Marshall, No. 452, £13.

The Passion of Our Lord. B. 3–18.

16 plates, namely:—

The Man of Sorrows. B. 3.
Christ praying in the Garden. B. 4.
Christ seized by the Jews. B. 5.
Christ before Caiaphas. B. 6.
Christ before Pilate. B. 7.
The Flagellation. B. 8.
The Crowning with Thorns. B. 9.
Ecce Homo. B. 10.
Pilate washing his Hands. B. 11.
The Bearing of the Cross. B. 12.
The Crucifixion. B. 13.
The Descent from the Cross. B. 14.

DÜRER, ALBRECHT, *continued.*

The Entombment. B. 15.

The Descent into Limbo. B. 16.

The Resurrection. B. 17.

St. Peter and St. John healing the Cripple at the Gate of the Temple. B. 18.

*** *From Otto's collection; but the set is not uniform,—the impressions are not all alike.*

Christ seized by the Jews. B. 5.

A duplicate from "The Passion."

Superb impression, from the collection, and signed with the name, of "P. Mariette, 1660."

Christ praying in the Garden. B. 19.

Etched on iron.

Common impression and pasted down.

The Man of Sorrows. B. 20.

Impression of the greatest delicacy and brilliancy.

From Otto's collection.

The Prodigal Son. B. 28.

1*st state* (see Hausmann), *with the scratch in the air, on the left over the roof, and with the slight perpendicular stroke through the swine. This copy is not in perfect condition, and is pasted down.*

The Virgin with Long Hair and Bandlet. B. 30.

Impression of great freshness and vigor.

From Otto's collection.

The Virgin with Short Hair and Bandlet. B. 33.

Delicate but cold impression, on thin paper.

From Ackermann's collection.

The Virgin suckling the Child. B. 34.

Delicate and clear impression, with the stamp of Böhm on the back of the print.

Harrach, No. 661, 435*fr.*

The Virgin embracing the Child. B. 35.

From Weber's sale, No. 112.

The Virgin nursing the Child. B. 36.

From Weber's sale, No. 113.

The Virgin crowned by an Angel. B. 37.

From Weber's sale, No. 115.

The Virgin, with Child swaddled. B. 38.

DÜRER, ALBRECHT, *continued.*

Of extraordinary freshness and vigor, on firm paper.

Purchased of Mr. Weber in Bonn.

The Virgin crowned by Two Angels. B. 39.

The Virgin sitting by a Wall. B. 40.

From Ackermann's collection, No. 131. Lehrs, No. 95, 46 *th.*

The Virgin with a Pear. B. 41.

Paper mark, an Anchor within a circle.

From Ackermann's collection.

The Virgin with a Monkey. B. 42.

From Geissler's collection. Drugulin's sale, London, 1866, No. 288, £ 9.

The Virgin with a "Butterfly." B. 44.

1st state, before the figure of the Virgin was changed.

From Weber's sale, No. 123.

St. Simeon. B. 49.

With the name "Jules Meunier, Lyon, 1821," *written on the back of the print.*

St. George on Horseback. B. 54.

St. Hubertus, or St. Eustachius. B. 57.

This impression, though not old nor strong, is clear and harmonious. It is on late paper, with the watermark of the single-headed German eagle.

From Otto's collection.

Drugulin's sale, London, 1866, No. 295, "early impression with the watermark of the high crown," £ 33; Marshall, No. 486, £ 46.

St. Jerome in his Cell. B. 60.

Probably the paper with the watermark of the High Crown, as appears from its texture and the wire lines.

From Ackermann's collection, and with another collector's mark, I. A. joined and surmounted with a five-pointed crown.

St. Jerome in Penitence. B. 61.

Watermark a Pineapple.

St. Genevieve, or the Penance of St. Chrysostom. B. 63.

Watermark of the large Bull's Head.

From Weber's sale.

The Witch. B. 67.

Powerful and brilliant impression.

The Effect of Jealousy. B. 73.

Early impression, but pasted down.

Melancholy. B. 74.

DÜRER, ALBRECHT, *continued.*

Fine and powerful impression, with the face of the female and of Cupid lighter.

The same. B. 74.

Fine and powerful impression, with the faces of the two figures darker; the whole, however, of a silvery tone.

Marshall, No. 502, £11 10*s.*; Lehrs, No. 96, 80*th.*

The "great" Fortune. B. 77.

*Mended through the middle of the print.**

The "little" Fortune. B. 78.

Lady on Horseback. B. 82.

The same. B. 82.

Impression of great freshness. Watermark, the High Crown.

Purchased from Messrs. Evans for £5 5*s.* Harrach, No. 701, 300*fr.*; Marshall, No. 510, £5 18*s.*

The Peasant and his Wife. B. 83.

The Hostess and the Cook. B. 84.

Very fine impression.

The Oriental with his Wife and Child. B. 85.

Uncommonly vigorous impression, very fresh, and very delicate. The paper appears, by its firmness, to be rather that with the watermark of the High Crown than that of the Large Bull's Head.

Purchased of Messrs. Evans for £5 5*s.* Marshall, No. 513, £6 10*s.*

Three Peasants in Conversation. B. 86.

The Standard-Bearer. B. 87.

From Ackermann's collection.

Peasants at Market. B. 89.

From Geissler's collection.

Offers of Love. B. 93.

Watermark of the Small Bull's Head.

Cut close. From Wm. Esdaile's and Ackermann's collections, and with three more marks of collectors.

Gentleman and Lady walking, Death lurking behind a Tree. B. 94.

Perfect impression on paper with the watermark of the Large Bull's Head.

With a collector's stamp, "C. P.," the letters joined. From the collection of Baron Verstolk.

Marshall, No. 522, £33.

* I have repeatedly met with impressions that seemed to have been torn in the middle, and afterwards carefully put together again.

DÜRER, ALBRECHT, *continued.*

The Knight of Death, or Franz von Sickingen. B. 98.

The same. B. 98.

Perfect impression.

From the De Bammeville collection, No. 367; bought at the sale for £ 32. Formerly in the collection of Cardinal Fesch.

The same. B. 98.

Still more vigorous impression.

Bought from Messrs. Evans for £ 50. An impression "of unsurpassed beauty," Quandt, No. 208, a, 149⅙ *th.*; Drugulin's sale, London, 1866, No. 317, £ 30.

The Great Cannon, etched on iron. B. 99.

The same, copy by J. Hopfer.

The Shield of Arms with a Death's-Head. B. 101.

The same. B. 101.

Superb impression.

From the collection and signed with the name of P. Mariette. 1666.

Purchased for £ 14 14 *s.* Harrach, No. 721, "épreuve de la plus grande beauté," 1,150 *fr.*

P Archbishop Albert of Mayence. "The Little Cardinal." B. 102.

Superb impression, of silvery tone.

From the collection and with the stamp of Prince de Paar. Quandt, No. 212, 53 *th.*

P. Frederic, Elector of Saxony, called the Wise. B. 104.

Though from the original plate, the impression is not equal to the rest in this collection.

P. Melanchthon. B. 105.

From the De Bammeville collection. Harrach, No. 725, 170 *fr.* B. 106.

P. Bilibald Pirkheimer.

Very vigorous impression. Paper with the watermark of the arms of Nuremberg.

P. Erasmus. B. 107.

Fine and powerful impression on paper, with the watermark of a Crowned Shield having fleurs-de-lis in it.

From the collection of Baron Verstolk. Marshall, No. 536, £ 14.

After DÜRER.

The Entombment: "Sicut in Adā omnes moriuntur," *etc.*

Heller, No. 2254.

Probably engraved by Willem de Passe (born at Utrecht in 1590).

1*st state, before address.*

DÜRER, ALBRECHT, *continued.*

Woodcuts.

The Life of the Virgin. A set of 20 plates (B. 76–95), bound; namely:—

Madonna on a Crescent, giving suck to the Infant. B. 76.

With text on the back. See Nagler, *Künstler-Lex.* III. p. 541.

The High Priest refusing the Offering of Joachim. B. 77.

With text on the back. Paper apparently that which has the watermark of a Flower with a stroke and a triangle over it. Hausmann's plates, fig. 28.

The Angel appearing to Joachim. B. 78.

With text. Watermark, a Flower with a stroke and a triangle over it. Hausmann, No. 28.

The Meeting of Joachim and St. Anna. B. 79.

With text. Watermark, Hausmann, No. 28.

The Birth of the Virgin. B. 80.

With text. Watermark, Hausmann, No. 28.

The Child Mary received by the High Priest at the Entrance of the Temple. B. 81.

Without text. Watermark an ornamented Gothic 𝔓. *Hausmann, fig.* 38.

The Marriage of the Virgin. B. 82.

With text. Watermark, Hausmann, No. 28.

The Annunciation. B. 83.

With text. Paper apparently of the watermark Hausmann, No. 28.

The Meeting of Mary and Elizabeth. B. 84.

Without text. Watermark, a Crowned Double Eagle. Hausmann, No. 51.

The Nativity, with the Adoration of the Shepherds. B. 85.

Proof, before the text. Watermark the Large Bull's Head with flower upon a single line. Hausmann, No. 19.

The Circumcision. B. 86.

With text. Watermark, a Tower surmounted by a crown. Hausmann, No. 27.

The Adoration of the Magi. B. 87.

Without text. Watermark a kind of Fish-bladder with the letters I. M. *in it. Hausmann, No.* 42.

The Presentation. B. 88.

Proof before the text. Watermark, the Large Bull's Head, with flower upon a single line. Hausmann, No. 19.

The Flight into Egypt. B. 89.

With text. Paper apparently of the watermark Hausmann, No. 28.

The Sojourn of the Holy Family in Egypt; Joseph working at his trade. B. 90.

DÜRER, ALBRECHT, *continued.*

With text. Watermark, Hausmann, No. 28.

Christ among the Doctors in the Temple. B. 91.

With text. Watermark, a Tower surmounted by a crown. Hausmann, No. 27.

Christ taking leave of his Mother, previous to his Passion. B. 92.

Without text. Watermark, a Shield with a cross bar. Hausmann, No. 46.

The Death of the Virgin. B. 93.

With text. Paper apparently of the watermark Hausmann, No. 28.

The Assumption of the Virgin. B. 94.

Proof before text. Watermark, the Large High Crown. Hausmann, No. 21.

The Worship of the Madonna. B. 95.

Without text. Watermark, a Shield with a cross bar. Hausmann, No. 46.

Harrach, No. 740, "Suite de vingt estampes, B. 76 – 95, superbes épreuves de la première édition avant le texte," 615 *fr.*

The Rhinoceros. B. 136. Heller, 1904.

3d impression, with the inscription in Flemish; six lines of inscription on the top of the print have been cut off. The crack in the block extends to the fore feet.

DUTTENHOFER, CHRISTIAN FRIEDRICH, landscape designer and engraver, born at Gronau in Würtemberg in 1778, died at Heilbronn in 1846. A pupil of Klengel.

CLAUDE LORRAIN *pinx.* The Temple of Diana at Nemi.

Painted for the Constable Colonna. Inscription on the plate, *Das Original ist im Palast Colonna in Rom.* According to Smith, *Cat. rais.* 175, now in the Royal Museum at Naples.

DUVET, JEAN, "The Master of the Unicorn," painter, goldsmith, and engraver, born at Langres in 1485, worked till 1561. Bartsch, VII. Robert-Dumesnil, V.

A King on Horseback and Suite, fleeing from the Attack of an Unicorn. B. 40. R.-D. 55.

From Weber's sale, No. 346.

Unicorn led in Triumph by a King and a Queen. B. 41. R.-D. 58.

From Weber's sale, No. 347.

DYCK, ANTONI VAN, painter and etcher, born at Antwerp in 1599, died at London in 1641. A pupil of H. van Balen and Rubens. Carpenter, *Pictorial Notices . . . of Sir Anthony Van Dyck,* London, 1844. Weber, *Catalogue raisonné d'une collection de portraits gravés par et d'après Antoine Van-Dyck,* Bonn, 1852.

DYCK, ANTONI VAN, *continued.*

TITIAN *inv.* "Titian and his Mistress."

See Carpenter, p. 127. There is an oil painting on canvas of this composition in the collection of James Morris, Esq., London, which Waagen, *Galleries and Cabinets,* or *Treasures* IV. p. 110, ascribes to a scholar of Titian.

3*d state.* "A Bonenfant excu."

The 1st state is before the artists' names; the second, before address.

"ANTONI VAN DYCK *in.*" Holy Family.

See Carpenter, p. 129. It is doubtful whether the plate was etched by Van Dyck.

4*th state, with Bonenfant's address.*

Portraits, painted and etched by Van Dyck.

P. Breughel, Jan (de Velour), painter.

See Smith, *Cat. rais.* No. 27. Munich Gallery. Carpenter, p. 85, No. 1. Weber, p. 21.

5*th state, after the address* "G[illis] H[endricx]" *had been effaced from the plate. Watermark of the paper, Fleur-de-lis and letter W.*

P. Breughel, Pieter (le Drôle), painter.

See Smith, 798. A picture corresponding with this print is in the collection of the Earl of Egremont. Carpenter, p. 87, No. 2; Weber, p. 22.

5*th state. Watermark, letters ending in* OR.

P. Cornelissen, Antoni, amateur.

Van Dyck etched the head and hand of this plate, which was finished by L. Vorsterman. Carpenter, p. 89, No. 3; Weber, p. 22. *See* VORSTERMAN.

P. Dyck, Antoni van.

Van Dyck etched the head himself, and just indicated the coat; the plate was finished by J. Neeffs. Carpenter, p. 92, No. 4; Weber, p. 23. *See* NEEFFS.

P. Erasmus, Desiderius.

See Smith, 718; Carpenter, p. 93, No. 5; Weber, p. 24.

4*th state, after the address* "G. H." *had been effaced from the plate. Watermark, Two Crescents.*

Franck, Frans, painter.

See Smith, 799; Carpenter, p. 95, No. 6; Weber, p. 24.

6*th state, after the address* "G. H." *had been effaced. Watermark, the arms of Amsterdam.*

P. Momper, Jodocus de, painter.

See Smith, 756; Carpenter, p. 97, No. 7; Weber, p. 26.

5*th state, after the address* "G. H."; *if not, perhaps* 3*d state, before these letters. Watermark, the letter* K.

DYCK, ANTONI VAN, *continued.*

P. Noort, Adam van, painter.

See Smith, 796; Carpenter, p. 99, No. 9; Weber, p. 28.

5th state, after the address "G. H." *was effaced. Watermark, some letters.*

P. Pontius, or Du Pont, Paul, engraver.

See Smith, 789; compare also 788; Carpenter, p. 101, No. 10; Weber, p. 29.

6th state, after the address "G. H." *was effaced.*

P. Snellinx, Jan, painter.

See Carpenter, p. 105, No. 13; Weber, p. 30.

5th state, after the address "G. H." *had been effaced. Watermark, Fleur-de-lis.*

P. Snellinx, Jan, painter. Second plate.

See Smith, 28; Carpenter, p. 106; Weber, p. 30. Van Dyck etched Snellinx's portrait a second time, differing but little from the first plate, but executed more delicately; it was finished with the graver by Pieter de Jode the younger. *See* JODE.

P. Snyders, Frans, painter.

See Smith, 329; Carpenter, p. 107, No. 15; Weber, p. 31. Van Dyck etched the head and coat; the plate was finished by Neeffs. *See* NEEFFS.

P. Suttermans, Justus, painter.

See Smith, 797; Carpenter, p. 111, No. 17; Weber, p. 32.

5th state, after the name had been corrected from "Jodocvs Citermans" *into* "Jvstvs Svttermans," *and the address* "G. H." *effaced. Paper without watermark.*

P. Triest, D. Antoni, Bishop of Ghent.

Van Dyck etched the head, and nearly finished the hand, also some of the drapery; the plate was finished by Pieter de Jode the younger. Carpenter, p. 113, No. 18; Weber, p. 33. *See* JODE.

P. Vorsterman, Lucas, engraver.

See Smith, 786; Carpenter, p. 115, No. 19; Weber, p. 33.

5th state, after the address "G. H." *had been effaced. Watermark, Fleur-de-lis.*

P. Vos, Willem de, painter.

Van Dyck etched the head and coat; the plate was finished by S. à Bolswert. Carpenter, p. 117, No. 20; Weber, p. 34. *See* BOLSWERT.

P. Vos, Paul de, painter.

The picture is in the collection of the Prince of Saxe-Coburg. *See* Smith, *Cat. rais.* 355.

Van Dyck etched the head and coat, and some background; the plate

DYCK, ANTONI VAN, *continued.*

was first unsatisfactorily, and afterwards better finished by S. à Bolswert. Carpenter, p. 119, No. 21; Weber, p. 35. *See* BOLSWERT.

P. Wael, Jan de, painter.

See Smith, 800; Carpenter, p. 121, No. 22; Weber, p. 36.

5th state, after the address "G. H." *had been effaced. No watermark.*

P. Wouwer, Jan van den, Councillor of the Archduke Albert.

See Smith, 303, and Appendix, p. 383, No. 53. The picture is in the Imperial Gallery at St. Petersburg. Van Dyck etched the head and coat; the plate was finished by P. Pontius. Carpenter, p. 123, No. 23; Weber, p. 37. *See* PONTIUS.

E.

EARLOM, RICHARD, designer, etcher, and the greatest engraver in mezzotinto, was born in Somersetshire in 1728, and died in 1794, according to Nagler, Haake, Heller, and Le Blanc. Bryan, in his *Dictionary*, 1816, does not give the date of his birth, but speaks of him as still living; Stanley says, in the new edition of this work, 1849, that Richard Earlom died in 1822.

VAN DER WERFF *pinx.* Bathsheba bringing Abishag to David.

The picture is in the Imperial Gallery of St. Petersburg. Engraved for the *Houghton Gallery.*

Proof before letters, having only the names of the artists and the publishers etched in outline, and with the coat of arms.

RUBENS *pinx.* The Feast of Simon with Mary Magdalene.

The picture is in the Imperial Gallery of St. Petersburg. Engraved for the *Houghton Gallery.* Smith, *Cat. rais.* 549.

RUBENS *pinx.* The Descent from the Cross.

Altar-piece in the Cathedral of Antwerp. Waagen, *Handbook,* II. p. 266; Smith, *Cat. rais.* 5, and *Supplement,* p. 244. Published by Boydell in 1800.

RUBENS *pinx.* Meleager and Atalanta, Boar-hunt.

The picture is in the Imperial Gallery of St. Petersburg. Smith, *Cat. rais.* 548. Engraved for the *Houghton Gallery.*

Proof, having only the artists' names traced in outline, and the coat of arms.

J. WRIGHT *pinx.* A Blacksmith's Shop.

Proof before letters, with only the names of the artists and the address traced in outline.

J. WRIGHT *pinx.* An Iron-forge.

MARIO DAI FIORI *pinx.* The Concert of Birds.

The picture is in the Imperial Gallery of St. Petersburg. Engraved for the *Houghton Gallery.*

EARLOM, RICHARD, *continued.*

QUENTIN MATSYS *pinx.* The Misers.

The picture is at Windsor Castle. Waagen, *Handbook*, I. p. 116.

FR. SNYDERS *pinx.* The Game-Market.
" " The Fish-Market.
" " The Herb-Market.
" " The Fruit-Market.

These four pictures are in the Imperial Gallery of St. Petersburg. They were engraved for the *Houghton Gallery.*

HUYSUM *pinx.* "A Flower Piece."
" " "A Fruit Piece."

Both pictures are in the Imperial Gallery of St. Petersburg. They were engraved for the *Houghton Gallery.*

Both are proofs, with the artists' names traced only, and the coat of arms.

RUBENS *pinx.* **P.** "Rubens's Son and Nurse."

The picture is in the collection of the Marquis of Bute, Luton House. Waagen, *Treasures*, III. p. 475; Smith, *Cat. rais.* 915.

REMBRANDT *pinx.* **P.** Rembrandt when about 56 years of age.

See Smith, *Cat. rais.* 215. Engraved from a picture then in the collection of the Duke of Montague.

Proof before letters, with only the artists' names, the address of the publisher, and the coat of arms.

*** All the above engravings are in mezzotinto.

SIR JOSHUA REYNOLDS *pinx.* **P.** General Eliott, Lord Heathfield.

Vernon Gallery. Waagen, *Treasures*, I. p. 365.

Engraved in the stippled manner.

EDELINCK, GERARD, designer and engraver, born at Antwerp in 1640, died at Paris in 1707. He received his first instruction from C. Galle, the younger, but his great talents were developed afterwards by François de Poilly in Paris. Robert-Dumesnil, VII.

PHIL. DE CHAMPAGNE *pinx.* Moses with the Tables of the Law. R.-D. 2.

Commenced by Nanteuil, and finished by Edelinck, who did the face and hands. The picture was in the collection of M. de Lalive, in Paris.

3d state, with Drevet's address.

"1ère épreuve, avant les noms: *Champagne pinxit, Nanteuil et Edelinck sculp.* 1699, et avant la dédicace," Debois, No. 302, 201 *fr.*

RAPHAEL *pinx.* Holy Family of Francis I. R.-D. 4.

See Passavant, II. 233. In the Gallery of the Louvre.

EDELINCK, GERARD, *continued.*

2d state, with letters, but before the coat of arms of Colbert was engraved in the plate in the foreground of the picture.

Debois, No. 296, 605 *fr.*; Maberly, No. 137, £12 12 *s.*; Archinto, No. 184, 290 *fr.*; Johnson, No. 61, £13 10 *s.*; Marshall, No. 682, £10 15 *s.*; Lehrs, No. 98, 95 *th.*

The 1st state is before any letters, and before the arms. Of this state but two copies are known to exist; one in the Imperial Cabinet of Engravings at Vienna, and the other in the Imperial Cabinet of Engravings in Paris; which latter the French government bought at the sale of the Duke of Buckingham's collection in 1834, No. 3252, for £73 10 *s.* — The 3d state has the coat of arms.

RAPHAEL *pinx.* The same. R.-D. 4.

4th state, with the coat of arms erased, and the traces of the erasure, with the new lines drawn over it, visible.

J. STELLA *pinx.* Madonna raising the Veil from the Sleeping Child. R.-D. 6.

1st state, before the escutcheon on the cradle.

GUIDO *pinx.* "La Couseuse." Madonna sewing, while the Child is asleep. R.-D. 7.

This little picture, 11½ by 9 inches, was in the old Royal Collection at Paris, but is not now in the Gallery of the Louvre. Waagen, *Kunstwerke und Künstler in Paris*, p. 69 and p. 776.

1st state, with the words "A Paris chez" *before the address of N. Poilly.*

In the 2d state these words are taken away, leaving "*N. de Poilly ex. cum priuil. Re.*"

From Otto's collection.

LE BRUN *pinx.* Holy Family at Table, called the Benedicite. R.-D. 8.

According to an inscription on the plate the picture was, when engraved, in the church of St. Paul in Paris.

3d and last state, with the address of J. Audran.

The 1st state is before letters, the 2d before address.

LE BRUN *pinx.* The Crucifixion. "Le Christ aux Anges." R.-D. 17.

The picture is in the Gallery of the Louvre. Villot, No. 62. Engraved on two plates.

3d state, with Drevet's address.

The 1st state is before the address, and with the misspelling of *k* instead of *ck* in the last syllable of the engraver's name; — the 2d is also before the address, but with the correction into *ck.*

LE BRUN *pinx.* **P.** St. Louis, King of France, in Penitence. R.-D. 28.

LE BRUN *pinx.* **P.** St. Charles Borromeo, praying. R.-D. 29.

EDELINCK, GERARD, *continued.*

In the St. Nicholas Church in Paris.

4th and last state, with the shorter address, "ce vend à Paris chez P. Dreuet."

The 1st state is before the inscription. — The 2d state has the inscription, consisting of four metrical lines and dedication to Ch. Le Brun, but no address. — The 3d state has the address, *Se vend à Paris chez P. Dreuet rue du Foin deuant les Mathurins, auec priuil. du Roy.*

LE BRUN *pinx.* **P.** Magdalen renouncing the Vanities of the World. Portrait of Mme. de La Vallière. R.-D. 32.

The picture is in the Gallery of the Louvre. Villot, No. 66. It was formerly in the church of the Carmelites at Paris.

2d state, before the border *formed of several lines, with but* ONE line below, close under which *are the artists' names. Our copy has also the inscription of four verses, in two columns, which, according to Robert-Dumesnil, accompany the 3d state,* with *the border; it forms, therefore, a state between his 2d and 3d.*

P. The same. R.-D. 32.

3d state, with the border, so *that the artists' names appear* between lines, *with the above-mentioned four lines of verses in two columns. Before address.*

P. The same. R.-D. 32.

4th state, with the address, "se vend à Paris chez P. Dreuet rue du Foin deuant les Mathurins, auec priuilege du Roy."

The 5th state, instead of *rue du Foin deuant les Mathurins,* has *aux galleries du Louvre.* The 1st state is before the border, and with the artists' names only slightly traced with the point; in the 2d state they were strengthened. 1st state, Logette, No. 53, 900 *fr.*

LE BRUN *pinx.* The Tent of Darius: the Family of Darius at the Feet of Alexander. R.-D. 42.

The picture, with "The Battles of Alexander," is in the Gallery of the Louvre. It was engraved on two plates to be joined, to complete the series of Le Brun's Battles of Alexander, engraved by Gérard Audran.

4th state, with the name of Goyton, engraved in dots, and 9 points after it, of which 5 are effaced in the present print.

The 1st state is before the inscription of four lines, which ends on *each* plate, with 1661; — the 2d state has these four lines, but not Goyton, the publisher's name; — the 3d state has Goyton's name in dots on each plate; — in the 4th state this name is followed by 9 points; — in the 5th state, Goyton's name is traced in reverse; — in the 6th state Goyton's name is scarcely visible, but there are 20 dots on the right.

PIERRE MIGNARD *pinx.* Alexander in the Tent of Darius. R.-D. 43.

Engraved on two plates, finished by P. Drevet. The picture is in the Imperial Gallery of St. Petersburg.

EDELINCK, GERARD, *continued.*

LEONARDO DA VINCI *pinx.* The Combat of four Horsemen for the Standard. R.-D. 44.

See Rigollot, No. 59. Engraved after a copy of the celebrated Cartoon, drawn in red chalk by Rubens, which Edelinck found at Antwerp.

2d state, with the inscription in the plate, "L. d' la finse pin. G. Edelinck Sc.," *and before the three points on the blade of the sword of the second horseman.*

The 1st state is before any letters. Logette, No. 50, 252*fr.*; Archinto, No. 189, 575*fr.*; Marshall, No. 683, £14.

In the 3d state, the retouched plate has still the misspelled inscription, — which was never corrected, — and three points on the sword, placed thus ⁚ ·

PHILIPPE DE CHAMPAGNE *pinx.* **P.** Arnauld, Antoine, Doctor of the Sorbonne. R.-D. 140.

Bust in oval.

1st state, before address.

The 2d state has the address, *A Paris chés la Ve de F. Chereau,* etc.

JEAN BAPTISTE DE CHAMPAGNE *pinx.* **P.** The same person. R.-D. 141.

Three quarters length, sitting.

RUBENS *pinx.* **P.** Joanna, Grand Duchess of Austria, wife of Francesco de' Medici. R.-D. 143.

The picture is in the Gallery of the Louvre. Villot, No. 456. Engraved for Nattier's *Galerie Luxembourg.*

2d state, before the 6 *in the margin at the right below.*

The 1st state is before letters.

CLAUDE LE FÈVRE ("LE FEBURE") *pinx.* **P.** Bussy, Roger de Rabutin, Comte de. R.-D. 162.

TESTELIN *pinx.* **P.** Carcavy, Pierre de, Librarian to the King. R.-D. 163.

P. DE CHAMPAGNE *pinx.* **P.** Champagne, Philippe de. R.-D. 164.

The picture is in the Gallery of the Louvre. Villot, No. 89; Waagen, *Handbook,* II. p. 300.

1st state, before the perpendicular slip of the graver near the trunk of the tree, back of the person.

In the Imperial collection at Paris, which also possesses the copperplate, there is an artist's proof of this engraving before letters, and before the cross-hatching on the trunk of the tree, etc. It was purchased for 1,417*fr.* 50*c.*, and came from the Debois collection, No. 320, in which it was sold for 1,350*fr.*; it had been before in the collection of Scitivaux.

P. The same. R.-D. 164.

2d state, with the slip of the graver.

EDELINCK, GERARD, *continued.*

EDELINCK *del.* **P.** Madame Chauvin as St. Elizabeth. R.-D. 167.
In 8vo.

1*st state, "très rare," with the inscription* "Elisabet."

The 2d state has the corrected form *Elisabeth.*

EDELINCK *del.* **P.** Coffeteau, Nicolas, Bishop of Dardania. R.-D. 169.

FR. HALS *pinx.* **P.** Descartes, René. R.-D. 181.

The picture in the Gallery of the Louvre (Villot, No. 190) nearly corresponds with this engraving, but in that painting the person is represented with a hat in his hand.

1*st state, before the address.*

The 2d state, *Se vend à Paris chez Chêreau le jeune,* etc.

HYAC. RIGAUD *pinx.* **P.** Des Jardins (*French name of* van den Bogaert), Martin, sculptor. R.-D. 182.

The picture is in the Gallery of the Louvre. Villot, No. 479.

2*d state, before address.*

The 1st state is before letters; the 3d has *Se vend à Paris chez,* to which in the 4th is added the name *Dreuet.*

HYAC. RIGAUD *pinx.* **P.** Fléchier, Esprit. R.-D. 205.

EDELINCK *del.* **P.** Goltzius, Henricus. R.-D. 216.

Without the name of the painter.

3*d state, with letters.*

The 1st state is before letters, and before the figure on the copperplate in the hands of Goltzius; the plate is blank. — The 2d state has the figure on the plate, but is still before letters.

VIVIEN *pinx.* **P.** Hameau, André, Doctor of the Sorbonne. R.-D. 221.

1*st state, before the verses on the console.*

The 2d state has 4 metrical lines; the 3d has the addition, *E. Desrochers ex.*

J. GALLIOT *pinx.* **P.** Mme. Helyot, "La belle Religieuse." R.-D. 223.

3*d state,* "G. Edelinck sculpsit et ex. cum pri. regis."

The 1st state, before letters, is very rare; — the 2d has *G. Edelinck sculpsit et ex.*; — the 4th, *G. Edelinck sculpsit.*

LARGILLIÈRE *pinx.* **P.** Huet, Pierre Daniel, Bishop. R.-D. 224.

1*st state, with* "Suessionensis" *in the inscription.*

In the 2d state "Suessionensis" is changed to "Abrincensis."

RICHART *pinx.* **P.** La Quintinie, Jean de. R.-D. 236.

LARGILLIÈRE *pinx.* **P.** Le Brun, Charles. R.-D. 238.

The picture is in the Gallery of the Louvre. Villot, No. 320.

EDELINCK *del.* **P.** Le Fèvre, Nicolas. R.-D. 240.

EDELINCK, GERARD, *continued.*

LE FÈVRE *pinx.* **P.** Le Nain de Tillemont, Sébastien. R.-D. 241.

HYAC. RIGAUD *pinx.* **P.** Léonard, Frédéric, Printer to the King. R.-D. 242.

2d state.

Of the 1st state, before the banderole with the device of the coat of arms, Robert-Dumesnil knew but one copy, which was then in the collection De La Salle. It was not, however, in that collection when it was sold, in 1856.

EDELINCK *del.* **P.** Lulli, Jean-Baptiste, Superintendent of Music to the King. R.-D. 262.

VIVIEN *pinx.* **P.** Mansart, Jules Hardouin. R.-D. 267.

The portrait of Mansart in the Gallery of the Louvre is a different picture; it was painted by *Rigaud*, and likewise engraved by Edelinck. R.-D. 268.

1st state, before Consilijs *was corrected into* Consiliis.

The 2d state has the correction.

RUBENS *pinx.* **P.** Medici, Francesco de', Grand Duke of Tuscany, father of Maria de' Medici. R.-D. 271.

The picture is in the Louvre. Villot, No. 455. Engraved, together with No. 143, for Jean Marie Nattier's *Galerie Luxembourg.*

2d state, before the 5 *in the lower margin on the right.*

The 1st state is before any letters.

CLAUDE MELLAN *del.* **P.** Mellan, Claude, engraver. R.-D. 272.

PIERRE MIGNARD *pinx.* **P.** Mignard, Pierre. R.-D. 274.

2d state.

The 1st state, before any letters, is very rare.

DE TROY *pinx.* **P.** Moréri, Louis, Doctor of Theology. R.-D. 280.

2d state.

The 1st state, before any letters, is very rare.

DE TROY *pinx.* **P.** Mouton, Charles. R.-D. 281.

2d state, with "De Troy pinx." *at the left, and* "Edelinck sculps. cum priuil. Regis. A Paris rue S. Iacques au Seraphin" *on the right; before J. Audran's address.*

The 1st state, before the names of the artists, is very rare. It has four Latin verses in two columns:—

"Hoc ore, hoc . . . reddere posse sonum!"

Cat. Lamotte Fouquet, by H. Weber, No. 221.

Impressions occur of the 2d state with four French verses in two columns:—

"Cher Mouton à te voir . . . je crois t'entendre."

The 3d state has the inscription, all on the left side, *De Troy pinxit.*

EDELINCK, GERARD, *continued.*

Edelinck Sculp. à Paris chez I. Audran graveur du Roy au gobelins. — In the 4th state is the inscription, also all on the left side, *De Troy Pinxit. Edelinck sculp. A Paris chés Buldet rue de Gesvres.* — In the 5th state the inscription is again divided as in the 2d, but, besides the difference of the impressions, the paper is different.

HYAC. RIGAUD *pinx.* **P.** Noailles, Anne Jules, Duc de. R.-D. 284.

1st state, with the verses, "Dans des apres Rochers . . . pour son Roy." In the 2d state the verses are changed to *Ce Vainqueur,* etc.

EDELINCK *del.* **P.** Ossat, Cardinal d'. R.-D. 186.

J. TORTEBAT *pinx.* **P.** Perrault, Charles. R.-D. 292.

Engraved as frontispiece for Perrault's *Les hommes illustres qui ont paru en France pendant ce siècle, avec leurs portraits,* Paris, Dezallier, 1690, 2 vols. fol., containing 101 portraits.

Impression in which the lines between which the name was engraved are still visible.

HYAC. RIGAUD *pinx.* **P.** Rigaud, Hyacinthe. R.-D. 303.

1st state, before "C. P. R."

HYAC. RIGAUD *pinx.* **P.** Rigaud, Hyacinthe. R.-D. 303.

2d state, with "C. P. R."

EDELINCK *del.* **P.** Saint-Evremond, Charles Marguetel de St. Denis, Chevalier seigneur de. R.-D. 306.

In 8vo.

EHRENSTRAHL *pinx.* **P.** Ulrica Eleonora, Queen of Sweden. R.-D. 331.

3d and last state, with arms and verses.

From John Barnard's collection.

The 1st state is before letters and arms; — the 2d, with the arms and the name and titles of the queen; also of the verses merely the first two lines, traced with the needle.

SIMON FRANÇOIS *pinx.* **P.** Vincent de Paul, St. R.-D. 338.

EDELINCK, NICOLAS, designer and engraver, born at Paris about 1680, where he died in 1768. He was a son and pupil of Gerard, but very inferior to his father.

RAPHAEL *pinx.* **P.** Half figure of a Young Man about 20 years of age.

See Passavant, II. No. 51, and III. p. 96. In the Gallery of the Louvre. Villot, No. 318, ascribes the picture to Francesco Francia. Engraved for the *Cabinet Crozat,* No. 11.

RAPHAEL *pinx.* **P.** Count Baldassare Castiglione.

In the Gallery of the Louvre. *See* Passavant, No. 120. Engraved in reverse, for the *Cabinet Crozat.*

EICHENS, FRIEDRICH EDUARD, designer and engraver of the present day, in Berlin, his native city. He studied first under Buchhorn, and afterwards with Toschi.

RAPHAEL *pinx.* The Vision of Ezekiel.

See Passavant, II. 118. The picture, of the same size as the engraving, is in the Gallery of the Pitti palace.

Proof before letters, with the names of the artists, of the publisher, and the coat of arms.

The 1st or artist's proof has only the coat of arms, and the name "Eichens" traced with the needle.

RAPHAEL *pinx.* The Adoration of the Kings.

A guazzo painting, in the Berlin Gallery. Passavant, II. No. 14. The picture is now considered to be the work of Lo Spagna, the fellow-pupil of Raphael under Perugino. *See* Passavant, III. p. 84.

TITIAN *pinx.* **P.** Titian's Daughter, bearing a Dish with Fruit.

In the Berlin Gallery.

Artist's proof, having merely on the left side, in the lower margin, slightly traced with the needle, "Eduard Eichens gez. in Venedig Septbr. 1829. gest. in Berlin Septbr. 1849."

EICHENS *del.* **P.** Paolo Toschi, engraver.

EICHENS, HERMANN, a German engraver of the present day.

MURILLO *pinx.* "La Vierge de Seville."

Gallery of the Louvre. Stirling, *Annals*, III. p. 1422 ; Villot, No. 548. Engraved in mezzotinto, in the modern mixed manner.

Proof, before letters.

ELLIS, WILLIAM, engraver, a pupil of Woollett, born at London, 1747.

T. HEARNE *pinx.* Two Scenes from the Vicar of Wakefield.

Two plates in oval, engraved by Ellis conjointly with W. Woollett, who engraved the figures.

ELSTRACKE, RENOLD, engraver in London, born about 1590.

P. Sir Richard Whittington with his Cat.

2d state, with the Cat, and with the address: "Are to be sould by P. Stent."

In the 1st state the hand is placed upon a Skull, instead of upon the Cat, and the address is *Compton Holland.*

ENDLICH, PHILIPP, designer and engraver, born at Amsterdam about 1700. A pupil of B. Picart.

ENDLICH *del.* **P.** John Taylor, ophthalmic physician.

EPISCOPIUS, or **BISCHOP, JOHANNES,** a distinguished Dutch lawyer, and an excellent designer and etcher. He was born at the Hague in 1646, and died at Amsterdam in 1686. The following is his principal work:—

Paradigmata Graphices variorum Artificium, per Joh. Episcopium.

It contains 57 plates, including a title by Gérard Lairesse. There is a 2d part of 45, making in the whole 102 plates; to which, in the 2d edition, Nic. Visscher added 11 more.

EREDI, BENEDETTO, engraver and publisher, born at Florence, 1750.

NANTEUIL *pinx.* **P.** Robert Nanteuil.

ESQUIVEL DE SOTOMAYOR, MANUEL, a Spanish engraver of the beginning of the nineteenth century.

RAPHAEL *pinx.* Madonna dell' Impannata.

See Passavant, II. 261. In the Gallery of the Pitti palace in Florence.

RAPHAEL *pinx.* The same.

Open letter proof.

BENVENUTO *pinx.* Mater Dolorosa.

The Virgin contemplating a crown of thorns. Engraved in 1817.

ESTEVE, or **ESTEVAN, DON RAFAEL D',** a Spanish engraver of the present time who studied in Paris and in Italy.

GUERCINO *pinx.* Jacob blessing the Sons of Joseph.

"Se halla en la Real Calcografia." The picture is not, however, according to Madrazo, in the Royal Gallery of Madrid. Engraved in 1808.

MURILLO *pinx.* "La Sed." Moses striking the Rock.

Engraved in 1839 from the picture in the Church of the Hospital of Charity in Seville. Passavant, *Christl. Kunst. in Spanien,* p. 109; Stirling, *Annals,* III. p. 1416.

Proof, with only the artists' names traced, on India paper.

Purchased for 30 guineas. Debois, 1843, No. 325, 155 *fr.*; Thorel, 1853, No. 46, 330 *fr.* In Debois' collection was also an artist's proof, before any letters, on India paper, No. 324, which sold for less than the proof just mentioned, with the artists' names, for 133 *fr.*—Archinto, 1862, No. 205, "Superbe épreuve avant toutes lettres, sur papier de Chine, seulement *les noms d'artistes tracées,*" 830 *fr.*

EVERDINGEN, ALDERT VAN, painter and etcher, born at Alkmaar in 1621, died there in 1675. A pupil of R. Savery and P. Molyn.

94 pieces, including 4 duplicates, while 4 of the series are wanting.

Old impressions, but with the sky done with the burin.

Small oval landscape, upright. B. 1.

EVERDINGEN, ALDERT VAN, *continued.*

First small oval landscape, oblong. B. 2.

The second small oval landscape, oblong, very rare, is wanting. B. 3.

Round (oval) landscape. B. 4.

In the very rare 1st state it is rounder.

Two Figures under a Tree. B. 5.

The Man on the Wooden Bridge. B. 6.

The Cascade. B. 7.

2 impressions.

The Swine Drover. B. 8.

Landscape, with a Millstone. B. 9.

The Chapel. B. 10.

The two Barrels before the Hut. B. 11.

The Pilgrim. B. 12.

The Fisherman's Hut. B. 13.

Marine Piece, with three Figures. B. 14.

The Dilapidated Hut. B. 15.

The Great Church on the Hill. B. 16.

The Hamlet on the Declivity of a Hill. B. 17.

The Rock. B. 18.

The Hamlet on a Hilly Ground. B. 19.

The Landing of Barrels. B. 20.

The Carpenter's Trestle. B. 21.

The Horseman on the Stone Bridge. B. 22.

2 impressions.

The two Floating Joists. B. 23.

The Goatherd. B. 24.

The Hamlet on the Rock. B. 25.

The Big Tree. B. 26.

The Remnants of the Fence. B. 27.

The three Figures on the Rock. B. 28.

The House with the Pointed Turret. B. 29.

The Hut seen from behind. B. 30.

The High Rock, night-piece. B. 31.

Two small Boats, approaching. B. 32.

The Winding River. B. 33.

The Rock rising from the Water. B. 34.

The three Goats on the Edge of the Water. B. 35.

The Huts on the Border of a Torrent. B. 36.

The two Pine Trees near a Hut. B. 37.

EVERDINGEN, ALDERT VAN, *continued.*

The Dilapidated Hut. B. 38.
The Man at the Entrance of the Dilapidated Fence. B. 39.
The Rock in the Middle of the River. B. 40.
The three Huts on the Top of a Rock. B. 41.
2 impressions.
The two Figures below a Peaked Rock. (*Wanting.*) B. 42.
The Herd of Swine. B. 43.
The River at the Foot of a Steep Rock. B. 44.
The little Covered Bridge. B. 45.
The two Men on the Elevated Terrace. B. 46.
A Marine View seen through a Hollow of a Rock. B. 47.
The two Men at the Door. B. 48.
The Village Carpenter. B. 49.
The Horseman on the little Bridge. B. 50.
The Goat on the little Bridge. B. 51.
2 impressions.
The Row-boat drawn up on the Shore. B. 52.
The little Wooden Bridge. B. 53.
The two Gentlemen sketching. B. 54.
The Inscription on the Rock. B. 55.
The two Rafters in the Water. B. 56.
The Cart in the Defile. B. 57.
The two Vessels on a large River. B. 58.
The Pines in a Ravine. B. 59.
The two Empty Boats. B. 60.
The Boat among the Rushes. B. 61.
The Peaked Rocks bordering the Water. B. 62.
The Sketchers. B. 63.
The Watermill at the Foot of a Mountain. B. 64.
Barrels and Planks on the Shore of a River. B. 65.
The Boat under the Hollow of a Rock. B. 66.
Two Men riding along Rocks. B. 67.
The Pines in the Water. B. 68.
The Peasant on Horseback. B. 69.
Three Travellers at the Foot of a great Rock. B. 70.
The two Peasants on the Hillock. B. 71.
Three Travellers followed by a Porter. B. 72.
The Freight Wagon. B. 73.
The Peaked Rock. B. 74.

EVERDINGEN, ALDERT VAN, *continued.*

The Woman watching the Boat. B. 75.
The sinking Hut. B. 76.
The Wheel under a movable thatched Roof. B. 77.
The Mill under the Waterfall. B. 78.
The Branch of a Tree. B. 79.
The Peasant followed by a Dog. B. 80.
The Forest. (*Wanting.*) B. 81.
The Great River. B. 82.
A movable thatched Roof in front of a Cottage. B. 83.
The Bell Tower. B. 84.
The two Carts. B. 85.
Landscape with three Men carrying Burdens. B. 86.
The Shepherd. B. 87.
The Boat among the Willows. B. 88.
The Dense Forest. B. 89.
The two Ladders. B. 90.
Landscape "en manière noire," very dark. (*Wanting.*) B. 91.
The Huts. B. 92.
The Man between two Pines. B. 93.
The Rocky Quarter. B. 94.

⁂ The 4 Numbers wanting, 3, 42, 81, and 91, are rare, and commonly wanting in the collections.

Illustrations to Reinecke Fuchs, 57 pieces. Retouched plates, from Gottsched's edition, with the German text on the reverse of them.

F.

FABER, JAN, the younger, designer and engraver in mezzotinto, born in Holland about 1684. He worked in England, where he died in 1756.

G. Kneller *pinx.* **P.** François Couplet, a Jesuit Missionary in China. In Chinese costume, whole figure. The picture is at Windsor Castle.

"Of all his works, Kneller was most proud of this portrait." Walpole, *Anecdotes.*

FABRI, LUIGI (or **ALOIS,** as he writes on his plates), was born at Rome about 1778, and died there about 1835.

Michel-Angelo *pinx.* Frescos in the Sistine Chapel.

Fabri engraved 13 of the 40 plates. See under Cunego.

Raphael *pinx.* The Oath of Leo III.

Fresco in the Stanza del Incendio in the Vatican. Passavant, ii. 121. *Open letters.*

FABRI, LUIGI, *continued.*

RAPHAEL *pinx.* The Coronation of Charlemagne.

Fresco in the same room. Passavant, II. 122.

Open letters.

RAPHAEL *pinx.* The Defeat of the Saracens at Ostia.

Fresco in the same room. Passavant, II. 124.

Open letters.

RAPHAEL *pinx.* The Donation of Rome.

Fresco in the Sala di Costantino. Passavant, II. 248.

Open letters.

RAPHAEL *pinx.* The Battle of Constantine.

Fresco in the Sala di Costantino. Passavant, II. 246.

Proof before letters.

FACIUS, GEORG SIGMUND, and **JOHANN GOTTLIEB,** brothers. They were born at Ratisbon about 1750, and went to England in 1776, where they engraved in the dotted manner.

P. POTTER *pinx.* "The Cowherd."

The famous "Young Bull" in the Gallery of the Hague. Smith, *Cat. rais.* 1.

FAIRLAND, WILLIAM, lithographer in London.

WEEKES *pinx.* **P.** Francis Chantrey.

FAITHORNE, WILLIAM, the elder, painter and engraver, born at London in 1620, died there in 1691. A pupil of Peake, and influenced by Nanteuil, whose instruction he received. *See* Walpole's *Anecdotes,* edition of 1849, III. p. 909 *et seqq.*

LA HIRE *pinx.* Holy Family.

Engraved while in Paris. *See* Walpole, III. p. 916.

Watermark of the paper, a pineapple. With the address of Herman Weyen.

SIR P. LELY *pinx.* **P.** Mrs. Sarah Gilly.

See Walpole's *Anecdotes,* 1849, III. p. 914.

"SOUSE *pinx.*" * **P.** William Sanderson.

Walpole, III. p. 912. — Impressions of this plate were prefixed to Sanderson's *Graphice; the Use of Pen and Pensill, in Designing, Drawing, and Painting; in two Parts.* London, 1658. fol.

* Instead of "Soust." The name of this portrait-painter is also sometimes spelled "Zoust." The correct form of the name seems to be "Soest." He was a native of Westphalia, where there is a town of this name.

FALCK, JEREMIAS, engraver, born at Dantzic in 1629, whence he called himself POLONUS; died there in 1709.

PALMA VECCHIO *pinx.* Holy Family with other figures in a landscape, the young Tobias offering a Fish.

Engraved for the *Cabinet Reynst.*

Proof before letters, that is, before address.

From Otto's collection, No. 752.

D. BECK *pinx.* **P.** Christina, Queen of Sweden.

With the inscription: *Jer. Falck sculp. et excu.*

FANOLI, M., lithographer.

AUG. GENDRON *pinx.* The Willis.

L'on voit, pendant la nuit, ces mortes fiancées
Renaitre au sein des bois, accourir aux plaisirs,
Voltiger sur le lac, entr'elles enlacées
Et tromper par leurs jeux l'élan de leurs désirs.

FARJAT, BENOÎT, engraver, born at Lyons in 1646, died about 1720. A pupil of Chateau.

BAROCCIO *pinx.* Sta. Michelina of Pesaro in Ecstasy.

The original picture is in the Gallery of the Vatican. Platner and Bunsen, II. ii. p. 431.

FAUCCI, RAIMONDO, an engraver in the latter half of the last century.

RAPHAEL *del.* PINTURICCHIO *pinx.* Narrazione delle geste di Enea Sylvio Piccolomini poi Pio II., rappresentate nelle pareti della libreria corale del Duomo di Siena dal Pinturicchio, con schizze e cartoni di Rafaello d'Urbino. Siena, 1771. fol.

(This title is wanting.)

Designed by Raphael, and painted in fresco by Pinturicchio by order of the Cardinal Francesco Piccolomini, afterwards Pope Pius III. Passavant, *Rafael,* I. p. 71.

10 plates, namely: —

1. Departure of the young Æneas Sylvius with the Cardinal Domenico da Capranica for the Council of Basle.
2. His speech before James I., King of Scotland.
3. He is crowned with Laurel by the Emperor Frederic III.
4. Pope Eugenio IV. nominates him Antistes.
5. The Marriage of the Emperor Frederic III. with Leonora of Portugal.
6. Pope Calixtus III. nominates him Cardinal.
7. Æneas Sylvius is elected Pope, as Pius II.
8. Pius II. at the Council of Mantua.

FAUCCI, RAIMONDO, *continued.*

9. The Canonization of Catherine of Siena.

10. Preparations at Ancona for the Expedition against the Turks.

This last is a proof before the names of the artists.

Bound with these are *proof impressions* of 2 plates printed on one sheet, — the bridal group of Frederic III. and Leonora, and a design of the magnificently carved Choir of the Cathedral of Siena, *Antonio Verico inv., Giuseppe Colignon Dirett. dell' Acc. di Siena diresse.*

FELSING, JACOB, engraver, born at Darmstadt in 1802. A pupil of his father Johann Conrad, and of Longhi.

DAN. CRESPI *pinx.* Christ bearing the Cross.

Engraved in 1826.

ANDREA DEL SARTO *pinx.* Madonna del Trono, or Madonna di San Francesco.

The picture is in the Tribune of the Uffizj Gallery at Florence. Alfred Reumont, p. 95. Engraved in 1834.

Artist's proof, before letters and arms, artists' names only traced with the needle.

The 2d state has the coat of arms; — the 3d has open letters.

At Macready's sale, No. 33, occurred a proof before any letters; it was purchased by Messrs. Amsler & Ruthardt of Berlin for £10 10 *s.*

OVERBECK *pinx.* Madonna and Child, with St. Elizabeth and St. John, and a Lamb.

The picture is in the Gallery of Modern Paintings in Munich. E. Förster, *Gesch. der deutschen Kunst,* IV. p. 187. Engraved in 1839.

1*st artist's proof, before* "Inst. Bibl. exc." *In the middle of the lower margin, traced only:* "J. Felsing sculp."

The 2d state has the address of the Bibliographic Institute at Hildburghausen, and the names of both artists. The 3d has the title in open letters; in the 4th the letters are shaded. The Bibliographic Institute having sold the plate, the latest impressions are without its address.

CORREGGIO *pinx.* Marriage of St. Catherine.

From the picture at Naples. Coxe, p. 42. Engraved in 1831.

1*st artist's proof, before letters, with the names of the artists, and before the coat of arms.*

In the 2d artist's proof the coat of arms is added. Macready, No. 34, £3 6 *s.* The 3d state, proof, has open and traced letters; the 4th, finished letters. There occur false proofs, which may be recognized by the artists' names being engraved with the burin.

MÜCKE *pinx.* St. Catherine's Body borne by Angels.

FELSING, JACOB, *continued.*

The picture is in the Wagner Gallery of Modern Paintings in Berlin.

Artist's proof, with only the names of the artists slightly traced with the needle.

Macready, No. 37, £6. There occur false artist's proofs, without inscription and without the coat of arms, with merely the names of the artists; but these are engraved with the burin, and the impressions are made by covering up the inscription while under the press, like the false proofs of the preceding print.

The 2d state has the artists' names engraved, and the coat of arms; the 3d has the inscription.

LEONARDO DA VINCI *pinx.* Mater Dolorosa.

The picture was formerly owned by Longhi; it is a fragment of a larger picture. The engraving was made under the direction of Longhi.

STEINBRÜCK *pinx.* St. Genoveva of Brabant, with her Child.

The picture is in the Gallery of Darmstadt. Engraved in 1839.

Artist's proof, before any letters, and before the border was shaded. In the lower part of the border, in Gothic letters, is the word "Genoveva."

The 2d state is before letters, but with the finished border; the 3d state is with letters.

KÖHLER *pinx.* Poesia.

Engraved for the Düsseldorf Art-Union for 1839–40.

Proof, with only the names of the artists and the address of the printer.

RAPHAEL *pinx.* The Violin Player.

The picture is in the Sciara palace in Rome. Passavant, II. 238.

Artist's proof, before "Il Suonatore di Violino" *in open letters, with merely the artists' names and the address.*

Macready, No. 40, £3 18*s.* There are still earlier proofs, before the address; and at the sale of Schenck and Gerstäckers, Leipzig, 1857, No. 557, there occurred an impression before any letters.

The 2d state has open letters; in the 3d state the letters are filled. The plate afterwards became the property of the Bibliographic Institute in Hildburghausen.

DRÄGER *pinx.* Girl playing the Mandoline.

Engraved for the Leipzig Art-Union for 1842.

BENDEMANN *pinx.* Maidens at the Fountain.

The painting is owned by Mme. Moll in Cologne. E. Förster's *Geschichte der deutschen Kunst,* V. p. 363. It was engraved for the Düsseldorf Art-Union for 1832–34.

Proof, with only the names of the artists and "H. Felsing impr."

BENDEMANN *pinx.* Jeremiah sitting amidst the Ruins of Jerusalem.

FELSING, JACOB, *continued.*

The painting is owned by the King of Prussia. Engraved for Count Raczynski's *Histoire de l'art moderne dans l'Allemagne.*

With open letters.

FEOLI, VINCENZO, engraver at Rome in the beginning of this century.

RAPHAEL *pinx.* Three of the seven plates, The Frescos of the Farnesina.

1. Venus showing Psyche to Cupid.
2. Cupid showing Psyche to the Graces.
3. a. Venus, Juno, and Ceres.
   b. Venus going to Olympus.

For the entire work, see under RICCIANI.

FERDINAND, LOUIS, painter and etcher, son and pupil of the portrait-painter Ferdinand van Elle, who had removed from Malines to Paris, and whose baptismal name he adopted. He was born at Paris in 1612, and died there in 1689. Compare Villot, *Notice des Tableaux du Louvre,* III. p. 117, under Ferdinand (the son of our artist), where he gives the fullest account of the family.

VAN ELLE *pinx.* **P.** Poussin, Nicolas.

"V[an] E[lle] pinxit. L. Ferdinand fecit. P. Ferdinand excudit cum privilegio Reg."

FERRERI, CESARE, an engraver of the present day in Italy.

VELAZQUEZ *pinx.* **P.** Philip IV.

Engraved for D'Azeglio's *Reale Galleria di Torino.*

Proof before any letters.

FERRETTI, L., an engraver of the present time in Rome.

RAPHAEL *pinx.* La Moderazione.

See Passavant, II. No. 249, b. p. 375.

RAPHAEL *pinx.* La Fede.

See Passavant, II. No. 249, p. 376.

RAPHAEL *pinx.* La Prudenza.

See Passavant, II. No. 249, e. p. 377.

In the Sala di Costantino, of the Vatican Stanze, are the representations of 8 popes, from St. Peter to Gregory VII., one on each side of the great frescos. They have at their sides allegorical figures, expressive of their characteristic qualities, 14 in number. Two of them, Meekness and Justice, have been engraved by Strange, and are in this collection. (*See* STRANGE.) The other 12 have been published by the Papal Calcografia of the Stamperia camerale in Rome. R. Weigel, *Kunst-Catalog,* XIV. No.

FERRETTI, L., *continued.*

13203, specifies them, with the affixed price of $19\frac{1}{2}$ *th.* They were engraved by L. Ferretti, C. Pestrini, and F. Cenci. The three mentioned above are part of these.

FICQUET, ÉTIENNE, engraver, born at Paris in 1731, died in 1794. A pupil of G. F. Schmidt and of Le Bas.

P. Chennevière.

Impression before the word "cincere" *was corrected into* "sincere."

LE BRUN *pinx.* **P.** Corneille, Pierre.

AVED *pinx.* **P.** Crébillon, Joliot de.

FR. HALS *pinx.* **P.** Descartes, René.

Æ. *pinx.* **P.** Farnese, Alexander.

2d state, with Odieuvre's address.

The 1st state is without this address, and in the 3d state the address is effaced.

HYAC. RIGAUD *pinx.* **P.** La Fontaine, Jean de.

With the vignette of a Wolf and Lamb below.

NANTEUIL *pinx.* **P.** Le Vayer, François de la Mothe.

P. MIGNARD *pinx.* **P.** Maintenon, Françoise d'Aubigné, Marquise de.

C. COYPEL *pinx.* **P.** Molière, Jean-Baptiste Poquelin de.

DUMOUSTIER *pinx.* **P.** Montaigne, Michel de.

AVED *pinx.* **P.** Rousseau, Jean-Baptiste.

DE LA TOUR *pinx.* **P.** Rousseau, Jean Jacques.

*** All the above portraits by Ficquet are in 8vo. The impressions are without any address.

FILLŒUIL, PIERRE, an engraver of the middle of the last century.

REMBRANDT *pinx.* **P.** Coppenol, Liven.

Called "The Writing-Master." *See* Smith, under No. 306. Engraved from a picture then in the Gallery of Count Brühl in Dresden. It is *not* the picture in the Gallery of Cassel; there the person is mending his pen, here he is merely looking up.

FINIGUERRA, TOMMASO. See under BOTTICELLI, Sandro.

FIORONI, ADOLFO, engraver. A pupil of Longhi.

RAPHAEL *pinx.* Riposo in Egitto.

The picture is in the Vienna Gallery. Passavant, II. 262.

FIORONI, ADOLFO, *continued.*

1st proof, before the title, but with the names of the artists, etc.

The 2d proofs have the title : *Riposo in Egitto, Adolfo Fioroni dis. ed inc.* 1829, in open letters.

FISCHER, JOSEPH, landscape-painter (pupil of Brand), and engraver (pupil of Schmutzer); born at Vienna in 1769, died there in 1822.

SPAGNOLETTO *pinx.* Christ disputing with the Doctors.

The picture is in the Vienna Gallery. Engraved in 1793.

With one line of inscription in shaded letters, and the coat of arms; before the dedication.

The 1st proofs are before the inscription.

"CORREGGIO *del.*" P. "Correggio's own portrait."

Etching in 8vo. With a croquis in the lower margin, on the left, of three heads.

FISHER, EDWARD, an English mezzotinto engraver, who was born about 1730, and died in London in 1785.

SIR JOSH. REYNOLDS *pinx.* P. Bunbury, Lady Sarah.

SIR JOSH. REYNOLDS *pinx.* P. Garrick between Tragedy and Comedy.

SIR JOSH. REYNOLDS *pinx.* P. Tavistock, The Marchioness of, at Hymen's Altar.

The picture is in the Duke of Bedford's collection at Woburn Abbey. Waagen, *Galleries and Cabinets,* or *Treasures,* IV. p. 333.

Artist's proof.

FITTLER, JAMES, engraver, born at London in 1758, died in 1835.

CLAUDE LORRAIN *pinx.* The Embarcation of St. Ursula.

The picture is in the National Gallery. Waagen, *Treasures,* I. p. 339; Smith, No. 54.

Proof, open letters.

CLAUDE LORRAIN *pinx.* The Arch of Constantine.

See Smith, 301. The picture is in the Grosvenor Gallery, formerly in the Agar Collection. Not sufficiently identified in Waagen's *Treasures.*

GASP. POUSSIN *pinx.* The Hurricane.

The figures were engraved by Bartolozzi.

RUBENS *pinx.* Spanish Officer.

See Smith, 793. The picture is in the collection of Lord Kinnaird.

G. H. HARLOW *pinx.* Benjamin West.

With a dedicatory inscription in open letters, and only the name "Benjamin West, P. R. A.," *shaded.*

FLIPART, JEAN CHARLES, engraver, born at Paris toward the close of the seventeenth century.

RAPHAEL *pinx.* Christ's Agony in the Garden.

Predella of the altar-piece for the cloister S. Antonio di Padova in Naples.

See Passavant, II. No. 31, a, and III. p. 87. From the collection of the poet Rogers, now owned by Miss Burdett Coutts. Engraved for the *Cabinet Crozat.*

FLIPART, JEAN JACQUES, engraver, son of the preceding,. born at Paris in 1723, died there in 1782. A pupil of L. Cars.

GREUZE *pinx.* L'Accordée du Village.

See Smith, No. 16. The picture is in the Gallery of the Louvre. Villot, No. 260.

The print has the signature of the painter and engraver on the back.

GREUZE *pinx.* Le Paralytique servi par ses Enfans.

See Smith, No. 146. The picture is in the Imperial Gallery of St. Petersburg.

The print has the signature of the artists on the back.

JOS. VERNET *pinx.* Storm and Shipwreck, by day.

JOS. VERNET *pinx.* Storm by night.

Impression on India paper.

FOKKE, SIMON, engraver, born at Amsterdam in 1712, died in 1784.

SPAGNOLETTO *pinx.* Jacob tending the Flock of Laban.

The picture is in the Dresden Gallery. Engraved for the *Rec. d'est. de la Gal. de Dresde,* I. No. 27.

FOLKEMA, JACOB, engraver, born at Dokkum in 1692, died at Amsterdam in 1767. A pupil of his father, Johan Jacob, and of B. Picart.

CASPAR NETSCHER *pinx.* Le Médecin du Village.

FRANCESCO FRANCIA *pinx.* Religion rebuking a Naval Hero.

An allegorical subject. The hero is supposed to be Prince Doria.

The picture is in the Dresden Gallery. Engraved for the *Rec. d'est. de la Gal. de Dresde,* II. No. 17.

HANS HOLBEIN *pinx.* **P.** Morett, goldsmith to Henry VIII.

Dresden Gallery. When engraved for the *Rec. d'est. de la Gal. de Dresde,* II. No. 5, the picture was considered to be by Leonardo da Vinci, and to represent the Duke Sforza il Moro, of Milan.

FOLO, GIOVANNI, engraver, born at Bassano in 1764, died at Rome in 1836. A pupil of Volpato and influenced by R. Morghen.

FOLO, GIOVANNI, *continued.*

TITIAN *pinx.* Adam and Eve.

The picture was owned when it was engraved by the banker Schultheis in Rome.

Proof, with verses in open and traced letters, before the dedication.

GUIDO *pinx.* The Archangel St. Michael vanquishing the Dragon.

The picture is in the Church of Santa Maria della Concezione in Rome. Platner and Bunsen, III. ii. p. 593. A copy in mosaic is in St. Peter's.

Proof, with open and traced letters.

RAPHAEL *pinx.* Holy Family. "La Bénédiction."

The picture is in the Gallery of Madrid. Passavant, II. No. 99, c. Repetition of the Holy Family of the Pio family in the Gallery of Naples. Engraved for the *Coleccion de las estampas de los cuadros . . . pertenecientes al Rey de España.*

SASSOFERRATO *pinx.* "Mater Amabilis."

Proof before letters, with only the artists' names.

DOMENICHINO *pinx.* The Martyrdom of St. Andrew.

The picture is in the Church of St. Gregory, in the chapel dedicated to St. Andrew, Rome. Platner and Bunsen, III. i. p. 485.

GUERCINO *pinx.* The Martyrdom of St. Sebastian.

The picture was owned, when engraved, by the Marchese Alessandro Lepri.

TITIAN *pinx.* Danaë.

The picture is in the Gallery of Naples; it was originally painted for the Duke Ottaviano de' Medici.

Proof, with open and traced letters.

RUBENS *pinx.* The Triumph of Silenus.

See Smith, *Cat. rais.* 564. The picture is now in the collection of Sir Robert Peel; formerly in those of Cardinal Richelieu, of Prince Lucien Buonaparte, and of the Chevalier Bonnemaison.

FONTANA, PIETRO, engraver, born at Bassano in 1763, died at Rome in 1837. He formed his style after Volpato and Morghen.

GUIDO *pinx.* The Daughter of Herodias carrying the Head of St. John on a Charger.

With a head-dress like a turban, concealing her hair in the manner of a Jewish married woman. Three quarters length.

The picture is in the Corsini palace in Rome. Platner and Bunsen, III. iii. p. 610. Engraved in 1797.

TITIAN *pinx.* The Marriage of St. Catherine.

A composition of four figures.

FONTANA, PIETRO, *continued.*

RAPHAEL *pinx.* **P.** The Fornarina in the Barberini Palace.

See Passavant, II. 87.

Proof, with open letters.

FONTANALS, FRANCISCO.

"RAPHAEL *pinx.*" Holy Family.

"Rafael Sanzio Pintò. Francisco Fontanals Dibujò y en Parta Gravò. Dn. Iuan Rivera concluyò." *See* RIVERA. *Coat of arms, and* "A. S. M. C. la Reyna Nuestra Señora Da. Maria Cristina de Borbon Regente de España. Por su mas humilde y reconocida Subdita Teresa Fontanals D. D. D. — Su Original existe en la Real Galeria de Madrid. — Florencia en Casa de Dn. Iuan Rivera." Large folio.

A round picture. In the foreground of a landscape, with a city and mountains in the distance, stands the Virgin; with her left arm she holds the Child, who is partly lying on a cushion, supported by an entablement and stretching out his arms; with her right she touches the inscription, *Ecce Agnus Dei*, of the scroll on the cross of the little St. John, who has approached to kiss the Saviour's toe. On the opposite side stands Joseph, resting both his hands and his head upon his staff. Three quarters length figures.

An apocryphal picture, not identified by Passavant as the one from the Vestry of the Escurial (Passavant, II. 267, and III. p. 168), nor by Richard Ford (*Handbook for Travellers in Spain*, II. p. 694). The "Agnus Dei" of the Madrid Gallery has ruined architecture in the background. and corresponds more with Passavant, II. 267, b, Mr. Munro's picture, which has been engraved by Forster.

FORSTER, FRANÇOIS, engraver, born in 1790 in Locle in French Switzerland, recently (since 1861) deceased in Paris. A pupil of Langlois.

LEONARDO DA VINCI *pinx.* La Vierge au Bas-relief.

See Rigollot, No. 25. The picture is in the collection of the Countess Warwick at Gatton Park. Waagen, *Galleries and Cabinets*, or *Treasures*, IV. p. 343. Lately owned by Lord Monson. Engraved in 1835.

Proof, No. 68, *before letters, with merely the artists' names traced with the point.*

Debois, No. 337, 540*fr.*; Johnson, No. 64, £14; Lehrs, No. 121, proof, No. 34, 60*th.*; *ibid.* No. 122, artist's proof, before the border line, and with only the engraver's name cut with the needle, on India paper, 165*th.*

The prints have the title in open letters, and the earliest impressions of them have the stamp of the engraver's initials and the stamp of the initials of the first publisher, Pierri-Bénard, both in white.

RAPHAEL *pinx.* La Vierge de la Maison d'Orléans.

FORSTER, FRANÇOIS, *continued.*

The smaller Madonna of the Orleans Gallery. Passavant, II. 45, and III. p. 93. The picture is owned by M. Benjamin Delessert; it was previously in the Aguado Gallery. Engraved in 1838.

Proof, No. 81, *before letters, with merely the names of the painter and the engraver.*

Schletter, No. 26, proof No. 102, 20 *th.*

The artist's proofs have only *Forster sculp*[t]. 1838, slightly cut with the needle, in the middle of the lower margin, and they are likewise numbered. Artist's proof No. 22, Lehrs, No. 126, 30 *th.*

RAPHAEL *pinx.* La Vierge à la Legende.

A square picture. Both children holding a scroll. Passavant, II. 267, b. The picture is in the collection of H. A. J. Munro, Esq., London. Waagen, *Treasures,* II. p. 132. Engraved in 1847.

Proof before letters, No. 115. *On India paper.*

Artist's proofs are before any letters, except in the middle of the lower margin, *F. Forster sculp.*, delicately cut with the needle. Johnson, No. 65; George Smith, No. 701, £6; Archinto, No. 215, 140*fr.*; Lehrs, No. 119, 70 *th.*

DELAROCHE *pinx.* St. Cecilia.

Engraved in 1840.

Proof, before the inscription on the tablet, having only the names of the artists and address of publishers below.

An artist's proof before any letters. Schletter, Leipzig, 1855, No. 28.

RAPHAEL *pinx.* Urania.

Bust, from the Parnassus. Passavant, II. 66. Engraved in 1839.

Proof before letters. On India paper.

RAPHAEL *pinx.* The Three Graces.

See Passavant, II. 48, and III. p. 96. The picture is in the collection of Lord Ward. Engraved in 1841.

Proof before letters No. 11, *with only the names of the artists, the publishers, and printers, and within a border of two lines.*

The artist's proofs are before any letters; they have merely *F. Forster sculpsit,* and the date, slightly traced with the point, in the *middle* of the lower margin. They are, further, before any border line to the plate, and are likewise numbered. Debois, No. 340, 300*fr.*; Johnson, No. 63, £10; G. Smith, No. 702, £11.

RAPHAEL *pinx.* **P.** Raphael at the age of about 23.

The picture is in the Painters' Portrait Gallery in Florence. Passavant, II. 47. Engraved in 1836.

Proof before letters, with the names of the artists, before the inscription on the tablet, which is shaded gray.

FORSTER, FRANÇOIS, *continued.*

The artist's proofs are before any letters; they have merely *Forster sculp.*, 1836, slightly traced with the point in the middle of the lower margin. The tablet is entirely blank, and they are numbered. Wilcox, No. 94, artist's proof, No. 9, £ 6 4 *s.* An impression of this state, No. 14, is priced 40 *th.* by Messrs. Amsler and Ruthardt of Berlin.

RAPHAEL *pinx.* **P.** "Raphael at the age of 15."

The portrait in the Louvre — a lovely youth with fair hair and large liquid eyes, resting his head on his hands — probably represents some young artist-friend of Raphael. Passavant, II. No. 61, and III. p. 101.

Proof, before any letters, except the address of the publishers. Numbered 36.

Macready, No. 31, a proof of this state, with the number 2, bought by Messrs. Amsler and Ruthardt for £ 5 5 *s.*

TITIAN *pinx.* **P.** "La Maîtresse du Titien."

The picture in the Louvre is supposed to represent the Duke Alfonso I. of Ferrara and Laura Bianti.

With the name of Ramboz as printer, and the address of Artaria and Fontaine.

Rare earlier impressions have the engraver's own address. The extremely rare proofs of this plate have open letters. Messrs. Amsler and Ruthardt, in Berlin, had such a proof in 1868, the price of which was about 30 *th.* Archinto, No. 216, "Très rare épreuve avant toutes lettres. Elle n'est pas entièrement terminée." Bought by Mr. Colnaghi for 155 *fr.*

DÜRER *pinx.* **P.** Albrecht Dürer's own portrait, after the picture in the Munich Gallery.

Proof, that is, with the inscription in open letters.

DÜRER *pinx.* **P.** The same.

Engraver's proof, before any letters, with the inscription on the background in white, and in the lower margin a croquis, a cluster of three stones.

George Smith, No. 708, £ 5 5 *s.*

FR. PORBUS *pinx.* **P.** Henry IV. of France.

Engraved in 1834 for Bettoni's *Le Panthéon des Nations.*

STEUBEN *pinx.* **P.** Alexander von Humboldt.

ANN. CARACCI *pinx.* The Nativity.

Engraved in conjunction with Lips. *See* LIPS.

FOSSEYEUX, JEAN BAPTISTE, born at Paris in 1782, died there in 1824.

"RAPHAEL *pinx.*" The Hours of the Night and Day.

See Passavant, II. p. 422, and III. p. 173.

Twelve plates, each with a female figure floating in the air, upon a black

FOSSEYEUX, JEAN BAPTISTE, *continued.*

ground, under which is a small socle with animals and other symbolic figures. They are not by Raphael, but are imitations of the small antique pictures from the walls of Pompeii, now in the Museum at Naples, reproduced in the spirit of the School of Raphael. It is not known where the pictures are from which these engravings were made, — whether they were ever executed as frescos in some palace in Rome, or merely designed for these engravings, which appeared in 1805 and 1806. Some sets were published in colors by Ag. Maestri. They were engraved by Fosseyeux in conjunction with Bourgois, Lavallée, L. F. Mariage, J. F. Ribault, F. Hubert, L. Croutelle, N. Tomas, L. Petit, and F. J. Dequevauvillier.

Ora prima di notte.

The figure carries poppy-pods in one hand, and an owl in the other.

Ora seconda di notte.

Carrying an hour-glass.

Ora terza di notte.

Carrying a squirrel.

Ora quarta di notte.

Carrying an owl.

Ora quinta.

Figure with wings of a libellula, pouring dew from an urn (like one of the three figures preceding the chariot of Aurora, painted by Guercino in the Villa Ludoviso in Rome).

Ora sesta.

Figure with wings of a libellula, carrying a swan.

Ora prima di giorno.

Figure carrying a torch.

Ora seconda di giorno.

Figure stretching out her arms toward the luminary.

Ora terza di giorno.

The figure which carries a censer is evidently taken from Raphael's Galatea in the Villa Farnesina in Rome.

Ora quarta di giorno.

Carrying a sun-dial.

Ora quinta di giorno.

The figure stretches her hand towards the sun.

Ora sesta di giorno.

Carrying a bat.

FRANCK, JOSEPH, an engraver of the present day.

FRANCK, JOSEPH, *continued.*

LEONARDO DA VINCI *pinx.* The Madonna with a Flower.

Of the Pourtalès collection, "formerly in the Gallery of the kings of Spain." Rigollot, No. 33.

The composition is different from that engraved by Juster; Rigollot, No. 96. The Virgin holds with one hand the Child, standing before her on a table on which is a book, with the other a flower (not a lily). Engraved while in the collection of Count Pourtalès in Paris, which was dispersed in the spring of 1865. The engraving was begun by Aristide Louis.

Proof, before letters, with the names of the artists and publishers. On India paper.

FRANCO, GIOAN-BATTISTA, called SEMOLEI, painter and engraver, was born at Udine in 1498 or 1510, and died in 1580. Bartsch, XVI.

The Ark of the Lord, placed by the Philistines in the Temple of Dagon. B. 6.

3d and last state, with the letters "B. F. V. F." *replaced, and* "Franco forma" *added.*

The 1st state has the letters *B. F. V. F.*; in the 2d these letters are effaced.

FRANÇOIS, ALPHONSE, engraver, born at Paris in 1811. A pupil of Henriquel-Dupont.

DELAROCHE *pinx.* A Mother holding up a Book to her Child.

Proof before letters, with only the names of the artists, publishers, and printers.

DELAROCHE *pinx.* **P.** Bonaparte crossing the Alps.

The picture, owned by John Dillon, Esq., was in the Manchester Exhibition, 1857, No. 659. "The property of Mr. John Naylor (Leighton Hall). The Queen possesses at Osborne a reduction of this picture, made by Delaroche himself." (*Fine Arts Quarterly Review*, May, 1864, II. 299 *n.*)

"Le Général Bonaparte franchissant les Alpes" *is in open and traced letters. On India paper.*

TITIAN *pinx.* **P.** "Titian's Portrait."

In reality this is the portrait of an unknown person, probably some Venetian nobleman.

Proof before letters.

FRANÇOIS, CHARLES REMY JULES, engraver, born at Paris in 1809. A pupil of Henriquel-Dupont.

DELAROCHE *pinx.* Les Pélerins.

"Tiré de la galerie du Cte. Raczynski."

Proof before letters, with only the names of the artists, publishers, and printers.

FREDERIC WILLIAM III., King of Prussia.

A Trooper leading a Pack-horse.

Amateur etching. Weigel, *Kunst-Catalog*, No. 11876; Nagler, *Die Monogrammisten*, II. p. 929.

FRENZEL, JOHANN GOTTLIEB ABRAHAM, engraver, principally of landscapes, was born at Dresden in 1782, and died at that place in 1855. A scholar of Darnstedt.

JAC. RUYSDAEL and W. ROMEYN *pinx.* Der Abend.

Engraved from the picture in the collection of Count Lamberg in Vienna, a duplicate of which, formerly in the possession of Baron Badenfeld in Bohemia, is owned by the Hon. Charles Sumner in Washington.

With the engraver's autograph dedication.

FREY, JOHANN JACOB, designer and engraver, born at Lucerne in 1681, died at Rome in 1752. A pupil of Carlo Maratti and of Westerhout.

NIC. POUSSIN *pinx.* The Sacrifice of Noah.

See Smith, *Cat. rais.* 5. The picture is in the Lichtenstein Gallery in Vienna.

GUIDO *pinx.* The Daughter of Herodias.

Herodias's daughter, followed by two maids, receives from a kneeling page the head of St. John on a platter; a third maid in front is pushing a curtain aside for her exit. Whole length figures. Engraved in 1745 from a picture then in the Colonna Gallery. There is such a picture in the collection of Lord Yarborough in London.

CIGNANI *pinx.* Joseph and Potiphar's Wife.

The composition is *not* the same as that of the picture of the same subject in the Dresden Gallery.

C. MARATTI *pinx.* The Adoration of the Kings.

"In Eccle. S. Marci Romae," but not mentioned by Platner and Bunsen as being there now.

DOMENICHINO *pinx.* The Communion of St. Jerome.

From the picture in the Gallery of the Vatican.

GUIDO *pinx.* The Doctors of the Church.

The picture is in the Imperial Gallery of St. Petersburg.

DOMENICHINO *pinx.* The Martyrdom of St. Sebastian.

Fresco painting, removed from St. Peter's to Santa Maria degli Angeli in Rome, and replaced by a copy in mosaic. Platner and Bunsen, III. ii. p. 356.

C. MARATTI *pinx.* St. Andrew, on his Way to Execution, sees his Cross.

GUERCINO *pinx.* The Burial of St. Petronella.

FREY, JOHANN JACOB, *continued.*

The picture is in the Gallery of the Vatican. Platner and Bunsen, III. i. p. 132.

SECCHI *pinx.* St. Romuald. "The White Friars."

Altar-piece, painted for the Church of the Camaldulensi in Rome, now in the Gallery of the Vatican. Platner and Bunsen, II. ii. p. 435.

C. MARATTI *pinx.* Cleopatra dissolving the Pearl.

"MICHEL-ANGELO" *sculp. in marm.* Statue of Venus.

"In the Museum of the Capitol."

C. MARATTI *pinx.* **P.** Carlo Maratti.

1*st state*, "Jo. Jac. Frey Incidit."

The 2d state has "Romae Apud Jo. Jacob Frey incidit." (Heller.)

FREY, JAN PIETER VAN, or **DE,** designer and engraver, born in 1770 at Amsterdam, died at Paris in 1834, according to Defer in Cat. Debois. A pupil of Jacob Lauwers.

BREKELENKAMP *pinx.* A Hermit in the Wilderness, reading.

In small 4to.

REMBRANDT *pinx.* Les Syndics de la Halle aux Draps.

The five trustees of the building called the *Staathof*, devoted to the Company of Clothweavers. The picture is now in the Amsterdam Gallery. Smith, *Cat. rais.* 141; Waagen, *Handbook*, II. p. 342.

REMBRANDT *pinx.* **P.** Nicol. Tulp delivering a Lecture on Anatomy.

Painted for the Anatomical Institute at Amsterdam, now in the Gallery of the Hague. Smith, *Cat. rais.* 142; Waagen, *Handbook*, II. p. 341.

FREY, MARTIN R., engraver, born at Wurzach in Swabia in 1769. A pupil of J. G. von Müller.

RAPHAEL *pinx.* Madonna with the Child sleeping, "Madonna del Velo."

Engraved from the round picture in the Gallery of Prince Esterhazy in Vienna. Passavant, II. 57, a.

One of the repetitions of this composition, also in a round, which King William II. of the Netherlands bought in 1847 for his Gallery, and which at the sale of the same, in 1850, found no purchaser, and is still in the possession of the Royal Family, was engraved in 1854, by Achille Martinet, as "La Sommeil de Jésus." A composition in a square was engraved by Longhi, and finished in 1834 by Toschi. *See* LONGHI.

FUSINATI, G., an Italian engraver, born about 1803.

TITIAN *pinx.* **P.** Magdalen.

The picture, formerly in the Barbarigo palace in Venice, the original of

FUSINATI, G., *continued.*

many repetitions, is now in the Imperial Gallery of St. Petersburg. A fine repetition is in the Gallery of the Pitti palace in Florence.

Artist's proof, with merely the engraver's name in the middle of the lower margin.

G.

GAILLARD, ROBERT, engraver, born at Paris in 1722, died in 1785.

HYAC. RIGAUD *pinx.* **P.** Castanier, François.

GERARD DOW *pinx.* **P.** Galilei, Galileo.

GALLE, CORNELIS, the elder, designer and engraver, born at Antwerp in 1570, died about 1641. A pupil of his father Philip.

RUBENS *pinx.* The Four Fathers of the Church.

Whole length figures, seated, with a crosier, with a burning heart, and with a beehive; hovering over them are a dove and three angels. The picture is in the Berlin Gallery. Attributed to the School of Rubens by Waagen, *Verzeichniss*, No. 773. Basan, 2.

2d state, the enlarged plate, two additional strips having been soldered on; and with the coat of arms.

VAN DYCK *pinx.* **P.** Artus Wolfaerts, painter.

See Smith, *Cat. rais.* 758. The grisaille painting is in the collection of the Duke of Buccleugh. Engraved for Martin van den Enden, *Van Dyck's Iconographia*, No. 10. Weber, *Cat. rais.* p. 56.

5th state, after the erasure of the letters "G. H." *from the plate.*

GALLE, CORNELIS, the younger, son and pupil of Cornelis the elder, born at Antwerp in 1600.

VAN DYCK *pinx.* **P.** Jan Meyssens, painter.

Engraved for Meyssens's collection of portraits after Van Dyck. Weber's *Cat. rais.* p. 111.

2d state; the name "Meysens" *has been changed into* "Meyssens," *and the name of the engraver, in the 1st state in the middle, has been effaced, and placed at the right below.*

VAN DYCK *pinx.* **P.** Baron Engelbert Taie, Chevalier.

The full inscription is "Dominvs Engelbertvs Taie Eqves Baro Wemmelivs, etc. Depvtatvs ordinarivs inter nobiles statvs Brabantiae."

Engraved for Meyssens's collection of portraits after Van Dyck. Weber, *Cat. rais.* p. 112.

An oil painting corresponding with this engraving, costume and all, but with the omission of the hands and the sword, is in the Dresden Gallery;

GALLE, CORNELIS, *continued.*

Hanfstängl gives a lithograph of it, a reverse of this engraving which is the reverse of the picture. Smith, *Cat. rais.* 703, describes only this engraving, without mentioning any picture. Matthäi, *Gemälde-Gallerie zu Dresden*, p. 35, No. 206, calls it the portrait of Martin Engelbrecht. Hübner, in his Catalogue of the Dresden Gallery, p. 209, No. 937, calls it the portrait of "the painter Engelbrecht," without giving a Christian name.

1st state, before the address of Joannes Meyssens was effaced. Watermark, the Large Foolscap.

GANDOLFI, MAURO, designer and engraver, born at Bologna in 1771, died in 1834. A pupil of Longhi.

ALLORI *pinx.* Judith with the Head of Holofernes.

The original is in the Gallery of the Pitti palace. Engraved for the *Musée Français.*

Proof, before letters, with only the artists' names. The paper has the watermark: "Musée Napoléon publié par Henri Laurent."

ALLORI *pinx.* The same picture.

Engraved in 1819; the second, larger plate.

Open letter proof.

GUIDO *pinx.* Virgin and Child with St. John.

Engraved from a picture in the Tanaro collection at Bologna.

Proof before letters, with merely the artists' names traced with the needle.

RAPHAEL *pinx.* St. Cecilia.

The picture is in the Gallery of Bologna. Passavant, II. 117. Engraved in 1834.

Artist's proof before letters, with merely the names of the artists and publisher traced with the needle.

GANDOLFI *del.* Cupid sleeping under a Tent.

Engraved in 1820.

GARAVAGLIA, GIOVITO, engraver, born at Paris in 1789, died in 1835. A pupil of Faustino Anderloni.

GUERCINO *pinx.* David with the Head of Goliath.

A corresponding picture is in the Duke of Sutherland's collection at Stafford House. Waagen, *Treasures*, II. p. 65.

Artist's proof, before any letters or arms.

An artist's proof, R. Weigel, *Kunst-Cat.* No. 16515. — The proofs have the artists' names; the 2d proofs have *lettres grises.*

BAROCCIO *pinx.* Hagar and Ishmael.

One of the repetitions of this pleasing subject after Correggio.

GARAVAGLIA, GIOVITO, *continued.*

Engraved in 1823 from the picture in the Dresden Gallery, of the size of the engraving.

1st state, artist's proof before any letters.

Wilcox, No. 102, £ 7. — The 2d state is with the names of the artists. — The 3d is with open letters and before the dedication; Arndt, I. No. 1824. — The 4th has closed letters, with *L' originale esiste nell' Imp. e Reale Galleria di Dresda* in small letters as the first line of the inscription. — The 5th has closed letters, with *L'originale existe nella R. Galleria di Dresda* in larger letters, and as the last line of the inscription. Even of this last state the good impressions are becoming rare, as the plate of this lovely engraving is worn out.

APPIANI *pinx.* Jacob and Rachel.

The picture is at the Parochiale at Alzano. Engraved in 1831.

Proof, with one line of open letters and the coat of arms, before the dedication. Below, in the middle, the white stamp of the engraver's initials.

LUINI *pinx.* The Daughter of Herodias with the Head of St. John.

Engraved after a picture in the Scarpa collection. There is a similar one in the Brera Gallery in Milan.

There are proofs before letters, and with open letters.

RAPHAEL *pinx.* Holy Family, with a Lamb.

Engraved in 1817, after a picture in the collection of the Marchese Malaspina da Sannazaro in Pavia, the original of which is in the Madrid Gallery. Passavant, II. 63. Compare Passavant's *Christliche Kunst in Spanien*, p. 154.

Proof, before letters, with the white stamp of the engraver's initials in the middle under the print.

RAPHAEL *pinx.* Madonna della Sedia.

In the Pitti palace in Florence. Passavant, II. 226. Engraved in 1828.

Lamotte Fouquet, No. 233, "Épreuve d'artiste avec remarque : Avant la lettre et avant les armes, seulement le nom du graveur écrit à rebours et tracé à la pointe ; le ruban, attaché à la petite croix que St. Jean tient, y est encore en blanc," 76 *th.* Same state, George Smith, No. 724, £18; Johnson, No. 69, £ 20; Wilcox, No. 105, £20 10 *s.*; Goddard, No. 235, £19 19 *s.*

The proofs are before letters, with merely the names of the artists and the coat of arms; of these there are two kinds, the first before the date, following the name Garavaglia, the second with the date, 1828. Debois, No. 342, "Épreuve avant la lettre, seulement les armes et les noms d'auteurs," 200 *fr.* It is not stated whether the impression was also before the date.

GARAVAGLIA, GIOVITO, *continued.*

GIMIGNANO *pinx.* Virgin and Child.

From the picture in the Dresden Gallery.

Proof, open letters, and before the dedication.

Artist's proofs are before any letters.

GUIDO *pinx.* The Assumption of the Virgin.

The engraving was finished by Faustino Anderloni. The picture is in Genoa, in the Church of St. Ambrose.

Proof, before letters, with only the artists' names.

Artist's proofs are before any letters; Debois, No. 343; George Smith, No. 727.

GUIDO *pinx.* **P.** "Beatrice Cenci."

From the picture in the Gallery of the Barberini palace in Rome. Platner and Bunsen, III. II. p. 434.

Proofs have the title, "Beatrice Cenci," in open letters, with the names of the artists and the address traced with the needle. Hösel, No. 96, 12½ *th.* R. Weigel, *Kunst-Cat.* No. 14996, 8 *th.* (Present price 25 *th.*) Artist's proofs are before any letters. Debois, No. 344, 65 *fr.*; the same copy afterwards, Johnson, No. 70, £5 10 *s.*; another copy of the same state, G. Smith, No. 719, £4; another, Goddard, No. 226, £5 5 *s.*; also Macready, No. 46, £7.

GARAVAGLIA *del.* **P.** Giuseppe Parini.

Engraved for the *Vite e ritratti di illustri Italiani.*

GARNIER, FRANÇOIS, engraver in Paris, born at Brest. A pupil of Bervic.

LEONARDO DA VINCI *pinx.* La Vierge aux Balances.

See Rigollot, No. 40. The picture is in the Gallery of the Louvre, Villot, No. 487.

Proof, with open letters.

Artist's proofs are before any letters. — The 3d state is with shaded, or filled letters.

LEONARDO DA VINCI *pinx.* Bacchus.

See Rigollot, No. 53. The picture is in the Gallery of the Louvre. Villot, No. 485.

GARNIER, HIPPOLYTE LOUIS, engraver in the modern mixed style of mezzotinto, born in 1803, died at Paris in 1855.

MURILLO *pinx.* "La Vierge de Madrid," Our Lady of the Conception.

Three quarters figure. Around the head is a glory of six cherubim, three on each side. Across her body is a large crescent, pointing upwards. A corresponding picture is in the Gallery of Madrid. Madrazo's *Catálogo*, No. 275.

GAYWOOD, ROBERT, an English etcher of the middle of the seventeenth century. A pupil of W. Hollar.

VAN DYCK *pinx.* Antoni van Opstal, portrait-painter.

See Smith, *Cat. rais.* 794. The plate has no name of engraver in any of its states. Weber, *Cat. rais.* p. 116, "Portraits divers d'après A. van Dyck," ascribes the engraving neither to J. Morin, nor W. Hollar, nor N. de Helt Stoccade, but to Robert Gaywood. It likewise calls to mind the style of Louis Ferdinand.

2d state, before the address of Jac. de Man, which appears in the 3d state, but with the retouch in the folds of the cloak, the absence of which constitutes the 1st state. Watermark, the arms of Amsterdam.

GAULTIER, LÉONARD, designer and engraver, born at Mentz in 1552 or 1560, worked at Paris, and died about 1641.

MICHEL-ANGELO *pinx.* The Last Judgment.

Fresco in the Sistine chapel.

1st state, before Mariette's address.

GAULTIER *del.* Christ sending forth his Disciples.

In 8vo. Engraved for a French Prayer-Book.

GHIGI, P., engraver at Rome at the beginning of this century.

RAPHAEL *pinx.* Two plates of the frescos of the Farnesina, namely,—Venus before Jupiter, and Psyche with the Vase. *See* RICCIANI.

GHISI, GIORGIO, painter and engraver, born at Mantua in 1520, died there in 1582. A son and pupil of G. B. Ghisi. Bartsch, XV.

RAPHAEL *pinx.* The Virgin lifting the Veil from the Child, Joseph standing by; composition known by the name of the "Madonna of Loretto." B. 5.

Passavant, II. 88, and III. pp. iii., 182.

1st state of the plate, with the year 1575.

The 2d state, 1602. *See* Passavant, II. p. 128.

RAPHAEL *pinx.* Theology. B. 23.

Fresco painting of the Camera della Segnatura, usually called "La Disputa del Sacramento." Passavant, II. 65, and, engraving, II. p. 98. Engraved in 1552, on two plates, to be joined.

Old, but 2d impression, with the retouch, and after Hier. Cock's address was erased.

RAPHAEL *pinx.* Philosophy. B. 24.

Fresco painting of the Camera della Segnatura, usually called "The School of Athens." Passavant, II. 67, and, engraving, II. p. 106. Engraved in 1550, on 2 plates, to be joined.

GHISI, GIORGIO, *continued.*

1st impression, before the retouch, and before the address of Hier. Cock was erased.

The engraver gave the plate this inscription: *Paulus Athenis per Epicuræos et Stoicos quosdam Philosophos adductus,* etc., mistaking the composition for a dispute of the Apostle Paul with the Stoics and Epicureans.

MICHEL-ANGELO *pinx.* Prophets and Sibyls. B. 17–22.

Fresco paintings in the Sistine chapel. A suite of 6 plates, namely:—

Jeremias. B. 17.

2d state, with the 1st address, of Nic. van Aelst.

Joel. B. 18.

2d state, 1st address, of Nic. van Aelst.

Sibylla Persica. B. 19.

2d state, 1st address, of Nic. van Aelst.

Sibylla Delphica. B. 20.

2d state, 1st address, of Nic. van Aelst.

"Another Sibyl." Sibylla Erythræa. B. 21.

3d state, in which to the address of Nic. van Aelst is added, in the tablet under the Sibyl, which did not contain her name, the 2d address, "Ioanes Iacobvs de Rvbeis formis Romæ alla pace."

"A Prophet." Ezekiel. B. 22.

3d state, in which to the address of Van Aelst is added, in the left corner of the plate, the 2d address, "Gio. Giacomo Rossi Formi Roma alla Pace."

The 1st state is before any address.

TEOD. GHISI *inv.* Venus embracing Adonis after the Chase. B. 42.

2d state, with the drapery and with Rossi's address.

GIULIO ROMANO *pinx.* The Birth of Memnon. B. 57.

Before the address of Honervogt.

GIULIO ROMANO *pinx.* The Prison. B. 66.

In reality engraved by George Pencz.

MICHEL-ANGELO *pinx.* **P.** Michel-Angelo's own portrait. B. 71.

GIACONI, VICENZO, engraver, born at Padua. A pupil of Marco Pitteri, in whose style — perpendicular lines without crossing — the following engraving is executed:—

MATTEINI *del.* **P.** Paolo Sarpi.

Engraved for the *Vite e ritratti di illustri Italiani.*

GIBBON, BENJAMIN PHELPS, engraver, born in 1802, died at London in 1851. A pupil of Robinson.

GIBBON, BENJAMIN PHELPS, *continued.*

Ed. Landseer *pinx.* The Shepherd's Chief Mourner.

"From the picture in the possession of John Sheepshanks, Esq."

Proof, open and traced letters.

Ed. Landseer *pinx.* The Shepherd's Grave.

"From the picture in the possession of William Wells, Esq., of Redleaf near Tonbridge."

Proof, open and traced letters.

Ed. Landseer *pinx.* "Suspense."

Dog watching at the door. "From a picture in the possession of John Sheepshanks, Esq."

Proof, open and traced letters.

GIBERTI, ANTONIO, engraver, a pupil of Longhi.

Luini *pinx.* The Presentation in the Temple.

Fresco in the Church of Our Lady in Saronna, near Milan. Engraved in 1815.

With the inscription, "Et Simeon accepit Jesum in ulnas suas et benedixit." *With the coat of arms and dedication.*

Luini *pinx.* The same.

Proof, before the inscription, with the dedication in open traced letters, and with the coat of arms.

Artist's proofs are before any letters.

GILLER, WILLIAM, an English engraver of the present day in the modern mixed style of mezzotinto.

Granet *pinx.* Franciscans at Morning Service in the Choir of their Church.

The picture is in Buckingham Palace (Waagen, *Treasures,* II. 24), and there are numerous repetitions.

Ed. Landseer *pinx.* Favorites; a Horse and Dog.

Open letter proof, India paper.

GIRARDET, ABRAHAM, engraver, born at Locle in the county of Neuchatel in 1764, died at Paris in 1823. A pupil of B. A. Nicolet.

Raphael *pinx.* The Transfiguration.

See Passavant, II. 244. The picture is in the Gallery of the Vatican. Engraved in 1806.

Rare and curious engraver's proof, where the landscape is not yet finished.

The 1st state of the finished plate is before letters. Rigal, 67*fr.*; Durand, 110*fr.*

GLASER, A., a German engraver of the present day.

FRANCESCO FRANCIA *pinx.* The Adoration of the Magi.

The picture, of the size of the engraving, is in the Dresden Gallery.

Artist's proof, before any letters.

The proofs have the names of the artists, the printer, and the publisher.

TITIAN *pinx.* The Tribute Money.

The picture, painted for the Duke Alfonso I., of Ferrara, is in the Dresden Gallery.

Inscribed, in open uncial letters, "Der Zinsgroschen," *and in current letters,* "Den Mitgliedern des Kunstvereins für die Rheinlande und Westphalen in Düsseldorf."

TITIAN *pinx.* The same.

Artist's proof before any letters.

GLEDITSCH, PAUL, engraver, born at Vienna in 1793. A pupil of Leybold.

PERUGINO *pinx.* Virgin and Child, with St. Magdalen and St. Catherine.

In Count Harrach's collection at Vienna.

RUBENS *pinx.* **P.** Helena Forman, second wife of Rubens, wrapped in a furred robe and prepared to enter a bath.

The picture, in the Gallery of Vienna, is known under the name of "La Pelisse." Smith, *Cat. rais.* 300.

GLOCKENTON, ALBRECHT, the elder, miniature-painter and engraver, born at Nuremberg in 1432. (Rud. Weigel.) A scholar or imitator of Martin Schongauer. Bartsch, VI.

Christ before Caiaphas. B. 6.

From "The Passion of Our Lord," a series of 12 pieces. B. 2 – 13.

1*st state, before the retouch and before the monogram of the Master* "I. S.," *but on later paper than the following.*

Christ descending into Limbo, redeeming our First Parents and the Patriarchs. B. 12.

Also from the Passion.

1*st state, before retouch and the monogram of the Master* "I. S." *On paper with the watermark of the High Crown.*

GMELIN, FRIEDRICH WILHELM, designer and landscape engraver, born at Badenweiler in Breisgau in 1745, died at Rome in 1821. A pupil of Mechel.

GMELIN *del.* Mare Morte, near Naples.

Engraved in 1798.

2*d proof, lettre grise, not open letters, with Gmelin's name* not *close under the plate. With Frauenholz's address and a white stamp of initials.*

GMELIN, FRIEDRICH WILHELM, *continued.*

Nic. Poussin *pinx.* I Sepolcri del Pussino.

Engraved in 1814 "d' appresso il quadro una volta in Roma nel Palazzo Falconieri."

Gasp. Poussin *pinx.* Il Temporale del Pussino.

The picture is in the Bridgewater Gallery; it was formerly in the Palazzo Colonna. Waagen, *Treasures*, II. p. 38. Engraved in 1813.

Claude Lorrain *pinx.* The Flight into Egypt.

The picture is in the Dresden Gallery. Smith, *Cat. rais.* 110.

Claude Lorrain *pinx.* Acis and Galatea.

The picture is in the Dresden Gallery. Smith, *Cat. rais.* 141.

Claude Lorrain *pinx.* The Temple of Venus.

The picture, in the Colonna palace at Rome, was painted in 1672 for the Constable Colonna. Smith, *Cat. rais.* 178. Engraved in 1804.

Claude Lorrain *pinx.* The Mill.

The famous picture in the Gallery of the Doria palace in Rome. Platner and Bunsen, III. iii. p. 548. Engraved in 1805.

GODEFROY, FRANÇOIS, engraver, born at Rouen in 1743 or 1748, died at Paris in 1819. A pupil of Descamps and Le Bas.

Teniers *pinx.* Les Amusemens de Brabant.

See Smith, *Cat. rais.* 164. In 1774 in the collection of Count Dubarri.

Teniers *pinx.* La Fête du Hameau.

See Smith, *Cat. rais.* 156. The picture was in the collection of Van Loo in 1772; in 1791 in Le Brun's collection.

GODEFROY, JEAN, painter and engraver, born at London of French parents in 1771, died at Paris in 1839.

Gérard *pinx.* The Battle of Austerlitz.

The picture is in the Historical Gallery at Versailles. Engraved in 1813, in the stippled manner.

Proof, the names of the artists and address slightly traced with the needle.

GOLE, JACOB, designer and engraver with the burin and in mezzotinto, born at Amsterdam in 1660, died about 1730.

Dusart *inv.* The Village Barber.

Mezzotinto, copy of Dusart's plate, B. 18.

GOLTZIUS, HENDRIK, painter and engraver, born at Mühlbrecht in the Duchy of Jülich in 1558, died at Haarlem in 1617. A pupil of Dirk Coornhert. Bartsch, III.

"The Six Masterpieces of Goltzius." B. 15 – 20.

GOLTZIUS, HENDRIK, *continued.*

Impressions before any address.

The 1st address is Nic. Visscher; the 2d, Peter Schenck, jun.

From the collections and with the stamp of De Graaf in Amsterdam and of Ackermann in Dresden.

Ackermann, II. No. 523, 62 *th.*

Namely: —

The Annunciation. B. 15.
"In Raphael's style." Engraved in 1594.
With the dedication to William, Duke of Bavaria; and without number.

The Visitation. B. 16.
"In Parmegianino's style." Engraved in 1593.
With the number 2.

The Adoration of the Shepherds. B. 17.
"In Bassano's style." Engraved in 1594.
With the number 3.

The Circumcision. B. 18.
"In Dürer's style." Engraved in 1594.
With the number 4.

The Adoration of the Magi. B. 19.
"In Luke of Leyden's style."
Without number.

The Holy Family. B. 20.
"In Baroccio's style." Engraved in 1593.
Without number.

The Adoration of the Magi. B. 22.
In 4to.
"*Goltzius sc. et exc.*"

Mars and Venus surprised. "Ut Phœbus nitido," etc. B. 139.
"*Goltzius sculps. et divulgavit.*"

The Farnese Hercules. B. 143.
The Emperor Commodus as Hercules. B. 144.
Apollo Pythius. B. 145.

GOLTZIUS *pinx.* **P.** Coornhert, Dirk Volckertsz. B. 164.
2d state, with the passe partout border.

GOLTZIUS *pinx.* **P.** Goltzius's own portrait, size of life. B. 172.
The margin and the inscription below are cut off, and the print is pasted down.

M. HEEMSKIRK *pinx.* **P.** Zurenus. B. 189.

GOLTZIUS, HENDRIK, *continued.*

3d state, having the coat of arms.

With the signature of P. Mariette and the stamp of Ackermann's collection.

The 1st state is before letters (R. Weigel); the 2d state is before the coat of arms.

GOLTZIUS *del.* 𝔓. "The Dog of Goltzius," with the Son of Dirk de Vries. B. 190.

Maberly, No. 164, £ 7 5 *s.*; G. Smith, No. 746, £ 8.

GOLTZIUS *del.* 𝔓. N. de la Faille. B. 212.

1st state, proof before the inscription in the oval, and before the motto "Jamais Faille" *was altered.*

With the signature of P. Mariette. Purchased for £ 2 2 *s.*

PALMA GIOVANE *pinx.* St. Jerome penitent. B. 266.

2d state, with address of Nic. Visscher.

After Goltzius, by an anonymous disciple:—

GOLTZIUS *del.* St. Peter. B. p. 96. No. 7.

Full length.

GOLTZIUS *del.* St. Paul. B. p. 96. No. 8.

Full length.

GONZENBACH, CARL ARNOLD, engraver in Paris, born at St. Gallen, Switzerland, in 1806. A pupil of Lips and of Forster.

KAULBACH *del.* 𝔓. Franz Liszt.

The inscription is in open letters.

GOODALL, EDWARD, engraver, born at Leeds in 1795.

CUYP *pinx.* Evening.

The picture is in the National Gallery.

Open letter proof.

GAINSBOROUGH *pinx.* The Market Cart.

The picture is in the Vernon Gallery. Waagen, *Treasures,* I. p. 368.

Open letter proof.

GOUDT, HENDRIK VAN, Count Palatine, amateur painter and engraver, born at Utrecht in 1585, died about 1630. His work consists of the following 7 plates after Abraham Elsheimer. (Two variations of the plate "Tobias with the Angel" are also ascribed to him.)

1. The Angel leading the young Tobias through the Water, called "The Little Tobias."

GOUDT, HENDRIK VAN, *continued.*

2. The Angel leading the young Tobias through a Landscape, called "The Great Tobias."

   From the picture in the collection of Hon. Edmund Phipps. Waagen, *Handbook,* I. p. 256.

3. The Flight into Egypt.

   From the picture in the Munich Gallery. Waagen, *Handbook,* I. p. 256.

4. The Beheading of St. John the Baptist.

5. Ceres changes the son of Metanira, Stellio, into a Lizard; called "The Sorcery."

   Such a picture is in the Berlin Gallery. Waagen's *Verzeichniss,* No. 696.

6. Jupiter and Mercury, as guests of Philemon and Baucis.

   A picture nearly corresponding is in the Dresden Gallery. Hübner's *Verzeichniss,* No. 1723.

7. The Dawn of Day.

GRATELOUP, JEAN BAPTISTE, amateur designer and engraver in the aquatinta manner, born at Dax in Gascony in 1735, died in 1815.

RIGAUD *pinx.* **P.** Bossuet.

After H. Rigaud's picture and P. I. Drevet's engraving. In small 8vo.

GRAVES, ROBERT, an English engraver of the present day.

MURILLO *pinx.* Madonna of the Rosary.

See Stirling, *Annals,* III. p. 1421. The picture is in the Dulwich Gallery. Engraved in 1851.

Open letter proof. On India paper.

ED. LANDSEER *pinx.* Monkey using a Cat's Paw to get Chestnuts off a Stove.

In 8vo.

THOMAS PHILLIPS *pinx.* **P.** Lord Byron.

Open letter proof.

GREEN, VALENTINE, designer and engraver in mezzotinto and in the aquatinta manner, born in Warwickshire in 1739, died at London in 1813.

MURILLO *pinx.* The Adoration of the Shepherds.

The picture is in the Imperial Gallery of St. Petersburg. Engraved for the *Houghton Gallery.*

RUBENS *pinx.* The Deposition from the Cross.

The altar-piece in the Cathedral of Antwerp. Smith, *Cat. rais.* 5.

Proof, with open letters, slightly traced with the needle.

VAN DYCK *pinx.* **P.** Danvers, Henry, Earl of Danby.

GREEN, VALENTINE, *continued.*

The picture is in the Imperial Gallery of St. Petersburg. Smith, *Cat. rais.* 647. Engraved for the *Houghton Gallery.*

GREGORJ, CARLO, engraver, born at Florence in 1719, died in 1759. A pupil of J. Frey.

RAPHAEL *inv.* The Virgin fainting before the Sepulchre, with the three Holy Women and St. John.

Engraved in 1759 after a drawing in the Gallery of the Uffizj at Florence. Passavant, II. p. 481, No. 110.

GREGORJ, FERNANDO, designer and engraver, born at Florence in 1743, died about 1804. A pupil of his father, Carlo Gregorj, and of Vangelisti.

GUIDO *pinx.* St. Sebastian, tied to a Tree.

Engraved in 1756 for *Raccolta de' quadri dei Granduchi di Toscana.* Not now in the galleries of Florence.

MICHEL-ANGELO *pinx.* The Three Fates.

The picture is in the gallery of the Pitti palace in Florence. Engraved in 1770 for *Raccolta de' quadri dei Granduchi di Toscana,* No. XVII.

GRÉVEDON, PIERRE LOUIS, called **HENRI,** painter and lithographer, born at Paris in 1782.

GRÉVEDON *del.* **P.** Mme. Malibran-Garcia.

GRIBELIN, SIMON, the son, painter and engraver, born at Paris in 1662, came to England in 1680, and died there about 1733. A son of Simon Gribelin the elder, painter and engraver at Blois.

RAPHAEL *pinx.* The Hampton Court Cartoons.

See Passavant, II. p. 250, and 256, c. 8 plates, 4to.

The 8th plate, the title, is a representation of the apartment in Hampton Court, with the paintings on the wall. Above, in a medallion, is Raphael's portrait after Pontius's engraving; below, a medallion with the portrait of Queen Anne, on the left side of which is the inscription, *The Seven Famous Cartoons of Raphael Urbin,* etc., and Dedication, which is repeated in Latin on the right.

PAOLO DE MATTEIS *pinx.* Hercules between Virtue and Pleasure.

GRIMM, LUDWIG EMIL, painter and etcher, born at Hanau in 1792. A pupil of Carl Hess.

P. Friedrich Müller, "Maler Müller," the painter and poet.

GRUNER, LUDWIG, painter and engraver, born at Dresden in 1801. A pupil of Krüger, and of Longhi and Anderloni.

GRUNER, LUDWIG, *continued.*

OVERBECK *pinx.* Moses at the Well, defending the Daughters of Jethro.

"Original owned by J. Hatfield, Esq."

OVERBECK *pinx.* Hagar in the Desert.

Proof before letters. On India paper.

RAPHAEL *pinx.* Christ's Agony in the Garden.

Predella of the altar-piece for the cloister San Antonio di Padova in Naples. *See* Passavant, II. 31, a, and III. p. 90. From the collection of the poet Rogers, owned by Miss Burdett-Coutts. Engraved in 1849. Gruner engraved this subject before, after the picture in Mr. Fuller Maitland's collection, for the *Abbildungen zu Passavant's Rafael von Urbino*, Leipzig, 1839.

RAPHAEL *pinx.* Madonna of the Family Ansidei.

See Passavant, II. 32. In the Marlborough Collection at Blenheim.

Proof before letters, that is, with the inscription, "Raphael pinx.t — L. Gruner del.t & sculp.t," *an empty space for the title, and, below,* "From the original picture in the possession of His Grace the Duke of Marlborough"; *below this,* "Imp.ie de Drouat, Rue du Fouarre 11, Paris."

The artist's proofs are before any letters; they have only, in the middle of the lower margin, *L. Gruner del. & sculp.* cut with the needle.

Gruner engraved this picture before, on a smaller scale, for *Abbildungen zu Passavant's Rafael von Urbino*, Leipzig, 1839.

OVERBECK *pinx.* Dead Christ and Virgin.

Proof before letters. On India paper.

OVERBECK *pinx.* Christ as the Good Shepherd.

Proof before letters. On India paper.

FRA FIESOLE *pinx.* St. Bonaventura.

The picture is in the Chapel of Nicholas V. in Rome. Engraved for the Arundel Society, 1850–51.

RAPHAEL *pinx.* The Vision of a Knight.

See Passavant, II. 19, and III. p. 87. The picture, of the size of the engraving, was bought for the National Gallery for £1,050. Engraved in 1847.

VELAZQUEZ *pinx.* A Shepherd.

Engraved in 1826.

RAPHAEL *pinx.* **P.** Cardinal Bernardo Dovizio da Bibbiena.

After the picture in the Madrid Gallery (Passavant, II. 116), where it passed for the portrait of Cardinal Granvella. Engraved in 1835 as the portrait of Giulio de' Medici (afterwards Pope Clement VII.).

Proof, with traced and open letters, coat of arms, and dedication. On India paper.

GRUNER, LUDWIG, *continued.*

RAPHAEL *pinx.* The ceiling of the Camera della Segnatura.

Fresco in the Vatican. Passavant, I. p. 137 *et seqq.*, II. p. 94 *et seqq.*, and III. p. 105. Printed in colors under the direction of L. Gruner, with the inscription : *Coved Ceiling of the "Stanza della Segnatura," in the Vatican. By Raphaele d' Urbino. Published by L. Gruner*, 183 *Regent Street.*

RAPHAEL *pinx.* The ceiling of the Stanza d' Eliodoro.

Fresco in the Vatican. Passavant, II. p. 152 *et seqq.*, and III. p. 119.

Printed in colors under Gruner's direction, with the inscription : *Paintings from the ceiling of the "Stanza dell' Eliodoro" in the Vatican. By Raphaele d' Urbino.* No address.

MICHEL-ANGELO *pinx.* The ceiling of the Sistine Chapel of St. Peter's.

Painted in fresco.

J. Storch fec. Pratesi del. L. Gruner dir. Printed in colors at the Lithographic Institute of Winkelmann and Sons in Berlin in 1852–53, under the direction of L. Gruner.

RAPHAEL *des.* The Mosaics of the Cupola in the Cappella Chigiana of Santa Maria del Popolo in Rome. London, 1850. fol.

See Passavant, II. p. 448. Title, text (pp. iii.), and 11 plates, namely :—

1. The whole ceiling in outline.
2. The Moon, Diana.
3. Mercury.
4. The Firmament of Stars.
5. Venus.
6. The Sun, Apollo.
7. Mars.
8. Jupiter.
9. Saturn.
10. God, with Cherubs, the centre-piece.
11. The whole ceiling colored.

Abbildungen zu J. D. Passavant's Rafael von Urbino und sein Vater Giovanni Santi. Leipzig, 1839. fol.

Engraved in conjunction with the engravers F. A. Krüger and Witthœft, and the lithographer Zöllner.

14 plates, namely :—

1. Raphael's Birthplace in Urbino. Witthœft *sc.*
2. Giovanni Santi *pinx.* Altar of the Buffi Family. L. Gruner *sc.*
3. Giovanni Santi *pinx.* **P.** Raphael at 13 years of age. Krüger *sc.*
4. Raphael *del.* **P.** His own portrait, from a drawing. Zöllner *lith.*
5. Raphael *pinx.* **P.** His own portrait. } On one sheet. Gruner *sc.*
6. Raphael *pinx.* **P.** Raphael's Mistress. The real "Fornarina." } On one sheet. Gruner *sc.*

GRUNER, LUDWIG, *continued.*

7. Raphael *pinx.* 𝔓. Juliano de' Medici. Gruner *sc.*
8. Raphael *pinx.* The Crucifixion, from the Gallery of Cardinal Fesch. Gruner *sc.*
9. Raphael *pinx.* The Knight's Dream. Gruner *sc.*
10. Raphael *pinx.* Christ's Agony in the Garden. After the picture in Mr. Fuller Maitland's collection. Gruner *sc.*
11. Raphael *pinx.* Madonna of the Family Ansidei. Gruner *sc.*
12. Fac-simile of a sonnet of Raphael. Zöllner *lith.*
13. Façade of Raphael's Palace. } On one sheet. Zöllner *lith.*
14. Raphael's ground-plan for St. Peter's. }

Die Bas-reliefs an der Vorderseite des Doms zu Orvieto. Marmorbildwerke der Schule der Pisaner. Mit erläuterndem Texte von Emil Braun, herausgegeben von Ludwig Gruner. Leipzig, 1858. 80 *plates.*

GUÉRIN, CHRISTOPHE, designer and engraver, born at Strassburg in 1758. A pupil of Jolin and Wille.

RAPHAEL *pinx.* The Angel Raphael leading the Young Tobias.

See Passavant, II. 4, and III. p. 82. Engraved from a copy in the possession of M. Favier in Strassburg, of which the original was recently bought of the Duca Melzi in Milan by the National Gallery in London.

Proof, before letters.

CORREGGIO *pinx.* Venus taking away Cupid's Bow.

The painting, when engraved, was owned by M. Mayno in Strassburg.

GUIDETTI, a modern Italian engraver in Rome. A pupil of R. Morghen.

RAPHAEL *pinx.* Madonna with the Child standing.

Engraved in 1827 from a repetition of the larger Madonna of the Orleans Gallery. The original was lately in the collection of the poet Rogers, after whose death it was purchased by R. James Mackintosh, Esq., in London. Passavant, II. 98, and III. p. 115. The background of this repetition is dark and has no landscape, as the original; the figures are also reversed.

1*st proof, before letters, with only the names of the artists.*

2d proofs have open letters.

GUIDO RENI, painter and etcher, born at Bologna in 1575, died there in 1642. A pupil of Calvaert and Lodovico Caracci. Bartsch, XVIII.

GUIDO RENI *inv.* Holy Family. B. 10.

2*d state, with Guido Reni's name.*

The 1st state is before the name of the artist.

ANN. CARACCI *inv.* Holy Family and St. Clara. B. 50.

3d *state, with* "Annib. Carracci fecit" *on the left below.*

The 1st state is before the address of Nic. van Aelst; the 2d has this address; the 3d has the inscription on the left below, as stated.

GUIDO RENI, *continued.*

ANN. CARACCI *inv.* Madonna and Child. B. 51.

ANN. CARACCI *pinx.* The Alms of St. Roch. B. 53.

The painting is in the Dresden Gallery. Guido added to the composition the two old men on the right.

2d state, with "Anibal Car. inuent. P. Stephanonius formis cum Priuilegio. — 1610."

The 1st state before this inscription is "*extrêmement rare.*"

GUNST, PIETER VAN, engraver, born at Amsterdam in 1667, where he died about 1730.

KNELLER *pinx.* **P.** Queen Anne of England.

M. SORG *pinx.* **P.** Episcopius, Simon.

VAN DER WERFF *pinx.* **P.** Lesley, Bishop of Rosse.

GUTTENBERG, HEINRICH, engraver, born at Nuremberg in 1749, where he died in 1818. A pupil of his brother, Carl Gottlieb, and of Wille.

TENIERS *pinx.* The Card-players.

Composition of 7 figures. Engraved for the *Musée Français,* while in the Louvre. Since 1815 it has been returned to the King of Sardinia. Smith, *Cat. rais.* 103.

Proof before letters, having merely in the middle below, written with the point in very small letters, "H. Guttenberg sc."

GUTTENBERG, HERMANN, a German engraver, who worked about the middle of the last century.

TENIERS *pinx.* Départ pour le Sabat.

A witch scene. The picture is in the Dresden Gallery. Smith, *Cat. rais.* 19. Engraved from the collection of Count de Vence.

H.

HAAS, JOHANN MENO, painter and engraver, born at Copenhagen in 1752, died at Berlin in 1833. A pupil of J. M. Preisler.

L. WOLF *del.* **P.** Frederic the Great. Frederic II. of Prussia on horseback in the Garden of Sans Souci.

Engraved in 1808. *See* Nagler, *Künstler-Lexicon,* XXII. p. 55.

HAHN, lithographer in the "Lithographische Anstalt" of P. C. Stern in Frankfort.

VEIT *pinx.* The Two Marys at the Grave.

"The original painting is in the possession of M. E. Bernus du Fay."

HAID, JOHANN ELIAS, designer and engraver in mezzotinto, a pupil of his father Johann Jacob Haid, was born at Augsburg in 1739, where he died in 1809.

COCHIN *del.* **P.** Franklin.

Copy in mezzotinto and in reverse, made in 1780, of the engraving by Saint-Aubin, designed and published by C. N. Cochin.

HAINZELMANN, ELIAS, engraver, born at Augsburg in 1640, died there in 1693. A pupil of François de Poilly.

SÉB. BOURDON *pinx.* The Rest in Egypt.

The Virgin at a brook is washing the swaddling-clothes. "Ommi tempore sint vestimenta vestra candida."

With the engraver's address.

From Otto's collection.

HAINZELMANN, JOHANN, designer and engraver, brother of Elias, born at Augsburg in 1641, died at Berlin in 1693. A pupil of François de Poilly.

P. Jean-Baptiste Tavernier, the great traveller.

A whole length figure in the costume presented to him by the Shah of Persia in 1665.* Often called, erroneously, "The Persian Ambassador." Engraved in 4to in 1679. (John Hainzelmann engraved in 1686, on three plates, small fol., the three Siamese Ambassadors at the court of Louis XIV.)

HALDENWANG, CHRISTIAN, landscape engraver, pupil of Christian von Mechel, but forming his style after Woollett, was born at Durlach in 1770, and died at Rippoldsau in 1831.

J. RUYSDAEL *pinx.* A Waterfall.

See Smith, *Cat. rais.* "Ruysdael," No. 14. The picture is in the Gallery of Cassel. Engraved, while in the collection of the Louvre, for the *Musée Français.*

Proof, with only the artists' names.

HALEN, AREND VAN, painter and engraver in mezzotinto, born about 1690, worked at Amsterdam, and died in 1732. He calls himself Aquila on his plates, translating the meaning of his Christian name into Latin.

"A. VAN BLOMMEN" *pinx.* **P.** Van Somer the painter, with a round hat, sitting in an arm-chair.

See Laborde, *Histoire de la gravure en manière noire*, Paris, 1839, p. 169, where a copy is given.

* Jean Baptiste Tavernier was born at Paris in 1604, where his father, Melchior Tavernier, engraver and geographer, had a very extensive establishment for engraving and publishing maps. He died in Moscow in 1689, on his way to the East.

HALEN, AREND VAN, *continued.*

P. The same.

A drawing in red chalk on parchment. From the collection of Baron Rumohr, No. 4015.

HALL, JOHN, engraver, born at Wivenhoe, near Colchester, Essex, in 1739, died at London in 1797.

B. WEST *pinx.* William Penn treating with the Indians.

Artist's proofs are before the letters; proofs have open letters.

REYNOLDS *pinx.* **P.** Richard Brinsley Sheridan.

Open letter proof.

HANFSTÄNGL, FRANZ, painter, designer, and lithographer, born at Bayernrain in Bavaria in 1804. A pupil of Mitterer and of Langer.

GIORGIONE *pinx.* Jacob greeting Rachel.

PAOLO VERONESE *pinx.* Susanna.

REMBRANDT *pinx.* The Feast of Ahasuerus.

PAOLO VERONESE *pinx.* The Adoration of the Magi.

FERD. BOL *pinx.* Rest on the Flight into Egypt.

PAOLO VERONESE *pinx.* The Marriage Feast at Cana.

PAOLO VERONESE *pinx.* Christ bearing the Cross.

PAOLO VERONESE *pinx.* The Concina Family before the Madonna.

TITIAN *pinx.* Holy Family, with Alfonso I. of Ferrara, his Wife, Lucrezia Borgia, and their young son, in Adoration.

TITIAN *pinx.* The Virgin and Child, with St. John represented as a grown-up man, St. Paul, St. Jerome, and a young married woman as Magdalen.

CORREGGIO *pinx.* Holy Family, with St. George.

Coxe, p. 32.

PALMA VECCHIO *pinx.* Madonna and Child, with St. John and St. Catherine.

PALMA VECCHIO *pinx.* Holy Family, with the infant St. John and St. Catherine.

RAPHAEL'S SCHOOL. Virgin and Child with St. John.

The children are holding a scroll; a round picture. Passavant, II. 267, a.

RUBENS *pinx.* Le Jardin d'Amour.

TENIERS *pinx.* The Alchemist.

TERBURG *pinx.* The Trumpeter.

FRANS MIERIS *pinx.* The Trumpeter in the Guard-room.

HANFSTÄNGL, FRANZ, *continued.*

METZU *pinx.* The Game-vender.

METZU *pinx.* The Lace-maker.

P. DE HOOGH *pinx.* Girl reading in the Sunlight at the Window.

FRANS MIERIS *pinx.* **P.** Frans Mieris and Wife, in his Studio.

REMBRANDT *pinx.* **P.** Rembrandt's Daughter.

*** All the above lithographs are from pictures in the Dresden Gallery, and drawn on stone for Hanfstängl's *Die vorzüglichsten Gemälde der kön. Sächs. Gallerie in Dresden,* 1835 et seqq.

MURILLO *pinx.* Madonna and Child.

The picture is in the Leuchtenberg Gallery in Munich. Stirling, *Annals,* III. p. 1422.

PH. FOLTZ *pinx.* Des Sängers Fluch.

After Uhland's poem. The picture is in the Museum of Cologne. E. Förster, *Geschichte der deutschen Kunst,* V. p. 81. Lithographed for the Cologne Art Union, 1839–40.

HAWARD, FRANCIS, engraver in the stippled manner in London in the second half of the eighteenth century.

SIR JOSHUA REYNOLDS *pinx.* The Infant Academy.

Printed in red.

Proof before letters, with the names of the artists.

SIR JOSHUA REYNOLDS *pinx.* **P.** Mrs. Siddons as the Tragic Muse.

The picture is in the Grosvenor Gallery. Waagen, *Treasures,* II. p. 172.

HEATH, JAMES, engraver, born in 1765.

TITIAN *pinx.* **P.** Titian's Daughter bearing a Casket.

The picture, owned by Earl Grey, was formerly in the Orleans Gallery. Waagen, *Treasures,* II. p. 85.

JAN BREUGHEL *pinx.* Adam and Eve in Paradise.

J. Heath assisted Middiman in this engraving. *See* MIDDIMAN.

HEATH, CHARLES, engraver, born about 1785.

SIR JOSHUA REYNOLDS *pinx.* Puck.

Painted for Boydell's *Shakespeare Gallery.* The picture is now owned by Lord Fitzwilliam, who bought it at the sale of the late poet Rogers, in 1856, for 980 guineas.

HENRIQUEZ, BENOÎT LOUIS, engraver, born at Paris in 1732, died in 1806. A pupil of C. Dupuis.

HENRIQUEZ, BENOÎT LOUIS, *continued.*

Paolo Veronese *pinx.* The Finding of Moses.

Proof before letters, with only the artists' names.

HERZ, JOHANN DANIEL, painter and engraver, born at Augsburg in 1693, died in 1754.

The Adoration of the Shepherds.

See Nagler, *K.-L.* vi. p. 139, art. "J. D. Herz," No. 3.

Very large sheet.

HESS, CARL ERNST CHRISTOPH, engraver and etcher, born at Darmstadt in 1755, died at Munich in 1828.

Jan van Eyck *pinx.* The Adoration of the Wise Kings.

The picture is in the Gallery of Munich, and in reality painted by Rogier van der Weyden the elder. Waagen, *Handbook,* i. p. 89. The standing king is the portrait of Charles the Bold of Burgundy. Engraved in 1828.

Artist's proof, before any letters.

The 2d state is with open letters; the 3d, with finished letters.

"Raphael *pinx.*" St. Jerome writing.

See Passavant, ii. p. 418. The picture, really painted by Palma vecchio, is in the Munich Gallery.

Gerard Dow *pinx.* The Quack Doctor.

See Smith, *Cat. rais.* 108. The picture is in the Munich Gallery.

Proof, with open letters, the address of Valentin Green, and the year 1792.

The prints have shaded letters and the date 1794, when the plate was retouched. Artist's proofs are before any letters.

Rubens *pinx.* **P.** Rubens and his First Wife, Elizabeth (or Isabelle) Brant.

The picture is in the Munich Gallery. Waagen, *Handbook,* ii. p. 265; Michiels, *Catalogue des tableaux et dessins de Rubens,* No. 1021.

Proof, open letters.

Titian *pinx.* **P.** The Emperor Charles V.

Bust.

Kügelgen *pinx.* **P.** Goethe.

HESS, PETER, painter and etcher, born at Düsseldorf in 1792.

The Painters in a Cow-house in the Alps.

Rembrandt *inv.* Portrait of a Young Man with a Hat.

HOFFMANN, A., engraver of the present day, in Düsseldorf.

Giulio Romano *pinx.* Holy Family with a Basin.

HOFFMANN, A., *continued.*

The picture is in the Dresden Gallery. Engraved in 1847.

Open letters. On India paper.

There are proofs before letters with the names of the artists, and before any letters.

RAPHAEL *pinx.* Madonna with St. Jerome and St. Francis.

See Passavant, II. 16. The picture is in the Berlin Gallery. Engraved in 1862.

Proof, before letters, with the names of the artists and the printer.

Artist's proofs are before any letters.

LESSING *pinx.* A Congregation of Hussites.

The picture is owned by the King of Prussia.

Proof before letters, with the names of the artists, the publisher, and the printer.

BLANC *pinx.* Die Kirchgängerin.

Engraved for the Düsseldorf Art Union.

HOGARTH, WILLIAM, painter, etcher, and engraver, born at London in 1698, died at Chiswick in 1764.

A Modern Midnight Conversation.

Engraved in 1733.

1*st state, before the cross-hatching on the cover of the pot in the right corner, and other retouches.*

The Harlot's Progress.

Two of the six of Hogarth's paintings of this series are owned by Mr. Munro, the others were destroyed by fire when in the possession of Mr. Beckford. Waagen, *Treasures*, II. p. 140.

6 plates. Engraved in 1734.

1*st state, before retouch, and the mark of a cross on each plate.*

The Rake's Progress.

Hogarth's eight paintings of this subject are in the Soane Museum in London. Waagen, *Treasures*, II. p. 321.

8 plates, engraved in 1735.

1*st state, before the retouch of* 1763.

The Distressed Poet.

Hogarth's painting of this subject is in the Grosvenor Gallery. Waagen, *Treasures*, II. p. 172.

Engraved in 1736.

1*st state, with Pope thrashing Curll.*

The Four Times of Day.

4 plates. Engraved in 1738.

HOGARTH, WILLIAM, *continued.*

1st state; in which, in the 3d plate, Evening, the man has blue hands, his wife a red face. Engraved by B. Baron.

Strolling Actresses dressing in a Barn.

Engraved in 1738.

1st state. The woman greases her hair with a tallow candle, and there is a hole in the roof. With Hogarth's address.

The Enraged Musician.

1st state, impression before retouch; the horse's head is white. With the inscription: "Design'd, Engrav'd, & Publish'd by Wm Hogarth Nov^{br} the 30th 1741. According to Act of Parliament."

Marriage à la Mode.

Hogarth's paintings of the same subject are in the Vernon Gallery. Waagen, *Treasures,* I. p. 363.

6 plates, engraved by G. Scotin, B. Baron, S. Ravenet, and R. F. Ravenet, in 1745.

Impressions before retouch.

The March to Finchley.

Hogarth's painting of this subject is in the Foundling Hospital in London. Bürger, *Trésors,* p. 373.

Engraved by L. Sullivan in 1745. *See* SULLIVAN.

Election. 4 plates, namely:—

1. An Election Entertainment.

   1st state. "Painted and the Whole Engraved by Wm Hogarth."

The same.

   2d state. "Painted and ... Engraved by Wm. Hogarth," *the word* "Whole" *covered with cross-hatching.*

2. Canvassing for Votes.

   Engraved by C. Grignion.

3. The Polling.

   Engraved by Hogarth and Le Cave.

4. Chairing the Members.

   Engraved by Hogarth and F. Aveline.

Sigismunda.

Hogarth's painting is owned by Mr. J. H. Anderson. Bürger, *Trésors,* p. 374.

Engraved in mezzotinto by Dunkarton. *See* DUNKARTON.

Analysis of Beauty.

2 plates. "Designed, Engraved, and Publish'd by Wm Hogarth, March 5th 1753, according to Act of Parliament."

HOGARTH, WILLIAM, *continued.*

𝔓. John Wilkes.

"Drawn from the life and etched in aqua forti by Willm Hogarth. Published according to Act of Parliament, May 16, 1763."

𝔓. Bishop Hoadly.

Engraved by Baron. *See* BARON.

HOLBEIN, HANS, the younger, a pupil of his father of the same name, born at Augsburg in 1498, lived in Basle and in London, at which latter place he died in 1554. The woodcuts that bear his name are now believed to have been engraved by professional carvers in wood; his best works, the Dance of Death, and the Portrait of Erasmus with the Terminus, by Hans Lützelburger, a person of whom very little is known beyond his name.

HOLBEIN *del.* 𝔓. Erasmus, with the Statue of Terminus.

2d state, with an inscription of four lines.

The 1st state has but two lines of inscription; — the 3d state is without, and the 4th with the additional inscription, *Erasmi Roterodami Effigies edita ex lignea Tabula, quae Basiliae in Museo Feschieno asservatur.* Very recently new impressions have been made of the original block for A. Woltmann, *Holbein und seine Zeit*, Leipzig, 1866 – 67.

See further under HONDIUS.

HOLLAR, WENCESLAUS, designer, etcher, and engraver, born at Prague in 1607, died at London in 1677. A pupil of Matth. Merian. Gustav Parthey, *Wenzel Hollar*, Berlin, 1853, and *Nachträge*, 1858.

H. HOLBEIN *pinx.* 𝔓. Anne Boleyn, Queen of Henry VIII., represented as Faith, also called St. Barbara. P. 176.

From Otto's collection.

RAPHAEL *pinx.* 𝔓. St. Catherine of Alexandria. P. 177.

Passavant, *Rafael*, II. No. 239, p. 338. Portrait of the real "Fornarina."

P. VAN AVONT *pinx.* A Nymph of Diana, sitting. P. 276.

Engraved in conjunction with Pontius.

1st state, before "J. Meyssens exc.," *after* "P. van Avont inu." *Compare Apell, No.* 822.

F. CLEYN *del.* Briseis led from Achilles's Tent. P. 286.

F. CLEYN *del.* Five Chiefs before Troy. P. 287.

F. CLEYN *del.* Agamemnon and the two Ajaxes. P. 288.

HOLLAR, WENCESLAUS, *continued.*

F. CLEYN *del.* Æneas and Diomed. P. 289.

*** These four plates were engraved for Ogilby's Homer.

MANTEGNA *del.* Four Antique Figures at an Altar. P. 465.

"Secundum originale quod conservatur in aedibus Arundelianis Londini."

With the stamp of Ackermann's collection.

GIULIO ROMANO *pinx.* Seleucus and his Son. P. 527.

W. HOLLAR *del.* The Seasons.

2d set, three quarters length, namely:—

Spring. P. 610.
Summer. P. 611.
Autumn. P. 612.
Winter. P. 613.

Before "Ciartres exc."; *see Apell's and Ackermann's 2d Catalogue.*

HOLLAR *del.* View of the West Front of Antwerp Cathedral. P. 824.

1st state, before the 2d and 3d line of inscription.

Purchased for £4 14*s.* 6*d.*

P. VAN AVONT *pinx.* Abbey of Rothendael. P. 886.

1st state, before any address, and with the year. See Apell, No. 924.

W. HOLLAR *del.* Strassburg Minster. P. 892.

Elizabeth Castle at Jersey. P. 922 – 925.

The set of 4 plates.

THOMAS JOHNSON *del.* North View of Canterbury. P. 961, a.

BONAVENTURA PETERS *pinx.* Louving in Ireland. P. 1090.

1st state, with Meyssens's address.

The small views of the Environs of Genoa. A set of 6 plates. P. 1095 – 1100.

1st impression, before the address of A. Tooker.

J. VAN ARTOIS *pinx.* View of two Cottages on a Hill. P. 1205.

1st impressions, with Meyssens's address, and the year.

J. VAN ARTOIS *pinx.* The Shepherd in the Wood, landscape. P. 1206.

2d state, without the year; address cut off.

J. VAN ARTOIS *pinx.* The Beggar, landscape. P. 1211.

1st state, with P. van Avont's address, and the year.

J. BREUGHEL *pinx.* The Angler, a landscape. P. 1214.

1st state, before the No. 7, *and before* "Buyten Brussel."

HOLLAR, WENCESLAUS, *continued.*

J. Breughel *pinx.* The Four Windmills, a landscape. P. 1215.
1st state, before Galle's address.

Titian *pinx.* 𝔭. Giovanni della Casa. P. 1339.
1st state, with the name of "Bindo Altovitii" [*sic*] *as the person represented. Watermark of a Crowned Shield, with a Lion.*

𝔭. The same. P. 1339.
3d state, with the substitution of the name "Monsigre Gio della Casa" *and the addition* "Antuerpiæ," *in the address.*

Titian *pinx.* 𝔭. Aretino, Pietro. P. 1348.
1st state, before "Antuerpiæ," *and before the later address.*
Watermark, a Crowned Shield, with a Lion.
From Ackermann's collection, No. 378.

J. van Balen *pinx.* 𝔭. Balen, J. van. P. 1356.
2d state, with the word "commensement" *corrected into* "commencement."
Engraved for De Bie's *Het gulden Cabinet.*

Titian *pinx.* 𝔭. Barbaro, Daniello. P. 1359.
Watermark, a Crowned Shield, with a Lion.

Sebastiano del Piombo *pinx.* 𝔭. Vittoria Colonna. P. 1379.
"Ex collectione Johannis et Jacobi van Verle."
The paper has the watermark of the Foolscap.

Albrecht Dürer *pinx.* 𝔭. Dürer, Albrecht, the father. P. 1389.
The picture was, at the time of the engraving, in the collection of the Earl of Arundel; it is now in that of the Duke of Northumberland at Sion House. Waagen, *Handbook*, i. p. 145, and Waagen's *Galleries and Cabinets*, or *Treasures*, iv. p. 267.
Watermark, a Small Double Eagle.
From John Barnard's and Ackermann's collection, No. 382.

J. Meyssens *pinx.* 𝔭. Elsheimer, Adam. P. 1397.
Engraved for De Bie's *Het gulden Cabinet.*
1st state, with Meyssens's address, and before the text on the back.
From Ackermann's collection, No. 383.

J. Meyssens *pinx.* 𝔭. Es, Jacob van. P. 1399.
Engraved for De Bie's *Het gulden Cabinet.*
1st state, with Meyssens's address.

H. Holbein *pinx.* 𝔭. Hans von Zürich, goldsmith. P. 1411.
With J. A. Boerner's name on the back.

H. Holbein *pinx.* 𝔭. Holbein, Hans. P. 1418.
1st state, before address.

HOLLAR, WENCESLAUS, *continued.*

W. HOLLAR *del.* Homer's Statue. P. 1422.

Engraved for Ogilby's Homer.

H. HOLBEIN *pinx.* **P.** Queen Jane Seymour. P. 1427.

There is a portrait of this queen, in rich attire, in the Belvedere Gallery at Vienna. Waagen, *Handbook*, I. p. 200.

From Ackermann's collection, No. 388.

PALMA VECCHIO *pinx.* **P.** Queen Catherine Cornara. P. 1455.

3d state, with the correction of the name, "Catarina Cornara" *instead of* "La Bella Lavra del Petrarca," *and the addition of* "Antu.piæ" *in the address.*

The 1st state has the inscription; the 2d has the correction, but not *Antu.piæ* in the address.

VAN DYCK *pinx.* **P.** Malderus, Johannes, Episcopus. P. 1463.

The picture is in the Antwerp Academy.

1st state, with Meyssens's address, which was afterwards erased, when the plate was added by a later publisher to Van Dyck's Iconographia. *I. von Szwykowski,* A. van Dyck's Bildnisse bekannter Personen, *Leipzig,* 1859, *p.* 264. *Watermark, Small Foolscap.*

H. HOLBEIN *pinx.* **P.** Morett, Thomas. P. 1470.

"W: Hollar fecit, ex Collectione Arundeliana, A.º 1647. 31 Dece:" The finished picture of this portrait of Thomas Morett, goldsmith to Henry VIII., is in the Dresden Gallery, where it till recently passed for the portrait of the Duke Sforza il Moro of Milan, painted by Leonardo da Vinci.

1st state, before the addition in the inscription.

From Ackermann's collection, No. 391.

J. MEYSSENS *pinx.* **P.** Peeters, Bonaventura. P. 1480.

1st state, with Meyssens's address, and before the text on the back.

Engraved for De Bie's *Het gulden Cabinet.*

RAPHAEL *pinx.* **P.** Raphael. P. 1486.

Passavant, II. p. 625, a.

W. HOLLAR *del.* **P.** Reede, Johan de. P. 1487.

W. HOLLAR *del.* **P.** Roelans, Johan. P. 1496.

W. HOLLAR *del.* **P.** Spottiswoode, Archbishop. P. 1505.

Engraved for Spottiswoode's *History of the Church of Scotland.*

TITIAN *pinx.* **P.** Titian's Daughter. P. 1511.

From the collection and with the signature of P. Mariette.

Watermark, arms of the city of Amsterdam.

ADR. VAN VENNE *pinx.* **P.** Venne, Adriaan van. P. 1514.

1st state, before the 4th bird, seen in the air through the window, was added.

Engraved for De Bie's *Het gulden Cabinet.*

HOLLAR, WENCESLAUS, *continued.*

A. Dürer *pinx.* Half length Portrait of a Female with Braided Hair. P. 1536.

"Also bin ich gestalt in achcehe jor altt 1497." Engraved when in the Arundel collection; now in the Speck collection in Leipzig. Von Eye, pp. 124, 125.

Watermark, the Small Foolscap.

H. Holbein *pinx.* Portrait of a Young Man with a slit cap and embroidered standing collar. P. 1543.

The thin paper has the watermark of a Foolscap.

H. Holbein *pinx.* Bearded Old Man with a Link Chain. P. 1548.

H. Holbein *pinx.* 𝔓. Catherine of Aragon, Queen of Henry VIII. P. 1549.

Also called Lady Leicester.

H. Holbein *pinx.* 𝔓. Lady Butts, Wife of the Physician of Henry VIII. P. 1553.

1*st state, before the number* 7 *at the right below.*

"Mazulino * *inv.*" Female Head, Hair adorned with Pearls. P. 1611.

1*st state, before the inscription above on the left,* "Mazulino inv. W. Hollar fecit."

Martin Schongauer *pinx.* Half length Portrait of a Woman with a Wreath of Oak Leaves. P. 1641.

J. Felix Biler *pinx.* Female Bust with Double-tongued Neckerchief. P. 1656.

1*st state, before the number.*

W. Hollar *del.* Bust of a Female, with a Flat Stomacher. P. 1664.

1*st state, before the number.*

W. Hollar *del.* Female Head, with a Fur Cap, and Millstone Collar in Outline. P. 1666.

1*st state, before the number.*

W. Hollar *del.* Female bust, with a delicately figured Neckerchief. P. 1708.

W. Hollar *del.* Hollar's Wife, seen from behind. P. 1717.

Female Heads in round.

See Parthey, Nos. 1912 – 1944. — All, except the first, from Ackermann's collection.

W. Hollar *del.* Lady, with Ribbons tied to her Hanging Curls. P. 1912.

W. Hollar *del.* Woman with uncombed Hair. P. 1918.

* Meant for Mazzolino, i. e. Francesco Mazzuoli il Parmegianino, or Parmegiano.

HOLLAR, WENCESLAUS, *continued.*

W. Hollar *del.* Female with Millstone Collar and Laced Bodice. P. 1919.

W. Hollar *del.* Female with Millstone Collar and Buttons on her Bodice. P. 1920.

W. Hollar *del.* Female with Millstone Collar, and Buttons on her Shoulder. P. 1921.

W. Hollar *del.* Female with Millstone Collar, and Hair-pin on her Forehead. P. 1922.

W. Hollar *del.* Female with a Disc Collar, and two Rows of Buttons on her Bodice. P. 1923.

W. Hollar *del.* Female with a Lace Cap fastened on her Ear with a Bodkin. P. 1926.

Haskins *del.* Bust; Lace Cap with a turned-up Border. P. 1928.

W. Hollar *del.* Woman of Strassburg with a Globular Cap, and sixfold plaited Millstone Collar. P. 1935.

W. Hollar *del.* Female with a Globular Cap and High Neckerchief. P. 1937.

W. Hollar *del.* Noble Woman of Vienna, with a Four-cornered Dark Fur Cap, flat at the Top, and a Disc Collar. P. 1939.

W. Hollar *del.* A Citizen's Wife of Antwerp; on her Forehead a Disc with a Tuft. P. 1944.

W. Hollar *del.* Muff, with Brocade Band. P. 1946.
From Ackermann's collection, No. 411.

W. Hollar *del.* Muff and Tippet. P. 1947.

W. Hollar *del.* Five Muffs, two lace-bordered Neckerchiefs, two Gauntlets, a Fan, a Feather Fan, a Needle-cushion, and a Half-mask. P. 1951.
From Ackermann's collection.

W. Hollar *del.* Head of a young Negro. P. 2005.

W. Hollar *del.* "Unus Americanus ex Virginia, aetatis 23." P. 2009.
"W. Hollar ad viuum delin. et fecit 1645."

W. Hollar *del.* Turk with Figured Waistcoat, or The Turkish Ambassador. P. 2010.

Peter Boel *pinx.* A dead Hare, suspended. P. 2058.
1st state, before address.

Bassano *pinx.* An Ass, standing. P. 2090.

Albrecht Dürer *pinx.* A Lion, couching. P. 2094.

HOLLAR, WENCESLAUS, *continued.*

W. HOLLAR *del.* Cat's Head. P. 2109.

The middle-sized head, "*Dobrá kočka,*" etc.

ANDREA MANTEGNA *del.* Communion Chalice. P. 2643.

From Count Sternberg's collection. Purchased for £ 6 6 *s.*

HONDIUS, HENDRIK, the elder, designer and engraver, born at Duffel in 1575, died in 1610. A pupil of Hans Vredeman and Johan Wierx.

H. HOLBEIN *pinx.* The Virgin, with the Child in her arms, to whom she offers an apple.

Three fourths length figure.

Te propter matris nunc paruulus hæret in vlnis,
Quem non Cœlorum machina vasta tenet.
Induit illo tuos vt te sibi jungeret artus,
Indue tu firmo rursus amore Deum.

Ioannes Holbein In: *Ex: H: cum priv:* 1593.

Shows an affinity with, or the influence of, Leonardo da Vinci. *See* Waagen, *Handbook,* I. p. 190.

From Otto's collection.

HONDIUS, HENRY, the younger, designer and engraver, born at London about 1580, died about 1642.

VAN DYCK *pinx.* **P.** Mich. Mierevelt, painter.

Engraved for M. van den Enden's *Iconographia of Van Dyck,* No. 9. Weber, p. 55.

1*st state, with the name of H. Hondius as engraver, and the address of Martin van den Enden.* "*Extrêmement rare.*"

Really engraved by W. Delff. *See* DELFF.

HONDIUS, WILLEM, designer and engraver, born at the Hague about 1600. A pupil of his father, Henry Hondius the younger.

VAN DYCK *pinx.* **P.** Frans Franck, the younger, painter.

The grisaille painting for this engraving is in the collection of the Duke of Buccleugh. Engraved for Martin van den Enden, Van Dyck's *Iconographia,* No. 11. Weber, p. 57.

4*th and last state, after the letters* "G. H." *were effaced.*

Watermark, the arms of Amsterdam.

VAN DYCK *pinx.* **P.** Willem Hondius, engraver.

Engraved for Martin van den Enden, Van Dyck's *Iconographia,* No. 12. Weber, p. 58.

4*th and last state, after the letters* "G. H." *were effaced. Fine impression on old paper, with the watermark of the letters* "K. I. K."

HONECK, engraver in Dresden at the beginning of this century.

PAOLO VERONESE *pinx.* The Presentation in the Temple.

The picture is in the Dresden Gallery, and not otherwise engraved. This engraving is in 8vo, and is a mere outline.

HOSEMANN, THEODOR, painter, etcher, and lithographer of the present day, in Berlin.

GIOVANNI LO SPAGNA *pinx.* The Birth of Christ.

A lithograph. With the name of Raphael as painter. The picture, which is in the Gallery of the Vatican, is, however, by Giovanni lo Spagna. *See* Passavant, II. 2, and III. p. 81. Mary and Joseph are kneeling in adoration at the side of the Child, which lies on the ground; behind and above are angels.

HOUBRAKEN, JACOB, designer and engraver, born at Dordrecht in 1698, died at Amsterdam in 1780. He was a pupil of his father, Arnold, but formed his style more after the works of Drevet, Edelinck, and Nanteuil.

REMBRANDT *pinx.* Manoah's Sacrifice.

See Smith, *Cat. rais.* 35. Engraved for the *Rec. d'est. de la Gal. de Dresde,* II. No. 47.

C. TROOST *del.* Divertissiment de la foire d'Amsterdam.

"Le dessin original est dans la collection de M. D. Neyman."

PAOLO VERONESE *pinx.* **P.** Barbaro, Daniello.

Engraved for the *Rec. d'est. de la Gal. de Dresde,* II. No. 10.

JAN WANDELAAR *pinx.* **P.** Barbeyracius, Joannes.

QUINKHARD *pinx.* **P.** Burmann, Dr.

P. Goes, Antoni van der, Advocate General of Holland.

No name of painter mentioned. Engraved in 8vo, in 1541.

Proof before any letters.

From Gawet's collection.

MIEREVELT *pinx.* **P.** Grotius (de Groot), Hugo.

The larger engraving. The picture is in the Hotel de Ville at Delft. Waagen, *Handbook,* I. p. 239.

From Krone's collection, with his name.

CHRISTOPH MÜLLER *pinx.* **P.** Heineccius.

VAN DER MY *pinx.* **P.** Honert, Johannes van den, the son, Professor of Theology.

H. POTHOVEN *del.* **P.** Houbraken, Jacobus.

Small fol.

MIERIS *pinx.* **P.** Loon, Gerard van.

HOUBRAKEN, JACOB, *continued.*

FOURNIER *pinx.* **P.** Missy, J. Rousset de.

POTHOVEN *del.* **P.** Orange, Willem Karel Hendrik Friso, Prince of.

ANT. PESNE *pinx.* **P.** Sophia Dorothea of Brunswick-Lunenburg, Queen of Prussia.

DE KEYSER *pinx.* **P** Van Waveren, Antoni Oetgens, Burgomaster of Amsterdam.

Large 8vo.

VAN DER MY *pinx.* **P.** Vitriarius, Juris Professor.

WANDELAER *del.* **P.** Anna, Empress of Russia.

The following portraits were engraved for Thomas Birch's *Heads of Illustrious Persons of Great Britain*, London, published by J. and P. Knapton, 1743.*

P. Chaucer, with an Inkhorn on his Button.

The portrait must originally have been taken from the miniature in the Occleve MS.

Engraved from a picture in the collection of Sir Hans Sloane, Bart.

HOLBEIN *pinx.* **P.** Anne Boleyn.

HOLBEIN *pinx.* **P.** Anne of Cleves.

In 1826 the picture was in the possession of T. Brydges Barret, Esq. Walpole, *Anecdotes*, ed. 1849, I. p. 72.

HOLBEIN *pinx.* **P.** Catharine of Aragon.

HOLBEIN *pinx.* **P.** Catharine Howard.

HOLBEIN *pinx.* **P.** Essex, Thomas Cromwell, Earl of.

HOLBEIN *pinx.* **P.** Fisher, John, Bishop of Rochester.

A very fine portrait was formerly in Lord Northwick's collection. Waagen, *Handbook*, I. p. 196; *Treasures*, III. p. 210.

HOLBEIN *pinx.* **P.** Henry VIII.

The original picture is in Warwick Castle, and there are numerous repetitions. Waagen, *Treasures*, III. 215; W. Bürger, *Trésors*, p. 145.

HOLBEIN *pinx.* **P.** More, Sir Thomas.

HOLBEIN *pinx.* **P.** Somerset, Edward Seymour, Duke of.

HOLBEIN *pinx.* **P.** Wolsey, Cardinal.

SIR ANTHONY MORE *pinx.* 1562. **P.** Thomas Howard, Duke of Norfolk.

The picture was sold in 1842, at the sale of the Strawberry Hill collection, to P. Howard, Esq. Walpole, *Anecdotes*, ed. 1849, I. p. 143.

* Vertue engraved also for this collection.

HOUBRAKEN, JACOB, *continued.*

Proof, before any letters.

ZUCCARO *pinx.* **P.** Bacon, Sir Nicholas.

ZUCCARO *pinx.* **P.** Howard, Charles, Earl of Nottingham.

The original is at Hampton Court.

VAN DYCK *pinx.* **P.** Strafford, Thomas Wentworth, Earl of.

ZUCCARO *pinx.* **P.** Walsingham, Sir Francis.

The original was sold, at the sale of the Strawberry Hill collection, to B. Botfield, Esq. Walpole, *Anecdotes*, ed. 1849, I. p. 164.

VAN DYCK *pinx.* **P.** Warwick, Robert Rich, Earl of.

There is a whole length portrait, dressed in armor, in the collection of Warwick Castle. Waagen, *Treasures*, III. p. 214.

CORNELIS JANSSENS, improperly called "Johnson," *pinx.* **P.** Robert, Earl of Lindsey.

PAULUS VAN SOMER *pinx.* **P.** Sir Francis Bacon.

The picture is in Earl Cowper's collection at Panshanger. Waagen, *Treasures*, III. p. 17.

SAMUEL COOPER *pinx.* **P.** Cromwell, Oliver.

A miniature, now in the possession of Lady Frankland, widow of Sir Thomas, a descendant of Cromwell. Walpole, *Anecdotes*, ed. 1849, II. p. 529, note.

SAMUEL COOPER *pinx.* **P.** Fairfax, Lord.

SAMUEL COOPER *pinx.* **P.** Ireton, General.

SAMUEL COOPER *pinx.* **P.** Thurloe, John.

ROBERT WALKER *pinx.* **P.** Fleetwood, Lieutenant-General.

ROBERT WALKER *pinx.?* **P.** Hampden, John.

"Picture in the possession of Sir Rich. Ellys, Bart." No name of painter.

ROBERT WALKER *pinx.* **P.** Lambert, Lieutenant-General.

M. BEAL *pinx.* **P.** Otway, Thomas.

SIR P. LELY *pinx.* **P.** Sydenham, Dr. Thomas.

SIR P. LELY *pinx.* **P.** Temple, Sir William.

SIR P. LELY *pinx.* **P.** Vane, Sir Henry.

SIR G. KNELLER *pinx.* **P.** Addison, Joseph.

SIR G. KNELLER *pinx.* **P.** Dryden, John.

SIR G. KNELLER *pinx.* **P.** Garth, Dr. Samuel.

SIR G. KNELLER *pinx.* **P.** Newton, Sir Isaac.

HOUBRAKEN, JACOB, *continued.*

The picture is at Petworth. Walpole, *Anecdotes*, ed. 1849, II. p. 587, note. *Manchester Exhibition*, 1857, No. 222, "Earl of Portsmouth."

SIR G. KNELLER *pinx.* 𝔓. Schomberg, Frederic, Duke of.

SIR G. KNELLER *pinx.* 𝔓. Steele, Richard.

SIR G. KNELLER *pinx.* 𝔓. Tillotson, Archbishop.

A. POND *pinx.* 𝔓. Pope, Alexander.

HOUSTON, RICHARD, designer and engraver in mezzotinto, born in England about 1728, died in London in 1775.

PENNY *pinx.* The Tailor in the Smith's Shop.

SIR JOSHUA REYNOLDS *pinx.* 𝔓. Ancaster, Mary, Duchess of.
Artist's proof, before any letters.

HOARE *pinx.* 𝔓. Pitt, William, Earl of Chatham.
With engraver's address.

HUBERT, FRANÇOIS, engraver, born at Abbeville in 1740. A pupil of Beauvarlet.

GERARD DOW *pinx.* 𝔓. "La Tante de Gérard Dow." An elderly woman about to water a flower-pot at the window-sill.

The picture is in the Vienna Gallery. Smith, *Cat. rais.* Suppl. p. 14, No. 42.

HUDSON, HENRY, engraver, worked in London in the last half of the eighteenth century.

SIR JOSHUA REYNOLDS *pinx.* 𝔓. Sir William Hamilton, surrounded by Etruscan Vases.

The picture is in the Vernon Gallery. Waagen, *Treasures*, I. p. 365.
Proof, with open letters.

HUFFAM, A. M., an English mezzotinto engraver of the present day.

GRANET *pinx.* Interior of a Chapel, with the Ceremony of a Nun taking the Veil.

HUMPHRYS, WILLIAM, the younger, engraver of the present day in London.

CORREGGIO *pinx.* Magdalen reading.

A copy of Longhi's engraving.

LESLIE *pinx.* Sancho Panza and the Duchess.

The picture is in the Vernon Gallery. Waagen, *Treasures*, I. p. 378.

HUMPHRYS, WILLIAM, *continued.*

Another, from which this engraving was made, is in the collection of Col. Egremont Wyndham, at Petworth. Waagen, *Treasures*, III. p. 37.

Proof, lettre grise.

I.

INGOUF, PIERRE CHARLES, engraver, born at Paris in 1746, died in 1800.

A pupil of Flipart.

P. A. WILLE *del.* **P.** Johann Georg Wille.

INGOUF, FRANÇOIS ROBERT, a brother of the preceding Pierre Charles, and surpassing him as an engraver, was born at Paris in 1747 and died there in 1812. A pupil of Flipart.

SPAGNOLETTO *pinx.* The Adoration of the Shepherds.

The picture is in the Gallery of the Louvre. Villot, No. 553. Engraved for the *Musée Français.*

IRELAND, SAMUEL, amateur etcher in London towards the end of the last century, and author of "Graphic illustrations of Hogarth, from Pictures, Drawings, and scarce Prints in the possession of Samuel Ireland," London, 1794 – 99, 2 vols. royal 8vo. There is also an edition in 4to, 1801, illustrated with the etchings and proofs. The following print is probably from this work, which must not be confounded with John Ireland's "Hogarth Illustrated," London, 1791 – 98, 3 vols. with plates.

HOGARTH *pinx.* **P.** Hogarth's own portrait.

With a palette. Bust with shoulders, but without hands. With the inscription, *Hogarth pinx^t. — W^M. HOGARTH died Oct^r.* 26th. 1764. *Aged* 67 —*Etch'd by Saml. Ireland from an Original Portrait in oil by HOGARTH in his possession.* 4to.

J.

JACOB, LOUIS, engraver, born in 1712, died in Paris in 1802.

PAOLO VERONESE *pinx.* Rebecca and Eliezer.

Engraved for the *Cabinet Crozat*, while in the collection of M. Bibron de Cormeri.

JARDINIER, CLAUDE DONAT, engraver, born at Paris in 1725, where he died in 1774. A pupil of Le Bas, N. Dupuis, and Laurent Cars.

ANN. CARACCI *pinx.* The Genius of Fame.

The picture is in the Dresden Gallery. Engraved for the *Rec. d'est. de la Gal. de Dresde*, II. No. 10.

JARDINIER, CLAUDE DONAT, *continued.*

GREUZE *pinx.* A Mother with Three Children.

She hushes the elder, to prevent his disturbing the sleep of the younger ones with his trumpet. Smith, *Cat. rais.* 57. The picture is in Buckingham Palace. Waagen, *Treasures,* II. p. 24.

Proof, before any letters.

JEANNERET, CHARLES, engraver of the present day.

"RAPHAEL *pinx.*" The Last Supper.

A fresco painting in the secularized Convent of San Onofrio in Florence, discovered in 1845. *See* Passavant, III. p. 160, who ascribes the picture to Perugino. See also Crowe and Cavalcaselle, *History of Painting in Italy,* III. p. 247.

JEAURAT, EDME, engraver, born at Paris in 1672 (or 1688), where he died in 1738. A pupil of Bernard Picart.

PAOLO VERONESE *pinx.* The Finding of Moses.

Engraved for the *Cabinet Crozat.* "Tableau dans le Cabinet du Roy." The picture is not now in the Gallery of the Louvre.

A. PESNE *pinx.* P. Nicolaus Vleughels Parisiensis, Pictor Regius.

JENTZEN, FRANZ, lithographer in Berlin.

ADR. VAN DER WERFF *pinx.* The Dismissal of Hagar.

The picture is in the Dresden Gallery.

JESI, SAMUELE, engraver, born at Correggio in 1800, died recently. A disciple of Longhi.

GUERCINO *pinx.* Abraham dismissing Hagar.

The picture is in the Brera Gallery in Milan. Engraved in 1821.

Artist's proof, before any letters or arms.

FRA BARTOLOMMEO *pinx.* Madonna della Catedrale di Lucca.

Madonna in trono with St. John and St. Stephen. *See* Crowe and Cavalcaselle, III. p. 449. Engraved in 1834.

Artist's proof, before any letters.

Purchased for £ 7 7 *s.* Proofs have the artists' names, and the inscription of the title in open letters.

RAPHAEL *pinx.* Madonna di casa Tempi.

See Passavant, II. 56. The picture is in the Munich Gallery.

Proof, with coat of arms, and dedication to the Empress of Austria in traced and open letters. The words "Raffaello da Urbino dipinse. S. Jesi disegnò ed incise," *are delicately cut with the needle. On the right corner, close under the print, is the white stamp of the engraver's initials.*

JESI, SAMUELE, *continued.*

RAPHAEL *pinx.* The same, second plate.

Artist's proof, without arms and letters, except "Raffaello Sanzio da Urbino dipinse. Samuele Jesi dis. nel 1824 ed inc. nel 1837," *delicately cut with the needle.*

Johnson, No. 78, £4 4 *s.*

The finished plate has a different dedication from the first (not to the Empress of Austria), and has no coat of arms.

DELAROCHE *pinx.* La Vierge à la Vigne.

The picture, in the collection of Thomas Baring, Esq. (Waagen, *Treasures*, II. p. 192), was burned in 1854. *Fine Arts Quarterly Review*, May, 1864, II. 290, note.

Open letter proof.

VASARI *del.* **P.** Benvenuto Cellini.

RAPHAEL *pinx.* **P.** Leo X. attended by the Cardinals Giulio de' Medici (afterward Pope Clement VIII.) and Lodovico de' Rossi.

The picture is in the Gallery of the Pitti palace in Florence. Passavant, II. 237. Engraved in 1840.

Open letters, with Jesi's autograph in pencil.

RAPHAEL *pinx.* **P.** The same.

Engraver's proof, not quite finished, with the hands, book, and bell on the table only in outline.

RAPHAEL *pinx.* **P.** Female Portrait in the Tribune at Florence.

It passed for the portrait of the Maddalena Strozzi-Doni until the authentic portrait was obtained in 1826.

See Passavant, II. 41, and comp. 40.

Artist's proof before any letters.

JESI *del.* **P.** Giuseppe Longhi.

With a dedication to P. Anderloni.

Proof, with open and traced letters.

JODE, PIETER DE, the elder, designer and engraver, born at Antwerp in 1570, died there in 1634. A pupil of Goltzius.

TITIAN *pinx.* "The Great Holy Family."

The Virgin and Child in a Landscape, St. Elizabeth with the infant St. John, St. Joseph, and St. Zacharias, or St. Jerome, who points to a passage in the Scriptures which an angel holds up.

2d state, with Bonenfant's address.

TITIAN *pinx.* The Marriage of St. Catharine.

A composition of seven figures.

JODE, PIETER DE, the younger, designer and engraver, born at Antwerp in 1606. A pupil of his father.

VAN DYCK *pinx.* 𝔓. Halmalius, Paulus, Senator of Antwerp.

Engraved for Martin van den Enden's *Iconographia of Van Dyck*, No. 16. Weber, p. 60.

2d state, with the name of the engraver under the name of the painter (the 1st state is before the name of the engraver), *but, like the 1st, with M. van den Enden's address* (which in the 3d state was changed for the address *G. H.*). *Watermark of the paper the "Croix de Lorraine No. 1" of the table of fac-similes by Dr. Wolff; in the* Archiv für die zeichnenden Künste, Jahrg. X., Leipzig, 1864.

VAN DYCK *pinx.* 𝔓. The same.

4th and last state, after the 2d address "G. H." *was erased, or 3d state without the* "G. H." *Paper with the watermark of a kind of beehive.*

VAN DYCK *pinx.* 𝔓. Jordaens, Jacob, painter.

Engraved for Martin van den Enden's *Iconographia of Van Dyck*, No. 17. Weber, p. 60.

4th and last state, after "G. H." *was effaced. Papermark, a kind of beehive.*

VAN DYCK *pinx.* 𝔓. Nole, Andreas Colyns de, sculptor.

Engraved for Martin van den Enden's *Iconographia of Van Dyck*, No. 18. Weber, p. 61.

A portrait of this person, half figure, is in the Munich Gallery. Dillis' Cat. p. 85, No. 327. The grisaille for this engraving is in the collection of the Duke of Buccleugh.

4th and last state, after "G. H." *Papermark, the coat of arms of the city of Amsterdam.*

VAN DYCK *pinx.* 𝔓. Poelenburg, Cornelis, painter.

Engraved for Martin van den Enden's *Iconographia of Van Dyck*, No. 19. Weber, p. 61.

5th and last state, after the second address "G. H." *had been effaced. Papermark, arms of Amsterdam.*

VAN DYCK *pinx.* 𝔓. Snellinx, Jan, painter.

Van Dyck painted and etched this portrait twice. This is the finished plate of his second etching. Carpenter, p. 106; Weber, p. 30.

Good impression of the 5th and last state after the effacing of the second address, "G. H." *On fine ribbed paper, with the watermark* CCo.

VAN DYCK *pinx.* 𝔓. Triest, Antoni, Bishop of Ghent.

Van Dyck painted and etched the head, also part of the hand and drapery. Carpenter, p. 113, No. 18; Weber, p. 33. It is No. 22 of M. van den Enden's *Iconographia.* See also under VAN DYCK.

JODE, PIETER DE, *continued.*

3d state, with M. van den Enden's address. Papermark, two interlaced C's, crowned, and with an inverted cross between them.

Signed with the name J. A. Boerner, and with the stamp of Ackermann's collection.

There is a portrait of this bishop in Sir Abraham Hume's collection. Smith, *Cat. rais.* 307.

VAN DYCK *pinx.* **P.** Tulden, Diodor, Professor of Jurisprudence at Louvain.

Engraved for M. van den Enden's *Iconographia* of Van Dyck, No. 23. Weber, p. 63.

4th and last state after "G. H.," *or perhaps 3d, without these letters. Papermark, a circle, wreath, with scrolls.*

VAN DYCK *pinx.* **P.** Albert, Count Wallenstein, Duke of Friedland.

The chiar-oscuro painting is in the Munich Gallery. Engraved for M. van den Enden's *Iconographia of Van Dyck,* No. 24. Weber, p. 63.

3d and last state, after the second address "G. H." *was effaced. Paper with the watermark of the Small Foolscap.*

VAN DYCK *pinx.* **P.** Hendrik Liberti of Groningen, Organist of the Cathedral of Antwerp.

Weber, p. 121, "Portraits divers d'après A. van Dyck." The plate has but one state.

Early impression, showing still the lines for the inscription. Watermark, a Shield with a kind of Agnus Dei. Wolff, in Naumann's Archiv, x. plate No. 27.

The original of the picture is in the Munich Gallery (Smith, *Cat. rais.* 49), and there are numerous repetitions, one in the Madrid Gallery (Passavant, *Christl. Kunst in Spanien,* p. 175 ; Madrazo, *Catálogo,* No. 1447), a very fine one in the collection of the Duke of Grafton, one in the Vienna Gallery, and one is owned by Mr. Hodgshon in Amsterdam.

VAN DYCK *pinx.* **P.** Quintin Simons, painter of Brussels.

Weber, p. 121, "Portraits divers d'après A. van Dyck."

2d state, with the additional inscription "Bruxellensis pictor historiarum," *but before the retouch of the plate.*

JONES, JOHN, engraver in mezzotinto and in the stippled manner, born in London about 1740, died in the early part of this century.

SIR JOSHUA REYNOLDS *pinx.* **P.** Erskine, Thomas Erskine, Lord.

In mezzotinto.

SIR JOSHUA REYNOLDS *pinx.* **P.** Fox, Charles James.

In mezzotinto.

JORDAN, FRANCISCO.

VINCENTE LOPEZ *del.* El Santo Caliz, "The Holy Chalice of Valencia."

The cup of agate, mounted with gold and enriched with gems, believed to have been used by our Saviour at the Last Supper. W. Stirling, *Annals*, I. p. 361. Engraved in 1806.

JOUILLON, FRANÇOIS, engraver and publisher, born at Paris in 1700, died there about 1790.

PAOLO VERONESE *pinx.* Apollo and Marsyas.

Crozat owned the picture, and it was engraved for the *Cabinet Crozat.*

PAOLO VERONESE *pinx.* Mercury turns into stone Aglauros, who attempts to prevent his access to her sister Herse.

The picture is in the Fitzwilliam Collection at Cambridge; it was formerly in the Orleans Gallery. Waagen, *Treasures*, III. p. 447. Engraved for the *Cabinet Crozat.*

JUSTER, JOSEPH, engraver, worked in Venice about 1690.

LEONARDO DA VINCI *pinx.* Virgin and Child, both holding Flowers, the Child a large Lily.

The picture was painted for Francis I. Nagler, *Künstler-Lexicon*, VI. p. 511 *; Rigollot, p. 107, No. 96. Engraved for Charlotte Catherine Patin's *Tabellæ selectæ ac explicatæ*, Patavii, 1691, fol. Nagler, XX. p. 331. The picture was then in the collection of her father, the celebrated Charles Patin. It is different in composition from the one engraved from the collection of Count Pourtalès in Paris, by Aristide Louis and Joseph Franck. According to Ernst Förster, in a note to the German edition of Vasari, 1843, III. i. 32, the picture, identified with Juster's engraving, is in the Albani palace in Rome; Platner and Bunsen, however, do not mention it.

K.

KAUFFMAN, MARIA ANNA ANGELICA, painter and etcher, born at Chur in the Grisons in 1741, died at Rome in 1807. A pupil of her father Joseph.

Juno.

Etched, and washed with bistre, 1770.

Hebe.

Etched, and washed with bistre, 1770.

KEATING, GEORGE, engraver in mezzotinto and in the stippled manner, born about 1750, worked at London.

* Where, by mistake, it is stated that the picture was painted for Francis II. The engraving has the inscription: *Iesvs lvdens in gremio sanctissimæ matris, lilivm tenens. Opus absolutissimum Leonardi Vincij pro Christianissimo Rege Francisco I. In ædibus Patinianis.*

KEATING, GEORGE, *continued.*

Sir Joshua Reynolds *pinx.* **P.** The Duchess of Devonshire and her Child.

The picture is in the collection of the Duke of Devonshire at Chatsworth. Waagen, *Treasures*, III. p. 352.

KELLER, JOSEPH, designer and engraver, born at Linz, lives in Düsseldorf.

Raphael *pinx.* The Trinity.

Fresco in San Severo in Perugia. *See* Passavant, II. 35.

Artist's proof, in the right corner only the inscription in reverse, traced with the needle: "Jos. Keller. Düsseldorf. 1845." *On India paper.*

E. Deger *pinx.* Virgin with a Crown, standing.

She holds in her arms the Child, who extends his hands in blessing.

Proof, with merely the inscription "Himmels Königin" *in open letters, before the inscription was changed to* "Den Mitgliedern des Kunstvereins für die Rheinlande und Westphalen," *in open letters.*

Düsseldorf Art Union Distribution for 1840, 1841.

E. Deger *pinx.* Virgin seated in the Clouds, with Crown and Sceptre.

She holds the Child on her knee, who raises his right hand in blessing. Inscribed, in open letters, *Regina Coeli. — Das Original befindet sich in der Kapelle des Grafen von Spee zu Heltorf.*

Düsseldorf Art Union Distribution.

J. Hübner *pinx.* Roland delivering the Princess of Galicia from the Robbers' Cave.

The picture is owned by Prince Frederic of Prussia.

Düsseldorf Art Union Distribution for 1838.

Open letters.

KELLY, T.

Stuart *pinx.* **P.** Washington at Dorchester Heights.

Engraved from the picture in Faneuil Hall in Boston, U. S., which is painted after Stuart. Line engraving, "published by the Franklin Print Company. D. H. Craig, Agent."

KESSEL, THEODOR VAN, engraver, born in Holland about 1620.

Rubens *pinx.* Meleager and Atalanta, killing the Calydonian Boar.

A picture corresponding with this engraving is in the Vienna Gallery. Smith, 929; Michiels, 584; Nagler, *Künstler-Lexicon*, XIII. p. 573. A similar one, in which the animals are by Snyders, was formerly in the Düsseldorf Gallery, and is now in Munich. It has been engraved by Corn. Bloemaert. Michiels, 1115; Nagler, *ut supra.*

KILIAN, LUCAS, designer and engraver, born at Augsburg, 1579, died in 1637.

ROTTENHAMMER *pinx.* The Adoration of the Shepherds.

Copy of Kilian's plate, without the name of the engraver. Signed with Mariette's name, and from Otto's collection.

KILIAN, PHILIPP, designer and engraver, born at Augsburg in 1628, died there in 1693. A son and pupil of Wolfgang.

PHILIPP KILIAN *pinx.* **P.** Bartholomæus Kilian, engraver.

Engraved in 1685.

KILIAN, PHILIPP ANDREAS, designer and engraver, born at Augsburg in 1714, died in 1759. A pupil of J. A. Friedrich and of Martin Preisler.

J. PONTE BASSANO *pinx.* Christ driving the Dealers from the Temple.

The picture is in the Dresden Gallery. Engraved for the *Rec. d'est. de la Gal. de Dresde,* II. No. 13.

DOSSO DOSSI *pinx.* The Four Fathers of the Church.

The picture is in the Dresden Gallery. Engraved for the *Rec. d'est. de la Gal. de Dresde,* II. No. 7.

KLAUBER, IGNAZ SEBASTIAN, engraver, born at Augsburg in 1754, died at Petersburg in 1820. A pupil of his father Johann Baptist, and of Wille.

A. GRAFF *pinx.* **P.** Bause, the engraver.

Proof, open letters.

KLEIN, JOHANN ADAM, painter and etcher, born at Nuremberg in 1792. A pupil of H. von Bemmel and Ambr. Gabler.

A Saxon Wagon.

Lazzarone; Est! Est!

Spanish Pilgrim at St. Peter's in Rome.

KLUGE, MORITZ ERWIN, engraver, born at Dresden in 1802. A pupil of Toschi.

AGOST. CARACCI *pinx.* Venus guiding Æneas to the Shores of Italy.

Proof before any letters.

KNOLLE, JOHANN HEINRICH FRIEDRICH LUDWIG, engraver, born at Brunswick in 1807. A pupil of P. Anderloni.

TITIAN *pinx.* The Tribute Money.

The picture is in the Dresden Gallery.

Artist's proof, before any letters. On India paper.

CORREGGIO *pinx.* Magdalen reading.

KNOLLE, *continued.*

The picture is in the Dresden Gallery.

Proof before letters.

CORREGGIO *pinx.* The Madonna of Count Sœder.

Proof before letters.

Artist's proofs are before all letters, and before the border.

CARLO DOLCE *pinx.* St. Cecilia.

The picture is in the Dresden Gallery.

Artist's proof, before any letters.

KOBELL, WILHELM VON, landscape painter, etcher, and engraver in the aquatinta style, born at Mannheim in 1766. A pupil of his father, Ferdinand.

WOUWERMANS *pinx.* The Riding School.

Aquatinta engraving. Nagler, *Künstler-Lexicon*, XXII. p. 107.

KONING, CORNELIS, painter and engraver, born at Haarlem in 1624.

J. VAN CAMPEN *del.* **P.** Laurence Coster. "Laurentius Costerus Harlemensis, Typogr. Invent."

2d state, with the address of Hugo Allardt added to the first address, which reads, "C. Koning sculps. et exc. Harl."

KRAUS, JOHANN ULRICH, designer and engraver, born at Augsburg in 1645, where he died in 1719. A pupil of Melchior Küssel.

KRAUS *del.* The Interior of St. Peter's at the Jubilee in 1700, under Clement XII.

1st state, or 1st plate. Above, on the right, the inscription is: "In Rom die Peterskirche im Vatican."—*In the smaller representations below the Holy Gate is open, and the explanatory inscription is in Italian.*

KRAUS *del.* The same.

2d state, or 2d plate. The inscription above, on the right, is "Jubel Jahr auf das 1700 Jahr." *The Holy Gate is walled up, and the lower inscription is in German.*

KRÜGER, EPHRAIM GOTTLIEB, designer and engraver, born at Dresden in 1756, died there in 1834. A pupil of Hutin and Camerata.

FERDIN. BOL *pinx.* Joseph presenting his Father to Pharaoh.

The picture is in the Dresden Gallery. Waagen, *Handbook*, II. p. 350. Engraved for the *Rec. d'est. de la Gal. de Dresde*, III. No. 9.

CASP. NETSCHER *pinx.* **P.** "Casp. Netscher and his Wife."

A gentleman at a window, accompanying the singing of a lady with the lute. The picture is in the Dresden Gallery. Engraved for the *Rec. d'est. de la Gal. de Dresde*, III. No. 10.

KRÜGER, EPHRAIM GOTTLIEB, *continued.*

ANGELICA KAUFFMAN *pinx.* Hebe with the Eagle.

In 8vo.

Proof.

JORDAENS *pinx.* Twelfth Night Feast. "Le Roi boit."

The picture is in the Gallery of the Louvre. Villot, No. 255. Engraved for the *Musée Français.*

Artist's proof, before any letters.

KRÜGER, FERDINAND ANTON, engraver, born at Dresden in 1793, where he died in 1856. A pupil of his uncle, E. G. Krüger, of J. G. von Müller, and of Longhi.

GUIDO *pinx.* Ecce Homo.

The picture is in the Dresden Gallery. Engraved for the *Rec. d'est. de la Gal. de Dresde,* III. No. 26.

Proof, with open letters. On India paper.

LUINI *pinx.* Christ bearing the Cross.

The original is in the Vienna Gallery, under the name of Leonardo da Vinci, and a still finer exemplar is in the Lichtenstein collection in Vienna.

1*st state, with the inscription in uncial letters.*

The 2d state has an inscription differently worded, and in cursive letters.

OVERBECK *pinx.* Sophronia and Olindo on the Funeral Pile.

Clorinda as deliverer arrives on horseback; in the background, King Aladin of Jerusalem on his throne. Fresco in the Villa Massina, formerly Giustiniani, in Rome. Platner and Bunsen, III. i. p. 562. The cartoon from which this was engraved was owned by the late Herr von Quandt in Dresden.

Proof before letters, with only the names of the artists, of the publisher, and the printer. On India paper.

KÜCHLER, C., designer and engraver. He studied drawing with C. Vogel.

J. HÜBNER *pinx.* 𝔓. W. Schadow.

L.

LABRUZZI, CARLO, painter and etcher, born at Rome in 1765.

MASACCIO *pinx.* Le Pitture di Masaccio esistenti in Roma nella Basilica di San Clemente, colle teste lucidate dal Sig. Carlo Labruzzi e pubblicate da Giovanni dalle Armi. Roma, 1809. fol.

See Platner and Bunsen, III. i. p. 582.

This is the 1st edition, containing 37 plates in outline (the 2d, published in 1830, contained 43 plates). Bound in the same volume are 8 additional plates by Aloysio del Medico. *See* MEDICO.

LANDINI, DOMENICO, Italian aquatinta engraver at the commencement of the nineteenth century.

The Cathedral of Milan.

Engraved in aquatinta.

FRULLANI *del.* View of the Interior of the Campo Santo of Pisa.

Engraved in aquatinta. Additional plate to Lasinio's *Pitture a fresco del Campo Santo di Pisa,* Firenze, 1812. *See* LASINIO.

LANDSEER, THOMAS, designer and engraver in the modern mixed style of mezzotinto, born towards the close of the last century; a son of the engraver and author John Landseer.

ED. LANDSEER *pinx.* Favorite Pony and Spaniel.

Open letter proof.

ED. LANDSEER *pinx.* Sleeping Bloodhound.

"From a picture in the possession of Jacob Bell, Esq."

Open letter proof.

ED. LANDSEER *pinx.* Head of a Dog. "Odin."

Open letter proof.

LANE, RICHARD, engraver and lithographer of the present day, in London.

SIR THOMAS LAWRENCE *pinx.* **P.** Lady Nugent.

A lithograph.

SIR THOMAS LAWRENCE *pinx.* **P.** Fanny Kemble.

A lithograph.

LANGER, T., a German engraver of the present time.

JULIUS SCHNORR *pinx.* Siegfried's Body carried to Worms.

From the frescos in Munich representing the story of the Nibelungen.

JULIUS SCHNORR *pinx.* Chriemhilde exciting the Huns to Vengeance.

From the frescos of the Nibelungen in Munich.

LANGLOIS, PIERRE GABRIEL, engraver, born at Paris in 1754, died in 1810. A pupil of Simonet.

DOMENICHINO *pinx.* **P.** Domenichino.

The picture is in the Artists' Portrait Gallery in Florence. Engraved for Wicar's *Galerie de Florence et du Palais Pitti.*

LARCHER, ANTOINETTE, engraver, born at Paris in 1635. She received instruction from François de Poilly.

"RAPHAEL *pinx.*" Judith.

See Passavant, II. 252. The picture, now in the Imperial Gallery of St. Petersburg, was really painted by Alessandro Bonvicino, called il Moretto. Engraved, in reverse, for the *Cabinet Crozat,* under the name of Raphael.

LARMESSIN, NICOLAS DE, the younger, designer and engraver, born at Paris in 1684, where he died in 1756. A pupil of his father.

RAPHAEL *pinx.* The Vision of Ezekiel.

See Passavant, II. 118. The picture from which this engraving was made was bought by Nicolas Poussin in Bologna for M. de Chantelou. From the collection of De Launay it passed into the Orleans Gallery, at the sale of which Lord Berwick bought it; it is now in the collection of Sir Thomas Baring at Stratton. Baron Rumohr (*Italienische Forschungen*, III. p. 119) considers it, mentioning this very engraving, a very fine repetition or duplicate, and by no means a mere copy, of the well-known picture in the Pitti palace in Florence. Engraved, of the size of the picture, for the *Cabinet Crozat*, No. 28.

"RAPHAEL *del.*" The Entombment.

Joseph of Arimathea supports the sitting body of Christ; opposite are four holy women, two standing, two kneeling. The design is in reality by Parmegiano. *See* Passavant, II. p. 634. The drawing was in the Arundel collection.

RAPHAEL *pinx.* **P.** Frederic Carondelet, Archdeacon of Bitonto and Neapolitan Envoy in Rome.

See Passavant, II. 279. The picture was a present of the United States of Holland to Lord Arlington, and has ever since remained in the family of the Dukes of Grafton. Engraved for the *Cabinet Crozat*, No. 35.

LE GROS *pinx.* **P.** Claude Hallé, painter.

Engraved for his admission into the Academy.

LASINIO, IL CONTE CAVALIERE CARLO, the father, designer and engraver, born at Trevigi in 1757. He engraved, besides the following, some of the plates in Lastri's *Etruria Pittrice.* (The rest are by F. Gregori, G. Vascellini, Gaetano and G.-B. Cecchi, G. F. Ravenet, C. Colombini, B. Eredi, etc.)

Pitture a fresco del Campo Santo di Pisa, intagliata. Firenze, 1812.

First edition. With the extra plate of Landini's View of the Interior. 41 plates, namely:—

Nicolini *del.* View of the Quadrangle with three sides of the Arcades, and background, showing the Cathedral, the Battisterio, and the Leaning Tower.

Giotto (1276–1336) *pinx.* 1. The Misfortunes of Job: The Almighty giving Audience to Satan.

Francesco da Volterra (fl. 1370) *pinx.* 2. The Misfortunes of Job: Job's Friends.

Spinello Aretino (1308–1400) *pinx.* 3. The Presentation of St. Ephesus to the Emperor Diocletian.

LASINIO, CARLO, *continued.*

Spinello Aretino *pinx.* 4. The Combat of St. Ephesus against the Pagans of Sardinia.

Spinello Aretino *pinx.* 5. The Martyrdom of St. Ephesus and St. Politus.

Simone Memmi (d. 1344) *pinx.* 6. The Conversion of St. Ranieri, the Patron Saint of Pisa.

Simone Memmi *pinx.* 7. St. Ranieri assuming the Dress of a Hermit.

Simone Memmi *pinx.* 8. The Miracles of St. Ranieri.

Antonio Veneziano (d. 1383) *pinx.* 9. The Return of St. Ranieri.

Antonio Veneziano *pinx.* 10. The Death of St. Ranieri.

Antonio Veneziano *pinx.* 11. Miracles of the dead Ranieri.

Pietro di Lorenzo (fl. 1342) *pinx.* 12. Life of the Hermits in the Wilderness.

Andrea Orcagna (1329 – 1389) *del.* Bernardo Orcagna *pinx.*
13 a. The Last Judgment. }
13 b. Hell. }

Andrea Orcagna *pinx.* 14. The Triumph of Death.

Buonamico Buffalmacco (d. 1350) *pinx.* 15. The Crucifixion.

"Buffalmacco" (*rather* Pietro da Orvieto) *pinx.* 16. The Creation.

"B. Buffalmacco" (*rather* Pietro da Orvieto) *pinx.*
17. The Death of Abel.

"B. Buffalmacco" (*rather* Pietro da Orvieto) *pinx.*
18 a. The Ark of Noah. }
18 b. The Deluge. }

⁂ According to Ciampi, Agincourt, and Quandt, the pictures of the three plates, 16, 17, 18, are by Pietro da Orvieto, who flourished at the beginning of the fourteenth century.

Benozzo Gozzoli *pinx.* 19. The Inebriation of Noah.
Gozzoli painted in the Campo Santo, 1469 – 1484.

Benozzo Gozzoli *pinx.* 20. The Malediction of Ham.

Benozzo Gozzoli *pinx.* 21. The Tower of Babel.
P. With portraits of the Medici.

Benozzo Gozzoli *pinx.* 22. Abraham and the Worshippers of Belus.

Benozzo Gozzoli *pinx.* 23. Abraham and Lot in Egypt.

Benozzo Gozzoli *pinx.* 24. Abraham Victorious.

Benozzo Gozzoli *pinx.* 25. Departure of Hagar from Abraham.

Benozzo Gozzoli *pinx.* 26. The Burning of Sodom.

Benozzo Gozzoli *pinx.* 27. The Sacrifice of Abraham.

Benozzo Gozzoli *pinx.* 28. The Nuptials of Rebecca and Isaac.

Benozzo Gozzoli *pinx.* 29. The Birth of Jacob and Esau.

Benozzo Gozzoli *pinx.* 30. The Nuptials of Jacob and Rachel.

LASINIO, CARLO, *continued.*

Benozzo Gozzoli *pinx.* 31 a. The Meeting of Jacob and Esau.
Benozzo Gozzoli *pinx.* 31 b. The Abduction of Dinah.
Benozzo Gozzoli *pinx.* 32. The Innocence of Joseph.
Benozzo Gozzoli *pinx.* 33. Joseph discovering himself to his Brethren.
Benozzo Gozzoli *pinx.* 34. Infancy and Early Prodigies of Moses.
Benozzo Gozzoli *pinx.* 35. The Passage of the Red Sea.
Benozzo Gozzoli *pinx.* 36. The Tablets of the Law.
Benozzo Gozzoli *pinx.* 37 a. The Rod of Aaron.
37 b. The Brazen Serpent.
Benozzo Gozzoli *pinx.* 38 a. The Fall of Jericho.
38 b. The Giant Goliath.
Benozzo Gozzoli *pinx.* 39. The Adoration of the Magi.
Franc. Frullani *del.* Additional plate. View of the Interior of the Campo Santo.

Engraved in mezzotinto by Domenico Landini. *See* LANDINI.

Affreschi celebri del XIV. e XV. secolo, incisi dal Cav. Carlo Lasinio sui disegni del Cav. Paolo suo figlio con illustrazioni. Firenze, 1841. fol. (Usually called the *Quatrocentisti Fiorentini.*)

All impressions of the 1*st edition, and with the first numbers on the plates.*

31 plates of the first edition, with the title, text (pp. 41), and 1 additional plate of the second edition, as follows: —

CHAPEL BRANCACCI OF THE CHURCH DEL CARMINE.

Masaccio *pinx.* I. 1. Crucifixion of St. Peter.
2. St. Peter and St. Paul before Nero.
Masaccio *pinx.* II. St. Peter and St. Paul raising the Youth from the Dead.
Masolino *pinx.* III. Christ calls St. Peter and St. Andrew.
Masolino *pinx.* IV. 1. St. Peter healing the Cripple at the Gate of the Temple.
2. St. Peter healing Petronella, his daughter.
Masolino *pinx.* V. 1. St. Peter in Prison.
2. St. Peter delivered from Prison.
3. Adam and Eve driven from Paradise.
4. The Transgression of the First Parents.
Fra Filippo Lippi *pinx.* VI. 1. Miracles of the Apostles St. Peter and St. John: the healing of the Cripple.
2. Miracles of the Apostles St. Peter and St. John: St. Peter giving Alms to the Poor and healing the Sick.
Fra Filippo Lippi *pinx.* VII. 1. St. Peter preaching to the Heathen.
2. St. Peter baptizing the Heathen.

LASINIO, CARLO, *continued.*

CHURCH SAN AMBROGIO.

Cosimo Rosselli *pinx.* VIII. The Elevation of the Holy Host.

The picture is on a side wall of the Chapel del Miracolo, and represents the solemn procession at the bearing of the Miraculous Host from the church San Ambrogio to the Episcopal palace.

CHAPEL SASSETTI IN SANTA TRINITÀ.

Domenico Ghirlandajo *pinx.* IX. A Little Boy of the Spina Family, killed by his falling from a window, is restored to life by the apparition of St. Francis.

Domenico Ghirlandajo *pinx.* X. Pope Honorius III. approves the Order of the Minorites, presented by St. Francis.

Domenico Ghirlandajo *pinx.* XI. 1. St. Francis renounces his parental inheritance and clothing, and throws himself naked at the feet of the Bishop of Assisi.

2. St. Francis walking before Sultan Sorio through the Fire.

Domenico Ghirlandajo *pinx.* XII. Death of St. Francis.

XXVII., afterwards XIII. See below, XXVII.

THE OLD REFECTORY DE' FRATI DI SANTA CROCE.

Giotto *pinx.* XIII. The Lord's Supper.

CHAPEL BURONCELLI, NOW CHAPEL GIUGNI IN SANTA CROCE.

Taddeo Gaddi *pinx.* XIV. 1. The High-priest driving St. Joachim from the Temple.

2. The Angel appearing to St. Joachim.

Taddeo Gaddi *pinx.* XV. 1. Meeting of St. Joachim and St. Anne at the Golden Gate.

2. The Birth of the Virgin.

Taddeo Gaddi *pinx.* XVI. 1. The Annunciation of the Shepherds.

2. The Birth of the Saviour.

3. The Annunciation of the Magi.

4. The Adoration of the Magi.

Taddeo Gaddi *pinx.* XVII. 1. The Virgin descending the Stairs of the Temple.

2. The Espousals of the Virgin.

THE CHOIR OF SANTA MARIA NOVELLA.

Domenico Ghirlandajo *pinx.* XVIII. St. Joachim driven from the Temple.

XIX. The Visitation.

LASINIO, CARLO, *continued.*

P. With the portrait of Ginevra Benci (the celebrated beauty of her time).

Domenico Ghirlandajo *pinx.* XX. The Birth of the Virgin.

Domenico Ghirlandajo *pinx.* XXI. The Birth of St. John the Baptist.

Domenico Ghirlandajo *pinx.* XXII. The Angel appearing to Zacharias.

Domenico Ghirlandajo *pinx.* XXIII. Zacharias writes that the Boy shall be called John.

Domenico Ghirlandajo *pinx.* XXIV. The Virgin mounting the Stairs of the Temple.

Domenico Ghirlandajo *pinx.* XXV. The Marriage of the Virgin.

Spinello Aretino *pinx.* XXVI. (afterwards XXXII.) The Fall of the Rebellious Angels.

A fresco, now whitewashed over, in the Church of St. Angelo in Arezzo.

Further Frescos in the Choir of Santa Maria Novella, by Domenico Ghirlandajo.

Domenico Ghirlandajo *pinx.* XXVII. (afterwards XIII.) St. Francis receiving the Stigmata.

Domenico Ghirlandajo *pinx.* XXVIII. St. John the Baptist preaching to the People.

Domenico Ghirlandajo *pinx.* XXIX. The Baptism of Jesus Christ.

Domenico Ghirlandajo *pinx.* XXX. The Adoration of the Magi.

Engraved in 1826.

Domenico Ghirlandajo *pinx.* XXXI. The Feast of Herod.

Engraved in 1827.

Added from the later edition.

Domenico Ghirlandajo *pinx.* XXXII. The Death of the Virgin.

Also in Santa Maria Novella. Engraved in 1833.

Single plates from the preceding work:—.

Masaccio *pinx.* I. 1. The Crucifixion of St. Peter.

2. St. Peter and St. Paul before Nero.

Taddeo Gaddi *pinx.* XIV. 1. The High-priest driving St. Joachim from the Temple.

2. The Angel appearing to Joachim.

Taddeo Gaddi *pinx.* XV. 1. Meeting of St. Joachim and St. Anne.

2. The Birth of the Virgin.

Taddeo Gaddi *pinx.* XVII. 1. The Virgin descending the Stairs of the Temple.

2. The Espousals of the Virgin.

LASINIO, GIOVANNI PAOLO, designer and engraver, son and pupil of Carlo.

RUBENS *pinx.* A Wild Boar at Bay, with three Dogs.

The picture is in the Gallery of Turin. Engraved for D' Azeglio's *La Reale Galleria di Torino*, Torino, 1836 *et seqq.*

Le tre porte del Battisterio di San Giovanni di Firenze.

45 plates. The title-page only wanting.

1ST GATE.

Andrea Pisano (b. 1270) began this work in 1330.

1. General View.
2 a. Archangel appearing to Zacharias.
2 b. Zacharias going out speechless.
3 a. The Visitation.
3 b. Birth of St. John the Baptist.
4 a. Zacharias naming his son John.
4 b. St. John in the Desert.
5 a. St. John preaching to the Pharisees.
5 b. St. John preaching to his Disciples and the People.
6 a. St. John baptizing in the Jordan.
6 b. St. John baptizing Christ.
7. Hope. — Faith.
8. Fortitude. — Temperance.
9 a. St. John before Herod.
9 b. St. John sent to Prison.
10 a. Jews questioning St. John in Prison.
10 b. St. John foretelling Christ.
11 a. The Daughter of Herodias asking for St. John's Head.
11 b. Beheading of St. John.
12 a. Feast of Herod.
12 b. Herodias' Daughter brings John's Head to her Mother.
13 a. St. John's Disciples carrying his Head.
13 b. Entombment of St. John.
14. Charity. — Humility.
15. Justice. — Prudence.

2D GATE.

Finished by Lorenzo Ghiberti (b. 1378, d. 1455) in 1414.

1. General View.
2 a. Christ bearing the Cross.
2 b. The Crucifixion.
3 a. Praying in the Garden.
3 b. Christ betrayed and taken.
4 a. Transfiguration.

LASINIO, GIOVANNI PAOLO, *continued.*

4 b. Resurrection of Lazarus.
5 a. Baptism of Christ.
5 b. Temptation in the Desert.
6 a. Annunciation.
6 b. Nativity.
7. St. Matthew. — St. John the Evangelist.
8. St. Ambrose. — St. Jerome.
9 a. Resurrection.
9 b. Descent of the Holy Spirit.
10 a. Christ scourged.
10 b. Christ before Pilate.
11 a. Christ entering Jerusalem.
11 b. Last Supper.
12 a. Christ expelling the Dealers from the Temple.
12 b. Christ walking on the Sea.
13 a. Adoration of the Magi.
13 b. Christ among the Doctors.
14. St. Luke. — St. Mark.
15. St. Gregory. — St. Augustine.

3D GATE.

Finished by Lorenzo Ghiberti in 1424.

1. General View.
2. Creation of Adam and Eve.
3. Cain and Abel.
4. Noah's Sacrifice.
5. Three Angels visiting Abraham.
6. Jacob and Esau.
7. Joseph sold by his Brethren.
8. Moses receiving the Tables of the Law.
9. Passing the Jordan.
10. David and Goliath.
11. Queen of Sheba visiting Solomon.
12. Four figures reclining, the Seasons, and four standing.
13. Eight figures standing.
14. Eight figures standing.

*** Nos. 12 – 14 are in the border. The twenty figures standing represent characters of mark in the Old Testament.

L. Ghiberti *fec.* 15. Sacrifice of Isaac.
Brunelleschi *fec.* 15. Sacrifice of Isaac.

Ghiberti and Brunelleschi were competing to be employed in making the third gate. Ghiberti was preferred, and most justly. This third gate is that which Michel-Angelo said was fit to be the Gate of Paradise.

LASINIO, GIOVANNI PAOLO, *continued.*

ANDREA DEL SARTO *pinx.* Pitture a fresco di Andrea del Sarto nel chiostro della Compagnia dello Scalzo [in Florence].

Engraved in conjunction with A. Verico, Ernestine Langermayr, Em. Lapi, I. Migliavacca, and M. Zignani.

1. The Angel Gabriel appearing to Zacharias in the Temple. C. Lasinio *sc.*
2. The Visitation. C. Lasinio *sc.*
3. The Birth of St. John. Ant. Verico *sc.*
4. (Franciabigio *pinx.*) The Child St. John meeting the Christ Child on the way. C. Lasinio *sc.*
5. St. John preaching. Ernestine Langermayr *sc.*
6. St. John baptizing the People. Emil Lapi *sc.*
7. St. John taken Prisoner. C. Lasinio *sc.*
8. The Dance of Herodias. C. Lasinio *sc.*
9. The Beheading of St. John. Innoc. Migliavacca *sc.*
10. Herodias receiving the Head of St. John. C. Lasinio *sc.*
11. Faith. — Hope. (*Wanting.*)
12. Justice. — Charity. M. Zignani *sc.*

LASTMAN, NICOLAS, painter, designer and engraver, born at Haarlem, where he worked from 1602 to 1648. A pupil of Jan Pinas.

GOLTZIUS *pinx.* **P.** Carl van Mander *aetatis* 56.

Bryan says "after John Saenredam," but J. Saenredam's picture is after Goltzius.

LAUGIER, JEAN NICOLAS, designer and engraver, born at Toulon in 1785. A pupil of Girodet.

TITIAN *pinx.* **P.** Hippolyte d' Este, Cardinal de' Medici, in Hungarian Costume.

The picture is in the Gallery of the Pitti palace in Florence. Engraved for the *Musée Français.*

LAURENT, PIERRE LOUIS HENRI, son and pupil of Pierre, designer and engraver, was born at Paris in 1779.

TITIAN *pinx.* The Martyrdom of St. Peter the Dominican.

The picture was in San Giovanni e Paolo in Venice, recently destroyed by fire. Engraved for the *Musée Français.*

DOMENICHINO *pinx.* The Communion of St. Jerome.

The picture is in the Gallery of the Vatican. Engraved for the *Musée Français.*

LAUTENSACK, HANS SEBALD, painter and engraver, born at Bamberg about 1507, died at Nuremberg in 1560. A pupil of his father Paul. Bartsch, IX.

LAUTENSACK, HANS SEBALD, *continued.*

𝔓. Dr. Georgius Roggenbach, jurisconsultus. B. 9.

Engraved in 1554. The plate is still in existence.

An old impression.

LAUWERS, CONRAD, engraver, a younger brother of Nicolas Lauwers, born in Leuze, in Hainault, in 1623. He worked at Antwerp.

RUBENS *pinx.* Elijah in the Desert, fed by an Angel.

See Smith, *Cat. rais.* 386. The picture is in the Gallery of the Louvre. Villot, No. 426; Basan, 26.

With Lauwers's own address.

LAUWERS, NICOLAS, engraver, born at Leuze, in Hainault, in 1620; a pupil of P. Pontius. He worked at Antwerp.

VAN DYCK *pinx.* 𝔓. Fra Lelio Blancatcio (Brancaccio), Commander of Malta.

See Smith, *Cat. rais.* 673. Engraved for Martin van den Enden, *Van Dyck's Iconographia,* No. 26. Weber, *Cat. rais.* p. 65.

4th and last state, after the erasure of the second address "G. H." *from the plate. Thick paper without watermark.*

LAVIGNE, MARIN, a lithographer of the present day residing in Paris.

MURILLO *pinx.* The Immaculate Conception.

The original is probably in Seville.

MURILLO *pinx.* "La Vierge de Seville."

The picture is in the Gallery of the Louvre. Villot, No. 548; Stirling, *Annals,* III. p. 1422.

LE BAS, JACQUES PHILIPPE, designer and engraver, born at Paris in 1707, died in 1783. A pupil of Herisset and Tardiou.

TENIERS *pinx.* The Temptation of St. Anthony.

At the time of the engraving the picture was owned by the Duc de Valentinois. Smith, *Cat. rais.* 56.

TENIERS *pinx.* 𝔓. A Flemish Festival with Teniers's Family.

The inscription is cut off.

RUYSDAEL *pinx.* View of the Coast of Scheveningen.

See Smith, *Cat. rais.* 19. The picture is now in the collection of Mr. Mildmay, London. Waagen, *Galleries,* etc., or *Treasures,* IV. p. 154.

CLAUDE LORRAIN *pinx.* "Ancien port de Messine."

A seaport with setting sun. The picture is in the Gallery of the Louvre. Villot, No. 222.

LE BAS, JACQUES PHILIPPE, *continued.*

BERGHEN *pinx.* View of the environs of Siena.

Engraved in conjunction with WEISBROD. *See* WEISBROD.

LE CLERC, SÉBASTIEN, designer and engraver, born at Metz in 1637, died at Paris in 1714. A pupil of his father, Laurent. Jombert, *Catalogue raisonné de l'œuvre de Séb. Le Clerc,* Paris, 1774, 2 vols. 8vo.

The Siege of Mons. J. 246.

The Miracle of the Loaves. J. 251.

Elijah taken up in a Chariot of Fire. Above the "Niagara Falls." J. 293.

The Young Tobit with the Angel. J. 298.

LECOMTE, NARCISSE, engraver, born at Paris in 1794. A pupil of J.-B. Regnault and of Lignon.

RAPHAEL *pinx.* Holy Family called "La Perla."

See Passavant, II. 231, and III. p. 137. The picture is in the Madrid Gallery. Engraved in 1845.*

Proof, before letters, with the names of the artists. On India paper.

Artist's proofs are before all letters, and with the two white round spots on the edge of the cradle.

LEEUW, WILLEM VAN DER, engraver, born at Antwerp in 1600 or 1602, died about 1665. A pupil of P. Soutman.

RUBENS *pinx.* Mater Dolorosa with a Dagger in her Bosom, assisted by two Angels.

Basan, 64.

LEFÈVRE, ACHILLE DÉSIRÉ, engraver, born at Paris in 1798.

MURILLO *pinx.* The Annunciation.

The picture is in the collection of the Marquis of Hertford. Waagen, *Treasures,* II. p. 156. Engraved for the *Aguado Gallery* while in that collection.

Proof before letters.

Artist's proofs are before any letters.

MURILLO *pinx.* The Conception.

The great picture of the Soult collection, now in the Louvre, painted for the church Los Venerables in Seville, from which the Marshal took it. Stirling, *Annals,* II. p. 883; Villot, No. 546 bis. Engraved in 1859.

Proof, before letters, with the names of the artists and the address engraved with the burin.

* M. Le Blanc omitted this very important engraving in the 8th livraison, 1856, of his *Manuel de l'amateur d'estampes.*

LEFÈVRE, ACHILLE DÉSIRÉ, *continued.*

The artist's proof has the artists' names merely traced with the needle, and lower down in the margin.

MURILLO *pinx.* Virgin and Child.

Engraved for the *Aguado Gallery.*

Proof before letters.

CORREGGIO *pinx.* "La Notte." The Holy Night with the Birth of Our Saviour.*

See Coxe, p. 81. The picture is in the Dresden Gallery.

Proof, before letters, with only the names of the artists, the publisher, and the printer. On India paper.

CORREGGIO *pinx.* The same.

Artist's proof, before any letters, having merely in the middle, below, "Ach. Lefèvre sc. 1852," *slightly traced with the needle.*

CORREGGIO *pinx.* Madonna and Child in a glory, with St. Sebastian, St. Geminianus, and St. Roch.

See Coxe, 90. The picture is in the Dresden Gallery.

Proof before letters, with the names of the artists, the publisher, and the printer, engraved with the burin. On India paper.

CORREGGIO *pinx.* The same.

Artist's proof, the names of the artists very slightly traced with the needle, and lower down in the margin.

The piece is arched; the prints in which the two upper corners are shaded are later impressions from the retouched plate.

RAPHAEL *pinx.* St. Cecilia.

See Passavant, II. 117. The picture is in the Gallery of Bologna. Engraved in 1857.

Proof before letters, with the names of the artists engraved with the burin.

Artist's proofs have the artists' names traced with the needle, and lower down in the margin.

RAPHAEL *pinx.* **P.** Joan of Aragon.

See Passavant, II. 236, and III. p. 144. Only the bust to the waist, without hands, and without the background of the picture in the Gallery of the Louvre, which represents the figure down to the knees, and has also a background. For an engraving of the *whole* picture, see R. MORGHEN.

Artist's proof, before the border lines; and in the middle below only the words, A. Lefèvre sculpt. d'après Rafael Paris 1843," *slightly traced with the needle.*

* This is another plate omitted by M. Le Blanc in his *Manuel de l'amateur d'estampes,* 8e livraison, Paris, 1856, but such omissions occur too frequently to be mentioned any further.

LEFÈVRE, ACHILLE DÉSIRÉ, *continued.*

Proofs have the border line, and the names of the artists engraved in the usual way. — 2d proofs have an inscription in open letter.

WINTERHALTER *pinx.* **P.** Helen of Mecklenburg, Duchess of Orleans, with the Young Count of Paris in her arms.

Inscription in open and traced letters.

LE GRAND, HYACINTHE, engraver, born in Lorraine in 1755, worked at Paris.

RENOU *pinx.* Jupiter and Io.

LE MIRE, NOEL, designer and engraver, born at Rouen in 1723, died at Paris in 1801. A pupil of Le Bas.

PARMEGIANO *pinx.* Madonna, with St. Sebastian in the foreground.

The picture is in the Dresden Gallery. Engraved for the *Rec. d'est. de la Gal. de Dresde,* I. No. 5.

TENIERS *pinx.* Latona avenged.

See Smith, *Cat. rais.* 84, and Suppl. p. 456, No. 152. Sold in the collection of the Marquis Camden in 1841, and bought by Mr. Norton.

P. Joseph II., Emperor of Germany.

With no name of painter. In 16mo.

P. DE SAINT-AUBIN *pinx.* **P.** Poullain de St. Foix.

In 8vo.

LEMPEREUR, LOUIS SIMON, engraver, born at Paris about 1725, died in 1796. A pupil of Aveline.

GUERCINO *pinx.* Cephalus and Procris.

The picture is in the Dresden Gallery. Engraved for the *Rec. d'est. de la Gal. de Dresde,* II. No. 22.

ANN. CARACCI *pinx.* L'Attente du Plaisir.

RUBENS *pinx.* Le Jardin d'Amour.

See Smith, *Cat. rais.* 576, 457, and 274. The picture is in the Dresden Gallery, a repetition of the one in the Madrid Gallery.

PALAMEDES *pinx.* Festin Espagnol.

The picture was, at the time of the engraving, in the collection of "M. de Pille."

LEONETTI, GIOVANNI BATTISTA, engraver, worked at Rome.

RAPHAEL *pinx.* Mercury with a Trumpet.

RAPHAEL *pinx.* Mercury carrying Psyche to Olympus.

Two plates of the frescos of the Farnesina. See under RICCIANI.

Stampe del Duomo di Orvieto. Roma, 1791. fol.

LEONETTI, GIOVANNI BATTISTA, *continued.*

Sculptures and paintings of Nicolò Pisano and Luca Signorelli, etc. Edited by Guglielmo della Valle, who also wrote a text in 4to, which is here wanting.

Engraved by G. B. Leonetti, conjointly with Giovanni Ottaviani, Francesco Morelli, and others. 38 pieces on 32 sheets, namely : —

ARCHITECTURE.

Lorenzo Maitani *inventò.* Pianto del Duomo. Engraved by Domenico Pronti.

C. T. P. *del.* 2. La Facciata vecchia. Engraved by Hier. Frezza.

Giuseppe Barberi *del.* 3. La Facciata nuova. Engraved by Domenico Pronti.

Fran Panini *del.* 4. Spaccato vecchio. Engraved by Domenico Pronti.

Giuseppe Barberi *del.* 5. Spaccato nuova. Engraved by Domenico Pronti.

BAS-RELIEFS BY NICOLÒ PISANO AND HIS SCHOOL.

6. Creazione de' Pesci e de' Volatili.
7. Creazione de' Quadrupedi.
8. Formazione di Adamo.
9. Adamo animato ed estrazione della di lui costa.
10. Formazione di Eva.
11. Precetto del frutto vietato.
12. Peccato di Adamo e di Eva.
13. Adamo ed Eva nascosti.
14. Adamo ed Eva cacciati dal Paradiso.
15. Adamo ed Eva al lavoro.
16. Sacrifizio di Abele e di Caino.
17. Caino uccide Abele.
18. Risurrezione de' Morti.
19. Inferno.

*** The bas-reliefs are all engraved by G. B. Leonetti.

SCULPTURES.

Ugolino da Siena *fece.* 20. Tabernacolo del SS. Corporale. Engraved by Giuseppe Pozzi.

Ugolino da Siena *fece.* 21. Four Enamels on the Tabernacle. Engraved by Domenico Pronti.

Ugolino da Siena *fece.* 22. Four Enamels on the Tabernacle. Engraved by Domenico Pronti.

Ippolito Scalza *scolpi.* 23. S. Tommaso Apostolo. Statues. Engraved by Giovanni Ottaviani.

LEONETTI, GIOVANNI BATTISTA, *continued.*

Giovanni da Bologna *scolpi.* 24. S. Matteo Apostolo. Statue. Engraved by Giovanni Ottaviani.

Francesco Mochi *scolpi.* 25. L' Annunziata. Statue. Engraved by Pietro Bombelli.

Francesco Mochi *scolpi.* 26. L' Angelo Gabriele. Statue. Engraved by P. Bombelli.

Ippolito Scalza *scolpi.* 27. Gruppo marmoreo della Pietà. Engraved by Luigi Cunego.

Alessandro Scalza *fece.* 28. Musaico della Facciata. Engraved by G. B. Leonetti.

FRESCOS.

Luca Signorelli *dipinse.* 29. Anticristo. Engraved by Luigi Cunego.

Luca Signorelli *dipinse.* 30. Fulminati. Engraved by Alessandro Mochetti.

Luca Signorelli *dipinse.* 31. Risurrezione. Engraved by G. B. Leonetti.

Giovanni da Fiesole *dipinse.* 32. Cristo Giudice. Engraved by Alessandro Mochetti.

Luca Signorelli *dipinse.* 33. Inferno. Engraved by G. B. Leonetti.

Luca Signorelli *dipinse.* 34. Paradiso. Engraved by Francesco Morelli.

Luca Signorelli *dipinse.* 35. Angeli del Paradiso. Engraved by Alessandro Mochetti.

Luca Signorelli *dipinse.* 36. Angeli del Paradiso. Engraved by Alessandro Mochetti.

Madonna di S. Brizio, di antico incerto pennello. 37. Engraved by Huberto Vincent.

Sangallo *inv.* 38. Pianta e profili del Pozzo di Orvieto. No name of engraver given.

LEPRI, GIOACHIMO, Italian engraver of the first half of this century.

VASARI *pinx.* **P.** Michel-Angelo.

A three quarters length portrait, showing one hand. With the inscription *Bonnarotus ego: ne tendas, Icare, tantum,* — the coat of arms and dedication to the Prior Orlandini, and the address of Niccolò Pagni e figlio.

LEROUX, JEAN MARIE, engraver, born at Paris in 1788. A pupil of David, but at a later period influenced by Desnoyers.

CORREGGIO *pinx.* "La Vierge du Musée de Parme." Madonna della Scala. Coxe, p. 80. Engraved in 1837, after Desnoyers's design.

Proof, open letters, No. 110.

LEROUX, JEAN MARIE, *continued.*

MURILLO *pinx.* "La Vierge aux Anges."

Madonna and Child in a glory, surrounded and borne up by angels. "Tiré de la galerie du Maréchal Soult." The sketch for this picture is in the collection of Lord Overstone. Waagen, *Galleries*, etc., or *Treasures*, IV. p. 145.

Artist's proof, before any letters, having merely, in the middle of the lower margin, "Leroux sc.," *in letters formed of dots. On India paper.*

LEONARDO DA VINCI *pinx.* Leda.

She stands in a landscape, with the swan and two children by her side. Engraved in 1835 from a picture then in the possession of the engraver. In 1824 there was a picture in the Gallery Sommariva in Paris corresponding with this. According to Lamazzo the original of this picture was at Fontainebleau. Rigollot, *Leonardo da Vinci*, No. 54.

Proof, open letters.

Artist's proof, with merely the names of the artists, R. Weigel, *Kunst-Catalog*, No. 14394, 20 *th.* The same state, "proof before letters on India paper," George Smith, No. 895, £ 2 3 *s.* I have met with spurious proofs, where the inscription "Leda," in letters formed of two lines, had been covered up while under the press.

LERPINIÈRE, DANIEL, engraver, born about 1745, died in 1785. A pupil of Vivares, worked at London.

CLAUDE LORRAIN *pinx.* The Israelites worshipping the Golden Calf. Landscape.

See Smith, *Cat. rais.* 129. In the Grosvenor Gallery, London. Waagen, *Treasures*, II. p. 171.

Proof before letters, with only the artists' names and address slightly traced with the needle, the coat of arms, and Boydell's address a second time, "John Boydell excudit 1782."

LEVASSEUR, JEAN CHARLES, engraver, born at Abbeville in 1734, died in 1804. A pupil of Daullé and Beauvarlet.

LUCA GIORDANO *pinx.* Apollo and Daphne.

"Le Tableau est au Cabinet de M. de Damery, Paris."

LEVEAU, JEAN JACQUES, engraver, born at Rouen in 1729, died in 1785. A pupil of Le Bas.

DEBUCOURT *pinx.* Le Juge, ou la Cruche cassée.

Proof with only one line of inscription and the coat of arms.

LEVI, SAMUEL. "Polacco."

LEVI, SAMUEL, *continued.*

TITIAN *pinx.* **P.** "Catherine Cornaro Reine de Cypre."

The picture is in the Mamfrini Gallery in Venice.

LEVILLAIN, GÉRARD RENÉ, engraver, born at Paris in 1740, died in 1836.

PHILIPPE DE CHAMPAGNE *pinx.* **P.** Les Religieuses.

The oldest daughter of Ph. de Champagne, a nun in Port Royal, under the name of Sister Catherine de Sainte Suzanne, ill with fever, is praying with Mother Catherine Agnes Arnauld. A votive picture of the father. Removed from Port Royal to the Gallery of the Louvre. Villot, No. 83. Engraved for the *Musée Français.*

LEYBOLD, JOHANN FRIEDRICH, miniature painter and engraver, born at Stuttgart in 1755, died at Vienna in 1838. A pupil of J. G. von Müller.

LEYBOLD *pinx.* **P.** Adam Bartsch.

LEYBOLD, GUSTAV, engraver, son and pupil of the preceding, born at Stuttgart in 1792.

HOLBEIN *pinx.* Virgin praying.

The picture is in the collection of Count Czernin in Vienna.

LIEVENS, or **LIVENS, JAN,** painter and etcher, born at Leyden in 1607, died at Antwerp in 1663. He was a pupil of G. van Schooten and of P. Lastman, but formed his style after Rembrandt. Bartsch, *L'œuvre de Rembrandt,* Vol. II.

P. Ephraim Bonus, a Jewish physician. B. 56.

2d state, with the 1st address, "Clement de Jonghe."

P. The same. B. 56.

Same state. The margin is cut off.

P. Justus van Vondel, poet. B. 57.

3d state, with the two Latin distichs and the 2d address, "Th. Matham."

With the stamp of Ackermann's collection.

P. Daniel Heinsius, Professor at Leyden. B. 58.

1st state, with Martin van den Enden's address.

With the stamp of Dr. Frank's collection.

P. Jacob Gouters, Musician of Charles I. B. 59.

1st state, with the engraver's address, before that of Meyssens.

With the stamp of Dr. Frank's collection.

LIGNON, ÉTIENNE FRÉDÉRIC, engraver, born at Paris in 1781. A pupil of Morel.

LIGNON, ÉTIENNE FRÉDÉRIC, *continued.*

RAPHAEL *pinx.* Madonna with the Fish.

The picture is in the Madrid Gallery. Passavant, II. 100, and III. p. 116. Engraved in 1822.

Proof before letters; with the stamp of the engraver's initials.

Later proofs have open letters.

RAPHAEL *pinx.* **P.** Leo X. attended by the Cardinals Giulio de' Medici (afterwards Pope Clement VIII.) and Ludovico Rossi.

The picture is in the Gallery of the Pitti palace in Florence. Passavant, II. 237. Engraved for the *Musée Français.*

Proof before letters, with only the artists' names. On India paper.

DOMENICHINO *pinx.* St. Cecilia, with a Violin.

Half length. The picture is not in the Louvre; when engraved in 1812, it was owned by "M. le Comte Français."

MME. CHERADAME *pinx.* **P.** Comtesse de Genlis.

GÉRARD *pinx.* **P.** Mademoiselle Mars.

LINNEL, J., a lithographer of the present day.

FRA FIESOLE *pinx.* St. Thomas.

A fresco in the chapel of Nicholas V. in the Vatican. Publication of the Arundel Society, 1850–51.

LIPS, JOHANN HEINRICH, designer and engraver, born at Kloten, near Zürich, in 1758, died at Zürich in 1817. A pupil of Schellenberg.

ANN. CARACCI *pinx.* The Adoration of the Shepherds.

The picture is in the Louvre. Villot, No. 135. Engraved, in conjunction with Forster, for the *Musée Français.*

LIVENS, JAN. *See* LIEVENS.

LIVY, F., engraved for V. Marchese, "San Marco in Firenze."
See under MARCHESE.

LOMMELIN, ADRIAAN, engraver, born at Amiens in 1637, worked at Antwerp.

VAN DYCK *pinx.* **P.** "Maria Dei gratiâ Princeps Comes Arenbergiæ, Princeps Barbansonia etc^{a}."

See Smith, *Cat. rais.* No. 364.

Without address and without any trace of an erasure on the plate.

Not in Weber, *Catalogue rais. de portraits gravés par et d'après Van Dyck. See* Szwykowski, *A. van Dyck's Bildnisse,* No. 162, p. 316.

Old paper, the watermark not plain.

LONGHI, GIUSEPPE, designer and engraver, born at Monza in 1766, died at Milan in 1831. A pupil of Vangelisti.

RAPHAEL *pinx.* The Vision of Ezekiel.

The original, of the size of the engraving, is in the Gallery of the Pitti palace in Florence. Passavant, II. 118. Engraved in 1803–08 for the *Musée Français.*

Artist's proof before letters, the artists' names only cut with the needle in very small letters.

Purchased from Messrs. Evans, in London, for £12 12*s.* — Archinto, No. 229, 250 *fr.*

Proofs are before letters, having the artists' names in larger letters, engraved with the burin, and the additional name of the printer.

RAPHAEL *pinx.* Vision of Ezekiel.

Engraved in conjunction with Anderloni. *See* ANDERLONI.

"GERARD DOW" *pinx.* The Beheading of St. John the Baptist.

In reality painted by Gerard Honthorst, who was in Italy called Gherardo dalle Notti. Ascribed to Dow by mistake. A picture, figures life size, corresponding with this engraving, is in Santa Maria della Scala in Rome. Smith, *Cat. rais.* I. p. 45, No. 137. Platner and Bunsen, *Rom,* III. iii. p. 678, give a detailed description. Etched in 1806.

Proof, with merely the artists' names etched in small letters.

PROCACCINI *pinx.* The Rest in Egypt.

The picture, of the size of the engraving, was owned by John Key, Esq., London. Longhi, *Calcografia,* Appendix by Longhena, p. 409. Engraved in 1801–03.

Artist's proof, before any letters, only "Longhi sc." *in very small letters, written with the needle. On the right, below, is the white stamp of the initials of the publisher, Domenico Artaria.*

Proofs, before letters, have the names of the artists engraved with the burin.

RAPHAEL *pinx.* Lo Sposalizio.

The Marriage of the Virgin, according to the Apocryphal books of the New Testament. Passavant, II. 22, and III. p. 87. The picture — after Perugino's prototype, now in the Museum at Caen in Normandy — is in the Brera Gallery in Milan; it was painted for the church San Francesco in Città di Castello. Engraved in 1812–20.

Subscription copy, before the inscription on the middle arch of the temple "RAPHAEL URBINAS. MDIIII.," *and with the name of Bardi as printer, — before the name of Lissant. On the left, below, is the small stamp* "G. L." *in white, and on the right the white stamp with the helmeted head of Minerva. Over the coat of arms in the margin, in the plate, in a round field, is the subscription number* 34, *written with ink.*

LONGHI, GIUSEPPE, *continued.*

RAPHAEL *pinx.* The same.

1st proof, or artist's proof, before letters and before the coat of arms, with only the names of the artists, — like Debois, No. 459. *With the two white stamps, as in the preceding.*

There are proofs before *any* letters, but they are not as satisfactory as those with the artists' names. The latter, however, are usually called "proofs before all letters," to distinguish them from the second proofs with the four verses, which the catalogues have as "avant la lettre." In Thorel's sale in Paris, December, 1853, there was an impression, No. 77, before any letters, as well as one with merely the artists' names, No. 78, the latter of which, formerly in the Debois collection, sold for double the price of the first, — No. 77 for 520 *fr.*, No. 78 for 1110 *fr.* The artist's proof, with artists' names, Johnson, No. 87, £84; Macready, No. 59, £74. Beretta, *Della vita,* etc. *del Cav. Longhi,* p. 85, states that Longhi was obliged to go to Florence to have the proofs of the Sposalizio taken, not being satisfied with the few first impressions taken in Milan. — The 2d or common proofs are before the coat of arms and the dedication; they have an inscription of four lines of verses in open letters. The small white stamp is on the left of the lower margin, the large on the right. Archinto, No. 228, 900 *fr.*; Lehrs, No. 172, 200 *th.* The first 1200 prints, according to Heller, *Praktisches Handbuch für Kupferstichsammler,* Leipzig, 1850, were numbered for the subscribers; they are before the inscription on the temple, and with Bardi's address. They were followed by 1200 more, *without* numbers, still without the inscription on the temple, and with Bardi's address. — The plate was then entirely retouched, and the impressions have the name of Lissant as printer. Very recently the plate has been again entirely retouched, and the new impressions are frequently met with.

REMBRANDT *pinx.* The Good Samaritan.

See Smith, *Cat. rais.* 118; Waagen, *Handbook,* II. p. 344. The picture is in the Gallery of the Louvre; Villot, No. 405. The composition differs from Rembrandt's etching of this subject, B. 90. Goethe confounds the two compositions. See his *Sämmtliche Werke,* Stuttgart, 1850–51, 8vo, XXV. p. 310. — Engraved in 1808 for the *Musée Français.*

RAPHAEL *pinx.* The Holy Family in Naples, Madonna of the Pio family; also called "La Bénédiction."

See Passavant, II. 99. The original is in the Gallery of Naples, and there are numerous repetitions. Engraved in 1827, after a school copy, then in the possession of the engraver, ascribed to Gianfrancesco Penni.

RAPHAEL *pinx.* The same.

LONGHI, GIUSEPPE, *continued.*

Artist's proof, before any letters, with merely "Longhi sc." *on the left below, in very small letters traced with the needle.*

Proofs have open letters, and are before the arms and dedication.

There also occur proofs with merely the names of the painter and the engraver. Lehrs, No. 178.

LEONARDO DA VINCI *inv.*, MARCO D' OGGIONE *pinx.* Madonna del Lago.

See Longhena, in Longhi's *Calcografia*, Appendix, p. 420; Beretta, *Vita di Longhi*, p. 91. In the Earl of Harrington's collection, Kensington, is a "small early copy on wood of Leonardo da Vinci's Madonna del Lago, known by Longhi's engraving," which Waagen attributes to Marco d' Oggione. Waagen, *Galleries*, etc., or *Treasures*, IV. p. 238. Engraved in 1825.

Nearly finished engraver's proof before any letters, and before the shading of the infant's figure.

The 1st state of the finished plate is the proof before any letters. Johnson, No. 91, £15 10 *s.* — The 2d state is the proof before letters, with merely the names of the artists. Wilson, *Catalogue raisonné*, p. 81, No. 191, "proof before any letters, the artists' names excepted; in which state six impressions only are said to have been taken." — The 3d state, proof, has but one line of inscription in open letters: *Madonna del Lago.* Archinto, No. 231, 80 *fr.*; Hösel, No. 109, 23½ *th.*; Lehrs, No. 173, 50 *th.* — The 4th state, still called proof, has the title in shaded letters and eight verses in Italian; it is before the coat of arms and the dedication. — The 5th state is the print, with coat of arms and dedication.

RAPHAEL *pinx.* Madonna with the Sleeping Child, "Madonna del Velo."

A square picture. Passavant, II. 57. Engraved from the painting owned by Sig. Brocca in Milan, one of the eight different repetitions and copies, some round and some square, of which the original is not known. Raphael's cartoon is in the Florentine Gallery. Engraved by Longhi in 1829, and finished by Toschi in 1834.

Artist's proof of the plate as finished by Toschi, before letters and before the coat of arms, with merely the artists' names traced with the point: "Raffaello dip:^{se} Raggio dis:^{o} Longhi inc^{o} Toschi ultimò." *On India paper. With the small white stamp of the initials* "G. L."

The proofs have, besides the artists' names, the coat of arms of the Prince of Prussia. — There are also artist's proofs of the plate as Longhi left it, almost finished and quite harmonious; they are without any letters.

LEONARDO DA VINCI *pinx.* Madonna di San Onofrio.

Longhi *dir.*, Marri *sc.* *See* MARRI.

GUIDO *pinx.* St. Joseph with the Infant Christ in his Arms.

LONGHI, GIUSEPPE, *continued.*

"Dal quadro ... esistente nella Galleria Arcivescovile di Milano."

Small piece, oval in a square border, $2\frac{1}{3}$ inches high, $1\frac{3}{4}$ inches broad; engraved in 1812 as a pendant to R. Morghen's plate, of the same size, of Lodovico Caracci's "Madonna col Bambino."

CORREGGIO *pinx.* Magdalen, reading.

See Coxe, p. 125. Engraved in 1809, of the size of the original in the Dresden Gallery. A repetition, or rather copy, is in the collection of Lord Ward. Waagen, *Treasures,* II. p. 234. "The figure ... is entirely worthy of Correggio; at the same time the many details in the landscape ... testify the hand of a skilful Netherlandish painter."

Artist's proof, before letters and coat of arms, having only: "Correggio pin. Joseph Longhi sc." *traced with the needle in very small letters. With the white stamp of the initials of the publisher, Dom. Artaria.*

Purchased from Messrs. Evans for £35. — Debois, No. 457, 585*fr.*; Johnson, No. 90, £21; Archinto, No. 232, 1010*fr.*; Marshall, No. 1075, £27.

Proofs are with the artists' names engraved with the burin, and the coat of arms. Debois, No. 458, 345*fr.*

CORREGGIO *pinx.* The same.

Old impression before retouch and on the first, thin paper of the print, with coat of arms and full inscription.

CORREGGIO *pinx.* The same.

Old impression of the print with the first retouch.

The current modern impressions are from the repeatedly and entirely retouched plate.

ALBANI *pinx.* Galatea.

See Longhi's *Calcografia,* Appendix by Longhena, p. 406. Engraved in 1813 from a picture then owned by the engraver. Such a picture is in the collection of the Earl of Leicester at Holkham. Waagen, *Treasures,* III. p. 419.

Impression of the print, with the title, the dedication, and coat of arms of Prince Beauharnais. With the white stamp of the engraver's initials.

ALBANI *pinx.* The same.

Artist's proof, with merely the names of the artists. With the white stamp of the engraver's initials in the middle of the lower margin.

Purchased for £9 9 *s.* Marshall, No. 1074, £10. Proofs have one line of open letters.

LONGHI *del.* Pan and Syrinx.

Etched in 1816.

Proofs are before letters.

LONGHI, GIUSEPPE, *continued.*

GUIDO *pinx.* The Genius of Music conquering Love.

Cupid is bound to a tree, while a youth burns his arrows. The picture, formerly in the Orleans Gallery, is now owned by T. Hope, Esq. Waagen, *Treasures,* II. p. 113. Engraved in 1794.

GUIDO *pinx.* The same.

Artist's proof, with the names of the artists in very small letters, cut with the needle.

RUBENS *pinx.* Bust of a Negro.

Etched in 1801, after a picture in the collection of Cavaliere Melzi. Longhi, *Calcografia,* Appendix by Longhena, p. 409.

REMBRANDT *pinx.* Filosofo in Contemplazione.

"P. Caronni incise. Gp^{e}. Longhi diresse e terminò. L' originale esiste nel Museo di Parigi." Longhi, *Calcografia,* App. p. 412; Villot, No. 408.

REMBRANDT *pinx.* Filosofo in Meditazione.

"Gpe. Cozzi inc. Gp^{e}. Longhi dir. e terminò. L' originale esiste nel Museo di Parigi." Longhi, *Calcografia,* App. p. 412; Villot, No. 409.

Both plates have in the right-hand corner, below, the stamp in white of a helmeted Minerva, with the inscription, "Di Giuseppe Longhi."

REMBRANDT *pinx.* An Oriental Figure.

Whole length, with a long-stemmed pipe in one hand. Etched in 1796. *See* Smith, *Cat. rais.* Nos. 410 and 433, which two numbers belong to the same picture, described twice from the present engraving by Longhi.

There is such a picture in the Gallery of Cassel.

REMBRANDT *pinx.* Borgomastro Olandese.

Longhi, *Calcografia,* Appendix by Longhena, p. 412.

Etched in 1807–11, from a picture in the "Casa Mamfrini."

SCHOOL OF REMBRANDT. A Man with Book and Cane.

Etched in 1804. Longhi, *Calcografia,* Appendix by Longhena, p. 411.

LONGHI *del.* Bust of an Old Woman.

Etched in 1807–08. Longhi, *Calcografia,* Appendix by Longhena, p. 413.

LONGHI *del.* Bust of a Man with Feathers in his Cap.

Etched in 1811.

GÉRARD *pinx.* **P.** Eugène Beauharnais, Viceroy of Italy.

Whole length figure. Engraved in 1812–14. Longhi, *Calcografia,* Appendix by Longhena, pp. 415, 416.

With open letters, which all the prints have.

GÉRARD *pinx.* **P.** The same.

LONGHI, GIUSEPPE, *continued.*

Proof before the border and before any letters, having merely "G. Longhi" *traced with the point.*

With a stamp in black: *E. N.*

MICHEL-ANGELO *pinx.* **P.** Buonarroti, Michel-Angelo.

Engraved in 1815 for *Vite e Ritratti di illustri Italiani.*

MICHEL-ANGELO *pinx.* **P.** The same.

Proof, i. e. *with open letters.*

MICHEL-ANGELO *pinx.* **P.** The same.

Earliest artist's proof, before any letters.

SIR THOMAS LAWRENCE *pinx.* **P.** Lady Burghersh and her Infant.

Engraved in 1823, with the inscription *Le Delizie materne.*

Artist's proof, before all letters, with merely "Longhi sc." *in very small letters on the right below.*

The proofs have one line of open letters.

P. Dandalo, Enrico, Doge of Venice.

Engraved in 1816 for *Vite e Ritratti di illustri Italiani.*

The proofs have the name *Enrico Dandalo* in open letters.

P. The same.

Artist's proof, before letters, with only the inscription, "Teodoro Matteini dis. Giuseppe Longhi inc."

P. The same.

Still earlier proof, with merely "Longhi sc." *traced in very slender letters.*

SCHIAVONI *pinx.* **P.** Francis I., Emperor of Austria.

SCHIAVONI *pinx.* **P.** The same.

Artist's proof, before the broad border of the plate and before any letters, with only "J. Longhi sc." *in very small letters in the right lower margin.*

LE GROS *pinx.* **P.** Napoleon Bonaparte at Arcole.

Engraved in 1798.

LE GROS *pinx.* **P.** The same.

Proof, with one line of inscription, "Bonaparte," *in slightly shaded uncial letters, and the artists' names in very small letters, traced with the needle.*

P. Napoleon I. as King of Italy, with a Crown of Laurel.

Bust in profile.

Proof, with "Jos. Longhi del. et scul. 1806," — *no further inscription.*

The print (finished plate) has the lettering, "J^{ph} Longhi delin. et sculp. 1806. — Napoleon I. Gall. Imp. Ital. Rex."

Engraved for Napoleon's *Code Civile*, published in Milan by the Stamperia Reale in 1806. Longhi, *Calcografia*, Appendix by *Longhena*, p. 412.

LONGHI, GIUSEPPE, *continued.*

𝔭. Napoleon I. as King of Italy, with the Iron Crown.
"Giuseppe Longhi disegnò ed incise 1812."
The letter N, *in a flaming star, is shaded.*
Engraved for *Vite e Ritratti di illustri Italiani.*

𝔭. The same.
Proof; the letter N *is open, formed of two lines.*

G. Bossi *dis.* 𝔭. Porta, Gian Battista dalla.
"G. Bossi dis. p̃ Bettoni — Beceni inc. G. Longhi dir."
Engraved for Bettoni's *Vite e Ritratti di illustri Italiani.*

Rembrandt *pinx.* 𝔭. Rembrandt.
Etched in 1815 in conjunction with P. Caronni. *See* Caronni.

Stuart *pinx.* 𝔭. Washington, George.
The portrait is in the Athenæum of Boston, U. S. Engraved in 1817 for Nicolò Bettoni's Collection of portraits entitled *Panteon delle Nazioni.* Longhi, *Calcografia,* Appendix by Longhena, p. 418; Beretta, *Della vita* etc. *del Cav. Longhi,* pp. 73, 74.
Proof, with open letters.
Later impressions have the letters shaded.
Very rare artist's proofs are before any letters.

LONGUEIL, JOSEPH DE, engraver, born at Lille in 1736, died at Paris in 1790.

Le Prince *pinx.* Les Modèles.
Proof, with only the artists' names and the coat of arms.

LORENZINI, GIOVANNI ANTONIO, painter and engraver, born at Bologna in 1665, died in 1740.

Raphael *pinx.* Madonna del Baldachino.
See Passavant, ii. 62. The picture is in the Gallery of the Pitti palace. Engraved for the *Raccolta de' quadri dei Granduchi di Toscana.*

Andrea del Sarto *pinx.* Madonna and Child appearing to Six Saints: Onufrius, Laurentius, James, and Sebastian, standing, Magdalen and John the Baptist kneeling.
See Alfred Reumont, pp. 179, 180. In the Gallery of the Pitti palace. Engraved for the *Raccolta de' quadri dei Granduchi di Toscana.*

LORICHON, CONSTANT LOUIS, engraver, born at Paris in 1800. A pupil of Forster.

Raphael *pinx.* Madonna of the Bridgewater Gallery.
See Passavant, ii. 97. Formerly in the Orleans Gallery.

LORICHON, CONSTANT LOUIS, *continued.*

Artist's proof; "Raphael Sanzio pinxit C. Lorichon sculpt 1832" *delicately traced with the needle and in the middle under the print. With the white stamp of the engraver's initials,* "C. L." *On India paper.*

With the engraver's autograph in pencil. Purchased for £5 10*s.*

"The ordinary proofs" have the inscription of the title in open letters. The plate afterwards became the property of the Bibliographic Institution in Hildburghausen.

CORREGGIO *pinx.* The Marriage of St. Catherine.

The picture is in the Gallery of the Louvre; half figures, natural size. Coxe, p. 43; Villot, No. 27.

Proof, with open and traced letters in a border shaded with horizontal lines. With a stamp of the engraver's initials.

LOUIS, ARISTIDE, engraver in Paris, recently deceased. A pupil of Dupont.

SPAGNOLETTO *pinx.* Mater Dolorosa.

Engraved from a picture in the collection of Count Pourtalès, dispersed in the spring of 1865.

The inscription in the border is in open letters.

There are proofs before this inscription, before the artists' names and any letters; and still earlier ones before the border.

GREUZE *pinx.* Innocence.

A girl with a lamb. Engraved from a picture in the collection of Count Pourtalès in Paris, dispersed in the spring of 1865.

Proof before letters, No. 43.

The artist's proofs are before any letters and before the border line.

ARY SCHEFFER *pinx.* Mignon regrettant la Patrie.

Proof before letters, No. 44.

ARY SCHEFFER *pinx.* Mignon aspirant au Ciel.*

Proof before letters, No. 44.

DELAROCHE *pinx.* **P.** Napoleon I.

After the picture in the Standish collection, three quarters length.

Proof before letters, with only the names of the artists, the painters, and the publishers. On India paper.

Artist's proofs are before any letters.

DELAROCHE **P.** *pinx.* Delaroche, Paul.

Proof before any letters.

* The figure of Mignon is the portrait of the artist's daughter. Mrs. Grote, *Memoirs of Ary Scheffer,* p. 85.

LOWRY, WILSON, engraver, born about 1755, worked in London, and died in 1824. A pupil of John Browne.

CLAUDE LORRAIN *pinx.* The Musical Shepherdess.

The picture is in the Grosvenor Gallery. Smith, *Cat. rais.* 124.

A somewhat similar picture is described under 153, but the engraving by Lowry, there mentioned, is after the present picture; and that by Wm. Wilson represents the one described under 93, also engraved by Vivares.

Proof before letters, with the names of the artists, the address, and the coat of arms.

LÜDERITZ, GUSTAV, engraver, born at Berlin in 1804. A pupil of C. Hübner, of Buchhorn, and of Richomme.

RAPHAEL *pinx.* The Archangel Michael vanquishing the Dragon.

From the picture in the Gallery of the Louvre. Passavant, II. 232. The larger representation of the subject.

Open letter.

VELAZQUEZ *pinx.* **P.** The Infanta Margarita. P.

Engraved in mezzotinto, after the picture in the Louvre. Villot, No. 555.

Open letter proof.

KRÜGER *pinx.* **P.** Thorwaldsen. P.

Mezzotinto.

Proof. With Thorwaldsen's signature.

LUKAS VAN LEYDEN, LUKAS JACOBSZ. (i. e. Jacob's son) of Leyden, painter and engraver, born at Leyden in 1494, died there in 1533. A pupil of his father, Hugo Jacob, and of Cornelis Engelbrechtsen. Bartsch, VII.*

Eve presenting the Apple to Adam. B. 10.

From Ackermann's collection.

Cain killing Abel. B. 13.

David playing before Saul. B. 27.

The Adoration of the Magi. B. 37.

Christ bearing the Cross. B. 72.

Christ appearing to Magdalen in the Garden. "Noli me tangere." B. 77.

The Return of the Prodigal Son. B. 78.

The Virgin in a Glory, standing on a Crescent. B. 82.

St. Matthew. B. 101.

St. Jerome near a Rock. B. 112.

* It has been repeatedly stated that the family name of this artist was Damesz, but this is an error. Lukas Damesz was the name of the son of his only daughter. See Bartsch, VII. p. 334.

LUKAS VAN LEYDEN, *continued.*

St. Jerome in his Chamber. B. 114.
Harrach, No. 1209, 110 *fr.*

The Dance of Magdalen. B. 122.
Quandt, No. 858, 300 *th.*; Harrach, No. 1217, 970 *fr.*

The Monk Sergius killed by Mohammed. B. 126.
With the initials and from the collection of William Edwards.
Debois, No. 473, 350 *fr.*; Harrach, No. 1221, 710 *fr.*

Virgil the Magician suspended in a Basket. B. 136.
Maberly, No. 329, £8 8*s.*; Harrach, No. 1225, 430 *fr.*

Ensign with a Banner. B. 140.
The Promenade. B. 144.
Gentleman and Lady. B. 145.
A Man and a Woman seated in a Landscape; he is handing her a Vase. B. 148.

The Milkmaid. B. 158.
From the collection and with the initials of François Debois.

P. Lukas van Leyden. B. 173.

*** All the impressions of the above prints of Lukas van Leyden are before any address.

LUTMA, JAN, the younger, goldsmith, etcher and engraver in mezzotinto and with the punch, "opus mallei," born at Groningen about 1609, died at Amsterdam in 1689. A pupil of his father of the same name.

P. P. C. Hooft, "Alter Tacitus."
"Opus Mallei per J. Lutma." Represented as a sculptured bust.

LUTZ, PETER, engraver, born at Munich in 1799. A pupil of Langer and of C. Hess.

CORREGGIO *pinx.* Madonna of St. Francis.
The picture is in the Dresden Gallery. Coxe, p. 30. Engraved in 1834.

CORREGGIO *pinx.* The same.
Proof, with the title in cursive writing and before the coat of arms and dedication.
The artist's proofs have merely the artists' names; and a very few impressions were taken before any letters.

BAGNOCAVALLO *pinx.* Madonna in a Glory, with four Saints.
The picture is in the Dresden Gallery. Engraved in 1829.
The proofs are before letters; the artist's proofs before any letters.

AUGUST RIEDEL *pinx.* Judith.

LUTZ, PETER, *continued.*

The picture is owned by the King of Bavaria. Nagler, *K.-L.* XIII. p. 154.
Artist's proof before any letters. On India paper.

M.

McARDELL, JAMES, mezzotinto engraver, born in Ireland about 1710, died in London in 1765.

VAN DYCK *pinx.* Time clipping the Wings of Love.

The picture is in the Marlborough collection at Blenheim. Smith, *Cat. rais.* No. 262; Waagen, *Treasures,* III. p. 122.

SIR JOSHUA REYNOLDS *pinx.* Lady Fenhoulet, when Ann Day.

Proof, with the names of the artists and the address, but without the name of the person represented.

McINNES, EDWARD, English mezzotinto engraver of the present day.

MISS MARGARET GILLES *pinx.* **P.** William Wordsworth.

Proof.

MAJOR, THOMAS, English engraver, born about 1715, died in 1768.

TENIERS *pinx.* The Village Surgeon.

See Smith, *Cat. rais.* 419.

TENIERS *pinx.* Grand Village Festival.

See Smith, *Cat. rais.* 495. Engraved in 1752 from a picture then in the possession of B. Cleve, Esq.

The entire margin and inscription of the plate is cut off.

MALLERY, KAREL VAN, designer and engraver, born at Antwerp in 1576. He followed the style of the Wierxes.

The Virgin and Child.

In 8vo.

With four lines of inscription "Gaudia matris . . . tonanti." *Without the engraver's name, but with* "Joa. Galle exc."

MANDEL, JOHANN AUGUST EDUARD, designer and engraver, born at Berlin in 1809. A pupil of Buchhorn.

RAPHAEL *pinx.* Madonna della Sedia, or della Seggiola.

In the Gallery of the Pitti palace in Florence. *See* Passavant, II. 226. Engraved in 1865.

Proof before letters, with the names of the artists and of the publisher.

There are artist's proofs, before any letters, with merely the engraver's name slightly traced in the middle, and *épreuves de remarque,* with a very

MANDEL, JOHANN AUGUST EDUARD, *continued.*

small white spot left on the cross of St. John, of which state only 25 impressions were taken. These were published for 100 thalers, but a few months after fetched 160 thalers.

RAPHAEL *pinx.* Madonna of the Colonna Family.

See Passavant, II. 59, and III. p. 100. The picture is in the Berlin Gallery.

Proof before letters, with the names of the artists, of the printer, and the publisher.

The artist's proofs are before any letters, with merely, *E. Mandel fec.* 1853, slightly cut with the needle.

RAPHAEL *pinx.* **P.** "Raphael at the age of Fifteen."

The portrait in the Louvre, — a lovely youth with fair hair and large eyes, resting his head on his hand. It probably represents some young artist-friend of Raphael. Passavant, II. 61, and III. p. 101.

Artist's proof, before any letters, with merely, "E. Mandel fec. 1860," *slightly cut with the needle.*

BEGAS *pinx.* Die Lurlei.

Engraved for the Berlin Art Union for 1839–40.

Open letters.

LÉOP. ROBERT *pinx.* La Vedova.

Robert's last painting; in the collection of M. Marcotte d'Argenteuil.

Proof before letters, with only the names of the artists, of the publishers, and the printer. On India paper.

The artist's proofs have only *Mandel fecit* slightly traced with the needle in the middle under the plate.

POLLACK *pinx.* Italian Goatherd Boy.

Proof with open letters, formed of two lines. On India paper.

Debois, No. 482, "Épreuve d'artiste avant toutes lettres, seulement on lit, *Mandel fecit Paris* 1840 tracé à la pointe; elle est sur papier de Chine," 120 *fr.*; George Smith, No. 941, £ 7 10 *s.*

HILDEBRANDT *pinx.* The Warrior and his Child.

The picture is in the Wagner Gallery of Modern Paintings in Berlin.

Proof with open letters.

An artist's proof, before letters, Colnaghi's sale, May, 1865, No. 1191, £ 3 6 *s.*

TITIAN *pinx.* **P.** Titian.

The picture is in the Berlin Gallery. Engraved in 1843.

1*st engraver's proof, before the border. The portrait is represented in a frame in which, below, there is a tablet for the name; this impression is before the frame, and before any letters. On India paper.*

MANDEL, JOHANN AUGUST EDUARD, *continued.*

"Artist's proofs" have the ornamented border, with the tablet left white, and below it, in the middle of the margin, merely the name *Mandel* traced with the needle. — Proofs have only the names of the painter and the engraver, and the tablet left blank.

VAN DYCK *pinx.* **P.** Van Dyck.

The picture is in the Gallery of the Louvre. Villot, No. 152. Engraved in 1840.

Proof before letters, having merely the names of the artists, the publishers, and printer, and the tablet slightly shaded with horizontal lines, without inscription. On India paper.

Artist's proofs are before any letters and with the tablet white. G. Smith, 1861, No. 938, £ 6.

VAN DYCK *pinx.* **P.** Charles I.

From the picture in the Dresden Gallery, a three fourths length portrait. Engraved in 1851.

Artist's proof, with merely "Mandel fec." *in the middle of the lower margin, traced with the point. On India paper.*

G. Smith, 1861, No. 936, £ 6 10 *s.* — Present price £ 10.

Proofs have the artists' names.

DORIS STOCK *del.* 1789. **P.** Mozart.

Engraved in 1858 en medallion.

MANTEGNA, ANDREA, painter and engraver, born at Padua in 1431, died at Mantua in 1506. A scholar of F. Squarcione. Bartsch, XIII.

The Entombment. B. 3.

One of the earliest delicate impressions, made by means of a roller, by hand.

Marshall, No. 1084, £ 11 10 *s.*; Harrach, No. 1421, 315 *fr.*

Triumphal Procession, Roman Senators. B. 11.

Triumphal Procession, Elephants and Torches. B. 12.

Triumphal Procession, Soldiers and Trophies. B. 13.

*** These pieces Mantegna engraved from his studies for the famous Triumphs of Cæsar, a series of nine pictures, painted in distemper, and now at Hampton Court.

MARATTI, CARLO, painter and etcher, born at Camurano in the Marquisate of Ancona in 1625, died at Rome in 1713. A pupil of Andrea Sacchi. Bartsch, XXI.

Virgin and Child with Magdalen. B. 6.

MARATTI, CARLO, *continued.*

With the inscription, "Carolus Maratus inuen. et fecit Romae."

The proofs are before this inscription.

MARC-ANTONIO, (full name, Marc-Antonio RAIMONDI,) goldsmith, niellist, and engraver, born at Bologna about 1488, died in his native town in 1534. He was first a pupil of the painter and goldsmith Francesco Francia, then studied the works of Dürer and Lukas van Leyden, and finally gave himself up to the school of Raphael, whose drawings he multiplied with the graver. Bartsch, xiv.

*** *All the following impressions are before any retouch and before address, except when the contrary is expressly stated.*

Raphael *del.* Adam and Eve. B. 1.

Very early impression, in perfect condition.

From the collections and with the marks of Sir Peter Lely and Wm. Esdaile; this same copy was also sold in the Ottley collection, No. 1444. Purchased for £63 from Messrs. Evans; B. Delessert, No. 36, 1520 *fr.*; Marshall, No. 1570, £86; Goddard, No. 121, £132.

Raphael *del.* David cutting off the Head of Goliath. B. 10.

3d state of the plate, with the 1st address, that of Antonio Salamanca.

The 2d address is that of Van Aelst. — The rare 1st state of the plate is before the tablet with the monogram of the engraver; the 2d state has the monogram, but is before any address.

Raphael *del.* The Massacre of the Innocents: with the Fir Tree. B. 18.

2d state of the plate, with Raphael's name and Marc-Antonio's monogram, but before any retouch, and before the address of Salamanca.

Our impression is soiled, mended, and pasted down.

A fine impression, Johnson, No. 136, £61; Drugulin's sale, London, 1866, No. 1265, £52.

Raphael *del.* The Massacre of the Innocents, without the Fir Tree. B. 20.

Fine impression of the 1st state, before Salamanca's address.

Maberly, No. 414, £35; George Smith, No. 1073, £44; Goddard, No. 126, £50.

Raphael *del.* The Saviour at the Table of Simon the Levite. B. 23.

1st state, before the retouch, before the parqueted floor, and before the address of Lafreri.

From Otto's collection.

Raphael *del.* The Deposition from the Cross. B. 32.

Fine and very early impression.

From Otto's collection. — Delessert, No. 49, 910 *fr.*; Marshall, No. 1575, £ 22 10*s.*

MARC–ANTONIO, *continued.*

Raphael *del.* "La Vierge au bras nu." The Dead Christ at the Feet of Mary. B. 34.

Fine and early impression.

Passavant says (*Rafael von Urbino*, II. p. 631) of this engraving, that it surpasses in delicacy of expression everything we know of Marc-Antonio so much, that he is inclined to ascribe it to another highly gifted master, of whom no other work is known. Weigel, *Kunst-Catalog*, No. 16504, calls it "a truly divine work," but considers it engraved by Marc-Antonio, in the time of his plate of Lucretia, and attributes its eminent superiority to *Raphael's own drawing on the plate.* Wellesley, No. 346, £38.

Raphael *del.* Paul Preaching at Athens. B. 44.

Impression before the retouch and before address, but not one of the earliest of this state.

A fine impression, Maberly, No. 418, £15.

Raphael *del.* La Vierge à l'escalier. B. 45.

Very early and powerful impression.

Raphael *del.* La Vierge assise sur les nues. B. 47.

Very early and perfect impression.

Our copy was purchased from Messrs. Evans in 1855 for £35. It has the stamp of Thomas Lloyd, to whose collection it formerly belonged, catal. No. 832, and from which it was purchased in 1825, together with Marc-Antonio's print B. 45, for £3 1*s.* by W. Y. Ottley; from Ottley's collection, 1837, No. 1460, it was purchased by Molteno for £3 5*s.* He sold it again, and an impression like ours occurs again in Thorel's sale, Paris, Dec. 1853, No. 87, where it was purchased by Messrs. Evans for 610 *fr.* Delessert, No. 54, 510 *fr.*

Raphael *del.* La Vierge à la longue cuisse. B. 57.

1st state, before address.

From Otto's collection.

Raphael *del.* Holy Family, the Child sucking. B. 60.

Fine and harmonious early impression.

Quandt, No. 1727, 90 *th.*

Raphael *del.* La Vierge au berceau. B. 63.

1st state, before Salamanca's address.

Harrach, No. 1884, 505 *fr.*

Baccio Bandinelli *del.* The Martyrdom of St. Lawrence. B. 104.

Raphael *del.* The Five Saints. B. 113.

Early and powerful impression.

From Otto's collection.—Wellesley, No. 366, £20; a fine impression,

MARC-ANTONIO, *continued.*

Johnson, No. 132, £66; Delessert, No. 67, 500 *fr.*; Harrach, No. 1889, 2,000 *fr.*

RAPHAEL *del.* St. Cecilia. B. 116.

One of the earliest impressions, with the very dark shade under the chin of the saint, resembling a necklace.

From Otto's collection. — Thorel, No. 90, 1086 *fr.*; Delessert, No. 69, 870 *fr.*; Lasalle, No. 318, 1350 *fr.*; Goddard, No. 136, £ 75 10 *s.*

RAPHAEL *del.* "The Martyrdom of St. Felicitas"; more correctly, of St. Cecilia. B. 117.

See Passavant, III. p. 151.

1*st state, before address.*

G. Smith, No. 1069, £ 21; Wellesley, No. 367, £33; Goddard, No. 142, £ 33.

RAPHAEL *del.* Dido. B. 187.

Early harmonious impression.

From the collection of De Bammeville, No. 479; bought for £ 12. It was previously in the collection of Cardinal Fesch. — Goddard, No. 146, £ 36.

RAPHAEL *del.* The same. B. 187.

Impression of the retouched plate.

RAPHAEL *del.* Lucretia. B. 192.

Early harmonious impression.

From the collection of De Bammeville, No. 48; bought for £ 20 10 *s.* It was previously in the collection of Cardinal Fesch. — Wellesley, No. 306, £ 76 13 *s.*

RAPHAEL *del.* Cleopatra, or, more correctly, Ariadne. B. 199.

Raphael took the motive from the antique, formerly in the garden of the Belvedere, now in the Museo Pio-Clementino in Rome.

Very fine impression of this beautiful plate.

From Otto's collection. — Debois, No. 530, 201 *fr.*; Goddard, No. 150, £ 68.

RAPHAEL *del.* Alexander puts Homer's Works in the Tomb of Achilles. B. 207.

Fine impression of the 1*st state, before Salamanca's address.*

From Otto's collection. — Debois, No. 531, 141 *fr.*; Maberly, No. 427, £ 43.

GIANANTONIO RAZZI *del.* The Triumph of Titus. B. 213.

The original drawing by Gianantonio Razzi, formerly attributed to Andrea Mantegna, also to Fr. Francia, is in the Musée Impérial in Paris.

A very fine and powerful impression.

MARC-ANTONIO, *continued.*

Our copy was successively in the collections of Dènon, Debois (No. 533, 240*fr.*), and Lasalle (No. 322, 460*fr.*). It was purchased from Messrs. Evans for £ 30. — Harrach, No. 1902, 800*fr.*

Two Fauns carrying the Infant Bacchus in a Basket. B. 230.

From a drawing probably by Raphael, after an antique bas-relief "on a sarcophagus found in Crete." (*Catalogue of the Manchester Exhibition in* 1857, Suppl. p. 31.)

From the collection of De Bammeville; purchased for £ 15 10 *s.*

RAPHAEL *del.* The Judgment of Paris. B. 245.

Impression of the retouched plate with the address of Salamanca, which has been erased on the print.

A good impression, of course before address, Wellesley, No. 406, £ 63; Goddard, No. 269, £ 67; a very fine one, Johnson, No. 135, £ 320.

RAPHAEL *del.* Parnassus. B. 247.

Clear and powerful impression.

From the collection of De Bammeville, No. 495; purchased for £ 33 10 *s.* — Lasalle, No. 327, 600*fr.*; Goddard, No. 271 (formerly in Sir P. Lely's collection), £ 170.

RAPHAEL *del.* A Faun with a Child, who seems to ask him to play the Flute. B. 296.

With the names of De Valois (whose collection was sold in Paris, 1801), and Dom. Artaria on the back. Purchased from Messrs. Evans for £ 9 9 *s.*

RAPHAEL *del.* Venus wiping her Left Foot, after leaving the Bath. B. 297.

Fine impression, but with two small oil spots.

From the Otto collection. Goddard, No. 280, £ 37.

RAPHAEL *del.* The Vintage. B. 306.

Perfect impression.

From the collection of De Bammeville, No. 507; purchased for £ 11 11 *s.* — Lasalle, No. 329, 650*fr.*; Marshall, No. 1585, £ 12 15 *s.*; Goddard, No. 283, £ 30.

Designer not known. Cupid and Three Infants. B. 320.

Good old impression.

Purchased for £ 7 7 *s.* — Debois, No. 558, 103*fr.*; Harrach, No. 1917, 600 *fr.*

RAPHAEL *del.* Cupid and the Three Graces. B. 344.

Drawn for the frescos in the Chigi palace (the Farnesina).

Very early and powerful impression, uncommonly fine.

From the Otto collection. Goddard, No. 298, £ 26.

MARC-ANTONIO, *continued.*

RAPHAEL *del.* Galatea. B. 350.

Drawn for the fresco in the Farnesina.

Before the address, but not a very early impression.

From the Otto collection. — A good impression, Wellesley, No. 445, £ 44.

RAPHAEL *del.* "Quos ego." Neptune quelling the Storm. B. 352.

1st state, before retouch and before the address (of Salamanca). Superb impression, in fine condition and with margin.

Logette, 1817, No. 91, 380*fr.* Another impression before the retouch and before address, in the collection of Van Putten, was bought in 1820 for 500*fr.*, for the Imperial Library in Paris.

La Femme au Croissant. B. 354.

According to Bartsch, "apparently after Fr. Francia's design"; according to Passavant, *Rafael von Urbino,* I. p. 581, the design is by a pupil of Raphael.

Fine impression.

Debois, No. 572, 155*fr.*

GIORGIONE *del.* "Raphael's Dream." B. 359.

Not from a design by Raphael, but evidently by Giorgione or his school.

Impression before retouch.

Wellesley, I. No. 448, £ 26.

RAPHAEL *del.* Prudence. B. 371.

From Prince de Paar's collection, No. 2008.

RAPHAEL *del.* The Two Sibyls with the Zodiac. B. 397.

From Prince de Paar's collection, No. 2013.

RAPHAEL *del.* The Pestilence. B. 417.

Without address, but not a very early impression.

A fine impression, Debois, No. 591, 399*fr.*; Goddard, No. 446, £ 20.

MICHEL-ANGELO *del.* Two Naked Men. B. 464.

Early and powerful impression.

Goddard, No. 573, £ 8 8 *s.*

MARCENAY DE GHUY, ANTOINE, amateur painter and etcher, born at Arnay-sur-Aron in 1722, died at Paris in 1811.

J. PAROCEL *pinx.* Fight of Cavalry.

Without coat of arms or letters, only with the artists' names and date, traced very small, and the number 13.

TINTORETTO *pinx.* 𝔓. Tintoretto.

Engraved from a picture then in the collection of the Count de Vence.

MARCHESE, VINCENZO.

S. Marco Convento dei Padri Predicatori in Firenze illustrato e inciso principalmente nei dipinti del B. Giovanni Angelico, con la vita dello stesso pittore, e un sunto storico del convento medesimo del P. Vincenzo Marchese. Firenze, 1853. fol. 163 pages of text, including index, besides half-title, title-page, and preface.

Painters.	Title.	Engravers.
D. Cellesi.	1. Interior of the Second Cloister.	D. Chiossone.
Fra Angelico.	2. St. Peter Martyr.	F. Livy.
Fra Angelico.	3. Pietà.	F. Livy.
Fra Angelico.	4. Crucifixion and Saints.	D. Chiossone.
Fra Angelico.	5. Crucifixion.	F. Livy.
Fra Benedetto min.	6. St. Agnes.	S. Martelli.
Fra Benedetto.	7. Christ blessing the Virgin and Martyrs.	R. Bettazzi.
Fra Benedetto.	8. Virgins singing.	D. Chiossone.
Fra Eustachio.	9. David praying.	F. Zannoni.
Fra Angelico.	10. The Annunciation.	D. Chiossone.
Fra Angelico.	11. Same subject, different composition.	F. Livy.
Fra Angelico.	12. Nativity.	R. Bettazzi.
Fra Angelico.	13. Adoration of the Magi.	Bonaini.
Fra Angelico.	14. Presentation in the Temple.	D. Chiossone.
Fra Angelico.	15. Baptism of Christ.	D. Chiossone.
Fra Angelico.	16. Christ in the Desert.	D. Chiossone.
Fra Angelico.	17. Sermon on the Mount.	D. Chiossone.
Fra Angelico.	18. Transfiguration.	D. Chiossone.
Fra Angelico.	19. Institution of the Sacrament.	D. Chiossone.
Fra Angelico.	20. Prayer in the Garden.	F. Livy.
Fra Angelico.	21. Treachery of Judas.	D. Chiossone.
Fra Angelico.	22. Christ mocked.	F. Livy.
Fra Angelico.	23. Christ going to Calvary.	F. Livy.
Fra Angelico.	24. Crucifixion.	F. Livy.
Fra Angelico.	25. Wound with the Spear.	Bonaini.
Fra Angelico.	26. Crucifixion and Saints.	P. Nocchi.
Fra Angelico.	27. Descent from the Cross.	F. Livy.
Fra Angelico	28. Entombment.	A. Perfetti.
Fra Angelico.	29. Descent to Limbo.	D. Chiossone.
Fra Angelico.	30. The Marys at the Sepulchre.	F. Livy.
Fra Angelico.	31. Noli me tangere.	E. Damele.
Fra Angelico.	32. Christ and Pilgrims to Emmaus. "L'Ospitalità."	F. Livy.

MARCHESE, VINCENZO, *continued.*

Fra Angelico.	33. Coronation of the Virgin.	F. Livy.
Fra Angelico.	34. Virgin and Saints.	F. Livy.
Fra Angelico.	35. Virgin and Saints.	F. Livy.
Fra Bartolommeo.	36. Virgin and Saints.	S. Martelli.
Fra Angelico.	37. Crucifixion and St. Dominic.	F. Livy.
Ghirlandajo.	38. Last Supper.	D. Chiossone.
Fra Bartolommeo.	39. Christ in Emmaus.	A. Perfetti.
Fra Bartolommeo.	40. Virgin and Child.	F. Livy.

MARCK, QUIRIN, designer and engraver, born at Littau in Moravia in 1753, died at Vienna in 1811. A pupil of Schmutzer.

RUBENS *pinx.* Diogenes and Alexander.

Engraved in 1784 after a picture then owned by M. Ch. de Lackner in Vienna.

MARCO DA RAVENNA, that is, Marco Dente of Ravenna, where he was born in the latter half of the fifteenth century; he died at Rome in 1527. A scholar and assistant of Marc-Antonio. Bartsch, XIV.

F. SALVIATI *del.* Jupiter with the Thunderbolt in his Hand. B. 216.

Early impression, without address, on thin paper.

RAPHAEL *del.* Venus, Juno, and Ceres. B. 327.

Drawn for the frescos in the loggia of the Chigi palace (the Farnesina).

Early impression, without address.

A Youth extracting a Thorn from his Foot. B. 480.

After the antique in the Capitol.

Early impression, without address.

GIULIO ROMANO *inv.* The Siege of Carthage.

A copy of G. Pencz's engraving. It is attributed to Marco. Nagler, *Künstler-Lexicon*, art. "Marco da Ravenna," No. 44. *See* PENCZ.

MARRI, GIUSEPPE, engraver, born at Milan about 1798. A pupil of Longhi.

LEONARDO DA VINCI *pinx.* Madonna of San Onofrio with the Child blessing the Donor.*

See Rigollot, No. 19. Platner and Bunsen, III. iii. p. 585. Fresco, now under glass, in the cloister of San Onofrio, on the Gianiculo in Rome.

Proof before any letters.

MARTELLI, L., an Italian engraver of our own time.

* Supposed to be the papal Datarius Baltasar Turini of Brescia, or, more probably, the founder of the cloister, Niccolò di Forca Palena.

MARTELLI, L., *continued.*

BRONZINO *pinx.* **P.** Maria de' Medici, when a young girl.

The engraving has a white stamp below, with the inscription, *Società edit. . . . della Galleria di Firenza.*

MARTELLI, S., an Italian engraver of the present day.

See V. MARCHESE, "San Marco," etc., plates 6 and 36.

MARTINET, ACHILLE LOUIS, designer and engraver, born at Paris in 1806. A pupil of Pauquet, Forster, and Heim.

RAPHAEL *pinx.* Holy Family called "La Vierge au Palmier."

The picture is in the Bridgewater Gallery. Passavant, II. 38. Engraved in 1844.

Artist's proof before any letters. On India paper.

Purchased for £ 7 7 *s.*

Proofs are before letters, with only the artists' names engraved.

RAPHAEL *pinx.* Madonna with the Goldfinch, "Madonna del Cardellino."

See Passavant, II. 36. The picture is in the Tribune of the Uffizj Gallery in Florence. Engraved in 1838.

Proof before letters, with merely, "Peint par Raphael Sanzio, gravé par Achille Martinet," *and, below, the names of the printer and publisher. On India paper.*

Artist's proofs have, slightly traced with the needle, *Peint par Raphael Sanzio, Dessiné et gravé par Achille Martinet.* There are still earlier proofs with merely the engraver's name traced with the needle in the middle of the lower margin of the plate.

RAPHAEL *pinx.* Madonna di Granduca.

See Passavant, II. 27. The picture is — or was — in one of the ducal apartments in the Pitti palace in Florence. Engraved in 1838. A slightly shaded engraving.

Has open letters. On India paper.

The proofs are before letters.

RAPHAEL *pinx.* La Vierge à la Redemption.

See Passavant, II. p. 410, g, and III. p. 171, a. A picture of Raphael's school, formerly owned by Count Verme in Milan, now by Sig. Tosoni, in the same place. Engraved in 1845.

Has open letters.

Proofs are before letters ; artist's proofs before all letters.

DELAROCHE *pinx.* "Mary in the Desert," or Hagar and Ishmael.

The picture is in the collection of the Marquis of Hertford. Waagen, *Galleries,* etc., or *Treasures,* IV. p. 85.

MARTINET, ACHILLE LOUIS, *continued.*

Proof before letters, with only the names of the artists, the publisher, and the printer. On India paper.

DELAROCHE *pinx.* Charles I. in the Guard Room of Cromwell's Soldiers.

The picture is in the Bridgewater Gallery. Waagen, *Treasures,* II. p. 54.

Proof before letters, with only the names of the artists, the publisher, and the printer. On India paper.

Artist's proofs have merely the name of the engraver, in the middle of the lower margin, traced with the point.

L. GALLAIT *pinx.* The Last Moments of Count Egmont in Prison.

The picture is in the Museum in Brussels.

Proof before letters, with only the names of the artists, the publisher, and the printer.

MARTINET, ALPHONSE.

WINTERHALTER *pinx.* A Little Girl (evidently a portrait), leaning on a Dog, in a Landscape.

Modern mezzotinto engraving.

Proof before letters, with only the names of the artists and the publisher.

MARTINI, PIETRO ANTONIO, designer and engraver, born at Parma in 1739, died at London in 1797. He studied in Paris under Le Bas.

H. RAMBERG *del.* The Exhibition of the Royal Academy in London in 1787.*

MASON, JAMES, English landscape engraver, born in 1710, died in 1780.

CLAUDE LORRAIN *pinx.* The Landing of Æneas in Italy; or, The Morning of the Roman Empire.

See Smith, *Cat. rais.* 122. In the collection of the Earl of Radnor, Longford Castle. Waagen, *Treasures,* III. p. 140, and IV. p. 358.

CLAUDE LORRAIN *pinx.* Evening, the Sun setting.

In an oval. Engraved in 1771 from a picture then in the possession of Sir Richard Lyttleton. Smith, *Cat. rais.* 308.

Proof, before letters.

With the initials and from the collection of Dr. E. Peart.

HOBBEMA *pinx.* The Rural Village.

See Nagler, VIII. p. 395, No. 3; Smith, *Cat. rais.* 65. The picture is in the Grosvenor Gallery.

Proof before letters, with merely "Hobbima Pinxit ... James Mason Sculpsit ... Publish'd Feb. 20th 1786 by John & Josiah Boydell in Cheapside London," *very slightly traced with the point; and, close under the print, the address repeated,* "John & Josiah Boydell, excudit (sic) London 1786."

* Le Blanc calls it, erroneously, "Exposition au Salon du Louvre en 1787."

MASQUELIER, CLAUDE LOUIS, engraver, born at Paris in 1781, died in his native place in 1852. A pupil of his father, Louis Joseph Masquelier, and of Langlois.

RAPHAEL *pinx.* The Entombment.

See Passavant, II. 54 and III. p. 98. Engraved in 1848, from the picture in the Gallery of the Borghese palace. Without the predella, painted in chiar-oscuro, representing the Three Cardinal Virtues, which is now separated from it, and in the Gallery of the Vatican.

Artists' proof before letters, having merely the names of the artists traced slightly with the needle. On India paper.

Purchased for £ 14.

The proofs have the names of the artists in uncial letters, engraved with the burin.

RAPHAEL *pinx.* Madonna di Casa Colonna.

See Passavant, II. 59. The picture is in the Berlin Gallery. Engraved in 1820.

MASSARD, JEAN-BAPTISTE, the father, engraver, born at Bélesme in Perche in 1740, died at Paris in 1822.

VAN DYCK *pinx.* Madonna nursing her Child. "La plus belle des Mères."

Engraved from the collection of M. Corsivart. Not mentioned by Smith.

With the engraver's address.

VAN DYCK *pinx.* **P.** Charles I. with his Queen and Children.

The picture is in Windsor Castle; Waagen, *Treasures,* II. p. 426; and there is a duplicate in the possession of the Duke of Richmond. Smith, *Cat. rais.* 224. Engraved in 1784.

Artist's proof, before any letters.

GREUZE *pinx.* La Mère bien aimée.

See Smith, *Cat. rais.* 142.

With the signature of the artists on the back of the print.

GREUZE *pinx.* La Cruche cassée.

In the Gallery of the Louvre. Villot, 263; Smith, *Cat. rais.* 42.

Impression with the address of Greuze.

MASSARD, J.-B. RAPHAEL-URBAIN, the son, engraver, born at Paris in 1775. A pupil of his father.

RAPHAEL *pinx.* St. Cecilia.

See Passavant, II. 117. The picture is in the Gallery of Bologna. Engraved in 1810.

1st artist's proof before letters, having only the names of the artists, in larger letters, formed of dots.

MASSARD, J.-B. RAPHAEL-URBAIN, *continued.*

RAPHAEL *pinx.* The same.

2d artist's proof before letters, with only the names of the artists, written in smaller letters (not formed of dots).

The proofs are before the coat of arms and before the dedication.

LEONARDO DA VINCI *pinx.* **P.** La Gioconda.

See Rigollot, No. 60. The picture is in the Gallery of the Louvre. Villot, No. 484. Engraved for the *Musée Français.*

Proof before letters, with only the artists' names.

LEONARDO DA VINCI *pinx.* The same.

Artist's proof, the names of the artists in uncial letters, formed of dots.

FABRE *pinx.* **P.** Clarke, Duc de Feltre.

MASSARD, L., a French engraver of the present day.

MURILLO *pinx.* The Conception.

From the great picture in the Louvre, painted for the church Los Venerables at Seville, from which Marshal Soult carried it off. Stirling's *Annals,* II. p. 883; Villot, No. 546 bis.

Proof before letters.

L. MASSARD *del.* **P.** Horace Vernet.

MASSÉ, JEAN-BAPTISTE, painter and engraver, born at Paris in 1687, died there in 1767.

COYPEL *pinx.* **P.** Antoine Coypel.

Engraved in 1717, for his admission into the Academy.

MASSON, ANTOINE, painter and engraver, born at Loury, near Orleans, in 1636, died at Paris in 1700. Robert-Dumesnil, II.

TITIAN *pinx.* The Supper at Emmaus. R.-D. 5.

The picture is in the Gallery of the Louvre. Villot, No. 462. It passed from the collection of the Duke of Mantua into that of Charles I., after whose death it was purchased by Eberhard Jabach of Cologne, banker in Paris, who afterwards sold it to Louis XIV. There is a tradition that the person on the right of the Saviour is the portrait of Charles V.; that on the left of Cardinal Ximenes and the page, Philip II. The engraving is called "La Nappe," from the exquisite work of the tablecloth.

3d state, the finished plate. Early impression, before the eye of the Saviour had suffered, and before the retouch in the air, etc.

In the 1st state, "*unique, peut-être,*" the nails on the feet of the Saviour

MASSON, ANTOINE, *continued.*

are white; — in the 2d state, "*rare,*" the building in the background on the right is covered only with a few strokes.

N. MIGNARD *pinx.* **P.** Brisacier, Guillaume de, Secrétaire des Commandemens de la Reyne. R.-D. 15.

The engraving is known under the name of "The Gray-headed Man." Engraved in 1664.

2d state with the two misspellings, "Brisasier" *and* "Segretaire."

N. MIGNARD *pinx.* The same. R.-D. 15.

4th state, with both misspellings corrected.

The 1st state is before the inscription in the oval border. Debois, No. 641, 430 *fr.*; Duke of Buckingham, No. 1681; Archinto, No. 242, 315 *fr.*; Marshall, No. 1101, £8 8 *s.*; Colnaghi, May, 1865, No. 584, £10 15 *s.* — The 3d state has one misspelling, Segretaire.

T. BLANCHET *pinx.* **P.** Charrier, Gaspard, Lieutenant, criminel au présidial de Lyon. R.-D. 16.

2d state, with the border, the arms, and the inscription finished.

In the 1st state these parts are not finished, the inscription is only indicated; — in the 3d, the tassel is parted in two.

P. MIGNARD *pinx.* **P.** Cureau de la Chambre, Marin, médecin ordinaire du roi. R.-D. 24.

Engraved in 1665.

1st state, before the cross-hatching on the left cheek.

Von Rumohr, No. 2236, 22 *th.*; Von Quandt, No. 1566, 24 *th.*

The 2d state has the cross-hatching; — the 3d has it over the whole face; — the 4th has *E. Desrochers* below in the oval; — in the 5th, the address was erased again and the plate was ruined.

N. MIGNARD *pinx.* **P.** Dupuis, Pierre, peintre de fleurs. R.-D. 25.

Engraved in 1663.

2 impressions.

P. MIGNARD *pinx.* **P.** Guise, Marie de Lorraine, Duchesse de. R.-D. 32.

Engraved in 1684.

3d state, before the rabbit after the word "pinxit," "*rare.*"

The 1st state is before letters and border, "*très rare*"; — the 2d, with unfinished border and before the letters, "*très rare aussi*"; — the 4th with the word *Roma*, and the rabbit, and the point after the word *pinxit* forms a zero.

N. MIGNARD *pinx.* **P.** Harcourt, Henri de Lorraine, Comte d', called Le Cadet La Perle. R.-D. 34.

Engraved in 1667.

MASSON, ANTOINE, *continued.*

1st state, before the figure resembling the number 4 on the left margin of the plate.

The 2d state has this 4; — in the 3d the figure is again erased, but there is a strange retouch visible over the head in the hair.

MASSON *del.* ? **P.** Helyot, Madame. R.-D. 36.

In 8vo. Without the name of the painter.

MASSON *pinx.* **P.** Le Fèvre d'Ormesson, Olivier. R.-D. 58.

Engraved in 1665.

2d state, with the correction in the curls.

In the 1st state the hair forms an arch over the brow; the figure is less finished.

MASSON *pinx.* **P.** Medavy, François Rouxel de. R.-D. 51.

2d state, with the letters.

The 1st state is before letters. Engraved in 1677.

MASSON *pinx.* **P.** Patin, Gui. R.-D. 59.

Engraved in 1678.

2d state, before the address of the engraver.

The 1st state is before letters; the 3d state has, on the right hand: *a Paris rue St. Germain de l'Auxerrois Proche lespée de Bois.*

MASSON *del.* **P.** Patin, Charles. R.-D. 60.

Engraved in 1670.

Impression with the inscription from a separate plate, "In effigiem V. C. Caroli Patin," *etc., and four Latin verses.*

MASSON *pinx.* **P.** Turgot, Antoine, de St. Clair. R.-D. 66.

MASSON, ANTOINE, an engraver of the present day.

TITIAN *del.* The Entombment.

Engraved in 1846. The picture is in the Gallery of the Louvre. Villot, No. 465. It is a repetition of the one in the Mamfrini Gallery in Venice, and was successively in the collections of the Duke of Mantua, Charles I., Eberhard Jabach, and Louis XIV.

Proof before letters, with artists' names and address.

MASTER OF THE CADUCEUS. *See* CADUCÉE.

MASTER OF THE DIE, whose real name probably was Dado or Daddo, and who adopted the mark of the die as an emblem of his name, has been called Beatrizet, or Beatricius the elder. *See* BEATRIZET.

MASTER OF THE UNICORN. *See* DUVET.

MASTER [monogram]. Brulliot, *Dict.* I. No. 1291.

Christ teaching the Doctors.

Already mentioned at the end of letter C.

MASTER E. S., 1466, goldsmith and engraver; supposed to be the first who used a rolling press, and made the engraving of copper plates his regular occupation; though his skill in handling the graver, and the number of his works, more than 200, prove sufficiently that he could not have been the first who attempted this pursuit. In his design he followed the school of Jan van Eyck. According to Harzen, Naumann's *Archiv für die zeichnenden Künste*, Jahrg. 1859, p. 1 *et seq.*, the letters "E. S." stand for Egidius (Gilles) Stechin, or Steclin (Stecher, i. e. engraver). He was a son of Hans, and a native of Cologne. The family name is not known. Bartsch, VI.

"Solomon adoring the Idols." B. 8.

In reality the Tiburtine Sibyl showing to the Emperor Augustus (who, in the costume of the Dukes of Burgundy, does homage and swings the censer) the apparition of the Holy Virgin with the Child in the air, as the true object for his worship. This engraving reproduces part of the representation of the right wing of an altar-piece by Rogier van der Weyden in the Berlin Gallery. Waagen, *Verzeichniss*, No. 535; compare his *Treasures*, I. p. 295. — Purchased for £ 30.

MATHAM, JACOB, painter and engraver, step-son and pupil of Hendrik Goltzius, was born at Haarlem in 1571, and died there in 1631. Bartsch, III.

FRANCESCO ROSSI, called CECCHINO DE' SALVIATI, *pinx.* The Visitation. B. 199.

Engraved in reverse, from the fresco in San Giovanni della Misericordia in Rome. Not mentioned by Platner and Bunsen. Nagler, XIII. p. 431.

2d state, with N. Visscher's address.

TITIAN *pinx.* The Virgin and Child with St. John (as a man) and St. Catherine. B. 208.

With C. Visscher's address.

TINTORETTO *pinx.* The Miracle of St. Mark, who appears to and delivers a tortured Christian slave. B. 192.

Painted for the School of San Marco in Venice, and now in the Gallery there. The original sketch was in the collection of the poet Rogers; it was purchased by Miss Burdett-Coutts.

MATHAM, THEODORUS, painter and engraver, born at Haarlem in 1589. A pupil of his father, Jacob, and of Corn. Bloemaert.

PAOLO VERONESE *pinx.* The Marriage of St. Catherine, Angels making Music, and St. John presenting the Ring.

MATHAM, THEODORUS, *continued.*

Engraved for the *Cabinet Reynst.*

The margin is cut off.

VAN DYCK *pinx.* **P.** Michel Le Blon, Agent of Sweden to the Court of England.

The original was sold in March, 1869 (Delessert's coll.), for £ 615.

See Weber, *Cat. rais.* p. 123, "Portraits divers d'après A. van Dyck."

MATHIEU, JEAN, engraver, born in 1749, died at Fontainebleau in 1815. A pupil of Longueil.

RUYSDAEL *pinx.* A Watermill, with the Dwelling adjoining; in the distance two Houses of the Village, and Trees.

"Ruisdael. J. Mathieu sc. 1772," without further inscription. Small folio, oblong. Nagler, *Künstler-Lexicon,* VIII. p. 437, No. 16.

MAUTORT, DE, engraver at Paris about 1750.

SCHALKEN *pinx.* "La Vieille inquiete."

A woman at a window with a lighted candle.

With Basan's address.

MAYER, CARL, painter and engraver, born at Nuremberg in 1798. For the last thirty years principally an engraver of small steel plates, portraits, etc. for books; also a publisher and printer.

LUCAS CRANACH *pinx.* The Woman taken in Adultery.

Engraved in stipple, after the picture in the Moritz-Kapelle in Nuremberg.

SCHMIDT *del.* **P.** Dr. David Friedrich Strauss.

MECHAU, JACOB WILHELM, landscape painter and etcher, born at Leipzig in 1745, lived for a long time in Rome, where he etched, with Dies and Reinhart, the *Collection de vues pittoresques d'Italie.* He died at Dresden in 1808. *See* REINHART.

MECKEN (or **MECKENEN**), **ISRAEL VAN,** the elder, sometimes miscalled van Mecheln, painter, goldsmith and engraver, probably a native of Mecken, a small town on the Moselle. He engraved after the Master E. S. 1466, and Franz van Bocholt, and even older models, and lived at Bocholt, where his name occurs in documents from 1482 to 1498. He died in 1503.* Bartsch, VI.

Christ scourged; from the Passion. B. 13.

* Zani, Ottley, Von Quandt, and Renouvier have come to the conclusion that there was a second, a younger Israel, perhaps the son and pupil of the elder, and that he continued to work till 1527, and copied a great deal, even after Dürer.

MEDICO, ALOYSIO DEL, engraver.

MASACCIO *pinx.* Frescos in the Church of San Clemente.

According to Vasari painted by Masaccio, though Schorn, in his notes to Vasari, ascribes the work to Giotto. Platner and Bunsen, III. i. p. 582. 8 plates in outline, namely, The Evangelists, the Fathers of the Church, the Apostles, the Annunciation, and St. Christopher with the Christ-child. These plates are added to Labruzzi's *Le Pitture di Masaccio esistenti in Roma nella Basilica di San Clemente.* See under LABRUZZI.

MELINI, CARLO DOMENICO, engraver, born at Turin about 1740, worked at Paris, in the style of Beauvarlet, towards the end of the last century.

DROUAIS *pinx.* **P.** The Two Children of Prince Turenne.

Represented as Savoyard boys, one with a marmot, the other with a hurdy-gurdy.

The picture is *not* in the Louvre.

MELLAN, CLAUDE, painter and engraver, born at Abbeville in 1601, died at Paris in 1688. He was a pupil of Simon Vouet; for engraving he studied Egidius Sadeler and Fr. Villamena. Montaiglon, *Catalogue raisonné de l'œuvre de Claude Mellan,* Abbeville, 1856.

CLAUDE MELLAN *del.* **P.** Mellan, Claude. M. p. 77.

1st state, before Odieuvre's address.

TINTORETTO *pinx.* Jacob and Rachel at the Well. M. 3.

From Otto's collection, No. 790, where it is called "Capitalblatt, vor der Adresse." *

Holy Family, or, rather, Rest in Egypt. M. 13.

3d state, with the coat of arms of Bishop Beaumanoir and the words "cum privilegio Regis" *after the engraver's name.*

The 1st state is before the arms; — the 2d with the arms, but before *cum privilegio Regis*; — in the 4th the arms are effaced, and the place on the stone where they were is shaded.

Christ praying in the Garden. M. 22.

2d state, with the dedication.

The 1st state is before dedication.

The Sudarium of St. Veronica, with the Face of the Thorn-crowned Saviour.† M. 25.

There are three different copies of this print.

* Nagler, under No. 18, mentions a state "before the mark of the artist" (it is not a mark, but the full names of both artists) of which Montaiglon does not speak. Heller enumerates this print twice, first as "Jacob and Rachel," then under the title "Rebecca," which mistake Le Blanc has repeated.

† Nagler, under No. 1, mentions a state "before the letter." Heller has "1st state before letters, 2d state, before address," — which Le Blanc copies after him. I have not met with any *avant la lettre,* and have seen even very late impressions without any address.

MELLAN, CLAUDE, *continued.*

The Corpse of our Saviour prepared for Burial by the Virgin; St. John and the Holy Women mourning. "Factvs obediens vsqve ad mortem." M. 32.

St. Alexius Romanus, represented as dead. M. 49.

1st state, before "cum p. R." *on the right, below.*

St. Francis. M. 71.

The saint, in the robe and hood of a capuchin, is kneeling before a cross placed on the ground; in the background is another figure of a capuchin in a hood. Inscription: *Cum priuilegio . . . Cl. Mellan Gall. inuen. et sc. . . . Eminentissimo S. R. E. Card. de la Rochefovcavlt Tit. S. Calisti hanc S. Francisci effigiem Patroni S. E. in obseqvii monvmentvm offert. d. d. Clavd. Mellan,* 1638.*

St. Ignatius in Ecstasy. M. 79.

Over the saint's head are the words "Ego vobis Romae propitivs ero."

3d state, having in place of the dedication, "Solicitvdinis patris pro bono familiae vigilantis. — C. Mellan in. et sc."

The 1st impressions are before the inscription, *Ego vobis.*

Perseus delivering Andromeda. M. 121.

1st state, before the dedication to Giustiniani, like Paignon-Dijonval's.

The 2d state is with the dedication; the 3d is retouched in the water.

Sim. Vouet *pinx.* Lucretia with the Dagger. M. 122.

P. Bentivoglio, Cardinal. M. 169.

From the collection of P. Mariette. Superb impression.

P. Gassendi, Pierre. M. 189.

P. Habert de Montmor, Henri Louis. M. 194.

A late impression, with the address "A Paris chez Vanheck" (*erased*).

Nagler mentions, under No. 265, "1st impression, before the mark of Mellan," which Le Blanc copies. The "mark," however, is, *Claud. Mellan Gall. del. et sculp.*

P. Giustiniani, Vincenzo. M. 197.

2d state.

The 1st state is before letters.

P. The Capuchin Father Joseph. M. 196.

In 8vo. From Gawet's collection.

P. Peyresc, Fabri de. M. 223.

1st state, before the plate was reduced.

The plate was afterwards cut down for Odieuvre's portraits.

* Heller describes the 1st state as with the year 1627, the 2d as with the year 1638 and having the eyes shut, the 3d as having the eyes open, which Le Blanc, No. 65, repeats. Montaiglon has but one state.

MELLAN, CLAUDE, *continued.*

P. Séguier, Pierre. M. 231.

1st state, before the additional inscription, "anno aetat. suae 51."

The 2d state has the inscription.

POUSSIN *del.* Apollo crowning Virgil. M. 303.

See Smith, *Cat. rais.*, Poussin, No. 283.

1st state, before any letters.

The 2d state is also without the names of the artist, but on an escutcheon stands

"VIRGILII MARONIS OPERA,"

and below

"PARISIIS E TYPOGRAPHIA REGIA
ANNO MDCLI."

MERCURJ, PAOLO, painter and engraver, born at Rome in 1804, works at Paris.

DELAROCHE *pinx.* St. Amelia, Queen of Hungary.

The picture was in the Oratory of Louis Philippe's Queen Amélie. Engraved in 1841.

Artist's proof; the plate has merely the names of the artists slightly traced with the point, in very small and irregular letters.

The 2d proofs have the artists' names in the same words, *re*-engraved, also in delicate letters, but regularly and calligraphically written; they have further the inscription *Sainte Amélie* in open letters, and, below, the names of the publisher and printer. — In the 3d state, *Reine de Hongrie* is added to the inscription.

LÉOP. ROBERT *pinx.* The Reapers in the Pontine Marshes.

The picture is in the Gallery of the Louvre. Engraved in 1831, with the aid of etching and the aquatinta manner, for the Paris journal *L'Artiste.*

Proof before letters, having merely the engraver's name, "P. Mercurj dis. e inc. Parigi 1831," *and the name of the printer,* "imprimé par Chardon ainé," *traced with the point.*

There is one impression on record, "Première épreuve d'artiste; on lit seulement: *P. Mercurj dis. e inc. Parigi* 1831," and before the name of the printer, Debois, 1843, No. 678, 365 *fr.*; it occurred again at Thorel's sale, Paris, 1853, No. 103, 361 *fr.*, and again at Schletter's, Leipzig, 1855, No. 73.

P. Columbus, "after an old cotemporary picture."

Proof before any letters, except very slightly written with the needle, "P. Mercurj inc. 1843."

P. Tasso.

In 8vo.

Impression on India paper; below is the address "Goupil et Vibert."

Earlier impressions are without this address.

MERZ, JACOB, painter and engraver, born in the Canton of Zürich in 1783, died at Vienna in 1807. A pupil of Lips.

P. Canova.

Engraved in 1805 in folio.

Has open letters.

Proofs are before any letters.

MICHEL, JEAN-BAPTISTE, engraver, born at Paris in 1748, died at London in 1804.

TENIERS *pinx.* A Flemish Kitchen.

Smith, *Cat. rais.* 507. In the Imperial Gallery of St. Petersburg. Engraved for the Houghton Gallery.

Open letter proof.

LEONARDO DA VINCI *pinx.* **P.** La Gioconda, undraped.

See Rigollot, under No. 60, p. 67. The picture is in the Imperial Gallery of St. Petersburg. Engraved for the Houghton Gallery.

MIDDIMAN, SAMUEL, designer and engraver, principally of landscapes, born in 1746, died at London in 1818. A scholar of Woollett and of Bartolozzi.

CIPRIANI et G. BARRETT *pinx.* Scene from Shakespeare's Tempest, Act I.

Landscape in an oval; figures by Bartolozzi.

CIPRIANI, G. BARRETT, et GILPIN *pinx.* Scene from Shakespeare's As You Like It.

Landscape in an oval; figures by Bartolozzi.

JAN BREUGHEL *pinx.* Adam and Eve in Paradise.

"Picture in the Royal Palace at Windsor." Engraved in 1799, in conjunction with James Heath.

Open letter proof.

MIGER, SIMON CHARLES, engraver, born at Paris in 1747, died in 1805. A pupil of Cochin the younger.

VANLOO *pinx.* **P.** Louis Michel Vanloo, painting the portrait of his Father, Jean-Baptiste Vanloo.

Painted in 1762. Engraved in 1799.

MILLER, WILLIAM, an English engraver of the present day.

TURNER *pinx.* Venice from the Canale Grande.

Proof before letters, with only the names of the artists and publishers slightly traced. On India paper.

GAINSBOROUGH *pinx.* The Watering Place.

The picture is in the Vernon Gallery. Waagen, *Treasures*, I. p. 368.

Open letter proof. On India paper.

MIRICENUS, MERICENUS, or **A MYRICINIS, PETRUS,** a Dutch engraver of the second half of the sixteenth century, whose real name Renouvier has ascertained to be Pieter van der Heyden. His monogram is composed of the letters A M E united, and surmounted by a P. Renouvier, *Des types et des manières des maîtres graveurs*, II. p. 148.

ANDREA DEL SARTO *pinx.* Herod ordering the Imprisonment of St. John the Baptist.

After the fresco in the Chiostro della Compagnia dello Scalzo in Florence. Cock *exc.*

PIETER BREUGHEL, the elder, *pinx.* Landscape with Grotesque Devilry.

In the foreground is a female figure praying with a cross in her hands, sitting on a stone from which hangs a chain, and with shackles at her feet; under it the inscription *Patientia.* On the left, *H. Cock excude* 1557, on the right the monogram of the engraver, and, *Brueghel* [sic] *inuent;* below, in the margin, *Patientia est malorum quæ aut inferuntur, aut accidunt, cum æquanimitate perlatio. Lact. inst. Lib.* 5.

MOCHETTI, ALESSANDRO, a pupil of Volpato, born at Rome in 1760.

RAPHAEL *pinx.* See under MONTAGNANI, "Picturae Peristyli Vaticani," Nos. 17–20, 22, 29–32.

RAPHAEL *pinx.* a. Psyche giving the Vase to Venus.
b. Cupid and Jupiter.

One plate from Raphael's frescos in the Farnesina. See under RICCIANI.

MOGALLI, COSMO, engraver, born at Florence in 1667, died in 1730.

TITIAN *pinx.* The Virgin and Child, St. Elizabeth, and the infant St. John.

The Christ-child is represented as taking the globe from a kneeling Emperor, Charles V.

Engraved for the *Raccolta de' quadri dei Granduchi di Toscana.*

The picture, formerly in the Gallery of the Uffizj, is not now in either of the Florentine Galleries.

MOITTE, PIERRE ÉTIENNE, engraver, born at Paris in 1722, died in 1780. A pupil of Beauvarlet.

ANDREA DEL SARTO *pinx.* Holy Family, with a Go-cart.

In the Dresden Gallery. Engraved for the *Rec. d'est. de la Gal. de Dresde,* I. No. 7.

RUBENS *pinx.* The Judgment of Paris.

The picture is in the Dresden Gallery; it corresponds with the picture formerly in the Brühl collection, and is probably the same, though that is not stated in Hübner's catalogue. This plate seems also to be the same

MOITTE, PIERRE ÉTIENNE, *continued.*

that was, as No. 30, in the *Recueil d'estampes gravées d'après les tableaux de la Galerie et du Cabinet de S. E. M. le Comte de Brühl,* etc., I[e] partie, 1754. Royal fol. 50 pl. (No more appeared.) It had the inscription "Peint par P. P. Rubens. Gravé à l'Eau forte par P. F. Tardieu" (all on the left side), the coat of arms of Count Brühl, an inscription, "Gravé d'après le tableau original ... qui est dans la Galerie de ... le Comte Brühl." When the picture came into the Electoral Gallery, Moitte retouched the plate, and changed the inscription, supplying the Electoral coat of arms, and it forms thus No. 35 of the third, the interrupted, volume of the *Rec. d'estampes de la Gal. de Dresde.*

Another picture of the same subject, about four times as large in size, but smaller in composition, otherwise corresponding with the Dresden picture, only painted in a bolder and broader style, is in the National Gallery in London, having been previously in the Orleans and Penryce collections. Smith, *Cat. rais.* 748 ; Waagen, *Treasures,* I. p. 317.

Trial impression on thinner paper and before the number.

MONTAGNANI, PIETRO PAOLO, engraver and publisher, born at Rome in 1740.

RAPHAEL *pinx.* Picturae Peristyli Vaticani manus Raphaeli Sanci ... expressae ... Opus ... quod Honori Pii VI. Pontificis Maximi ... Petr. Paulus Montagnanus dedicat ... Romae, [1790.] Oblong fol.

Fresco paintings in the 13 cupolas of the arcade of the Loggie, known under the name of "Raphael's Bible." (See also under OTTAVIANI and VOLPATO.) Passavant, II. p. 207, i. ; Platner and Bunsen, *Rom,* II. i. p. 302, *et seqq.* ; Kugler, *Handbook of Painting,* II. p. 361. Montagnani was only the publisher ;* the names of the several engravers are mentioned on the plates. This is the 1st impression, the 2d was published in 1795.

The 52 plates are as follows : —

GIULIO ROMANO *pinx.* Cupola I. The Creation.

1. God dividing Light from Darkness. Passavant, II. 128.
2. God dividing Water from Earth. P. II. 129.
3. Creation of Sun and Moon. P. II. 130.
4. Creation of Animals. P. II. 131.

*** Nos. 1 – 4 were engraved by Aloysio Cunego.

GIULIO ROMANO *pinx.* Cupola II. History of Adam and Eve.

5. God leading Eve to Adam. P. II. 132.
6. Temptation and Fall. P. II. 133.
7. Expulsion from Paradise. P. II. 134.

* Le Blanc and Nagler incorrectly speak of him as the *engraver* of 52 plates of Raphael's Loggie.

MONTAGNANI, PIETRO PAOLO, *continued.*

8. Adam and Eve at Labor. P. II. 135.

*** Nos. 5 – 8 were engraved by Giovanni Petrini.

GIULIO ROMANO *pinx.* Cupola III. History of Noah.

9. Building of the Ark. P. II. 136.
10. Deluge. P. II. 137.
11. Leaving the Ark. P. II. 138.
12. Noah's Offering. P. II. 139.

*** Nos. 9 – 12 were engraved by Carattoni.

FRANCESCO PENNI *pinx.* Cupola IV. History of Abraham and Lot.

13. Abraham and Melchizedek. P. II. 140.
14. Calling of Abraham. P. II. 141.
15. Abraham meeting Three Angels. P. II. 142.
16. Lot leaving Sodom. P. II. 143.

*** Nos. 13 – 15 were engraved by Carattoni; No. 16 by G. Morghen.

FRANCESCO PENNI *pinx.* Cupola V. History of Isaac.

17. God appearing to Isaac. P. II. 144.
18. Isaac embracing Rebecca. P. II. 145.
19. Isaac blessing Jacob. P. II. 146.
20. Esau asking a blessing. P. II. 147.

*** Nos. 17 – 20 were engraved by Alessandro Mochetti.

PELLEGRINO DA MODENA *pinx.* Cupola VI. History of Jacob.

21. Jacob's Ladder. P. II. 148.
22. Jacob and Rachel at the Well. P. II. 149.
23. Jacob suing for Rachel. P. II. 150.
24. Jacob returning to Canaan. P. II. 151.

*** Nos. 21, 23, 24 were engraved by Aloysio Cunego; No. 22, by Alessandro Mochetti.

GIULIO ROMANO *pinx.* Cupola VII. History of Joseph.

25. Joseph telling his Dream. P. II. 152.
26. Joseph before Pharaoh. P. II. 155.
27. Joseph and Potiphar's Wife. P. II. 154.
28. Joseph sold by his Brethren. P. II. 153.

*** Nos. 25 and 26 were engraved by Giacomo Bossi; Nos. 27 and 28 by Francesco Cecchini.

PERINO DEL VAGA *pinx.* Cupola VIII. History of Moses.

29. The Finding of Moses. P. II. 156.
30. Moses before the Burning Bush. P. II. 157.
31. Passage of the Red Sea. P. II. 158.
32. Moses striking the Rock. P. II. 159.

MONTAGNANI, PIETRO PAOLO, *continued.*

The first representation, "The Finding of Moses," was painted, according to Vasari, by Giulio Romano.

*** Nos. 29 – 32 were engraved by Alessandro Mochetti.

RAFFAELINO DAL COLLE *pinx.* Cupola IX. History of Moses, continued.

33. Moses receiving the Tables of the Law. P. II. 160.
34. The Golden Calf. P. II. 161.
35. Moses kneeling before the Cloudy Pillar. P. II. 162.
36. Moses showing the Tables of the Law. P. II. 163.

*** Nos. 33 – 36 were engraved by Francesco Pozzi.

PERINO DEL VAGA *pinx.* Cupola X. History of Joshua.

37. Crossing the Jordan. P. II. 164.
38. Fall of Jericho. P. II. 165.
39. Joshua's Victory. P. II. 166.
40. Joshua dividing the Land. P. II. 167.

*** Nos. 37 – 40 were engraved by Giovanni Petrini.

PERINO DEL VAGA *pinx.* Cupola XI. History of David.

41. David anointed King. P. II. 168.
42. David conquering Goliath. P. II. 169.
43. David's Triumph over the Syrians. P. II. 170.
44. David and Bathsheba. P. II. 171.

*** Nos. 41 and 42 were engraved by Camillo Tinti; Nos. 43 and 44, by J.-B. Dasori.

PELLEGRINO DA MODENA *pinx.* Cupola XII. History of Solomon.

45. Solomon anointed King. P. II. 172.
46. Judgment of Solomon. P. II. 173.
47. Queen of Sheba visiting Solomon. P. II. 174.
48. Building of the Temple. P. II. 175.

*** Nos. 45 – 48 were engraved by Francesco Cecchini.

PERINO DEL VAGA *pinx.* Cupola XIII. From the New Testament.

49. Adoration of the Shepherds. P. II. 176.
50. Adoration of the Kings. P. II. 177.
51. Baptism of Christ. P. II. 178.
52. Last Supper. P. II. 179.

According to Vasari, the painter was Perino del Vaga; according to others, Giulio Romano.

*** Nos. 49 – 52 were engraved by Giacomo Bossi.

MONTMORILLON, LUDWIG ALBERT VON, designer and engraver, born at Erlangen in 1794.

ANDREA DEL SARTO *pinx.* Holy Family.

MONTMORILLON, LUDWIG ALBERT VON, *continued.*

After the picture in the Munich Gallery. Alfred Reumont, p. 81; Nagler, *K.-L.* art. "Montmorillon," No. 1. A similar picture is in the Vienna Gallery. Alfred Reumont, p. 77.

Proof before letters, with only the artists' names.

MORACE, ERNST, engraver, born at Stuttgart in 1776, died, according to Nagler, in Stuttgart, about 1820, according to Heller, in Paris in 1808; Le Blanc has followed Nagler. He was a pupil of J. G. von Müller.

GIULIO ROMANO *pinx.* Venus and Vulcan.

The picture is in the Gallery of the Louvre. Villot, No. 296. Engraved for the *Musée Français.*

SIR JOSHUA REYNOLDS *pinx.* **P.** Angelica Kauffman.

Proofs have the name in the socle in open letters. — Artist's proofs have no letters in the socle, and no names of the artists nor of the publisher.

MOREL, ANTOINE ALEXANDRE, engraver, born at Paris in 1765, died there in 1829. A pupil of Massard the elder, and, in drawing, of David.

RAPHAEL *pinx.* **P.** Pope Julius II.

Engraved for the Orleans Gallery, from a copy in that collection, which was sold in England, with the other pictures, in 1800. Passavant, II. No. 83, h. The original of many repetitions and copies is the picture in the Gallery of the Palazzo Pitti in Florence.

RUBENS *pinx.* **P.** "Les quatres philosophes." Portraits of Hugo Grotius, Justus Lipsius, Philip Rubens, and P. P. Rubens.

In the Gallery of the Palazzo Pitti in Florence. Smith, No. 521. Engraved for Wicar, *Tableaux de la Galerie de Florence et du Palais Pitti.*

MORELLI, FRANCESCO, engraver, born about 1768, and a pupil of Volpato; he was a Frenchman by birth, and his name was Morel, but he usually added the Italian termination (Nagler, IX. p. 459).

Temples of the Sibyl and of Vesta.

"Francesco Morel, 1797."

Castle of St. Angelo.

"Francesco Morelli, 1796."

Tomb of Cæcilia Metella.

"Fr. Morelli, 1796."

Temple "delle Tosse," on the way to Tivoli

"Morel, 1798."

MORGHEN, GIOVANNI ELIA, engraver, a brother of Filippo, the father of Raphael Morghen, was born at Florence in 1721.

MORGHEN, GIOVANNI ELIA, *continued.*

GUIDO RENI *pinx.* St. Cecilia.

"E tabula Romae Burghesianis in aedibus asservata." — "Romae apud Montagnani, in Platea Pasquini." The picture seems not to be now in the Borghese Gallery; we do not remember to have seen it there, nor do we find it recorded as being there.

GUTTENBRUN *pinx.* **P.** J. F. Reifenstein.

"Si vende a Napoli da Ernesto Morace." With a white stamp of the letters *E. M.*, which probably do not stand for Elia Morghen, but are the initials of the publisher.

MORGHEN, G., engraved the 16th plate of Montagnani's Bible of Raphael. (*See* MONTAGNANI.) Le Blanc ascribes it also to Giovanni Elia Morghen; Nagler mentions this uncle, as well as a Guglielmo, a brother of Raphael Morghen, as engravers for Montagnani's work, though there is but this one plate engraved in the work by *G.* Morghen. No particulars are known about the life of Guglielmo, and it is possible that he is the engraver of the two plates mentioned above, under Giovanni Elia.

MORGHEN, RAFFAELLO, designer and engraver, born at Portici in 1758, died at Florence in 1833. A pupil first of his father Filippo, and then of Volpato. Palmerini, *Catalogo delle opere d' intaglio di Raffaello Morghen,* Ediz. 3[a], Firenze, 1824.

GUERCINO *pinx.* Lot and his Daughters. Palm. 130.

Engraved from a picture now in the possession of the Rev. T. Staniforth at Storrs. Waagen, *Galleries*, etc., or *Treasures*, IV. p. 426. Different from the composition of the same subject in the Louvre.

Proof before letters, with only the artists' names.

In this state the plate remained a considerable time, and a great number of impressions were taken before letters; then an inscription was made in open letters, which in the next state were shaded.

RAPHAEL MENGS *pinx.* Adoration of the Shepherds. Palm. 163.

From the picture in the Gallery of Madrid. Engraved for the *Coleccion de las estampas ... de los cuadros ... pertenecientes al Rey de España.*

The proofs are before letters, having only the names of the artists.

N. POUSSIN *pinx.* Rest on the Flight into Egypt. Palm. 131.

In the Palazzo Rospigliosi.

Proof, before the inscription, "Butirum et mel," etc., *with the artists' names and the dedication traced with the needle.*

RAPHAEL *pinx.* The Transfiguration. Palm. 209.

Painted for the Church San Pietro in Montorio; now in the Gallery of the Vatican. Passavant, II. 244. Engraved in 1812.

MORGHEN, RAFFAELLO, *continued.*

Subscription copy, signed with ink, " N. Quattro cento tre. R. Morghen," *and having the white stamp of the engraver's initials in the right-hand corner.*

There were 600 impressions taken of this state.

The artist's proofs of the plate which are finished, except the book in the hands of St. Andrew, which has no cross-hatching, are before any letters. There are 15 impressions known of this state. " Première épreuve avant toutes lettres, au livre blanc," Logette, No. 105, 472 *fr.*; Wilcox, No. 193, £ 80. — There were also impressions taken from the unfinished plate, beginning with the first etch-proof, which are properly to be considered curiosities, and not as "states" of the engraving.

The proofs of the plates are entirely finished. I could not find any additional work on the book, or " the leaves of the book," distinguishing the prints from the proof presently to be described, as Palmerini states, and Heller, Nagler, Le Blanc, etc. after him. The regular proofs are before the coat of arms and the dedication; they have only the inscription *Raph. Sanctius pinxit, Steph. Tofanelli delin. Raph. Morghen sculpt."*; — in open, traced uncial letters, *Et transfiguratus est ante eos. Mat. C.* XVII. *v.* 2; — below, on the left, *Aloysius Bardi excudit*; — in the middle, in uncial letters, *Exstat in Imperiali Museo Parisino*; — and, in the right corner, the white stamp with the initials of the engraver. Thorel, No. 106, 910 *fr.*; Archinto, No. 258, 975 *fr.*; G. Smith, No. 1021, £ 30. An artist's proof with the white book, Duke of Buckingham, 1834, No. 1103, £ 21, and a proof of the finished plate, No. 1102, £ 24 3 *s.*

In the prints the artists' names remain the same, only to *Raphael Morghen sculpt.* is added, in a line below, *Florentiae* 1811. The line *Transfiguratus est ante eos. Matth. C.* XVII. *v.* 2 is newly engraved; the letters are again open, but smaller, and *Matth.* stands instead of *Mat.* Under the coat of arms and the dedication to " Napoleon le Grand " stands, below, on the left, *Déposé à la Bibliothèque Impériale à Paris* 6 *Décembre* 1811. *Emprimé* [sic] *par Louis Bardi*"; in the middle, in written cursive letters, *Le Tableau existe au Muséum Impérial à Paris*, and, on the right, *Par son très humble et très obéissant serviteur et sujet Raphael Morghen.*

LEONARDO DA VINCI *pinx.* The Last Supper. Palm. 180.

See Rigollot, No. 14. The well-known painting in oil, not fresco, on the wall of the refectory of the convent of the Dominicans in Santa Maria delle Grazie, in Milan. Engraved in 1800, after the drawing of Teod. Matteini.

Impression of the 1st state of the print, before the mark, resembling a comma, after the word vobis, *and the dot under the* R *of the engraver's name.*

In the 2d state the comma and dot are found, and in the 3d the plate is retouched.

The proofs have the artist's name, then an empty space, where in the

MORGHEN, RAFFAELLO, *continued.*

prints the inscription stands, *Amen dico vobis*, etc., and under this the coat of arms and dedication, *Ferdinando III.*, etc., traced with the needle. Harrach, No. 1523, 1200 *fr.*

Impressions of the etching occur in which a small part of the background is finished with the graver.

There are eleven artist's proofs, before any letters, and in which the dish next to the Apostle Simon is drawn only in outline, and the shadow of the bread thereon is before the cross-hatching. Such a one is described in Thomas Wilson's *Catalogue*, No. 180; another was sold in Johnson's collection, in London, 1860, No. 96, for £316. Same state, Archinto, Paris, 1862, No. 256, "magnificent proof of the first state of the finished plate, before all letters, and with the coat of arms; with the white dish, on which is the monogram R. M." (these letters are *not* on *all* the impressions). It was sold for 8,400 *fr.*, and 5 per cent addition, and bought by Messrs. Amsler and Ruthardt, printsellers in Berlin. At the sale of Macready's prints there occurred, No. 74, a "proof with the white plate"; it was bid in by Mr. Colnaghi for £110.

LEONARDO DA VINCI *pinx.* Head of the Saviour. Palm. 207.

"Engraved in 1809, from a picture, of the size of the plate, in the possession of the Trivulzio family in Milan."

BAROCCIO *pinx.* Christ appearing to Magdalen in the Garden: "Noli me tangere." Palm. 222.

The picture, now in England, was formerly in the collection of the Duke of Lucca. Mrs. Jameson, *Sacred and Legendary Art.*

Engraved in 1816.

Old impression with the white stamp of the initials of the publishers: "A. E. L(api)."

Proofs have *lettres grises;* artist's proofs have one of the canes in the foreground left white, and are before any letters. La Motte Fouquet, No. 320, 58 *th.*; George Smith, No. 1018, £9; Marshall, No. 1166, £7 7 *s.*; Lehrs, No. 239, 31½ *th.*

ANDREA DEL SARTO *pinx.* Madonna del Sacco. Palm. 175.

Fresco in the cloister of the Serviti in Florence. Alfred Reumont, p. 153; Crowe and Cavalcaselle, III. p. 572; Nagler, *Künstler-Lexicon*, XIX. p. 400. Engraved in 1795.

Old impression, before the additional flourishes of the letters of the inscription, which the late impressions have.

Proofs have, besides the artists' names and the coat of arms, only one line of dedication in uncial open letters, *A sua Eccellenza, il Signor Generale Marchese Mamfrini;* which in the prints is shaded, and has two additional lines added in cursive letters.

MORGHEN, RAFFAELLO, *continued.*

Artist's proofs are before any letters. Archinto, No. 265, 115 *fr.*

TITIAN *pinx.* Madonna watching over the Sleeping Child. Palm. 177.

Engraved in 1797 for the painter Head. In 1814 it formed one of the plates of the "Select engravings published by Stone under the direction of Wm. Buchanan, Esq."

Proof with the artists' names, and the inscription "Parce somnum rumpere" *in open letters; and with the English address. On India paper.*

In the 1st state of the print the inscription is shaded, but there is still the English address; — the 2d has the address of Artaria in Mannheim. — There are artist's proofs with only the names of the artists (Johnson, No. 106, £ 26), and still earlier ones without any letters. Duke of Buckingham, No. 1091; Marshall, No. 1169, £ 29 10 *s.*; Archinto, No. 262, 610 *fr.*; Lehrs, No. 234, 70 *th.*

GAROFALO *pinx.* Madonna and Child. Palm. 219.

Engraved in 1815.

1st proof, before letters, with only the artist's names in very small letters.

The 2d proofs have open letters. — Artist's proofs are before any letters.

ANDREA DEL SARTO *pinx.* Madonna col Bambino. Palm. 124.

Virgin and Child with St. John. The picture was in the collection of Count Fries in Vienna, now dispersed. Alfred Reumont, p. 84. Engraved in 1787.

Impression before the address.

The 1st proof is before letters, with only the artists' names; — the 2d has the inscription with the misspelling *Rambino;* — the 3d is with the correction, but is before the address; — the 4th has Artaria's address.

RAPHAEL *pinx.* Madonna del Granduca: "Pulcra est," etc. Palm. 251.

The picture is (or was) in one of the Duke's private apartments of the Pitti palace. Passavant, II. 27. Engraved in 1823.

Artist's proof before any letters, with merely the two letters "R. M." *traced with the needle in the middle below.*

Purchased for £ 7 7 *s.* — Proofs have open letters.

LOD. CARACCI *pinx.* Madonna col Bambino. Palm. 198.

Small piece, oval in a square border, two and one third inches high, one and three quarters inches broad, engraved in 1804 after a picture of the same size in the possession of the Gini family in Bologna.

Impression with the misspelling "Rambino" *instead of* "Bambino" *in the inscription.*

Proofs are before letters, with only the artists' names: Thomas Wilson, No. 188; Hillig, No. 296. Palmerini mentions that a very few artist's proofs were taken from the plate before the shading that made the oval square.

MORGHEN, RAFFAELLO, *continued.*

RAPHAEL *pinx.* Madonna del Cardellino, Madonna with the Goldfinch. "Mater pulchrae dilectionis." Palm. 213.

See Passavant, II. 36. The picture is in the Tribune of the Uffizj Gallery in Florence. Engraved in 1814.

Proofs are with open letters. — Lehrs, No. 233, "Proof before letters, with only the names of the artists," 43 *th.*

Artist's proof before any letters, Thomas Wilson, No. 187. — Artist's proof before any letters, with the white book, Marshall, No. 1167, £ 35.

RAPHAEL *pinx.* Madonna della Sedia, or della Seggiola. Palm. 165.

From the picture in the Pitti palace. Passavant, II. 226. Engraved in 1793.

Proof, with "Raffaelle da Urbino dipinse, Raffaelle Morghen dis. e inc. in Firenze. A sua Eccelz[a] il Sig[r] March[se] General Manfredini ec. ec.," *in open uncial letters; the coat of arms; a white space left for the further inscription of the dedication, and below, on the left,* "In Firenze per Nicolò Pagni e Gius. Bardi"; *on the right,* "Raffaelle Morghen le sue Toscane Primizie D. D. D.," *all traced with the needle.*

Purchased for £ 9. A similar impression, Lehrs, No. 227, 63 *th.*

RAPHAEL *pinx.* The same.

A print impression with the full inscription, and all engraved with the burin. *The artist's names as well as all the writing in current letters are thicker, and the letters which were open in the proof are shaded. The impression has the 2d address of Nicolò Pagni, and is of that state which has the misspelling* A SUA ECCLL[za] *in the dedication.*

After the mere etch-prints come: — 1st state, finished proof before any writing, Thomas Wilson, No. 177; — 2d state, before letters, with merely the artists' names and the arms of Manfredini, Debois, No. 690, 405 *fr.*; — 3d state, proof with one line of inscription, dedication to Manfredini, in open letters traced with the needle as described above; — 4th state, the letters of the inscription shaded, and the dedication written out in full with the graver, the address still Pagni e Bardi; — 5th state, with only *Pagni's* name as address, the inscription, that is, the dedication, erased, and only the coat of arms left. — The 6th state has Pagni's address, and again one line of inscription in open uncial letters, the dedication, with the misspelling "ECCLL[za]." Palmerini describes this state with the misspelling and but one line of inscription, and so do the manuals of engraving after him. I have never met with such an impression, nor found one described in a catalogue of a collection. — The 7th state would then be the print with the full inscription engraved with the burin and the uncial letters shaded, but with the misspelling ECCLL[za]; such I have seen repeatedly, and our second copy is such, though I do not find it described before Rudolph

MORGHEN, RAFFAELLO, *continued.*

Weigel in the catalogue of Von Quandt, whose collection was sold in 1860. No. 2179, "Alter schöner Abdruck mit ECCLL[za] und der Adresse von N. Pagni (on the left side below), auch Nic. de Antonj's Name als Drucker" (in the lower corner on the right). — 8th state, still Pagni's address, with the misspelling corrected; — 9th state, address of Bettelini, Rome.

There are still later impressions with Antoni's address on the left side below; and very recently the whole plate has been re-engraved, and these new impressions have again put the misspelling in the dedication, calculated to deceive: they are, however, without Pagni's address; those that I have seen had no address at all.

RAPHAEL *pinx.* The same Madonna della Seggiola.

A small plate, in 16mo, engraved in 1832, shortly before Morghen's death, when he was 74 years old. Not enumerated in Palmerini's catalogue, of which the 3d and last edition appeared in 1824.

An impression before any letters, Johnson, No. 122; "before the R. M.," Marshall, No. 1161.

MURILLO *pinx.* Magdalen. (Whole figure, kneeling.) Palm. 188.

Different from the picture in the Doria palace, Rome, which is half figure. *See* Alfred de Reumont, *Römische Briefe*, II. p. 210; Platner and Bunsen, III. iii. p. 551.* Engraved in 1800.

Artist's proof of the finished plate, before any letters, Th. Wilson, No. 181; Debois, No. 696; Johnson, No. 102, £35; Duke of Buckingham, No. 1085; Marshall, No. 1170, £17; Goddard, No. 342, £24 10*s.*

Proof before letters, with only the artist's names, George Smith, No. 1014, £11 11*s.*; Macready, No. 66, £15 10*s.*

CARLO DOLCE *pinx.* Magdalen. Palm. 249.

With the box of ointment and with the inscription: *Fides salvam fecit.* The picture is in the Uffizj Gallery, Florence.

The proofs have open letters. — Artist's proofs are before any letters. "Before all letters, with the white jewel," Johnson, No. 116.

RAPHAEL *pinx.* The Mass of Bolsena. Palm. 63.

Fresco of the Stanze, Sala d' Eliodoro; Passavant, II. No. 106.

* William Stirling, in his *Annals of the Artists in Spain*, in the Catalogue of the works of Murillo, III. p. 1439, says: "St. Mary Magdalen, possibly the picture from which Sir Robert Strange's and G. Balestra's engravings were executed. ROME, D. of Bracciano, Bracciano Palace." The Gallery of the Duke of Bracciano came into the Orleans Gallery, and the latter was sold in England in 1798. The banker Torlonia is now Duke of Bracciano, through the purchase of the fee of the Orsini Odescalchi. I do not know of such a picture in his palace; perhaps the Doria palace was meant. The only Magdalen engraved by Giovanni Balestra that I know of is after Francesco Vanni. Sir Robert Strange did not engrave a Magdalen after Murillo; Raphael Morghen must have been meant, who engraved our Magdalen, a whole length figure; while the picture in the Doria palace, of which, as far as I know, there is no engraving, is half figure.

MORGHEN, RAFFAELLO, *continued.*

Old impression before the retouch, with the mended crack in the plate barely visible over the heads of the persons on the stairs (see Palmerini, p. 43, *under* 4), *and with trial marks of the graver in the margin.*

Proofs are before letters, with only the artist's name.

RAPHAEL *pinx.* The Three Allegorical Figures, Attributes of Jurisprudence, — Prudence, Fortitude, and Moderation. Palm. 49.

Passavant, II. No. 68. Fresco of the Stanze, Camera della Segnatura.

Proofs are before letters, with only the artist's names.

RAPHAEL *pinx.* Allegorical Figure. Theology. Palm. 48.

Fresco on the ceiling of the Camera della Segnatura, Stanze of the Vatican. Passavant, II. 71. Engraved in 1781.

Impression before the retouch of the plate.

RAPHAEL *pinx.* Allegorical Figure. Poetry. Palm. 47.

Fresco on the ceiling of the Camera della Segnatura, Stanze of the Vatican. Passavant, II. 72. Engraved in 1781.

Before the retouch.

RAPHAEL *pinx.* Allegorical Figure. Philosophy. Palm. 67.

Fresco on the ceiling of the Camera della Segnatura, Stanze of the Vatican. Passavant, II. 73. Engraved in 1784.

Before the retouch.

RAPHAEL *pinx.* Allegorical Figure, Justice. Palm. 68.

Fresco on the ceiling of the Camera della Segnatura, Stanze of the Vatican. Passavant, II. No. 74. Engraved in 1784.

Before the retouch.

*** The proofs of these four pieces have only the artists' names. Of the two first there are also rare artist's proofs, before any letters; Debois, No. 699.

CARLO DOLCE *pinx.* La Poesia.

The picture is in the Corsini Gallery, Florence. Engraved in 1827. It is not contained in Palmerini's catalogue of R. Morghen's engravings, as the last (third) edition was published in 1824. Nagler, *Künstler-Lexicon*, No. 162.

Artist's proof before letters and before the coat of arms, with only the artists' names. In the corner is the white stamp of the engraver's initials.

The proofs have the coat of arms. There are also earliest artist's proofs before any letters. "Proof before any letters, with the white buckle," Johnson, No. 114.

GAV. HAMILTON *pinx.* Poetry. Palm. 39.

Engraved in 1780.

With the 1*st address,* Rome.

MORGHEN, RAFFAELLO, *continued.*

GAV. HAMILTON *pinx.* Painting. Palm. 38.

Engraved in 1779.

With the 1*st address,* Rome.

⁂ Of these two prints the 2d state has the address *Naples;* the 3d the address *Florence.* — The proofs, which are very rare, have the title in open letters and the coat of arms, and are before the dedication.

GÉRARD *pinx.* Les Trois Ages. Palm. 238.

The picture is owned by the royal family of Naples; there is a copy in the Palais Royal in Paris. Engraved in 1820.

The proofs have open letters.

"CORREGGIO *pinx.*" Caritas. Palm. 166.

A mother with three children. "Pulchriores Charitum pingunt charitatis amorem." Engraved in 1795.

The picture was in reality painted by Ignatius Unterberger, born at Cavalese in 1748, a successful student of Correggio's works, like Mengs, whose friend and associate he was in Rome. On his departure from that city he left this picture behind unfinished and neglected, and his brother Christoph Unterberger sold it in 1786 – 87, with some other trumpery, to a picture-dealer and restorer, Lovera, who, after the necessary preparation, brought it forward as a newly discovered original of Correggio. The English painter Day purchased the privilege of making a drawing from it, and having it engraved by Morghen, which spread the fame of the picture. In the same year in which the engraving came out, Prince Nic. Esterhazy, then in Rome, bought the picture, by the advice of Hofrath Hirt, but when it arrived in Vienna, Ignatius Unterberger, who then resided there, identified it as the picture which he had left behind him in Rome twenty-five years before. It was returned to Rome in 1796, and is now forgotten.

Proofs are before letters, with only the names of the artists. There occurs a counterfeit copy of this plate without any letters.

NIC. POUSSIN *pinx.* The Dance of the Hours to the Tune of Time. Palm. 132.

See Smith, *Cat. rais.* "Poussin," No. 279. Engraved in 1789, when "in the Palazzo Rospigliosi." Waagen, *Treasures,* II. p. 156, mentions it as in the Marquis of Hertford's collection: "The celebrated Dance of the Seasons, from the collection of Cardinal Fesch, and generally known by Raphael Morghen's elegant engraving."

1*st state of the print, before the inscription* "In aedibus Rospigliosis."

Proofs have merely the coat of arms and dedication to Ferdinand of Austria, and the names of the artists, traced. They are also before the inscription *In aedibus Rospigliosis.*

DOMENICHINO *pinx.* La Caccia di Diana. Palm. 115.

MORGHEN, RAFFAELLO, *continued.*

Diana presiding over the prize-shooting of her Nymphs. The picture is in the Borghese Gallery in Rome. Platner and Bunsen, III. iii. p. 279. Engraved in 1784.

Early impression before the crack in the plate. On stout paper.

From the collection of Carmesina.

The late impressions show a stroke, like a large comma, where the printer's ink went into a crack, between *et* and *Sua* in the dedication. — The proofs are on paper of a bluish tint, showing the lines of the paper wire, and have no inscription, except the names of the artists, and these scarcely perceptible, in very small letters traced with the needle. — The early impressions of the print are on stout, not very white paper, which, according to Palmerini, — I have not found it, — has the watermark of the name of Pietro Miliani.

GUIDO RENI *pinx.* Aurora with Apollo and the Hours. Palm. 125.

Aurora scatters flowers before the chariot of the Sun-god Apollo, which is drawn by four steeds and accompanied by the dancing Hours. A fresco on the ceiling of the casino in the garden of the Palazzo Rospigliosi in Rome. Platner and Bunsen, III. ii. p. 400. Engraved in 1792.

Impression before the retouch and on the old paper.

The proofs are before letters, the artists' names excepted. Wilcox, 191, £51; Johnson, No. 99, £50; Archinto, No. 259, 1300*fr.*; Lehrs, No. 255, 300 *th.* — The first rare impressions of the print are before the inscription on the left below; *In aedibus Rospigliosis.* Archinto, No. 260, 360*fr.*; Lehrs, No. 254, 100 *th.* After many retouches the plate became the property of the "Stamporia Camoralo" in Romo, which issued impressions again without that inscription. Recently the plate has been entirely re-engraved, and the impressions look like a new engraving.

AFTER AN ANTIQUE CAMEO. Head of Jupiter. Palm. 142.

Engraved in 1790, for E. A. Visconti, *Osservazioni sopra un antico cameo rapp. Giove Egioco,* Padova, 1793.

1*st impression with* "effosus" *instead of* "effossus."

The very rare proofs are before letters.

RAPHAEL *pinx.* **P.** Joan of Aragon. Palm. 239.

Joan was the daughter of Ferdinand of Aragon, Duke of Montaldo, married to Ascanio Colonna, Constable of Naples, and mother of Marc-Antonio Colonna, the hero of Lepanto. Vasari calls her, erroneously, Vice-queen of Naples. She was one of the most remarkable women of the sixteenth century for her intellect and her beauty; she was celebrated by more than three hundred poets, and she was of spotless fame.

The picture in the Louvre is the original of numerous school repetitions. The portrait. in the Doria Gallery in Rome is by a scholar of Leonardo da

MORGHEN, RAFFAELLO, *continued.*

Vinci after Raphael's picture. Passavant, II. 236, and III. p. 144. Engraved for the *Musée Français.*

Impression of the unretouched plate.

The proofs of this plate are before letters, with the names of the artists. Johnson, No. 120, £5 10*s.* — Artist's proof, before any letters, Duke of Buckingham, No. 974, £5 5*s.*; Maberly, No. 356, £9 5*s.*; Wilcox, No. 198, £16 10*s.*

CANOVA *sculps. in marm.*, SALESA *del.* Theseus conquering the Minotaur. Palm. 122.

Proof before letters, with only the artists' names and the coat of arms.

MORGHEN *del.* Portrait of a Nun. Palm. 173.

The plate never had any inscription, except "Raphael Morghen sc."

TOFANELLI *del.* **P.** Ariosto, Lodovico. Palm. 208.

Engraved for the folio edition of *Orlando Furioso,* Pisa, dalla tipografia della Società letteraria, 1809.

With L. Bardi's address.

The proofs have open letters. — Artist's proofs are before letters, with only the names of the artists; George Smith, No. 996. A still earlier proof of this portrait, with those of the other great Italian poets, Dante, Petrarca, Ariosto, and Tasso, before any letters, Johnson, No. 107, together £15.

BARTOLINI *del.* **P.** Boccaccio, Giovanni. Palm. 243.

Engraved in 1822, and inserted in the folio edition of the *Decamerone* which F. Didot published in 1816, in conformity with the Pisa edition of the great Italian poets, and which originally had only a small head of Boccaccio, in a round, engraved by Rosaspina.

With the address "L. Bardi & C° Borgo degli Albizzi."

The proofs have open letters. — The set of the poets Dante, Ariosto, Petrarca, Tasso, and Boccaccio, proofs before any letters, Duke of Buckingham, No. 971. — Portrait of Boccaccio, proof before letters with the white book, George Smith, No. 999, £6.

SANTARELLI *del.* **P.** Buonarroti, Michel Angelo. Head, profile view in a medallion. Palm. 226.

Engraved in 1817. The plate was afterwards used to insert in *Rime de Michel-Angelo Buonarroti con comento di G. Biagioli,* Paris, presso l' editore, 1821, 8vo.

Proof impression. With only the words "Raffaelle Morghen inciso" *cut with the needle in very small letters.*

MORGHEN *del.* **P.** Buonarroti, Michel Angelo.

MORGHEN, RAFFAELLO, *continued.*

Face view, bust. Engraved in 1829, therefore after Palmerini's catalogue (of 1824).

Proof, with merely the words "Raffaello Morghen disegnò e inc. 1829."

VASARI *pinx.* 𝔓. Cellini, Benvenuto. Palm. 245.

Engraved in 1822 in 8vo.

VASARI *pinx.* 𝔓. The same.

Impression before the line forming a square border round the oval.

VASARI *pinx.* 𝔓. The same.

Artist's proof before any letters, as well as before the lines forming a square.

TOFANELLI *del.* 𝔓. Dante Alighieri. Palm. 192.

Engraved for the folio edition of *La Divina Commedia,* Pisa, dalla tipografia della Società letteraria, 1804.

Impression without the address of L. Bardi.

The different states of proofs are like those of the portrait of Ariosto.

TOFANELLI *del.* 𝔓. Dante Alighieri. Palm. 203.

In 8vo. A repetition of the preceding on a reduced scale. Engraved for Gaetano Poggiali's edition of Dante's *Divina Commedia,* 4 vol. 1807 – 13, large 8vo.

RAPHAEL *pinx.* 𝔓. "La Fornarina," in reality the portrait of Beatrice Pio da Ferrara. Palm. 215.

The famous picture in the Tribune at Florence. Passavant, II. No. 95, III. p. 114. Engraved in 1805.

An early impression, with the white stamp of the engraver's initials in the right-hand corner below.

Proofs have one line of inscription, *Raphaelis amicitia celeberrima La Fornarina,* in open letters, the artists' names, the coat of arms, no dedication, and on the right below the white stamp *R M.* Lehrs, No. 285, $43\frac{1}{8}$ *th.* — Artist's proof before letters, but with the artists' names, Johnson, No. 112, £ 11 15 *s.*, and G. Smith, No. 1007, £ 7. — A still earlier finished proof before any writing, Wilson, No. 186. — Impression of the plate in which the bust is finished except the bosom, but the arm is only traced, Wilson, No. 185; Quandt, No. 2157; Hillig, No. 307. — There is also a copy of this engraving by Antonio Morghen, with Antonio's name as engraver; impressions before any letters of this plate may be easily mistaken for an artist's proof of the original Raffaello Morghen, and, no doubt, are often confounded.

RAPHAEL *pinx.* 𝔓. The Head of the Figure in the Transfiguration. Palm. 204.

Kneeling in the foreground; designated by the name of the "Fornarina." Engraved on a piece of silver. Very rare.

MORGHEN, RAFFAELLO, *continued.*

P. Fulger, Madame. Palm. 174.

Engraved in 1794 in 8vo. It has, like all the prints of this state, merely the name of the engraver, not the name of the person represented.

Proofs are before any letters; Palmerini knew of but one such impression; one occurred in Schenck and Gerstäcker's sale, Leipzig, Jan. 12, 1857, No. 220.

P. Guicciardini, Francesco. Palm. 235.

Without name of the painter or designer. Engraved in 1819 for Gio. Rosini's edition of Guicciardini's *Storia d' Italia*, Pisa, 4to. It was also inserted in Nicolò Capurro's edition of the *Storia*, Pisa, 1822, 4to.

Impression before the line forming a square round the oval.

Proofs have open letters. — Artist's proof before any letters, Johnson, No. 104.

ANGELICA KAUFFMAN *pinx.* **P.** Hamilton, Lady, represented as the Comic Muse. Palm. 141.

Engraved in 1790.

The rare proofs are before letters.

ANGELICA KAUFFMAN *pinx.* **P.** The Holstein-Beck Family. Palm. 168.

Engraved in 1794.

Proof before letters, with only the names of the artists and the coat of arms.

Before any letters, Duke of Buckingham, No. 963.

"SIMONE MEMMI" *pinx.* **P.** Laura, Madonna. Palm. No. 234 and p. 97.

From a miniature by Francesco Scotto after a picture in the possession of the Bellanti family in Siena, attributed to Simone Memmi. Engraved in 1819 for Marsand's edition of *Le rime di Petrarca*, 2 vol. Padova, 1819–20, large 4to.

RAPHAEL *pinx.* **P.** Leo X. Palm. 218.

The bust merely of the pope, from Raphael's celebrated picture in the Pitti palace, representing Leo sitting at a table and attended by the Cardinals Giulio de' Medici and Lodovico de' Rossi. Passavant, II. 237. Engraved in 1815 for Bettoni's *Vite e Ritratti di illustri Italiani.*

Open letter proof with the white stamp "P. C."

RAPHAEL *pinx.* **P.** The same.

Artist's proof before letters with only the artists' names, and the white stamp "P. C."

RAPHAEL *pinx.* **P.** The same.

Still earlier finished trial proof, before any letters, and without stamp.

A. BRONZINO *pinx.* **P.** Machiavelli, Nicolò. Palm. 171.

MORGHEN, RAFFAELLO, *continued.*

There is a portrait of Machiavelli by Bronzino in the Palazzo Doria (formerly Pamfili). Platner and Bunsen, III. iii. p. 542. Engraved in 8vo for the works of Machiavelli, Livorno, 1797.

The prints have open letters.

A. BRONZINO *pinx.* The same.

Proof before letters, with only the artists' names.

VASARI *pinx.* **P.** Medici, Lorenzo de'. Palm. 236.

With the address, "L. Bardi & C°."

Proofs have open letters. — Artist's proofs are before letters, but with the artist's name. Wilcox, No. 186.

VAN DYCK *pinx.* **P.** Moncada, Francisco de, on Horseback. Palm. 162.

Engraved in 1793. The picture is in the Gallery of the Louvre. Villot, No. 146; Smith, *Cat. rais.* 143; Waagen, *Handbook,* II. p. 287.

Impression before the cross-hatching on the cuirass.

The cross-hatching was made after the plate began to wear, and constitutes the 2d state. — The proofs are before the inscription, *Imago equestris Francisci de Moncada,* etc., for which a place is left blank; they have the names of the artists, the coat of arms, and the dedication in open and traced letters, "lettre grise," Debois, No. 704, 320 *fr.* — Finished proof before the inscription and with the date 1792, Thomas Wilson's *Cat. rais.*, No. 176; — an artist's proof, before letters and arms, Sir. J. Hippisley, London, 1857, No. 111, £ 23 10 *s.*

The title-inscription of the prints "with letters" is in open letters.

GÉRARD *pinx.* TOFANELLI *del.* **P.** Napoleon I. Emperor of France, in his Imperial Robes. Palm. 206.

Engraved in 1808.

Open letter proof, 4th state of the finished plate.

GÉRARD *pinx.* **P.** The same.

Print, old impression with the 2d address.

The states of the finished plate are as follows: — 1st, proof before any letters and before the motto round the star of the Legion of Honor, Johnson, No. 111; Marshall, No. 1158. — 2d, proof before letters, with only artists' names, Debois, No. 705; Marshall, No. 1156. — 3d, proof with the artists' names and only the name "Napoléon" in open uncial letters, without further inscription and without address. There were but one hundred impressions taken in this state, to be inserted in a magnificent folio edition of the *Code Napoléon,* for which this plate was expressly engraved, and which was published by Molini, Landi & Co. in the style of the Pisa edition of the Italian poets. — 4th, proof, in which to the name, in open letters, are added the titles in cursive letters, and,

MORGHEN, RAFFAELLO, *continued.*

traced with the needle, *Empereur des François, Roi d'Italie et Protecteur de la Confédération du Rhin.* Without address. — 5th, *print,* with shaded and stronger letters, and still before the address. — 6th, with the address of Molini, Landi, & Co. — 7th, with the address of L. Bardi & Co.

TOFANELLI *del.* **P.** Neri, San Filippo. Palm. 190.

TOFANELLI *del.* **P.** Petrarca, Francesco. Palm. 200.

Engraved for *Rime di Francesco Petrarca,* Pisa, dalla tipografia della Società letteraria, 1805.

Impression with L. Bardi's address.

The different states of the proofs are like those of the portrait of Ariosto.

RAPHAEL *pinx.* **P.** Raphael. Palm. 191.

In reality the portrait of Bindo Altoviti, whose family kept it as such for more than two centuries, until, about the middle of the last century, Bottari, misunderstanding a passage in Vasari, "for Bindo Altoviti he painted his portrait while he was young," pronounced it Raphael's own portrait. As such it was engraved in 1803, and as such it was in 1808 bought by Louis of Bavaria, then Crown Prince. It is now in the Munich Gallery. Passavant, II. 96. Herman Grimm, however, maintains that it is the portrait of Raphael, and so did Baron Rumohr.

RAPHAEL *pinx.* **P.** The same.

Proof, with the artists' names, coat of arms, one line of dedication in letters traced with the needle, an open space for one line, and, below, one line in small letters.

Lehrs, No. 283, 38 *th.* — Artist's proof, Johnson, No. 115, before letters, but with the artists' names, £ 17 10 *s.* — A still earlier proof, "finished proof before any writing," Wilson, No. 182.

CATENI *del.* **P.** Rossini, Gioacchino. Palm. 242.

Engraved in 1822, after a marble bust, by Bartolini.

P. ERMINI *del.* **P.** Tasso, Torquato. Palm. 205.

Engraved for *La Gerusalemme Liberata,* Pisa, dalla tipografia della Società letteraria, 1807.

With L. Bardi's address.

The different states of the proofs are like those of Ariosto.

Raphael Morghen engraved the portrait of this poet a second time, in profile view and of 8vo size (Palm. 254), which was inserted in the *Gerusalemme Liberata* edited by Giuseppe Molini, 1818.

MIEREVELT *pinx.* **P.** "William II., Prince of Nassau." Palm. 66.

This is not the portrait of William of Nassau, but of an unknown person, and as such engraved by Morghen in 1784 at Rome. After Mr. Artaria,

MORGHEN, RAFFAELLO, *continued.*

the publisher at Mannheim, had bought the plate, he caused impressions to be made from it with the inscription "Wilhelmus II., Princeps Nassoviae."

This impression is before that inscription.

F. Vieira *pinx.* 𝔓. Turchi, Deodato, Bishop of Parma. Palm. 181.

Engraved in 1800.

1st state of the print, with the titles of the prelate, and before Bardi's address.

The proofs are before letters. — "Proof before any letters," Duke of Buckingham, No. 969.

Leonardo da Vinci *pinx.* 𝔓. Leonardo da Vinci. Palm. 224.

Engraved in 1817, after the picture in the Painters' Portrait Gallery in Florence. Rigollot, No. 84.

Artist's proof before any letters, with merely the artists' names.

Purchased for £ 8. G. Smith, No. 991, "fine and rare proof before any letters," £ 10 10 *s.* — Proofs have open letters.

Angelica Kauffman *pinx.* 𝔓. Volpato, Giovanni. Palm. 186.

Engraved in 1801. Proofs have open letters. — Engraver's proof not quite finished, the waistcoat still white, Quandt, No. 2028.

Fra Bartolommeo *pinx.* Virgin and Child, with a Book and Two Angels. Palm. ed. 1824, p. 154.

Inscription on the plate, *Ricavato dal quadro originale esistente nella Galleria di S. E. Milord Clive in Londra.* Engraved by Raphael Morghen and Giovanni Volpato in conjunction. There is no engraver's name, only the address *Apud Joan. Volpato.*

MORIN, JEAN, painter and etcher, born at Paris at the beginning of the seventeenth century, died in 1666. A pupil of Philippe de Champagne. Robert-Dumesnil, ii.

Ph. de Champagne *pinx.* 𝔓. Borromeo, Cardinal Carlo. R.-D. 46.

Profile to the right, in an oval border without inscription, also no inscription below, except the artist's name.

From the collection and with the signature of John Barnard.

Franck *pinx.* 𝔓. Franck, Jérôme. R.-D. 52.

In an oval border, without inscription; the bust rests upon a socle, and is surrounded by a shaded square. The socle has the inscription, on a slip of paper of greenish hue, pasted on the print, *Jérôme Francque, peintre du Roi. Francque Pin. Morin sculp.* This is pasted over and covers the inscription, *Henri IV. Roi de France et de Navarre. Ferdinand pinx. Morin sculp.* The portrait *is*, however, that of the painter, as Ferdinand's picture of the King represents him in cuirass, only a passe-partout was

MORIN, JEAN, *continued.*

used in printing which contained the other name. *A Paris chez Bligny, Lancier du Roi, md d' estampes*, etc.

VAN DYCK *pinx.* **P.** Opstal. *See* GAYWOOD.

MOUZIN, or **MOZIN, MICHEL,** painter and engraver, born at Amsterdam about 1630.

LIEVENS *pinx.* **P.** "Joan van Galen, Admiral der Holl. Vlote in de Middelandsche Zee."

With twelve Dutch verses in two columns, divided by a coat of arms, commencing: *Dus ziet men Galen in 't gedrang der Britten woeden,* and ending *Zyn Krygsroem . . . eewig staan.* Jan Vos. "J. Livius Pinxit. — F. de Wit excudit."

Without "Michiel Mozyn sculpsit." *With the address of F. de Wit, not mentioned by Bartsch,* L'œuvre de Rembrandt, II. *p.* 174, *No.* 94, *nor by Claussin,* L'œuvre de Rembrandt, II. *p.* 165, *No.* 95, *who give the address of Cornelis Danckertsz.*

This impression is also without the coat of arms in the plate, on the left above, where the space for it is left unshaded.

The 1st state has Danckertsz's address; the 2d has the address of Allardt. Le Blanc, after Heller's *Handbuch,* art. "Mouzin," 21.

MOYREAU, JEAN, engraver, born at Orleans in 1691, died at Paris in 1762. A pupil in drawing of Bon de Boulogne.

P. VERONESE *pinx.* Rebecca and Eliezer.

The picture, probably not painted by Paolo Veronese, but from his school, is in the Gallery of the Louvre. Villot, No. 110.

Engraved for the *Cabinet Crozat.*

WATTEAU *pinx.* La Collation.

PH. WOUWERMANS *pinx.* Grande Chasse au Cerf. No. 20.

See Smith, *Cat. rais.* No. 14. When engraved, in 1736, the picture was owned by the Countess de Verrue; it is now in the Dresden Gallery. There is a repetition in the Gallery of the Louvre; Villot, No. 569.

La Fontaine de Bacchus. No. 22.

According to Smith, *Cat. rais.* No. 35, in the Dresden Gallery, but not identified in Hübner's Catalogue of that Gallery; when engraved in 1736, it was owned by Mr. de Fontpertuis.

PH. WOUWERMANS *pinx.* La Présent du Chasseur. No. 31.

Not in Smith, *Cat. rais.* A party returned from the chase, in front of a chateau; on the left a statue of Diana, on the right a fountain. When engraved, in 1738, the picture was in the collection of the Duke of Orleans, to whom the plate is dedicated.

MOYREAU, JEAN, *continued.*

PH. WOUWERMANS *pinx.* La petite Foire aux Chevaux. No. 33.

See Smith, *Cat. rais.* 26. When engraved, in 1738, the picture was in the collection of Prince Victor Amadeus of Savoy, Prince de Carignan, to whom the plate is dedicated; it is now in the Gallery of the Louvre, Villot, No. 576, under the title "Halte de militaires."

PH. WOUWERMANS *pinx.* Le Defilé d'Equipages. No. 44.

See Smith, *Cat. rais.* 204. When engraved, in 1742, the picture was in the possession of the Prince d'Issenghien, to whom the plate is dedicated; it was afterwards in the collections of D'Argenville, Praslin, Prince Talleyrand, and is now in that of A. Baring, Esq.

PH. WOUWERMANS *pinx.* Gardes de Cavalerie. No. 45.

See Smith, *Cat. rais.* 342. When engraved, in 1742, the picture was in the collection of M. Dinet; in 1827 in that of M. Van Loone in Amsterdam.

PH. WOUWERMANS *pinx.* Les Marchands Forains. No. 60.

See Smith, *Cat. rais.* 354. When engraved, in 1748, the picture was in the Gallery of Count Brühl in Dresden, the greater part of which was bought by Catharine II., for her Gallery at St. Petersburg.

PH. WOUWERMANS *pinx.* Départ pour la Chasse à l'Oiseau. No. 80.

See Smith, *Cat. rais.* 357. When engraved, in 1756, the picture was in the collection of the Marquis de Marigny, to whom the plate is dedicated.

*** These engravings form part of the "*Œuvre de Philippe Wouvermans, Hollandois, gravées d'après les meilleurs tableaux,* Paris, 1737," containing 89 plates. The plates are numbered, and the numbers used above refer to this work. Treuttel and Würtz, Paris, published a new edition, the plates of which are not desirable.

TITIAN *pinx.* **P.** François I.

The picture is in the Gallery of the Louvre; Villot, No. 469.

MÜCKE, HEINRICH CARL ANTON, painter and etcher, born at Breslau in 1806, lives in Düsseldorf. A pupil of his father and of König.

Two Friars leaning over a Parapet by a Lake.

In 8vo. Etched in 1840.

MULLER, JAN, designer and engraver, born at Amsterdam about 1570, flourished from 1589–1625. A follower of Goltzius. Bartsch, III.

SPRANGER *pinx.* "Apotheosis of the Fine Arts." B. 76.

Painting, Sculpture, and Architecture, fleeing from Barbarism, are received in Olympus. A great Allegory, engraved on two plates.

Impression with the 1st address, that of Harman Muller.

MULLER, JAN, *continued.*

The 2d address was that of Ger. Valck.

ALDEGREVER *sculps.* **P.** Johan van Leyden, King of the Anabaptists.

A copy of the engraving of Aldegrever (Bartsch, No. 182).

MÜLLER, JOHANN GOTTHARD VON, painter and engraver, born at Bernhausen near Stuttgart in 1747, died at Stuttgart in 1830. A pupil of Wille, and father and teacher of Johann Friedrich Wilhelm Müller, the engraver of the Sistine Madonna. *See* A. Andresen, *Johann Gotthard von Müller und Johann Friedrich Wilhelm Müller, beschreibendes Verzeichniss ihrer Kupferstiche*, Leipzig, 1865.

RAPHAEL *pinx.* Madonna della Sedia.

The well-known picture is in the Pitti palace. Passavant, II. 226. Engraved in 1804 for the *Musée Français.*

Old impression, with the name of Ramboz as printer.

The later ones have Durand's name.

RAPHAEL *pinx.* The same.

Artist's proof before any letters.

Rigal, No. 560; Bause, No. 2855.

The proofs have merely the artists' names; Rigal, No. 562. — 2d proofs have open letters.

DOMENICHINO *pinx.* FR. MÜLLER FILS *del.* St. Cecilia with a Basso.

The picture, formerly in Jabach's collection, is in the Gallery of the Louvre. Villot, No. 494. Engraved in 1809 for the *Musée Français.*

Proofs have merely the artists' names.

Artist's proofs are before any letters; they have, however, Müller's name very slightly traced on the *top* of the plate. Hösel, No. 126, 38 *th.*

"LEONARDO DA VINCI *pinx.*" St. Catherine with Two Angels.

The picture is by a follower of Leonardo da Vinci's school. Engraved in 1817, after one of the repetitions of the picture, owned by M. Frauenholz, a picture-dealer in Nuremberg. The best of these repetitions is in the Royal Gallery of Copenhagen. Rigollot, No. 48.

Artist's proof before any letters.

The 1st proof has the names of the artists merely; — the 2d has the inscription in open letters.

N. R. JOLLAIN *pinx.* The Nymph Erigone.

Engraved in 1773.

Proofs are before letters, having merely the name of the engraver; the 1st are *before* the coat of arms, the 2d with it.

J. TRUMBULL *pinx.* The Battle of Bunker Hill.

Lettre grise proof. Close under the plate, in open traced letters stands the inscription: "Painted by J. Trumbull, Esq. London, Published Feb. 1798,

MÜLLER, JOHANN GOTTHARD VON, *continued.*

by A. C. de Poggi, No. 91 New Bond Street. Engraved by J. G. Müller." *The next line is the title,* "The Battle of Bunker's Hill," *in open uncial letters. No further letters.*

The states of the plate, after the etching, are as follows: 1st, before any letters, from the larger plate before it was made smaller. — 2d, before letters, with only *J. G. Müller* slightly traced with the needle, the letters formed of two lines, open letters; Rigal, No. 565; Bause, I. No. 2864. — 3d, before letters, with the names of the painter and engraver; Debois, No. 747. — 4th, before letters, the name of the publisher added; Hillig, No. 327. — 5th, *lettre grise;* Schwarzenberg, No. 1085, and our copy. — 6th, with finished letters.

P. A. WILLE *pinx.* La Mère Brigide.

Engraved in 1772.

P. A. WILLE *pinx.* La Petite Javotte.

Engraved in 1772.

⁂ The proofs of these two plates are before all letters.

F. TISCHBEIN *pinx.* **P.** Dalberg, Carl Theodor Anton Marie Freyherr von.

Engraved in 1798.

Proof, i. e. lettre grise.

Artist's proofs are before all letters.

LOUIS TOCQUÉ *pinx.* **P.** Galloche, Louis, painter.

Engraved in 1776, as a second plate for his admission into the Academy.

LOUIS TOCQUÉ *pinx.* **P.** The same.

Proof, before all letters; it also has not the engraver's name traced on the top of the plate.

A. GRAFF *pinx.* **P.** Graff, Anton.

The picture is in the Dresden Gallery. Engraved in 1795.

Open letter proof.

A. GRAFF *pinx.* **P.** The same.

Artist's proof, before letters, with merely the artists' names.

There are still earlier artist's proofs, without any letters, having, however, the engraver's name traced on the top of the plate.

MME. KINSON *del.* **P.** Jérôme, Roi de Westphalie. In his Regal Robes.

Half length. "Dessiné à Cassel par Mde. Kinson." Engraved in 1813 by J. G. Müller, in conjunction with his son Friedrich Müller, who did the face and the lace kerchief.

A print; "Jérôme Napoléon" *in shaded German text,* "Roi de Westphalie, Prince Français" *in cursive letters.*

MÜLLER, JOHANN GOTTHARD VON, *continued.*

MME. KINSON *del.* **P.** The same.

An open letter proof, i. e. the first line, "Jérôme Napoléon," *is in open German text.*

MME. KINSON *del.* **P.** The same.

Artist's proof, before any letters.

N. S. A. BELLE *pinx.* **P.** Leramberg, Louis, sculptor.

Engraved in 1775, as the first plate for his admission into the Academy. Proofs are before all letters; Bause, No. 2875.

F. TISCHBEIN *pinx.* **P.** Loder, Professor of Anatomy.

Engraved in 1801.

Proof; the name is in cursive letters, traced with one line.

The rare artist's proofs are before any letters.

DUPLESSIS *pinx.* **P.** Louis XVI. King of France.

Engraved in 1793.

Open letter proof, 4th state.

The different impressions of this plate are:—

1. Before any letters; Rigal, No. 567.—2. With only the name *LOUIS SEIZE* traced with the needle, before letters, before Müller's name at the right below.—3. The same, but *with* Müller's name at the right below.—4. With the full inscription, the name *LOUIS SEIZE*, however, only traced, i. e. in open letters, before Ramboz's name, and with the traced address: *à Nuremberg chez Frauenholz.*—5. With the full inscription, engraved with the burin: *LOUIS SEIZE*, and below it: *Il voulut le bonheur de sa nation, et en devint la victime;* at the left, *Peint d'après nature par Duplessis;* at the right, *Gravé par J. G. Müller Prof. ... de l'Acad. des Arts à Paris,* and in the margin, at the left, *Imprimé à Nuremberg par Ramboz;* in the middle, *Se vend chés J. Fr. Frauenholz à Nuremberg.*

FRISCH *pinx.* **P.** Mendelssohn, Moses.

Engraved in 1787.

With the names of the artists and the dedication.

GREUZE *pinx.* **P.** Wille.

Engraved in 1776.—The original was sold at Paris in March, 1869, (Delessert's collection,) for £1,218.

2d impression, with the address of the engraver.

The 1st impressions are before the address. The proofs of the finished plate are before any letters; they have also not the engraver's name on the top of the plate.

MÜLLER, JOHANN FRIEDRICH WILHELM (*not* Christian Friedrich), son and pupil of the preceding Johann Gotthard, was born in 1782. After leaving the school of his father at Stuttgart, he studied for

MÜLLER, JOHANN FRIEDRICH WILHELM, *continued.*

several years at the Academy in Paris, was made Engraver to the King of Würtemberg, and afterwards Professor at the Academy of Dresden. His great work of the Sistine Madonna places him at the head of all modern engravers, and upon this plate he bestowed all his energies to the end of his life. He may be said even to have sacrificed life itself for it; he died at the Sonnenstein near Dresden, where he was confined, in the gloomiest depression of insanity, in 1816. A. Andresen, *Johann Gotthard von Müller und Johann Friedrich Wilhelm Müller*, Leipzig, 1865.

RAPHAEL *pinx.* Adam and Eve.

Engraved in 1812, after the fresco on the ceiling of the Camera della Segnatura of the Stanze in the Vatican. Passavant, II. 75.

Artist's proof of the finished plate, before any letters, with merely "Raf. Sanzio pinx. F. Müller sculp.," *traced in very thin letters.*

The artists' names were afterwards re-engraved differently.

A proof before any letters, even before the names of the artists, Lehrs, No. 330, 14$\frac{5}{6}$ *th.*

RAPHAEL *pinx.* The same.

Lettres grises. With the artists' names differently engraved. With the inscription "Was sich . . . im Leben," *in open, and the whole inscription in traced letters, with the dedication, and with the engraver's own address. Andresen's 4th state.*

The 5th state has shaded letters; — the 6th has Frauenholz's address added; — the 7th has the address taken out, and it has only the name Felsing as printer; — the 8th is with the address of the Bibliographic Institution in Hildburghausen.

RAPHAEL *pinx.* Madonna di San Sisto.

The picture, now the pride of the Dresden Gallery, was painted for the Gray Friars of the order of St. Benedict of the cloister of St. Sixtus in Piacenza, as a drapellone (according to Rumohr), a banner to be carried round in procession, and for this reason on canvas, which otherwise was very seldom used instead of panel in the Roman and Tuscan schools. It must soon, however, have been withdrawn from this use, as Vasari already found it secured on the principal altar of their church. In 1753 it was bought for Augustus III., Elector of Saxony, after protracted negotiations, and an old copy by Paris Nogari put up in its place. When, in 1827, the celebrated restorer Palmeroli of Rome was called to clean, line, and varnish the picture, which had become dim and dry, he at the same time unrolled the upper end of the canvas, which had been turned over the frame in such a manner that the top of the curtain with the rod and rings was concealed. These parts were not brought to view at the time of this engraving. They are represented in Steinla's engraving of the year 1847.

MÜLLER, JOHANN FRIEDRICH WILHELM, *continued.*

A proof etching of the plate, containing the whole design. The Madonna and Child are WITHOUT, *the two Saints* WITH, *a halo. Below the print are traces of small letters in reverse.*

RAPHAEL *pinx.* The same.

Artist's proof before any letters. The Madonna and Child are without a halo, though St. Sixtus and St. Barbara have one, as in the etching. At the right below there are still the traces of letters in reverse, very slightly written with the needle: "gef. d. 26 Merz. geätzt 24 Jul 1810."

From the collection of the father of the engraver, J. G. von Müller.

Other recorded exemplars of this very rare state of the plate: — Durand, 1821 (sold for 550 *fr.*); Révil, 1845, No. 118 (sold for 1,750 *fr.*), where it is said that but five impressions are known to exist of this state of the plate; but it is there stated that, besides these, there occur some impressions without any letters, *with* the halos on the heads of the Madonna and Child (these, of course, would also be without the traces of the letters in reverse); they were taken from the plate after the first inscription of the proofs (*Madonna di S. Sisto di Rafaele,* in traced letters) and the artists' names had been erased to make room for the inscription in uncial letters and the coat of arms, and dedication of the prints. I never saw such a spurious artist's proof. — Th[orel], 1853, No. 111, this identical exemplar of the Révil collection, "l'une des cinq épreuves tirées de cet état," 2,550 *fr.* The same copy, of the Révil and Thorel collections, occurred again in the sale of the engravings of M. Thieme, Leipzig, Jan. 28, 1867, No. 51, and was purchased by Messrs. Amsler and Ruthardt of Berlin for 185 thalers. I saw the print at that time, and ascertained that it corresponds exactly with the impression in the Gray collection, the Virgin and Child wanting the halo in both, and both having the somewhat indistinct inscription, or rather traces of an inscription, in reverse, at the bottom of the plate. — Johnson, 1861, No. 126, £126; Archinto, 1862, No. 293, 3,000 *fr.*; Marshall, 1864, No. 1190, "first finished proof before any letters, and before the aureoles over the heads of the Virgin and Child," £86.

RAPHAEL *pinx.* The same.

Proof, before the coat of arms and dedication, with only the names of the artists, of the publisher, and printer, and the title "La Madonna di S. Sisto di Rafaele," *in open cursive letters.*

On the back, written in pencil, the name H[ermann] Weber (of Bonn).

Bought from Mr. M. M. Holloway, for £50. — Debois, No. 750, 1,300 *fr.*; Quandt, Leipzig, 1860, No. 219, 416 *th.*; Lehrs, Berlin, 1866, No. 323, on India paper, 740 *th.* In the autumn of 1867 a similar impression was sold in Dresden by Mr. Ernst Arnold to C. F. Harris, Esq., of Providence, R. I., for 800 thalers.

MÜLLER, JOHANN, FRIEDRICH WILHELM, *continued.*

After this state, twelve impressions of the print were struck off with letters and arms, in which the word *servo* in the dedication was omitted on the plate. Our collection does not possess one of these.

RAPHAEL *pinx.* The same.

Impression of a print with the letters, that is, the artists' names, coat of arms, title in uncial letters, and dedication. An early impression on India paper, like R. Weigel's, Kunst-Catalog, No. 11008.

Purchased for 200 thalers. These first impressions on India paper precede those on plain paper, and are highly esteemed; they are said to have been taken only in very small numbers and for presentation copies. It seems, however, that later, after the several retouches of the plate, some new impressions on India paper were made. I know of one with the retouch of Desnoyers, and have seen one even of a very late and very wretched retouch.

RAPHAEL *pinx.* The same.

Impression with the first retouch, by Bervic.

The second and more extensive retouch was by Desnoyers; and after him there are retouches without number. Impressions after a thorough re-engraving of the plate are within the last two years.

DOMENICHINO *pinx.* St. John the Evangelist.

Engraved in 1808, after a picture, then in the possession of M. Fromman, in Stuttgart, of whom Prince Narishkin bought it, and sold it afterwards to the Emperor Alexander I. of Russia for 60,000 rubles. It is a repetition of the picture of the Orleans Gallery, now in the collection of the Earl of Carlisle at Castle Howard.

1*st state; with* "Dom*i*nichino pinx.," *with the date* 1808 *after the name of the engraver, with the name of Ramboz as printer, and, in the dedication to his father, the words* "von seinem Sohne." *The inscription* "Da gerieth ich am Tage des Herrn," *etc. in uncial letters is shaded, in this state as well as in the originals of the* 2*d state.*

DOMENICHINO *pinx.* The same.

Engraved in 1808.

DOMENICHINO *pinx.* The same.

Engraved in 1812.

The plate, after being ground down, was very carefully retouched, and, after an excellent water-color drawing by Müller's pupil Esslinger, especially of the head, was engraved anew by the latter and Müller.

2*d state of the print. The spelling of the painter's name in the inscription is changed to* "Domenichino," *and the date has been altered to* 1812. *The dedication ends with the words* "von dem Verfasser" *instead of* "gewidmet

MÜLLER, JOHANN FRIEDRICH WILHELM, *continued.*

von seinem Sohne," *and the name of Ramboz as printer is wanting; having been covered up in printing.*

Good impressions of the original plate of 1812 are almost as rare as those of 1808.

DOMENICHINO *pinx.* The same.

Still with the year 1812.

3d state of the print. A quite new, entire re-engraving of the plate. The work is boldly and cleverly done. The light place under the forefinger of the right hand of St. John is gone over with continued diagonal strokes; the light place over the scroll is almost filled up by continued diagonal strokes. The reflection of light in the eyes is closed towards the outside, while it was open in the former impressions. The inscription "Da gerieth ich," *etc. appears again in open letters. The paper is, of course, fresh and new.*

Besides this, there is the following, an older, counterfeit copy of this plate.

DOMENICHINO *pinx.* The same.

With the date 1812.

M. Rudolph Weigel, who furnished this copy, describes it minutely in his Kunst-Lager Catalog, No. 14288, *to which I refer. I would only add that the print is more feebly engraved, and that the inscription,* "Da gerieth ich," *etc. is in open letters formed of two lines without shading. The paper is of a bluish white tint.*

Proof, Wilson, No. 443, "first finished impression, with the inscription only traced, with the text in open letters, and before the address [*sic*] of Ramboz," and, in a note, "The inscription, it is said, was erased after a few of these impressions were taken, and some were then printed without letters. These, and a few in an unfinished state, are, it is believed, the only ones without writing." — Same state, Debois, No. 751; Th[orel], Nos. 113 and 114; Johnson, No. 125, £ 38; G. Smith, No. 1026, £ 21; Sir J. Hippisley, No. 116, £ 29 8 *s.*; Marshall, No. 1189, £ 24 3 *s.*; Lehrs, No. 328, 126 *th.*

At Goddard's sale, No. 355, occurred "a proof before any letters"; it was bid in by Mr. Colnaghi for £ 30.

See, however, Andresen, quoted at the head of the article Müller, who describes the following states: 1st, before any letters, of which there are (a) 50 impressions made in Stuttgart, which are not so satisfactory, and (b) 50 more made by Ramboz in Paris, which are the rare and precious impressions. — 2d state, with the names of the artists. — 3d state, with the full inscription, of which, however, the two first lines are only traced in open letters, like Wilson's. In the fall of 1867 an impression of this state was sold by Mr. Ernst Arnold in Dresden for 250 thalers, about £ 37, to C. F. Harris, Esq., of Providence, R. I.

MÜLLER, JOHANN FRIEDRICH WILHELM, *continued.*

F. MÜLLER *del.* **P.** Hebel, Johann Peter, author of *Allemannische Gedichte, Schatzkästlein,* etc.

In 8vo.

First proof etching, the portrait only in an octagon, and before any letters.

F. MÜLLER *del.* **P.** The same.

The finished engraving. Shaded from the octagon to a square border, with the inscription, and the address of Artaria and Fontaine.

F. TISCHBEIN *pinx.* **P.** Hufeland, Professor of Medicine in Berlin.

Engraved in 1802 as a pendant to J. G. von Müller's portrait of Loder.

Proof, the name traced in cursive letters.

Artist's proofs are before all letters.

MME. KINSON *del.* **P.** Jerome, King of Westphalia. *See* MÜLLER, J. G.

F. MÜLLER *pinx.* **P.** William, Crown Prince of Würtemberg.

Engraved in 1806.

AFTER THE ANTIQUE. The Venus of Arles.

Engraved for the *Musée Français.*

Proof before letters; under the right-hand corner below stands merely "F. Müller fils," *written in small letters formed of dots.*

AFTER THE ANTIQUE. The same.

Artist's proof, before any letters.

MÜLLER, JOHANN FRIEDRICH, an engraver of the present day, born at Weimar, son of the engraver Johann Christian Ernst Müller.

RAPHAEL *pinx.* **P.** Raphael at the age of 23 years.

From the picture in the Artists' Portrait Gallery at Florence. Passavant, II. No. 47, and p. 621, No. 5. Engraved in 1834, after a drawing by his brother Moritz (Müller, called) Steinla.

Proof, with cursive letters traced with the needle. On India paper.

Artist's proofs are before letters.

HOLBEIN *pinx.* **P.** Calvin.

The original is in the Council-chamber of the Consistory in Dresden.

MÜLLER, F.*

P. "Friedrich Josias Prinz v(on) Coburg, Kaisl. Oestr. Feldmarschall."

"F. Müller gest.," without the name of the painter. Engraved in a square, small 4to. There is another engraving of this prince by Johann

* This seems to be a different artist from the two just mentioned, inferior to Friedrich Wilhelm, the son of Johann Gotthard, and older than Johann Friedrich, son of Johann Christian Ernst. Nagler, IX. p. 548, mentions another Christian Friedrich Müller, born at Copenhagen in 1744, and a pupil of Preisler, who engraved subjects of natural history, and a Christian Ferdinand Müller, who engraved in Leipzig the latter half of the last century, principally for booksellers.

MÜLLER, F., *continued.*

Christian Ernst Müller, father of Johann Friedrich, in an oval, fol. Nagler, No. 6; Le Blanc, No. 22.

P. "B[enjamin T[hompson] Graf v[on] Rumford."

"F. Müller gest.," without the name of the painter.

MÜLLER, CARL, an engraver of the present day at Frankfort.

PH. VEIT *pinx.* The Years of Plenty.

After Veit's cartoon in Städel's Museum at Frankfort. Engraved for Count Raczynski's *Histoire de l'art moderne dans l'Allemagne,* Vol. I. 1836.

Open letters.

MUNTANER, F., engraver at Madrid in the latter half of the last century.

MURILLO *pinx.* The Virgin appearing to St. Bernard.

The picture is in the Gallery of Madrid. Stirling's *Annals,* II. p. 914, and III. p. 1435. Engraved for the *Coleccion de las estampas de los cuadros . . . pertenecientes al Rey de España.*

MURPHY, JOHN, engraver in mezzotint, born in 1748, worked in London, and died at the beginning of this century.

TITIAN *pinx.* The Son of Titian led by his Nurse.

The picture is in the Imperial Gallery of St. Petersburg. Engraved for the Houghton Gallery.

MUSI, AGOSTINO DE'. *See* AGOSTINO VENEZIANO.

MÜTZEL, HEINRICH, landscape painter and lithographer at Berlin, known since 1830.

LESSING *pinx.* The Smugglers.

A landscape.

N.

NANTEUIL, ROBERT, painter and engraver, born at Rheims in 1630, died at Paris in 1678. A pupil of Regnesson and Ph. de Champagne, and of A. Bosse. Robert-Dumesnil, IV.

PH. DE CHAMPAGNE *pinx.* Moses. R.-D. 1.

Engraved in conjunction with G. Edelinck.

3d state, with Drevet's address.

See EDELINCK.

Mater Dolorosa. R.-D. 5.

A bust.

Without the inscription on the banderole, "Ante te omne Desiderium

NANTEUIL, ROBERT, *continued.*

meum," *but with the crochet in place of the year* 1654, *therefore in the 3d state, with the inscription taken out.*

LE SUEUR *pinx.* The Four Evangelists. R.-D. 7.

The later impressions, 3d state *et seqq.*, were used to adorn C. Savreux's *Historia et Concordia Evangelica,* Paris, 1653, 12mo.

1*st state,* "très rare," *before the inscription on the banderole,* "Unus atque idem Spiritus."

From Otto's collection.

MIGNARD *pinx.* 𝔓. Anne of Austria, Queen of Louis XIII. R.-D. 22.

3*d state of* 5, *before the No.* 15 *over the coat of arms.*

NANTEUIL *pinx.* 𝔓. Anne of Austria. R.-D. 23.

Life size.

2*d state, with the crochet after the year.*

NANTEUIL *del.* 𝔓. Barberini, Cardinal. R.-D. 29.

2*d state, with the additional shading on the right side of the plate.*

NANTEUIL *pinx.* 𝔓. Bartillat, Étienne Johannot de. R.-D. 32.

1*st state,* 1666.

The 2d state has the date 1668.

NANTEUIL *del.* 𝔓. Beaumanoir, Bishop of Mans. R.-D. 35.

1*st state* (*of* 5), 1660.

NANTEUIL *del.* 𝔓. The same. R.-D. 35.

2*d state,* 1666.

LE BRUN *pinx.* 𝔓. Bellièvre, Pomponne de. R.-D. 37.

2*d state, with the crochet after* "sculpebat."

From Otto's collection.

In the Harrach collection, sold at Paris, Feb. 1867, occurred a very fine impression of the 2d state, No. 1621, which sold for 200 *fr.*

1st state before the crochet, Archinto, No. 299, 1055 *fr.* The identical impression, Marshall, No. 1238, £44.

NANTEUIL *del.* 𝔓. Blondeau, François. R.-D. 40.

From the collection and with the name of "G. Storck à Milan 1797" on the back of the print.

NANTEUIL *del.* 𝔓. Bragelogne, Marie de, Veuve de Claude Le Bouthillier. R.-D. 57.

4*th state, with two dots and a stroke, in a perpendicular line between the two coats of arms under the plate, which has no inscription, except the name of the artist.*

NANTEUIL *del.* 𝔓. Charles de Lorraine. R.-D. 63.

From Otto's collection.

NANTEUIL, ROBERT, *continued.*

BOURDON *pinx.* **P.** Christina of Sweden. R.-D. 67.
3d state, with the mark ? after esclaues.

NANTEUIL *del.* **P.** Clermont-Tonnerre, Bishop of Noyon. R.-D. 68.
1st state (of 3), before the pastoral cross.

NANTEUIL *del.* **P.** The same. R.-D. 68.
2d state, with the pastoral cross.

NANTEUIL *del.* **P.** Coislin, Cardinal. R.-D. 69.
1st state, with the date 1658.
The 2d state has 1664.

CHAMPAGNE *pinx.* **P.** Colbert, J.-B. R.-D. 72.
2d state (of 3). The two dots after the crochet are separated by a perpendicular stroke.
In the 3d state a laurel wreath was substituted for the inscription.

NANTEUIL *del.* **P.** Colbert, J.-B. R.-D. 74.
Life size.
5th state (of 7), with three dots.

NANTEUIL *pinx.* **P.** Colbert, J. N., Abbas, etc. R.-D. 77.
Life size.
2d state, having in the middle of the upper margin a mark like ?

NANTEUIL *del.* **P.** Condé, Louis de Bourbon (IIe du nom), Prince de.
R.-D. 79.

CHAMPAGNE *pinx.* **P.** Henri de Guénégaud. R.-D. 106.
1st state, before the order of the Holy Spirit.

NANTEUIL *del.* **P.** Hesselin, Louis. R.-D. 110.
Engraved by Nanteuil alone, and in the manner of Mellan.
2d state, with the name of the person inscribed on the socle.

NANTEUIL *del.* **P.** Jeannin, Pierre. R.-D. 112.

NANTEUIL *del.* **P.** La Masle, Michel. R.-D. 126.
1st state, with the date 1658.
The 2d has 1661.

CHAMPAGNE *pinx.* **P.** Le Tellier, Michel. R.-D. 128.
2d state, with the names of the artists.

NANTEUIL *del.* **P.** Le Tellier, Michel. R.-D. 129.
1st state, with 1658.
The 2d has 1659.

NANTEUIL *del.* **P.** Le Tellier, Michel. R.-D. 135.
2d state, with the crochet after the word "Regis."
The 1st state is before the crochet.

NANTEUIL, ROBERT, *continued.*

P. Le Vayer, François de la Mothe. R.-D. 143.

2d state, with the year between marks of quotation.

NANTEUIL *del.* **P.** Loménie de Brienne, Henri Auguste de. R.-D. 148.

1st state, before the name of the person on the socle.

CHAMPAGNE *pinx.* **P.** Longueville, Henri d'Orléans, (IIe du nom,) Duc de. R.-D. 149.

NANTEUIL *del.* **P.** Loret, Jean, poet. R.-D. 150.

2d state, with the crochet after the year, as well as a period. "*Rare.*"

The 1st state, "very rare," has only a period. — The comma after the name *Loret* in the first verse of the inscription indicates the 3d state.

From Otto's collection.

NANTEUIL *del.* **P.** Longueil, René de, Marquis de Maisons. R.-D. 166.

4th state (*of* 5), *with* 1662.

With the names of P. Mariette and Amann on the back, and from Baron Friesen's collection, No. 2278.

NANTEUIL *del.* **P** Maridat de Serrière, Pierre de. R.-D. 168.

In 8vo.

NANTEUIL *del.* **P.** Novion, Nicolas Potier de. R.-D. 207.

1st state, before the crochet after the year.

Harrach, No. 1730, 50*fr.*

NANTEUIL *del.* **P.** Ormesson, André Le Fèvre d'. R.-D. 209.

1st state, before the year (1654) *was erased.*

NANTEUIL *pinx.* **P.** Poncet, Pierre. R.-D. 215.

1st state (*of* 3), *before the change in the collar, or rather band.*

The 2d state shows the knot below.—The 3d state has 1673 instead of 1660.

From Baron Friesen's collection, No. 2312, with the names of P. Mariette and H. Schmidt on the back.

NANTEUIL *del.* **P.** Regnauldin, Claude. R.-D. 216.

1st state (*of* 5), *the year* 1658 *followed by a dot.*

The 2d state is denoted by a crochet; the 3d has the date 1661; the 4th, 1663; the 5th has a crochet after the year.

With the signature and from the collection of John Barnard.

NANTEUIL *del.* **P.** Sarrasin, Jean François. R.-D. 220.

2d state (*of* 4), *with one perpendicular stroke in the lower margin.*

From Otto's collection.

The 1st state is before any stroke. "*Très rare.*" Harrach, No. 1740, 106*fr.* — The 2d state has two strokes; the 3d three.

NANTEUIL *del.* **P.** Scuderi, George de. R.-D. 221.

1st state, before the plate was reduced.

NANTEUIL, ROBERT, *continued.*

From Geissler's collection.

NANTEUIL *del.* **P.** Seguier de Saint-Brisson, Pierre. R.-D. 224.

DUCHASTEL *pinx.* **P.** Steenberghen, Johan Baptist van, " L'Advocat de Hollande." R.-D. 226.

1st state (of 4), with " Duchastel pinxit."

With the collector's stamp, the letters *F. A.* with a crown over them.

DUCHASTEL *pinx.* **P.** The same. R.-D. 226.

2d state, with " nob. D. F. Duchastel pinxit."

In the 3d state " nob. D. F." is effaced, but the traces are still visible; — in the 4th, on the socle in open letters are the words : *Ioan. Bapt. van Steenberghen.*

NANTEUIL *pinx.* **P.** Tvrenne, Henricvs de La Tovr Davvergne, Princeps et Vicecomes de. R.-D. 233.

Of the size of life.

4th state (of 6), with the stroke or line, " barre," *between* " R." *and* " Nanteuil"; *no longer showing the little stroke between* " privilegio " *and* " Regis," *and the* ,, *after the crochet* ∾ *at the end of the inscription, which were to be seen in the 3d state; — before the three dots* ∴ *following the crochet* ∾, *which indicate the 5th state.*

In the 6th state these dots, as well as the " barre " between " R." and " Nanteuil," have disappeared.

With P. Mariette's name on the back. Purchased for £ 14 14 *s.*

NARDINI, modern Italian engraver.

TITIAN *pinx.* The Virgin and Child in a glory, with St. John.

The original was formerly in the Giustiniani Gallery.

Proof before any letters.

NARGEOT, JEAN DENIS, engraver, was born at Paris in 1795, and died there. A pupil of Roger and of Benoist.

MURILLO *pinx.* The Virgin in a glory of Angels, with Four Saints below.

The picture is in the Marquis of Hertford's collection. Waagen, *Treasures,* II. p. 156. Engraved for the *Aguado Gallery.*

Proof before letters. On India paper.

NATALIS, MICHEL, designer and engraver, born at Liége in 1606 or 1609, died about 1680. A pupil of Mallery and Joachim von Sandrart.

RUBENS *pinx.* Christ at the House of Simon the Pharisee.

Basan, 55; Smith, No. 549. The picture is in the Imperial Gallery of St. Petersburg; it was formerly in the Houghton Gallery.

The impression has the address of Abraham a Diepenbeke; like Brandes's and Winckler's.

NATALIS, MICHEL, *continued.*

TITIAN *pinx.* **P.** Marquis del Guasto, and a Female to whom Cupid, Flora, and Zephyr bring Offerings.

The picture is in the Gallery of the Louvre. Villot, No. 470.

Proof before letters.

NEEFFS, JACOB, engraver, born at Antwerp in 1630.

RUBENS *pinx.* St. Michael vanquishing the rebellious Angels.

Basan, No. 2. Smith mentions this engraving under No. 1024; the composition, however, corresponds better with No. 173.

1st state, with the sparks from the inferno on the left (which in the later impressions are spots), and with the first address of G. Hendricx. Inscription of one line.

RUBENS *pinx.* Martyrdom of St. Thomas, the Apostle.

See Basan, 48; Smith, *Cat. rais.* 147; Michiels, No. 188.

Old impression on firm thin paper, of rough texture, without address.

VAN DYCK *pinx.* **P.** Martin Ryckaert, landscape painter of Antwerp.

Ryckaert was born in 1591. He painted with his left hand, as he was without a right arm. He died at Paris in 1636. — The picture is in the collection of the Earl of Warwick, Warwick Castle (in the "Red room"), and it is the portrait of Martin Ryckaert, not David, as is sometimes stated, by mistake, e. g. by Smith, *Cat. rais.* 741. Engraved for G. Hendricx's *Iconographia;* Weber, p. 104.

2d and last state, the address "G. H." *effaced. Early paper, no watermark perceptible.*

VAN DYCK *pinx.* **P.** Van Dyck.

Etched by Van Dyck, finished by Neeffs. Carpenter, p. 92, No. 4; Weber, p. 23. (See further under VAN DYCK, p. 107.) The original picture is in the Florentine Gallery; the grisaille for this engraving is in the collection of the Duke of Buccleugh. Smith, *Cat. rais.* 159.

3d state, with "G. Hendricx exc.," *but the year* 1645 *effaced; before Verdussen's address. Papermark, the arms of Amsterdam.*

VAN DYCK *pinx.* **P.** Frans Snyders, painter.

Van Dyck etched the head and coat. Carpenter, p. 107, No. 15; Weber, p. 31. (See further under VAN DYCK, p. 108.)

3d state, with the address "G[*illis*] H[*endricx*]." *Paper with the watermark of a Fool's-cap.*

In the 4th and last state the two letters are effaced.

Engraved after the picture in the collection of the Earl of Carlisle, at Castle Howard, "one of the finest of the master, — and of all portraits," with a change in the position of the hands. Waagen, *Handbook,* II. p. 287; Smith, *Cat. rais.* 329. A similar picture is in the Munich Gallery. Smith, *Cat. rais.* 54.

NICOL, WILLIAM, published in 1851 a lithograph:

𝔓. Shakespeare.

Head, and neck to below the collar. With the words "Gul. Shakspeare 1597. R. B." in fac-simile of the writing of that date, and the further inscription: "A fac-simile in all but colour of the remains of a Portrait on pannel of William Shakspeare, by Richard Burbage, his fellow-player and partner. Published as the act directs June 4th 1851, for the Proprietor, William Nicol, of the Shakspeare Press by W. N. Wright, Bookseller to The Queen, 60 Pall Mall."

NICOLET, BERNARD ANTOINE, engraver, born at St. Immier, in the ancient bishopric of Basle, in 1740, died at Paris in 1807. A pupil of Boily and Cochin.

RAPHAEL *pinx.* Madonna del Baldacchino.

The picture is in the Gallery of the Pitti palace, Florence. Passavant, II. 62. Engraved in 1802 for Wicar's *Galerie de Florence.*

NIELLO. See under BOTTICELLO, Sandro.

NOCCHI, P., engraved for V. Marchese, "San Marco in Firenze."

FRA FIESOLE *pinx.* Crucifixion and Saints.

See under MARCHESE.

NOEL, ALPHONSE LEON, lithographer, born at Paris in 1807. A pupil of Gros and Hersent.

PALMA VECCHIO *pinx.* The Three Daughters of Palma vecchio.

The picture is in the Dresden Gallery.

RAPHAEL *pinx.* Head of the Angel in Raphael's Madonna of the Fish.

Passavant, II. 100.

NORBLIN DE LA GOURDAINE, JEAN PIERRE, painter and etcher, born at Misy-Faut Yonne (Basse Bourgogne) in 1745. He was a pupil of Franc. Casanova in Dresden; adopted the style of etching of Rembrandt; worked from 1774 to 1804 in Poland, when he returned to France, and died there in 1830.

The (little) Rat-catcher.

In 8vo.

The Offering of the Crown of Poland to Piast.

NOVELLI, FRANCESCO, engraver, born at Venice in 1764. A pupil of his father Pietro Antonio Novelli.

REMBRANDT *inv.* The Descent from the Cross.

A copy of Rembrandt's etching.

O.

OBERTHÜR, F. J., an engraver of the present time at Strassburg.

F. GÜNTHER *del.* The Cathedral of Strassburg.

Engraved in 1827.

OLESZCYNSKI, ANTON, Polish painter and engraver in Paris, in the earlier part of this century.

RAPHAEL *inv.* A Man sawing.

An academic study from Raphael's fresco in the Vatican, "The building of the Ark."

Presentation copy to Count Potocki, with the engraver's autograph.

OLMÜTZ, WENZEL VON, goldsmith and engraver, a scholar or imitator of Martin Schongauer. Bartsch, VI.

St. Sebastian. B. 30.

OSTADE, ADRIAAN VAN, painter and etcher, born at Lubeck in 1610, moved to Amsterdam in 1662, where he died in 1685. A pupil of Frans Hals. Bartsch, I., and Weigel's Supplement.

The Smokers. B. 13.

3d and last state, with the border line.

The Smoker and the Drinker. B. 24, appendix.

2d state (of 3).

The Humpbacked Fiddler. B. 44.

2d and last state.

The Fiddler and Hurdy-Gurdy Boy. B. 45.

3d and last state.

OTTAVIANI, GIOVANNI, engraver, born at Rome about 1735, died in 1808. A pupil of Wagner in Venice.

FR. SMUGLIEWICZ *del.* "The Aldobrandine Marriage." The Nuptials of Thetis and Peleus.

From the antique picture, found in 1606 in the Villa Aldobrandini, now preserved in the Appartamento Borgia in the Vatican.

RAPHAEL *pinx.* Le Loggie.*

* The Loggie in the Vatican are three stories of galleries or corridors, running round three sides of an open court. The first side, which is next to the staircase of the second story, and leads to the Stanze, contains the Loggie of Raphael. Since 1813 it has been closed with glass. It is an arcade, the roof of which is formed of thirteen cupolas, each containing four paintings of connected subjects, the whole fifty-two forming "Raphael's Bible." (*See* MONTAGNANI.) Ottaviani, in Part II., gives only the principal representation of each cupola. These rest on pilasters, richly ornamented in

OTTAVIANI, GIOVANNI, *continued.*

Kugler, II. 361; Passavant, III. 202; Platner and Bunsen, *Rom*, II. i. p. 302 *et seqq.* Engraved in conjunction with Giovanni Volpato. 46 plates large folio, in 3 parts, namely: —

I.

19 plates, namely: —

Title to Part I., Perspective View of the Loggie; above is the portrait of Raphael in a medallion; below, the inscription, "Loggie di Rafaele nel Vaticano. Pĕtrus Camporesi delin. Joannes Volpato sculp."

Text, headed by a vignette of griffins, etc., and at the bottom of the second page, "A Rome 1772 (not 1782) chez Marc Pagliarini." One sheet of two pages, each in two columns.

Section through the centre "Spaccato per il longo," etc.

Door A of the Loggie.

Door B of the Loggie.

The doors were carved in wood by Gian Barile, after designs by Raphael.

I. Ornament ("Arabesque") resting on a Mask.
II. Ornament with a Saddled Horse in the middle.
III. Ornament with a Deer at the bottom.
IV. Ornament with Fame sitting on a Globe.
V. Ornament with Climbing Vine.
VI. Ornament with Diana of Ephesus.
VII. Ornament with a Bird-catcher.
VIII. Ornament with Sporting Children.
IX. Ornament with Climbing Vine.
Pendant to V.
X. Ornament resting on a Group of three Figures.
XI. Ornament resting on a Porcupine.
XII. Ornament resting on a Vase.
XIII. Ornament with the Temple of Diana in the centre.
XIV. Ornament with Landscapes and Hunting Pieces.

*** These are all engraved by Ottaviani.

color and stucco; as is the space round the representations in the arches. The space round the windows leading from the Stanze into the Loggie is ornamented with flowers and fruit. The ornaments are in the style of the antique grotesque, — so called from the rooms of an antique building where this kind of ornament was found having become subterranean grottos, through the rising of the surrounding ground. For all these pictures, reliefs, and ornaments Raphael made the designs in sepia; Giulio Romano superintended their execution, the decorative department being under the direction of Giovanni da Udino and Perino del Vaga. These ornaments are often, not quite correctly, called Arabesques of Raphael. The arabesque proper is a geometrically constructed design, excluding the representation of men and animals, originated by the Arab patterns of weaving and embroidery, which, even when painted, were intended to represent their rich tapestry. Comp. Quandt, *Verzeichniss meiner Kupferstich-sammlung*, p. 273.

OTTAVIANI, GIOVANNI, *continued.*

II.

Seconda parte delle logge di Rafaele nel Vaticano che contiene XIII. volte ed i loro respettivi quadri. Pubblicata in Roma l' anno 1776.

The 13 Arches and the pictures over them (Raphael's Bible).

14 plates, namely :—

1. God dividing Light from Darkness. P. II. 128.
2. Adam and Eve at Work out of Paradise. P. II. 135.
3. Building of the Ark. P. II. 136.
4. Three Angels appearing to Abraham. P. II. 142.
5. God appearing to Isaac. P. II. 144.
6. Jacob's Ladder. P. II. 148.
7. Joseph telling his Dream. P. II. 152.
8. The Finding of Moses. P. II. 156.
9. Moses showing the Tables of the Law. P. II. 163.
10. The Fall of Jericho. P. II. 165.
11. David's Triumph over the Syrians. P. II. 170.
12. The Judgment of Solomon. P. II. 173.
13. The Last Supper. P. II. 179.

*** These are all engraved by Ottaviani.

III.

Terza ed ultima parte delle logge di Rafaele nel Vaticano che contiene il compimento degli ornati e de' bassirilievi antichi, esistenti nelle logge medesime. Pubblicata in Roma l' anno 1777.

13 plates, namely :—

1. Ornament with Fishes in the middle.
2. Ornament with Venus and Diana.
3. Ornament with Musical Instruments.
4. Ornament with Three Girls dancing, at the bottom.
5. Ornament with a Faun and his Wife tilting.
6. Ornament with Landscape with ruins.
7. Ornament with Sporting Children supported by two Satyrs.

* 8. Ornament with the Four Seasons.

Compare Waagen, *Treasures,* II. p. 382 ; Passavant, II. p. 208.

* 9. Ornament with the Three Fates. P. II. p. 208.

* 10. Ornament with Day and Night : Apollo and Diana with a Dial.

Compare Waagen, *Treasures,* II. p. 389 ; Passavant, II. p. 208.

* 11. Ornament with Faith, Hope, and Love.

* The designs of the five numbers marked with an asterisk are from *tapestries for the Sistine Chapel,* strips for the decoration of the pillars which separated the large Arras-hangings after Raphael's designs.

OTTAVIANI, GIOVANNI, *continued.*

Compare Waagen, *Treasures,* II. p. 379; Passavant, II. p. 208.

* 12. Ornament with Heaven — Hercules, who has taken the Celestial Sphere from Atlas — and Earth.

See Waagen, *Treasures,* II. p. 389; Passavant, II. p. 208.

⁂ These are all engraved by Volpato.

OUTKYN, NIKOLAUS, engraver in St. Petersburg. A pupil of Klauber and Bervic.

DOMENICHINO *pinx.* Æneas saving Anchises.

The picture is in the Louvre, where it is now ascribed to Spada. Villot, No. 409. Engraved for the *Musée Français.*

P.

PALMERINI, NICCOLÒ, engraver in Florence. A pupil of R. Morghen. He is the author of *Opere d' intaglio del cav. Raffaello Morghen raccolte ed illustrate,* Firenze, 1810, 8vo. — 3ª ed., Firenze, 1824, 8vo.

𝔓. Ginevra Benci.

After a picture in the Pandolfi family in Florence which Rigollot (*Catalogue de l'œuvre de Leonardo da Vinci,* p. 74) attributes to Sandro Botticelli. Palmerini engraved it as the *portrait of Petrarch's Laura,* but identified it afterwards as that of Ginevra, by Domenico Ghirlandajo's fresco, the Visitation in Santa Maria Novella, in which this celebrated beauty is introduced (see Vasari). There is another portrait of her, by Leonardo da Vinci, in the Gallery of the Pitti palace (Rigollot, No. 67). The portrait of Laura, from a miniature in a MS. in the Laurentian Library in Florence, by Simone Memmi, is engraved by Bridoux. *See* BRIDOUX.

PANNIER, an engraver of the present day in Paris.

VELAZQUEZ *pinx.* 𝔓. Bust of a Young Man.

Engraved in 1846 as Velazquez's own portrait.

Open letter.

The picture is in the Historical Museum at Versailles. The engraving is mentioned in Stirling's *Velazquez,* p. 251, Catalogue.

PARMEGIANO, that is **FRANCESCO MAZZUOLI,** called PARMEGIANO, or PARMEGIANINO, painter and etcher, born at Parma in 1503, died at Casal Maggiore in 1540. Bartsch, XVI.

The Entombment. B. 5.

The Resurrection of Christ. B. 6.

PASSE, WILLEM DE, designer and engraver, son and pupil of Crispin, born at Utrecht in 1590. See under DÜRER, p. 104.

PAVON, IGNAZIO, engraver in Florence. A pupil of R. Morghen.

PERUGINO *pinx.* The Temptation.

DOMENICHINO *pinx.* Communion of St. Jerome.

The picture is in the Gallery of the Vatican.

Proof before letters, with only the artists' names, "Dom. Zampieri dito il Domenichino dip. Luigi Durantini dis. Ignazio Pavon inc."

SASSOFERRATO *pinx.* Mater Amabilis.

"RAPHAEL *pinx.*" La Vierge au Papillon.

See Passavant, II. p. 410, s. A picture of Raphael's school. — (To judge from the engraving without having seen the painting, I should be inclined to attribute it to Sassoferrato.)

PENCZ, GEORG, painter and engraver, born at Nuremberg in 1500, died at Königsberg in 1550. A pupil of Albrecht Dürer; he went to Italy and worked with Marc-Antonio. Bartsch, VIII.

Abraham receiving Hagar. B. 1.

Abraham dismissing Hagar. B. 3.

Joseph sold by his Brethren. B. 11.

From Geissler's collection.

Thomyris with the Head of Cyrus. B. 70.

Death of Lucretia. B. 79.

Sophonisbe. B. 82.

Artemisia. B. 83.

From Otto's collection.

The Siege of Carthage. B. 86.

After Giulio Romano.

1*st state, before any address.*

Quandt, No. 415, 32 *th.*

The 2d state has the address of Ant. Salamanca; — the 3d, that of Nic. van Aelst; — the 4th, that of J. B. de Rossi.

The same.

A copy of the engraving, two plates joined in the middle.

The inscription on the upper, middle battlement of the original, "Julius Romanus inventor," *is wanting, and on the lower battlement on the left, which in the original is without inscription, stands* "Carthago," *and below this* "R," *the same mark that Marco da Ravenna used. — Below, in the middle, it has not the monogram of Pencz, nor the shield with the inscription* "Georgius Pencz pictor Nurnberg [sic] faciebat Anno MDXIXXXIX," *but has instead,* "EXCUDEB. ANT. SALAMANCA MDXL." *not* 1560 (*as is stated in Sternberg,* I. No. 3224), *and over this is added,* "Joannis Orlandi formis Romæ

PENCZ, GEORG, *continued.*

1602." *The banner in the middle of the composition, which is white in the original, has here the letters,* "R Q P S" *in this reversed order.*

Compare Quandt, No. 417, and Durand's Catalogue quoted there.

A Woman wading through a Stream towards Soldiers. B. 94.

P. John Frederic, Elector of Saxony, called the Magnanimous. B. 126.

Quandt, No. 423, 40 *th.*

PERFETTI, ANTONIO, engraver, born at Florence in 1790. A pupil of R. Morghen.

RAPHAEL *pinx.* The (larger) Madonna of Lord Cowper.

Formerly of the Nicolini family in Florence.

The picture is now in the Gallery of Lord Cowper at Panshanger near Hertford. Passavant, II. 58. Engraved in 1831.

Proof before letters and arms, with the names of the artists.

There are proofs before any letters and before the coat of arms.— 2d proofs have the artists' names merely, as ours. — The 3d proofs are with the names of the artists and the coat of arms.

RAPHAEL *pinx.* Madonna della Sedia.

The painting is in the Gallery of the Pitti palace in Florence. Passavant, II. 226, and III. p. 133.

Artist's proof before any letters. On India paper. With a statement, written in pencil, and signed with the name of M. Steinla, that this copy was selected and sent by Perfetti to M. Steinla for the King of Saxony, who, however, had received already a similar copy from his sister the Duchess Dowager of Toscany.

MURILLO *pinx.* Madonna and Child.

The picture is in the Gallery of the Palazzo Pitti in Florence.

Proof before letters, with the names of the artists and the address. On India paper.

ANDREA DEL SARTO *pinx.* Birth of the Virgin.

A fresco in the vestibule of the Chapel of the Annunciation of the Serviti in Florence. A. Reumont, p. 57; Crowe and Cavalcaselle, III. p. 555.

Artist's proof before any letters, "with the white Jewel." With the engraver's autograph.

GUIDO RENI *pinx.* Sibylla Persica.

The picture is in the Uffizj Gallery in Florence.

Artist's proof, before any letters.

DOMENICHINO *pinx.* "La Sibylla."

PERFETTI, ANTONIO, *continued.*

The picture is in Prince Poniatowski's collection, in Florence. Engraved in 1832.

1st proof, before letters, and without the artists' names.

The 2d proof has open letters.

DOMENICHINO *pinx.* "Sibylla Cumæa," or, more correctly, St. Cecilia.

The original is in the Gallery of the Borghese palace in Rome. Platner and Bunsen, III. iii. p. 288, No. 38. Engraved in 1828.

GUERCINO *pinx.* Sibylla Samia.

The picture is in the Tribune of the Uffizj Gallery in Florence. Engraved in 1833.

Artist's proof, before letters or arms, with only the artists' names, in small letters traced with the needle.

ALLORI *pinx.* **P.** Cosimo de' Medici.

The picture is in the Turin Gallery. Engraved for D'Azeglio's *La Reale Galleria di Torino.*

Proof before any letters.

TITIAN *pinx.* "La Bella di Tiziano."

The picture, in the Sciara palace in Rome (Platner and Bunsen, III. iii. p. 190), is ascribed to Palma vecchio; Passavant, *Christliche Kunst in Spanien,* p. 163, note.

Proof, before letters, with coat of arms and the names of the artists and printer.

Engravings for V. Marchese, "San Marco in Firenze." See under MARCHESE.

PERSICHINI, RAFFAELLO, a modern Italian engraver.

RAPHAEL *pinx.* The Presentation in the Temple.

See Passavant, II. 17, c. p. 23. Engraved, of the size of the original in the Vatican, for the Calcografia Camerale in Rome.

PETERSEN, HEINRICH LUDWIG, painter and engraver at Nuremberg, was born at Altona in 1806. A pupil of Kroymann and Rosmäsler.

RAPHAEL *pinx.* Madonna della Sedia.

In the Gallery of the Pitti palace in Florence. Passavant, II. 226, and III. p. 133. Engraved in 1838.

The inscription "La Madonna della Sedia" *is in open uncial letters, and, as well as the artists' names, traced with the needle.*

PETHER, WILLIAM, painter and mezzotint engraver, born at Carlisle in 1731, died at London about 1795. A pupil of Thomas Frye.

REMBRANDT *pinx.* "A Warrior."

PETHER, WILLIAM, *continued.*

An officer (portrait of Rembrandt himself), with a sword of state. *See* Smith, *Cat. rais.* No. 273; Waagen, *Treasures*, III. p. 448. The picture is in Fitzwilliam College at Cambridge.

Proof before letters.

REMBRANDT *pinx.* A Standard-bearer.

Described by Smith, *Cat. rais.* No. 201, and Supplement, p. 798, No. 23. The picture, lately in the collection of Lady Clarke, Oak Hill, is now in that of Baron Rothschild. Smith's description does not entirely correspond; the features are not those of Rembrandt's own portrait, and the person wears no steel cuirass.

Proof before letters.

REMBRANDT *pinx.* A Jewish Rabbi.

Smith, *Cat. rais.* 290.

The picture is in the collection of the Duke of Devonshire.

Proof before letters.

PETIT, GILLES EDME, designer and engraver, born at Paris in 1696, where he died in 1760.

MEYTENS *pinx.* **P.** Marie Thérèse, Reine de Hongrie, etc.

"Née le 13. May 1717, peint à Vienne en 1742, gravé à Paris en 1743."

PETIT, J. LOUIS, designer and engraver, born at Paris in 1760, died about 1812. A pupil of N. Ponce.

RAPHAEL *pinx.* St. George with a Sword.

See Passavant, II. 25. The picture is in the Gallery of the Louvre. Engraved for the *Musée Français*, of the size of the original. Villot, No. 381. Vorsterman's engraving, which is quoted there, by the side of this, is from a *different* picture, which is now in St. Petersburg, "St. George with a *Lance.*" See under VORSTERMAN.

Waagen, *Kunstwerke und Künstler in Paris*, p. 435, states likewise, by mistake, that this picture was engraved by Vorsterman.

PETRINI, GIOVANNI, engraver, born about the middle of the eighteenth century. Engraved for Montagnani, "Raphael's Bible." See under MONTAGNANI.

PICART, ÉTIENNE, designer and engraver, born at Paris in 1632, died at Amsterdam in 1721. He seems to have been a pupil of François de Poilly; he went to Rome, where he stayed some time, and after his return to Paris was called "Le Romain."

CORREGGIO *pinx.* The Marriage of St. Catherine.

The picture is in the Gallery of the Louvre; Coxe's *Sketches*, p. 43;

PICART, ÉTIENNE, *continued.*

Villot, No. 27. This is the second plate, with the Martyrdom of St. Sebastian in the background, which was omitted in the first. *See* Coxe, p. 66, and Otto's catalogue, by R. Weigel, II. No. 580.

PICART, BERNARD, designer and engraver, born at Paris in 1673, died at Amsterdam in 1733. A pupil of his father Étienne and of Sébastien Le Clerc.

J. VAN SCHUPPEN *del.* 𝔓. Prince Eugene.

1st state before address; Nagler, 23.

KNELLER *pinx.* 𝔓. Duke of Marlborough.

PICCHIANTI, GIOVANNI DOMENICO, designer and engraver, born at Florence about 1670. A pupil of Giovanni-Battista Foggini.

TITIAN *pinx.* Madonna with the Child holding Pears in his Hands.

The picture is no longer in the Galleries of Florence. Engraved for *Raccolta de' quadri dei Granduchi di Toscana.*

PICHLER, JOHANN PETER, mezzotint engraver, born at Botzen in 1765, died at Vienna in 1806. A pupil of Schmutzer and Jacobé.

PERUGINO *pinx.* Madonna with the Veil of Stars.

The picture is, perhaps more properly, attributed to Pinturicchio. Some have also ascribed it to Francesco Francia.

Impression without any letters.

BATTONI *pinx.* St. Magdalen in the Desert.

The picture is in the Dresden Gallery.

RUBENS *pinx.* 𝔓. The Two Sons of Rubens.

After the picture in the Lichenstein Gallery in Vienna, which, according to Smith, *Cat. rais.* No. 327, is by Rubens himself, though on the engraving it is stated to be by Van Dyck. The duplicate in the Dresden Gallery, Smith, *Cat. rais.* No. 259, engraved by Daullé, is there considered the original.

PICKERING, F.

𝔓. General Riego.

From a bust. "Printed by C. Hullmandel."

PIERACCINI, FRANCO, a lithographer of the present time in Florence.

RAPHAEL *pinx.* 𝔓. Angelo Doni.

The picture is in the Gallery of the Pitti palace. Lithographed in 1829. Passavant, II. 39.

PILSEN, FRANZ, painter and engraver, born at Ghent in 1676. A pupil of Robert van Audenaerde.

PILSEN, FRANZ, *continued.*

RUBENS *pinx.* The Conversion of St. Bavo.

The picture is in the Cathedral of St. Bavo at Ghent. Smith, *Cat. rais.* No. 105.

PIOTTI–PIROLA, CATARINA, engraver, born at Milan in 1800. She was a pupil of Longhi, at the Brera.

LUINI *pinx.* Adoration of the Infant Christ by Mary and Joseph, and two Angels making music.

The picture is in the collection of Gozzi in Milan. Engraved in 1827.

Unfinished artist's proof before any letters, and before the shading of the infant's figure.

GUERCINO *pinx.* Semiramis, at her Toilet, receives the Message of the Revolt.

"Semiramide risponsò al nunzio: La mia bellezza calmera la sedizione." Engraved in 1830.

Artist's proof before any letters; with the white stamp of the engraver's initials.

GUERCINI *pinx.* The same.

Artist's proof unfinished, the figure of Semiramis and her attendant only in outline.

PIRANESI, GIAMBATTISTA, architect, designer and engraver, born at Rome in 1707, where he died in 1778. His son Francesco, who was born at Rome in 1756, and died in 1810, assisted him in the following engravings: —

View of the interior of Santa Maria degli Angeli, in the Baths of Diocletian.

View of the Column of Antonine.

View of the Column of Trajan.

View of the Colosseum, exterior.

View of the Colosseum, interior.

View of the Pantheon, exterior.

View of the Pantheon, interior.

View of St. Peter's, exterior.

View of St. Peter's, interior.

View of St. Peter's, back view.

View of St. Paul fuor dei muri, exterior.

View of St. Paul fuor dei muri, interior.

View of Santa Maria Maggiore.

View of the Quirinal Palace.

PIRANESI, GIAMBATTISTA, *continued.*

View of the Arch of Constantine.

View of Acqua Felice.

View of the Palazzo dell' Academia Francese.

PITAU, NICOLAS, engraver, born at Antwerp in 1633, came early to Paris, where he died in 1676, a follower of François de Poilly.

SIMON FRANÇOIS OF TOURS *pinx.* The Christ Child seated on the Globe in Clouds, adored by Angels.

1st state, with the engraver's address.

The 2d has Mariette's address.

CLAUDE LE FÈVRE *pinx.* **P.** Alexandre Pitau (Petavius), Senator in Parliament.

PITTERI, GIOVANNI MARCO, designer and engraver, born at Venice in 1703, where he died in 1786. A pupil of Giuseppe Baroni and Antonio Faldoni. His style of engraving was, however, his own; he engraved by single strokes without crossing them; they run from top to bottom, and the shadows for the design are produced by strengthening the line. (Claude Mellan, who engraved some pieces with single lines, did not draw them in such a mechanical way.)

ELSHEIMER *pinx.* Flight into Egypt.

A night piece. In 8vo.

SPAGNOLETTO *pinx.* St. Peter delivered from Prison.

The picture is in the Dresden Gallery. Engraved for the *Rec. d'est. de la Gal. de Dresde,* II. No. 34.

C. F. RUSCA *pinx.* **P.** Count Schulenburg.

PIAZETTA *pinx.* **P.** Goldoni.

A head, life size.

PIZZI, LUIGI, designer and engraver, seems to be a pupil or follower of R. Morghen, at least in the second of the two pieces here mentioned, which is worthy of that master; in the first, seventeen years earlier, he is not so clear and pure in the lines.

RAPHAEL *pinx.* The Transfiguration of our Saviour.

See Passavant, II. under 244. Differing somewhat in the composition as well as in drawing and expression from the picture in the Vatican. Christ is represented in a glory of elliptical form, and the two deacons on Mount Tabor are absent.

"Rafaele Sanzio d' Urbino dipinse in Oglio a chiaroscuro. Luigi Pizzi Veronese disegnò dall' originale ed incise in Roma l' anno 1795." *No further inscription, and the margin full of trial marks of the graver.*

PIZZI, LUIGI, *continued.*

There is no account as to where the original of this engraving is, nor do I find this plate mentioned. The composition corresponds with that of the engraving of Marc-Antonio's school, Bartsch, xv. p. 187, No. 6, and is the same with the cartoon in black chalk (Passavant, II. p. 362, m.), purchased by Pope Clement IX. (Albani), and seen in the Albani palace, Rome, as late as 1826. This cartoon was engraved by Francesco Pozzi in 1779.* Bettelini (see our catalogue under BETTELINI) afterwards retouched or re-engraved this plate, and then put his own name on it; " Rafaele Sanzio d' Urbino inv. Stefano Tofanelli dires. Pietro Bettelini perf[ettò]. Transfigurazione del Signore, curata dal cartone del famoso quadro di Raffaele ove si scorgono le mutazione fatte dall' autore nell' essecuzione del quadro. — A William Hamilton Nisbet, Esq., grand' amatore delle belle arti. — In Roma presso il d° de Sanctio — Francesco de Sanctis D. D." See also Passavant, II. p. 363, n. and Nagler, *Künstler-Lexicon*, XIV. pp. 404, 405, and p. 473, No. 198.

PAOLO VERONESE *pinx.* The Feast at the House of Simon.

The picture is in the Brera Gallery in Milan. Christ as a pilgrim with a scallop-shell on his cape; sitting between a pope and a cardinal; — three colonnades, the middle arched. *Paolo Veronese dipinse a olio in tela a Monte Borio di Vicenza. Il quadro è lungo piedi di Parigi* 27, *poll.* 3, — *alto* 14, *poll.* 10. *Trovasi ora nella R. Pinacoteca in Milano* 1811. — *Luigi Pizzi Veronese, Professore nella Università di Padova, disegnò dall' originale et incise* 1808. A coat of arms, and the inscription, *A sua Altezza Imperiale il Principe Eugenio Napoleone di Francia, Arcicancelliere di state dell' Impero Francese, Vice Re d' Italia e Principe di Venezia.* Largest folio, oblong.

PLANER, GUSTAV, an engraver of the present day at Dresden.

"GIOVANNI BELLINI *pinx.*" Salvator Mundi.

The picture, in the Dresden Gallery, is now attributed to Cima da Conegliano.

"GIOVANNI BELLINI *pinx.*" The same.

Artist's proof, before any letters and with the croquis of a helmeted head in the left margin.

CORREGGIO *pinx.* Magdalen reading.

In the Dresden Gallery. *See* Coxe, p. 125.

Artist's proof before any letters. With a dedication to Professor A. Krüger, in pencil, by the engraver.

* N. B. There is another engraving of the Transfiguration by Francesco Pozzi with the same date, representing the composition of Raphael's picture in the *Vatican*, "Raffael da Urbino inv. e dip. Pietro Paolo Panci dis. Francesco Pozzi inc. Roma 1779. Et evigilantes viderunt maiestatem ejus. S. Luc. Cap. IX. v. 32. Ext. venal. apud Stephanus [sic] Coppa." An inferior print. *See* POZZI.

POILLY, FRANÇOIS DE, designer and engraver, born at Abbeville in 1622, died at Paris in 1693. A pupil of Daret and follower of C. Bloemaert.

LE BRUN *pinx.* The Visitation: "Fecit mihi magna qui potens est. Lucae I."

A piece in oval.

GUIDO RENI *pinx.* The Adoration of the Shepherds.

The picture is in the Imperial Gallery of St. Petersburg; it was formerly in the Houghton Gallery. The picture in the Grosvenor Gallery, mentioned by Waagen, *Treasures*, II. p. 170, corresponds also with this engraving.

2d state, with the two angels above, and the shaded border. With the engraver's own address.

In the 1st state the place of the two angels is left white, and the octagon border is only in outline, not shaded. *See* Paignon-Dijonval, No. 1114, also Valois, No. 214; Alibert, No. 288, and Debois, No. 907.

RAPHAEL *pinx.* The Virgin praying.

Bust, nearly life size, from the Holy Family di Casa Pio in Naples, also called La Bénédiction; Passavant, II. 99.

With the engraver's address.

GUIDO RENI *pinx.* The Flight into Egypt.

The picture was in the old Royal French collection, but it is not now in the Louvre. *See* Waagen, *Kunstwerke und Künstler in Paris,* p. 69 and p. 777.

2d state, with the coat of arms of Colbert, but before address.

ANN. CARACCI *pinx.* The Virgin and Child adored by two Angels.

See Hecquet, 17; Brandes, I. p. 57.

1st state, with the inscription on a stone in the landscape, "Annibal Carratius Pinxit. F. Poilly Sculpsit cum Pr. Re. A Paris, rue St Jacques a l'Image St Benoist."

From Otto's collection, II. No. 1131.

SÉBASTIEN BOURDON *pinx.* Holy Family.

Proof, before any letters.

With the signature of P. Mariette.

LE BRUN *pinx.* St. John at Patmos.

The picture is in the Gallery of Munich; Dillis's Catalogue, No. 424.

Proof before letters.

P. MIGNARD *pinx.* St. Carlo Borromeo administering the Communion to the Plague-stricken.

From the now ruined picture at Rome.

3d state; the saint is represented as using his right hand, and the address is added, "A Paris chez Jean, rue de Beauvais, No. 10."

POILLY, NICOLAS DE, designer and engraver, born at Abbeville in 1626, died at Paris in 1696. A pupil of his brother François.

BEAUBRUN *pinx.* 𝔓 Marie Thérèse, Infante d'Espagne, Reine de France. (Queen of Louis XIV.)

Bust, life size.

2d state, with the lace kerchief.

POLLAJUOLO, ANTONIO DEL, sculptor, painter, goldsmith, niellist, and engraver, born at Florence in 1426, where he lived till 1484, when Pope Sixtus called him to Rome, where he died in 1498. He was a pupil of the celebrated goldsmith Bartoluccio Ghiberti, whose still more famous son Lorenzo he assisted in his gates of the Battisterio in Florence. Bartsch, XIII.

Hercules combating the Giants. B. 3.

Purchased for 15 guineas.

POLLET, a French engraver of the present day.

RAPHAEL *pinx.* The Violin-player.

The picture is in the Sciara palace in Rome.

See Passavant, II. 238.

Artist's proof before any letters, with ten crosses scratched in the margin.

POMAREDE, SILVESTRO, engraver, who worked in Rome and Florence about 1742 – 1768.

TITIAN *pinx.* The Triumphs, after Petrarch.

4 plates engraved 1748 – 50 for Giovanni Michilli, who owned the originals. The Triumph of Time. — The Triumph of Fame. — The Triumph of Death. — The Triumph of the Christian Religion.

PONTIUS, or **DUPONT, PAULUS,** designer and engraver, born at Antwerp in 1596. He was a pupil of Vorsterman, but is, with the latter and the two Bolswerts, to be considered as a scholar of Rubens.

TITIAN *pinx.* The Entombment.

2d state, figures entire.

In the 1st state the figures extend to the knees. — The original, in which they are three fourths size, is in the Vienna Gallery.

RAPHAEL *pinx.* 𝔓. Raphael.

See Passavant, II. 86, p. 124, and p. 622, No. 6, also III. p. 66 and p. 111.

The original of this engraving was purchased at Venice in 1807 by Prince A. Czartoryski, after whose death Mr. Samuel Woodburn bought it at St. Petersburg, and brought it to London in 1850. The French translation of Passavant's *Rafael,* however, has a modern copy by F. Girard of this engraving as frontispiece to Vol. I., in the inscription of which it is said to

PONTIUS, or **DUPONT, PAULUS,** *continued.*

be "from the collection of Prince A. Czartoryski in Paris." From this it would appear that the family had bought the picture back.

An old copy is in the collection of the Countess Warwick at Gatton Park; Waagen, *Galleries*, etc., or *Treasures*, IV. p. 344.

2d state, with Meyssens's address.

RUBENS *pinx.* The Adoration of the Shepherds.

One of the shepherds has a bagpipe stuck in his girdle. An upright piece, arched: "*Ecce Virgo concipiet et pariet Filium. Isaiae 7.— G. Hendricx exc.*" The picture is in the Munich Gallery. Smith, *Cat. rais.* 170; Basan, 10.

1st address; the paper appears rather late.

RUBENS *pinx.* The Massacre of the Innocents.

The picture is in the Munich Gallery. Smith, *Cat. rais.* 218; Basan, 32.

Engraved on two sheets.

1st state, before any address.

From the collection and with the signature of P. Mariette. Purchased for £ 4.

The 2d state has Blooteling's address.

RUBENS *pinx.* The Presentation in the Temple.

Painted on the inside of one of the doors that cover the picture of the Deposition from the Cross in the Cathedral of Antwerp. Smith, *Cat. rais.* 5; Basan, 34.

1st state, before any address.

Purchased for £ 4.

The 2d state has the 1st address, of G. Huberti; — the 3d state, the 2d address, of Corn. van Merlen.

RUBENS *pinx.* Christ bearing the Cross.

Painted for the Abbey Church of Afflegem; now in the Museum at Brussels. The engraving omits a female with an infant on the left, and the two thieves guarded by two soldiers in the lower part of the picture; two children are substituted in their place. Smith, *Cat. rais.* 159; Basan, No. 75.

1st state, before address.

RUBENS *pinx.* Le Christ au Capucin.

The dead Christ wept over by his friends, two angels and a capuchin (St. Francis). Painted for the Church of the Capuchins, to whom it was presented by the Duke of Aremberg. Now in the Museum at Brussels. Smith, *Cat. rais.* 139; Basan, No. 101.

Without any address.

RUBENS *pinx.* The Virgin and Child enthroned before a green bower.

PONTIUS, or **DUPONT, PAULUS,** *continued.*

With St. Bonaventura in adoration, St. Jerome, St. George, St. Magdalen, and two other holy women. Altar-piece in the chapel of the tomb of Rubens, where it was placed by his widow, in the Church of St. Jacques at Antwerp. Smith, *Cat. rais.* 15; Basan, 17.

1*st state, with Gillis Hendricx's address.*

There are proofs before the inscription *Laudate Dominum in Sanctis Ejus. Psalm.* 150, and before *Tabula epitaphii*, etc., with merely the names of the artists.

RUBENS *pinx.* St. Roch interceding for the Sick with the Plague.

The picture is in the Church of St. Roch at Alast. Smith, *Cat. rais.* 121; Basan, 44.

Old impression on firm, thin paper, without address; watermark, Fleur-de-Lis in a Crowned Shield.

RUBENS *pinx.* Thomyris causing the Head of Cyrus to be immersed in Blood.

The picture was in the Orleans Gallery, and is now in the collection of the Earl of Darnley at Cobham. Waagen, *Treasures*, III. p. 23. A painting of the same subject, but treated differently, is in the Gallery of the Louvre. Villot, No. 433; Smith, *Cat. rais.* 745; Basan, 22.

1*st state, before address.*

Proofs are before the letters: *Satia te sanguine quem semper sitisti.* The 2d state is with the address of Van Merlen; the 3d has Huberti's address.

RUBENS *pinx.* **P.** After Velazquez. Gaspar Gusman Count Olivares, Duke of St. Lucar.

A bust in an oval, supported by two genii, holding, the one a Medusa's head, the other a club and lion's skin of Hercules, surrounded by emblems and ornaments. Engraved from a copy in grisaille by Rubens, made for the purpose and with additional ornaments, which is now in the collection of the Duke of Hamilton. Smith, *Cat. rais.*, "Rubens," 1151; Stirling, *Velazquez*, p. 249.

1*st impression, with the short beard, reaching only to the shirt-collar.*

Harrach, No. 1843, 100*fr.*

In the 2d state the beard reaches to the six parallel buttons of the cuirass. *See* Bartsch's *Anleitung*, II. p. 215.

RUBENS *pinx.* **P.** Philip IV. of Spain.

Engraved from the picture in the Munich Gallery, with the omission of the hands. Michiels, No. 994; Basan, No. 16.

1*st state, before address.*

The 2d state has Hendricx's address, and the mustache was also increased.

PONTIUS, or **DUPONT, PAULUS,** *continued.*

RUBENS *pinx.* **P.** Elizabeth of Bourbon, Queen of Philip IV. (daughter of Henry IV.). B. 17.

Engraved from the picture in the Munich Gallery, with the omission of the hands. Michiels, No. 841; Smith, *Cat. rais.* 230.

1st state, before address.

Hendricx's address designates the 2d state.

RUBENS *pinx.* **P.** Rubens.

He is represented with hat and cloak; the top of the plate is arched. (Another portrait of Rubens, engraved by Pontius after a painting by *Van Dyck,* is in the *Iconographia.*) The original of this plate is in Windsor Castle, from the collection of Charles I. Waagen, *Treasures,* II. p. 436; Smith, *Cat. rais.* 558; Basan, No. 48.

P. Pontius sc. et exc. 1630.

A proof before any letters, Marshall, No. 1565, £ 40 10 *s.*

LIEVENS *pinx.* Daniel Seghers, e Societate Jesu.

Bartsch, "Rembrandt," II. Appendix, p. 176, No. 96.

1st state, before the name of the engraver.

VAN DYCK *pinx.* The Virgin, looking on high, with the Child in her Arms, which is standing.

With two lines of inscription, "Virgo tuum stringens . . . crede Deum," *four verses in two columns, then an open space for the dedication, below the artists' names; before any address.*

The 2d state has a dedication to Antoni Triest; the 3d has the address of Bonenfant. Nagler, XI. p. 504, No. 100.

The picture is in the collection of Lord Francis Leveson Gower at Bridgewater House. There is another in the Marlborough collection at Blenheim, and still another in the Dulwich Gallery; there was also one in the Gallery of Salzdahlum, and one in the collection of Count de Vence, which latter is engraved by Salvador Carmona. Smith, *Cat. rais.* 263.

VAN DYCK *pinx.* The Coronation of St. Rosalia.

The Virgin and Child with St. Peter and St. Paul, the Infant Saviour crowning St. Rosalia with a chaplet of roses.

Painted for the hall of the congregation of Jesuits at Antwerp. It is now in the Gallery of Vienna. Smith, *Cat. rais.* 2; Waagen, *Handbook,* II. p. 286.

Without any address.

VAN DYCK *pinx.* **P.** Carignan. Francis Thomas of Savoy, Prince of Carignan.

The larger plate; figure three fourths length. He wears a richly embroidered collar and cuffs, and stands at a table. The picture is in the Berlin Gallery; Waagen's *Verzeichniss,* No. 782. (It was in 1840 also

PONTIUS, or **DUPONT, PAULUS,** *continued.*

engraved by Caspar.) A similar picture, with slight deviation, is in the collection at Windsor Castle. Smith, *Cat. rais.* 213; Waagen, *Treasures,* II. p. 427.

The plate is larger than those of Van Dyck's *Iconographia,* in which occurs another portrait of this Prince. See below.

1st state; Van der Stock's name stands under the dedication on the plate, where afterwards G. Hendricx's address was placed.

The 2d state has *Gillis Hendrix excudit Antu.*

VAN DYCK *pinx.* 𝔓. Orange, Frederic Henry, Prince of, Count of Nassau.

A larger plate than those of the *Iconographia.* The picture is in the Royal Gallery of the Hague. R. Weigel's *Kunst.-Catalog,* No. 491; Smith, *Cat. rais.* 711. A grisaille for the engraving in the collection of the Duke of Buccleugh.

1st state, 1st address: Van der Stock.

2d address: *Gillis Hendricx. See* Szwykowski, *A. van Dyck's Bildnisse bekannter Personen,* Leipzig, 1859, p. 312.

VAN DYCK *pinx.* 𝔓. Rubens's and Van Dyck's portraits on one plate, in a border.

"Ant. van Dyck pinx. Er. Quellinus del. Fr. Huberti excudit." Smith, *Cat. rais.* 484. The picture is in the collection of the Duke of Devonshire, Devonshire House. Waagen, *Treasures,* II. p. 94.

PORTRAITS CONTAINED IN VAN DYCK'S ICONOGRAPHIA AND ITS CONTINUATIONS.

VAN DYCK *pinx.* 𝔓. Aremberg, Mary, Countess of, Princess of Barbançon.

Engraved for J. Meyssens. Weber, p. 113.

2d state, Meyssens's address effaced.

Smith, *Cat. rais.* 363. (Also engraved by Lommelin. Smith, *Cat. rais.* 364.)

VAN DYCK *pinx.* 𝔓. Basan, Don Alvaro, Marquis of Santa Cruz.

Engraved for Martin van den Enden's *Iconographia,* No. 28. Weber, p. 66.

4th state, after the 2d address, of G[illis] H[endricx], was effaced. Water-mark, Small Foolscap.

Smith, *Cat. rais.* 671. The grisaille for the engraving is in the collection of the Duke of Buccleugh.

VAN DYCK *pinx.* 𝔓. Breuck, Jacob de, architect.

Engraved for Martin van den Enden's *Iconographia,* No. 29. Weber, p. 67.

2d state, like the first, with but one line of inscription and Van den Enden's address, but with the addition of the name of the engraver.

PONTIUS, or **DUPONT, PAULUS,** *continued.*

VAN DYCK *pinx.* **P.** The same.

4th state, after the 2d address, "G. H.," *was effaced. Watermark, Small Foolscap.*

Smith, *Cat. rais.* 734, describes only this engraving; the picture is not known.

VAN DYCK *pinx.* **P.** Carignan. Francis Thomas of Savoy, Prince of Carignan.

The smaller plate. Figure half length, with a plain linen collar and no cuffs; there is no table in the picture. Engraved from the grisaille in the Munich Gallery, Cabinets, No. 346, which Smith, *Cat. rais.* 83, quotes, but the description differs a little. Engraved for Martin van den Enden, No. 48. Weber, p. 80.

1st state (of 3), with the 1st address, "Mart. vanden Enden excudit. Cum privilegio." "*Très rare.*"

VAN DYCK *pinx.* **P.** Colonna, Don Carlo.

Engraved for Martin van den Enden, No. 30. Weber, p. 68.

4th state, after the 2d address, "G. H.," *was effaced. Watermark, the coat of arms of the city of Amsterdam.*

Smith, *Cat. rais.* 672. The grisaille for the engraving is in the collection of the Duke of Buccleugh.

VAN DYCK *pinx.* **P.** Geest, Cornelis van der, a great lover of Art.

Engraved for Martin van den Enden, No. 33. Weber, p. 70.

4th state, after the 2d address, "G. H.," *was effaced. Watermark, Small Foolscap.*

Smith, *Cat. rais.* 782. The grisaille is in the collection of the Duke of Buccleugh. The portrait of this gentleman in the National Gallery, commonly called *Gevartius*, is one of the finest of the master. *See* Waagen, *Handbook*, II. p. 287.

VAN DYCK *pinx.* **P.** Gerbier, Balthasar, English Envoy at the Court of Brussels.

Compare Smith, *Cat. rais.* 237; Weber, "*Portraits divers d'après A. van Dyck,*" p. 124.

3d state, before the address of P[eter] S[tent].

The 4th state has the address *P. S.*; the 1st and 2d are "*extrêmement rare.*" — Watermark, Small Fleur-de-lis.

VAN DYCK *pinx.* **P.** Guzman, Don Diego Phelipe de, Marquis de Leganes.

Engraved for Martin van den Enden, No. 35. Weber, p. 71.

3d state, after the 2d address, "G. H.," was effaced. *Watermark, the arms of the city of Amsterdam.*

PONTIUS, or **DUPONT, PAULUS,** *continued.*

See Smith, *Cat. rais.* 670. The grisaille is in the collection of the Duke of Buccleugh.

VAN DYCK *pinx.* **P.** Gustavus Adolphus, King of Sweden.

Engraved for Martin van den Enden, No. 36. Weber, p. 72.

3d state, with the 2d address, "G. H." *Watermark, Large Foolscap.* "Beau et rare."

The sketch in chiar-oscuro is in the Munich Gallery. Smith, *Cat. rais.* 81.

VAN DYCK *pinx.* **P.** Honthorst, Gerard, painter.

Engraved for Martin van den Enden, No. 37. Weber, p. 73.

5th state, after the effacing of the 2d address, "G. H." *Watermark, two C's interlaced (one pointing to the right, the other to the left), surmounted with a crown.*

VAN DYCK *pinx.* **P.** Huygens, Chevalier Constantin.

Engraved for Martin van den Enden, No. 38. Weber, p. 73.

3d state; the 2d address, "G. H.," *effaced. Watermark, the arms of the city of Amsterdam.*

VAN DYCK *pinx.* **P.** Maria de' Medici.

Weber, p. 84, No. 56. Engraved for Martin van den Enden's *Iconographia.* Smith, *Cat. rais.* 75. The original for this print is a grisaille, a sketch on wood, brown and white, in the Munich Gallery. Dillis's *Verzeichniss der Pinakothek,* p. 240. Cabin. XIII. No. 335.

4th state, after the effacing of the 2d address. Watermark, Foolscap.

VAN DYCK *pinx.* **P.** Miræus, Aubertus (Aubert Le Mire), Elder of the Cathedral of Antwerp.

Engraved for Martin van den Enden, No. 39. Weber, p. 74.

3d state; the 2d address, "G. H.," *effaced. Watermark, the arms of the city of Amsterdam.*

See Smith, *Cat. rais.* 540. A portrait of the same person, slightly differing from this, is in the collection of the Duke of Bedford. Waagen, *Treasures,* III. p. 464.

VAN DYCK *pinx.* **P.** Mytens, Daniel, painter.

Engraved for Martin van den Enden, No. 40. Weber, p. 74.

5th state, after effacing "G. H.," *the 2d address. Watermark, the arms of the city of Amsterdam.*

See Smith, *Cat. rais.* 763.

VAN DYCK *pinx.* **P.** Nassau-Siegen, John, Count of.

Engraved for Martin van den Enden, No. 41. Weber, p. 75.

4th state, after "G. H.," *the 2d address, was effaced. Watermark, Small Foolscap.*

PONTIUS, or **DUPONT, PAULUS,** *continued.*

Smith, *Cat. rais.* 77. A chiar-oscuro sketch is in the Munich Gallery, and a very similar one, only with a plain collar, *and without the order of the Golden Fleece,* is owned by Alex. Baring, Esq. Smith, *Cat. rais.* 374.

VAN DYCK *pinx.* **P.** Palamedes. The painter Stevens, so called.
Engraved for Martin van den Enden, No. 42. Weber, p. 76.
4th state, the 2d address, "G. H.," *effaced. Watermark, Small Foolscap.*
Smith, *Cat. rais.* 80. A chiar-oscuro sketch is in the Munich Gallery.

VAN DYCK *pinx.* **P.** Pontius, or Du Pont, Paulus, engraver.
Engraved for Martin van den Enden, No. 43. Weber, p. 76.
4th state, after the 2d address, "G. H.," *was effaced. Watermark, the arms of the city of Amsterdam.*
Smith, 788. The grisaille is in the collection of the Duke of Buccleugh.

VAN DYCK *pinx.* **P.** Ravestein, Jan van, painter.
Engraved for Martin van den Enden, No. 44. Weber, p. 77.
3d state, with the 2d address, G[illis] H[endricx]. *Watermark, Foolscap.*
Smith, 774. A grisaille is in the collection of the Duke of Buccleugh.

VAN DYCK *pinx.* **P.** The same.
4th state, "G. H." *effaced. Watermark, the arms of the city of Amsterdam.*

VAN DYCK *pinx.* **P.** Rockox, Nicolas.
Weber, p. 105.
4th state, "très rare," *with only* "Paul. Pontius sculpsit 1639," *before* "Pet. Paul. Rubenius" *in a line above the name of the engraver* (which line marks the 5th state). *Watermark, Small Foolscap.*
The 6th state adds *Obiit XII Dec. MDCXL.*
The 7th state has *Ant. van Dyck pinx. Paul. Pontius sculpsit* (without date), and the address of the six preceding states, *H. de Neyt,* is changed to *G. H.*
Smith, *Cat. rais.* 25, says that "the picture formerly adorned the Hall of the Assembly at Antwerp."

VAN DYCK *pinx.* **P.** The same.
Weber, p. 106.
8th state, in which the address "G. H." *is effaced. Watermark, the arms of the city of Amsterdam.*

VAN DYCK *pinx.* **P.** Rombouts, Theodorus, painter.
Engraved for Martin van den Enden, No. 45. Weber, p. 77.
4th state, after the "G. H." *of the 2d address was effaced. Watermark, the arms of the city of Amsterdam.*
Smith, *Cat. rais.* 777, describes the engraving merely.

VAN DYCK *pinx.* **P.** Rubens, Pieter Paul, painter.
Engraved for Martin van den Enden, No. 46. Weber, p. 78.

PONTIUS, or **DUPONT, PAULUS,** *continued.*

5th state, after effacing the 2d address, "G. H." *Watermark, apparently the arms of the city of Amsterdam.*

Smith, *Cat. rais.* 482. A grisaille is in the collection of the Duke of Buccleugh.

VAN DYCK *pinx.* **P.** Scaglia, Cæsar Alexander, Abbot of Staphard.

Engraved for Martin van den Enden, No. 47. Weber, p. 79.

1st state (of 6), "presque unique," *before the name of the engraver. On the left stands* "Ant. Van Dyck pinxit," *on the right* "Mart. vanden Enden excudit Cum priuilegio." *Before the changed inscription of the title, etc. Watermark, in the very thin paper, a Small Fleur-de-lis. Superb impression.*

The grisaille for this engraving is in the Munich Gallery; Smith, *Cat. rais.* 78. The whole length picture, of which the preceding is a copy, is in the Academy of Antwerp (Kugler, *Handbuch,* 2ᵉ *Aufl.* II. *p.* 416); and a duplicate (Smith, *Cat. rais.* 295), "one of the finest productions of this master, is now owned by Sir Thomas Baring, valued 600 guineas."

VAN DYCK *pinx.* **P.** Seghers, Gerard, painter.

Engraved for Martin van den Enden, No. 49. Weber, p. 80.

4th state, after the erasure of the 2d address, "G. H." *Watermark, Small Foolscap.*

Smith, *Cat. rais.* 747, describes the engraving.

VAN DYCK *pinx.* **P.** Steenwyck, Hendrik, painter.

Engraved for Martin van Enden, No. 51. Weber, p. 81.

4th state; the 2d address, "G. H.," *effaced. Watermark, Fleur-de-lis.*

Smith, *Cat. rais.* 766, describes the engraving.

VAN DYCK *pinx.* **P.** Vanloon, Theodorus, painter.

Engraved for Martin van den Enden, No. 52. Weber, p. 82.

3d state (of 4), *with 2d address,* "G. H."; "beau et rare." *Watermark, two interlaced Cs (one to the right, the other to the left), with an inverted cross between them, and surmounted with a crown.*

Smith, *Cat. rais.* 778, describes the engraving.

VAN DYCK *pinx.* **P.** The same.

4th state, the letters of address effaced. Thick paper, watermark not plain.

VAN DYCK *pinx.* **P.** Vos, Simon de, painter.

Engraved for Martin van den Enden, No. 53. Weber, p. 83.

3d state (of 4), *with 2d address,* "G. H."; "beau et rare." *Watermark not distinguishable.*

Smith, *Cat. rais.* 752. The grisaille for this engraving is in the collection of the Duke of Buccleugh.

VAN DYCK *pinx.* **P.** Wouwer, Jan vanden (Joannes Woverius), Councillor of the Archduke Albert.

Van Dyck etched the head and doublet.

PONTIUS, or **DUPONT, PAULUS,** *continued.*

Carpenter, p. 123, No. 23; Weber, p. 36.

5th state, after the erasure of the 2d address, "G. H." Watermark a kind of beehive.

Added as No. 54 to Martin van den Enden's *Iconographia.* Smith, *Cat. rais.*

The picture is in the Imperial Gallery of St. Petersburg. See further under VAN DYCK, p. 109.

VAN DYCK *pinx.* **P.** Wildens, Jan, painter.

Engraved for Martin van den Enden, No. 55. Weber, p. 83.

4th state, with the 2d address, "G. H.," effaced. Watermark, Foolscap.

Smith, *Cat. rais.* 772, describes the engraving.

PORPORATI, CARLO ANTONIO, designer and engraver, born at Turin in 1741, died there in 1816. A pupil of Wille, Chevillet, and Beauvarlet.

VAN DER WERFF *pinx.* Adam and Eve Weeping over Abel.

The picture is in the Gallery of Turin.

With the engraver's own address.

There are impressions before all letters.

CORREGGIO *pinx.* Madonna with the Rabbit, "La Zingarella." *

So called on account of the Egyptian head-dress. *See* Coxe, p. 40.

The Virgin resting with the Child in the desert under a palm-tree, with angels hovering over her. Sometimes called "Rest in Egypt," and also, very appropriately, "Hagar and Ishmael." The original is in the Gallery of Naples, and there are numerous repetitions, copies, and imitations. There is a very pleasing imitation in the Dresden Gallery, there ascribed to Baroccio, and called "Hagar and Ishmael"; it is engraved by G. Garavaglia.

Impression with letters.

Longhi observes, in his *Calcografia,* that he has met only with proofs of this plate; such are before any letters, and seem to be more frequent than the prints with letters.

CORREGGIO *pinx.* The Bath of Leda.†

The original picture, of which this engraving represents but a part, is in the Gallery of Berlin. The entire composition is engraved by Duchange. *See* DUCHANGE.

Proof before letters, with only the names of the artists and the coat of arms. (Like Debois, No. 924.)

* Ferrario enumerates this plate twice, pp. 271 and 272, once as "Madonna del Caniglio," and then again as "Zingarella."

† In Bryan's Dictionary, edition of 1849, this plate is mentioned three times under Porporati: first as Jupiter and Leda, and then again, in Stanley's addition to the article, once as Leda and the Swan, and then as Leda bathing. In the same place, the preceding plate is also enumerated twice, once as "Madonna with the Rabbit," and again as "Zingarella."

PORPORATI, CARLO ANTONIO, *continued.*

Of the prints with letters, the first have the engraver's address; the second the address of Tessari.

ANGELICA KAUFFMAN *pinx.* "Garde à vous." A Cupid.

Proof with one line of inscription and coat of arms, before dedication.

At Goddard's sale, No. 375, occurred a "fine proof," which was bought by Mr. Colnaghi for £ 8.

CARLE VANLOO *pinx.* Preparing for Bed. "Le Coucher."

Impression of the 2d state, with Buldet's address.

The 1st impressions are before this address.

Proofs are before any letters; there occur counterfeit proofs, made by covering the inscription of the plate, while under the press.

GREUZE *pinx.* The Little Girl with a Dog.

Smith, *Cat. rais.*, "Greuze," 21. The picture, owned by Richard Forster, Esq., was formerly in the collection of the Duc de Choiseul.

With the address, "chés J. B. Greuze Peintre du Roi rue Thibautodé, la première Porte cochere à droite en entrant par l'Arche Marion."

Proof before letters, Thorel, No. 925, 205 *fr.*; George Smith, No. 1059, £ 11.

POSSELWHITE, an English engraver of the present day.

C. R. LESLIE *pinx.* Griselda.

Engraved in the modern English mixed mezzotinto manner.

Proof before letters.

POUSSIN, GASPAR, landscape painter and etcher, whose real name was DUGHET, but he adopted the name of his brother-in-law and teacher Nicolas Poussin. He was born at Rome in 1613, and died there in 1675. Robert-Dumesnil, I.

Rocky Landscape with Water in the foreground, three Trees and two Men. R.-D. 3.

POZZI, FRANCESCO, engraver, born in Rome in 1750, died there in 1805. A pupil of his relation Rocco Pozzi.

RAPHAEL *pinx.* The Transfiguration.

See Passavant, II. 244. The picture is in the Gallery of the Vatican. Engraved in 1779.

This engraving is not to be confounded with one by the same artist and of the same year, from a cartoon in black chalk, made after Raphael's first design, *without the two deacons* on the mount. *See* under PIZZI.

PRADIER, CHARLES SIMON, designer and engraver, born at Geneva about 1785, where he died in 1847. He was a pupil of Desnoyers and worked at Paris.

RAPHAEL *pinx.* La Vierge aux Ruines.

See Passavant, II. 266. Engraved after a picture owned by the Marquis de Marialva, probably the same which is now in the collection of the Marchese Malaspina di Sannazaro in Pavia, of which the original, attributed to Raphael, was in the sacristy of the Escurial. Compare Passavant, *Christliche Kunst in Spanien*, p. 161, note.

Proof, with open letters.

ST. OURS *pinx.* **P.** H. B. de Saussure.

PREISLER, JOHANN MARTIN, designer and engraver, born at Nuremberg in 1715, died at Copenhagen in 1794. A pupil of his father Johann Daniel and his brother Georg Martin.

PAOLO VERONESE *pinx.* Christ bearing the Cross.

The picture is in the Dresden Gallery. Engraved for the *Rec. d'est. de la Gal. de Dresde*, I. No. 16.

GUIDO RENI *pinx.* Semiramis taking the Crown from Ninus.

The picture is in the Dresden Gallery. Engraved for the *Rec. d'est. de la Gal. de Dresde*, II. No. 20.

PRENNER, ANTON JOSEPH VON, designer and engraver, born at Vienna in 1698, died in 1761.

CHRISTOPH AMBERGER *pinx.* Herodias's Daughter receives from the Executioner the Head of St. John the Baptist.

The picture is in the Vienna Gallery. Engraved in 4to, upright, for the *Theatrum Artis pictoriæ*, etc., 4 vols., each containing 40 plates, Vindobonæ, 1728 – 33. Compare Nagler, *Künstler-Lexicon*, under "Prenner."

RAPHAEL *pinx.* St. Margaret.

The picture is in the Vienna Gallery; it was formerly in the collection of the Archduke Leopold William, Governor of the Spanish Netherlands, who left it by will to the Emperor Leopold I. It was previously engraved, in 1660, by John Troyen, for the "Teniers" Gallery, *Theatrum Artis pictoriæ*, Bruxellæ, 1669. For the different editions of the Teniers Gallery, *see* under STEEN. Engraved in 1733 for Prenner's *Theatrum Artis pictoriæ*. Passavant, II. 234, B. p. 317.

PREVOST, ZACHARIAS, engraver in line and mezzotinto with aqua-fortis, and in the aquatinta manner, born at Paris in 1797.

PAOLO VERONESE *pinx.* The Marriage Feast at Cana.

PREVOST, ZACHARIAS, *continued.*

With the **Portraits** of Francis I., Soliman I., Vittoria Colonna, Charles V., and of Titian and Paolo himself.*

Formerly in the refectory of San Giorgio Maggiore at Venice. The great picture is now in the Gallery of the Louvre; Villot, No. 103. Line engraving.

Open letters. On India paper.

PAOLO VERONESE *pinx.* The Feast in the House of Simon.

The picture, originally painted for the refectory of the Servites in Venice, was presented by the city of Venice to Louis XIV., and is now in the Gallery of the Louvre. Villot, No. 104. Line engraving.

Has likewise open letters.

LÉOP. ROBERT *pinx.* Fête à la Madonna de l'arc à Naples.

The picture is in the Gallery of the Louvre; Villot, No. 494. Etching and aquatinta, etc., the modern mixed style.

Open letter proof. On India paper.

LÉOP. ROBERT *pinx.* Les Moissonneurs dans les Marais Pontins.

The painting is in the Gallery of the Louvre; Villot, No. 493. Etching and aquatinta, modern mixed style.

Open letters. On India paper.

LÉOP. ROBERT *pinx.* Les Pêcheurs de l'Adriatique.

Etching and aquatinta, etc., the modern mixed style. *The letters of the inscription are formed of three lines. Not on India paper.*

PRIMAVESI, JOHANN GEORG, landscape painter and etcher, born at Heidelberg in 1776.

JAC. RUYSDAEL *pinx.* The Cemetery.

In the Dresden Gallery. Goethe, *Ruysdael als Dichter*, in his *Sämmtl. Werke*, edit. in 30 vols., 1851, Vol. xxv. p. 153. Hübner, catalogue of the Dresden Gallery, No. 1366; Waagen, *Handbook*, p. 441. — Smith, *Cat. rais.* 60, mentions that a duplicate which was imported into England about 1815, for £800, is in the collection of Mr. Mackintosh. Engraved in 1808.

Proof before letters.

PYE, JOHN, the elder, engraver in London, was born about 1745.

CLAUDE LORRAIN *pinx.* Hagar directed by the Angel to the Well.

"Claude Lorraine pinxt. John Pye sculpsit. Hagar directed by the Angel to the Well. Engraved from an Original Painting, by Claude Lorraine, in the possession of Wm. Baillie, Esq. To whom this Plate is dedicated by his Obliged humble Servant J. Pye. Published according to Act

* "For this colossal chef d'œuvre the artist received not more than 90 ducats" (about 180 dollars). Waagen, *Kunstwerke und Künstler in Paris*, p. 480.

PYE, JOHN, *continued.*

of Parliament, and sold by H. Parker, No. 82 Cornhill, & J. Pye, at Mr. Edward's, Duke Street, Lincoln's Inn Fields, 1770."

Nagler, XVIII. p. 36, mentions, under Swanevelt, an engraving, "Hagar directed by the Angel to the Well," engraved by J. Pye. Our plate looks more like Swanevelt than Claude; is it not, perhaps, the same plate?

PYE, JOHN, the younger, engraved in London about 1830.

CLAUDE LORRAIN *pinx.* Cephalus and Procris.

See Smith, *Cat. rais.* No. 91. Waagen, *Treasures,* I. 341. The picture is in the National Gallery; it was previously in the Angerstein collection.

Open letters.

Q.

QUAGLIO, SIMON, architectural painter and lithographer, born at Munich in 1795. A pupil of his father, Joseph.

Palazzo Pitti, detto Palazzo Vecchio, in Firenze.

Engraved in 1818.

Il Duomo di Como.

Engraved in 1817.

QUAST, PIETER, painter and etcher, born at the Hague about 1600 or 1602.

Beggars.

4 plates from the suite of 26, in 4to.

R.

RAGGIO, TOMMASO, designer and engraver, born at Reggio in 1804. A pupil of the Brera in Milan.

LUINI *pinx.* The Virgin and Child.

Engraved in 1831.

RAHL, CARL HEINRICH, painter and engraver, born at Hofen near Heidelberg in 1779, lived in Vienna, where he died in 1843.

CORREGGIO *pinx.* "La Notte"; The Holy Night, with the Birth of our Saviour.

See Coxe, p. 81. The picture is in the Dresden Gallery.

Proof before letters, with the names of the artists.

FRA BARTOLOMMEO *pinx.* The Presentation in the Temple.

The picture is in the Vienna Gallery; there is a sketch in the Gallery of the Uffizj, Florence. *See* Crowe and Cavalcaselle, III. p. 470.

RAHL, CARL HEINRICH, *continued.*

Artist's proof before any letters. On India paper.

From R. Weigel, *Kunst-Cat.* No. 17144. Bought for 48 *th.*

PERUGINO *pinx.* The Virgin in a Landscape, adoring the Child, who is supported by an Angel.

The picture is in the Lichtenstein Gallery, Vienna. Engraved in 1825.

Proofs are before the letters, but have the artists' names. Arndt, I. No. 542.

RAPHAEL *pinx.* Saint Margaret.

Engraved after the picture then in Vienna, in private possession, formerly in the celebrated Jabach collection. It is a copy of the picture in the Louvre (Passavant, II. No. 234, p. 317, a), which is different from the picture in the Vienna Gallery, engraved by Prenner. *See* PRENNER.

Proof with traced cursive letters. On India paper.

"PORDENONE *pinx.*" Sancta Justina.

The kneeling figure beside her represents Duke Hercules of Ferrara.

The picture, in the Vienna Gallery, was in reality painted by Alessandro Bonvicino, il Moretto.

Proofs are before letters, with only the artists' names in small letters.

Artist's proofs are before any letters. Hillig, No. 343.

FR. MILLET *pinx.* Landscape with Waterfall.

Engraved in 1807.

Proof before letters.

RAIMBACH, ABRAHAM, designer and engraver, born at London in 1776, died there in 1843.

WILKIE *pinx.* Distraining for Rent.

From the picture in the collection of William Wells, Esq. Engraved in 1828.

RAINALDI, FRANCESCO, engraver, born at Rome in 1770, died in 1805. A pupil of Bettelini and of R. Morghen.

PAOLO VERONESE *pinx.* The Rape of Europa.

The picture is in the Gallery of the Capitol at Rome. Platner and Bunsen, III. i. p. 134.

RAMPOLDI, CARLO, designer and engraver, born at Milan about 1775. A pupil of Longhi.

LUINI *pinx.* The Nativity.

Fresco in the Church of Our Lady at Saronna.

LUINI *pinx.* Christ disputing with the Doctors.

Fresco at Saronna.

RAMPOLDI, CARLO, *continued.*

Proof before letters, with merely the artists' names very small and slightly traced.

There occur false proofs made by covering the inscription while printing, which may be recognized by the different letters of the artists' names.

LONGHI *del.* **P.** Giotto.

Engraved for the *Vite e Ritratti di illustri Italiani.*

MATTEINI *del.* **P.** Vettor Pisani.

Engraved for the *Vite e Ritratti di illustri Italiani.*

RASP, CARL GOTTLIEB, engraver, born at Dresden in 1752, died there in 1807. A pupil of Zucchi.

ANT. PESNE *pinx.* The Pigeon-Girl.

The picture is in the Dresden Gallery. Engraved for the *Rec. d'est. de la Gal. de Dresde,* III. No. 17.

VAN DYCK *pinx.* **P.** "Ryckaert, David, painter."

It seems that this name is now generally adopted for that beautiful portrait in the Dresden Gallery, I do not know if upon sufficient authority. David Ryckaert was born in 1615, and died in 1677. Van Dyck was born in 1599; he went to England in 1632, and died in 1641. The portrait represents a man of about 35 or 40 years of age, but if Van Dyck painted it as the likeness of David, it ought to be from 10 to 15 years younger. Moreover, if it was the portrait of that renowned painter, it probably would not be wanting in his *Iconographia.* There is no doubt that the picture is by Van Dyck, and it is probable that the writer of the Catalogue of the Dresden Gallery, after the death of the Director Matthäi, first called it the portrait of the painter Ryckaert, induced by some remote resemblance in the costume of the person, in his beard and fur cap, to the portrait of *Martin* Ryckaert, the one-armed painter, in the collection of the Earl of Warwick (Waagen, *Treasures,* III. p. 214, where, however, it is called *David* Ryckaert by mistake, for the picture *there* is *Martin* Ryckaert, and Waagen's description — "marked features," etc. — is that of Martin), engraved by Neeffs, for the *Iconographia.* As the Dresden picture, however, shows two arms, the name of *Martin* Ryckaert could not be retained; and it was called David, the more readily as there is an elder David, the father of our artist, of whom nothing further is known.*

* There seems to have been a time when names were given to pictures in Dresden with more readiness than criticism, as, for instance, to Van Dyck's portrait of Chevalier Taie, which is still called in the official catalogue the portrait of the painter Engelbrecht (see the present catalogue, *art.* GALLE); and Holbein's portrait of Morett, the goldsmith, which, till recently, passed for a painting of Leonardo da Vinci, and as representing the Duke Sforza of Milan, etc.

RASP, CARL GOTTLIEB, *continued.*

Matthäi, in his official catalogue of the Dresden Gallery, No. 204, describes the picture, without naming the subject of the portrait. The next official catalogue, under No. 405, says: "Portrait of the painter David Ryckaert, sitting in an easy-chair." Hübner, in his official catalogue, No. 936, says merely, "Portrait of the painter David Ryckaert."

Engraved for the *Rec. d'est. de la Gal. de Dresde*, III. No. 15, under the name, "Transylvain." Smith, *Cat. rais.* No. 192, describes the picture in the Dresden Gallery, without mentioning the name of the person represented in the portrait. Passavant, *Christliche Kunst in Spanien*, p. 175, mentions in the Madrid Gallery (Madrazo, *Catálogo*, No. 1233) "the exquisite portrait of the artist David Ryckaert, in his loose fur robe." Waagen, also, *Galleries*, etc., or *Treasures*, IV. p. 518, describes in the collection of the Earl of Hardwicke at Wimpole, Cambridgeshire, a repetition of this picture as a portrait of "the painter David Ryckaert in a fur cap and furred dress, and red waistcoat. Bust picture on wood. Of the frequent repetitions of this portrait, the best, which is to the knees, is in the Dresden Gallery." How many of these repetitions are from the picture in Dresden, or perhaps from that in the collection of the Earl of Warwick, I cannot judge.

VAN DYCK *pinx.* **P.** "Cromwell."

A man in armor with a baton in his hand, and a scarf round his other arm; miscalled "Portrait of Cromwell."

Engraved for *Rec. d'est. de la Gal. de Dresde*, III. No. 16, "Buste d'un général, connu comme le portrait de Cromwell."

VAN DYCK *pinx.* **P.** The same.

Proof before any letters, with only the coat of arms of Saxony.

RAVENET, SIMON FRANÇOIS, the father, engraver, born at Paris in 1721 (according to Basan); died at London in 1774. A pupil of Le Bas.

SALVATOR ROSA *pinx.* The Prodigal Son.

The picture is in the Imperial Gallery at St. Petersburg. Engraved for the Houghton Gallery.

1*st state, with the year* 1767.

The 2d state has the date 1781.

PAOLO VERONESE *pinx.* Venus and Adonis.

Engraved for the *Cabinet Crozat*, while in the collection of M. Dupille.

TITIAN *pinx.* The Three Stages of Life.

The picture is in the Bridgewater Gallery. In the Borghese Gallery is a fine copy by Sassoferrato. Engraved, while in the Orleans Gallery, for the *Cabinet Crozat.* Waagen, *Treasures*, Orleans Gallery, II. p. 496; Bridgewater Gallery, *ibid.* II. p. 30, where he justly remarks, that the picture reminds one rather of Giorgione.

RAVENET, SIMON FRANÇOIS, *continued.*

LUCA GIORDANO *pinx.* The Death of Seneca.

The picture is in the Marlborough collection at Blenheim palace. Waagen, *Treasures,* III. p. 131.

RAVENET, SIMON FRANÇOIS, the son, born at London about the year 1775. A pupil of the preceding and of F. Boucher.

CORREGGIO *pinx.* Martyrdom of Saint Placidus and Saint Constantia.

After the fresco in San Giovanni in Parma. Coxe, p. 76.

RAVENNA, MARCO DA, that is, Marco Dente of Ravenna.

See MARCO.

REINDEL, ALBRECHT CHRISTOPH, designer and engraver, was born at Nuremberg in 1784. A pupil of Zwinger and Heinrich Guttenberg.

LEONARDO DA VINCI *pinx.* Madonna of Count Schönborn at Pommersfelden.

See Passavant, *Rafael,* II. p. 412; Rigollot, *Cat. de l'œuvre de Léonard de Vinci,* No. 47; Quandt, *Verzeichniss meiner Kupferstich-Sammlung,* No. 2200, C. Engraved in 1844.

Proof before letters, having the artists' names and date only, very slightly traced with the needle.

HEINRICH MARIA HESS *pinx.* Christ blessing the Little Children.

Fresco in the Church of All Saints in Munich. Engraved for Count Raczynski's *Histoire de l'art moderne dans l'Allemagne.*

Open letters.

STIELER *pinx.* **P.** Ludwig I., King of Bavaria.

Whole length figure in royal robes. With the dedication on a separate plate.

REINHART, JOHANN CHRISTIAN, landscape painter and etcher, born at Hof in 1761, made Rome his residence in 1789 and died there in 1847. A pupil of Œser.

"Collection de vues pittoresques d'Italie, dessinées d'après nature et gravées à l'eau forte à Rome, par C. A. Dies, Ch. Reinhart, et J. Mechau. Nuremberg, chez J. Fr. Frauenholz, 1799."

Etched in connection with C. A. Dies and J. Mechau, 72 plates (see DIES and MECHAU), each contributing 24 plates, which were collected under the above-mentioned title, here wanting:—

REINHART.

a. Pallazzola.
b. Castell Gandolfo.

REINHART, JOHANN CHRISTIAN, *continued.*

Proof before letters.

c. Sepolcro dei Orazii e Curiazii a Albano.
d. Avanzo del Teatro a Albano.
e. A Tivoli.
f. Ponte Acquoreo a Tivoli.
g. A Subiaco.
h. The same, another view.
Proof before letters.
i. The same, another view.
Proof before letters.
k. Vicino a Subiaco.
l. Rovine della Villa di Ventidio Basso a Tivoli.
m. Tempio della Tosse a Tivoli.
n. Avanzi della Bibliotheca in Villa Adriana.
o. In villa Mecenate a Tivoli.
p. Aricia.
q. Nel Colosseo.
r. The same, another view.
s. In Villa Borghese.
t. Vicin' al Circo di Caracalla.
u. Sepolcro a Falerium, città Etrusca ditrutta.
v. In villa Mecenate a Tivoli.
w. A Cività Castellana.
x. The same, another view.
y. The same, another view.

MECHAU.

a. Castella [*sic*] Gandolfo.
b. Entrata nel bosco di Marine.
c. Romitorio a Albano.
d. Ponte Salaro.
Proof before letters.
e. Caduta del Velino a Papigno vicino a Terni.
f. Papigno vicino a Terni.
g. Vicino a Subiaco.
h. Francesco fuori di Subiaco.
i. Ospitaletto di St. Francesco fuori Subiaco.
k. Arco della Torretta vicin' a Tivoli.
l. Fontana Blandusia [a Tivoli].
m. Sotto a Ponte Lupo a Tivoli.
n. Avanze dell' Aqua Marzia, Claudia, e dell' Aniene vecchio.
Proof, letters traced.

REINHART, JOHANN CHRISTIAN, *continued.*

o. Porta di Giovanni.
p. La Fontana Egeria.
q. Sito . . . dei Pittori Fiaminghi . . . a monte testaccio.
r. Porta di St. Paolo.
s. Arco di Druso.
t. Ponte Molle.
u. Porta di Falerium.
v. Ponte antico a Cività Castellana.
w. A Cività Castellana.
x. Ponte Cellio a Cività Castellana.
y. Arco di Druso.

DIES.

a. Nomi.
b. A piè del monte Catillorr.
c. Situatione del Tempio di Vesta a Tivoli.
d. Ponte lupo a Tivoli.
e. Cascatella di Tivoli.
Proof, before letters.
f. Porta scura, o sia Entrata nella Villa Mecenate.
g. Tivoli.
h. Tempj della Sivilla [*sic*] e di Vesta a Tivoli.
i. Cascata, e Ponte di St. Rocco a Tivoli.
k. Sepolcro di L. Cellio a Tivoli.
l. Cascatella di Tivoli.
m. Villa Mecenate.
n. Ruderi a Tivoli del Piano inferiore della villa di Cassio.
o. Rovine del Piano superiore della Villa di Cassio a Tivoli.
p. Sepolcro di Plauzio vicin' a Tivoli.
q. Terme publiche in Villa Adriana.
r. Tempio di Giove Olimpico in Villa Adriana.
s. In Villa Mecenate.
t. Avanzi della Villa di M. Bruto a Tivoli.
u. Lago di Nemi.
Proof, letters traced.
v. Terme di Caracalla.
w. Muro torto preso in Villa Borghese.
Proof, letters traced.
x. Lago in Villa Borghese.
Proof, letters traced.
y. Cascatella Superiore a Tivoli.

REMBRANDT VAN RYN, painter and etcher, born near Leyden in 1608, died at Amsterdam in 1669. He was instructed by Jacob Isaaksen van Swanenburg, P. Lastman, J. Pinas, and Joris van Schooten. The full name of this remarkable artist was Harmens Rembrandt Gerritszen ; he was called van Ryn from the canal of the Rhine, on which was his father's mill, where the painter was born. The baptismal name Paul, which is frequently given to him by writers, appears not to have belonged to him. Bartsch, *Catalogue raisonné*, 2 vols., Vienna, 1797 ; Claussin, *Catalogue raisonné*, 2 vols., Paris, 1824 ; [T. Wilson], *A Descriptive Catalogue of the Prints of Rembrandt, by an Amateur*, London, 1836. Comp. also Ch. Blanc, *L'œuvre complet de Rembrandt*, 2 tom., Paris, 1859 – 61.

*** The Roman numerals denote the state of the plate.

𝔓. Head of Rembrandt, with frizzled hair. B. 8, Cl. 8, III., W. 8, III.

3d state of 5, from the reduced plate, with the additional work of the deep shadows near the nose.

From Ackermann's collection.

In the 4th state the crown of the head was covered with strokes ; in the 5th the plate is entirely retouched with the burin, and the hair behind shortened.

𝔓. Bust of Rembrandt, with a fur cap and robe. B. 14, Cl. 14, W. 14.

With the stamp of Ackermann's collection.

𝔓. Rembrandt and his Wife. B. 19, Cl. 19, W. 19.

With the collector's stamp "E. F." and that of Ackermann.

𝔓. Rembrandt, bust in an oval. B. 23, III., Cl. 23, III., W. 23, III.

In the 1st state, of which there exist but four impressions, the figure extends to the knees ; in the 2d "there is a kind of square formed by an outline at each extremity of the oval, before the plate was cut to the latter shape." (Wilson.)

With the stamp of Ackermann's collection.

Abraham entertaining the Three Angels. B. 29, Cl. 35, W. 36.

On the back of the print is the name "E. Faesch" written with ink; there is also the stamp "E. F." and that of Ackermann's collection.

Abraham caressing Isaac. "An Old Man with a Boy." (Wilson.)
B. 33, Cl. 38, W. 135.*

Impression of the first state, before any retouch in the shaded parts, and with the strokes of the dry point on the right above very distinct.

Abraham's Sacrifice. B. 35, Cl. 36, W. 39.

Beautiful impression, with burr.

From Otto's collection.

Jacob lamenting the Death of Joseph. B. 38, Cl. 42, W. 42.

One of the earliest impressions.

REMBRANDT VAN RYN, *continued.*

From Otto's collection.

The Triumph of Mordecai. B. 40, Cl. 44, W. 44.

Superb impression, full of burr.

The Presentation in the Temple, with the Angel.
B. 51, II., Cl. 55, II., W. 56, II.

Early impression, with the lower margin unburnished.

From Ackermann's collection, but without his stamp.

In the very rare 1st state the plate has a margin at the top beyond the representation, which gives to the impression a white margin; this is cut away in the 2d state.

The Flight into Egypt; a night piece. B. 53, II., Cl. 57, II., W. 58, II.

Wilson's 2d state of 4. The light reflects upon the front of the figure of Joseph, from the knees upwards, likewise on the head, neck, and legs of the ass, and on the right cheek of the Virgin. The bottle and luggage are distinctly seen, not so the landscape.

With the stamp of Ackermann's collection.

The 1st very rare impressions are little more than pure etching, without the additional work of the graver.

Rest in Egypt. B. 58, Cl. 62, W. 63.

Most delicate and distinct impression.

From the collections of Otto and Ackermann, and with the stamp of the latter.

Return from Egypt; or, "Jesus found by his Parents, in their Journey to Jerusalem." (Wilson.) B. 60, Cl. 64, W. 64.

Impression full of burr.

With the stamp and from the sale of H. Weber.

Virgin and Child on Clouds. B. 61, Cl. 65, W. 65.

Early impression, with some smut on the plate.

From Otto's collection.

Christ preaching, called "Le petit La Tombe."
B. 67, II., Cl. 71, II. W. 71, II.

Impression on Japan paper, full of burr. The man with the turban, standing upon the left, has the sleeve of the right arm very dark.

With the initials and from the collection of John Barnard.

Purchased from Messrs. Evans for £ 12 12 *s.*

In the 1st state, *of which only one impression is known*, that in the Imperial collection at Paris, the corner of the wall behind the Saviour is not visible, the man with a high turban in the background to the left has his beard only shaded with a single stroke; the man holding his thumb to his mouth, on the same side, has only two buttons on his coat, slightly ex-

REMBRANDT VAN RYN, *continued.*

pressed, instead of five distinct ones; the child lying down has no top near him. (Compare, however, Guichardot, *Catalogue Van den Zande*, p. 249.) The 3d and last state is without any burr; the sleeve of the man on the left, with the turban, is white.

The Tribute Money. B. 68, III., Cl. 72, III., W. 72, III.

The 1st extremely rare state is clearer than the others, especially the head of the Rabbi sitting on the right is less wrought upon; — in the 2d state the head and clothes of the Rabbi are more shaded; — the 3d and last state is worked over throughout, especially on the little archway in the left corner, over which two figures are sitting.

Christ driving the Money-changers from the Temple.

B. 69, II., Cl. 73, II., W. 73, II.

A state between the 1st and 2d. From Otto's collection, where it was designated, No. 1555, as 1st state. The face and the sole of the foot of the man dragged by the cow, as also the belly of the latter, have not the stronger shading of the 2d state, but the mouth is enlarged by additional strokes, so that the lower lip is not distinctly visible.

Christ and the Samaritan Woman. B. 71, Cl. 75, W. 75.

The second, upright, plate of the subject.

1st state, with the part of the well near the Saviour's foot clearer, and before the light parts on the left side of the plate were filled by work brought to the edge.

This additional work constitutes the 2d state; — in the 3d state the plate is retouched, and in the shadows resembles the work of mezzotinto.

Christ healing the Sick, called the Hundred Guilder Piece.

B. 74, I., Cl. 78, II., W. 78, II.

An impression, not strong nor early, of Bartsch's 1st state of the plate, with a pear-shaped arch or vault in the background over the Saviour's head.

Maberly, 1851, No. 498, "most superb impression of the 2d state of Wilson, £ 71; Harrach, 1867, No. 2010, "magnifique épréuve du 1er état de Bartsch," 8,000 *fr.*

Bartsch did not know of the 1st state of Claussin and of Wilson. In this the neck of the ass in the right corner is light, not shaded with diagonal lines; and in the group on the left, especially the hands of the tall figure, holding a cane behind him, the dog, and in front, near the middle of the foreground, the dry branch, and the cord of the mattress on which is the sick woman, are full of burr. "This impression is most clear, brilliant, and transparent, and of inestimable value: it is to be found in the British Museum, in the Imperial Collection at Paris, in the Museum at Amsterdam, and in the collections of Denon, Lord Aylesford, and Mr. Esdaile." (Wilson.)

REMBRANDT VAN RYN, *continued.*

In the collection of Sir Charles Price, sold in London, February 21, 1867, there occurred, catalogue No. 395, an "impression of the 1st state (of Claussin and Wilson) before the diagonal lines on the neck of the ass, etc., of which not more than eight impressions are believed to be known, viz., two in the British Museum, — one, owned by Mr. Holford, — one by the Duke of Buccleugh, — the other three in the public collections of Paris, Vienna, and Amsterdam." This impression was on Japan paper, and was purchased by C. J. Palmer, Esq., for £ 1,180.

The same. B. 74, II., Cl. 78, III., W. 78, III.

With additional work by Rembrandt, before the retouch of Captain Baillie. The additional shading of the background covers the design of the arch. Brilliant impression, full of burr.

The 3d state of Bartsch, 4th of Claussin and of Wilson, is entirely retouched by Captain Baillie, with great care; he had purchased the plate from the engraver Greenwood. — After the Captain had taken a limited number of impressions, he cut the plate into four pieces, of different size, from which the 4th impressions of Bartsch (the 5th of Claussin and Wilson) are made.

Ecce Homo. B. 77, II., Cl. 82, II., W. 82, II.

The 1st state of the finished *plate. The right cheek of the head above that of the man holding the reed is only etched with a single stroke. "Extremely rare." (Claussin and Wilson.)*

From the collection of Dr. E. Peart, with his initials on the face of the print, and with H. Weber's on the back.

In the 3d state the cheek is crossed with diagonal lines, to give it more shade. Of this state also the good impressions are rare. Drugulin's sale, London, 1866, No. 1354, early impression in the 3d state, £ 25 10 *s.* — The 1st state, trial proof, may be regarded as *presque unique.* The figures of Pilate and the principal persons are merely traced, the rest, though nearly finished, is less wrought upon than in the later impressions. Two impressions in this state, one of them retouched with bistre, are in the British Museum. (Wilson.)

Our Lord crucified between the Two Thieves. "The Three Crosses."
B. 78, III., Cl. 81, III., W. 81, III.

In this 3d state the composition is entirely changed, only the Saviour and the thief on the left remain the same. Powerfully shaded. The whole plate covered with large strokes. Name and date invisible.

With the stamp of Ackermann's collection.

In the 1st state, the head of the afflicted man, whom they are leading toward the left, is merely in outline. Without name or date. "Extremely rare." — In the 2d state the name and date are added; the head

REMBRANDT VAN RYN, *continued.*

of the old man is finished; and there is some additional work and shading. "Very rare."

The Deposition from the Cross. B. 81, II., Cl. 83, II., W. 84, II.

In the 1st state, which is very rare, the legs of the men below, supporting the body of Christ, are shaded with only a single stroke; — in the 2d state, the legs of these men are shaded with cross strokes; — in the 3d state, the address of Hendricus Ulenburgensis is added; — the late 4th state has Danckertsz's address.

Debois, No. 953, 451 *fr.*; and No. 954, 465 *fr.*; both 2d state.

The Descent from the Cross. B. 82, Cl. 86, W. 87.

Impression with burr, especially in the group in the left corner.

With the stamp of Ackermann's collection.

The Good Samaritan. B. 90, III., Cl. 94, IV., W. 95, IV.

The composition is different from that of the picture in the Louvre, which was engraved by Longhi.

Good impression of the last state. With name and date in the lower margin.

In the 1st state, the tail of the horse is white and the wall on the landing of the steps is not shaded. The plate is larger on the left. "Extremely rare." Debois, No. 957, 1,800 *fr.*

In the 2d state the horse's tail is shaded, but not the wall. "It is more scarce than the first."

In the 3d, both the horse's tail and the wall are shaded; — in the 4th, the name and date are added.

The Return of the Prodigal Son. B. 91, Cl. 95, W. 96.

Brilliant impression, with some burr, and with smut of the plate.

Saint Jerome, sitting by a Tree. B. 100, Cl. 103, W. 105.

With the stamp of Ackermann's collection.

Saint Jerome, kneeling. B. 102, Cl. 105, W. 107.

Saint Jerome in his Chamber; a night piece.

B. 105, II., Cl. 108, II., W. 110, II.

With the curtain of the window drawn back at the bottom, so as to form a curve.

On the back the name "Gawet, 1818."

The 1st state is "very scarce." The right half of the window is concealed by the curtain, which falls straight down.

A Young Couple walking, surprised by Death.

B. 109, Cl. 111, W. 113.

Impression with some burr on the plate.

From Otto's collection, and with Ackermann's stamp.

REMBRANDT VAN RYN, *continued.*

The Star of the Three Kings; a night piece. B. 113, Cl. 115, W. 117.

With Ackermann's stamp.

The Nail-cutter; or, Bathsheba.

B. 127. (Cl. Supplément, "pieces douteuses," No. 3. W. omits it.)

From Otto's collection and Ackermann's, with the latter's stamp.

The Man drawing from a Bust. B. 130, Cl. 131, W. 133.

From Otto's collection.

A Jew with a High Cap. B. 133, Cl. 133, W. 135.

Very early impression.

From Otto's collection.

A Man playing Cards. B. 136, Cl. 136, I., W. 137, I.

Before the retouch and with the white places on the right and on the top.

With H. Weber's stamp.

The same. B. 136, Cl. 136, II., W. 137, II.

With Watelet's retouch; the ground especially is darker and the white spots filled in.

The Blind Fiddler, led by his Dog. B. 138, I., Cl. 137, I., W. 138, II.

2d state, before the retouch with the burin.

With the stamp of Ackermann's collection.

In the 1st state, the figure of the fiddler is less wrought upon in the neck and drapery; — the 3d is retouched with the burin, and highly finished.

A Pole, with Cane and Sword. B. 141, II., Cl. 140, II., W. 141, IV.

A fine old impression, but of the retouched plate.

From Weber's sale, with the stamp of his initials.

Bartsch and Claussin describe two states: the 1st very slightly etched, and "rare"; — the 2d more worked upon, especially in the shadows; the stick which in the 1st was formed of two lines is now shaded. — Wilson describes four states: the 1st is slightly etched, the sabre belt is scarcely defined where the sword passes through; — in the 2d the belt is more defined, the plate is irregular, and the edges dirty; — the 3d is worked upon throughout, and the contour of the stick defined on one side by a double line, which in the preceding state is single; and the plate is cut and cleaned; — the 4th is retouched throughout with the burin, and the shadows rendered black and disagreeable.

The Scholar meditating by his Lamp.

B. 148, III., Cl. 145, III., W. 146, III.

From Otto's collection.

The 1st state is "very scarce"; the light of the lamp is large, and all the parts are somewhat indistinct, as in a haze; — in the 2d the rays of the

REMBRANDT VAN RYN, *continued.*

lamp are less diffused, and the subject is better defined and clearer; — in the 3d the cap of the man is larger, and the whole plate of a crude blackness; — in the 4th the rays of the lamp are again more diffused, as in the 1st state, and the curtain is more worked upon, so that the folds are hardly to be seen.

The Persian. B. 152, Cl. 149, II., W. 150, II.

Very rich and beautiful impression of the finished plate, with burr, and some smut of the plate.

From Otto's collection.

Claussin's and Wilson's 1st state is $\frac{4}{10}$ of an inch larger on the right, and it is less worked upon, having no richness of effect. "Extremely rare."

A Beggar Couple by a Mound. B. 165, a state between the 3d and 4th; Cl. 162, between the 3d and 4th; W. 162, between the 3d and 4th.

According to plate I. fig. 6 *of Bartsch,* Catalogue raisonné de l'œuvre de Rembrandt; *and pl. IX. fig.* 110 *of Bartsch,* Anleitung zur Kupferstichkunde, *the altered form of the mound, or rock, would show it to be of the 4th state, but it is before the cheek of the woman was covered with shadows which are harsh and indistinct. Though from the reduced plate, after Rembrandt's monogram was cut off, the impression is delicate and harmonious.*

With the stamp of Ackermann's collection, from which it was obtained at the sale in Leipzig in 1853, under No. 689 as the 3d state, and with the name of Dr. Petzold of Vienna on the back, in whose collection it occurred in that part which was sold in Dresden in 1848, No. 2339, also as 3d state; and also with Robert-Dumesnil's mark (the letters R. D. in a small oval, printed in white) on the face of the print; see p. 15 of that part of his catalogue which was issued in 1835.

The Beggar Family at the Door of a House.

B. 176, Cl. 173, W. 173, II.

With the name and date, but a very curious impression in red.

From H. Weber's sale, No. 285.

Bartsch and Claussin mention that there are impressions, "extremely rare," before the name of Rembrandt and the date; such constitute Wilson's 1st state.

A Woman sitting before a Stove. B. 197, IV., Cl. 194, IV., W. 194, V.

The woman is without a cap, and there is a key (damper) in the pipe of the stove.

From Weber's sale, No. 311.

Woman preparing to dress after bathing.

B. 199, II., Cl. 196, II., W. 196, II.

Though in the 2d state, with the flat cap, the impression is full of burr. On Japan paper.

REMBRANDT VAN RYN, *continued.*

From Weber's sale, No. 314, and with the name "J. Chalon" on the back.

In the 1st state the cap is high.

Landscape with a Sportsman. B. 211, I., Cl. 208, I.,—W. 208, who reverses the order of the two states.

Before the house and barn beyond the two figures on the eminence to the left. Impression with some burr and smut of the plate.

From Ackermann's collection, No. 697.

The Three Trees. Landscape. B. 212, Cl. 209, W. 209.

Charming and brilliant impression, with burr in the sky, but with an artificial margin.

With the stamp and from the collection of Ackermann.

A Village near the Highroad. "Le paysage aux Trois Chaumières." B. 217, I. (of two states), Cl. 214, I. (of three states), W. 214, II. (of four states).

Arched plate.

A most superb impression, full of burr.

With John Barnard's initials and William Esdaile's on the back, and the latter's also twice on the face of the print.

Purchased for £ 36.

Wilson says: "*First impression.* The great tree on the right has very little foliage. This impression, which is *presque unique*, is in the Cambridge [England] collection.

"*Second impression.* The shading before the door of the first cottage is only with a single stroke, and the roof of the nearest cottage is not so much shaded as in the next impression. In every part of the road are spaces quite white: the great tree has more foliage, but the dry point with which it is added is in heavy patches, as it is in some remoter parts of the subjects over the houses. It is extremely rare.

"*Third impression.* The road is lightly shaded with dry point in all those parts which in the preceding impression are clear; the patches are softened, but the door of the cottage is still only shaded with the single stroke.

"*Fourth impression.* The door of the first cottage is shaded with cross strokes; the roof of the third also is more shaded.

"All the impressions, even those in the fourth state, when fine, are full of bur."

Landscape, with the Draughtsman. B. 219, Cl. 216, W. 216.

From the collection and with the stamp of Prince de Paar.

Landscape with a Mill, a Sail seen above a Cottage. "La chaumière au grande arbre." B. 226, Cl. 223, W. 223.

REMBRANDT VAN RYN, *continued.*

Restored in the white part of the print.

Rembrandt's Mill. B. 233, Cl. 230, W. 230.

Powerful impression, with burr, and with smut of the plate in the background.

From P. Mariette's collection, with his name, and Prince de Paar's, with his stamp.

Landscape, with a Cow drinking. B. 237, Cl. 234, W. 234, II.

With less burr.

A Man under a Trellis. B. 257, Cl. 254, W. 258.

Very fine impression.

From Otto's and Ackermann's collection.

Old Man with large Beard and Fur Cap. B. 262, Cl. 259, I., W. 264, I.

Before retouch. The print is mended in the upper part.

With Petzold's name and Ackermann's stamp on the back.

Man with a Square Beard and Split Fur Cap. B. 265, Cl. 262, W. 267.

From Otto's collection.

A Young Man musing. B. 268, Cl. 265, W. 270.

Superb and brilliant old impression.

From Ackermann's collection, without his stamp.

Doctor Faustus. B. 270, Cl. 267, W. 272.

Impression rich with burr, on thin paper.

With the stamp "v. E.," and that of Ackermann.

P. Ansloo, Renier. B. 271, Cl. 268, W. 273.

Superb impression, very delicate and very rich with burr.

On the back is the autograph "T. Philips." Purchased from Messrs. Evans for £ 26.

P. Jonghe, Clement de. B. 272, I., Cl. 269, I., W. 274, I.

With the white seam under the upper cross-bar of the arm-chair.

For a distinct identification of the five states of this plate, see Bartsch, *Rembrandt*, plates, figs. 16 – 20, also Bartsch, *Anleitung zur Kupferstichkunde*, plates, figs. 105 – 109.

P. Fransz, Abraham. B. 273, II., Cl. 270, II., W. 275, between III. and IV.

With the hair still light, but with the trees seen through the window. Impression on thick parchment, — hog-skin.

From Weber's sale, No. 388.

P. Young Haaring. B. 275, IV., Cl. 272, IV., W. 277, IV.

Impression of the last state, from the reduced plate.

P. Lutma, Jan. B. 276, II., Cl. 273, III., W. 278, III.

REMBRANDT VAN RYN, *continued.*

The finished plate, with the window, and the names of Lutma and of Rembrandt. Not quite so much worked upon as the following copy, — showing more of the linen under the man's chin.

P. The same. B. 276, II., Cl. 273, III., W. 278, III.

More worked upon and darker. Powerful impression.

With the name of P. Mariette and the stamp of Prince de Paar.

P. Sylvius, Cornelius. B. 280, Cl. 277, W. 282.

Most delicate and rich impression, full of burr, and of perfect freshness.

Purchased from Messrs. Evans for £ 26.

P. Uytenbogaert. "The Gold-weigher." B. 281, II., Cl. 278, II., W. 283, II.

1*st state with the finished face of the portrait. Before the money in the cask. Impression of* "the greatest brilliancy," *full of burr, and with smut of the plate in the margin.*

Purchased from Messrs. Evans for £ 31 10 *s.*

The 1st state of the plate, extremely rare, has the face blank, except two or three strokes for the features. — The 3d is entirely retouched, and the print appears heavy and muddy; most impressions are on thick Japan paper.

P. Coppenol. B. 283, II., Cl. 280, III., W. 285, III.

The large portrait.

Before the darker shading of the background, and before the darker shading of the sleeves and the forepart of the garment in general; before the additional folds in the curtain. Superb impression, very rich.

Purchased from Messrs. Evans for £ 31 10 *s.*

Bartsch describes three states of the plate, as follows :-

The 1st, of the greatest rarity; the ground is white, except that a column reaching to the top of the plate on the left is partly shaded with single strokes; the right sleeve of the coat is little worked upon. — In the 2d the whole ground is covered with hatches; one does not see any column, but a great curtain. The coat is more shaded, especially on the left arm. — In the 3d the plate is cut down, showing only the bust.

Claussin and Wilson describe five states : —

The 1st is almost unique. The background is white, except that a column reaching to the top of the plate on the left is only shaded with single strokes to the middle of its height; the right sleeve is white.

The 2d is of extraordinary rarity. The background is still white, but the sleeve, clear in the preceding impression, in this is shaded with light single lines, and the shadow of the column extends beyond three fourths of its height.

REMBRANDT VAN RYN, *continued.*

These impressions are found in the Imperial collection at Paris.

The 3d is very scarce. The background is covered with etching; the column is not seen, but a large curtain is introduced, which reaches nearly to the extremity on both sides; and the habit, particularly on the left arm, is more shaded.

The 4th also is scarce. The background is darker, the curtain has more folds, and in general the sleeves and the forepart of the habit are more shadowed.

In the 5th, the plate is reduced, leaving only the bust.

P. The Burgomaster Six.

B. 285, between I. and II., Cl. 282, II., W. 287, II.

Impression on Japan paper, before the inscription in the margin at the left corner: "Jan Six. Æ. 29." *With Rembrandt's name in the right corner and the year* 1647, *the two middle figures of which stand reversed.* (*The* 1*st state is without any inscription.*) *The window-sill, which in the* 1*st extends half-way up the arm of the Burgomaster, is suppressed. Rare and precious impression, in fine condition.*

Purchased from Messrs. Evans for £ 55.

Bartsch describes but two states, and his designations are insufficient. Claussin and Wilson distinguish three states:—

The 1st state is of the very greatest rarity. The name and age of the Burgomaster, and Rembrandt's name and the date are wanting; the window has a stone sill extending half-way up the arm of the portrait. Superb impressions in this state are in the Museum at Amsterdam and in the Imperial collection at Paris.

The 2d is of very great rarity. The window-sill is suppressed, but some traces of it are visible near the arm of the Burgomaster; the name of Rembrandt is added in the margin in the right corner, with the date 1647, the two middle figures reversed. This impression, when in good condition, on Japan paper, is as beautiful in effect as the first.

In the 3d state the name and age of the Burgomaster are added in the margin at the left corner; the middle figures of the date are effaced, and inserted in the right direction. The hat, stick, matting, and various parts of the background are more worked on. Impressions in this state are extremely rare, and as beautiful as those in the 2d state; in these the name and age of the Burgomaster are full of burr. There are also modern, faint impressions, sometimes washed over with India ink.

Oriental Head, the first of the three; also called the portrait of Cats.

B. 286, Cl. 283, W. 288.

Impression with smut of the plate.

From Ackermann's collection.

REMBRANDT VAN RYN, *continued.*

Old Man with Large Beard and Fur Cap.

B. 312, Cl. 308, II., W. 313, II.

Impression of the plate after the edges were smoothed and the work carried to the bottom of it.

With Ackermann's stamp.

Old Man with Bald Head. B. 324, II., Cl. 317, II., W. 322, II.

Good impression of the second state; with some additional shading on the cheek, and the damaging retouch on the neck. With smut of the plate.

With the stamp of Ackermann's collection, in the catalogue of which it was erroneously called 1st state; it was previously in Otto's collection, in which it is correctly recorded as "2d state, with smut of the plate."

St. Catherine, frequently called "The Little Jewish Bride."

B. 342, Cl. 332, W. 338.

Superb impression, with a little burr.

From Otto's collection.

Portrait of an Old Woman sitting with her hands crossed before her, looking to the right.

B. 343, I., Cl. 333, and Appendix p. 37, III., W. 339, III.

Impression before the plate was cut oval.

Portrait of an Old Woman, sitting, with her hand on her breast.

B. 348, II., Cl. 338, II., W. 343, II.

The shadow in the background, which in the rare 1st state goes higher than the head, is effaced to the height of the shoulder.

The Head of an Old Woman, called "Head of Rembrandt's Mother."

B. 351, II., Cl. 341, II., W. 346, II.

Extending only to the chin.

The 1st state is extremely rare; the plate is a quarter inch deeper at the bottom, which makes the shape more agreeable, by the subject not ending so abruptly under the chin. (Wilson.)

RENI, GUIDO. *See* GUIDO.

RETZSCH, FRIEDRICH AUGUST MORIZ, painter and etcher, born at Dresden in 1779, where he died in 1857. A pupil of Grassi.

The Chess-players.

A proof impression before the border.

Venus and Cupid.

Three Children attempting to catch a Butterfly.

REYHER, R., engraver of the present day in Berlin, a pupil of Mandel.

REYHER, R., *continued.*

RAPHAEL *pinx.* **P.** Raphael at the age of about 23.

Engraved, under Mandel's direction, after the picture in the Painters' Portrait Gallery in Florence. Passavant, II. 47.

Proof before letters, with the names of the artists, and the address in traced letters.

Artists' proofs are before any letters.

G. O. MAY *pinx.* 1779. **P.** Goethe.

Engraved in 1860. Medallion.

RHEIN, NICOLAUS, engraver in mezzotinto, born at Vienna in 1767, died there in 1819. A pupil of Jacobé.

RUBENS *pinx.* Tigress in a Rocky Landscape, suckling her three Cubs.

The picture is in the Vienna Gallery; it was formerly in Count Lamberg's collection.

RIBAULT, JEAN FRANÇOIS, engraver, born at Paris in 1767, died in 1820. A pupil of Ingouf.

TITIAN *pinx.* The Crowning with Thorns.

The picture is in the Gallery of the Louvre. Villot, No. 464. Engraved for the *Musée Français.*

RIBERA, JOSEF, called **SPAGNOLETTO.**

See SPAGNOLETTO.

RICCIANI, ANTONIO, designer and engraver, born at Rome in 1775.

LEONARDO DA VINCI *pinx.* Magdalen.

See Rigollot, No. 49. Engraved from the picture of the Aldobrandini palace in Rome, from which it came into the possession of the Counsellor Adamowich in Vienna.

Open letter proof.

CANOVA *sculp. in marm.* **P.** Statue of Napoleon, represented as Jupiter.

Proof before letters.

RAPHAEL *pinx.* The Fable of Cupid and Psyche.

Frescos in the Villa Farnesina in Rome.

Engraved in conjunction with Feoli, Ghigi, Leonetti, Mochetti, and Campanella, 10 plates:—

1. Venus points out Psyche to Cupid. Passavant, II. p. 344, 1.

Engraved by Vincenzo Feoli. Dedicated to Ferdinand IV., King of the Two Sicilies.

2. Cupid points out Psyche to the Graces. P. II. p. 345, 2.

Engraved by Vincenzo Feoli. Dedicated to Ferdinand IV.

3. a. Venus, Juno, and Ceres. P. II. p. 345, 3.

RICCIANI, ANTONIO, *continued.*

b. Venus going to Olympus. P. II. p. 345, 4.

Engraved by Vincenzo Feoli. Dedicated to Ferdinand IV.

4. Venus before Jupiter. P. II. p. 345, 5.

Engraved by P. Ghigi. Dedicated to Ferdinand IV.

5. Mercury with a Trumpet. P. II. p. 345, 6.

Engraved by J. B. Leonetti. Dedicated to Sig. Luigi Marconi.

6. Psyche with a Vase. P. II. p. 346, 7.

Engraved by P. Ghigi. Without dedication.

7. a. Psyche giving the Vase to Venus. P. II. p. 346, 8.

b. Jupiter and Cupid. P. II. p. 346, 9.

Engraved by Al. Mochetti. Without dedication.

8. Mercury carrying Psyche to Olympus. P. II. p. 346, 10.

Engraved by J. B. Leonetti. Dedicated to Luigi Marconi.

9. The Assembly of the Gods. P. II. p. 346, 11.

Engraved by A. Ricciani. Dedicated to Ferdinand IV.

10. The Nuptial Feast. P. II. p. 347, 12.

Engraved by A. Campanella. Dedicated "Agli Amatori delle belle Arti."

RICHOMME, JOSEPH THÉODORE, engraver, born at Paris in 1785. A pupil of Regnault and Coiny.

RAPHAEL *pinx.* Adam and Eve.

Engraved in 1814 after the fresco painting on the ceiling of the Camera della Segnatura of the Stanze in the Vatican. Passavant, II. 75.

Artists' proofs have only the names of the artists traced. Proofs have open letters.

J. Smith, No. 1134, £7; Macready, No. 96, £7.

RAPHAEL *inv.* The Five Saints.

The picture, in the Gallery of the Academy in Parma, is the work of a pupil of Raphael, after the drawing known through Marc-Antonio's engraving, with some small deviations. Passavant, II. 271, b.

Engraved for the *Musée Français.*

The artist's proofs "avant toutes lettres" have only very delicately traced with the needle the words *Raphael pinxit. Dessiné par Bouillon. Jph Tre Richomme Sculpt anno* 1819. The proofs have *lettres grises.*

ANNIBALE CARACCI *pinx.* La Silence.

The picture is in the Gallery of the Louvre. Villot, No. 137. Engraved in 1838.

The Art Union of Baden gave this print as a premium in 1838.

Proof before letters, with only the names of the artists, of the publishers, and of the printer; on India paper, with the number 72.

RICHOMME, JOSEPH THÉODORE, *continued.*

Artist's proofs are before any letters. Debois, No. 1021.

RAPHAEL *pinx.* "La Vierge au Livre."

Engraved in 1836 after an old school copy, in the Gallery of the Louvre, of the Madonna Staffa in the possession of the Count Connestabile della Staffa in Perugia. Passavant, II. 18.

The finished artist's proofs have no letters, except the title "La Vierge au Livre," in dark shaded letters, in the socle under the picture. — The proofs have the names of the artists traced under this socle, an empty space, and then, below, the names of the publisher and the printer. The common prints have in the above-mentioned space the inscription, "Dessiné d'après un tableau de Raphael et gravé par Tre Richomme."

RAPHAEL *pinx.* La Vierge de Lorette.

Engraved in 1813, after a repetition, attributed to Giulio Romano. There are twenty repetitions and copies known; one in the Louvre, Villot, No. 389; Passavant, II. No. 88, and III. pp. 111 and 182. It is supposed now that the picture in the possession of Sir Walter Kennedy Lawrie in Florence is the original, long lost sight of.

Proofs have open letters; they have the stamp TR. in the right corner below, as well as the prints. — Messrs. A. E. Evans & Sons, London, had in 1857 an artist's proof before any letters, with the engraver's signature.

RAPHAEL *pinx.* The Holy Family of Francis I. The Great Holy Family of Paris.

See Passavant, II. 233, and III. 141. Engraved for the *Musée Français.*

Proofs are before letters, with only the names of the artists. Lehrs, No. 358, 17 *th.* — Debois, No. 1018, "Premiere épreuve d'artiste, avant la lettre, seulement les noms d'auteurs à la pointe." It is stated in the same place that there occur impressions without any letters, fraudulently made by covering up the inscription of the plate while under the press. — Debois' copy occurred again in Th(orel)'s sale in Paris, 1853, and at Schletter's in Leipzig, 1855. A similar one, with only the artists' names *cut with the needle*, Lehrs, No. 359, 69 *th.*

RAPHAEL *pinx.* The same painting, engraved in a larger size.

Richomme began the engraving in 1839, but becoming disabled before he accomplished it, it was eventually finished by Dien.

Impression on India paper.

An artist's proof "de remarque," before all letters and with the white sandal, Schletter, No. 84; Wilcox, No. 250.

RAPHAEL *pinx.* The Triumph of Galatea.

Engraved in 1820, after the fresco in a saloon of the Villa Farnesina in Rome. Passavant, II. 113.

RICHOMME, JOSEPH THÉODORE, *continued.*

Old impression "with the stamp of the engraver's initials in the right corner," *which is found, however, even in the newest impressions.*

Proofs have open letters. Archinto, No. 378, 250 *fr.*; Macready, No. 96, £ 14 14 *s.* Artist's proofs are before any letters, having merely the artists' names traced with the needle; they have also a croquis, a sketch of a landscape, in the margin of the plate below. Debois, No. 1019; G. Smith, No. 1136, £ 35.

GIULIO ROMANO *pinx.* Neptune and Amphitrite.

Engraved in 1818. With the large white stamp of the *Société des Amis des Arts.*

Proofs have only the artists' names and the large white stamp just mentioned; Hösel, No. 198; Arndt, II. No. 1088; Lehrs, No. 362, 22 *th.*

GÉRARD *pinx.* 1803. **P.** Napoléon.

Engraved in 1835, and dedicated to Mme. Letitia Bonaparte by the publisher, N. Bettoni.

Proof, open and traced letters. India paper.

RIDINGER, JOHANN ELIAS, animal painter and etcher, was born at Ulm in 1695 and died at Augsburg in 1767. A pupil of his father of the same name.

RUBENS *pinx.* Landscape.

In the foreground a tigress suckling three cubs, and a lion standing near her; behind her a tiger approaching with a hare, and in the background a chase after a lion. The picture is in the Dresden Gallery. Engraved for *Rec. d'est. de la Galerie de Dresde,* II. *No.* 46.

RIEDEL, ANTON HEINRICH, painter and engraver, born at Dresden in 1763. A pupil of his father Johann Anton.

REMBRANDT *pinx.* The Feast of Ahasuerus.

Etched after the picture in the Dresden Gallery. Not mentioned by Smith, in his *Cat. rais.*

Proof, with the title in open traced letters, without the name of the engraver.

RIOLLET, MADEMOISELLE CAROLINE, afterwards the wife of Beauvarlet, her master, engraved in Paris, where she died in 1798.

TENIERS *pinx.* The Wicked Rich Man.

Smith, *Cat. rais.*, "Teniers," No. 260.

RIVERA, GIOVANNI, painter and engraver at Florence, born about 1776. A pupil of Raphael Morghen.

GUIDO RENI *pinx.* Cleopatra putting the Asp to her Bosom.

RIVERA, GIOVANNI, *continued.*

Three quarters length figure ; near her, on a small table, a basket with fruit. The picture is in the Gallery of Turin.

Proof before letters, with only the artists' names in small letters, and the arms of Sardinia unshaded.

TITIAN *pinx.* Flora.

The picture is in the Uffizj Gallery of Florence. Engraved in 1826.

Proof, that is, with open letters.

Artist's proofs are before any letters. G. Smith, No. 1137, £ 6 ; Lehrs, No. 365, 19$\frac{5}{6}$ *th.*

"RAPHAEL *pinx.*" Holy Family.

In conjunction with Fontanals. *See* FONTANALS.

ROBETTA, goldsmith and engraver, worked at Florence, from 1490 to 1520. Bartsch, XII.

The Adoration of the Magi. B. 6.

Probably after Filippino Lippi.

One of the earliest impressions.

From Otto's collection.

ROBINSON, JOHN HENRY, engraver in London, born about 1800.

MURILLO *pinx.* "The Spanish Flower-Girl."

The picture is in the Dulwich Gallery. Stirling, *Annals,* III. p. 1443.

Proof, with merely the inscription of the title in letters traced with the point, on the right hand of the lower margin. On India paper.

LANDSEER *pinx.* Little Red Riding Hood.

Lettre-grise *proof.*

LANDSEER *pinx.* Maria. Twelfth Night.

P. Portrait of the Marchioness of Abercorn.

Artist's proof, before letters, with only the names of the artists and the publisher. On India paper.

VAN DYCK *pinx.* **P.** James Stanley, seventh Earl of Derby, with his Wife and little Daughter, standing, in a landscape.

The original is in the collection of the Earl of Clarendon, as stated on the print. Smith, No. 562.

Proof, with the letters traced with the needle ; on India paper.

SIR THOMAS LAWRENCE *pinx.* **P.** Sir Walter Scott.

Engraved in 1833.

Proof before letters, only the names of the artists and publishers traced. On India paper.

ROCCA, CARLO DELLA, engraver of the present time in Milan. A pupil of Longhi.

ROCCA, CARLO DELLA, *continued.*

LUINI *pinx.* ANTONIO GIBERTI *dis.* The Adoration of the Magi.

A fresco in the Church of Our Lady at Saronna near Milan. With the inscription : " Vidimus Stellam ejus in Oriente et venimus cum muneribus adorare."

With the coat of arms and dedication.

LUINI *pinx.* The same.

Proof, before the inscription, with the dedication in open traced letters, and with the coat of arms.

Artist's proofs are before any letters.

ROCHEFORD, PIERRE DE, designer and engraver, born in France about 1675, died in Lisbon.

ÉLIZ. CHERON *pinx.* 𝔓. Louis Bourdaloue, de la Compagnie de Jésus, Prédicateur du Roy.

RODE, CHRISTIAN BERNHARD, painter and etcher, also engraver in line and in mezzotinto, was born at Berlin in 1725, and died there in 1797. A pupil of Pesne, Vanloo, and Restout.

Semiramis armata. Nagler, 86.

An etching.

Resurrection of a Christian. Nagler, 189.

An etching after a painting, in the Church of St. Mary in Berlin, dedicated to the memory of the artist's mother. (Nagler.)

ROLLS, CHARLES, designer and engraver in London, born about 1800.

SIR THOMAS LAWRENCE *pinx.* 𝔓. Benjamin West.

The picture is in the Vernon Gallery, London.

Open letter proof.

ROMANET, ANTOINE LOUIS, engraver, born at Paris in 1748, died in 1807. A pupil of Wille.

TITIAN *pinx.* Venus sleeping.

Nagler, *art.* "Romanet," No. 25.

LEONARDO DA VINCI *pinx.* La Colombine, also called Flora.

See Rigollot, No. 57.

Successively in the collection of Maria de' Medici, the Orleans Gallery, Mr. Udney's collection, and the Gallery of the King of the Netherlands; bought by the Emperor of Russia for 40,000 florins. — It was formerly believed to be the portrait of Diane de Poitiers. Engraved for the *Orleans Gallery.*

ROMANO, FRANCESCO GIANGIACOMO.

Fra Angelico da Fiesole *pinx.* Le pitture della Capella di Nicolò V., opere del Beato Giovanni Angelico da Fiesole, esistenti nel Vaticano, disegnate e incise a contorni da Francesco Giangiacomo Romano, in 16 rami. Roma, 1810. folio.

Sixteen outline engravings, including the title-page with the portrait of the painter.

ROSA, SALVATOR, painter and etcher, born at Borgo di Renella near Naples in 1615, died at Rome in 1673. A pupil of F. Francanzani, Falcone, and Spagnoletto. Bartsch, xx.

The Master's entire Work.

St. William the Hermit. B. 1.

On the right below : *S. Rosa.*

Saint Albert. B. 2.

On the left below : *S. Rosa.*

Plato and his Disciples. B. 3.

With the full name of the artist : *Saluator Rosa Inu. Scul.*

Alexander with Apelles. B. 4.

Saluator Rosa Inu. Scul.

Diogenes throwing away his Bowl. B. 5.

Saluator Rosa Inu. scul.

A corresponding picture, painted by Salvator Rosa, is in the Grosvenor Gallery. Waagen, *Treasures,* II. p. 170.

Alexander and Diogenes. B. 6.

Saluator Rosa Inu. scul.

Democritus meditating. B. 7.

Saluator Rosa Inu. scul.

The same. B. 7.

A corresponding picture by Salvator Rosa is in Grosvenor Gallery. Waagen, *Treasures,* II. 170.

The finding of Œdipus. B. 8.

Saluator Rosa Inu. pinx. scul.

The Death of Regulus. B. 9.

Saluator Rosa Inu. pinx. scul.

The Crucifixion of Polycrates. B. 10.

Saluator Rosa Inu. pinx. scul.

Combat of Tritons, with a Nymph. B. 11

The name of the artist on the right.

ROSA, SALVATOR, *continued.*

Another Combat of Tritons, with a Nymph. B. 12.

Name of the artist on the right.

Another Combat of Tritons, with a Nymph. B. 13.

Initials of the artist on the right.

Pan with his Flute and Two Fauns. B. 14.

The name of the artist is reversed, on the right.

Five Rivers. B. 15.

On the right the initials of the artist.

Five other Rivers. B. 16.

Initials on the left.

*** B. 11 – 16 are oblong pieces, in the form of friezes.

Apollo and the Cumæan Sibyl. B. 17.

The name *Rosa* written on the lyre.

Jason charming the Dragon. B. 18.

Name in the left corner.

A corresponding picture by Salvator Rosa is in the collection of Lord de Mauley (Waagen, *Treasures*, II. p. 84), and a duplicate in Earl Fitzwilliam's collection, Wentworth House. Waagen, *Treasures*, III. p. 338.

Ceres and Phytalus. B. 19.

Saluator Rosa Inu. scul.

Glaucus and Scylla. B. 20.

S. Rosa in the right corner.

A corresponding picture by Salvator Rosa in the collection of Lord Caledon. Waagen, *Galleries*, etc., or *Treasures*, IV. p. 148.

Fall of the Giants. B. 21.

Saluator Rosa Inu. pinx. scul.

Shepherd sitting on a Mound ; in one hand a flute, the other pointing towards the landscape ; behind, two other figures. B. 22.

Without the artist's name or mark.

A River-god charming a Warrior to sleep. B. 23.

In the left corner : *S. Rosa.*

The Genius of Salvator Rosa. B. 24.

With *Salvator Rosa* in the inscription.

Salvator Rosa Has Ludentis otij Carolo Rvbeo Singularis Amicitiæ pignus D. D. D. B. 25 – 86.

62 plates representing various figures and groups of warriors, and other men and women.

ROSA, SALVATOR, *continued.*

SOLDIERS, SINGLE FIGURES.

A man holding a square tablet with the title just mentioned, and pointing at it, behind him Envy. — With no mark. B. 25.

A soldier with the shaft of a lance, going to the left. — With the mark of the initials on the right. B. 26.

A soldier standing, with a shaft of a lance, pointing to the left. — With the mark on the right. B. 27.

A soldier standing, supporting his head and both hands upon his sword. — With the mark on the right. B. 28.

A soldier sitting, towards the right; behind him, on the left, his shield. — With the mark on the right. B. 29.

A soldier standing, resting both hands on his buckler with Jupiter's thunderbolt on it. — With the mark on the shield below. B. 30.

A warrior in antique Roman costume, standing with a staff in his hand, towards the right. — With the mark on the left. B. 31.

A soldier in profile, towards the right, a sword with cross-hilt at his side; in his right hand is a very long cane, with the left he is pointing at his breast. — The mark on the right. B. 32.

A soldier with the shaft of a lance on his shoulder, striding towards the left, and stretching out his hand in a gesture. — With the mark on the right. B. 33.

A variation, with two figures at the right on the ground. The plate is full of the blots of aqua-fortis. — No mark.

A cuirassed or armor-clad soldier, with a staff in his hand, bends over the rocky shore, to look into the water. — With the mark on the left. B. 34.

A standing soldier, grasping a lance in both hands, turned to the right, nearly a full back view. — Mark on the right. B. 35.

A standing soldier without hat, turned to the left, full face, in one hand a lance-shaft, in the other a shield on which is the artist's initials or monogram. B. 36.

A sitting soldier, towards the left, his head and his arms resting on his buckler. — Mark on the right. B. 37.

A standing cuirassed soldier, turned towards the right, seen in profile, both hands grasping the shaft of a lance. — Mark on the right below. B. 38.

A standing soldier in chain-cuirass, head-dress the skin of the head of a wild animal; in one hand he holds a buckler; the other holds a mace on his shoulder. — Mark on the right. B. 39.

A variation: instead of the mace, a sword is seen on the shoulder of the warrior. — Mark on the left.

A cuirassed soldier sitting on a stone, grasping the shaft of a lance with both hands, profile to the right. — The mark on the right. B. 40.

ROSA, SALVATOR, *continued.*

A standing soldier seen from behind, with the straps of his breastplate on his back, wearing an iron helmet and a short sword at his side; his left hand carrying a pole-axe with the head part up, in lieu of a walking-stick. — Mark on the right. B. 41.

A standing soldier, head and body dressed in shawls, with arms stretched to the left resting on the handle of a pole-axe, of which the head is downward. Full face view. — The mark on the right. B. 42.

A standing soldier, seen from behind, leaning on a rock; in his hand a lance-shaft. — The mark on the right. B. 43.

A standing soldier in cuirassed armor, towards the left, in one hand a buckler, in the other a halberd. — The mark on the right. B. 44.

A standing soldier looking on the ground, his right hand on his hip, with his left holding a lance-shaft on his shoulder. — The mark on the left. B. 45.

Soldiers and other Figures in Groups.

A soldier sitting on a mound, his right arm resting on his buckler, at his side a person beckoning him away. — The mark on the right. B. 46.

Two soldiers sitting on square stones; the one on the right shows his back, with a large sword; the other, seen in profile towards the right, wears a helmet with feathers, and carries a pole. — The mark on the left. B. 47.

A variation. The figure on the right sitting alone on a stone, twice as high and not so square, shows a scarf instead of a sword. The left figure is entirely different, not a soldier, but a man in a kind of Phrygian cap, with a cloak thrown over the shoulder; nearly full face view. — The mark on the right.

A cuirassed soldier sitting on a stone, his profile towards the left; his hands rest on the head of a pole-axe; beyond him sits another soldier on the ground, holding a pole-axe in his hands. — The mark on the right. B. 48.

An old soldier standing, speaking to his comrade, who is sitting at his left before him; both are clad in cuirass with helmet and lance; a little beyond the second soldier is a third young person standing. — The mark on the left. B. 49.

A man reclining on a stone, profile towards the right, is making signs to some one in the distance; next beyond him a soldier with helmet and breastplate, leaning on his buckler, appears to be asleep. — The mark on the right. B. 50.

A man reclining on a rock, profile towards the left, holding a long staff in his hands, is addressed by an old soldier, who points towards the left; on this side is also seen the head of a young person. — The mark on the left. B. 51.

A soldier with shield and a long staff, sitting on a square stone, showing his

ROSA, SALVATOR, *continued.*

back; on the left before him are two other soldiers, apparently in conversation with him. — The mark on the right. B. 52.

A soldier, nearly back view, sitting on a square stone on the left, turned towards the right; in one hand he holds a staff, in the other a large round buckler; before him are three other soldiers, one with a halberd. — Mark on the left. B. 53.

A soldier standing, turned towards the left, with one hand on his hip, and the other pointing into the distance; behind him on the left is another soldier, looking at him, with his hands resting on a round buckler with the head of Medusa upon it. — The mark on the left. B. 54.

A soldier, seen from behind, sitting at an improvised table, apparently playing dice with two other soldiers, one of them wearing a helmet, the other two showing bare heads. — This plate has no mark. B. 55.

A soldier, sitting on a stone, resting his left hand on a round buckler, with his right gesticulating, and turning his head towards another soldier with a head-dress of scale-armor, standing behind him. In front of him are two more persons. — The artist's name on the right. B. 56.

Two soldiers in conversation; one, standing, is seen full face, the other, sitting, with a cap of scale-armor, is seen from behind; on the right is another soldier, carrying a banner, on the left another young person. — The mark on the left. B. 57.

A soldier sitting on a square stone, and supporting himself on it with his left hand, while he points with his right to the distance; profile towards the left. Near him, a little back, are two more figures, of which one, in an ample cloak, points in an opposite direction. — The mark on the right. B. 58.

A variation. The same composition reversed; and between the heads of the two figures, back of the principal figure, the upper part of the head of a third figure, apparently a woman, is visible. The print is full of smut of the uncleaned plate. — The mark is, as the whole is reversed, on the left. (This plate seems to be a copy.)

A soldier sitting on a mound, turned towards the left, resting his head and hands on his raised right knee, his left leg extended, leaning from the spectator, so that nothing of his face is seen. He wears an iron helmet and scale-armor on his legs, the fastening of his breastplate is seen on his back, between his feet he has the shaft of his lance. On the left, a little back, is seen another soldier. — The mark on the left. B. 59.

A soldier, sitting on a mound, seen from behind, turned to the left, holding with his left hand his buckler before him, his head tied up in a handkerchief. Before him stand two soldiers with bare heads, one of them having a drawn sword on his shoulder. — The mark in the middle below. B. 60.

ROSA, SALVATOR, *continued.*

Five soldiers in conversation. One, with his feet hanging over a ledge towards the spectator, supports his drooping head with one hand, while the other hand rests on his knee. — The mark on the right. B. 61.

A soldier standing, seen from behind with a mace in his right hand, carried as a staff, gesticulating with his left to a comrade who carries a pole on his shoulder. — The mark on the right. B. 62.

Repetition, corresponding with the preceding, but with less shading, especially in the sword and mace of the principal figure. — Without the mark of the artist. (Seems to be likewise original.)

A standing soldier, face view, turned to the left, one hand resting on his buckler with the head of Medusa, the other pointing to the left, on which side, a little back, another soldier with a lance is seen. — The mark on the right. B. 63.

A standing soldier turned towards the right, seen from behind, leaning with his left arm on a mound, holding a staff in his right hand; farther back, towards the right, is another soldier, making a gesture with his hand. — The mark on the left. B. 64.

A soldier sitting on a stone, on the right, turned towards the left, leaning forward and turning his back; he holds a halberd in his hand. At his back are two other soldiers; one of them, with a long staff, is beckoning towards the right, in front of him, a little back, another soldier. — The mark on the right. B. 65.

A soldier sitting on a stone on the left, profile towards the right; he rests his right hand on the cross of his sword, and gesticulates with his left to a comrade standing before him with a halberd in his hand; farther back on the right is a bareheaded old man with a cloak on. — The mark on the left. B. 66.

A repetition in reverse. — The mark on the right; the lines of the work are finer.

Other Figures of Men.

An old peasant, sitting with folded hands on his knees at the foot of a rock; at his left, a little back, two other men. — The artist's name at the right. B. 67.

A man kneeling with his right knee on a stone, supports himself with both hands on a staff, profile towards the right; on the right of him, a little back, two men are sitting on the ground, one of whom is seen from behind. — The mark on the left. B. 68.

A man standing, seen from behind; he has a pole in his right hand and leans with his elbows on a ledge of rock; his left knee rests on a lower ledge. — The mark on the left. B. 69.

An old man, sitting on a mound at the left, speaks with uplifted hand to

ROSA, SALVATOR, *continued.*

three other men on the right before him, the youngest of whom stretches his hand towards him. — The mark on the right. B. 70.

A young man with a shaggy fur cap, sitting on a bank, speaks with uplifted hands to two persons on the left farther back. — The mark is on the right. B. 71.

A young man standing, in profile towards the right, his right hand on his hip, and contemplating a picture of the Ephesian Artemis, which he supports with his left hand. — The mark on the picture below. B. 72.

A variation. The same young man, but turned towards the left, with his left hand on his hip, and his right (in the position of the preceding print) on a pile of stones. — The mark on the right.

A man in profile towards the left, drawing in a fish-net. On the left, farther back, an old man with crossed arms, and a young person. — The mark on the right. B. 73.

A man in profile, dressed in a cloak, and making a gesture with his left hand, walking towards the right, followed by another man in the costume of a peasant. — The mark on the right. B. 74.

A man standing in a tattered garment with bare head and bare legs, carrying a gourd-bottle and a long staff, points at something on the ground before him. — The mark on the right. B. 75.

A man dressed in loose upper and under garments and wide cap with a long tail, walking towards the left and pointing at something in the distance. — The mark on the right. B. 76.

An old Oriental with high cap and long flowing garments, seen from behind, at his right two women. — The mark on the right. B. 77.

A young man wearing a cap with long ear-laps, with a book under his arm, walking towards the left. — The mark on the left. B. 78.

A man almost naked; with a fur cap of a Bashkir and a bow, pointing with his left hand at something on the ground. Face view. — The mark on the right. B. 79.

A man standing, turned towards the left, having a cloak hanging on his right shoulder, and pointing with his hand towards the left. Three quarters face view. — The mark on the left. B. 80.

WOMEN.

A nearly nude woman sitting on a mound at the foot of a tree, and clasping both arms round its trunk. — The mark on the left. B. 81.

An almost nude woman, drapery hanging to the ground, nearly full face view, stepping towards the right. — The mark on the right. B. 82.

A girl walking towards the right; she holds up her dress with her right hand, while she points with the finger of her left before her. — The mark on the right. B. 83.

ROSA, SALVATOR, *continued.*

A young woman walking towards the left, the right hand wrapped up in her garment, before her mouth, with her left holding up her dress. — The mark on the right. B. 84.

A nude woman, sitting in a wilderness, profile, towards the right; she sits on a stone, resting her head, supported by her hands, on another stone. Background, trees. — The mark on the left. B. 85.

A young mother carrying her infant, walking towards the left. — The mark on the left. B. 86.

PIECES NOT DESCRIBED BY BARTSCH.

A. Of the same size as the preceding series. — A man stepping towards the left. He wears a cap of the form of the Neapolitan fishers, and a loose cloak, drawn up under his arms with his right hand, so that it forms a kind of cape over the left arm, the hand of which is stretched out behind him. His head inclines a little. — The plate has no mark.

B. Also of the same size as the preceding series. — Landscape, and likewise an upright piece. A large tree, under and in front of which are rocks, on the largest of which and under the tree sits a shepherd, his profile towards the right. — The plate has no mark.

ROSASPINA, FRANCESCO, designer and engraver, born in 1762 at Rimini, died at Bologna in 1842. He studied after the works of Bartolozzi, Volpato, and Morghen.

CORREGGIO *pinx.* Christ deposited from the Cross, and wept over by St. John and the Holy Women.

The lower part of the cross with a ladder against it, and a man descending, is seen in the background. — From an oil painting, formerly in San Giovanni, now in the Gallery of Parma. Not mentioned by Coxe. One of the three great easel paintings of that place, — the Madonna of St. Jerome, or the Day of Correggio, and the Madonna della Scodella, or Rest in Egypt, being the other two.* Engraved in 1802.

The same.

Proof before any letters, with only the artists' names in very small writing.

ALBANO *pinx.* Dancing Amoretti, with the Rape of Proserpina.

An oval picture, formerly in the Sampieri collection in Bologna, now in the Gallery of the Brera in Milan.

Proof, with open letters.

Artist's proofs are before any letters.

* Heller, *Praktisches Handbuch,* quotes this engraving twice, first as "The Corpse of Christ wept over by the Holy Women and St. John," and then again, as "Pietà, a rich composition."

ROTA, MARTINO, designer and engraver, born at Sebenico in Dalmatia about 1532. He worked in Rome and Venice. Bartsch, XVI.

TITIAN *pinx.* The Martyrdom of Saint Peter the Dominican. B. 20.

The picture was in San Giovanni e Paolo in Venice, recently destroyed by fire.

1st state, with the address, "Lvcæ Gverinoni Formis."

MICHEL-ANGELO *pinx.* The Last Judgment. B. 28.

The great fresco in the Sistine Chapel.

"Ser^{mo} Emanueli Philiberto Sabaudiae Duci D." *on one tablet, and* "Martinus Rota Sebenicensis F. 1569," *on the other.*

2d state, with the 3d small white *tablet, instead of the address,* Lucae Guarinonij [*sic*] formis," *of the 1st state.*

From the collection of Professor Vogel von Vogelstein.

ROTHE, landscape painter and etcher in Dresden, where he was born in 1785. Nagler, *Künstler-Lexicon,* XIII. p. 467.

We find no notice of this artist, except by Nagler, who does not mention his Christian name, nor any etching of his.

JACOB RUYSDAEL *pinx.* A Waterfall with a rock in the foreground; in the distance, on a rocky height, a castle, and at the foot a farm-house among trees.

Etching. Without any letters.

The picture is in the Dresden Gallery. Matthäi, No. 185; Hübner, No. 1364.

ROULLET, JEAN LOUIS, designer and engraver, born at Arles in 1645, died at Paris in 1699. A pupil of Claude Mellan and François de Poilly.

P. MIGNARD *pinx.* The Visitation.

1st state, with dedication to Mme. la Dauphine, and with the engraver's own address.

In the 2d state the dedication and arms are erased, and it has the address of Drevet.

P. MIGNARD *pinx.* Madonna with the Grape.

The picture is in the Gallery of the Louvre; Villot, No. 349.

Proof, before dedication.

From W. Esdaile's collection.

P. MIGNARD *pinx.* The same.

2d state, with dedication to Mme. Maintenon.

In the 3d state the dedication is erased.

ANN. CARACCI *pinx.* The Virgin in a landscape with the Child standing on her knee; in her hand she holds the Book of Isaiah.

The inscription is, *Olim Deus ... Filio.* The same as Brandes, II. p. 56.

ROULLET, JEAN LOUIS, *continued.*

ANN. CARACCI *pinx.* The Three Maries and the Angel at the Sepulchre of our Lord.

Engraved from the picture then owned by the Philarmini family in Naples.

1st state, with Raillardi's address.

From Otto's collection, No. 1157. — The 2d state has the address of Dan. Herz, sen. — A proof before any letters, Johnson, No. 144.

ANN. CARACCI *pinx.* Pietà; "Les Cinq Douleurs."

The dead Christ is near the tomb on the lap of the Virgin, and three other holy women are weeping. — The picture, first in the collection of the Marquis de Seignelay, then in the Orleans Gallery, is now in the collection of the Earl of Carlisle at Castle Howard. Waagen, *Treasures,* III. p. 324.

Fine old impression of the 4th state.

The 1st state is with only the artists' names below in the plate itself, before *cum priuil. Regis,* and before the drapery which falls over the right arm of the Virgin is continued. Debois, No. 1028, 300*fr.*

The 2d state has *cum priuil. Regis,* in the plate itself. The drapery is extended. It is, like the preceding, before the inscription, *Tiré de la Galerie du Marquis de Seignelay.* Debois, No. 1029, 120*fr.*

The 3d state has on the right of the lower margin the inscription: *Tiré de la Galerie du Marquis de Seignelay.*

These three states may be considered as proofs.

The 4th state has the following, changed inscription in the *middle* of the lower margin: *Divino afflatu correptæ Christo justa persolvunt;* also, with small letters, on the left: *Se vend à Paris chez P. Drevet, avec priuil. du Roy,* and, on the right: *le Tableau est au Cabinet de son S. A. R. Monseigneur le duc d'orléans.*

GIRARDON *sculp.* **P.** Colbert, Édouard.

Engraved in 1698, after a bas-relief by Girardon. Nagler, XIII. "Roullet," No. 7.

POILLY *del.* 1680. **P.** Poilly, François de.

Engraved in 1699. Nagler, XIII. "Roullet," No. 15.

J. COTELLE *pinx.* **P.** Touchellée, Catherine, wife of M. Hilaire Clément, and, by second marriage, of M. Antoine Le Riche.

Bust in an oval, hair in long loose curls, dress open in the neck, fastened in front by two ornamental buckles. *Joan. Cotelle pinx.* 1667 — *Jo. Lud. Roullet sculpt.* 1693. The medallion rests upon a socle, on the front of which is a white circle with a chiffre of letters, interlaced with the same letters reversed, — without further inscription of the name of the person represented. Nagler, XIII. "Roullet," No. 17, and 18 (where, by mistake, the plate is enumerated a second time). Compare Winckler, IV. No. 3351.

ROULLET, JEAN LOUIS, *continued.*

R. LEVIEUX *del.* **P.** Saint André, Pierre de.

Nagler, XIII. "Roullet," No. 5.

ROUSSELET, GILLES, designer and engraver, born at Paris in 1614, died in 1686. He studied after the works of C. Bloemaert.

TITIAN *pinx.* The Entombment.

The picture is in the Gallery of the Louvre. It passed through the collections of the Duke of Mantua, Charles I., and the banker Eberhard Jabach in Paris, to Louis XIV. Villot, I. No. 465. A duplicate of this picture is in the Mamfrini Gallery in Venice, after which the engraving of Schiavoni was made.

RUSCHEWEYH, FERDINAND, designer and engraver, born at Neu-Strelitz in Mecklenburg in 1785, lived principally in Rome, and died in his native place in 1845.

BENDEMANN *pinx.* 1832. Captive Jews weeping by the Waters of Babylon.

Engraved in 1832.

India proof, with the inscription, in small letters: "Das Original ist vom Kunstverein für die Rheinlande und Westphalen einer öffentlichen Bestimmung gewidmet"; *and below:* "Gedr. von H. Felsing in Darmstadt."

RAPHAEL *pinx.* Christ and the Apostles.

See Passavant, II., under No. 127. After the paintings in fresco on the pillars of the Church SS. Vincenzo ed Anastasio alle Tre Fontane, near St. Paul, outside of Rome. 13 plates, engraved with the assistance of Marc-Antonio's engravings. Bartsch, XIV. No. 64 – 76.

DOMENICHINO *pinx.* The Miracle of Saint Nilus.

Fresco in Grotto-Ferrata, near Rome. Engraved in 1813.

Proof before letters, Heydeck, No. 1107.

CORNELIUS *inv.* "Bilder zu Goethe's Faust von P. Cornelius, Gestochen von F. Ruscheweyh. Frankfurt am Main bei F. Wenner. 1816."

1*st edition of the plates.*

12 plates, namely :—

1. Title-page.
2. Dedication to Goethe.
3. Students and Citizens leaving the gate of the city.
4. Faust offering his arm to Gretchen.
5. Scene in Auerbach's cellar.
6. Promenade in the Garden.
7. The Serenade.
8. Gretchen before the Mater Dolorosa.

RUSCHEWEYH, FERDINAND, *continued.*

9. Gretchen fainting at church.
10. Faust on the Blocksberg.
11. Faust and Mephistopheles passing the gallows.
12. Faust visiting Gretchen in prison.

RUYSDAEL, JACOB, landscape painter, a pupil of Berghem, etched 10 plates. He was born at Haarlem in 1635 and died at Amsterdam in 1681. Bartsch, I., and Weigel, *Suppléments.*

The Little Bridge. B. 1.

Old impression of the 3d state of the plate, with Basan's retouch. (R. Weigel, *Suppléments.*)

The Cottage on a Hill. B. 3.

Old impression of the 3d state of the plate, with Basan's retouch. (R. Weigel, *Suppléments.*)

RYCKEMAN, CLAS, engraver, born at Antwerp in 1600. A pupil of Pontius.

RUBENS *pinx.* Christ and the Apostles, including both Judas and Matthias.

14 plates, with the articles of the creed inscribed on them. Michiels's catalogue of engravings after Rubens, No. 300. — Rubens painted the 12 Apostles for the Palazzo Rospigliosi. — Smith, *Cat. rais.*, mentions only the engravings, No. 1070.

1*st state, with the address of Ryckeman.*

The 2d state has the address of Engel Koning.

S.

SADELER, EGIDIUS, painter and engraver, born at Antwerp in 1570, diod at Prague in 1629. A pupil of his Uncle Johan.

JACOPO DA PONTE BASSANO *pinx.* The Annunciation to the Shepherds.

See Nagler, XIV. *art.* "E. Sadeler," No. 77.

From Otto's collection, No. 759.

BAROCCIO *pinx.* The Entombment.

The picture belongs to the Fraternity of the Cross in Sinigaglia. Nagler, *Künstler-Lexicon,* I. p. 279, *art.* "Baroccio," and XIV. p. 158, *art.* "E. Sadeler," No. 112.

With the 1*st address, that of Marco Sadeler. See R. Weigel's Catalogue of the Otto collection,* II. No. 926.

JACOPO DA PONTE BASSANO *pinx.* St. Christopher with the Christ Child.

SADELER, EGIDIUS, *continued.*

See Nagler, *art.* "E. Sadeler," No. 128.

SPRANGER *pinx.* Hercules spinning.

See Nagler, *art.* "E. Sadeler," No. 142.

SPRANGER *pinx.* ? **P.** Pieter Breughel the elder.

See Nagler, *art.* "E. Sadeler," No. 61.

SADELER, JOHAN, designer and engraver, born at Brussels about 1550, died at Venice about 1610.

P. Sigismund Feyerabend.

Nagler's description (XIV. p. 140, No. 14), "Sigmund Feyerabend, berühmter Buchdrucker in Frankfurt a. M., Brustbild, *ohne Namen*, 1587, 4," must have been made from a copy that had the upper margin cut off. The plate has a margin at the top, and in it the inscription, *Sigismondvs Feyerabendivs Bibliopola Francofvrti ad Moenvm. Anno œtatis svœ LIX. Filivm Alloqvitvr.* He holds a book in his right hand on which stands the year 1587, and near his left is written, *Honoris ipsius causa ĩ œs* [sic] *incisus à I. Sadeler.*

SADELER, RAPHAEL, the father, designer and engraver, born at Brussels in 1555, died, not at Venice in 1617, as is usually stated, but with more probability in Munich, where he had a stroke of apoplexy, in 1628. A pupil of his brother Johan Sadeler. Nagler, *Künstler-Lexicon,* XIV.

JACOPO DA PONTE BASSANO *pinx.* The Adoration of the Magi.

See Nagler, *art.* "R. Sadeler the elder," No. 27.

FRANCESCO VANNI *pinx.* Virgin and Child.

In an oval 8vo, or rather small 4to.

With the inscription, "Lumen verbum," *etc.; below is the dedication,* "D^{ae} Adrianae Vberti, D^{i} Bonifacii Antelmi Vxori."

Not mentioned by Nagler.

From Otto's collection, No. 1192.

SADELER, RAPHAEL, the son, engraver, pupil of his father, worked at Venice after 1596.

TITIAN *pinx.* Venus urging Adonis to desist from the Chase.

From one of the numerous repetitions of this subject, of which the original is in the Barbarigo palace in Venice. Nagler, *art.* "R. Sadeler the younger," No. 17.

SAENREDAM, JAN, painter and engraver, born at Saerdam or Saenredam in 1565, lived at Assendelft, where he died in 1607. A pupil of J. de Gheyn and follower of Goltzius. Bartsch, III., and Weigel, *Suppléments.*

SAENREDAM, JAN, *continued.*

PAOLO VERONESE *pinx.* The Feast at the House of Simon.

Three arched colonnades. Engraved on three plates. The picture, formerly in the refectory of San Giovanni e Paolo, is now in the Gallery of Venice. B. 34, and Weigel, *Supplêments.*

1st state before address.

The 2d state has *Danker Dankertz excudit;* — the 3d has, in addition to the address just mentioned, *C. Dankertz excudit.*

PETER ISAAC *pinx.* 𝔓. Johan van Achen. B. 105.

With the engraver's address.

SAINT-AUBIN, AUGUSTIN DE, designer and engraver, born at Paris in 1736, died there in 1807. A pupil of L. Cars and Fessard.

TITIAN *pinx.* Venus Anadyomene; "Venus à la Coquille."

The picture is in the Bridgewater Gallery. Engraved for the *Orleans Gallery.* Formerly owned by Christina of Sweden.

C. N. COCHIN *inv.* Apollo and Venus, with the Muses and Graces. "Concert of the Graces and Nymphs."

In 8vo.

COCHIN *del.* 𝔓. Franklin with his spectacles and historical fur cap.

ST. AUBIN *del.* 𝔓. Gluck.

A medallion in 8vo.

ST. AUBIN *del.* 𝔓. Heineken.

L. M. VANLOO *pinx.* 𝔓. Helvetius.

DUPLESSIS *pinx.* 𝔓. Necker.

SAITER, GOTTFRIED, painter and engraver, born at Augsburg in 1717, died in 1800. A pupil of Ridinger and of G. M. Preissler.

PAOLO VERONESE *pinx.* The Marriage Feast at Cana.

Engraved on two plates, after the painting now in the Gallery of the Louvre. Villot, No. 103. Formerly in the refectory of San Giorgio Maggiore in Venice.

𝔓. With the portraits of Francis I., Soliman I., Vittoria Colonna, Charles V., Titian, and Paolo himself.

TITIAN *pinx.* Madonna with Six Saints.

The Virgin and Child within a glory of angels, adored by the Saints, St. Nicholas, St. Peter, St. Anthony of Padua, St. Francis of Assisi, St. Sebastian, and St. Catharine. The picture, taken from San Nicolò de' Frari della Latuca in Venice, is now in the Gallery of the Vatican. Platner and Bunsen, II. ii. p. 430.

SALANDRI, VINCENZO, engraver at Rome, about 1835.

"CORREGGIO *pinx.*" "Correggio painted by himself."

Erroneously ascribed to Correggio, and not his portrait.

RAPHAEL *pinx.* Constantine's Address to his Troops, or the Vision of the Cross.

Fresco of the Stanze, Sala di Costantino, in the Vatican. Passavant, II. 245.

RAPHAEL *pinx.* The Baptism of Constantine.

Fresco of the Stanze, Sala di Costantino, in the Vatican. Passavant, II. 247.

Proof before any letters.

SALVADOR. *See* CARMONA.

SANDRART, JOACHIM VON, author of the *Academia Tedesca*, etc., painter and engraver, born at Frankfort in 1606, died at Nuremberg in 1688. A pupil of Th. de Bry, M. Merian, and Eg. Sadeler.

TITIAN *pinx.* Flora.

The picture is in the Uffizj Gallery in Florence.

With the engraver's address.

SANTI BARTOLI, PIETRO. *See* under BARTOLI.

SAUNDERS, JOSEPH, engraver in London; a pupil of Longhi.

FRA BARTOLOMMEO *pinx.* Madonna della Misericordia, with the portraits of the family of Monte Catini.

Altar piece of San Romano in Lucca. *See* Crowe and Cavalcaselle, III. p. 462. The drawing is in England. Engraved in 1834.

Proof before letters, with the coat of arms. On India paper.

Purchased for £ 8.

ANDREA DEL SARTO *pinx.* **P.** Andrea del Sarto.

The picture was formerly in the Ricci Gallery in Florence; it was afterwards owned by Mr. J. Sanford. Alfred Reumont, p. 222. Engraved in Florence in 1824.

SAVART, PIERRE, engraver, born at Paris about 1750.

G. E. PETIT *pinx.* **P.** Bayle, Pierre.

In 8vo.

With the engraver's address.

DROUAIS *pinx.* **P.** Buffon.

In 8vo.

With the engraver's address.

SAVART, PIERRE, *continued.*

CHAMPAGNE *pinx.* **P.** Colbert, J.-B.

In 8vo.

With the engraver's address.

RIGAUD *pinx.* **P.** Louis XIV.

In 8vo.

With the engraver's address.

P. Louis XVI.

In 32mo.

Without address.

SANTERRE *pinx.* **P.** Racine, Jean.

In 8vo.

With the engraver's address.

SAVORELLI, PIETRO, engraver, born at Rome.

MICHEL-ANGELO *pinx.* Frescos in the Sistine Chapel.

See under CUNEGO.

SCALBERGE, PIERRE, painter and etcher at Paris in the first half of the seventeenth century.

RAPHAEL *pinx.* The Battle of Constantine.

Fresco of the Stanze, Sala di Costantino, in the Vatican. Passavant, II. 246. Engraved on 4 plates in 1637. Robert-Dumesnil, No. 12.

1st state, with Mariette's address, which was afterwards effaced.

SCHÄFFER, EDUARD EUGEN, designer and engraver, born at Frankfort in 1803. A pupil of Ulmer.

RAPHAEL *pinx.* Madonna della Sedia.

Half the size of the original picture, in the Gallery of the Pitti palace in Florence. Passavant, II. 226, and III. p. 133. Engraved in 1852.

Proof, with coat of arms and part of the dedication in traced and open letters. On India paper.

The different states of the plate are: (*a*) prints, with the whole inscription; (*b*) proofs with the coat of arms and part of the dedication; (*c*) numbered proofs, Nos. 1 – 100; (*d*) *Épreuves de remarque*, before any letters, 35 impressions taken; (*e*) *Épreuves de remarque*, before any letters, with the engraver's signature, 35 impressions taken.

GIOTTO *pinx.* Pietà.

A fresco in the chapel of Santa Maria della Arena in Padua. Published by the Arundel Society, 1851 – 52.

FRA FIESOLE *pinx.* St. Stephen before the Council.

SCHÄFFER, EDWARD EUGEN, *continued.*

A fresco in the chapel of Nicholas V. in the Vatican. Published by the Arundel Society, 1850 – 51.

FRA FIESOLE *pinx.* St. Lawrence before the Emperor Decius.

A fresco in the chapel of Nicholas V. Published by the Arundel Society, 1851 – 52.

VEIT *pinx.* Christianity introducing the Arts into Germany.

A fresco in Städel's Museum in Frankfort. Published by the Frankfort Art Union, for the year 1839.

SCHENCK, PETER, etcher, mezzotinto engraver and print publisher, was born at Elberfeld in 1645, and lived at Amsterdam, where he died in 1715.

RAPHAEL *pinx.* The Holy Family of Francis I. "The Great Holy Family in Paris."

The picture is in the Gallery of the Louvre. Passavant, II. 233. In mezzotinto. Small folio.

SCHIAVONETTI, LUIGI, designer and engraver, born at Bassano in 1765, died at London in 1810. A pupil of Bartolozzi.

MICHEL-ANGELO *inv.* The Cartoon of Pisa.

Engraved in 1808 after an old copy of the principal and largest part of the cartoon, painted in oil in chiar-oscuro in the collection of the Earl of Leicester at Holkham. Waagen, *Treasures,* III. p. 424.

Open letter proof.

There are proofs with merely the artists' names; G. Smith, No. 1147. Artist's proof before any letters, G. Smith, No. 1146.

SCHIAVONETTI, NICOLÒ, a younger brother of the preceding, likewise born at Bassano and a pupil of Bartolozzi, died soon after his brother.

RUBENS *pinx.* Madonna with the Child standing on her knee.

See Smith, *Cat. rais.* No. 794, and Suppl. p. 299; Waagen, *Treasures,* II. p. 451. In the collection of Richard Forster, Esq., Clewer Park, formerly in that of Sir Mark Masterman Sykes.

Lettres grises.

THOS. PHILLIPS *pinx.* **P.** Sir Joseph Banks.

Proof, open and traced letters.

SCHIAVONI, NATALE, painter and engraver, born at Chiozza in 1777. A pupil of R. Morghen and of F. Maggioto.

TITIAN *pinx.* The Entombment, after the picture in the Mamfrini Gallery in Venice, a duplicate of which is in the Louvre.

SCHIAVONI, NATALE, *continued.*

Proof before any letters, Johnson, No. 147, £9 10*s.*; Macready, No. 102, £11.

TITIAN *pinx.* Magdalen.

The picture, formerly in the Barbarigo Palace in Venice, the original of numerous repetitions, is now in the Imperial Gallery of St. Petersburg. A fine repetition is in the Gallery of the Pitti palace in Florence.

TITIAN *pinx.* The Assumption of the Virgin.

The picture is in the Gallery of the Academy of Venice; it was formerly in the Church Santa Maria Gloriosa dei Frari.

1*st impression with the three middle words of the inscription,* "Maria in Cœlum," *in open unshaded letters.*

TITIAN *pinx.* The same.

Artist's proof before any letters. The coat of arms of Russia in the lower margin has, by mistake, only St. George in the middle, instead of this Saint and the White Eagle of Poland on a divided shield, and the crown over the arms is only in outline.

Such a proof occurred in the Macready collection, No. 101, where it was erroneously described as "with the Polish eagle"; it was sold for £28 10*s.* Harrach, No. 2491, 620*fr.*

The proofs have the coat of arms re-engraved and corrected, also the names of the artists and the inscription, *Assumta est Maria in Cœlum. Gaudent Angeli,* and the dedication to the Emperor Alexander I.,—all in traced and open letters.

TINTORETTO *pinx.* **P.** Galilei, Galileo.

Engraved for the *Vite e Ritratti di illustri Italiani.*

SCHMIDT, HEINRICH FRIEDRICH THOMAS, engraver, born at Berlin in 1780.

From a marble bust. **P.** Baron Stosch.

JAGEMANN *pinx.* **P.** Dr. Gall.

Nagler, *Künstler-Lexicon,* xv. p. 339, No. 4.

SCHMIDT, GEORG FRIEDRICH, designer, etcher, and engraver, born at Berlin in 1712, worked at Paris, St. Petersburg, and Berlin, at which latter place he died in 1775. Jacobi, *Schmidt's Werke,* Berlin, 1815.

Works of the Graver,—Portraits.

ANTOINE PESNE *pinx.* **P.** Anhalt, Christian August, Prince of. J. 66.

Engraved in 1750.

FALBE *pinx.* **P.** Blume, Christian Friedrich. J. 65.

Engraved in 1748.

SCHMIDT, GEORG FRIEDRICH, *continued.*

SCHMIDT *del.* **P.** Count Brühl. J. 84.
A bust on a pedestal, without the name of the person represented. In 8vo. Engraved in 1762.

ERIKSEN *pinx.* **P.** Büsching, Anton Friedrich. J. 90.
Engraved in 1774. "Rare."

FONTAINE *pinx.* **P.** Caylus, Charles Gabriel de Tubières de, Évêque d'Auxerre. J. 40.
Engraved in 1739. "Rare."

ANT. PESNE *pinx.* **P.** Cocceji, Samuel, Baron de. J. 67.
Engraved in 1751.

TOCQUÉ *pinx.* **P.** Esterhasi de Galantha, Nicolas, Comte. J. 78.
Engraved in 1759.

1*st state, before the introduction of the graver on the socle at the right.* "Very rare."

TOCQUÉ *pinx.* **P.** The same. J. 78.
2*d state, with the graver on the socle.*

HYAC. RIGAUD *pinx.* **P.** Évreux, Louis de Latour d'Auvergne, Comte d'. J. 42.
Engraved in 1739. "Rare."

SCHMIDT *pinx.* **P.** La Mettrie, De. J. 76.
Engraved in 1757.

LA TOUR *pinx.* **P.** La Tour, Maurice Quentin de, called The Laughing Painter. J. 50.
Engraved in 1742. "Rare."

LA TOUR *pinx.* **P.** The same person represented with his hat on. J. 89.
Engraved in 1772.

HYAC. RIGAUD *pinx.* **P.** Mignard, Pierre, painter. J. 59.
Engraved by Schmidt in 1744, as a candidate for admission into the Academy at Paris.
1*st state,* before *the asterisk in the lower margin.* "Rare."

HYAC. RIGAUD *pinx.* **P.** The same. J. 59.
2*d state,* with *the asterisk in the lower margin.*

ANT. PESNE *pinx.* **P.** Pesne, Antoine, painter. J. 69.
Engraved in 1752.

SCHMIDT *del.* **P.** Prévost, Antoine François, Abbé. J. 61.
Engraved in 1745. "Rare."

SCHMIDT, GEORG FRIEDRICH, *continued.*

TOCQUÉ *pinx.* **P.** Rasoumowsky, Cyrillus, Comte de. J. 83.
Engraved in 1762. "Very rare."

AVED *pinx.* **P.** Rousseau, Jean-Baptiste. J. 44.
Wille engraved part of the accessories. Le Blanc, *Wille*, No. 131. Engraved in 1740. "Very rare."

LIOTARD *pinx.* **P.** Scarlati, Constantinus, Moldaviae Princeps. J. 39.
The name of the painter is not mentioned on the plate. Engraved in 1737 – 39. "Very rare."

HYAC. RIGAUD *pinx.* **P.** Silva, Jean-Baptiste, Med. Dr. J. 52.
Engraved in 1742.

FALBE *pinx.* **P.** Splittgerber, David. J. 87.
Engravod in 1766.

TOCQUÉ *pinx.* **P.** Woronzow, Michel, Comte de. J. 77.
Engraved in 1758. "Very rare."

Etchings, more or less finished with the Burin:—

SCHMIDT *del.* Bust of an Oriental, face view, with a thick beard and a high cap surmounted by a crescent. Jac. 114.
Etched in 1750, in the style of Castiglione. Dedicated to Count Algarotti.

SCHMIDT *del.* An old bearded Man with fur cap and breastplate. Jac. 116.
The plate bears no date, but was engraved in 1750.

REMBRANDT *pinx.* An old Persian with a cane. Jac. 120.
Three quarters length, looking to the right; he has a short beard, a rich turban, and a cloak fastened with a clasp. "Du Cabinet du Sieur Godskoffsky." Engraved in 1756.

REMBRANDT *pinx.* Bust of a Young Gentleman. Jac. 124.
Half length; he leans his left arm upon a wall; his flat cap surmounts a profusion of hair. "Du Cabinet de Monsieur le Comte de Kamcke." Engraved in 1763.

FLINCK *pinx.* Bust of a fine-looking Man with curly hair, mustache, and imperial, and with two feathers in his cap. Jac. 125.
Engraved in 1765. In an oval.

FLINCK *pinx.* Girl with a Pug-dog in her arms. Jac. 126.
Engraved in 1766, from the collection of M. César.

REMBRANDT *pinx.* Bust of a Man. Jac. 127.
Face view, with bare head, a mustache and imperial; his cloak is open,

SCHMIDT, GEORG FRIEDRICH, *continued.*

showing a chain with a medallion. Engraved in 1768. "Du Cabinet de Ms: le Con^{ller} Trible."

REMBRANDT *pinx.* La Juive Fiancée. Jac. 128.

Engraved in 1769. "Gravé d'apres le Tableau Original de Rembrandt, tiré du Cabinet de Monsieur le Comte de Kamcke, et dédié au dit Seigneur," *etc.* — Smith, *Cat. rais.*, "Rembrandt," No. 567, mentions the *print.*

SCHMIDT *fec. ad vivam.* **P.** Mme. Schmidt, sewing, looking towards the right. Jac. 135.

Engraved in 1753.

REMBRANDT *pinx.* The Duke Adolphus of Gueldres threatening his Imprisoned Father. Jac. 137.

See Smith, *Cat. rais.* 166, where he, however, misunderstands the meaning of the picture. From the picture in the Berlin Gallery, No. 802. Waagen, *Verzeichniss,* and Waagen, *Handbook,* II. p. 344. This etching omits the two negro attendants behind the prince, — they are represented in Berger's engraving. *See* BERGER.

Impression before the cross-hatching on the raised hand, on the shoulder of the cloak, etc., *and before the shading of the keyhole.*

The space under the plate remained blank in all the impressions, as the plate never had an inscription, except the artists' names. Engraved in 1756.

SCHMIDT *pinx.* **P.** Schmidt, G. F. Jac. 141.

The portrait with the *spider in the window,* on the inner wall of which hangs a thermometer.

"George Friderich Schmidt, se ipse fecit aqua forti Petropol. 1758."

The first impressions of this plate are before the cross-hatching on the lower part of the window wall, and on the thermometer. Weigel, *Kunst-Catalog,* VII. No. 7978 a.; described also in Prince Schwarzenberg's catalogue, and in Tschirschky's, No. 907.

SCHMIDT *del.* **P.** Schmidt's wife, reading. "Dorothée Louise Viedebandt, Femme de George Fréderic Schmidt." Jac. 142.

SCHMIDT *del.* **P.** Michel, Hirsch. Jac. 144.

Three fourths length, the face towards the right, a full beard, Oriental fur cap, caftan or easy gown of the Polish Jews, with fur cuffs and tied with a sash, the hands crossed over the stomach. In the background of the etching is the inscription, "G. F. Schmidt ad vivum fecieb. [*sic*] Berolini. 1762."

1*st state, with the inscription in the lower margin,* "Hirsch Michel, presentirt an Isaac Onis durch Aaron Monceca."

The later impressions are without this inscription.

SCHMIDT, GEORG FRIEDRICH, *continued.*

REMBRANDT *pinx.* "Princess of Orange." Jac. 147.

Portrait of a lady, half figure, turned towards the right; a string of pearls fastens her hair, and a clasp on her bosom secures her cloak. Engraved in 1767.

ANT. PESNE *pinx.* **P.** Dinglinger, jeweller in Dresden. Jac. 148.

In an oval. Engraved in 1769. With Boerner's and Geissler's names on the back.

REMBRANDT *pinx.* **P.** Rembrandt at the age of 28. Jac. 150.

Half figure, turned towards the right; face view. "Rembrandt p. 1634. G. F. Schmidt 1771. f. aqa [*sic*] forti. — Le Tableau Original est à Florence dans la Collection de Ms: le Marquis Gerini."

REMBRANDT *pinx.* **P.** Rembrandt at the age of about 60. Jac. 151.

Half figure, turned towards the left, nearly full face. "Dédié à Monsieur B. N. Le Sueur, par son ami Schmidt." Smith, *Cat. rais.* No. 218, states that the original is now in the Pitti palace. Nagler, *Künstler-Lexicon,* XV. p. 315, "Schmidt," No. 99, designates the picture in the Pitti palace as the one formerly owned by the Marquis Gerini (Jac. 150), representing Rembrandt at the age of about 30 years. Engraved in 1771.

In our copy the dedication is cut off.

G. FLINCK *pinx.* **P.** Cats instructing the young prince William Henry of Orange. Jac. 152.

The prince is in profile, with a wreath of laurels on his head; his old teacher wears a gold chain. Engraved in 1772.

A similar picture is in the Imperial Gallery of St. Petersburg. Waagen, *Die Gemäldesammlung in der Kaiserlichen Ermitage zu St. Petersburg,* München, 1864, p. 187, No. 842.

REMBRANDT *pinx.* Rembrandt's Mother. Jac. 153.

An old woman, three fourths face, half figure, in a fur-lined gown and with a kerchief over her head. She sits at a table covered with a rug, her folio Bible before her; her right hand supports her head, her left, holding a pair of spectacles, rests on the book, at the side of which stand several other books, a candlestick, and an inkstand. Engraved in 1774.

"Du Cabinet de Monsieur Glume." A corresponding picture is in the Gallery of the Hermitage at St. Petersburg, Room 12. Waagen, *Die Gemäldesammlung in der Kaiserlichen Ermitage zu St. Petersburg,* München, 1864, p. 183, No. 807. Nagler, *Künstler-Lexicon,* XII. "Rembrandt," p. 419, mentions such a picture in the Gallery of Gotha.

A. VAN OSTADE *pinx.* Two Boors drinking and smoking. Jac. 160.

"A. v. Ostade *pinx.* 1667. — G. F. Schmidt fecit Aqua forti. 1757." — All impressions have an open space in the lower margin, and no inscription.

SCHMIDT, GEORG FRIEDRICH, *continued.*

SASSOFERRATO *pinx.* Mater Amabilis. Jac. 163.

Dedicated to Count Esterhasy [*sic*], who owned the picture. Engraved in 1763.

REMBRANDT *pinx.* Hermit in a Grotto near a burning City; also called Anchises looking upon Troy, also Lot. Jac. 166.

With dedication to J. G. Lesser. "Tiré du Cabinet de Mr. César. R. van Ryn pinx. 1630. — G. F. Schmidt fec: aqua for: 1768." Smith, *Cat. rais.*, "Rembrandt," No. 190.

Impression with the white stamp of the engraver's initials.

DIETRICH *pinx.* The Presentation in the Temple. Jac. 167.

According to Defer, in *Catalogue Debois,* No. 1075, the original was in the Aguado Gallery in Paris, which was dispersed a few years ago. Engraved in 1769.

ANN. CARACCI *pinx.* Alexander and Timoclea. Jac. 169.

1st state, before any letters.

The 2d state is before the dedication to the Empress Catherine II.; the 3d, with the dedication.

REMBRANDT *pinx.* Lot and his Daughters. JAC. 173.

See Smith, *Cat. rais.*, "Rembrandt," 8. The picture was in the collection of Prince Henry of Prussia at the time of the engraving.

VAN DYCK *pinx.* Virgin and Child, with the infant St. John. Jac. 176.

The picture was, when engraved in 1773, in the collection of Prince Henry of Prussia.

The 1st state is without the inscription, "tiré de la Collection de S. A. R. Mgr. le Prince Henry de Prusse."

REMBRANDT *pinx.* Tobias and his Wife. Jac. 177.

Nagler, *K.-L.*, art. "Schmidt," No. 162; Smith, *Cat. rais.*, "Rembrandt," No. 48.

Impression with the white stamp of the engraver's initials.

SCHMUTZER, ANDREAS, and his brother Joseph, engravers, born at Vienna about the beginning of the eighteenth century. They usually worked conjointly on the same plate; Andreas died at Vienna in 1739, and Joseph in 1740.

RUBENS *pinx.* The High Priest dedicates the Veiled Consul, Decius Mus, to Death.

The third of the series, and the finest, of seven pictures illustrating the life of Decius Mus, in the Lichtenstein Gallery in Vienna. Smith, *Cat. rais.* No. 330. Waagen, *Handbook*, II. p. 270.

SCHMUTZER, ANDREAS, *continued.*

The brothers also engraved the two preceding pieces of this series, Decius addressing his soldiers (Smith, *Cat. rais.* No. 329), and Decius consulting the Augurs (Smith, No. 328). The four remaining pieces were engraved, two by G. A. Müller and two by Ad. Bartsch. Nagler, *K.-L.*, art. "Rubens," XIII. p. 579.

SCHMUTZER, JACOB MATTHIAS, son of Andreas, designer and engraver, born at Vienna in 1733, died there in 1811. A pupil of Wille.

RUBENS *pinx.* St. Ambrose refusing the Emperor Theodosius entrance into the Church.

The picture is in the Vienna Gallery. Smith, *Cat. rais.* No. 287. Engraved in 1784.

1*st state of the print with letters, inscribed* "Saint Ambroise et Théodose le Grand, *etc.*, à Paris chés Chéreau," *etc.*

RUBENS *pinx.* The same.

Proof before letters, with merely the names of the artists and the coat of arms.

RUBENS *pinx.* Mucius Scævola before Porsenna.

From the picture in Prince Esterhazy's collection, formerly in that of Prince Kaunitz in Vienna. Smith, *Cat. rais.* No. 1111. Engraved in 1776.

DIETRICH *pinx.* **P.** Chr. Wilh. Ernst Dietrich.

Engraved in 1764.

J. STEINER *pinx.* **P.** Prince Kaunitz, standing at a table.

SCHONGAUER (sometimes **SCHÖN**), **MARTIN,** painter and engraver, according to Passavant, *Peintre-graveur*, II. pp. 103, 106, born about 1420, at Colmar (or Augsburg), died at Colmar, February 2, 1499. Waagen, after Harzen, puts the date of his birth at about 1440. He formed himself after Jan van Eyck and Rogier van der Weyden the elder. "Martin Schongauer, the greatest German master of the fifteenth century, is historically known to have been a scholar of Rogier." Waagen, *Handbook*, I. p. 91. See also p. 130. — Bartsch, VI.

The Nativity. B. 4.

Very fine and harmonious impression. Paper with the watermark of the Profile of a Human Head.

With the stamp and from the collection of Prince de Paar.

Harrach, No. 2538, 400 *fr.*

The Flight into Egypt. B. 7.

Fine and early impression. Paper with the watermark of the Profile of a Human Head.

SCHONGAUER, MARTIN, *continued.*

The Crowning with Thorns. B. 13.

Retouched impression on somewhat later and thicker paper.

From Otto's collection.

Christ before Pilate. B. 14.

Powerful early impression.

The Bearing of the Cross with St. Veronica. B. 16.

Delicate, though not powerful impression. Paper with the watermark of the Gothic 𝔭.

The Crucifixion. B. 17.

A powerful impression.

From the collection of G. Storck, with his autograph on the back: "G. Storck. Milano 1799."

The Entombment. B. 18.

Early impression.

The Resurrection. B. 20.

Impression on somewhat later and thicker paper. Retouched.

From Otto's collection.

⁂ The six pieces described above, B. 13 – 20, are from the Passion of Christ, B. 9 – 20.

Virgin and Child, standing. B. 28.

Fine and powerful impression.

From Otto's collection. — Harrach, No. 2549, 305 *fr.*

The Virgin with the Child on a Crescent crowned by two Angels. B. 31.

Very fine and early impression. Watermark of the paper, Small Bull's Head.

From Weber's sale.

St. Anthony tormented by Demons. B. 47.

A copy of this rare print.

One of the Foolish Virgins. B. 87.

Half figure, face view, the lamp carried in both hands, and a braid of hair falling on her left shoulder. This is not one of the series of the five foolish Virgins, B. 82 – 86; it does not belong to any set.

Perfect impression of extraordinary power.

Watermark of the paper, Fleur-de-lis.

From the collections of John Barnard, sold in 1798; Fr. Debois, 1843, No. 1087, 50 *fr.*; B. Delessert, 1852, No. 265, 81 *fr.*; and H. Weber, 1855, No. 63, 20 *th.*

SCHREINER, JOHANN GEORG, lithographer, born at Mergelstetten in Würtemberg in 1801. He studied at the Academy in Munich.

HESS *pinx.* Adoration of the Magi and Shepherds.

Fresco in the church of All Saints in Munich.

HESS *pinx.* The Virgin enthroned.

Fresco in the church of All Saints in Munich.

RAPHAEL *pinx.* Portrait of a Cardinal.

From the picture in the Leuchtenberg Gallery in Munich. Passavant, II. 280.

SCHULTHEISS, ALBRECHT, engraver in Munich, of the present day.

PERUGINO *pinx.* The Entombment.

From Sta. Chiara in Florence ; now in the Gallery of the Pitti palace.

Proof before letters, with the names of the artists, the publisher, and the printer. On India paper.

SCHULZE, CHRISTIAN GOTTFRIED, engraver, born at Dresden in 1750, died there in 1819. A pupil of Camerata and of Wille.

RAPHAEL *pinx.* Madonna di San Sisto.

See Passavant, II. 240. The picture is in the Dresden Gallery. Engraved for the *Rec. d'estampes de la Gal. de Dresde*, III. No. 1.

Paris impression.

RAPHAEL *pinx.* The same.

Proof, with open traced letters. Artists' names very small, cut with the needle.

RAPHAEL *pinx.* The same.

Artist's proof, before letters, with the coat of arms and merely the artists' names, very small, cut with the needle.

ANN. CARACCI *pinx.* Head of Christ.

The picture is in the Dresden Gallery. Engraved for the *Rec. d'est. de la Gal. de Dresde*, III. No. 5.

ANGELICA KAUFFMAN *pinx.* A Vestal.

The picture is in the Dresden Gallery. Engraved for the *Rec. d'est. de la Gal. de Dresde*, III. No. 7.

ANGELICA KAUFFMAN *pinx.* The same.

Earliest impression ; a proof, though with the first inscription.

GUIDO RENI *pinx.* The Union of Drawing and Color.

The picture is in the Gallery of the Louvre. Villot, No. 334. Engraved for the *Musée Français.*

Artist's trial proof before any letters, not quite finished.

PORDENONE *pinx.* **P.** "Catterina Cornara Regina di Cipro."

SCHULZE, CHRISTIAN GOTTFRIED, *continued.*

The picture is in the Dresden Gallery. Engraved for the *Rec. d'est. de la Gal. de Dresde,* III. No. 3.

Artist's trial proof, before any letters, with the coat of arms.

KYMLI *pinx.* **P.** Joseph II. Empereur des Romains.

"Peint 1777, gravé 1778."

CASANOVA *pinx.* **P.** Count Beloselsky, Russian Ambassador in Dresden.

Artist's trial proof, before any letters.

A. GRAFF *pinx.* **P.** Palitzsch, the peasant-astronomer.

The original picture is owned by Mr. C. Schirmer, inspector of the Gallery in Dresden.

SCHUPPEN, PIETER VAN, designer and engraver, born at Antwerp in 1623, died at Paris in 1702. A pupil of Nanteuil.

F. VOUET *pinx.* **P.** Barbot de Lardeinne, Simon Joseph de.

Nagler, *Künstler-Lexicon,* art. "Schuppen," No. 88. Engraved in 1691.

MIGNARD *pinx.* **P.** Reynie, Messire G. N. de, Cons. du Roy.

Nagler, *K.-L.,* art. "Schuppen," No. 47.

SCOTIN, LOUIS GÉRARD, engraver, born at Paris in 1690.

WATTEAU *pinx.* Les Plaisirs du Bal.

"Ce tableau est dans le Cabinet de Mr Glucq, Conseil^{er} au Parlement." Nagler, *Künstler-Lexicon,* art. "Scotin," No. 16.

SCOTT, JOHN, a distinguished engraver of animals, born at Newcastle, died at London in 1828 at the age of 54.

R. R. REINAGLE *pinx.* The Spaniel.

Proof, with open and traced letters.

SCOTTO, GIROLAMO, engraver, born about 1780. A pupil of Longhi.

PAOLO VERONESE *pinx.* The Feast at the House of Simon.

The picture is in the Royal palace at Genoa.

"G. Scotto dis. in Genoa 1824, inc. Firenze 1830."

RAPHAEL *pinx.* Madonna del Duca di Terranuova.

See Passavant, II. No. 28, and III. p. 89. The picture was in 1855 bought from the Terranuova family in Naples, formerly of Genoa, for the King of Prussia for 30,000 thalers; it is now in the Berlin Gallery. Engraved in 1823. Nagler, *Künstler-Lexicon,* art. "Scotto," enumerates this engraving twice, No. 5 and No. 6 being the same.

Proof with open and traced letters.

SCOTTO, GIROLAMO, *continued.*

𝔓. Aldo Manuzio.

Engraved for the *Vite e Ritratti di illustri Italiani.*

SELMA, FERNANDO, engraver, born in 1748 at Madrid (according to Stanley, in Bryan's *Dictionary*, at Valencia). He studied under Carmona, and at Paris, and died in 1810, a Professor at the Academy of Madrid.

MURILLO *pinx.* St. Ildefonso receiving the Chasuble from the Hands of the Virgin.

The picture is in the Madrid Gallery. Stirling, *Annals*, II. p. 914, III. p. 1435. Engraved for the *Coleccion de las estampas de los cuadros pertenecientes al Rey de España.*

VAN DYCK *pinx.* 𝔓. Van Dyck and the Earl of Bristol in one picture.

The picture is now in the Madrid Gallery; Madrazo, *Catálogo*, No. 1407. While in the Royal palace it was engraved as the portraits of Van Dyck and Marshal Turenne, — "Retratos de Antonio Wandik y el Marisal Conde de Turena, cuyo original se halla en el Real Palacio di Madrid." Passavant, *Die Christliche Kunst in Spanien*, p. 174, says of this picture, . . . "but surpassing all are the portraits, combined in an oval (lengthwise), of Antony van Dyck and the Earl of Bristol, the latter dressed in white silk, the artist in black silk."

SEMLER, engraver of the present day, in Dresden. A pupil of Steinla.

MURILLO *pinx.* Madonna and Child, of the Dresden Gallery.

1st artist's proof, before the representation on the plate was changed from oval into square. Before any letters.

SCHEIDER *pinx.* 𝔓. Baron Rumohr.

SHARP, WILLIAM, engraver, born at London in 1746, died there in 1824. A pupil of B. West and of Bartolozzi.

WEST *pinx.* The Witch of Endor.

The picture was in the collection of Daniel Daulby, Esq. at the time of the engraving.

SIR JOSHUA REYNOLDS *pinx.* Holy Family.

The picture is in the Vernon Gallery. Waagen, *Treasures*, I. p. 366. This is the larger plate.

GUIDO RENI *pinx.* The Doctors of the Church.

The picture is now in the Imperial Gallery of St. Petersburg; at the time of the engraving it was in the Houghton Gallery.

Proof before letters, with the coat of arms, and with the artists' names only traced with the needle. The present impression is also before the address, which is ordinarily found traced in small letters under the coat of arms.

SHARP, WILLIAM, *continued.*

Artist's proofs are before arms or any letters. Johnson, No. 150; G. Smith, No. 1185, £15; Marshall, No. 1726, £4 1 *s.*

DOMENICHINO *pinx.* St. Cecilia.

The picture at the time of the engraving was in the collection of Mr. R. Udney.

Proof, with the inscription "St. Cecilia" in open letters.

In some of the earliest impressions of the proofs the inscription is merely "Cecilia," without the "St." Of the prints, those with the date 1790 are the first, the later ones have 1791.

"Artist's proof before any letters and before the border," G. Smith, No. 1191, £3 10 *s.*

DOMENICHINO *pinx.* The same picture engraved in 8vo.

Subscription ticket to "The second series of the select work of Engravings under the direction of Wm. Buchanan, Esq."

DOMENICHINO *pinx.* Circe.

Proof, with open and traced letters.

DOMENICHINO *pinx.* Lucretia.

Proof before letters, having only the artists' names and the address.

SALVATOR ROSA *pinx.* Diogenes in search of an Honest Man.

Engraved in 1792 from a picture then in the possession of Edward Knight, Esq.

WEST *pinx.* King Lear.

Engraved for Boydell's Shakespeare Gallery, for which also the picture was painted. The latter was brought to America by Fulton, and is now in the Gallery of the Athenæum, in Boston, Mass.

WEST *pinx.* The same.

Proof etching.

WEST *pinx.* King Alfred dividing his Loaf with a Beggar.

Proof, with the coat of arms, and only one line of inscription, the title, before the dedication.

TRUMBULL *pinx.* The Sortie from Gibraltar.

The picture is in the Gallery of the Athenæum in Boston, Mass.

Proof with open and traced letters. On India paper.

TRUMBULL *pinx.* The same.

Artist's proof before any letters, with only "J. Trumbull pinxt. W. Sharp sculpt." *traced with the needle.*

WOODFORTH *pinx.* Interview of Charles I. with his Children.

Artist's proof with no inscription except "Published by Wm. Sharp, London, May 16, 1818." *On India paper.*

SHARP, WILLIAM, *continued.*

The proofs have the inscription of the title in open letters, formed of two lines, to which, in the common prints, the shading of a third line is added.

VAN DYCK *pinx.* **P.** Charles I., the head in three positions.

Painted for Bernini, to assist him in making a bust of the King. Now at Windsor Castle. Waagen, *Treasures*, II. p. 428.

G. F. JOSEPH *pinx.* **P.** Sharp, William.

Open letter proof.

Artist's proof, before any letters, and before the border, G. Smith, No. 1160.

SIR J. REYNOLDS *pinx.* **P.** John Hunter.

The picture is in the collection of Glasgow University. Waagen, *Treasures*, III. p. 283.

1*st proof, before letters, with only the names of the artists and the address traced with the needle.*

The 2d proof has one line of open letters. Drugulin, *Allgemeiner Portrait-Catalog*, No. 9545.

R. HOME *pinx.* **P.** Hyde, John, Judge at Calcutta.

Proof, lettre grise ; *the letters are lightly shaded, but not filled.*

WEST *pinx.* **P.** Moore, Samuel.

Artist's proof before any letters.

ROMNEY *pinx.* **P.** Walker, Thomas, of Manchester.

Open letter proof.

First proofs are before letters, with merely the artists' names.

R. WILSON *pinx.* Niobe.

A landscape, the figures engraved by Sharp, the landscape by Samuel Smith. *See* SMITH.

SHERWIN, JOHN KEYES, designer and engraver, probably born in Essex about 1746, died at London in 1792. He was a pupil of Bartolozzi, and studied also after Woollett. Stanley, in Bryan's *Dictionary.*

FRANCISCO DE RIBALTA *pinx.* Christ bearing the Cross.

After the picture in the chapel of Magdalen College, Oxford, which has also been attributed to Morales el Divino, to Murillo, and even to Lodovico Caracci, Guido, and Guercino. Passavant says that the picture is Spanish, but not by Murillo. Wm. Stirling, *Annals*, I. p. 500, ascribes it, on the authority of Richard Ford, to one of the Ribaltas.*

* Francisco de Ribalta, the chief painter of the school of Valencia, was born at Castellon de la Plana in 1551, and died at Valencia in January, 1628. His son and pupil, Juan de Ribalta, was born at Valencia, 1597, where he died in October, 1628.

SHERWIN, JOHN KEYES, *continued.*

1st state of the plate, with the date 1779.

The 2d state has the year 1784.

STUART *pinx.* **P.** William Woollett.

The picture is in the Vernon Gallery.

1st state of the print, with an open window.

In the later impressions the window is shaded over. "Artist's proof before any letters," Marshall, No. 1729, £1 10*s.*

SICHEM, CARL or **KAREL VAN,** engraver at Amsterdam, of the seventeenth century.

GOLTZIUS *pinx.* ? **P.** Gvilelmvs D. G. Princ. Avraicæ Comes Nassaviæ Gvberna(tor) Belgicæ.

"C. V. Sichem (the three capitals interlaced) sculp. et ex."; in the right upper corner, "fol. 466."

Engraved for E. van Meteren's *Nederlandsche Historie*, Amsterdam, 1663, fol. Nagler, *K.-L.* XVI. p. 346, "Carl van Sichem," No. 14.

SICHLING, LAZARUS GOTTLIEB, engraver, born at Nuremberg in 1812, died at Leipzig in 1863. A pupil of Reindel and Amsler.

HOLBEIN *pinx.* **P.** Thomas Morett, goldsmith of Henry VIII.

See Waagen, *Handbook*, I. p. 198. This exquisite picture in the Dresden Gallery was formerly attributed to Leonardo da Vinci, and called the portrait of the Duke Sforza of Milan.

Proof before letters, with only the artists' names.

The artist's proofs are before any letters.

L. SEBBERS *pinx.* **P.** Hegel.

SICHLING *del.* **P.** Francis Calley Gray.

The former and donor of this collection.

Drawn and engraved by Lazarus Sichling, with the aid of a photograph by Whipple.

1st engraver's proof, before the name in fac-simile was engraved.

SIRANI, ELISABETTA, painter, of whom there are also known 10 etchings. She was born at Bologna in 1638, and died there in 1665, poisoned by her servant. She was a pupil of her father, Giovanni Andrea Sirani, but became a follower of Guido Reni in his best style. Bartsch, XIX.

Rest in Egypt. B. 5.

From Gawet's collection.

SLOANE, MICHEL, engraver at London. A pupil of Bartolozzi.

CORREGGIO *pinx.* The Adoration of the Shepherds, called "La Notte," The Holy Night.

SLOANE, MICHEL, *continued.*

The picture is in the Dresden Gallery. Coxe, p. 81. Engraved in the stippled manner.

SMITH, ANKER, engraver, born at London in 1759, died there in 1819. A pupil of Taylor, James Heath, and Bartolozzi. Stanley, in Bryan's *Dict.*

TITIAN *pinx.* Sophonisba.

Engraved December, 1817, for the "Select work of Engravings, published by Stone, under the direction of W. Buchanan Esqr."

SMITH, JOHN, designer and engraver in mezzotinto, born at London in 1654, died there in 1727. A pupil of Tillet, Becket, and Van der Vaart.

KNELLER *pinx.* **P.** Mrs. Cross, the actress. Represented as *St. Catherine.*

Whole figure, with the wheel. Nagler, *Künstler-Lexicon,* XVI. p. 517, No. 354.

HEEMSKIRK *pinx.* A Man and Woman drinking.

See Nagler, *K.-L.*, XVI. p. 519, No. 413.

KNELLER *pinx.* **P.** Henry Aldrich, Dean of Christ Church, Oxford.

The picture is at Christ Church College. Nagler, XVI. p. 511, No. 184.

2d state.

The 1st state has *J. Smith fec. et exc.*, to which in the 2d state is added, *Sold by Smith.*

SMITH, JOHN RAPHAEL, painter and engraver in the dotted manner and in mezzotinto, born at London in 1740, where he died in 1811. A pupil of his father, Thomas Smith.

SIR JOSHUA REYNOLDS *pinx.* **P.** Master Crew as Henry VIII.

Mezzotinto.

Proof before letters, having only the artists' names and address cut in open letters.

SIR JOSHUA REYNOLDS *pinx.* **P.** Lady Elizabeth Montague, child of the Duke of Buccleugh.

See Walpole's *Letters to Lady Ossory,* I. p. 251. Mezzotinto.

Proof before letters.

SIR JOSHUA REYNOLDS *pinx.* **P.** Louis Philippe, Duke of Orleans, "Egalité."

Mezzotinto.

SMITH, H. W., engraver of the present day in Boston, U. S.

HOYT *pinx.* **P.** Daniel Webster.

Proof.

SMITH, SAMUEL, landscape engraver, born at London about 1745, died about 1808.

ZUCCARELLI *pinx.* The Finding of Moses.

Nagler, *Künstler-Lexicon,* art. "Smith," states that the picture is in the collection of Hampton Court. Waagen does not mention it in his *Treasures.*

Proof before letters, with only the artists' names and the British coat of arms.

J. RUYSDAEL *pinx.* Waterfall.

The picture is in the collection of Colonel Hugh Baillie. Smith, *Cat. rais.* 170.

Proof, with only the title in open letters, the coat of arms, and the address.

R. WILSON *pinx.* Niobe.

From the first picture of this subject by Wilson, in the Vernon Gallery, differing somewhat from the composition that Woollett engraved (Waagen, *Treasures,* I. p. 367), and from the one in the Bridgewater Gallery (*ibid.* II. p. 53). The figures are engraved by Sharp.

Proof, with the title "Niobe" *in lettre grise, and the inscription,* "From the first picture on the subject painted by Richard Wilson, Esqr., R. A." *in letters traced with the needle, as are also the artists' names; with a coat of arms, but before dedication.*

SOTOMAYOR, MANUEL ESQUIVEL DE. *See* ESQUIVEL.

SOUTMAN, PIETER, painter and engraver, born at Haarlem about 1580, died about 1656. A pupil of Rubens.

RUBENS *pinx.* Wolf Hunt, with the portraits of Rubens and his Wife. Bas. 5.

The picture is in the collection of Lord Ashburton. Smith, *Cat. rais.* 925; Waagen, *Handbook,* II. p. 272; *Treasures,* II. p. 102.

Impression with the engraver's address.

RUBENS *pinx.* Hippopotamus and Crocodile Hunt. Bas. 11.

The picture is in the Palace at Schleissheim near Munich; Smith, *Cat. rais.* 238; Michiels, No. 1101.

Impression with the engraver's address.

SPAGNOLETTO, JOSEF RIBERA, so called, painter and etcher, born at Xativa, — the present San Felipe, — near Valencia, in 1588, died at Naples in 1656. A pupil of Michel-Angelo Caravaggio. Bartsch, XX.

St. Jerome. B. 4.

The smaller representation, — with an angel blowing a trumpet.

2d state, with Wyngaerde's address.

SPAGNOLETTO, JOSEF RIBERA, *continued.*

The 1st state is before address :— in the 3d state the address is effaced again. (Weigel.)

The Martyrdom of St. Bartholomew. B. 6.

SPIERRE, FRANÇOIS, painter and engraver, born at Nancy in 1643, died at Marseilles in 1681. A pupil of S. Vouet and François de Poilly.

FR. SPIERRE *del.* Christ in a glory, giving his blessing to Five Saints, recently (1671) canonized by Clement X.

The first, on the left, raises a monstrance; the next holds a crucifix and a horse-pistol in *one* hand; the third an open book and a pen; the fourth, a woman, holds the blessed Child in her arms; and the last one, on the right, with a tiara at his feet, holds a crucifix and a lily in his hand. Designed and engraved to commemorate the great event of this canonization, and dedicated to Cardinal Alfieri.

The Saints are: Cajetan of Thiene, born in 1480, the founder of the Regular Clergy "Theatines"; Francis Borgia, born in 1572, General of the Jesuits; Philip Benozzi (Benizzi or Beniti) though not one of the seven original founders, the principal saint of the Serviti, born in 1285; Lewis Beltran, or Bertrand, born in 1526, of the Dominican order of preachers, apostle in Peru; and Rosa di Lima, born at Lima in 1586, of the Dominican order, the patron saint of America.

On each side below in the margin of the plate the star of the Dominicans is engraved.

Nagler, *Künstler-Lexicon,* art. "Spierre" has No. 12, "Christ in a glory, adored by several Saints, after Spierre's own design," and No. 20, "Five Saints in adoration of the Saviour in the clouds, after Fr. Vanni." Under this last designation the print occurred in, and was purchased from, the Otto collection. Vanni cannot be the designer of this composition, because he lived a century before the canonization took place.

STEEN (sometimes **STEIN**), **FRANS VAN DEN,** painter and engraver, born at Antwerp in 1604.

ANN. CARAÇCI *pinx.* Pietà.

The dead Christ near the tomb, his head on the lap of his fainting mother, who is supported by two angels; on the tomb are seen the crown of thorns and nails. The picture is in the Gallery of Vienna. Engraved for the first edition of the old Brussels (Archduke Leopold's) Gallery, entitled: "Davidis Teniers Antverpiensis Pictoris ... Theatrum Pictorum ... Anno 1660. Antwerpiae apud Henricum Aertsens, Typographum." All the other editions are without this engraving.

The 2d edition was published "Antwerpiae apud Jacobum Peters 1684";

STEEN, FRANS VAN DEN, *continued.*

the 3d edition was entitled, "Theatrum pictorium Davidis Teniers ... Antwerpiae apud Henricum & Cornelium Verdussen, Typographos, sub leone aureo," undated; the 4th edition was entitled, "Le grand Cabinet des tableaux de l'Archiduc Léopold Guillaume, peint par des maîtres italiens & dessinés par David Teniers, . . . & gravés sous sa direction. A Amsterdam & Leipsic chez Arkstée & Mercus. 1704." Heineken, *Ideé générale*, pp. 45 – 48.

STEFANONI, or **STEPHANONI, PIETRO,** engraver, was born at Vicenza in 1589. He removed to Rome, where he established a printing-press, and became publisher of engravings, especially of the Caracci school. His mark, St. or Stephanoni f., means *usually*, even in the absence of the name of the artist, Stephanoni *formis*.

ANN. CARACCI *pinx.* Holy Family with a Cradle. Virgin and Child, and Joseph, St. John offering cherries.

"P. Stephanoni f[ecit]."

2d state, with the dark shadow on the Virgin's left cheek, the drawing of which has been corrected.

In the 1st state, before the correction, the cheek appears swollen. The comparison was made in the Royal Cabinet of Dresden.

The plate is dedicated to Prince Francesco Ludovisi, who owned the original painting.

STEINLA, MORITZ. His family name was Müller, but to distinguish himself from numerous contemporary artists of this name, he called himself after his birthplace, Steinla (near Hildesheim in Hannover) where he was born in 1791. He died in Dresden in 1858. A scholar of Morghen and of Longhi.

RAPHAEL *inv.* The Slaughter of the Innocents.

See Passavant, II. p. 528, No. 259. Engraved in 1836, after a drawing in the possession of the King of Saxony, and corresponding with Marc-Antonio's engraving, B. 20, the second plate, *without* the fir-tree.

Artist's proof before any letters, with the stamp of the engraver's initials. With Steinla's autograph; the sheet bears also the autograph of E. Mandel.

TITIAN *pinx.* "Cristo della Moneta." The Tribute Money.

The picture is in the Dresden Gallery; it was painted for the Duke Alfonso I. of Ferrara, and is the original of several copies.

Proof, with merely the inscription, "Il Christo [*sic*] della Moneta" *in open uncial letters; and, in very small cursive letters,* "Titian pinx. . . . M. Steinla sc." *On India paper. In the right corner of the lower margin is the white stamp of the letters A and R, surmounted with a crown* (*Antonius Rex*).

STEINLA, MORITZ, *continued.*

The plate was bought for the Royal Cabinet of Engravings in Dresden, to be added to Part III. of the *Rec. d'estampes de la Gal. de Dresde.*

TITIAN *pinx.* The same.

Artist's proof, 1st state of the finished plate before the title. With the inscription, "Titian gem. — gez. zu Dresden u. gest. z. Mailand u. Florenz v. Moritz Steinla 1827," *traced with the needle in larger letters than in any other state.*

There occur impressions of the plate without any letters, which were taken after the German notice about the artists just mentioned was erased, and before it was replaced by the short inscription, *Titian. pinx., M. Steinla sc.*, of the open-letter proofs. The prints have the notice about the artists in French, in small letters, *Peint par Tiziano Vecelli, gravé par M. Steinla à Florence;* the title, *Il Christo della Moneta*, is in shaded letters, under it are the arms of Saxony, and the further inscription, *Tableau de Tiziano Vecelli da Cadore de la Galerie Roiale de Dresde. Haut* 2 *pieds* 8 *pouces, sur* 2 *pieds de largeur.*

FRA BARTOLOMMEO *pinx.* Pietà.

Engraved in 1830 after the picture in the Gallery of the Pitti palace in Florence. *See* Crowe and Cavalcaselle, III. p. 471.

Artist's proof, before letters and arms, with only the names of the artists.

Some still earlier impressions are before any letters or arms. The proofs are also before letters, but they have the artists' names and the coat of arms.

MICHEL-ANGELO *pinx.* Madonna and Child, and the infant Saint John.

Engraved in 1829, after an oil painting, alleged to be by Michel-Angelo, in the possession of the Countess Camilla Farrari in Florence, for the *Antologia di Firenze* XXXV. *See* Nagler, *Künstler-Lexicon*, under "Buonarroti," p. 221.

Without inscription.

PALMA VECCHIO *pinx.* Madonna and Child, with the infant Saint John and Saint Catherine.

The picture is in the Dresden Gallery.

Artist's proof before any letters, with the croquis of the profile of the engraver, drawn with the needle in the right hand corner below.

RAPHAEL *pinx.* Madonna di San Sisto.

Engraved in 1847. Passavant, II. 240. The picture is in the Dresden Gallery; it was originally painted for the Grey Friars of St. Benedict in Piacenza. See further under MÜLLER, p. 257.

Proof, before letters, arms, or dedication, with only the artists' names. With the stamp of the engraver's initials.

STEINLA, MORITZ, *continued.*

Published for 40 *th.*; present price from 75 to 80 *th.*

RAPHAEL *pinx.* The same.

Artist's proof, before any letters, with the croquis on the left below; a female figure, engraving, and a head, Steinla's own profile.

Macready, No. 110, £ 19; bid in by Messrs. Amsler and Ruthardt, of Berlin.

Of the prints, those with open letters are the first, and before the plate was retouched,—the price of these is 30 *th.* now at the publishers, — and such of them as have the stamp of the engraver's initials are subscription copies. The impressions from the retouched plate have shaded letters.

HOLBEIN *pinx.* The Madonna of the Burgomaster Meyer, of Basle.

The Burgomaster is represented with his family in devotion before the Virgin and Child.

A full history of the picture (now in the Dresden Gallery) is given by G. Th. Fechner, in Naumann's *Archiv*, Jahrg. XII. p. 58, *et seqq.*, which corrects the former accounts, and the statements given by Hübner, in his *Verzeichniss der K. Gemälde-Gallerie zu Dresden.* A duplicate of this picture is in the possession of the Princess Charles of Hesse-Darmstadt, Waagen, *Handbook*, I. p. 192; A. von Zahn, in Naumann's *Archiv*, Jahrg. XI. p. 42, *et seqq.* Engraved in 1841.

1*st proof, before letters and before the coat of arms, with only the names of the artists.*

The 2d proofs, still before letters, have the coat of arms; and a very small number (it is said but 12) of engravers' proofs are before the arms and before any letters.

RAPHAEL *pinx.* **P.** Pope Julius II.

Passavant, II. No. 83. The original is in the Gallery of the Pitti palace in Florence, and there are numerous repetitions and copies.

Artist's proof before any letters. On India paper.

STEINMÜLLER, JOSEPH, engraver, born at Vienna in 1795, where he died in 1841. A pupil of Maurer.

RAPHAEL *pinx.* The Virgin in the Meadow, "Die Jungfrau im Grünen."

See Passavant, II. No. 37, and III. p. 91. The picture is in the Vienna Gallery. Engraved in 1841.

Proof before any letters.

PERUGINO *pinx.* Virgin and Child with two female Saints.

The picture is in the Vienna Gallery. Engraved for the Austrian Art Union in 1834.

LEONARDO DA VINCI *pinx.* Virgin and Child, with St. Catherine and St. Barbara.

STEINMÜLLER, JOSEPH, *continued.*

See Rigollot, No. 27. The picture is in the Esterhazy Gallery in Vienna. Engraved in 1827.

STOCK, ANDREAS, engraver, born in Holland about 1590, worked at the Hague and at Amsterdam. Supposed to be a pupil of Jac. de Gheyn.

VAN DYCK *pinx.* 𝔓. Snayers, Pieter, painter.

Smith, *Cat. rais.* No. 84. Munich Gallery.

Engraved for Martin van den Enden, Van Dyck's *Iconographia,* No. 57. Weber, p. 84.

2d and last state, with the name of the engraver (instead of "Martinus van den Enden excudit," of the 1st state). *Watermark, Small Foolscap.*

STÖLZEL, CHRISTIAN ERNST, designer and engraver, born at Dresden in 1792, died there in 1837. A pupil of his father, Christ. Friedr. Stölzel.

RAPHAEL *pinx.* The Coronation of the Virgin.

Altar-piece for the church of San Francesco in Perugia; now in the Gallery of the Vatican. Passavant, II. 17. Engraved in 1832.

1st state, with the name of Hultzsch as printer.

The proofs have open letters.

RAPHAEL *pinx.* An Angel, from the fresco in San Severo in Perugia, called "The Trinity."

See Passavant, II. 35. Engraved in 1836.

FRA FIESOLE *pinx.* Saint John the Evangelist.

From the fresco in the chapel of Nicholas V. in the Vatican. Engraved in 1825. On India paper.

FRA FIESOLE *pinx.* Saint Catherine.

The original, painted in tempera, is in the church of San Domenico in Perugia. Engraved in 1824. On India paper.

STÖLZEL, CHRISTIAN FRIEDRICH, designer and engraver, born at Dresden in 1751, died there in 1816. A pupil of Schenau and Canale.

GIORGIONE *pinx.* The Concert.

Two choristers, the one playing a clavecin, with a youth at his elbow, wearing a barret-cap with feathers; the other holding a violoncello. The picture is in the Gallery of the Pitti palace. Engraved in 1808, for the *Musée Français.*

Artist's proof; the engraver's name and the date slightly cut with the needle.

Villot, *Musée du Louvre,* I. p. 26, mentions this print (with a mistake in the name of the engraver, Hoelzel for Stoelzel), as an engraving of the picture in the Louvre, which, however, is entirely different. The other engraving he mentions, by N. Dupuis, is from that picture, representing a landscape with four figures, etc.

STÖLZEL, CHRISTIAN FRIEDRICH, *continued.*

RUBENS *pinx.* 𝔭. Rubens's first wife, Isabelle, or Elizabeth, Brant.

The picture is in the Dresden Gallery. Engraved for *Rec. d'est. de la Gal. de Dresde,* III. No. 13, where it is called, erroneously, the portrait of Helena Forman, the *second* wife of Rubens.

STORM, G. F., an English engraver of the present day.

𝔭. Shakespeare.

Mezzotinto, three quarters length, "from an original picture in the possession of C. U. Kingston, Esq., of Ashbourne, Derby."

Proof, with the inscription written with the needle.

G. STUART *pinx.* 𝔭. Nathaniel Bowditch.

The original is in the possession of the family of the late Dr. N. Bowditch, in Boston, U. S.

Proof.

STRANGE, SIR ROBERT, designer and engraver, born in one of the Orkney Islands in 1723, died at London in 1792. He was first instructed by Richard Cooper in Edinburgh, and went thence to Paris, to study with Le Bas. His work consists of 62 plates, and is described by Charles Le Blanc, *Catalogue de l'œuvre de Robert Strange,* Leipzig, 1848. About 1790 Strange selected 80 of the finest impressions of each of his plates, — with letters, for of those before letters but a very limited number were taken, — which he numbered and had bound up with an introductory essay on the progress of the art of engraving. For this collection he engraved his portrait, of which one sheet contains the proof etching and the finished print. These numbered copies have mostly been separated; they are recognized by the Roman numbers stamped in the margin.

GREUZE *del.* 𝔭. Sir Robert Strange. Le Blanc, 62.

Head in profile, in a medallion.

Two impressions, one of the pure etching, and the other of the finished plate. With the stamped numbers I. and II.

GUERCINO *pinx.* Abraham dismissing Hagar. Le Bl. 1.

The picture is in the Brera Gallery at Milan.

Proof, before any letters, Marshall, No. 1743, £4; A. E. Evans and Sons, sale catalogue, No. 4789, £12 12*s.*

GUERCINO *pinx.* Esther before Ahasuerus. Le Bl. 2.

The picture is in the collection of the Duke of Northumberland in Alnwyck Castle. Waagen, *Galleries,* or *Treasures,* IV. p. 470. It was formerly in the Camuccini collection in Rome. Platner and Bunsen, III. iii. p. 273.

With the stamped number XXIV.

STRANGE, SIR ROBERT, *continued.*

Proof, before any letters, Johnson, No. 156, £ 9.

GUIDO *pinx.* The Chastity of Joseph. Le Bl. 3.

The picture is in the collection of the Earl of Leicester at Holkham. Waagen, *Treasures,* III. p. 420.

With the stamped number XXV.

GUIDO *pinx.* Bust of the Virgin, with her hands crossed over her bosom. Le Bl. 4.

The picture was owned, at the time of the engraving, by Dr. Charles Chauncy.

GUIDO *pinx.* The Angel of the Annunciation. Le Bl. 5.

The picture was owned, at the time of the engraving, by Dr. Charles Chauncy.

GUIDO *pinx.* The Annunciation; the Angel Gabriel in the dress of a Carmelite. Le Bl. 6.

Painted for the Carmelite church in Paris; now in the Gallery of the Louvre. Villot, No. 321.

With the stamped number XLVI.

CORREGGIO *pinx.* Madonna of St. Jerome, Il Giorno, "The Day," of Correggio; Virgin and Child with St. Jerome, St. Magdalen, and two Angels. Le Bl. 7.

The picture is in the Gallery of Parma. Coxe, p. 86. Originally painted for a Parmesan lady, Donna Brisaide Colla, widow of Orazio Colonna, for 400 lire.

A proof, before any letters, in the Debois collection, No. 1114 — by mistake not described as such in the *Catalogue raisonné,* but in the sale catalogue called *Trois ordres de vacation,* . . . III. p. 17, — and by Piot, *Le Cabinet de l'amateur,* was sold for 1015 *fr.*

GUIDO *pinx.* The Offspring of Love. Le Bl. 8.

The picture is in the Grosvenor Gallery.

CARLO MARATTI *pinx.* "Parce somnum rumpere." The Infant Christ sleeping. Le Bl. 9.

The picture, when engraved, was owned by Dr. Charles Chauncy.

MURILLO *pinx.* The Infant Christ as the Good Shepherd, twisting a crown of thorns. Le Bl. 10.

This picture, when engraved, was owned by Dr. William Hunter. Waagen saw such a picture in the collection of Glasgow University, probably the same, *Treasures,* III. p. 283. Stirling, *Annals,* p. 1429.

VAN DYCK *pinx.* The Infant Jesus, sleeping. Le Bl. 11.

"In Pinacotheca regia Neapolitana," at the time of the engraving; the

STRANGE, SIR ROBERT, *continued.*

picture is not now in the Gallery of Naples. Smith, *Cat. rais.* "Van Dyck," No. 418, mentions this engraving, without any statement about the picture.

GUERCINO *pinx.* Christ apearing to his Mother. Le Bl. 12.

"Painting in the church of Il Nome di Dio at Cento."

With the stamped number XXXIII.

DOMENICHINO *pinx.* Saint Agnes. Le Bl. 13.

The picture is in Windsor Castle, Waagen, *Treasures,* II. p. 434. It was formerly in Kensington Palace.

With the stamped number XVI.

RAPHAEL *pinx.* Saint Cecilia. Le Bl. 14.

The picture is in the Gallery of Bologna. Passavant, II. 117.

CARLO MARATTI *pinx.* Saint Cecilia. Le Bl. 15.

The picture, formerly in the Houghton Gallery, is in the Imperial Gallery of St. Petersburg.

Impression on India paper.

GUIDO *pinx.* Saint Magdalen, standing, taking the pearls out of her hair. Le Bl. 16.

Owned, at the time of the engraving, by Roger Harenc, Esq.

GUIDO *pinx.* Saint Magdalen sitting in a Grotto; two Angels appear above. Le Bl. 17.

The picture is in the Sciara palace (formerly in the Barberini palace). Platner and Bunsen, III. iii. p. 191.

"Printed by Hocquet."

CORREGGIO *pinx.* Saint Magdalen reading. Le Bl. 18.

She is seen from the front, in an oval. — "1780. In Pinacotheca Hugonis Seton Armigeri conservata." — Le Blanc, p. 19, note: "dans le cabinet de Purling, écuyer."

SALVATOR ROSA *pinx.* King Laomedon refuses to Neptune and Apollo his tribute for the construction of the walls of Troy. Le Bl. 19.

The picture is in the collection of the University of Glasgow. Waagen, *Treasures,* III. p. 283. It was formerly in Dr. Hunter's collection.

GUERCINO *pinx.* Dido stabbing herself on the funeral pile. Le Bl. 20.

Engraved from the picture in the Palazzo Spada in Rome. Platner and Bunsen, III. iii. p. 449. There are numerous repetitions.

Proof, before any letters.

PIETRO DA CORTONA *pinx.* The Finding of Romulus and Remus. Le Bl. 21.

The picture, formerly in the City Hall at Toulouse, is now in the Gallery of the Louvre. Villot, No. 78.

STRANGE, SIR ROBERT, *continued.*

GUIDO *pinx.* Cleopatra, seated. Le Bl. 22.

The picture is in Windsor Castle. Waagen, *Treasures,* II. p. 434.

GUIDO *pinx.* Cleopatra, standing. Le Bl. 23.

The picture is now in the collection of H. A. J. Munro, Esq. Waagen, *Treasures,* II. p. 135.

With the stamped number XL.

Proof before any letters, Johnson, No. 157, £19; George Smith, No. 1203, £16; Marshall, No. 1750, £16 15 *s.*

PIETRO DA CORTONA *pinx.* Cæsar repudiating Pompeia, receives Calphurnia as his wife. Le Bl. 24.

The picture, at the time of the engraving, was in the City Hall at Toulouse; Le Blanc says, p. 26, note, that it is now in the Louvre, but incorrectly, as Villot's Catalogue does not mention it.

SALVATOR ROSA *pinx.* Belisarius. Le Bl. 25.

Engraved from the picture in the collection of Lord Townshend. Waagen, *Treasures,* III. p. 439, says, "Raynham Hall, seat of Lord Charles Townshend, contains Salvator Rosa's celebrated Belisarius." In the Doria palace in Rome there is (or was) a picture of the same subject; compare Platner and Bunsen, III. iii. p. 553.

ANDREA SACCHI *pinx.* Apollo rewarding Merit, and punishing Arrogance. Le Bl. 26.

"1755. In the collection of Henry Furnese, Esq." According to Le Blanc, "Ce tableau passa ensuite dans la collection du Cte. de Spencer."

TITIAN *pinx.* The Venus of the Tribune in Florence. Le Bl. 27.

TITIAN *pinx.* Venus blindfolding Cupid. Le Bl. 28.

From the picture in the Borghese Gallery at Rome. Platner and Bunsen, III. iii. p. 283, No. 35.

TITIAN *pinx.* Venus urging Adonis to desist from the Chase. Le Bl. 29.

Engraved from the picture in the Gallery of Naples, of which there are many repetitions; the one in the Madrid Gallery is considered the finest, and the original of all. Madrazo, *Catálogo,* No. 801.

GUIDO *pinx.* Venus attired by the Graces. Le Bl. 30.

The picture is in the National Gallery. Waagen, *Treasures,* I. p. 338.

GUIDO *pinx.* Cupid sleeping. Le Bl. 31.

At the time of the engraving, the picture was owned by Sir Lawrence Dundas.

SCHIDONE *pinx.* Cupid seated. Le Bl. 32.

STRANGE, SIR ROBERT, *continued.*

The picture is in the Gallery of Naples.
"Printed by Hocquet."

CARLE VANLOO *pinx.* Cupid, standing. Le Bl. 33.

NIC. POUSSIN *pinx.* The Judgment of Hercules. Le Bl. 34.

See Smith, *Cat. rais.*, "Nic. Poussin," No. 270. The picture is in the collection of Sir Richard Colt Hoare.

TITIAN *pinx.* Danaë. Le Bl. 35.

The picture is in the Gallery of Naples.

RAPHAEL *pinx.* Justice. Le Bl. 38.

See Passavant, II. No. 249, d, p. 376. Painted in oil on the wall of the Sala di Costantino of the Stanze in the Vatican.

RAPHAEL *pinx.* Meekness. Le Bl. 39.

See Passavant, II. No. 249, b, p. 375. Painted in oil on the wall of the Sala di Costantino of the Stanze in the Vatican.

GUIDO *pinx.* Liberality and Modesty. Le Bl. 40.

The picture is in the collection of the Earl of Darnley at Cobham Hall. Waagen, *Treasures*, III. p. 21. In 1755, when engraved, it was owned by Henry Furnese, Esq.

GUIDO *pinx.* Fortune, soaring over the Globe, while Cupid catches her flying lock. Le Bl. 41.

The picture is in the collection of the Capitol at Rome. Platner and Bunsen, III. i. p. 134. There is a repetition in the Grosvenor Gallery. "Ex tabula G. R. in pinacotheca Roberti Strange conservata. 1778."

SCHIDONE *pinx.* Two Little School Children, one holding a Tablet. Le Bl. 42.

Below, in the margin, is the inscription: *Imprimis venerare Deos. Virg. G.* 1. The picture is in the Naples Gallery.

WOUWERMANS *pinx.* Return from Market. Le Bl. 43.

The picture is now in the Gallery of R. S. Holford, Esq., of London. According to Smith, *Cat. rais.*, "Wouwermans," No. 77, it was, in 1829, in the collection of the Duchesse de Berri; when engraved, it was in the "Cabinet de M. Le Noir."

VAN DYCK *pinx.* **P.** Charles I. of England. Le Bl. 45.

The King, who wears a large hat, has just descended from his horse; the Marquis of Hamilton, as equerry, is holding the horse.

The original picture of this engraving is in the Gallery of the Louvre. Villot, No. 142; Waagen, *Handbook*, II. p. 288; Smith, *Cat. rais.*, "Van Dyck," No. 138.

STRANGE, SIR ROBERT, *continued.*

Proof, before any letters, Johnson, No. 153, £ 37; Marshall, No. 1752, £ 32 10 *s.* "Épreuve avec lettres tracées,"* Archinto, No. 390, 216 *fr.*

VAN DYCK *pinx.* **P.** The same. Le Bl. 45.

Proof before any letters.

VAN DYCK *pinx.* **P.** Charles I. of England. Le Bl. 46.

Full length figure, dressed in ermine and his royal robes.

The picture was owned, at the time of the engraving, by Strange himself; according to Le Blanc, p. 49, note, it passed into the possession of Sir Robert Dundas; it is at present in Windsor Castle, though not mentioned by Waagen, *Treasures.* Smith, *Cat. rais.*, "Van Dyck," No. 210.

Proof, before any letters, Debois, No. 1126, 1030 *fr.*; Sir J. Hippisley, No. 147, £ 44; Johnson, No. 152, £ 52; Marshall, No. 1751, £ 62.

VAN DYCK *pinx.* **P.** Henrietta Maria, Queen of Charles I., with her two Sons. Le Bl. 48.

"In Pinacotheca Regis Britannici conservata. 1784."

The engraving does not contain the whole composition of the picture in Windsor Castle (Smith, *Cat. rais.* III. "Van Dyck," No. 224; Waagen, *Treasures,* II. p. 426); it leaves out the portrait of King Charles I., seated in an arm-chair. Smith, *Cat. rais.*, Appendix, p. 377, No. 34, describes a picture in the collection of Earl Douglas at Bothwell Castle, a repetition of the one in Windsor Castle, with the omission of the King.

Proof, before any letters, and before the jewels on the table, Johnson, No. 154, £ 22.

VAN DYCK *pinx.* **P.** Children of Charles I. Le Bl. 49.

Charles Prince of Wales, James Duke of York, and Princess Mary. Two "King Charles" spaniels are seated at their feet.

See Smith, *Cat. rais.*, No. 211, and the correction of the description in the Appendix, p. 374, No. 25; Waagen, *Treasures,* II. p. 429. The picture is in Windsor Castle, and a repetition in the Dresden Gallery.

B. WEST *pinx.* Apotheosis of two young English Princes. Le Bl. 50.

The picture is at Hampton Court.

Proof, before any letters.

RAPHAEL *pinx.* **P.** "Ille hic est Raphael." Le Bl. 54.

In reality the portrait of Bindo Altoviti; Passavant, II. 96.

PARMEGIANO *pinx.* **P.** "Parmigiani Amica." Le Bl. 55.

The picture is in the Gallery of Naples.

"Printed by Hocquet."

MEDINA *pinx.* **P.** Archibald Pitcairn, M. D. Le Bl. 61.

* The proofs of Strange's plates are, as a rule, before any letters whatever.

STRANGE, SIR ROBERT, *continued.*

Bust in a medallion, with a border in which is the name as given above; it rests on a socle which *has no inscription;* on the ground in front lie an Æsculapius-staff with the snake, resting on a book, and a lyre with a branch of laurel. Below the border line, in the margin of the plate, are the following lines in traced letters: *To John Clerk M. D. President of the Royal College of Physicians in Edinburgh — This Head of his Celebrated Friend D^r. Archibald Pitcairn, is with the — Utmost Respect Humbly Inscrib'd by — His most Obedient and — very humble Servant — Robt. Strange. — J. Medina Eques Pinxit — R. Strange Sculp^t. Edin^r.* Le Blanc knows but one state of the plate, of which he gives the following description: "Archibald Pitcairn, Médecin et Poëte. D'après Jean Baptiste Medina. Buste dans un médaillon posé sur un socle, où se lit le distique suivant:

Scire potestates herbarum et tangere plectrum,
Pitcairno Phoebus munera magna dedit."

Ours would seem to be an earlier state.

STRIXNER, JOHANN NEPOMUK, designer and lithographer, born at Alt-Oetting in 1782, studied in Munich under Mitterer, Dorner, and Mannlich.

JAN VAN MABUSE *pinx.* Madonna in Trono.

At the left of the Virgin is a young princess with a book before her, offering a small globe; at her right another maiden with a book on her lap, and roses in her hair and in a basket before her.

MEMLING *pinx.* Saint Christopher.

The picture in the Gallery of Munich is attributed by Waagen, *Handbook,* I. p. 96, to Memling's master, Rogier van der Weyden the elder. — Engraved in 1821. This plate and the preceding were published in S. and M. Boisserée and J. Bertram's *Sammlung Alt- Nieder- und Ober-Deutscher Gemälde,* Stuttgart und München, 1822–36, containing 120 plates, including the supplement.

SUAVIUS, the Latin name of **LAMBERT SUSTERMAN,** or **SUTERMAN,** painter and engraver, born at Liége. He flourished 1544–55, and was a pupil of Lambert Lombard, with whom he is often confounded. See Jules Renouvier, *Des types et des manières des maîtres graveurs,* Montpellier, 1853–56, "Les élèves de Lambert Lombard." See also Bryan's *Dictionary,* Nagler's *Künstler-Lexicon,* and Heller's *Handbuch.*

SUAVIUS *del.* Saint Peter and Saint John healing the Cripple at the Gate of the Temple.

See Zani, IX. p. 179.

2d state, with "Inventore ac Caelatore Suavio, 1553," *but before* "M. Petri exc."

SUAVIUS, LAMBERT, *continued.*

From the collection and with the name of Gawet.

The 1st state has, instead of the above inscription, *Hujus Prototipi Inuen. Suauius.*

SUBLEYRAS, PIERRE, painter and etcher, born at Uzès in 1699, died at Rome in 1749. A pupil of his father, Matthieu Subleyras, and of A. Rivalz. Robert-Dumesnil, II.

SUBLEYRAS *pinx.* The Feast at the house of Simon, Magdalen washing Christ's feet. R.-D. 3.

The picture is in the Gallery of the Louvre, Villot, No. 504, where, under the following No., there is also a sketch for this picture; another sketch is in the Dresden Gallery.

2d state, before the inscription of two lines on the left below: "Observer que Subleyras n'a fait tirer," etc.

The 1st state is a pure aqua-fortis etching.

SULLIVAN, LUKE, miniature painter and engraver, born in Ireland.

He came, when young, to London, and became a pupil of Thomas Major.

HOGARTH *pinx.* The March to Finchley.

"Painted by Wm. Hogarth, and published in 1750, According to Act of Parliament."

With but one s *in Prussia in the dedication.*

SUMMERFIELD, JOHN, engraver at London, pupil of Bartolozzi.

RUBENS et SNYDERS *pinx.* 𝔓. "Rubens and his Wife."

He is represented as carrying game, a young stag, on his shoulder, and a basket with fowls; and she as carrying a basket with fruit on her head. The painting is owned by Lord Aylesford. Bürger, *Trésors*, p. 193.

Proof, with open skeleton letters and unshaded coat of arms; below, the address: "London, published by J. Summerfield at No. 9 Southampton Street, Strand, Feby 11, 1801."

The artist's proofs are before any letters; they have only below, cut with the needle, *London, published by Summerfield Nov.* 15, 1800.

SURUGUE, LOUIS, engraver, born at Paris in 1686, died in 1762. A pupil of Picart.

ANDREA DEL SARTO *pinx.* The Sacrifice of Abraham.

See Alfred Reumont, pp. 180–183. The picture is in the Dresden Gallery. Engraved for the *Rec. d'est. de la Gal. de Dresde*, I. No. 8.

RAPHAEL *pinx.* Saint Margaret.

SURUGUE, LOUIS, *continued.*

See Passavant, II. 234. The picture is in the Gallery of the Louvre. Engraved for the *Cabinet Crozat.*

SURUGUE, PIERRE LOUIS, engraver, son and pupil of Louis Surugue, born at Paris in 1717, died there in 1771.

CORREGGIO *pinx.* The Adoration of the Shepherds, called "La Notte," The Holy Night.

The picture is in the Dresden Gallery; Coxe, p. 81. Engraved for the *Rec. d'est. de la Gal. de Dresde,* II. No. 1.

SUYDERHOEF, JONAS, designer and engraver, is believed to have been born at Leyden about the year 1610, and died about 1669. He is of the school of P. Soutman. Joh. Wussin, *Jonas Suyderhoef, Verzeichniss seiner Kupferstiche,* Leipzig, 1861.

M. A. DA CARAVAGGIO *pinx.,* RUBENS *del.* The Entombment. W. 107.

The picture is in the Gallery of Prince Lichtenstein at Vienna.

2d state, before address.

The 1st state is before any letters, and a pure aqua-fortis etching, — the 3d, with the address of Carolus Allard, — the 4th, with a French inscription, *Christ mort,* etc. and the address, *à Paris chez Basan.*

RUBENS *pinx.* Bacchus, led by a Satyr and a Faun. He is preceded by two Bacchantes and a Panther. W. 108.

Smith, *Cat. rais.* 1090.

With the inscription "Visus Hebet, fumant Artus, Cerebrumq; Rotatur," etc.

4th state, without any address.

The 1st has the address, *P. Soutman Excud.,* — the 2d has the address, *Clement de Jonghe Excudit,* — the 3d, *F. de Wit exc.,* which is erased in the next state.

A. VAN OSTADE *pinx.* "The Big Broom." W. 124.

Peasants under an arbor in front of a tavern, with an old hostess. Smith, *Cat. rais.* 36. The picture was sold in the collection of Braamcamp in 1771, and in the sale of Walsh Porter, in 1810.

2d state, before address, with only the names of the artists.

The rare 1st state is before the artist's names; Verstolk, No. 1352, 110 *fl.* . . . The 3d state has the address of C. de Jonghe; — the 4th has *Leon Schenk Excudit,* on the left below.

A. VAN OSTADE *pinx.* "Jan de Moff." W. 121.

Three peasants in a tavern, one playing the violin. "*Als Jan de Moff sijn Veel doet spelen,*" etc., without artist's name. Smith, *Cat. rais.* 125; Waagen, *Treasures,* II. p. 343. The picture is in the Dulwich Gallery, No. 190.

SUYDERHOEF, JONAS, *continued.*

3d state, with " C. Visscher Excu." *The artists' names, in the print itself, about half an inch from the bottom on the right, are so covered up with hatches as to be hardly perceptible.*

From the collection, and with the name of Amann on the back.

The 1st state, very rare, is before the names of the artists and the verses in the margin; — the 2d has the names of the artists, and the verses, "*Als Jan de Moff sijn Veel doet spelen,*" etc., but is before the address. — In the 4th state, the address has been erased, but some traces of it are still perceptible. — The 5th state has the address "*J. Côvens et C. Mortier Excudit.*"

A. VAN OSTADE *pinx.* A Man with a Jug and Pipe. W. 116.

See Smith, *Cat. rais.*, " Ostade," No. 86.

1st state, with " A. v. Ostaden pinxit, J. Suyderhoef sculpsit, *without address.*

The 2d state has *Ex Formis Nicolai Visscher;* — the 3d has the same, with the addition, " *Cum Privil: Ordin: General: Belgii Fœderati.*"

TERBURG *pinx.* The Knife-fighters. W. 122.

The smaller composition; three boors fighting over their cards, a fourth coming up to take part.

2d state, with Clement de Jonghe's address.

The 1st state is with only the names of the artists, before the verses and before any address; — the 3d, with the address of F. de Wit; — the 4th, with the address of Marrebek.

A. VAN OSTADE *pinx.* The Knife-fighters. W. 127.

The larger composition, of 8 figures. Smith, *Cat. rais.* 220.

3d state, with Clement de Jonghe's address.

The 1st state is before much additional work and various changes, and before the address of Clement de Jonghe; — the 2d state is *with* the additional work, and still before the address; — the 3d is with the white chalk marks, scores, over the chimney, and the address, *Clemendt de Jonghe Excudit;* — the 4th has the address *F. de Wit excudit.*

TERBURG *pinx.* The Peace of Münster. W. 103.

Smith, IV. p. 115, No. 1; Waagen, *Handbook*, II. p. 363. Terburg was not willing, while he lived, to sell the picture, which is of the size of the engraving, for 6,000 *fl.* From his descendants it came into the collection of Van Leyden in Amsterdam, in which it was sold in 1804, and bought for Prince Talleyrand for 16,000 *fr.* After his pictures were sold in 1817, it came into the collection of the Duc de Berry, and when this was sold in 1837, it was bought by Count Anatole Demidoff for 45,500 *fr.* In April, 1868, it was sold again in Paris for the sum of 182,000 *fr.* A repetition of this picture, of larger size, is in the Gallery of Amsterdam.

There exist very rare proofs, 1st, before the two artists' names at the

SUYDERHOEF, JONAS, *continued.*

bottom in the plate itself, and before the inscription in the margin; and, 2d, still before the artists' names, but *with* the inscription.

TH. DE KEYSER *pinx.* The Four Burgomasters of Amsterdam. W. 102.

Anton Oetgens van Waveren, Albert Conradi Burgh, Pieter Hasselaer, and Abraham Boom, while deliberating about the reception of Queen Maria de' Medici, receive, through Cornelis van Davelaer, the news that she has already arrived.

The picture is in the Gallery of the Hague. The plate forms part of the work: *Blyde Inkomst ... van Maria de Medicis t' Amsterdam ... door K. van Baerle*, Amsterdam, 1639. fol.

The same. W. 102.

Impression of extraordinary freshness and power.

Purchased for £ 7 7 *s.*

There exist very rare proofs, 1st, before the names of the painter and engraver, and 2d, with merely the name of the painter.

AART VAN LEYDEN *pinx.* **P.** Aart van Leyden. W. 1.

3d state, with the address of P. Goos.

The 1st state is before the name of Suyderhoef, and before the address; the 2d state is *with* the name, but before the address.

J. DE VOS *pinx.* **P.** Beekerts van Thienen, Adriaan, Prof. Lugd. W. 9.

1*st state*, "C. Banheyningh excudit."

The 2d state has the address of Nic. Visscher.

J. VER SPRONK *pinx.* **P.** Bloemaert, Augustyn. W. 12.

J. DE VOS *pinx.* **P.** Cocceius, Joh., Theol. Prof. W. 20.

1*st state*, "C. Banheynigh excudit."

The 2d state has the address of Hugo Allardt.

H. GOLTZIUS *pinx.* **P.** Goltzius, Henricus. W. 30.

1*st state*, "P. Soutman Exc. cum Privil."

The 2d state has Visscher's address.

J. DE VOS *pinx.* **P.** Hegger, Rud. W. 34.

3*d state*, "Carolus Allard excudit."

The 1st state has the address of C. Banheyningh; the 2d state, that of Hugo Allerdt.

VAN DYCK *pinx.* **P.** Moncada, Francisco de. W. 57.

Head and part bust. The picture is in the Louvre; Villot, No. 147. A study for the great equestrian portrait in the same Gallery, No. 146.

Engraved after P. Soutman's design, with the embellished border of leaves and fruit.

FR. HALS *pinx.* **P.** Reves, Jacob de, Theol. Dr. W. 71.

SUYDERHOEF, JONAS, *continued.*

2d state, with the name of F. Hals as painter.

The 1st state — extremely rare — has *A. v. Dyk Pinsit* in the background of the plate.

DUBORDIEU *pinx.* **P.** Rivet, Andreas, Theol. Dr. W. 72.

1st state, before any address.

The 2d state has *Cornelus Banheinningh excud.*; the 3d state, *C. Allard* excud.

REMBRANDT *pinx.* **P.** Swalm, Eleazar. W. 84.

1st state, "P. Goos Excudit." *The inscription begins,* "Aldus draacht Swalmius een Kroon" *and ends* "van zyn wacht ontslaat."

2d state. The plate is cut smaller, the background, etc., altered, and has now the inscription, *Eleazar Swalmius, Ecclesiastes Harlemensis.*

SWANENBURG, WILLEM, designer and engraver, born at Leyden in 1581. A pupil of Isaak Klaaszen Swanenburg and of J. Saenredam.

TINTORETTO *pinx.* Christ blessing the Little Children.

From Otto's collection.

A. BLOEMAERT *pinx.* **P.** Abraham Bloemaert.

Excudit I. Covens.

SWANEVELT, HERMAN VAN, landscape painter and etcher, born at Woerden in 1620, lived principally at Rome, where he died in 1690. He was first instructed by G. Dow, but studied in Italy after Claude Lorrain. Bartsch, II. and Weigel, *Suppléments.*

The Camels. B. 26.

2d state (Weigel), *with the artist's name and the address of Audran.*

The 1st state is before letters.

The Fishers. B. 77.

Impression in which the words "ot oxc." *of the inscription in the 2d state,* "Herman Van Swaneuelt in. fe. et exc. Cum pr. Re," *have been erased from the plate, but before Bonnart's address.*

Weigel's 1st state, before any letters, and before some work in the sky, "presque unique." — 2d state, with the name and address of the artist. — 3d state, with the address of H. Bonnart. — 4th state, with this address erased.

T.

TANJÉ, PIETER. engraver, born at Bolswert in 1706, died at Amsterdam in 1760. He studied at Amsterdam, and followed the style of Houbraken.

GIUSEPPE PORTA DEL SALVIATI *pinx.* The Dead Body of Christ, supported and mourned over by three angels.

TANJÉ, PIETER, *continued.*

The picture is in the Dresden Gallery. Engraved for the *Rec. d'est. de la Gal. de Dresde*, II. No. 12.

PARMEGIANO *pinx.* "Flora."

A saint in a glory, crowned with flowers, and surrounded by angels bearing flowers. *Tanjé sc. et excudit* 1734, without further inscription or title, and usually called Flora. Nagler, *Künstler-Lexicon*, VIII. p. 518, and XVIII. p. 99, No. 77. Saint Rosalia would seem a better designation.

ALBANO *pinx.* Dancing Amoretti, with the Rape of Proserpina.

A *square* picture, in the Dresden Gallery. Engraved for the *Rec. d'est. de la Gal. de Dresde*, II. No. 21.

RUBENS *pinx.* Mars, trampling Silenus under foot, and turning his back to Venus, is crowned by Victory, in spite of Envy.

The picture is in the Dresden Gallery. Smith, *Cat. rais.* 177. Engraved for the *Rec. d'est. de la Gal. de Dresde*, II. No. 44; called "Charles V. couronné par la Vertu"!

A duplicate of this picture is in the Munich Gallery.

REMBRANDT *pinx.* Portrait of an Old Man with a cane; half figure, with both hands.

Smith, *Cat. rais.* 451. The picture is in the Dresden Gallery. Engraved for the *Rec. d'est. de la Gal. de Dresde*, II. No. 48.

M. A. CARAVAGGIO *pinx.* The Card-players.

The picture is in the Dresden Gallery. Engraved for the *Rec. d'est. de la Gal. de Dresde*, II. No. 28.

CORREGGIO *pinx.* **P.** "Correggio's Physician."

See Coxe's *Sketches*, p. 23. The picture is in the Dresden Gallery. Engraved for the *Rec. d'est. de la Gal. de Dresde*, II. No. 2.

DAVID KRAFT *pinx.* **P.** Charles XII.

MIEREVELT *pinx.* **P.** William I., Prince of Orange.

MIEREVELT *pinx.* **P.** Maurice, Prince of Orange.

TARDIEU, JACQUES NICOLAS, designer and engraver, born at Paris in 1718, where he died in 1795. A pupil of his father Nicolas Henri Tardieu.

TENIERS *pinx.* Le Médecin empirique.

Engraved while in the collection of Count de Vence; in 1824, it was in the collection of Joseph Barchard, Esq. Smith, 75.

TARDIEU, NICOLAS HENRI, designer and engraver, born at Paris in 1674, died in 1749. A pupil of J. Le Pautre and G. Audran.

TARDIEU, NICOLAS HENRI, *continued.*

TITIAN *pinx.* Christ appearing to Magdalen in the garden. "Noli me tangere."

The picture was bequeathed by the poet Rogers to the National Gallery. Waagen, *Galleries,* or *Treasures,* IV. p. 59. Engraved while in the Orleans Gallery, for the *Cabinet Crozat.*

Impression before the number.

WATTEAU *pinx.* L'embarquement pour l'isle de Cythère.

The picture is in the Gallery of the Louvre. Villot, No. 649.

TARDIEU, PIERRE ALEXANDRE, engraver, born at Paris in 1756, where he died in 1844. A pupil of his uncle J. N. Tardieu, but especially of Wille.

DOMENICHINO *pinx.* The Communion of St. Jerome.

The picture is in the Gallery of the Vatican.

1*st proof before letters, with only the artists' names, and the date* 1821.

The 2d proof has open letters.

FRANÇOIS *pinx.* **P.** Stanislaus Augustus [Leszczinski] Rex Poloniæ.

In 8vo.

Impression with the address of the engraver.

TARDIEU, PIERRE FRANÇOIS, engraver, born at Paris in 1720, died in 1772. A pupil of Nic. Henri Tardieu.

RUBENS *pinx.* The Judgment of Paris.

The picture was in the collection of Count Brühl in Dresden. See under MOITTE.

TAUREL, EDUARD, an engraver of the present day at Amsterdam.

MIEREVELT *pinx.* **P.** Prins Willem de Eerste.

Proof before letters, with only the artists' names, and the above inscription traced with the needle. On India paper.

TASSAERT, PIETER JOSEPH, painter and engraver, born at Brussels in 1736.

RUBENS *pinx.* Venus detaining Adonis from the Chase.

Smith, 378. The picture is in the Gallery at the Hague. Etched.

TENIERS, DAVID, the younger, painter and etcher, born at Antwerp in 1610, died at Brussels in 1694. He was a pupil of his father of the same name, and of Adriaan Brouwer.

Two Monkeys smoking.

TENIERS, DAVID, *continued.*

"D. Teniers in. et excud. cum privilegio." Probably etched by C. Boel.

TERWESTEN, AUGUSTIN, the elder, a painter, who also etched 10 plates. He was born at the Hague in 1649; in 1699 he founded the Academy of Fine Arts at Berlin, and died there in 1711.

PAOLO VERONESE *pinx.* The Finding of Moses.

The engraving corresponds with the picture in the Dresden Gallery.

2d state, with Blooteling's address.

TESTA, PIETRO, painter and etcher, born at Lucca in 1617, drowned in the Tiber at Rome in 1650. A pupil of Domenichino, and of Pietro da Cortona. Bartsch, xx.

Thetis causing the infant Achilles to be dipped into water from the River Styx.

1st state, before address.

TESTA, GIOVANNI CESARE, painter and etcher, died in 1655.

DOMENICHINO *pinx.* The Communion of St. Jerome.

The picture is in the Gallery of the Vatican.

1st state, with Colignon's address.

The 2d state is with Billy's address.

TESTI, DAVIDE, an Italian engraver of the present day. A pupil of Toschi.

"MICHEL-ANGELO *pinx.*" La Fortuna.

After a picture on panel, 97 centimetres high and 73 centimetres broad, in the possession of Signor Vincenzo Botti, the publisher of the plate. "Inc. in Firenze 1849."

GREENOUGH *sculp. in marm.* BANDINI *del.* P. Lafayette.

TEUCHER, JOHANN CHRISTOPH, engraver at Dresden, born in 1715, studied in Paris.

PARMEGIANO *pinx.* La Vierge à la Rose, Madonna della Rosa.

See Coxe's *Sketches*, p. 247. The Virgin with the Child, whose left hand rests on a globe, while his right hand holds a rose.

This picture was originally painted for Pietro Aretino, as Venus and Cupid, but eventually offered to Clement VII., who bought it on the condition that the Goddess of Love should be draped into a Madonna. It was purchased in 1752 from the Prelate Dion. Zani in Rome for 5,000 scudi, for the Dresden Gallery. Engraved for the *Rec. d'est. de la Gal. de Dresde*, II. No. 3.

THÄTER, JULIUS CÆSAR, designer and engraver, born at Dresden in 1804. A pupil of Reindel and Amsler.

KAULBACH *pinx.* Die Hunnenschlacht.

Engraved from the cartoon painted for Count Raczynski, now owned by the King of Prussia, for Raczynski's *Histoire de l'art moderne en Allemagne.* The finished fresco is in the Museum of Berlin.

Artist's trial proof, the right side of the upper part in outline. On India paper.

THÉVENIN, J. CHARLES, engraver at Paris of the present day.

ARY SCHEFFER *pinx.* L'Enfant charitable.

Open letter proof.

THOMASSIN, SIMON, designer and engraver, born at Troyes in 1652, died at Paris in 1732.

RAPHAEL *pinx.* The Transfiguration.

See Passavant, II. 244. The picture is in the Gallery of the Vatican. Engraved in 1680, on two plates, to be joined.

THOMSON, JAMES, an engraver of London, born about 1785.

CHANTREY *sculp. in marm.*, CORBOULD *del.* **P.** Washington.

THULDEN, THEODORUS or **DIRK VAN,** painter and etcher, born at Bois-le-Duc in 1607, died in 1686. A pupil of Rubens.

RUBENS *inv.* The Meeting between Ferdinand II., King of Hungary, and Ferdinand, Infant of Spain, previous to the battle of Nördlingen, 1634.

The picture is now in the Vienna Gallery; it formed part of the first triumphal arch after the battle. Smith, *Cat. rais.*, "Rubens," 288. Compare Smith, 92; Nagler, *Künstler-Lexicon*, "Thulden," pp. 447 and 450. This etching forms the 9th plate of the rare work, *Pompa trivmphalis introitvs honori Ferdinandi Austriaci Hispan. Infant. a S. P. Q. Antverp. decreta et adornata*, etc. *Iconum tabulas ex archetypis Rubenianis del. et sculps. Theod. à Tulden.* Antverpiæ apud Joannem Meursium, 1642. fol. pp. 189. With 43 plates. Text by Caspar Gevartius.

TIEPOLO, GIOVANNI-BATTISTA, painter and etcher, born at Venice in 1693, died at Madrid in 1770. A pupil of Lazarini.

The Conjurer.

See Nagler, 11.

A Rider.

From the *Varj Capricci* (10 plates). Nagler, 13.

TINTI, CAMILLO, engraver, born at Rome in 1738. A pupil of D. Cunego.

TINTI, CAMILLO, *continued.*

PERINO DEL VAGA *pinx.* David anointed King.

PERINO DEL VAGA *pinx.* David conquering Goliath.

Engraved for Montagnani's Bible of Raphael. *See* MONTAGNANI, Nos. 41, 42.

TISCHLER, ANTON, engraver, born at Vienna, 1721, where he died in 1780. A pupil of Camerata.

WOUWERMANS *pinx.* Les Voitures.

See Smith, 396. Engraved while in the Gallery of Count Brühl in Dresden.

WOUWERMANS *pinx.* Retard de Chasse.

See Smith, 384. Engraved while in the Gallery of Count Brühl in Dresden; now in the collection of the Earl of Lonsdale.

TOMBA, GIULIO, engraver at Bologna, born in 1780. A pupil of Rosaspina.

P. Torricelli.

Engraved for the *Vite e Ritratti di illustri Italiani.*

TORRE, FLAMINIO, painter and etcher, born at Bologna in 1621, died at Modena in 1661. A pupil of Cavedone, Guido, and Cantarini. Bartsch, XIX.

GUIDO *pinx.* Madonna with the Patron Saints of Bologna. B. 4.

The picture is in the Gallery of Bologna. It is known by the name "Il Pallione," because it was used as a banner to be carried round in processions, in commemoration of the delivery from the plague.

TOSCHI, PAOLO, designer and engraver, born at Parma in 1788, where he became director of the Academy of Fine Arts, and died in 1858. A pupil of Bervic.

CORREGGIO *pinx.* Madonna della Scodella, Rest on the Return from Egypt.

The picture is in the Gallery of Parma; it was formerly in the Church of San Sepolcro. Coxe, p. 78.

CORREGGIO *pinx.* The same.

Proof; the inscription in traced cursive letters, and before the dedication.

Artist's proofs are before any letters. George Smith, No. 1236.

RAPHAEL *pinx.* Madonna della Tenda.

See Passavant, II. 227. Engraved in 1832, after the picture in the Gallery of Turin, which is a repetition of the one in the Munich Gallery.

Artist's proof, with merely the names of the artists.

George Smith, No. 1235.

TOSCHI, PAOLO, *continued.*

RAPHAEL *pinx.* The same.

Still earlier finished proof, before any letters. On India paper.

Purchased for £ 9 10 *s.* Archinto, No. 400, 210 *fr.*

The proofs are before the coat of arms and dedication, and have the inscription in traced cursive letters.

RAPHAEL *pinx.* Lo Spasimo di Sicilia, Christ bearing the Cross.

See Passavant, II. 228. Painted for the church of the Olivetan cloister Santa Maria della Spasimo in Palermo; now in the Gallery of Madrid. Engraved in 1832.

2*d state,* "H. Felsing impr."

The 1st state has the name of L. Bardi as printer.

RAPHAEL *pinx.* The same.

Proof, before the coat of arms and dedication; the inscription is in traced cursive letters.

The finished artist's proofs are before letters, having merely the artists' names. G. Smith, No. 1242, £ 23; Archinto, No. 398, 1330 *fr.*; Colnaghi, May, 1865, No. 958, £ 37 10 *s.* Still earlier trial proofs are before the cross-hatching of some parts of the ground, and before any letters. Debois, No. 1165, 1050 *fr.*; G. Smith, No. 1241, £ 31. *Épreuve de remarque,* with "the white nail," Marshall, No. 1795, £ 43.

DANIELLO DA VOLTERRA *pinx.* The Descent from the Cross.

The fresco painting in the church Trinità de' Monti in Rome, detached from the wall and removed to the sacristy. Platner and Bunsen, III. ii. p. 599. There is an interesting account of the picture in the London *Athenæum,* Feb. 9, 1861, p. 197.

DANIELLO DA VOLTERRA *pinx.* The same.

Proof, before the coat of arms and dedication; the inscription is in traced cursive letters.

The finished artist's proofs are before any letters. G. Smith, No. 1238, £ 12 12 *s.* — Artist's proofs *avec remarque* are finished up to a little white square on the ladder, at the right. Wilcox, No. 275, £ 15 10 *s.*; Johnson, No. 162, £ 15 15 *s.*; G. Smith, No. 1237, £ 19 10 *s.*

ALBANO *pinx.* Venus and Adonis.

This is the principal part of the composition of the picture in the Gallery of the Louvre (Villot, No. 12); the one that belongs to a set of four, "The History of Venus," which was engraved by Steph. Baudet, in 1672, "au Cabinet du Roi," complete at that time, of which the other three seem to have been lost; they are not in the Louvre *now.*

Artist's proof, with merely the following inscription on the right below: "gravé en 1816, s[ous] l[a] d[irection] de M. Bervic," *slightly traced with the needle.*

TOSCHI, PAOLO, *continued.*

GÉRARD *pinx.* **P.** Entry of Henry IV. into Paris.

The picture is in the Gallery of the Louvre; Villot, No. 235.

Proof before letters of the finished plate, with merely the names of the artists and of the printer, Chardon fils. On India paper.

Lehrs, No. 406, artist's proof, before the names of the artists and before the work in the letter H in the banner, and "with the white collar," 145 *th.*

FABRE *pinx.* **P.** Alfieri, Vittorio.

Engraved in conjunction with A. Isac.

GÉRARD *pinx.* **P.** Decazes, le Duc.

On India paper.

GÉRARD *pinx.* **P.** The same.

Proof before letters, with only the names of the artists and the printer, and the coat of arms. On India paper.

SANTE DI TITO *pinx.* **P.** Machiavelli.

The proofs of these three portraits are before letters, and with the artists' names.

Tutti gli affresco del Correggio in Parma e quattro del Parmigianino, disegnati ed intagliati in rame da Paolo Toschi e dalla sua scuola. Parma, 1846 – 56. 24 plates.

Toschi did not live to complete the work; during his life and under his direction there appeared the following 13 numbers:

1ª dispensa: plate II. VI. XV. XVI.
2ª dispensa: plate XXVII.
3ª dispensa: plate XXV.
4ª dispensa: plate XXXV.
5ª dispensa: plate III. IV. XIV. XXIII.
6ª dispensa: plate XXXIX.
7ª dispensa: plate XXVIII.
8ª dispensa: plate XXIX.
9ª dispensa: plate XXXIII.
10ª dispensa: plate I. X. XVIII. XX.
11ª dispensa: plate V.
12ª dispensa: plate XXX.
13ª dispensa: plate XXIV. The Coronation of the Virgin.

Also two small plates without numbers, representing groups of children, from Agostino Caracci's copy. See p. 378.

FRESCOS OF PARMEGIANO IN SAN GIOVANNI.

Tav. I. S. Agata.
Tav. II. S. Luccia e S. Apollonia.

TOSCHI, PAOLO, *continued.*

Tav. III. Due Diaconi : San Lorenzo and San Vincenzo.

Tav. III. The same.

Artist's proof, before the number, and before any letters and with the croquis, an urn, etched in the left side margin. On India paper.

Tav. IV. San Giorgio.

Correggio's Fresco, now in the Gallery of the Academy.

Tav. V. Madonna della Scala ; Virgin and Child.

Originally painted on the wall of the house of a friend, the picture was removed to a chapel consecrated to Santa Maria della Scala, from which it was again removed, much injured, to its present place.

Correggio's Frescos in the Camera di San Paolo, a room in the Convent of Benedictine Nuns in Parma, painted for the Abbess Giovanna di Piacenza.

Over the projecting chimney Diana is represented as returning from the chase, in a chariot drawn by two white stags. The apartment represents an arbor of vines and flowers ; 16 stems, rising from consoles, form as many arcades by the interwoven branches and leaves, and leave in each an oval lunette, through which are seen a couple of sporting children. Under each lunette a niche is painted in chiaroscuro, an antique bas-relief of some mythological or allegorical subject.

Tav. VI. Diana in a Chariot, returning from the Chase.

"Camera di S. Paolo No. 2." On the wall over the chimney.

Tav. VI. The same.

Proof, before the number and before letters, with only the artists' names slightly traced with the needle. On India paper.

Tav. VI. The same.

Artist's proof, before the number and before any letters, and with the croquis etched in the lower margin, — a crouching child.

The Lunettes of the Arbor.

Tav. VII. VIII. IX. did not appear.

Tav. X. Camera di S. Paolo. No. 3. Due putti colla sottoposta lunetta.

Below, Fortuna with a cornucopia, a rudder and a globe.

Tav. XI. XII. XIII. did not appear.

Tav. XIV. Camera di S. Paolo, No. 7. Due putti colla sottoposta lunetta.

One of the children is carrying a stone on his head. Below, a youth with a cornucopia, bringing a libation to the altar.

Tav. XV. Camera di S. Paolo, No. 8. Due putti colla sottoposta lunetta.

TOSCHI, PAOLO, *continued.*

One of the children has a mask. Below, a woman reclining, holds in one hand a cornucopia with fruits, etc., in the other a scorpion; on her head is a rampant snake, and before her stands a basket with herbs and flowers, — Nature (dispensing blessings and poison); — otherwise, Summer.

Tav. XVI. Camera di S. Paolo, No. 9. Due putti colla sottoposta lunetta.

One child is embracing a dog. Below, Juno, suspended from heaven with an anvil under her feet.

Tav. XVII. did not appear.

Tav. XVIII. Camera di S. Paolo, No. 11. Due putti colla sottoposta lunetta.

One child holds a spear. Below, a bearded old man, sitting in a chair like Jove, and holding as a sceptre something like a twig with a sprout in his hand.

Tav. XIX. did not appear.

Tav. XX. Camera di S. Paolo, No. 13. Due putti colla sottoposta lunetta.

One of the children is harnessing a dog. The heads of two more children are seen behind. Below, the Parcæ.

Tav. XXI. XXII. did not appear.

Tav. XXIII. Camera di S. Paolo, No. 16. Due putti colla sottoposta lunetta.

One child is blowing a horn. Below, Pan blowing on a conch-shell.

Correggio's Frescos in the Church San Giovanni Evangelista.

Tav. XXIV. The Coronation of the Virgin.

The principal group of the original, now in the Library at Parma, to which it was transferred from the wall of the Tribune behind the altar, when this part was pulled down in 1584, to enlarge the church. The whole composition is known from Ann. Caracci's copy, now in the Gallery of Naples.

A. Group of Cherubs and Angels, with one head in the middle below.

From the choir of the church, copied by Agostino Caracci, before that part was broken down.

B. Second group, one having a violin.

From the same place, and likewise copied by Agostino Caracci.

Tav. XXV. Lunetta in San Giovanni: Joannes Evangelista.

Over the door of the sacristy.

Tav. XXVI. did not appear.

Tav. XXVII. Primo pennacchio della cupola in San Giovanni: San Giovanni Vangelista e San Agostino.

Tav. XXVIII. Secundo pennacchio della cupola in San Giovanni: San Matteo Evangelista e San Gerolamo.

TOSCHI, PAOLO, *continued.*

Tav. XXIX. Terzo pennacchio della cupola in San Giovanni : San Marco Evangelista e San Gregorio.

Tav. XXX. Quarto pennacchio della cupola in San Giovanni : San Luca Evangelista e San Ambrogio.

Tav. XXXI. XXXII. did not appear.

Tav. XXXIII. Secondo gruppo di Apostoli nella cupola di San Giovanni. One, St. Peter, is holding the keys.

Tav. XXXIV. Terzo gruppo di Apostoli nella cupola di San Giovanni has not appeared.

Tav. XXXV. Quarto gruppo di Apostoli nella cupola di San Giovanni. Two Apostles ; on the right, above, are two cherubs kissing each other.

Tav. XXXVI. XXXVII. XXXVIII. did not appear.

CORREGGIO'S FRESCO IN THE DUOMO.

Tav. XXXIX. Terzo pennacchio della cupola del Duomo. San Tommaso Apostolo.

The proofs of these plates are before letters, with merely the artists' names traced with the needle. — Artist's proofs (of which only 33 impressions were issued, previously subscribed for) are before any letters, and with croquis in the margin.

Artist's proofs of the 24 plates above enumerated were sold by Messrs. Christie and Manson, June 3, 1857, Hippisley, No. 156, for £ 44 2 *s.* Another set of these 24 plates, in the same state, to which was added Toschi's portrait by C. Raimondi, was sold by Messrs. Leigh, Sotheby, & Wilkinson, May 27, 1856, Wilcox, No. 276, for £ 56. A set of 30 pieces, also artist's proofs, consisting of the 24 here mentioned, Toschi's portrait, and 5 more of the frescos, engraved by Toschi's followers, were sold by Messrs. Leigh, Sotheby, & Wilkinson, April 18, 1860, Johnson, No. 164, for £ 80.

TROSSIN, ROBERT, designer and engraver in Königsberg, born about 1820, and a pupil of Buchhorn in Berlin.

P. Alexander von Humboldt.

Engraved in 1850, under the direction of Mandel, after a photograph.
Artist's proof before any letters, with a dedication in pencil by the engraver.

TROUVAIN, ANTOINE, engraver, born at Montdidier in 1650, died at Paris in 1710.

TORTEBAT *pinx.* **P.** R. A. Houasse.

One of the two plates engraved in 1707 for his admission into the Academy.

JEAN JOUVENET *pinx.* **P.** The painter's own portrait.

One of the two plates engraved by Trouvain in 1707 for his admission into the Academy.

U.

ULMER, JOHANN CONRAD, engraver, born at Beroldsheim near Ansbach in 1783, died at Frankfort in 1820. A pupil of J. G. von Müller.

RAPHAEL *pinx.* Madonna della Seggiola.

The picture is in the Gallery of the Pitti palace in Florence. Passavant, II. 226.

Artist's proof, before any letters.

Proofs have *lettres grises.*

B. VAN DER HELST *pinx.* The Distribution of Prizes for Archery.

The picture is in the Gallery of the Louvre, Villot, No. 197. There is also a repetition with some alterations, in the Gallery at Amsterdam. Engraved in 1812 for the *Musée Français.*

Artist's proof before any letters.

Rud. Weigel, *Kunst-Catal.* No. 3697, price 60 *th.*

Proofs are before letters, but with the names of the artists.

CARLO DOLCE *pinx.* **P.** Carlo Dolce.

The picture is in the Artists' Portrait Gallery of the Uffizj in Florence. Engraved for Wicar, *Tableaux . . . de la Galerie de Florence et du Palais Pitti.*

Proof before any letters.

TITIAN *pinx.* **P.** Cardinal Beccadelli.

The picture is in the Gallery of the Uffizj in Florence. Engraved for Wicar, *Tableaux . . . de la Galerie de Florence et du Palais Pitti.*

Proof before any letters.

V.

VAILLANT, WALLERANT, portrait painter and engraver in mezzotinto, born at Lille in 1623, died at Amsterdam in 1677. He was instructed in painting by Erasmus Quellinus; the art of scraping in mezzotinto he learned from Prince Rupert, to whom it was communicated by the inventor, Ludwig von Siegen.

RAPHAEL *pinx.* St. Barbara.

See Passavant, II. p. 643, d.; Nagler, *Künstler-Lexicon,* "Vaillant," No. 74.

2d state, in which, after "W. Vaillant fec. Ex.," *is added* "R. Thompson ex."

HOLBEIN *pinx.* **P.** Froben, the printer.

Nagler, "Vaillant," No. 33.

VALCK, GERARD, designer and engraver in line and in mezzotinto, and publisher, born at Amsterdam about 1626, where he died about 1680. A pupil of Blooteling.

VALCK, GERARD, *continued.*

Van der Werff *pinx.* **P.** William I., Prince of Orange.

Van der Werff *pinx.* **P.** Maurice, Prince of Orange.

Both this picture and the preceding are engraved in line.

Sir Peter Lely *pinx.* **P.** Nell Gwynne, with a Lamb, as a Shepherdess.

The picture is now owned by Colonel Meyrick. Engraved in line.

VALLÉE, SIMON DE LA, engraver, born at Paris in 1680. A pupil of P. Drevet.

M. A. Amerighi da Caravaggio *pinx.* The Death of the Virgin.

The picture is in the Gallery of the Louvre. Villot, No. 32. Engraved for tho *Cabinot Crozat.*

VALLET, GUILLAUME, engraver, born at Paris in 1636, where he died in 1704. Probably a pupil of François de Poilly.

Carlo Maratti *pinx.* **P.** Andrea Sacchi.

2d state, with Frey's address.

VANDERMEER, NOAH, the younger, designer and engraver at Amsterdam, born about 1745.

Steenwyck *pinx.* Interior of a Gothic Church.

"Tiré du cabinet de M. Le Brun."

VANDYCK. *See* under Dyck.

VANGELISTI, VINCENZO, engraver, born at Florence in 1738, where he died in 1798. A pupil of Wille.

"Raphael," in reality A. Solario, *pinx.* Le premier devoir des mères, "Madonna with the Green Cushion."

The picture is in the Gallery of the Louvre. Villot, No. 403.

Callet *pinx.* **P.** Charles Gravier, Comte de Vergennes.

Engraved in 1784.

In the inscription is the misspelling "Glavier," which has been corrected on a piece of thin paper laid over the letters "Gl."

VANNI, GIOVANNI-BATTISTA, painter, architect, and etcher, born at Pisa in 1599, died at Florence in 1660. A pupil of Cristoforo Allori. Bartsch, xx.

Paolo Veronese *pinx.* The Marriage Feast at Cana.

The great picture in the Louvre, Villot, No. 103; formerly in the refectory of San Giorgio Maggiore at Venice. It contains, among others, the **Portraits** of Francis I, Soliman I., Vittoria Colonna, Charles V., and of

VANNI, GIOVANNI-BATTISTA, *continued.*

Paolo himself, playing the violoncello, and Titian playing the contrabasso. Etched in 1637 on two plates. B. 17.

1st state, before address.

The 2d state has Rossi's address; proofs are before letters. New impressions are issued from the papal print-shop of the Stamperia Camerale in Rome.

VAN SOMPEL, PIETER, engraver with the burin and the needle, a pupil of Soutman, was born at Antwerp in 1600.

RUBENS *pinx.* **P.** Effigies Paracelsi Medici Celeberrimi.

Philippus Aureolus Theophrastus Bombast von Hohenheim, who translated his name, von Hohenheim, after the fashion of his time, into barbarous Græco-Latin, — Paracelsus.

2d state, with "P. P. Rubens pinxit. P. Soutman excudit."

The 1st state is before Rubens's name; — the 3d state has *P. Soutman invenit et excudit.*

VASQUEZ, BARTOLOMÉ, engraver at Madrid about 1785 – 1810.

ZURBARAN *pinx.* Pastorcita.

The good shepherdess with her crook; in the background a monster (Heresy). Engraved for *Coleccion de las estampas ... de los cuadros ... pertenecientes al Rey de España.*

VELDE, JAN VAN DE, painter and engraver, was born at Leyden in 1598, and is supposed to have been still living in 1679. A pupil of Moises van Uytenbroeck.

The Good Samaritan.

A night-piece.

1st state, with the artist's own address.

The 2d state has the address of Visscher; — the 3d, the address of De Wit.

P. Jac. Zaffius, Cathedr. Eccl. Harlem. Praepos.

Engraved in 1630. Nagler, "Jan van de Velde," No. 8.

1st state, with Proost's address.

From Otto's collection.

VENDRAMINI, GIOVANNI, engraver, born at Roncade, near Bassano, in 1769. At the age of nineteen he came to London, and studied with Bartolozzi; he died at the latter place in 1839. Stanley, in Bryan's *Dictionary.*

SEBASTIANO DEL PIOMBO *pinx.* The Raising of Lazarus.

VENDRAMINI, GIOVANNI, *continued.*

Painted after the drawing furnished by Michel-Angelo. Waagen, *Treasures*, I. p. 320, etc. The picture is in the National Gallery; it was formerly in the Orleans Gallery. Engraved in 1828.

Artist's proof, with merely the names of the artists traced.

PAOLO VERONESE *pinx.* Visione di S. Catterina.

London, published Jan. 1, 1820.

VERMEULEN, CORNELIS, engraver, born at Antwerp in 1644, where he died in 1710. He was a pupil of B. Picart, but followed afterwards the style of Edelinck.

GUIDO *pinx.* The Nymph Erigone.

The picture was in the Orleans Gallery.

Engraved for the *Cabinet Crozat.*

1st state, with coat of arms and six metrical lines BEFORE *the inscription Erigone, and the dedication.*

VAN DER WERFF *pinx.* **P.** Anna Boleyn, Queen of England.

Engraved for Larrey's *Histoire d'Angleterre*, etc. 4 vol. Rotterdam, 1707–13. fol.

ANN. CARACCI *pinx.* **P.** Annibal Caraccius.

"Ex Musæo de Bourdaloue."

VAN DER WERFF *pinx.* **P.** Catherine of Arragon, Queen of England.

Engraved for Larrey's *Histoire d'Angleterre*, etc.

P. MIGNARD *pinx.* **P.** Mignard, Pierre.

H. RIGAUD *pinx.* **P.** Montmorency, François, Duc de Luxembourg, Maréchal de France.

VERNON, T., an engraver of the present day.

FRA FIESOLE *pinx.* St. Matthew.

From the frescos in the chapel of Nicholas V. in the Vatican. Published by the Arundel Society, 1850–51.

VERTUE, GEORGE, engraver, born at London in 1684, died there in 1756. *See* Bryan's *Dictionary.*

VAN DYCK *pinx.* **P.** Dorset, Edward Sackville, Earl of.

Engraved for Birch's *Heads of Illustrious Persons of Great Britain*, published by Knapton.

HOLBEIN *pinx.* **P.** Henry VIII.

The original picture, of which there are many repetitions, is, according to W. Bürger, *Trésors d'art en Angleterre*, p. 145, owned by the Earl of Warwick. Waagen, *Treasures*, III. p. 215. Engraved in 8vo, as frontis-

VERTUE, GEORGE, *continued.*

piece to Vol. VII. of Rapin's *History of England, translated by N. Tindal,* London, James & John Knapton, 1729. 8vo.

P. Milton, John.

Joannes Milton ætat. 62, *A. D.* 1670, at the top of the print; below, *Geo. Vertue sculp.* 1725, without the name of the painter. On a socle below are 6 verses, beginning, *Three poets,* and ending, *the former two.* Under this is a dedication, *Illustrissimo* D^{no} D^{no} *Algernon Comiti de Hertford* D^{no} *Percy.*

Fol.

VILLAMENA, FRANCESCO, painter and engraver, born at Assisi about 1566, died at Rome in 1626. A pupil of C. Cort.

PAOLO VERONESE *pinx.* The Presentation in the Temple.

The picture is in the church of San Sebastiano at Venice. Nagler, *art.* "Villamena," No. 16.

1*st state of the impressions with inscription.*

There are impressions without the inscription; the late impressions have the address of C. Lossi, 1773.

BAROCCIO *pinx.* The Descent from the Cross.

The picture is in the Duomo at Perugia; Nagler, *art.* "Villamena," No. 31. Engraved in 1606.

1*st state, before address.*

The 2d state has "*Gio.* $Batt^{a}$ *Rossi formis in P. Navona;* the 3d has *apud Carolum Lossi, Anno* 1773.

VILLAMENA *del.* St. Francis in the Desert, praying before a Crucifix.

See Nagler, *art.* "Villamena," No. 36.

VISCHER, PETER, amateur designer and etcher, born at Basle in 1779, died there in 1851; he was a connoisseur and collector of engravings.

RUYSDAEL *pinx.* An old castellated Dutch building on the bank of a canal on which two fishermen in boats are throwing their nets.

"P. Vischer sc. [aqua forti] 1807." — "du Cabinet de mon père."

Small folio, oblong.

VISSCHER, CORNELIS DE, designer and engraver. It is usually assumed that he was born at Haarlem about 1629, and that he died about 1658. He was a pupil of Soutman, but formed a style of his own, which, especially in portraits, is unsurpassed in boldness and picturesque effect. Hecquet, in the Appendix of the 2d vol. of Basan, *Dict. des graveurs;* Nagler, *Künstler-Lexicon,* xx. p. 383, *seq.;* William Smith, *Catalogue of the Works*

VISSCHER, CORNELIS, *continued.*

of Cornelius Visscher, London, 1864, also printed in the *Fine Arts Quarterly Review*, London, Vol. I. 1863, *et seq.*

JACOPO DA PONTE BASSANO *pinx.* The Angel bidding Abraham quit his Country.

Engraved for the *Cabinet Reynst.* Nagler, 102. Hecquet, 1. W. Smith, 1.

With the figure of the Angel in the clouds. Without the name of painter or engraver.

From Otto's collection.

Nagler describes a 2d state : with the promises written in the plate in the place where the Angel was before (Nagler speaks of four angels, here is but one), and with the names of the artists. William Smith does not mention such a state.

GUIDO RENI *pinx.* Susannah and the Elders.

A picture of this subject is in the National Gallery (Waagen, *Treasures,* I. p. 338); it was formerly in the Lancelotti palace in Rome. The picture from which this plate is engraved was in the Orleans Gallery, see Basan; it was bought by Mr. Willett for £400. Waagen, *Treasures,* II. p. 495, No. 10. Engraved for the *Cabinet Reynst.* Nagler, 104. Hecquet, 3. W. Smith, 3.

1*st state, before any letters, i. e. before the names of the artists, and before address.*

From Otto's collection.

The second state is with the names of the artists; the 3d has the address of F. de Wit added.

TINTORETTO *pinx.* The Entombment.

Engraved for the *Cabinet Reynst.* Nagler, 105. Hecquet, 4. W. Smith, 8.

2*d state; within the print, at the bottom,* "Tintoretto pinxit. Corn. Visscher figuravit aqua forti."

From Otto's collection.

The first state is of great rarity, only two copies being known; it is before the inscription; — the 3d is with the address of Nicolaus Visscher; — the 4th, with the address of Danckerts.

PAOLO VERONESE *pinx.* The Ascension.

Engraved for the *Cabinet Reynst.* Nagler, 107. Hecquet, 5. W. Smith, 9.

1*st state, before the names of the artists and before address; like Verstolk, No.* 1161. — *The inscription* "Ego et pater vnv̄ svmvs *is on a scroll in the plate.*

From Otto's collection.

VISSCHER, CORNELIS, *continued.*

The 2d state is with the inscription: "*Corn. Visscher Shulp.* [sic.] *P. Veronees Pinxit. F. de Wit excudit.*" Verstolk, 1162.

TITIAN *pinx.* The Virgin and Child, with Tobias and the Angels in the background.

The original picture is now in Hampton Court palace. (William Smith.) Engraved for the *Cabinet Reynst.* Nagler, 108. Hecquet, 6. W. Smith, 4.

3d state, without any letters, i. e. "Tixianus pinxit" *in the margin at the left, effaced.*

From Otto's collection.

The 1st state is before any letters, Verstolk, No. 1163; the 2d has, in the margin beneath, on the left, *Tixianus pinxit.*

RUBENS *pinx.* The Last Judgment.

The picture is in the Munich Gallery; it was formerly at Schleissheim. John Smith, *Cat. rais.* 167. Engraved on two plates. Nagler, 133. Hecquet, 13. W. Smith, 36.

1st state, before Soutmann's address; like Verstolk, No. 1176.

The 2d state has the plate retouched, with the address of P. Soutman, Verstolk, 1178; — the 3d is with the additional address of F. de Wit, Verstolk, 1179; — the 4th has the address effaced.

PARMEGIANO *pinx.* "Artemisia."

According to Stanley, in Bryan's *Dictionary,* the original picture is in Hampton Court palace; it is not mentioned, however, by Waagen, in his *Treasures.* Engraved for the *Cabinet Reynst.* Nagler, 153. Hecquet, 28. W. Smith, 51.

1st state, before any letters, i. e. before Visscher's name and address; a painter's name was never put on the plate.

The 2d state is with *Corn. Visscher sculp.,* in the margin below, immediately under the engraving on the left; — the 3d, with the name of Visscher effaced, and in the right corner, at the bottom, *G. Valk ex.*

PIETER DE LAER *pinx.* A set of three Landscapes, engraved for the *Cabinet Reynst.* Namely: —

1. The Robbery of the Wagons, Le coche volé.
   Nagler, 168. Hecquet, 18, a. W. Smith, 67.
   1st state, before any letters.
2. The Fight with Pistols, Le coup de pistolet.
   Nagler, 169. Hecquet, 18, b. W. Smith, 68.
   1st state, before any letters.
3. The Kiln, Le four à briques.
   Nagler, 170. Hecquet, 18, c. William Smith, 69.
   1st state, before any letters.

VISSCHER, CORNELIS, *continued.*

The 2d state of the three plates has the artists' names and G. Valk's address; — in the 3d, the address is effaced.

VISCHER *del.* The Pancake Woman.

Nagler, 144. Hecquet, 14. W. Smith, 42.

Uncommonly fine and clear impression of the plate, described as the 7th and last state. It might be mistaken for an impression of the 3d state, but for the deeper shading in the foreground, where the inscription is. Perhaps an impression after the effacing of an earlier address than the last.

From Otto's collection.

The 1st state is before the handkerchief of the old woman and the hair of the old man were covered with cross strokes; — the 2d state, with these cross strokes added, but before those on the left hand of the old woman; — in the 3d state, cross strokes are introduced on the woman's left hand; — in the 4th state, on the left, within the print, in the same line with that of Visscher, we read: *Clemendt de Jonghe exc.*; — in the 5th state, the name of De Jonghe is effaced, and *J. Visscher* inserted; — in the 6th state, *J. Visscher* is effaced, and *N. de Visscher exc.* inserted; — in the 7th state, the address is entirely effaced, and the place in which it was is covered with diagonal lines proceeding from near the sticks, and continued almost to the margin. C. Visscher's name is not nearly so distinctly visible on account of the shadows having been strengthened. In this state the plate is retouched all over, and has a disagreeable black effect, instead of the silvery tone of the earlier impressions. Before address of Cl. de Jonghe, Debois, No. 1181, 255 *fr.*; Verstolk, No. 1180, 125 *fl.* With Cl. de Jonghe's address, Verstolk, No. 1181, 22 *fl.* Address effaced, Verstolk, No. 1182.

VISSCHER *del.* The Rat-catcher.

Nagler, 146. Hecquet, 16. W. Smith, 43.

3d state, with the inscription in the margin beneath: "Fele fugas mures! — felesque fugabo," *and under this, on the right,* "Clemendt de Jonghe excudit." *Within the print is a paper, represented as fastened to the wall on the right near the top, on which is slightly etched,* "C. Visscher Inv. et sculp. A° 1655."

In the 1st state the plate has no inscription in the margin below, nor in the 2d; but in this state there is more work on the right cheek of the man, and *exc.* has been added under *Inv.* on the paper represented in the print. "These 1st and 2d states are extremely rare." — In the 4th state, Cl. de Jonghe's address is replaced by *F. de Wit excudit*; — in the 5th, De Wit's address is effaced.

"Before any letters," Sternberg, No. 3075; Verstolk, No. 1185, 205 *fl.*; Johnson, No. 166, £18; Debois, No. 1183, 400 *fr.*

A. VAN OSTADE *pinx.* The Strolling Musicians.

VISSCHER, CORNELIS, *continued.*

See Smith, *Cat. rais.*, "Ostade," No. 219. The original picture was sold in 1795, in the collection of Baron Nagel. Nagler, 145. Hecquet, 15. W. Smith, 80.

2d state, with the names of the artists, before the address of Cl. de Jonghe. "A. v. Ostade pinxit, C. Visscher fecit aqua forti," *in two lines at the right of the lower margin.*

The 1st state is before any letters. Verstolk, No. 1184, 201 *fl.*; Johnson, No. 167, £5 5 *s.*; Debois, No. 1182, 550 *fr.* — The 3d state is with the address of Cl. de Jonghe. — The 4th is coarsely retouched all over, De Jonghe's address effaced, and strong, nearly perpendicular lines are introduced on the cap of the boy on the left.

A. VAN OSTADE *pinx.* The Skaters.

See Smith, *Cat. rais.*, "Ostade," No. 202. The original picture, of the size of the engraving, is in the collection of M. Six van Winter at Amsterdam. Nagler, 148. Hecquet, 23. W. Smith, 79.

3d state, with the inscription in the margin below, "Cornelius de Visscher sculpsit. Adr. van Ostade Pinxit. Nicolaus Visscher Excudit."

The 1st state is before any letters, and before the shading with diagonal lines, extending from right to left, was added to the perpendicular and horizontal lines of the chimney. Of this state one exemplar is known, formerly in the collection of Mr. Anthony Stewart, then in Verstolk's, catalogue No. 1203, sold for 180 *fl.*, and now in the British Museum. — The 2d state is also before the letters, but with the additional shadows and work. Weber, 1197, 45 *th.* — The 4th state is with the address of Clement de Jonghe.

VAN DYCK *pinx.* **P.** Henderik du Booys.

See Smith, *Cat. rais.*, "Van Dyck," 821. Waagen, *Galleries*, or *Treasures*, IV. p. 520, describes the original picture of this and the following engraving in the collection of the Earl of Hardwicke, at Wimpole, Cambridgeshire. Nagler, 18. Hecquet, 17. W. Smith, 88.

6th and last state, with "E. Cooper excudit. E collectione Nobilissimi Joannis Domini Somers."

The 1st state is before any letters; — the 2d, with the letters, but before Visscher's name and the address; — the 3d has the name of Visscher, but before address; — the 4th is with the address of Du Booys very slightly etched; — in the 5th, the address is strongly engraved; — in the 6th, Du Booys's address is effaced, and Cooper's put in its stead, and at the bottom is the notice that the picture is from Lord Somers's collection.

VAN DYCK *pinx.* **P.** Helena Eleonora de Sieveri, wife of H. du Booys.

See Smith, *Cat. rais.*, "Van Dyck," 723; Waagen, *Galleries*, or *Treasures*, IV. p. 520. The originals of this and of the preceding picture are in the

VISSCHER, CORNELIS, *continued.*

collection of the Earl of Hardwicke, at Wimpole, Cambridgeshire. Nagler, 18. Hecquet, 18. Wm. Smith, 117.

5th and last state, with "E. Cooper excudit. E Collectione Nobilissimi Joannis Domini Somers." *Watermark, a crowned shield with a fleur-de-lis.*

The 1st state is before any letters; — the 2d, with the inscription, but before Visscher's name; — the 3d has Visscher's name added, and the address of Du Booys slightly etched; — the 4th has the address strongly engraved; — the 5th has Du Booys's address changed for Cooper's, and, below, the notice that the picture is from the collection of Lord Somers.

These two plates, though corresponding in size, were never added to the different collections of Van Dyck's portraits, the *Iconographia.*

𝔓. Gellius de Bouma, Ecclesiastes Zutphaniensis.*

Nagler, 4. Hecquet, 4. William Smith, 89.

4th state, with the date.

In the 1st state, the leaves of the book on the table are entirely blank. Duke of Buckingham, No. 819; Révil, 1838, No. 247; Debois, No. 1194, which individual print was sold again, in the Marshall Coll. No. 1827; it had also the name of "Mariette 1670" inscribed on it, and sold for £ 26. Verstolk, No. 1246, sold for 180 *fl.* — The 2d shows on the upper leaf an inscription of 12 lines, 11 of which have no meaning, and are merely made to resemble letters; on the 12th line is distinctly written "Amst." — In the 3d, two more leaves are covered with hatchings to resemble writing; the further one a little below the middle, the one *this* side of the upper one in 5 paragraphs or sections. Still before date. Marshall, No. 1828, £ 10. — The 4th has the date 1656 in the centre of the lower margin of the plate at bottom. — The 5th has the date effaced, but is before address. — The 6th has in the centre at bottom the address: "Tot Amsterdam by Johannes Covens en Cornelis Mortier."

PALAMEDES *pinx.* 𝔓. Robertus Junius.

The smaller portrait, oval in a shaded square. Nagler, 34. Hecquet, 34. William Smith, 100.

2d state, with the first address, that of P. Goos.

The 1st state is before any address; Verstolk, No. 1301. — The 3d state is with the second address, of H. Focken.

𝔓. Guilliam de Ryck, Ophthalmist at Amsterdam.

Nagler, 5. Hecquet, 5. William Smith, 115.

* This portrait and that of De Ryck are called *The Great Beards,* and are, according to Hecquet, the finest of the master. Very frequently the portrait of Scriveri is put as a third, but *his* is not a *great* beard. In Wilson's and Debois' Catalogue, the portrait of Winius is mentioned as the third; this is of the greatest rarity, and occurs in French catalogues as *l'Homme au pistolet.*

VISSCHER, CORNELIS, *continued.*

3d state, with the upper part of the ear made light, and with the first inscription: "Den wel Eervaren Gvilliam de Ryck, Ooge Meester tot Amsterdam, *and twelve verses, in two columns, in Dutch:* "So ymant wiens gesicht en . . . isser geen gesicht."

The 1st state, "before *any* letters, and before the age and date in the background of the plate." (William Smith.)

First and rare proof *before* the title "Den wel Eervaren Guilliam de Ryck, Oogen Meester tot Amsterdam," before the twelve verses which are below, and before the work to lighten the beard and the left ear. Debois, No. 1195, 1020 *fr.* "Épreuve superbe et rare, avec l'oreille noire, 1r état," Verstolk, No. 1248, 275 *fl.*—The 2d state is *with* the letters (the first inscription stated above), Winckler, No. 6208; Marshall, No. 1831, £ 25 10 *s.*—In the 3d the letters of the 2d state remain. The upper part of the ear is made light, four hairs are introduced about the middle of it, extending behind it towards the left. Einsiedel, No. 3600; La Motte Fouquet, No. 397.—In the 4th, the *twelve lines* in two columns being *effaced, instead of them appears in large letters,* "Den wijdt beroemde en wel-eerwaren, Guilliam de Ryck Oculist ofte Ooge-Meester tot Amsterdam"; and, *on the right,* "Corn. de Visscher delinia. et sculp." . . . In the 5th, the mouth is half opened; both lips are distinctly marked. On the ear are some light portions which are only worked with a single hatching. The very strong wrinkles on the joints of the fingers are softened, and there are many alterations in the face. The collar is broader, measuring nine lines (nearly seven eighths of an English inch). Compare Bartsch, *Anleitung zur Kupferstichkunde.*

P. Soutman *pinx.* 𝔓. Petrus Scriverius, Harlemensis.

Nagler, 23. Hecquet, 23. W. Smith, 116.

3d state, with the correction Hæc, *but before the slip of the graver.*

From the collection and with the autograph of De Valois on the back.

The 1st state is before the name of Visscher;—the 2d, with his name, before the scratch on the cheek, and, in the last line but one, with the misspelling *Hac,* instead of *Hæc.* Marshall, No. 1832, £ 10 10 *s.*—In the 4th state a scratch appears on the mustache and beard on the right, caused by the graver slipping during the process of retouching the plate.

VISSCHER, CLAS JANSZ, (i. e. Jan's son,) born at Amsterdam about 1550, designer and engraver, but of more importance as a publisher; he continued the business of his father Jan Claessen Visscher, and was followed by Nicolas Visscher.

A. Bloemaert *pinx.* The Golden Age.

In the print, on a shield at the right: *A. Bloemaert inven. J. C. Visscher*

VISSCHER, CLAS JANSZ, *continued.*

excudit; below, in the margin, *Saturno sub rege œtas fuit aurea mundi; Omnia tunc tellus absq. labore tulit.* And sixteen Dutch verses: *Owaerde Gulden Eew . . . en in den Heemel leeft.* Compare Nic. de Bruyn's engraving.

VISSCHER, JAN DE, engraver, during the latter part of his life also painter, brother of Cornelis, was born at Amsterdam in 1636. Nagler, *Künstler-Lexicon*, XX. *art.* "Jan Visscher," p. 407, *et seq.*

A. VAN OSTADE *pinx.* The "small" Ball in a Barn.

A composition of 14 figures. Nagler, No. 22.

2d state, with the 1st address of N. Visscher.

The 1st state is before letters; — the 3d, with the address of F. de Widt; — the 4th with G. Valk's address.

A. VAN OSTADE *pinx.* Three Men smoking and drinking, and a Woman.

See Nagler, No. 23.

2d state, with the address of Justus Danckerts.

The 1st state is before address.

WOUWERMANS *pinx.* Le coup de pistolet.

Five horsemen before two tents. Smith, *Cat. rais.*, "Wouwermans," No. 158. The picture is in the collection at Buckingham palace. Waagen, *Treasures*, II. p. 18, No. 3. Nagler, No. 28, (4.)

With the address of Justus Danckerts.

BERGHEM *pinx.* Summer, landscape with cattle; a family sleeping

Nagler, No. 31.

4th state, address of Nic. Visscher.

The 1st state is before letters; — the 2d, before address; — the 3d, with the address of F. de Widt; — the 5th, with P. Schenk's address.

BERGHEM *pinx.* The Spinster, sitting by a rock, near her a man sleeping, etc.; landscape with cattle.

See Nagler, No. 36.

2d state, with the 1st address, of Frederick de Widt.

The 1st state is before letters; — the 3d, with Nic. Visscher's address.

BERGHEM *del.* The Seamstress, sitting at the foot of a large tree; landscape with cattle.

See Nagler, No. 37.

2d state, with the 1st address, of Frederick de Widt.

The 1st state is before letters; — the 3d, with Nic. Visscher's address.

BERGHEM *pinx.* The "great" Boors' Dance or Ball in a Barn.

See Nagler, No. 18. The picture, an imitation of A. van Ostade, was

VISSCHER, JAN, *continued.*

painted *en grisaille* by Berghem, for his friend Jan Visscher, who engraved it. Smith, *Cat. rais.*, "Berghem," No. 200.

In the collection of Lord Gwydyr in 1829; bought by Mr. John Smith.

3d state, Berghem pinxit. Johannes Visscher fecit. Justus Danckerts excudit.

A similar impression, Ploos van Amstel, 40 *fl.*

The 1st state is before letters, and but partly finished with the graver. Rigal, No. 828, 204 *fr.*; G. Smith, No. 1273, £ 12 10 *s.* — The 2d is before letters, and finished with the graver; Marshall, No. 1836, "proof before any inscription," £ 5. — The 4th adds to the inscription of the 3d state, *cum privilegio Ordin. Hollandiae et Westfrisiae.*

J. van der Helst *pinx.* **P.** Vander Hulst, Abraham, Viceadmirael van Hollant en Westvrieslant.

Nagler, No. 2.

The border, composed of palm leaves, has been cut off.

Jan van Noort *pinx.* **P.** Proëlius, Petrus, Ecclesiastes Amstelædamensis.

Nagler, No. 4.

2d state; "Joan van Noort pinxit. Nicolaus Visscher excudit."

With the stamp of Franck's collection.

The 1st state is before letters.

Van Dyck *pinx.* **P.** Rubens.

Nagler, No. 7.

2d state, with the address of Clem. de Jonghe.

The 1st state is before address; — the 3d with Marrebeeck's address.

VISSCHER, LAMBERT DE, engraver, brother of Cornelis and Jan, born at Amsterdam in 1633. In after life he went to Italy, where, about the year 1690, he engraved, in conjunction with Bloemaert, Spierre, and others, the plates from the frescos by Pietro da Cortona in the Pitti palace at Florence, where he died.

Pietro da Cortona *pinx.* Wisdom withdrawing a Youth from Love and Pleasures, and leading him to Labor.

A fresco on the ceiling in the Pitti palace. Room of Minerva.

2d state, with Rossi's address.

Ferd. Bol *pinx.* **P.** Cornelis Tromp, Admiral of Holland.

See Bartsch, *Rembrandt*, appendix, p. 172, No. 89; Claussin, *Rembrandt*, appendix, p. 163, No. 90.

With the address: "'t Amsterdam, Uytgegeven by Marcus Doornik."

VITALI, PIETRO MARCO, engraver, born at Venice about 1755, died about 1810. A pupil of Joseph Wagner, and afterwards of D. Cunego.

VITALI, PIETRO MARCO, *continued.*

GUIDO *pinx.* Cupid on the Sea-shore.

"P. Vitali delin. et sculp. Romae 1781. Apud Joh. Volpato."

VIVARES, FRANÇOIS, designer and landscape engraver, was born near Montpellier in 1709, and compelled by his father, who was a tailor, to follow the same occupation, till he succeeded in getting to England, where he placed himself under the tuition of J. B. Chatelain. He died in London in 1782.

REMBRANDT *inv.* Rembrandt's Windmill.

A copy of Rembrandt's etching.

CLAUDE LORRAIN *pinx.* A Herdsman instructing a Shepherdess to play on the Pipe.

"Claudio Gillée Lorenese pinxit, 1645. In the Collection of Thomas Walker, Esqr. Published by C. Knapton, 1741." Painted for M. Fontany. It was subsequently the property of Thomas Walker, Esq., and of Sir Eliab Harvey, from whom it descended by marriage to W. Lloyd, Esq. Smith, *Cat. rais.* 93.

Has been also engraved by William Wilson. *See* WILSON.

CLAUDE LORRAIN *pinx.* The Ford.

"Claudio Lorenese pinxit 1656. Vivares sculp. In the collection of Dr. Mead," 1741. Smith, *Cat. rais.* 8. Sold in Mead's collection in 1754.

CLAUDE LORRAIN *pinx.* The Flight into Egypt.

Engraved from a picture at that time (1757) in the possession of Rev. Dr. Newton. Smith, *Cat. rais.* 310.

HOBBEMA *pinx.* Village in a Wood, near Antwerp.

Nagler, No. 11. Smith, *Cat. rais.* 91, calls it "View of a Hamlet among Trees."

Artist's proof, with merely F. Vivares fecit 1777, *delicately cut with the needle.*

GEORGE SMITH *pinx.* The Hop-pickers.

Published by Fr. Vivares, 1760.

G. F. GRIMALDI, called BOLOGNESE, *pinx.* Castel Gandolfo.

"Vivares & Chatelain sculp. Jos. Goupy del. J. Boydell exc. 1769. In the collection of H. R. Highness the Princess of Wales."

VIVIANI, ANTONIO, an engraver of Venice, died recently.

TITIAN *pinx.* The Pesaro Family in Adoration before the Madonna, surrounded by St. Peter, St. George, St. Anthony of Padua, and St. Francis.

The picture, from Santa Maria Gloriosa de' Frari, is now in the Gallery of the Academy in Venice.

Artist's proof, before letters, with only the artists' names.

Proofs have open letters.

VOERST, ROBERT VAN, designer and engraver, born at Arnheim in 1596. He studied his profession at Utrecht, and formed his style after Egidius Sadeler. In 1626 he went to London, and the last date of his plates is 1635.

VAN DYCK *pinx.* **P.** Digby, Sir Kenelm.

See Smith, No. 220. The picture is in Windsor Castle. Waagen, *Treasures,* II. p. 428. Engraved for Martin van den Enden, No. 58. Weber, p. 85.

4th and last state, after the 2d address, "G. H.," had been effaced. Watermark, Large Foolscap.

VAN DYCK *pinx.* **P.** Inigo Jones.

Smith, *Cat. rais.* No. 223, mentions the picture, identified by this engraving in the list of Van Dyck, in "His Majesty's collection." Waagen, *Treasures,* does not mention it as in Windsor Castle. Engraved for Martin van den Enden, No. 59. Weber, p. 86.

4th state, after the 2d address, "G. H.," had been effaced. Watermark, Foolscap.

VAN DYCK *pinx.* **P.** Herbert, Philip, Earl of Pembroke.

See Smith, No. 518. The picture, of which this is only the half length, is in the collection of the Earl of Pembroke. Weber, p. 127, "Portraits divers," describes only this state of the plate. Weigel, *Kunst-Catalog,* No. 20,302, has a proof before all letters, price 15 *th.*

Watermark, Two interlaced C's, crowned, with no inverted cross between them.

VAN DYCK *pinx.* **P.** Voerst, Robert van, engraver.

See Smith, *Cat. rais.* No. 779. Engraved for Martin van den Enden, No. 60. Weber, p. 86.

4th state, after the second address, "G. H.," had been effaced. Watermark, Foolscap.

VAN DYCK *pinx.* **P.** Vouet, Simon, painter.

See Smith, *Cat. rais.* 765. Engraved for Martin van den Enden, No. 61. Weber, p. 87.

4th state, after the second address, "G. H.," had been effaced. Watermark, Arms of the city of Amsterdam.

VOET, ALEXANDER, engraver, born at Antwerp in 1613, supposed to have been a pupil of Pontius.

RUBENS *pinx.* Judith with the Head of Holofernes, which she is putting in a sack held by an attendant.

Called "The smaller Judith," Basan, 28. Smith, *Cat. rais.* No. 1002, mentions merely the engraving. This is not the composition of the picture

VOET, ALEXANDER, *continued.*

of the Salzdahlum collection, now in the Ducal Gallery of Brunswick, Cat. No. 431, in which the attendant holds a light.

2d state, without the engraver's name, with only "C. Galle excudit." *Fine impression on thin paper, with the watermark of the Arms of Amsterdam.*

The 1st state is without the engraver's name, and without address.

RUBENS *pinx.* Madonna and Child, in a landscape, with three Angels, two of them bringing fruit.

Smith, *Cat. rais.* 955, mentions only this engraving. Basan, 35.

With the engraver's address.

In the Dresden Gallery is a similar picture, Madonna sitting, in a landscape, with *one* angel bringing fruit. A small picture, on copper.

JORDAENS *pinx.* Fool with a Cat.

Basan, 22.

2d state, with Huberti's address.

The 1st state is with the engraver's name and address.

VOLPATO, GIOVANNI, designer and engraver, born at Bassano in 1738, died at Rome in 1803. He was a pupil of the engraver and publisher, Joseph Wagner, at Venice, at the same time with Bartolozzi, and in the drawing of both, the influence of the school of Amiconi, the master of Wagner, is very perceptible.

MICHEL-ANGELO *pinx.* Sibylla Erythraea.
MICHEL-ANGELO *pinx.* Sibylla Delphica.
MICHEL-ANGELO *pinx.* Sibylla Cumaea.

*** From the frescos in the Sistine Chapel.

GUERCINO *pinx.* Aurora. In a chariot drawn by two piebald steeds.

She is chasing Night and Stars before her, and leaving behind her old husband Tithonus, who follows her with eager looks. Fresco on the ceiling of a garden pavilion in the Villa Ludovisi at Rome. Platner and Bunsen, III. ii. p. 588.*

The proofs of this plate have, besides the artists' names, 4 verses, "Rore madens — suspirantem" in open traced uncial letters. These letters were shaded in the "prints," and a dedication to Angelica Kauffman was added.

In the same room with the picture just mentioned there are two lunettes, painted in fresco by the same master, and represented by the two following plates, also engraved by Volpato; they are smaller than the preceding.

GUERCINO *pinx.* Day, or Dawn; a youth with flowers in one hand, and a torch in the other, and

* Heller, *Praktisches Handbuch*, and also Nagler, *Künstler-Lexicon*, "Volpato," No. 36 and No. 37, enumerate this print twice, — first as Aurora, and then as Evening.

VOLPATO, GIOVANNI, *continued.*

GUERCINO *pinx.* Night; a sleeping mother, with two sleeping children.

GUIDO *pinx.* The Martyrdom of St. Andrew.

A fresco in the chapel of St. Andrew, of the church San Gregorio at Rome. Platner and Bunsen, III. i. p. 485.

Proofs have open letters.

CORREGGIO *pinx.* Christ praying in the Garden.

See Coxe, p. 122. The original is in the collection of the Duke of Wellington; a repetition in the National Gallery, another at St. Petersburg. Engraved for Hamilton's *Scuola Italica.*

The rare first impressions are on bluish ribbed paper.

RAPHAEL *pinx.* The Marriage of Alexander and Roxana.

See Passavant, II. 223. Fresco in the Villa Raffaelle. Engraved for Hamilton's *Scuola Italica.*

CARLO BIANCONI *inv.* The Sepulchral Monument of Count Algarotti in the Campo Santo at Pisa. (Erected by Frederic the Great.)

RAPHAEL *pinx.* The Stanze in the Vatican.

7 plates; the 8th, The Mass of Bolsena, was engraved by R. Morghen, who also added, as 9th plate, "The Attributes of Jurisprudence," three allegorical figures, Prudence, Fortitude, and Moderation. He further engraved from the Stanze (though in a different size, 4to), not belonging to this set, the four allegorical figures on the ceiling of the Camera della Segnatura: Theology, Poetry, Philosophy, and Jurisprudence. *See* MORGHEN. — The rest of the Stanze, beyond Volpato's plan, were afterwards engraved by FABRI and SALANDRI. See those names.

1. The School of Athens. Camera della Segnatura.

See Passavant, II. No. 67.

2. Disputa di S. Sacramento. Camera della Segnatura.

See Passavant, II. No. 65.

3. Heliodorus driven from the Temple. Sala di Eliodoro.

See Passavant, II. No. 105.

The same.

Unfinished etch print.

4. Defeat of Attila. Sala di Eliodoro.

See Passavant, II. No. 107.

5. Parnassus. Camera della Segnatura.

See Passavant, II. No. 66.

6. L'incendio del Borgo. Sala del Incendio.

See Passavant, II. No. 123.

7. The Deliverance of St. Peter from Prison. Sala di Eliodoro.

See Passavant, II. No. 108.

⁂ *Impressions before the retouch.*

VOLPATO, GIOVANNI, *continued.*

Still earlier impressions are printed on paper of a bluish tint. Proofs are before letters, i. e. before the dedication, "PIO SEXTO PONT. MAX." Debois, No. 1226, 870 *fr.*; George Smith, No. 1280, £ 26. — The late impressions have the white stamp of the papal print-shop, Stamperia Camerale, on the first plate of the set.

FRA BARTOLOMMEO *pinx.* Virgin and Child with a Book and Two Angels.

Without name of engraver; with only the address, "Apud Joan. Volpato."

Engraved in conjunction with R. Morghen. Palmerini, Catalogue of R. Morghen, p. 154. *See* MORGHEN.

RAPHAEL *pinx.* Loggie.

46 plates in three parts. — Engraved conjointly with Ottaviani. *See* OTTAVIANI.

ANN. CARACCI *pinx.* The Gallery of the Palazzo Farnese.

Three larger and three smaller plates. — Engraved conjointly with P. BETTELINI. Volpato etched the outline, which, in the copies to be colored, he carefully finished with water-colors, and gilded the stucco-work. For the impressions not to be colored, the plates were afterwards finished with the graver by P. Bettelini, to which class belong these impressions.

VORSTERMAN, LUCAS, the elder, painter and engraver. A pupil of Rubens. He was born at Antwerp in 1578; in 1623 he visited England, where he stayed till 1631, and enjoyed the patronage of Charles I. and the Earl of Arundel; after that he returned to Antwerp. The date of his death is not known.

RUBENS *pinx.* The Archangel St. Michael expelling the Bad Angels.

Basan, 1; Smith, *Cat. rais.* 173; comp. also 1024. The picture is in the Munich Gallery; it was formerly in Düsseldorf.

1*st state, before Huberti's address.*

The 2d state is with this address.

ERASMUS QUELLINUS *pinx.* The Beheading of St. John.

With Martin van den Enden's address, and a dedication by the same to Johann Christoph Butkens. Without the name of L. Vorstermann on the plate. (Nagler, xx. p. 548, No. 106.)

RUBENS *pinx.* The Adoration of the Magi, with two torches.

"Serenissimo et potentissimo Alberto Austriae Archiduco," etc. 1620.

Basan, 23. Smith, *Cat. rais.* 126. The picture is in the church of St. John of Malines, for which it was painted.

With Vorsterman's own address.

PARMEGIANO *pinx.* The Virgin adoring the Child.

VORSTERMAN, LUCAS, *continued.*

RAPHAEL *pinx.* Holy Family, called La Perla.

See Passavant, II. 231. The picture is in the Gallery of Madrid.

The engraving represents only the group in the foreground; the background is shaded black.

1st state, before "L. Vorsterman sc.," *his name being only in the dedication.*

RUBENS *pinx.* The Return from Egypt.

Basan, 30; Smith, *Cat. rais.* 830. The picture is in the Marlborough collection at Blenheim. Waagen, *Treasures*, III. p. 124; Waagen, *Handbook*, II. p. 266.

With Vorsterman's own address.

VAN DYCK *pinx.* Pietà.

The picture is in the Gallery of the Louvre. Villot, No. 138.

A state between the 2d and 3d; it has still the dedication, but the words "Regis" *after* "privilegio" *and* "et excudit" *after* "sculp." *have been erased.*

The first state is before the word *Regis* after *privilegio*, before *et excudit* after *sculp.*, and before the 3d line of inscription, the dedication. Wilson, *Catalogue raisonné*, No. 494; Debois, No. 1231, from the collections of Mariette, St. Yves, and Révil, 389*fr.*; Otto, III. No. 1232, 31 *th.* — The 2d state has *Lucas Vorsterman sculp. et excudit*, and a 3d line following the six verses (a dedication) *Perillustri apud Anglos Domino D. Georgio Gagi*, etc. — In the 3d state the word *excudit* and the dedication are erased. — The 4th has the address of Bonenfant.

RAPHAEL *inv.* The Entombment.

Engraved from a sepia drawing, formerly in the Arundel collection (Passavant, II. p. 491, No. 149), which was afterwards in the palace Borghese. Still later it was owned by Cavaliere Camuccini, and in 1829 bought by Hon. George John Warnon, England.

RAPHAEL *pinx.* St. George with a Lance.

The Saint-Knight wears a Garter of which the inscription "Honi" is visible. The picture was ordered by the Duke of Urbino, as a present to King Henry VII., who had bestowed that order upon him. At the time of the engraving, 1627, the picture was owned by the Earl of Pembroke; soon after it came into the collection of Charles I., and was sold with it. From the Crozat collection it was bought by Catherine II., and it hangs now like a votive picture, with an ever-burning lamp, before the portrait of the Emperor Alexander I. in the Hermitage at St. Petersburg. Passavant, II. No. 43.

M. A. AMERIGHI DA CARAVAGGIO *pinx.* St. Francis in Ecstasy.

With Vorsterman's name only under the dedication to J. van der Goes, and without address.

RUBENS *pinx.* St. Francis receiving the Stigmata.

VORSTERMAN, LUCAS, *continued.*

Basan, 11. According to Smith, *Cat. rais.* No. 110, the picture is in the Academy at Ghent, which statement Michiels, No. 430, corrects, assigning it to the Museum at Antwerp.

With Vorsterman's own address.

RUBENS *pinx.* The Martyrdom of St. Lawrence.

Basan, 37. Painted for the church of the Chartreux of Notre Dame de la Chapelle in Brussels, and now in the Munich Gallery. Smith, *Cat. rais.* 150.

With Vorsterman's own address.

PAOLO VERONESE *pinx.* St. Helena, seeing the Cross.

The picture is in the Gallery of the Vatican. Platner and Bunsen, II. ii. p. 430.

PIETER BREUGHEL THE ELDER *pinx.* Fight of Peasants at Cards.

"*Vorsterman exc.*"

TITIAN *pinx.* **P.** The Constable Bourbon.

The picture was, when engraved, in the Arundel collection.

TITIAN *pinx.* **P.** Isabelle of Este, wife of Duke Francis Gonzaga, at Mantua.

The picture is in the Vienna Gallery; it was formerly in the collection of Charles I. Engraved after a copy by Rubens.

The plate does not bear the engraver's name; it has "Rubens exc."

TITIAN *pinx.* **P.** Charles V., Emperor of Germany.

The picture is at present neither in the Gallery of Vienna, nor in Madrid; it is probably lost. Engraved after a copy by Rubens.

The plate does not bear the engraver's name; it has "Rubens exc."

HOLBEIN *pinx.* **P.** Desiderius Erasmus, Rotterodamus.

Nagler, *K.-L.* xx. p. 542, No. 30. *L. Vorsterman sc. c. pr.* is, however, not on the plate, the long dedication to Thomas Howard, Earl of Arundel, only has at the end, *hanc Erasmi effigiē amoris ergo humiliter Lucas Vorsterman sculptor D. D.*; and, in the right corner, *Cum Privilegio Reg.*

LIEVENS *pinx.* **P.** Hieronymus de Bran.

"Cæsaris Agenti Catholici exercitus Capitaneo ejusq. Annonae Prefecto generali in Belgio," etc., "D. D. Lucas Vorsterman sculptor." The engraver's name is merely at the foot of the dedication, not under the plate, nor is the painter's name mentioned; and as a later publisher put this plate with Van Dyck's *Iconographia*, the portrait has usually been ascribed to Van Dyck. So Nagler, *Künstler-Lexicon*, xx., under "Vorsterman," No. 29; also Smith, *Cat. rais.* III. No. 801, who describes this portrait, from the present engraving, as a picture by Van Dyck.

VORSTERMAN, LUCAS, *continued.*

The plate is without address, and never had one. Watermark of the old thin paper, letters, apparently K. I. R.

Szwykowski, *A. Van Dyck's Bildnisse bekannter Personen*, p. 319.

Harrach's cat., Paris, 25 Febr. 1867, "No. 2786, Vorsterman, Portrait de Jérôme de Bran, d'après J. Livens. Superbe épreuve du pr^{er} état, avec l'inscription en lettres italiques. No. 2787, Le même portrait. Belle épreuve, avec l'inscription changée, et avec le nom de Livens effacé." Both numbers were sold in one lot, and bid in by Messrs. Amsler and Ruthardt of Berlin, for 54 *fr.*

VAN DYCK *pinx.* **P.** Nicolas Rockox.

According to Smith, *Cat. rais.*, "Van Dyck," No. 293, a portrait, probably the same from which this engraving was made, was sold in 1749 in the collection of Van Halen. Weber, p. 127, "Portraits divers d'après A. van Dyck"; Szwykowski, p. 229, c. This plate was never added to the *Iconographia* and its continuations.

1*st state, before any letters in the lower margin, before the names of Plato and Seneca on the books, before the medals on the table, before the coat of arms in the background, in the place of which stands,* "A. van Dyck pinxit, L. Vorsterman sculp. et excud. Cum privilegio." *Watermark, Large Fleur-de-lis.*

The 2d state is with the names of Plato and Seneca, otherwise like the 1st state; — in the 3d the plate is cut down to the knees of the portrait; it has the medals on the table, and the arms in the background, and in the lower margin a dedication, 14 Latin verses, the artist's name, and the date 1625.

VAN DYCK *pinx.* Thomas Howard, Earl of Arundel.

Smith, *Cat. rais.* III. "Van Dyck," describes, under No. 627, a portrait from this engraving, without knowing the original. Weber, p. 127, "Portraits divers d'après Van Dyck." The plate is without address, and later impressions are not distinguished by a different state. It was added by a later publisher to Van Dyck's *Iconographia.*

Watermark, the Arms of the city of Amsterdam.

VAN DYCK *pinx.* **P.** Callot, Jacques, painter and engraver.

See Smith, *Cat. rais.* 791, who mentions merely this engraving. Engraved for Martin van den Enden, No. 63. Weber, p. 88.

5*th and last state after the* 2*d address,* "G. H.," *was effaced. Watermark, the Arms of the city of Amsterdam.*

VAN DYCK *pinx.* **P.** Coeberger, Wenzel, painter and architect.

See Smith, *Cat. rais.* 733, who mentions merely this engraving. Engraved for Martin van den Enden, No. 64. Weber, p. 88.

3*d state, with the* 2*d address,* "G. H." *Watermark, Large Foolscap.*

VORSTERMAN, LUCAS, *continued.*

VAN DYCK *pinx.* **P.** Cornelissen, Antoni, an amateur of pictures.

See Carpenter, p. 89, No. 3; Weber, p. 22. Van Dyck himself etched the head and hand.

5th state, after the address, " G. H.,*" had been effaced. Thin paper; watermark, a line of letters.*

VAN DYCK *pinx.* **P.** Van Dyck, Sir Anthony.

Engraved from a grisaille on paper, in the collection of the Duke of Buccleugh, — a slight modification of the painting in the Florence Gallery.

Smith, under No. 159. Engraved for Martin van den Enden, No. 567. Weber, p. 90.

4th state, after the 2d address, " G. H.,*" had been effaced. Watermark, Foolscap.*

VAN DYCK *pinx.* **P.** Eynden, Hubert van den, sculptor.

See Smith, *Cat. rais.* 793, who mentions merely this engraving. Engraved for Martin van den Enden, No. 68. Weber, p. 90.

2d state, with one line of inscription, with engraver's name (the 1st is before this), and M. van den Enden's address. Watermark, a Laurel Wreath.

From the collection and with the name of Gawet.

VAN DYCK *pinx.* Gentileschi, Orazio Lomi, painter.

Smith, *Cat. rais.* 760, mentions and describes this engraving, and remarks, "a drawing in chalks washed with Indian ink is now in the British Museum." Engraved for Martin van den Enden, No. 71. Weber, p. 92.

4th state, after the 2d address was erased on the plate; the " G. H.*" still visible on the print. Watermark, Small Foolscap.*

VAN DYCK *pinx.* **P.** Jode, Pieter de, the elder, engraver.

Smith, *Cat. rais.* 783, mentions and describes merely this print. Engraved for Martin van den Enden, No. 72. Weber, p. 93.

4th and last state, after the 2d address, " G. H.,*" was effaced. Watermark, Small Foolscap.*

VAN DYCK *pinx.* **P.** Lievens, Jan, painter and etcher.

Smith, *Cat. rais.* 754, mentions and describes merely this print. Engraved for Martin van den Enden, No. 73. Weber, p. 93.

State between Weber's 2d and 3d, after the address of M. van den Enden was erased, and G. Hendricx had a second line of inscription added, but before his initials. Szwykowski, p. 172. *Watermark, a Beehive.*

VAN DYCK *pinx.* **P.** Moncada, Francisco de.

See Smith, *Cat. rais.* 95. The grisaille for this engraving is in the collection of the Duke of Buccleugh. Engraved for Gillis Hendricx. Weber, p. 107.

VORSTERMAN, LUCAS, *continued.*

3d state, after the letters "G. H." *had been effaced. No watermark.*

VAN DYCK *pinx.* **P.** Peiresc, Nicolas Fabrice de.

See Smith, *Cat. rais.* 732. The grisaille for this engraving is in the collection of the Duke of Buccleugh. Engraved for Martin van den Enden, No. 77. Weber, p. 95.

4th and last state. Watermark, the Arms of the city of Amsterdam.

VAN DYCK *pinx.* **P.** Sachtleven, Cornelis, painter.

Smith, *Cat. rais.* 781, mentions and describes this engraving, and then remarks, "A study for the preceding portrait, done in bistre, is in the collection of the late Sir Thomas Lawrence." Engraved for Martin van den Enden, No. 78. Weber, p. 96.

4th and last state, after the 2d address, "G. H.," *had been effaced. Watermark, the Arms of the city of Amsterdam.*

VAN DYCK *pinx.* **P.** Schut, Cornelis, painter.

Smith, *Cat. rais.* 755, mentions and describes this engraving merely. Engraved for Martin van den Enden, No. 79. Weber, p. 96.

A state of the plate between Weber's 2d and 3d, with the 2d line of inscription, but before (not after) the address of "G. H." "Mart. van den Enden excudit" *is effaced on the plate, but is in this impression distinctly visible. Paper, thin and strong, with wire lines, but no watermark on this part of the sheet.*

VAN DYCK *pinx.* **P.** Spinola, Don Ambrosio, Duca di Sanseverino.

See Smith, *Cat. rais.* 702. The grisaille for this engraving is in the collection of the Duke of Buccleugh. Engraved for Martin van den Enden, No. 80. Weber, p. 97.

3d and last state. Watermark, the Arms of the city of Amsterdam.

VAN DYCK *pinx.* **P.** Stevens, Pieter, of the Senate of Antwerp, Treasurer of the Charity Fund.

See Smith, *Cat. rais.* 740. The grisaille for this engraving is in the collection of the Duke of Buccleugh. Engraved for Martin van den Enden, No. 81. Weber, p. 97.

4th and last state, after the effaced 2d address, "G. H." *Watermark, Large Fleur-de-lis.*

VAN DYCK *pinx.* **P.** Vos, Cornelis de, painter.

Smith, *Cat. rais.* 767, mentions and describes merely this engraving. Engraved for Martin van den Enden, No. 83. Weber, p. 99.

4th and last state after the 2d address, "G. H.," *was effaced. No watermark perceptible. Pasted down.*

VORSTERMAN, LUCAS, the younger, painter and engraver, son and pupil of the preceding.

VORSTERMAN, LUCAS, *continued.*

TITIAN *pinx.* **P.** Titian.

TITIAN *pinx.* **P.** Jacopo Sansovino, holding a model of Venus, according to Nagler, *Künstler-Lexicon ;* or, according to R. Weigel, *Künstler-Portraits,* No. 136, it is the portrait of Bandinelli.

This, and the portrait of Titian are in the Vienna Gallery of the Belvedere; they were engraved for the "Teniers Gallery," or *Theatrum artis pictoriae.*

W.

WAGNER, JOSEPH, engraver and publisher, born at Thalendorf on the Lake of Constance in 1706, died at Venice in 1780. He first studied painting with Ottavio Amiconi, who adopted him when he was but fourteen years old; afterwards he devoted himself to engraving under the tuition of L. Cars. He then joined Amiconi in England, and again removed with him to Venice, where he founded an extensive establishment as print publisher.

PAOLO VERONESE *pinx.* Madonna enthroned, with the infant St. John, St. Francis, St. Jerome, and St. Catherine.

The picture, from the Convent San Zacaria in Venice, is now in the Gallery of the Academy.

WAGSTAFF, CHARLES EDWARD, engraver, born at London in 1808.

ALLSTON *pinx.* The Witch of Endor.

The picture is in the family of the late Col. Perkins, in Boston, U. S. Engraved in mezzotinto, conjointly with Joseph Andrews.

Proof, on India paper.

WALKER, JAMES, engraver in the stippled manner, and in mezzotinto, born in 1748, studied in London, was sixteen years in St. Petersburg as engraver to the Empress Catherine II., and returned to London, where he died in 1808. (Nagler.)

SIR JOSHUA REYNOLDS *pinx.* The Infant Hercules strangling the Serpents.

The picture is in the Imperial Gallery of St. Petersburg. Engraved in mezzotinto.

WALKER, WILLIAM, engraver, born at Salisbury in 1725, studied at London, where he died in 1793.

F. LE MOINE *pinx.* Diana and Callisto, landscape.

The original was, when engraved in 1769, in the collection of Nath. Webb, Esq.

WALKER, WILLIAM, *continued.*

RUBENS *pinx.* Lions at Play.

The picture is in the Imperial Gallery of St. Petersburg; it was formerly in the Houghton collection, in which it was engraved. Smith, *Cat. rais.* 553.

LA TOUR *pinx.* **P.** Voltaire.

Narrow 4to, or 8vo.

WALKER, WILLIAM, engraver, born at London in 1800.

DOYLE *pinx.* "A Literary Party at Sir Joshua Reynolds."

The picture is owned by J. Prior, Esq. A mezzotinto engraving.

Open letter proof.

WARD, JAMES, mezzotinto engraver at London. A pupil of J. R. Smith. He was still living in 1810.

SIR JOSHUA REYNOLDS *pinx.* Mrs. Billington as St. Cecilia.

The picture is in the Marquis of Lansdowne's collection at Bowood. Waagen, *Treasures,* III. p. 160.

WARNER, W.

TRUMBULL *pinx.* **P.** Washington at the Battle of Trenton.

The original is at Yale College, New Haven, Connecticut, U. S.

WATERLOO, ANTONI, landscape painter,* and etcher, born near Utrecht (or Amsterdam) about 1618, died poor in the hospital of St. Job, at Utrecht, either in 1660, 1662, or 1679. Bartsch, II., and Weigel, *Suppl.*

The Great Mill. B. 119.

Retouched, and on thick paper.

The Little Bridge. B. 124.

Retouched, and on thick paper.

A set of six Landscapes, with Mythological Figures.

1. Alpheus and Arethusa. B. 125.

Before retouch, and on thin paper.

2. Apollo and Daphne. B. 126.

Retouched, and on thick paper.

3. Mercury and Argus. B. 127.

On thin paper.

4. Pan and Syrinx. B. 128.

Retouched, and on thick paper.

* So he is usually styled, though there exists not a single painting that can with certainty be assigned to him.

WATERLOO, ANTONI, *continued.*

5. Venus and Adonis. B. 129.

Before retouch, and on thin paper.

6. The Death of Adonis. B. 130.

Before retouch, and on thin paper.

WATSON, CAROLINE, engraver in the stippled manner and in mezzotinto, born at London in 1758, died in 1810.

Roslin *pinx.* 𝔭. Catherine II., Empress of Russia.

Engraved in the stippled manner, as frontispiece to the *Houghton Gallery.*

Sir Joshua Reynolds *pinx.* 𝔭. The Hon. Mrs. Stanhope.

Engraved in the stippled manner.

WATSON, JAMES, engraver in mezzotinto, born at London in 1740.

Sir Joshua Reynolds *pinx.* 𝔭. Amherst, Sir Jeffery, Governor of Virginia, Commander-in-Chief of His Majesty's Forces in North America from 1758 to 1764.

Sir Joshua Reynolds *pinx.* 𝔭. Burke, Edmund.

Sir Joshua Reynolds *pinx.* 𝔭. Granby, John, Marquis of.

The picture is in Col. Wyndham's Collection at Petworth. Waagen, *Treasures,* III. p. 41. Printed in brown.

Proof before letters, the artists' names slightly traced with the needle.

Van Dyck *pinx.* 𝔭. Wandesford, Lord Chief Baron.

The picture is in the Imperial Gallery at St. Petersburg (Smith, *Cat. rais.* 649), and was formerly in the Houghton Gallery. Engraved for the *Houghton Gallery.*

WATSON, THOMAS, engraver in the stippled manner and in mezzotinto, born at London in 1748, died in 1781.

Sir Joshua Reynolds *pinx.* 𝔭. Warren Hastings.

The picture is owned by J. P. Fearon, Esq. Mezzotinto.

WATT, J. H., an English line engraver of the present day.

Stothard *pinx.* The Procession for the Flitch of Bacon.

The original is "a drawing made in sepia." Mrs. Bray, *Life of Thomas Stothard,* p. 144, note.

Artist's proof. On India paper.

Landseer *pinx.* Highland Drovers departing for the South.

Open letter proof.

WATT, J. H., *continued.*

LANDSEER *pinx.* Horses drinking.

Artist's proof.

WATT, W. H., an English line engraver of the present day.

LESLIE *pinx.* The Manuscript of Sterne.

Lettre grise *proof.*

WEBER, FRIEDRICH, engraver, born at Listal, near Basle, in 1813. A pupil of Amsler.

HANS HOLBEIN *pinx.* **P.** Hans Holbein.

After the picture (a slightly colored drawing) in the Museum at Basle. Engraved in 1847.

WEINHOLDT, JOHANN GEORG, painter and lithographer of the present day, at Dresden.

MURILLO *pinx.* Madonna and Child.

The picture is in the Dresden Gallery.

MURILLO *pinx.* Mater Dolorosa.

The picture is in the possession of J. M. Escazena of Seville; Stirling, *Annals,* III. p. 1420.

WEISBRODT, CARL WILHELM, designer and etcher, born at Ludwigsburg, or, according to others, at Hamburg, in 1746, at which latter place he died in 1806. (Nagler.) A pupil of Wille.

TENIERS *pinx.* A Village Merry-making.

One man fiddling, six figures dancing, seven persons looking on. Smith, *Cat. rais.,* "Teniers," 578. Engraved from a picture then in the collection of the Duc de Cossé.

Proof before letters; with only "Weisbrodt sc. a. f." *etched very small, and coat of arms.*

BERGHEM *pinx.* View of the Environs of Siena.

Smith, *Cat. rais.,* "Berghem," 21.

Proof before letters; with only "Weisbrodt 1775 a. f.," *and coat of arms.*

BERGHEM *pinx.* The same.

The same print finished with the graver by Le Bas. Engraved in 1775, when in the collection of the Marquis de Brunoy. In 1828 it was in the collection of M. Zachary, Esq.

J. RUYSDAEL *pinx.* Wood near the Hague.

A woody landscape with water, a man with a pack leading a little boy. The picture was engraved in 1773, when in the collection of the Duc de Praslin; it was sold in 1793. Smith, *Cat. rais.,* "Ruysdael," 71.

WEISS, DAVID, engraver, born at Strigno in South Tyrol in 1775, died at Vienna in 1846. A pupil of Q. Mark.

ANN. CARACCI *pinx.* Head of Christ.

Engraved in 1808 from the original drawing, owned by Prince Esterhazy, the painting of which is in the Gallery of Dresden. Large fol. Engraved in the stippled manner.

WELCH, THOMAS.

STUART *pinx.* 𝔓. Head of Washington.

From the original in the Athenæum Gallery, Boston, U. S. Mezzotinto. *Artist's proof, before any letters.*

WHITFIELD, E. R., an engraver of the present day in London.

DOMENICHINO *pinx.* "Domenichino's Mistress."

Proof before letters, with only the names of the artists and of the publisher.

WILDT, CARL, designer and lithographer of the present day in Berlin.

BENDEMANN *pinx.* Jews weeping by the Waters of Babylon.

The picture is in the Wallraff Museum at Cologne.

GER. DOW *pinx.* The Hermit.

The picture is in the Dresden Gallery.

WILKIN, CHARLES, engraver in the stippled manner, born in England in 1730.

SIR JOSHUA REYNOLDS *pinx.* 𝔓. Lady Cockburn, with her three Children, as Cornelia.

WILLE, JOHANN GEORG, designer, etcher, and engraver, was born near the small town of Königsberg in the Grand-Duchy of Hesse-Darmstadt, in 1717. He learned originally the trade of a gunsmith, and the ornamental work belonging to this business led him to study the art of engraving plates. After finishing his apprenticeship, he wandered to Paris, where he became the founder of an important school of engravers, and died, after many vicissitudes of fortune, a very old and very poor man, in 1808.

Mr. Rudolph Weigel remarks in a note to p. 7 of Charles Le Blanc's *Catalogue de l'œuvre de J. G. Wille,* Leipsic, 1847, that he has met with modern spurious proofs of "La Mort de Marc-Antoine," "Les Musiciens ambulans," "Les Offres réciproques," "Le Concert de Famille," and "L'Instruction paternelle," in which the letters were covered up in making the impression, leaving merely the arms. I have met with some, especially of the latter plate, on very white, modern paper, and looking very harsh.

WILLE, JOHANN GEORG, *continued.*

DIETRICH *pinx.* Abraham receiving Hagar. Le Bl. 1.

3d state, 1st of the finished plate, before "20[te] Platte 1775," *and the name* "Wille" *written in reverse, were erased. On India paper.*

The erasure indicates the 4th and last state. The 1st artist's proof is before letters and arms; — the 2d state, proof, is before letters, but *with* the coat of arms.

DIETRICH *pinx.* Repos de la Vierge. Le Bl. 2.

3d state, with the title and the dedication.

The 1st state is before the title and the dedication; — the 2d state is *with* the title, but before the dedication.

BATTONI *pinx.* Death of Mark Antony. Le Bl. 4.

3d state (see additions to Le Blanc, who originally described it as 1st state), before any letters, but with the border lines and the coat of arms, and the latter surrounded by rays.

With the autograph inscription in pencil: "A Monsieur le Baron de Soursanvault de la part de son très humble serviteur Wille, 1778."

NETSCHER *pinx.* Death of Cleopatra. Le Bl. 5.

The picture, at the time of the engraving, was in the collection of the Count de Vence.

4th state, with the letters.

2d state, before the border of the plate below, before any letters, but with the coat of arms, Verstolk, No. 1558, 475 *fl.*; Debois, No. 1241, 1,080 *fr.*

DIETRICH *pinx.* Les Musiciens ambulans. Le Bl. 52.

The picture is in the National Gallery. Waagen, *Treasures*, I. p. 358; Waagen, *Handbook*, II. p. 524.

5th state, with the correction "Électorale" *in the inscription, instead of* "Électoral" *in the preceding state.*

"Épreuve avant toutes lettres (et avant les armes)," Debois, No. 1252; Verstolk, No. 1567, 310 *fl.*; Archinto, No. 414, 920 *fr.* Proof before any letters, but with the coat of arms, Wilcox, No. 309, £28.

DIETRICH *pinx.* Les Offres réciproques. Le Bl. 53.

4th state, before *the accent over the* a, *in the dedication.*

DIETRICH *pinx.* The same. Le Bl. 53.

5th state, with *the accent over the* a *in the inscription:* "Dédié à," *etc.*

SCHALKEN *pinx.* Le Concert de Famille. Le Bl. 54.

2d state, with the letters.

"Épreuve avant toutes lettres et avant les armes," Verstolk, No. 1576, 225 *fl.* — "Épreuve avant la lettre, seulement les armes," Debois, No. 1249,

WILLE, JOHANN GEORG, *continued.*

375 *fr.* Likewise, "fine and rare proof, with the arms," George Smith, No. 1298, £ 11.

TERBURG *pinx.* L'Instruction paternelle, "The Satin Gown." Le Bl. 55.

The picture is in the Gallery of Amsterdam. Smith, *Cat. rais.*, "Terburg," 4; Kugler, *Handbook, German and Dutch Schools*, I. p. 288; Waagen, *Handbook, German and Dutch Schools*, II. p. 364. Two excellent repetitions, in the Berlin Gallery, and in the Bridgewater Gallery.

4th state, with the letters.

"Épreuve avant toutes lettres et avant les armes," Debois, No. 1250, 1,100 *fr.* — "Épreuve avant la lettre (toutes lettres), avant les armes et *avant la bordure*," La Motte Fouquet, No. 462, 207 *th.* — "Épreuve avant la lettre et les armes, *avec la bordure*," Verstolk, No. 1580, 600 *fl.* — "Fine proof before the arms," Wilcox, No. 303, £ 37 10 *s.* — "Fine and rare proof before any letters," George Smith, No. 1299, £ 24 5 *s.*

A. VAN OSTADE *pinx.* Les Bons Amis. Le Bl. 56.

2d state, with letters.

SCHALKEN *pinx.* Le jeune Joueur d'Instrument. Le Bl. 57.

See Smith, *Cat. rais.*, "Schalken," 9, p. 272. Collection of M. Lormier at the Hague. When engraved, in 1762, it was in the collection of Chevalier Damery at Paris.

3d state, with letters and dedication.

GER. DOW *pinx.* La Tante de Gérard Dow. Le Bl. 60.

4th state; the finished plate, with letters, arms, and dedication.

GER. DOW *pinx.* La Dévideuse, Mère de Gérard Dow. Le Bl. 61.

The picture was, at the time of the engraving, in the collection of the Count de Vence.

2d state, with the letters, the coat of arms, and the address: "a Paris chez l'Auteur, Quai des Augustins, à côté de l'Hôtel d'Auvergne"; — *without a number.*

In the 3d and last state the coat of arms was erased, as well as the dedication and title, and the new inscription is only: "*La Dévideuse, Mère de Gérard Douw. A Paris chez l'Auteur, quai des Augustins, no.* 35.

GER. DOW *pinx.* La Liseuse. Le Bl. 62.

2d state, with the letters, with the dedication to J. M. Usteri, and before the number was added to the address.

In the 3d and last state the dedication is effaced, and the long inscription replaced by *La Liseuse. A Paris chez l'Auteur. Quai des Augustins, no.* 35.

FRANS MIERIS *pinx.* La Tricoteuse hollandaise. Le Bl. 64.

2d state, with letters.

WILLE, JOHANN GEORG, *continued.*

FRANS MIERIS *pinx.* L'Observateur distrait. Le Bl. 65.

A boy making soap-bubbles. Waagen, *Handbook,* II. p. 377, mentions such a picture in the Gallery of the Hague.

3d state, with arms and letters.

NETSCHER *pinx.* Le petit Physicien. Le Bl. 66.

A boy on the sill of a window, blowing soap-bubbles. Smith, *Cat. rais.,* "Netscher," 16. The picture is in the collection of Lord Ashburton. Waagen, *Treasures,* II. p. 104.

2d state, with arms and letters.

METZU *pinx.* La Cuisinière hollandaise. Le Bl. 67.

2d state, with arms and letters.

TERBURG *pinx.* La Gazetière hollandaise. Le Bl. 68.

2d state, with arms and letters.

SCHENAU *pinx.* La petite Écolière. Le Bl. 69.

3d state, with arms and letters.

P. A. WILLE *pinx.* La Maîtresse d'École. Le Bl. 70.

3d state, with arms and letters.

P. A. WILLE *pinx.* La bonne Femme de Normandie. Le Bl. 71.

3d state, with arms and letters.

P. A. WILLE *pinx.* Sœur de la bonne Femme de Normandie. Le Bl. 72.

3d state, with the finished border and the letters.

PARROCEL *pinx.* **P.** Louis XV. Le Bl. 104.

3d state, before the face of the person next to the king was changed from that of an old to that of a young man, and before the changed inscription.

In the 4th and last state, the person next to the king appears a *young* man, and the reading of the inscription is changed.

DAN. KLEIN *pinx.* **P.** Louis, Dauphin de France, fils de Louis XV. Le Bl. 106.

2d state, with the letters.

DAN. KLEIN *pinx.* **P.** Marie-Thérèse d'Espagne, Dauphine de France. Le Bl. 107.

2d state, with the letters.

PARROCEL *pinx.* **P.** Pierre de Guérin de Tencin, Cardinal. Le Bl. 109.

The larger plate.

2d state, with the letters, but with the cross [star] *in the coat of arms and the three balls left white.*

In the 3d state the cross and balls are shaded with dots.

PHIL. DE CHAMPAGNE *pinx.* **P.** Antoine de Singlin. Le Bl. 113, b.

2d state, with letters.

WILLE, JOHANN GEORG, *continued.*

CHEVALIER *pinx.* **P.** François de Neufville, Duc de Villeroy. Le Bl. 119.

2d state, with letters, before the dedication "Q(uesnay) off(erebat)" *in the middle of the lower margin, and before the correction of* "enc^{ne} Comp^{e}" *into* "anc^{ne} Comp^{e}," *in the titles of the Duke.*

The 3d state has the dedication; the 4th has the correction.

RIGAUD *pinx.* **P.** Ch. L. A. Fouquet de Belle-Isle. Le Bl. 120.

3d state, with letters and arms.

RIGAUD *pinx.* **P.** Maurice de Saxe. Le Bl. 121.

2d state, with letters.

J. L. TOCQUÉ *pinx.* **P.** Louis Phelypeaux, Count de Saint-Florentin. Le Bl. 124.

2d state, with letters, but before the word "Ministre" *in the titles, and with the white mallets in the coat of arms.*

Duplicate from the private collection of King Frederic Augustus of Saxony, with the stamp *F. A. R.*, surmounted by a royal crown.

Debois, No. 1270; La Motte Fouquet, No. 539. The 3d state is still before "Ministre," but the hammers or mallets are shaded. La Motte Fouquet, No. 540.

J. L. TOCQUÉ *pinx.* **P.** The same. Le Bl. 124.

4th state, with the title "Ministre Secrétaire" *and the shaded mallets.*

J. L. TOCQUÉ *pinx.* **P.** Abel François Poisson de Vandières, Marquis de Marigny. Le Bl. 125.

The picture is in the Gallery of Versailles. Defer, in his catalogue of the Debois collection.

4th state, with arms and letters, but before the additional inscription: "Gravé par Jean Georges Wille pour sa reception à l'Académie, 1761."

The 5th state is with this additional inscription.

RIGAUD *pinx.* **P.** Jean de Boullongne. Le Bl. 126.

3d state, with three lines of inscription.

RIGAUD *pinx.* **P.** Joseph Parrocel, painter. Le Bl. 128.

2d state, with letters.

J. L. TOCQUÉ *pinx.* **P.** J.-B. Massé, painter. Le Bl. 130.

The picture is in the Gallery of Versailles. Defer, in his catalogue of the Debois collection.

3d state, with letters, and with Wille's address.

The 2d state is before Wille's address.

AVED *pinx.* **P.** Jean-Baptiste Rousseau. Le Bl. 131, b.

Partly engraved by Wille.

See SCHMIDT (Jacobi, 44), whose name is on the plate.

WILLE, JOHANN GEORG, *continued.*

TOURNIÈRE *pinx.* **P.** P. L. Moreau de Maupertuis. Le Bl. 132.

Partly engraved by Wille.

See DAULLÉ, whose name is on the plate.

WILLE *del.* **P.** Briseux, Charles Étienne, architect. Le Bl. 135.

The proofs are before letters.

CHEVALIER *pinx.* **P.** François Quesnay, médecin. Le Bl. 138.

2d state, with letters.

LE SUEUR *pinx.* **P.** François Chicoyneau, médecin. Le Bl. 140.

In 8vo.

3d state, with the letters in three lines.

The 2d state has the letters in two lines.

LARGILLIÈRE *pinx.* **P.** Marguerite Élisabeth de Largillière, daughter of the painter. Le Bl. 146.

The proofs are before letters.

TOCQUÉ *pinx.* **P.** Charles, Prince of Wales. Le Bl. 148.

Painted and engraved in 1748.

The proofs are before letters.

A. PESNE *pinx.* **P.** Frédéric II., Roi de Prusse. Le Bl. 151.

2d state, with letters.

TOCQUÉ *pinx.* **P.** Tycho Hofman. Le Bl. 163.

4th state of the plate, with the inscription in Latin.

The 1st and 2d states are before letters; the 3d has the inscription in French, the 5th in Danish, the 6th in English.

WILLMORE, JAMES TIBBETTS, engraver at London, born in 1800. A pupil of Burke.

TURNER *pinx.* View of Oberwesel, on the Rhine.

"The picture is in the possession of Benj. Godfrey Windus, Esq."

Open letter proof on India paper.

JAC. THOMPSON *pinx.* A Ferry-Boat in the Highlands, with a Hunting Party.

Proof before letters, with only the names of the artists and the publishers, cut in with the needle. On India paper, with the engraver's autograph.

WILSON, WILLIAM CHARLES, engraver in London, born about 1750.

CLAUDE LORRAIN *pinx.* A Herdsman instructing a Shepherdess to play on the Pipe.

A pastoral landscape; on the left, high cliffs with overgrown bushes, surmounted by a castle; at the foot, a rustic bridge; in the middle a view of a distant city and hills; in the foreground, a rivulet and cattle pastur-

WILSON, WILLIAM CHARLES, *continued.*

ing; on the right, under a tree, a young shepherd, with bended knee, instructing a shepherdess, sitting on the ground, to play the pipe, while another is standing behind, leaning on her staff.

Painted for M. Fontany in 1645. Engraved while in the collection of Thomas Walker, Esq.; afterwards the property of Sir Eliab Harvey, from whom it descended to W. Lloyd, Esq. Smith, *Cat. rais.* No. 93. Also engraved by Vivares. *See* VIVARES.

WITDOECK (WITDOUCK, WITHOUC), JAN, designer and engraver, born at Antwerp in 1604. A pupil of Corn. Schut and Rubens.

RUBENS *pinx.* The Adoration of the Shepherds.

With a woman pouring milk into a can, and another with a basket on her head, the figures casting gigantic shadows on the wall. Basan, 11; Smith, *Cat. rais.* 117. Painted for the church of the Capuchins in Lille.

1st state, with Witdoeck's name as engraver, and with his address, before the additional drapery on the bosom, etc.

La Motte Fouquet, No. 623.

The 2d state is with Witdoeck's and Coeberch's (Coeberger's) address, with the extended drapery, and retouched.

RUBENS *pinx.* The same.

3d state.

Schelte à Bolswert retouched the plate throughout, and put his name on it, effacing both Witdoeck's name and Coeberger's address. An impression of this state of the plate is already mentioned under Bolswert.

RUBENS *pinx.* The Elevation of the Cross.

Painted for the church of Santa Walburga; now in the Cathedral of Antwerp. Waagen, *Handbook,* II. p. 266; Smith, *Cat. rais.*, "Rubens," 1; Michiels, No. 103. Engraved on three plates. Basan, 78.

Impression before Mariette's address.

RUBENS *pinx.* Christ at Emmaus.

The picture is in the Munich Gallery. Smith, *Cat. rais.*, "Rubens," 246; Basan, 114.

The 1st impression is before any letters. "Admirable épreuve avant toutes lettres; extrêmement rare, presque unique," H. Weber, I. 1292, 46 *th.*

There are very rare 1st impressions, shaded by the engraver with India ink in deep chiaroscuro. Perhaps Weber's copy was one of them.

RUBENS *pinx.* St. Ildefonso receiving the Chasuble from the hands of the Virgin.

Basan, 31. The picture is in the Vienna Gallery. Waagen, *Handbook,* II. p. 265; Smith, *Cat. rais.* 295.

WITDOECK (WITDOUCK, WITHOUC), JAN, *continued.*

Old impression, on rough paper, without address.

CORN. SCHUT *pinx.* Madonna and Child, with St. John.

Without address.

RUBENS *pinx* St. Cecilia playing the Harpsichord.

Basan, 24; Smith, *Cat. rais.* 350. The picture is in the Berlin Gallery, Waagen's Catalogue, No. 781.

1*st state,* "Jo. Witdoeck sculpsit, Joan. Witdoeck excud." *Otto's collection, Cat.* III. No. 769.

In the 2d state the plate is retouched by S. à Bolswert, who put his name on the plate in the place of Witdoeck's. — The 3d state has the address of Hendricx.

WOOD, JOHN, engraver, principally of landscapes; born at London in 1720, died about 1780.

REMBRANDT *pinx.* "A Fire-Light," night landscape.

See Smith, *Cat. rais.*, "Rembrandt," 603. When engraved, in 1774, the picture was in the collection of Henry Hoare, Esq.; it is now in that of Sir Richard Colt Hoare, Bart., Stourhead.

SALVATOR ROSA *pinx.* Rocky landscape, with a Hermit reading.

At the time of the engraving, in 1774, the picture was in the collection of William Kent, Esq.

WOOLLETT, WILLIAM, engraver, born at Maidstone, Kent, in 1735, died at London in 1785. He was a pupil of one John Tinney, and of Vivares, but formed a style of his own, successfully combining the use of aqua fortis, the dry point, and the burin.

WEST *pinx.* The Death of General Wolfe.

The picture is in the Grosvenor Gallery.

2d proof, lettre grise. Before the retouch in the smoke, and the cross-hatching on the butt of the gun. With "B. West pinx. W. Woollett sc." (*without their titles,* "historical painter and engraver to His Majesty") *in very small letters, and* "The Death of General Wolfe," *in open letters, without the dedication to the King. The place near the feet of the General, which in the preceding state forms a white spot, is shaded.*

"With the title in open letters, and with the names of the artists traced with the point," Rigal, No. 901, 496 *fr.*

The 1st, or artist's, proof is before the coat of arms, and before any letters, and with the white spot left at the feet of the General. Logette, No. 175, 850 *fr.*; Marshall, No. 1910, £ 11 15 *s.**

* Heller, *Prakt. Handbuch,* mentions, by mistake, the impression in Rigal's collection as a 1st proof. Nagler, *Künstler-Lexicon,* XXII. p. 77, "Woollett," No. 3, mentions Logette's impression, by mistake, as a 2d proof.

WOOLLETT, WILLIAM, *continued.*

WEST *pinx.* The Battle of La Hogue.

The picture is in the Grosvenor Gallery.

Choice impression, without the dots on the side of the plate, mentioned by Longhi in his "Calcografia" as indicating later impressions.

1st proof, before letters, with merely the artists' names, traced with the point, Johnson, No. 180, £18; Archinto, No. 426, 140*fr.*; Marshall, No. 1912, £10. — 2d proof, *lettres grises,* with the arms, the title in open letters, and the names of the artists and of the publishers in traced letters, Debois, No. 1281.

CLAUDE LORRAIN *pinx.* Jacob and Laban. "Il Ponte."

The picture is in Col. Egremont Wyndham's collection at Petworth. Waagen, *Treasures,* III. p. 33; Smith, *Cat. rais.,* "Claude," No. 134.

Proofs are before letters; they have only the arms, the names of the artists, and of the publisher, Boydell, traced with the needle. Debois, No. 1285, 195*fr.*

ANN. CARACCI *pinx.* Judah and Tamar, or St. John and Magdalen.

The picture, at the time of the engraving, was in the collection of John Pitt, Esq.

Proofs are before letters; artists' names traced with the needle. Debois, No. 1288, 135 *fr.*

R. WILSON *pinx.* Cicero at his Villa.

The picture is in the collection of Sir W. W. Wynn, Bart.

Impression with the address of the engraver and Green Street.

The impressions with Boydell's address are very inferior. — Proofs have the title in open letters, the coat of arms, and the artists' names and address traced with the point. Debois, No. 1297; Archinto, No. 428.

R. WILSON AND J. MORTIMER *pinx.* Apollo and the Seasons.

Proof before letters, with only the artists' names traced with the needle. This is the deceptive copy of Woollett's plate.

R. WILSON *pinx.* Niobe.

Engraved from the second picture of this subject by R. Wilson, differing somewhat from the first, which is engraved by Samuel Smith. A similar picture is in the Vernon Gallery (Waagen, *Treasures,* I. p. 367), and another in the Bridgewater Gallery (Waagen, *Treasures,* II. p. 53).

A "très rare épreuve avant la lettre, seulement les noms d'auteurs tracés à la pointe," Debois, No. 1301, was withdrawn from the sale of the collection. — "A most brilliant and finished proof of this exquisite plate, which may be declared all but unique," Johnson, No. 183, £70.*

* Stanley, in his edition of Bryan's *Dictionary,* 1849, says, "In a manuscript catalogue written by the late Alderman Boydell, mention is made of two proofs before the letter," and adds, "If such

WOOLLETT, WILLIAM, *continued.*

R. Wilson *pinx., figures by* Mortimer. Meleager and Atalanta.

Engraved in conjunction with Pouncy.

1*st proof, before letters, with only the names of the artists. On India paper. This is the deceptive copy of Woollett's plate.*

The 2d proof has the inscription, *Engraved from an original picture painted by R. Wilson and J. Mortimer.* Address, Sayer and Bennett. — The 3d state, the common print, has the inscription changed into "Meleager and Atalanta," artists' names, and the address of Laurie and Whittle.

R. Wilson *pinx.* Phaëton.

"In the collection of his Grace the Duke of Bridgewater."

Debois, No. 1300, "Épreuve avant toutes lettres,"* 90 *fr.* — Wilcox, No. 318, "Splendid proof before the letter," £ 10 10 *s.* George Smith, No. 1306, "Very fine proof," £ 10 5 *s.* Marshall, No. 1924, "Proof before any letters," £ 10 15 *s.*

Filippo Lauri *pinx.* Diana and Actæon.

When engraved, in 1764, the picture was in the collection of the Right Rev. Thomas, Lord Bishop of Bristol.

Proofs are before letters, but have the coat of arms and the names of the artists and of the publisher in traced letters. Debois, No. 1289.

Jones *pinx., figures by* Mortimer.

Figures engraved by Bartolozzi.

Dido and Æneas.

Proof, with merely the inscription, "Dido and Æneas," *in open letters, with the coat of arms, the names of the artists and of the publisher, and before the dedication.*

From the collection and with the initials of William Esdaile.

Artist's proofs are before the inscription of the title; they have merely the names of the artists and of the publisher in traced letters, and the coat of arms. Debois, No. 1305.

Claude Lorrain *pinx.* The Temple of Apollo.

See Smith, *Cat. rais.*, "Claude," 157. The picture is from the Altieri palace in Rome; now in the collection of John P. Miles at Leigh Court. Waagen, *Treasures*, iii. p. 181.

Proofs are before letters, with only the artists' names traced. Debois, No. 1283; Archinto, No. 427.

Claude Lorrain *pinx.* Roman Edifices in Ruins.

See Smith, *Cat. rais.* 82; Waagen, *Treasures*, iii. p. 140, and iv. or *Gal-*

are in existence, they are invaluable." M. Duchesne saw two proofs before letters (the same?) in the Duke of Buckingham's collection at Stowe. *Voyage d'un Iconophile*, p. 375.

* Nagler quotes this exemplar, by mistake, as a "lettre grise." *Künstler-Lexicon*, "Woollett," No. 13.

WOOLLETT, WILLIAM, *continued.*

leries, p. 359. The picture is in the collection of the Earl of Radnor at Longford Castle.

Proofs are before letters; they have the coat of arms and the names of the artists and of the publishers in traced letters. Debois, No. 1284, 285 *fr.*; Johnson, No. 181; Wilcox, No. 322, £ 8. — Artist's proof, before any letters, and before the coat of arms, Marshall, No. 1926, £ 19.

CLAUDE LORRAIN *pinx.* The Enchanted Castle.

The picture is in Lord Overstone's collection, Wickham Park, Bromley. Waagen, *Treasures,* III. p. 27, and IV. or *Galleries,* p. 140. Lately in the collection of William Wells, Esq., Redleaf. Smith, *Cat. rais.* 162. Engraved in conjunction with Vivares.

Proofs are before letters; they have only the names of the artists in traced letters. Debois, "Vivares," No. 1212, 81 *fr.* — Artist's proof, before any letters, Wilcox, No. 323, £ 4 15 *s.*

R. WILSON *pinx.* Celadon and Amelia.

Landscape, with stormy sea. Engraved in conjunction with Browne.

Impression with the address "Green Street"; *Heller's and Nagler's first address.*

Still earlier rare impressions have the address, not mentioned by Heller or Nagler, "Longs Court, Leicester Fields." — After the address "Green Street" follows the address "Charlotte Street." — Proofs have, besides the artists' names, but one line of inscription, the title, in common — not open — letters: they are before the verses. Debois, No. 1299; Marshall, No. 1937; Wilcox, No. 328, £ 7.

R. WILSON *pinx.* Ceyx and Alcyone.

Marine view with storm.

Proof; besides the artists' names, but one line of inscription, the title, in common — not open — letters; before the verses, also before the correction of i *into* y *in the last word,* "Ceyx and Alcione." (*Like Debois, No.* 1299; *Marshall, No.* 1922.)

Purchased for £ 8 8 *s.*

The 1st state of the print with the full inscription of four Latin and six English verses has still the misspelling "Alcione," and the address "Green Street." — The 2d state has the correction "Alcyone," the same inscription, and address "Charlotte Street."

ZUCCARELLI *pinx.* Macbeth meeting the Witches.

The picture was, when engraved in 1770, in the collection of William Lock, Esq.

1*st state, with the address* "Green Street."

The 2d state is with the address "Charlotte Street." — Proofs are before

WOOLLETT, WILLIAM, *continued.*

letters, with the names of the artists and of the publisher, in traced letters.

Debois, No. 1292, 75 *fr.*

Richards *pinx.* The First Scene of the Maid of the Mill.

2d state, with Charlotte Street.

The 1st state has "Green Street." — Proofs are before letters, with only the artists' names traced with the point. Debois, No. 1304, 131 *fr.* The same copy, Marshall, No. 1952, £ 1 15 *s.* Another copy of the same state, Archinto, No. 430, 58 *fr.*

Hearne *pinx.* Two Scenes from the Vicar of Wakefield.

Two plates, engraved conjointly with Ellis, in oval. *See* Ellis.

R. Wilson *pinx.* Solitude.

Engraved in conjunction with Ellis.

1st state, with the address "Green Street."

The 2d state is with the address "Charlotte Street." — Proofs have the title in open letters, the coat of arms, and the artists' names and address traced with the point. Debois, No. 1298; Wilcox, No. 326, £ 8 8 *s.*; Archinto, No. 429.

Gasp. Poussin *pinx.* A Forest, with Waterfall.

Etched by Browne. The picture was, when engraved, in the collection of Thomas Anson, Esq., to whom the plate is dedicated.

3d state, with the address "Charlotte Street."

The 1st state is with the address "Longs Court." (Heller and Nagler state that the address of Parrs is still earlier.) — The 2d state has "Green Street." — "Proof before letters, with only the words *G. Poussin pinx., J. Browne et W. Woollett sculp.*, traced with the point," Debois, No. 1286, 400 *fr.*; Marshall, No. 1950, £ 2 11 *s.*

Pillement *pinx.* Les Agréments de l'Eté.

1st state of the finished plate with letters: "Les Agréments de l'Été. Gravé par Wm Woollett d'apres Le dessein Original de Même grandeur inventé et dessiné par Jean Pillement. London Publish'd according to Act of Parliament June 26. 1760." *Without any address.*

Pillement *pinx.* The same.

3d state. With the same inscription as the 1st state, to which is added, in the right corner below, "a Paris chez Esnauts et Rapilly ruë St Jacques à la Ville de Coutances."

"De la collection de Leviez" (Nagler) is not on either copy. According to Nagler, *K.-L.* xxii. p. 84, "Woollett," No. 45, the 2d state has the address of Leviez, and the 4th that of Jean de Paris.

WOOLLETT, WILLIAM, *continued.*

R. Wilson *pinx.* Snowden Hill and the adjacent country in North Wales.

Published by J. Boydell in 1775.

C. Dusart *pinx.* The Jocund Peasants.

Engraved in conjunction with J. Browne, who etched this and the following plate. When engraved, in 1769, the picture was in the collection of Sir Joshua Reynolds.

1st state, with the address of Longs Court.

The 2d state has the address "Green Street"; — the 3d has the address "Charlotte Street." — Proofs are before arms and letters, except the artists' names in traced letters. Debois, No. 1293; Quandt, No. 1644; Marshall, No. 1946, £ 8.

C. Dusart *pinx.* The Merry Cottagers.

Engraved in conjunction with J. Browne, who etched this and the preceding plate.

The picture was, when engraved in 1765, in the possession of Mr. Bradford.

1st state, with the address, "Longs Court."

The different states of the plate are like the preceding. Proof, Debois, No. 1293; Quandt, No. 1645; Marshall, No. 1946, £ 8.

R. Wright *pinx.* The Fishery.

1st state, with the address "Green Street."

The 2d state has the address "Charlotte Street." Proof, before letters, with only the artists' names traced with the point, Debois, No. 1296, 800 *fr.*; George Smith, No. 1308, £ 23; Archinto, No. 425, 250 *fr.* — Artist's proof, "before any letters, on India paper, in the highest condition," Wilcox, No. 331, £ 26.

Stubbs *pinx.* The Spanish Pointer.

The picture, formerly in the collection of Mr. Bradford, is now in the private collection of the King of Bavaria. (Nagler.)

1st state, with the address, "Bradford, Fleet Street."

In the 2d state the address is "Bradford, Charlotte Street"; — the 3d state is with the address of "Boydell, Laurie, and Whittle." — Proof, before letters, with only the artists' names and the address of Bradford, 1768, traced with the point, Debois, No. 1294, 501 *fr.*; Archinto, No. 424, 145 *fr.* — Artist's proof, before any letters, Wilcox, No. 316, £ 15 15 *s.*

Stubbs *pinx.* Shooting.

Set of 4 pieces.

Proofs are before letters. Debois, No. 1295; Archinto, No. 433.

Wm. Pars *pinx.* Swiss Landscapes.

WOOLLETT, WILLIAM, *continued.*

1st state, address "Percy Street." 1773.

The 2d state has the address "Green Street"; — the 3d has the address of J. Boydell, 1783.

A series of 5, namely: —

1. The Valley of Luterbrun, in the Canton of Berne.
2. The Devil's Bridge, in the Canton of Uri.
3. The Valley and Glaciers of Grindelwald, in the Canton of Berne.
4. The Great Frozen Valley near Chamouny, in Savoy.
5. The Lower Part of the Valley and Glaciers of Chamouny.

VAN DYCK *pinx.* **P.** Rubens, represented as looking out of a Window.

See Smith, *Cat. rais.* 351. The picture is in the collection of Edward Gray, Esq.

Proofs have the name Rubens, and the names of the artists traced with the point. Debois, No. 1282, 95 *fr.*; Archinto, No. 436; Marshall, No. 1908, £ 1 13 *s.*

WORLIDGE, THOMAS, painter and etcher, born at Peterborough in Northamptonshire in 1700, died at Hammersmith in 1766. A pupil of Grimaldi and L. Boitard.

WORLIDGE *del.* **P.** John Lindsey, Earl of Craufurd.

WORLIDGE *del.* Portrait of a man, in Rembrandt's style.

A bust, nearly full face, in a fur cloak, with a head-dress of a plaid scarf, surmounted by fur, or feathers. Marked "Thos. Worlidge 1759," and numbered "58."

WORTHINGTON, WILLIAM HENRY, engraver in London, born about 1795.

PICKERSGILL *pinx.* **P.** Hannah More.

Proof before letters, with only the names of the artists and the address in traced letters.

WOUTERS, GOMAR, painter and etcher of Antwerp, flourished in Rome towards the end of the seventeenth century.

Piazza Navone in Rome.

WYNGAERDE, FRANS VAN DEN, engraver and publisher, born at Antwerp in 1612, died about 1660.

RUBENS *pinx.* The Marriage of Thetis and Peleus.

See Smith, *Cat. rais.* 1094; Michiels, 701.

Z.

ZAAL, J.,* a Flemish engraver and probably painter, of whom only this plate is known, flourished about 1670.

SNYDERS *pinx.* Wild Boar Hunt.

See Nagler, *art.* "Snyders," p. 544; Brandes, I. p. 512.

2d state, with the address of G. Valk.

The rare 1st state is before this address.

ZANNONI, F., engraver. See under MARCHESE.

ZIGNANI, MARCO, engraver of Florence. Died in 1829. A pupil of R. Morghen.

RAPHAEL *pinx.* Madonna with the Child standing.

See Passavant, II. 98, and III. p. 115. The larger Madonna of the Orleans Gallery, lately in the collection of the poet Rogers, after whose death it was purchased by R. James Mackintosh, Esq., of London.

Proofs have open letters.

RAPHAEL *pinx.* **P.** Maddalena Strozzi Doni.

See Passavant, II. 40. The picture is in the Gallery of the Pitti palace.

Artist's proofs are before the letters; they have only the names of the artists and the coat of arms. Proofs have open letters.

ZINGG, ADRIAN, designer and engraver, born at St. Gall in 1734, died at Dresden in 1816. A pupil of J. R. Holzbach and J. L. Alberti.

JAC. RUYSDAEL *pinx., figures by* ADR. VAN DE VELDE. The Stag Hunt.

The picture is in the Dresden Gallery. Waagen, *Handbook,* II. p. 439; Smith, *Cat. rais.* 230.

Artist's proofs have only the coat of arms, and are without any letters. Proofs have, besides the arms, the names of the artists traced with the needle. Bause, I. Nos. 2258 and 2259.

ZUCCHI, LORENZO, engraver, born at Venice in 1704, died at Dresden in 1779. A pupil of his father Andrea.

RUBENS *pinx.* Marriage of St. Catherine.

Engraved after a repetition of Rubens's picture, by Erasmus Quellinus, of the same size with the engraving.

ZULIANI, FELICE, engraver at Venice, flourished about 1828.

TITIAN *pinx.* The Martyrdom of St. Peter the Dominican.

* It is uncertain whether this stands for Jan or Isac.

ZULIANI, FELICE, *continued.*

The picture was in San Giovanni e Paolo in Venice, recently destroyed by fire.

Proof, with the coat of arms and traced letters, the artists' names written in pencil.

𝔓. Marco Polo.

Engraved for Bettoni's *Vite e Ritratti di illustri Italiani.*

𝔓. Paolo Manuzio.

Engraved for Bettoni's *Vite e Ritratti di illustri Italiani.*

ENGRAVER UNKNOWN.

GERARD DOW *pinx.*, apparently. An Old Woman eating from an Iron Pot on her knee.

She is sitting near a table, on which are a brass kettle, a jug, and a book; by her side is her spinning-wheel, near her head hangs a pouch. Beyond the table is a window, with a bird-cage at the side. The room is a basement, with a flight of stone steps on the left, terminating at a heavy open door. In the left corner lies a water-barrel with stop-cock, a pitcher placed before it, and a broom leaning against it. In the background hangs a lantern.

The plate is $14\frac{1}{2}$ inches high, $10\frac{5}{8}$ inches broad. Without name of engraver. Also without the name of the painter or any other inscription.

INDEX

TO

THE PORTFOLIOS, ETC.

INDEX

TO

THE PORTFOLIOS, ETC.

I. A.

TUSCAN SCHOOL, AND OTHERS.

GIOTTO *pinx.* [Giotto di Bondone.]
Pietà. . . . . E. E. Schäffer *sc.*

SIMONE MEMMI *pinx.* [Simone di Martino.]
P. Petrarch's Laura. . . . . Bridoux *sc.*
P. The same. . . . . R. Morghen *sc.*
P. "Petrarch's Laura." In reality the portrait of Ginevra Benci, painted by Sandro Botticelli. . . . . Palmerini *sc.* R. Morghen *dir.*

TADDEO GADDI *pinx.*
Saint Joachim driven from the Temple. . . . . . . Lasinio *sc.*
Angel appearing to Saint Joachim. . . . . . . Lasinio *sc.*
The Birth of the Virgin. . . . . Lasinio *sc.*
The Meeting of Saint Joachim and Saint Anna. . . . Lasinio *sc.*
The Virgin descending from the Temple. . . . . . Lasinio *sc.*
The Espousals of the Virgin. . . . . Lasinio *sc.*

FRA FIESOLE *pinx.* [Il Beato Fra Giovanni Angelico da Fiesole.]
St. Stephen before the Council. . . . . . E. E. Schäffer *sc.*
St. Matthew. . . . . T. Vernon *sc.*
St. John the Evangelist. . . . . Stölzel *sc.*
St. Thomas. . . . . J. Linnell *lith.*
St. Bonaventura. . . . . L. Gruner *sc.*
St. Lawrence before the Emperor Decius. . . . E. E. Schäffer *sc.*
St. Catherine. . . . . Stölzel *sc.*

MASACCIO *pinx.* [Tommaso Guidi, usually called Masaccio.]
The Martyrdom of St. Peter. . . . . Lasinio *sc.*

FRANCIA *pinx.* [Francesco Raibolini.]
The Adoration of the Magi. *Artist's proof.* . . . . . Glaser *sc.*

FRANCIA *pinx., continued.*

The Virgin adoring the Child amid Flowers. *Inscribed:* "Raphael pinx." J. Bernard *sc.*

Religion rebuking a Naval Hero. . . . . Folkema *sc.*

FRA BARTOLOMMEO *pinx.* [Baccio della Porta.]

The Presentation in the Temple. *Artist's proof.* . . . . Rahl *sc.*

Pietà. *Artist's proof.* . . . . Steinla *sc.*

Madonna della Misericordia. *Proof.* . . . . . Saunders *sc.*

Virgin and Child, with Book, and Two Angels. . Apud Joan. Volpato.

Madonna di Lucca. *Artist's proof.* . . . . S. Jesi *sc.*

MICHEL-ANGELO *pinx.* [Michelangelo Buonarroti.]

David cutting off the Head of Goliath. . . . . . B. Audran *sc.*

The same subject, opposite view. . . . . B. Audran *sc.*

Holy Family. . . . . Steinla *sc.*

The Cartoon of Pisa. *Proof.* . . . . Schiavonetti *sc.*

La Fortuna. . . . . D. Testi *sc.*

Atlas, a study. . . . . Bartolozzi *sc.*

Venus, from a statue. . . . . Frey *sc.*

The Tomb of Giulio de' Medici. . . . . C. Cort *sc.*

Frescos in the Sistine Chapel. *See* Portfolio I. C.

The Three Fates. . . . . F. Gregorj *sc.*

P. Michel-Angelo's own portrait, Bonasone *sc.*, and the same, G. Ghisi *sc.* *See* Portf. XVII.

For the following: — Les Grimpeurs, from the Cartoon of Pisa, Agostino Veneziano *sc.*; Two Naked Men, Marc-Antonio *sc.*; The Fall of Phaëton, Beatrizet the younger *sc.*; Tityus gnawed by the Vulture, Beatrizet the younger *sc.*; The Last Judgment, Martino Rota *sc.*, *see* Portf. XVII.; — for the Last Judgment, Gaultier *sc.*, *see* Portf. I. C.

DOSSO DOSSI *pinx.*

The Four Fathers of the Church. . . . . L. Kilian *sc.*

GAROFALO *pinx.* [Benvenuto Tisio, called Garofalo.]

Virgin and Child. . . . . R. Morghen *sc.*

SEBASTIANO DEL PIOMBO *pinx.* [Sebastiano Luciani, commonly called Sebastiano del Piombo.]

The Raising of Lazarus. *Proof.* . . . . Vendramini *sc.*

ANDREA DEL SARTO *pinx.* [Andrea Vannucchi, or Andrea d'Agnolo.]

The Sacrifice of Isaac. . . . . Surugue *sc.*

The Entombment. *Proof.* . . . . Bettelini *sc.*

The Birth of the Virgin. *Artist's proof.* . . . . . . Perfetti *sc.*

Madonna del Sacco. . . . . R. Morghen *sc.*

Holy Family. *Proof.* . . . . Montmorillon *sc.*

ANDREA DEL SARTO *pinx., continued.*

Holy Family with a Go-cart. . . . . Moitte *sc.*
Holy Family with the Marriage of St. Catherine. . . C. Bloemaert *sc.*
Madonna del Trono. *Artist's proof.* . . . . . . Felsing *sc.*
Madonna col Bambino. . . . . R. Morghen *sc.*
Madonna appearing to six Saints. . . . . . . Lorenzini *sc.*
St. John taken prisoner before Herod. . . . . . Miricenus *sc.*
Salvator Mundi. . . . . A. Dalco *sc.*
Charity. . . . . Audouin *sc.*
P. Andrea's own Portrait. . . . . Saunders *sc.*

DANIELE DA VOLTERRA *pinx.* [Daniele Ricciarelli.]

The Deposition from the Cross. . . . . Toschi *sc.*
The same. *Proof.* . . . . Toschi *sc.*

FRANCESCO ROSSI, called CECCHINO DE' SALVIATI, *pinx.*

The Visitation. . . . . J. Matham *sc.*

GIUSEPPE PORTA, called SALVIATI, *pinx.*

The Dead Body of Christ supported and mourned over by Three Angels. Tanjé *sc.*

CALISTO DA LODI *pinx.*

Christ bearing the Cross. . . . . P. Anderloni *sc.*

CRISTOFANO ALLORI *pinx.*

Judith with the Head of Holofernes. First plate. *Proof.* Gandolfi *sc.*
The same. Second plate. *Proof.* . . . . . . Gandolfi *sc.*

I. A. a.

ANDREA DEL SARTO *pinx.*

Pitture a fresco di Andrea del Sarto nel Chiostro della Compagnia dello Scalzo.

10 plates, subjects from the Life of St. John the Baptist, by Andrea del Sarto and Franciabigio, and 1 plate, Justice and Charity. 1 plate, Faith and Hope, is wanting. Engraved by C. Lasinio, and others. *See* LASINIO, p. 190.

I. B.

LEONARDO DA VINCI AND HIS SCHOOL; LUINI, ETC.

LEONARDO DA VINCI *pinx.*

The Last Supper. . . . . R. Morghen *sc.*
The Head of Christ. *See* Portfolio XXXII. . . . . R. Morghen *sc.*
La Vierge aux Rochers. . . . . Desnoyers *sc.*
The same. *Artist's proof.* . . . . Desnoyers *sc.*
La Vierge aux Balances. *Proof.* . . . . F. Garnier *sc.*
Virgin and child with St. Catherine and St. Barbara. . Steinmüller *sc.*

LEONARDO DA VINCI *pinx., continued.*

Madonna del Lago. *Engraver's proof.* . . . . . . Longhi *sc.*
Madonna of Count Schönborn. *Proof.* . . . . . . Reindel *sc.*
Madonna of San Onofrio. *Artist's proof.* . . . . . . Marri *sc.*
Holy Family with a Lamb. *Proof.* . . . . . . Benaglia *sc.*
Virgin and Child with a Pigeon. . . . . Bernardi *sc.*
The same. *Artist's proof.* . . . . Bernardi *sc.*
Madonna with the Child standing, holding a Flower. *Proof.* Jos. Franck *sc.*
Virgin and Child, both holding Flowers. . . . . . Juster *sc.*
Vierge au Basrelief. *Proof.* . . . . Forster *sc.*
Mater Dolorosa. . . . . Felsing *sc.*
Magdalen. *Proof.* . . . . Ricciani *sc.*
St. Catherine with Two Angels. *Artist's proof.* . . J. G. von Müller *sc.*
Leda and two Children. *Proof.* . . . . Leroux *sc.*
Bacchus. . . . . Garnier *sc.*
Vanity and Modesty. *Proof.* . . . . Campanella *sc.*
Vanity. . . . . M. Blot *sc.*
The Combat for the Standard. . . . . Edelinck *sc.*
P. La Gioconda. *Proof.* . . . . R. U. Massard *sc.*
P. The same. *Artist's proof.* . . . . . R. U. Massard *sc.*
P. The same, different picture. . . . . . J. B. Michel *sc.*
P. La Colombine. . . . . Romanet *sc.*
P. La Belle Ferronnière. *Proof.* . . . . Bridoux *sc.*
P. The same. *Artist's proof.* . . . . Bridoux *sc.*
P. "Duke Sforza," engraved by Folkema, is really Holbein's portrait of Morett. *See* HOLBEIN, Portfolio XI.
P. Leonardo da Vinci's own Portrait. *Artist's proof.* . R. Morghen *sc.*

BERNARDO LUINI, OR DI LUVINO, *pinx.*

The Nativity. . . . . Rampoldi *sc.*
The Infant Christ adored by Mary, Joseph, and two Angels. *Engraver's proof.* Catterina Piotti *sc.*
The Adoration of the Magi. . . . . Della Rocca *sc.*
The same. *Proof.* . . . . Della Rocca *sc.*
The Presentation in the Temple. . . . . . . Giberti *sc.*
The same. *Proof.* . . . . Giberti *sc.*
Christ teaching the Doctors. *Proof.* . . . . . . Rampoldi *sc.*
The Daughter of Herodias with the Head of St. John the Baptist. Garavaglia *sc.*
Christ bearing the Cross. . . . . A. Krüger *sc.*
Madonna with St. Anthony and St. Barbara. . . . . . Bisi *sc.*
The same. *Artist's proof.* . . . . Bisi *sc.*
Virgin and Child. . . . . T. Raggio *sc.*

ANDREA DA SOLARIO *pinx.*

Madonna with the Green Cushion. . . . . . Vangelisti *sc.*

The plate is inscribed "Raphael pinx."

I. B. a.

LEONARDO DA VINCI *pinx.*

Études de la Cène d'après Léonard de Vinci lithographiées par Chatillon, Professeur à l'École Royale et Militaire de St. Cyr. Paris. fol.

13 Heads.

I. C.

MICHEL-ANGELO BUONARROTI *pinx.*

Frescos in the Sistine Chapel, engraved by D. and A. Cunego, Carattoni, Fabri, and Savorelli.

40 plates, specified in the Catalogue of Engravers under CUNEGO. To which is added The Last Judgment, engraved by Gaultier, and the Representation of the Ceiling, a chromo-lithograph. "Pratesi delt — L. Gruner direxit. Executed and printed in colours under the direction of J. Storch at the Lithographic Institute of Winckelmann & Sons at Berlin, 1852 – 1853. Drawn on stone in colours, under the direction of C. Köpper." The Portfolio contains further G. Ghisi's 6 plates, The Prophets and Sibyls, and Volpato's engraving of the Sibylla Erythræa, Delphica, and Cumæa.

For Martino Rota's engraving of the Last Judgment, *see* Portf. XVII.

I. C. a.

MICHEL-ANGELO BUONARROTI *pinx.*

Illustrations of the Genius of Michael Angelo Buonarroti, with description of the plates by the Commendatore Canina, C. R. Cockerell and John S. Harford. London, 1857. fol.

18 plates.

I. D.

Le tre porte del Battisterio di San Giovanni di Firenze, opere in bronzo di Antonio Pisano (b. 1270) e di Lorenzo Ghiberti (b. 1378), incise ed illustrate da Giovanni Paolo Lasinio.

45 plates (46th, the title, wanting). *See* LASINIO, p. 188.

I. E.

Stampe del Duomo di Orvieto. Roma, 1791. fol.

38 pieces and 32 sheets. Edited by Guglielmo della Valle, and containing works of Nicolò Pisano (flourished in 1240), Ugolino di Siena (died in 1339), Fra Fiesole (1387 – 1455), and Luca Signorelli (1439 – 1521). Engraved by J. B. Leonetti and others. *See* LEONETTI, p. 195.

I. E. a.

Die Basreliefs an der Vorderseite des Doms zu Orvieto. Marmor-Bildwerke der Schule der Pisaner mit erläuterndem Texte von Emil Braun. Herausgegeben von Ludwig Gruner. Leipzig, 1858. fol.

80 plates, on India paper.

I. F.

Pitture a fresco del Campo Santo di Pisa intagliate da Carlo Lasinio, conservatore del medesimo. Firenze, 1812.

The larger edition. 41 plates; with Landini's View of the Interior, in place of title. Containing works of Giotto (1276 – 1336), Spinello Aretino [Spinello di Luca] 1308 – 1400), Simone Memmi (died 1344), Antonio Veneziano (died 1383), Pietro di Lorenzo (flourished 1342), Andrea Orcagna (1329 – 1389), Buonamico Buffalmacco (died 1350), and Benozzo Gozzoli (1400 – 1485). *See* LASINIO, p. 183.

I. G.

Affreschi celebri del XIV. e XV. secolo incisi dal Cav. Carlo Lasinio sui disegni dal Cav. Paolo suo figlio, con illustrazioni. Firenze, 1841. fol.

32 plates, with 41 pages text by P. Tanzini. "The Quatrocentisti Fiorentini," containing works of Giotto (1276 – 1336), Taddeo Gaddi (1300), Spinello Aretino (1308 – 1400), Masolino [da Panicale] (1378 – 1440), Masaccio (1401 – 1443), Fra Filippo Lippi (1412 –1469), Cosimo Roselli (1416 – 1496), and Domenico Ghirlandajo [*family name* Corradi] (1449 – 1498). *See* LASINIO, p. 185.

I. H.

MASACCIO *pinx.*

Le Pitture di Masaccio esistenti in Roma nella Basilica di S. Clemente, colle teste lucidate dal Sig. Carlo Labruzzi e pubblicate da Giovanni Dalle Armi. Roma, 1809. fol.

37 plates in outline. To these are added, bound in the same volume, 8 plates in outline by Aloysio del Medico. *See* LABRUZZI, p. 181, and MEDICO, p. 228.

I. I.

FRA FIESOLE *pinx.*

Le Pitture della Capella di Nicolò V., opere del Beato Giovanni Angelico di Fiesole, esistenti nel Vaticano, disegnate e incise a contorni da Francesco Giangiacomo Romano. In 16 rami. Roma, 1810. fol.

I. K.

FRA FIESOLE *pinx.*

Mariä Krönung und die Wunder des heiligen Dominicus, nach Johann

FRA FIESOLE *pinx., continued.*

von Fiesole, in fünfzehn Blättern; gezeichnet von Wilhelm Ternite [gestochen von Forsell]. Nebst einer Nachricht vom Leben des Mahlers und Erklärung des Gemähldes von August Wilhelm von Schlegel. Paris, 1817. fol.

15 plates.

I. L.

FRA FIESOLE *pinx.*

S. Marco Convento dei Padri Predicatori in Firenze illustrato e inciso principalmente nei dipinti del B. Giovanni Angelico, con la vita dello stesso pittore, e un sunto storico del convento medesimo del P. Vincenzo Marchese. Firenze, 1853. fol.

Text, with Index, 163 pages. 40 plates, engraved by D. Chiossone, F. Livy, S. Martelli, R. Bettazzi, F. Zannoni, G. Bonaini, P. Nocchi, A. Perfetti, E. Damele. *See* MARCHESE, p. 218.

RAPHAEL [RAFFAELLO SANTI (SANZIO) DA URBINO].

II. RAPHAEL A.

On the works of Raphael see particularly Passavant, *Rafael von Urbino*, u. s. w. 3 Theile, Leipzig, 1839–58, 8vo, and 1 vol. fol. (plates).

Adam and Eve. . . . . P. 75. Richomme *sc.*

The same. *Open letter proof.* . . . . P. 75. Friedr. Müller *sc.*

The same. *Artist's proof.* . . . . . P. 75. Friedr. Müller *sc.*

A man sawing. Study from The Building of the Ark, fresco in the Loggie. A. Oleszczynski *sc.*

The Lord appearing to Moses in the Burning Bush. *Proof.* P. 104. Gér. Audran *sc.*

The Vision of Ezekiel. *Artist's proof.* . . . . P. 118. Longhi *sc.*

The same. *Proof.* . . P. 118. Anderloni *sc.* Longhi *dir. et term.*

The same. *Proof.* . . . . P. 118. Eichens *sc.*

The same. . . . . P. 118. Nic. de Larmessin *sc.*

The Judgment of Solomon. *Proof.* . . . . P. 78. Anderloni *sc.*

The Archangel Raphael leading the young Tobias. *Proof.* P. 4. Guérin *sc.*

(In reality painted by Moretto.) Judith. P. 252. b. Toinette Larcher *sc.*

Heliodorus. *Proof.* . . . . P. 105. Anderloni *sc.*

The same. *Artist's proof.* . . . . . P. 105. Anderloni *sc.*

The Sibyls. *Proof.* . . . . P. 112. Dien *sc.*

St. John the Baptist. *Proof.* . . . . P. 243. Bervic *sc.*

The same. . . . . P. 243. Biondi *sc.*

The Marriage of the Virgin. *Artist's proof.* . . . P. 22. Longhi *sc.*

The same. *Subscription copy,* No. 34. . . . . . P. 22. Longhi *sc.*

The Visitation. *Proof.* . . . . P. 229. Desnoyers *sc.*

II. Raphael A., *continued.*

The Nativity. . . . . P. 2. Hosemann *lith.*

The Adoration of the Magi. . . P. II. p. 23, No. 17. b. A. Banzo *sc.*

The same subject, different picture. . . . . . P. 14. Eichens *sc.*

The same subject, Arras hanging, engraved on three plates by Pietro Santi Bartoli. . . . . P. 205.

The same. . . . . P. 205. Hieron. Cock *sc.*

The Slaughter of the Innocents.
P. II. p. 528, No. 259, and p. 628, No. 8. Aurelio Colombo *sc.*

The same. *Artist's proof.*
P. II. p. 528, No. 259, and p. 628, No. 8. Moritz Steinla *sc.*

The same subject. Different composition.
P. No. 203 B. p. 263. Campanella *sc.*

The Presentation. . . . . P. II. p. 23, No. 17 c. Persichini *sc.*

II. RAPHAEL B.

The Transfiguration. . . . . P. 244. Corn. Cort *sc.*

The same. . . . . P. 244. Sim. Thomassin *sc.*

The same. 1*st state before* "Eques." . . . . P. 244. Dorigny *sc.*

The same. 2*d state with* "Eques." . . . . P. 244. Dorigny *sc.*

The same. *Subscription copy,* No. 403. . P. 244. Raphael Morghen *sc.*

The same. *Engraver's proof.* . . . . . . P. 244. Girardet *sc.*

The same. *Proof. With key.* . . . . . P. 244. Desnoyers *sc.*

The same. . . . . P. 244. Francesco Pozzi *sc.*

P. The head of the woman in the foreground, usually called Fornarina. *A silver plate.* P. 244. R. Morghen *sc.* *See* Portfolio XXXII.

The Transfiguration. Composition somewhat differing. Engraved by the Master of the Die B. 6. P. 244. *See* Portfolio XVII. Earliest Italian Engravers.

The same. Composition similar to that engraved by the Master of the Die. *Proof.* . . . . P. 244. Luigi Pizzi *inc.*

The Transfiguration. The same composition. *Proof.*
P. 244. Bettelini *sc.*

Christ's Agony in the Garden. . . . . P. 31. a. J. Ch. Flipart *sc.*

The same. . . . . P. 31. a. L. Gruner *sc.*

The Last Supper. . . . . . P. III. p. 160. Ch. Jeanneret *sc.*

Christ carrying the Cross. . . . . P. 228. Toschi *sc.*

The same. *Proof.* . . . . P. 228. Toschi *sc.*

The Entombment. More correctly attributed to Parmegiano.
P. p. 634, No. 14. m. Nic. de Larmessin *sc.*

The same subject. Different composition.
P. p. 491, No. 149. Vorsterman *sc.*

II. Raphael B., *continued.*

The Entombment, or, more correctly, Pietà.
P. No. 31. c. Claude Duflos *sc.*

The Entombment. Different composition. . . . P. 54. Amsler *sc.*

The same. *Artist's proof.* . . . . . P. 54. Masquelier *sc.*

Faith, Hope, Charity. The Three Christian Virtues, Predella of the Entombment. . . . . P. 54, p. 78. Desnoyers *sc.*

The Virgin fainting before the Sepulchre, with the Three Holy Women, and St. John. . . . . . . P. p. 481, No. 110. C. Gregorj *sc.*

The Supper at Emmaus. . . . . . P. 210. A. Campanella *sc.*

The Archangel Michael vanquishing the Dragon. *Proof.*
P. 232. Chatillon *sc.*

The same. . . . . P. 232. Lüderitz *sc.*

The same subject. Different picture. . . P. 26. Claude Duflos *sc.*

The Death of Ananias. Cartoon. . . P. 196. Gér. Audran *sc.*

Paul and Barnabas at Lystra. Cartoon. . . P. 199. Gér. Audran *sc.*

(The Hampton Court Cartoons. *See* Portf. II., Raphael M.)

Christ and the Apostles. 13 plates. . . P. 127. Ruschweyh *sc.*

"The Five Saints," Christ, The Virgin, St. John Baptist, St. Paul, and St. Catherine. . . . . P. 271. b. Richomme *sc.*

The Coronation of the Virgin, of Monte Luce. . P. 251. Jac. Bossi *sc.*

The Coronation of the Virgin, of San Francesco in Perugia.
P. 17. E. Stölzel *sc.*

II. RAPHAEL C.

Holy Families with Four and more Figures.

"La Perla." *Proof.* . . . . . P. 231. Narcisse Lecomte *sc.*

The same, without the background. . . P. 231. Vorsterman *sc.*

Madonna del Passeggio. *Proof.* . . . . P. 263. P. Anderloni *sc.*

La Vierge aux Ruines. *Proof.* . . . . . P. 266. Pradier *sc.*

La Vierge au Poisson. 1*st impression.* . . P. 100. Desnoyers *sc.*

The same. 1*st impression on India paper.* . . P. 100. Desnoyers *sc.*

The same. *Proof.* . . . . P. 100. Lignon *sc.*

The same. . . . . P. 100. Bartolozzi *sc.*

The Angel Raphael, from The Madonna with the Fish. P. 100. Noel *lith.*

Madonna dell' Impannata. . . . P. 261. Esquivel de Sotomayor *sc.*

The same. *Proof.* . . . . P. 261. Esquivel de Sotomayor *sc.*

Holy Family of the House of Canigiani. *Proof.* . P. 52. Amsler *sc.*

La Vierge au Berceau. *Proof.* . . . . . P. 235. Desnoyers *sc.*

La Vierge à la Redemption. . . . . . P. p. 410. q. Martinet *sc.*

Madonna del Duca di Terranuova. *Proof.* . . . . P. 28. Scotto *sc.*

Madonna of the Family Pio, in Naples. . . . . P. 99. Longhi *sc.*

The same. *Artist's proof.* . . . . P. 99. Longhi *sc.*

II. Raphael C., *continued.*

The same, repetition in Madrid. . . . P. 99. c. Giov. Folo *sc.*
Bust of the Virgin from this picture. . . P. 99. l. Fr. de Poilly *sc.*
Rest in Egypt. *Artist's proof.* . . . . . P. 262. Fioroni *sc.*
Holy Family under the Oak Tree, Madrid Gallery. P. 230. Brebiette *sc.*
Repetition of the same, painted by Giulio Romano, in the Gallery of the Pitti palace. . . . . P. 230. a. Corot *sc.*
Madonna del Baldacchino. . . . . . P. 62. Lorenzini *sc.*
The same. . . . . P. 62. Nicollet *sc.*
Madonna and Child with St. Jerome and St. Francis. *Proof.* P. 16. Hoffmann *sc.*
Holy Family of Francis I. *Before the coat of arms of Colbert.* P. 233. Edelinck *sc.*
The same. *After the erasure of the arms.* . . . . P. 233. Edelinck *sc.*
The same. Mezzotinto. . . . . . . P. 233. P. Schenck *sc.*
The same. For the *Musée Français.* . . . P. 233. Richomme *sc.*
The same. The larger plate. . . P. 233. Richomme and Dien *sc.*
Madonna di Foligno. 1*st state, with stamp of two antique heads.* P. 92. Desnoyers *sc.*
The same. *Proof.* . . . . P. 92. Desnoyers *sc.*
Madonna di San Sisto. *Paris impression.* P. 240. Ch. Gottfr. Schulze *sc.*
The same. *Proof, open and traced letters.* P. 240. Ch. Gottfr. Schulze *sc.*
The same. *Artist's proof, before letters.* P. 240. Ch. Gottfr. Schulze *sc.*
The same. *Before Desnoyers' retouch.* . P. 240. Friedr. Müller *sc.*
The same. *Earliest impression on India paper.* P. 240. Friedr. Müller *sc.*
The same. *Proof, before the coat of arms and dedication.* P. 240. Friedr. Müller *sc.*
The same. *Artist's proof, before any letters.* P. 240. Friedr. Müller *sc.*
The same. *The first finished proof-etching.* P. 240. Friedr. Müller *sc.*
The same. *Proof.* . . . . P. 240. M. Steinla *sc.*
The same. *Artist's proof.* . . . . . P. 240. M. Steinla *sc.*
The same. . . . . P. 240. Desnoyers *sc.*
The same, Picture in Rouen. . . . . P. 240. Aubry-Lecomte *lith.*
Madonna of the family Ansidei. *Proof.* . . . P. 32. L. Gruner *sc.*

II. RAPHAEL D.

Madonnas with 3 Figures.

Madonna del Cardellino. *Proof.* . . . . P. 36. Martinet *sc.*
Madonna in the Meadow. *Proof.* . . . . P. 37. P. Anderloni *sc.*
The same. . . . . P. 37. Agricola *sc.*
The same. *Proof.* . . . . P. 37. Steinmüller *sc.*
La Belle Jardinière. . . . . . . P. 60. Jacq. Chéreau *sc.*

II. RAPHAEL D., *continued.*

The same. . . . . P. 60. Desnoyers *sc.*

The same. *Artist's proof.* . . . . . . P. 60. Desnoyers sc.

La Vierge au Palmier. *Artist's proof.* . . . . P. 38. Martinet *sc.*

Holy Family, Joseph beardless. . . . . . P. 44. J. Chéreau *sc.*

Holy Family with a Lamb. *Proof.* . . . . P. 63. Garavaglia *sc.*

La Vierge au Diadème, "La Vierge au Linge." . P. 91. Desnoyers *sc.*

The same. *Proof.* . . . . P. 91. Desnoyers *sc.*

Madonna del Velo. Round picture. . . . . P. 57. a. M. R. Frey *sc.*

The same subject. Square picture. *Artist's proof.* P. 57. c.
Longhi *inc.* Toschi *term.*

La Vierge de Lorette. . . . . P. 88. Richomme *sc.*

La Vierge de la Maison d'Albe. . . . . . P. 89. Desnoyers *sc.*

The same. *Proof.* . . . . P. 89. Desnoyers *sc.*

Madonna of the Aldobrandini family. *Proof.* . P. 90. Bridoux *sc.*

Madonna della Seggiola. . . . . . P. 226. J. G. von Müller *sc.*

The same. *Artist's proof.* . . . . P. 226. J. G. von Müller *sc.*

The same. *Artist's proof.* . . . . P. 226. Ulmer *sc.*

The same. *Proof.* . . . . P. 226. Raph. Morghen *sc.*

The same. *Impression with the misspelling in the dedication.*
P. 226. Raph. Morghen *sc.*

The same. The small plate. . . . . P. 226. Raph. Morghen *sc.*

The same. . . . . P. 226. Garavaglia *sc.*

The same. . . . . P. 226. Desnoyers *sc.*

The same. . . . . P. 226. Petersen *sc.*

The same. *Artist's proof.* . . . . . . P. 226. Perfetti *sc.*

The same. *Proof.* . . . . P. 226. E. E. Schäffer *sc.*

The same. *Proof.* . . . . P. 226. Mandel *sc.*

Madonna della Tenda. *Artist's proof, with merely the names of the artists.*
P. 227. Toschi *sc.*

The same. *Still earlier engraver's proof before any letters. On India paper.*
P. 227. Toschi *sc.*

"La Vierge à la Légende." Both children holding a Scroll. Square picture.
Proof. No. 115. . . . . P. 267. b. Forster *sc.*

The same subject. Round picture. . . . P. 267. a. Hanfstängl *lith.*

La Vierge au Papillon. . . . . P. p. 410. No. 270. s. Pavon *sc.*

II. RAPHAEL E.

MADONNA WITH 2 FIGURES.

Madonna of the Staffa Family in Perugia. *Proof.* . P. 18. Amsler *sc.*

"La Vierge au Livre," repetition of the Madonna Staffa, in the Gallery of the Louvre. . . . . P. 18. Richomme *sc.*

II. Raphael E., *continued.*

Madonna del Granduca. *Artist's proof.* . . . P. 27. R. Morghen sc.
The same. . . . . P. 27. Martinet sc.
"La Vierge de la maison d'Orléans." The smaller Madonna of the Orleans Gallery. *Proof.* No. 81. . . . . . P. 45. Forster sc.
Madonna di casa Tempi. *Proof.* . . . . . P. 56. Jesi sc.
The same. Second plate. *Artist's proof.* . . . P. 56. Jesi sc.
The (larger) Madonna of Lord Cowper. *Proof before letters and arms.* P. 58. Perfetti sc.
Madonna di casa Colonna. . . . . P. 59. C. L. Masquelier sc.
The same. . . . . P. 59. Caspar sc.
The same. *Proof.* . . . . P. 59. Mandel sc.
Madonna with the Pink. . . . . . . P. 55. J. Couvay sc.
The same. . . . . P. 55. Boulanger sc.
Madonna with the Child standing. . . . P. 98. M. Zignani sc.
The same subject. The background omitted. *Proof before letters.* P. 98. N. Guidetti sc.
Madonna of the Bridgewater Gallery. *Artist's proof.* P. 97. Lorichon sc.
Repetition in the Gallery of Naples. *Open letter proof.* P. 97. F. Anderloni sc.
The same. *Artist's proof before any letters.* . . P. 97. F. Anderloni sc.
Madonna dei Candelabri. . . . . . P. 264. P. Bettelini sc.
The same. *Proof.* . . . . P. 264. M. Blot sc.
The same, with but one Candelabre, and without the two angels' heads. *Proof.* . . . . P. 264. Bridoux sc.
La Belle Jardinière de Florence. *Proof.* . P. iii. p. 170. Desnoyers sc.

II. RAPHAEL F.

Saints, Mythology, Allegory, History and Portraits.

St. Luke painting the Virgin. . . . . P. 272. Corn. Bloemaert sc.
St. Jerome writing. In reality painted by Palma Vecchio. P. 273, p. 418. C. E. Hess sc.
St. George with a Sword. . . . . P. 25. Petit sc.
St. George with a Lance. . . . . . . P. 43. Vorsterman sc.
St. Catherine of Alexandria. . . . . . P. 53. Desnoyers sc.
The same. *Proof.* . . . . P. 53. Desnoyers sc.
St. Margaret. . . . . P. 234. Surugue sc.
The same. . . . . P. 234. Desnoyers sc.
The same. *Proof.* . . . . P. 234. Desnoyers sc.
The same. *Proof.* . . . . P. 234. a, p. 317. Rahl sc.
The same subject. Different composition. . . P. 234 B. Prenner sc.
St. Cecilia. 1*st Artist's proof.* . . . . P. 117. R. U. Massard sc.

II. Raphael F., *continued.*

The same. *2d artist's proof.* . . . . P. 117. R. U. Massard *sc.*

The same. *Proof.* . . . . P. 117. Lefèvre *sc.*

The same. *Artist's proof.* . . . . . P. 117. M. Gandolfi *sc.*

The same. P. 117. Strange *sc.* *See* Portfolio XXIX.

Martyrdom of St. Felicitas, or, more correctly, of St. Cecilia. P. 242, and III. p. 151. Delaulne *sc.*

St. Barbara. . . . . P. p. 643. d. W. Vaillant *sc.*

Trinity, fresco in San Severo in Perugia. *Artist's proof.* P. 35. Keller *sc.*

Angel from the fresco in San Severo. . . . . P. 35. Stölzel *sc.*

Theology, "Disputa del Sacramento." . . . . P. 65. G. Ghisi *sc.*

Philosophy, "The School of Athens." . . . . P. 67. G. Ghisi *sc.*

The same. . . . . P. 67. Cossin *sc.*

The same. *Proof.* . . . . P. 67. Cossin *sc.*

Venus extracting a Thorn from her Foot. *Artist's proof.* P. 218. Audouin *sc.*

The Three Graces. *Proof.* No. 11. . . . . . P. 48. Forster *sc.*

The Triumph of Galatea. . . . . . P. 113. Richomme *sc.*

A Nymph combing her Hair, "Pan and Syrinx." P. II. p. 281, No. 217. Campanella *sc.*

Urania, bust, from the Parnassus. *Proof.* . . . P. 66. Forster *sc.*

The Vision of a Knight. . . . . . . P. 19. L. Gruner *sc.*

The Rape of Helena. . . . . . P. p. 662, No. 79. Delaulne *sc.*

The Nuptials of Alexander and Roxana. . . P. 223. Volpato *sc.*

The Defeat of Attila. *Proof.* . . . . . P. 107. P. Anderloni *sc.*

P. Portrait of Julius II. . . . . P. 83. Morel *sc.*

P. The same. . . . . P. 83. Delfini *sc.*

P. The same. *Artist's proof.* . . . . . . P. 83. Steinla *sc.*

P. Portrait of Leo X., with the Cardinals Giulio de' Medici and Lodovico de' Rossi. . . . . P. 237. Jesi *sc.*

P. The same. *Unfinished proof, with the hands, book, and bell on the table left in outline.* . . . . P. 237. Jesi *sc.*

P. The same. *Proof.* . . . . P. 237. Lignon *sc.*

P. Bust of Leo X. *Proof with open letters.* P. 237, p. 332. R. Morghen *sc.*

P. The same. *Proof with only the artist's name.* P. 237, p. 332. R. Morghen *sc.*

P. The same. *Proof before any letters.* P. 237, p. 332. R. Morghen *sc.*

P. Raphael's own portrait. *Proof.* P. II. No. 47, compare II. p. 621, No. 5. Forster *sc.*

P. The same. *Proof.* P. II. No. 47, compare II. p. 621, No. 5. Friedr. Müller *sc.*

II. RAPHAEL F., *continued.*

𝔓. The same. *Proof.*
P. II. No. 47, compare II. 621, No. 5. Reyher *sc.* Mandel *dir.*

𝔓. Portrait of the "Fornarina" in the Barberini palace.
P. 87. D. Cunego *sc.*

𝔓. The same. *Proof.* . . . . P. 87. Fontana *sc.*

𝔓. Portrait of the "Fornarina" in the Pitti palace. P. 237. Gruner *sc.* *See* Atlas to Passavant's *Rafael*, plate VI. (Portf. II. RAPHAEL Q.)

𝔓. Portrait of the so-called "Fornarina" in the Tribune, supposed to be the portrait of Beatrice Pio da Ferrara. . . P. 95. R. Morghen *sc.*

𝔓. "Raphael's Mistress," in the Marlborough collection in Blenheim.
P. 281. Th. Chambers *sc.*

𝔓. "Raphael's Mistress." Repetition of the Blenheim picture, at Verona.
P. 281. J. Bernardi *sc.*

𝔓. Portrait of Raphael, in the collection of Prince Czartorysky in Paris.
P. II. No. 86, p. 122. Pontius *sc.*

𝔓. Raphael. . . . . P. II. p. 625. a. W. Hollar *sc.*

𝔓. Raphael et son Maître d'Armes. P. II. p. 424. No. 278. Audouin *sc.*

𝔓. "Raphael," in reality the portrait of Bindo Altoviti.
P. 96. Raph. Morghen *sc.*

𝔓. The same. *Proof.* . . . . . P. 96. Raph. Morghen *sc.*

𝔓. The same picture engraved by Strange. P. 96. *See* Portfolio XXIX.

𝔓. Portrait of Angelo Doni. . . . . . P. 39. Pieraccini *lith.*

𝔓. Portrait of Maddalena Strozzi Doni. . . P. 40. Zignani *sc.*

𝔓. Female Portrait in the Tribune, formerly under the name of Maddalena Strozzi Doni. *Artist's proof.* . . . . . . P. 41. Jesi *sc.*

𝔓. Bernardo Dovizio da Bibbiena, but engraved with the name of Giulio de' Medici. *Proof.* . . . . P. 116. Gruner *sc.*

𝔓. Carondelet. . . . . . P. 279. Nic. de Larmessin *sc.*

𝔓. Count Baldassare Castiglione. . . . P. 120. N. Edelinck *sc.*

𝔓. Joan of Aragon. . . . . . . P. 236. Raph. Morghen *sc.*

𝔓. Portrait of the same, only half figure, and without the background.
Artist's proof. . . . . P. 236. Lefèvre *sc.*

𝔓. Portrait of a youth, in the Louvre, incorrectly called Portrait of Raphael when 15 years of age. *Proof.* No. 36. P. p. 88, No. 61. Forster *sc.*

𝔓. The same. *Artist's proof.* . . . P. p. 88, No. 61. Mandel *sc.*

𝔓. Portrait of a young man of about 20 years, in the Louvre. Portrait of Domenico Alfani ? . . P. II. No. 51, and III. p. 96. N. Edelinck *sc.*

𝔓. The Violin-player, portrait in the Sciara palace in Rome. Portrait of Andrea Marone ? *Artist's proof.* . . . . . P. 238. Felsing *sc.*

𝔓. The same. *Artist's proof.* . . . . . P. 238. Pollet *sc.*

Portrait of a Cardinal, in the Leuchtenberg Gallery in Munich.
P. 280. Schreiner *lith.*

II. RAPHAEL G.

RAPHAEL'S STANZE.

Camera della Segnatura.

La Disputa del Sacramento. . . . . . . P. 65. Volpato *sc.*
The Parnassus. . . . . P. 66. Volpato *sc.*
The School of Athens. . . . . P. 67. Volpato *sc.*
The Attributes of Jurisprudence: Prudence, Fortitude, and Moderation,— three Allegorical Figures. . . . . . P. 68. R. Morghen *sc.*
The whole Ceiling, chromo-lithograph. . . P. 71–78. L. Gruner *dir.*

The Four Round Pictures on the Ceiling, Allegorical Female Figures, namely:—

Theology. . . . . P. 71. R. Morghen *sc.*
Poetry. . . . . P. 72. R. Morghen *sc.*
Philosophy. . . . . P. 73. R. Morghen *sc.*
Jurisprudence. . . . . P. 74. R. Morghen *sc.*

Stanza of Heliodorus.

Heliodorus driven from the Temple. . . . . P. 105. Volpato *sc.*
The same. Etch print. . . . . P. 105. Volpato *sc.*
The Mass of Bolsena. . . . . . . P. 106. R. Morghen *sc.*
The Defeat of Attila. . . . . P. 107. Volpato *sc.*
The Deliverance of St. Peter from Prison. . . . P. 108. Volpato *sc.*
The whole Ceiling, chromo-lithograph. . P. 101–104. L. Gruner *dir.*

Sala del Incendio.

The Oath of Leo III. . . . . P. 121. Fabri *sc.*
The Coronation of Charlemagne. . . . . . P. 122. Fabri *sc.*
L' Incendio del Borgo. . . . . P. 123. Volpato *sc.*
The Defeat of the Saracens at Ostia. . . . . P. 124. Fabri *sc.*

Sala di Costantino.

Constantine's Address to his Troops. . . . . P. 245. Salandri *sc.*
The Battle of Constantine. *Proof.* P. 246. Fabri *sc.* *See* Portfolio XIV.
The Baptism of Constantine. *Artist's proof.* . . P. 247. Salandri *sc.*
The Donation of Rome. . . . . P. 248. Fabri *sc.*

Allegorical Figures, on the Walls.

Comitas, "Meekness." P. 249. b. Strange *sc.* *See* Portfolio XXIX.
Moderazione. . . . . P. 249. b. Ferretti *sc.*
La Fede. . . . . P. 249. c. Ferretti *sc.*
Justice. P. 249. d. Strange *sc.* *See* Portfolio XXIX.
La Prudenza. . . . . P. 249. e. Ferretti *sc.*

II. RAPHAEL G. a.

The same with the above, except the Allegorical Figures. Modern impressions. Also, Battle of Constantine, engraved by P. Aquila in 4 plates.

II. RAPHAEL G. b.

The first 8 Stanze, reduced copies of Volpato's and Morghen's plates by Giuseppe Mochetti, viz., La Disputa — The Parnassus — School of Athens — Heliodorus — The Mass of Bolsena — Defeat of Attila — Deliverance of St. Peter from Prison — L' Incendio del Borgo.

II. RAPHAEL H.

Caryatides and Termini in the Stanza of Heliodorus in the Vatican, engraved by Gérard Audran. 13 plates.

II. RAPHAEL I.

Picturae Peristyli Vaticani, manus Raphaelis Sanci.

With dedication to Pius VI. by P. Montagnani. Romae, 1790. fol. 52 plates and engraved title. *See* MONTAGNANI, p. 233.

II. RAPHAEL K.

Loggie di Rafaele nel Vaticano. Jo. Volpato et Jo. Ottaviani *sc.* 3 vol. Roma, 1772–77. large fol. 43 plates. *See* OTTAVIANI, p. 269.

II. RAPHAEL K. a.

Logge del Vaticano. 12 plates by Carlo Lasinio and title by Rinaldi. Reduced copies of the above.

II. RAPHAEL L.

Socle-pictures and borders of fresco paintings and Arras-hangings in the Vatican, designed and etched by Pietro Santi Bartoli. 2 parts, each 15 plates. *See* BARTOLI, p. 19.

II. RAPHAEL M.

Pinacotheca Hamptoniana, etc., by Nic. Dorigny, 1719.

The Hampton Court Cartoons. 7 plates, the Cartoons, and 8th plate, title, with Dedication to George I. *See* DORIGNY, p. 93.

II. RAPHAEL M. a.

The Seven Famous Cartoons of Raphael Urbin, etc. by Gribelin. 7 plates, the Cartoons, and 8th plate, the title, with Dedication to Queen Anne.

II. RAPHAEL N.

Psyches et Amoris Nuptiae, etc., engraved by Nic. Dorigny. Romae, 1693. Frescos in the Farnesina in Rome, 10 plates. The Triumph of Galatea. 12 plates (with the title). Dorigny, p. 94.

II. RAPHAEL N. a.

The Fable of Cupid and Psyche. Frescos in the Farnesina in Rome. Dedicated to Ferdinand IV. King of the Two Sicilies. Engraved by V. Feoli, P. Ghigi, J. B. Leonetti, Mochetti, Ricciani, and Campanella, 10 plates. *See* Ricciani, p. 314.

II. RAPHAEL O.

La Favola di Amore e Psiche, inventata da Raffaelle da Urbino in 32 rami, incisi all' acquaforte da Luigi Fabri. 1811. 4to, oblong. Containing the title-page with the head of Raphael and 32 plates, copied from engravings by Agostino Veneziano and the Master of the Die. Bartsch, xv. p. 211 *et seqq.* No. 39 – 70; Passavant, *Rafael*, ii. p. 651.

II. RAPHAEL P.

The Mosaics of the Cupola in the Cappella Chigiana of Santa Maria del Popolo in Rome. London, 1850. fol. Containing title, text, and 11 plates, engraved by L. Gruner, — the 11th colored. Passavant, ii. p. 448.

Also 6 plates of the set of 9 by Dorigny, same subject.

II. RAPHAEL Q.

Atlas zu J. D. Passavant's Rafael von Urbino, und sein Vater Giovanni Santi. Leipzig, 1839. fol. 14 plates, engraved by L. Gruner, F. A. Krüger, and Witthoeft, and lithographed by Zöllner. *See* Gruner, p. 152.

II. RAPHAEL R.

Narrazione delle geste di Enea Sylvio Piccolomini poi Pio II. rappresentate nelle pareti della libreria corale del Duomo di Siena dal Pinturicchio, con schizze e cartoni di Rafaello d' Urbino. Siena, 1771. fol. 10 plates, engraved by Raimondo Faucci. Bound up with these are 2 plates by A. Verico, carvings of the Choir in the Cathedral of Siena. *See* Faucci, p. 123.

II. RAPHAEL S.

The planets in the Sala Borgia, in the Vatican. Engraved by P. Bonato, P. Fontana, G. Bortignoni, and P. Bettelini. 7 plates. *See* under Bonato, p. 52.

II. RAPHAEL T.

The Hours of the Night and Day; comp. Passavant, II. p. 422, and III. p. 173. 12 plates, by Fosseyeux, Bourgois, F. J. Dequevauvillier, Lavallée, L. F. Mariage, J. F. Ribault, F. Hubert, L. Croutelle, N. Tomas, and L. Petit. *See* FOSSEYEUX, pp. 133, 134.

II. RAPHAEL U.

Studio del disegno ricavato dall' estremità delle figure del celebre quadro della Transfigurazione di Raffaelle delineato dal Sr. Cav. V. Camuccini, inciso da Giov. Folo. Roma, *s. a.* fol. Lithographs, 31 plates and title.

II. RAPHAEL U. a.

Fac-similes of original drawings by Raphael, now in the Louvre, by Bein, Dien, and others. 15 plates.

II. V. PERUGINO AND SCHOOL, AND FOLLOWERS OF RAPHAEL.

PERUGINO *pinx.* [Pietro Vannucci.]

The Prophets and Sibyls in the hall of the Cambio in Perugia. *Artist's proof.* Cecchini *sc.*
The Temptation in the Wilderness. . . . . . . Pavon *sc.*
The Entombment. *Proof.* . . . . Schultheiss *sc.*
The same subject, different composition. . . . . C. Duflos *sc.*
The Virgin adoring the Child. . . . . Rahl *sc.*
The Virgin and Child with two female Saints. . . Steinmüller *sc.*
The Virgin and Child with Magdalen and St. Catherine. . Gleditsch *sc.*

PERUGINO (or PINTURICCHIO ?) *pinx.*

The Virgin, with a veil of stars, and Child. *Artist's proof.* . Pichler *sc.*

GIULIO ROMANO *pinx.* [Giulio Pippi.]

Madonna with the Basin. . . . . A. Hoffmann *sc.*
The Holy Family with the Lizard. Corot *sc.* Repetition of the Holy Family under the Oak Tree, by Raphael. *See* Portfolio II. RAPHAEL C.
Holy Family. . . . . Chatillon *sc.*
Venus and Vulcan. . . . . Morace *sc.*
Neptune and Amphitrite. . . . . Richomme *sc.*
Triumphal Procession of Bacchus. . . . . . J. Th. de Bry *sc.*

VINCENZIO DA SAN GIMIGNANO *pinx.*

Virgin and Child. . . . . Garavaglia *sc.*
The same. *Open letter proof.* . . . . Garavaglia *sc.*

BAGNOCAVALLO *pinx.* [Bartolommeo Ramenghi.]

Madonna with four Saints. . . . . Lutz *sc.*

PERINO DEL VAGA *pinx.* [Pierino Buonacorsi, called Perino del Vaga.]
The Muses and Pierides, now attributed to Rosso Rossi. *Proof.*
Desnoyers *sc.*

Inscribed RAPHAEL, but A. SCHIAVONE *pinx.* The Adoration of the Shepherds.
C. Bloemaert *sc.*

Inscribed RAPHAEL. Madonna of Madrid. . . Rivera and Fontanals *sc.*

III. A. CORREGGIO, PARMEGIANO, BAROCCIO, SCHIDONE, AND PROCACCINI.

CORREGGIO *pinx.* [Antonio Allegri.]
The Adoration of the Shepherds. "La Notte." . . Surugue *sc.*
The same. *Proof.* . . . . Rahl *sc.*
The same. . . . . Michel Sloane *sc.*
The same. *Proof.* . . . . Ach. Lefèvre *sc.*
The same. *Artist's proof.* . . . . Ach. Lefèvre *sc.*
The Virgin adoring the Child. *Proof.* . . . . Della Bruna *sc.*
Rest on the Return from Egypt. . . . . Toschi *sc.*
The same. *Proof.* . . . . Toschi *sc.*
Christ praying in the Garden. . . . . Volpato *sc.*
The Deposition from the Cross. . . . . . . F. Rosaspina *sc.*
The same. *Proof.* . . . . F. Rosaspina *sc.*
Madonna with a Rabbit, "La Zingarella." . . . . C. Porporati *sc.*
"La Vierge au Panier." . . . . F. Aquila *sc.*
Madonna col Divoto. . . . . P. Bettelini *sc.*
The Madonna of Count Sœder. *Proof.* . . . . . . Knolle *sc.*
The Virgin and Child, St. John bringing Fruit. . . . . N. Bazin *sc.*
Madonna della Scala. *Proof.* No. 110. . . . . . Leroux *sc.*
The same. Toschi *sc.* *See* Portfolio III. B.
Madonna of St. Francis. . . . . P. Lutz *sc.*
The same. *Proof.* . . . . P. Lutz *sc.*
Madonna of St. Jerome, "Il Giorno." . . . . . Bartolozzi *sc.*
Madonna of St. Jerome. Strange *sc.* *See* Portf. XXIX.
Madonna of St. George. . . . . Beauvais *sc.*
The same. . . . . Hanfstängl *lith.*
Madonna of St. Sebastian. *Proof.* . . . . . . Ach. Lefèvre *sc.*
The same. *Artist's proof.* . . . . Ach. Lefèvre *sc.*
The Martyrdom of St. Placidus and St. Constantia. . S. F. Ravenet *sc.*
The Marriage of St. Catherine, at Naples. *Artist's proof.* . Felsing *sc.*
The Marriage of St. Catherine, at Paris. . . . . . Picard *sc.*
The same. *Proof.* . . . . Lorichon *sc.*
Magdalen (bust only). . . . . Desnoyers *sc.*
Magdalen sleeping with a Cross. *Artist's proof.* Faustino Anderloni *sc.*
Magdalen reading. . . . . Daullé *sc.*

CORREGGIO *pinx.*, *continued.*

The same. *Before the number.* . . . . Daullé *sc.*
The same. *Proof.* . . . . Daullé *sc.*
The same, with Longhi's own retouch. . . . . . . Longhi *sc.*
The same, before the retouch. . . . . Longhi *sc.*
The same. *Artist's proof.* . . . . Longhi *sc.*
The same. *Proof.* . . . . Knolle *sc.*
The same. *Artist's proof.* . . . . Planer *sc.*
The same. . . . . Humphrys *sc.*
The same, seen from front. Strange *sc.* *See* Portf. XXIX.
Caritas, a Mother with Three Children. Was in reality painted by Unterberger. *See* R. MORGHEN, p. 244. . . . . . R. Morghen *sc.*
Jupiter and Antiope. . . . . Audouin *sc.*
Venus taking away Cupid's Bow. . . . . Guérin *sc.*
The Bed of Danaë. . . . . Duchange *sc.*
Io and Jupiter. . . . . Duchange *sc.*
The Bath of Leda. . . . . Duchange *sc.*
The Bath of Leda, a part of the preceding composition. *Proof.* Porporati *sc.*
P. Correggio's own portrait. . . . . Salandri *sc.*
P. Correggio's own portrait, different. . . . . . . Fischer *sc.*
P. Correggio's Physician. . . . . P. Tanjé *sc.*

PARMEGIANO *pinx.* [Francesco Maria Mazzola, called Parmegiano, also Parmigianino, or Parmesano.]

Holy Family : Virgin and Child with Joseph and an Angel, and with a Cow and an Ass. . . . . Agricola *sc.*
The Virgin adoring the Child. . . . . Vorsterman *sc.*
Madonna della Rosa. . . . . Teucher *sc.*
Madonna of St. Sebastian. . . . . Le Mire *sc.*
Venus nursing Cupid. *Proof.* . . . . . . P. Caronni *sc.*
"Artemisia." *Proof.* . . . . Corn. Visscher *sc.*
"Flora," perhaps more correctly St. Rosalia. . . . . . Tanjé *sc.*
Parmigiani Amica. Strange *sc.* *See* Portf. XXIX.

FEDERIGO BAROCCIO *pinx.*

Hagar and Ishmael. *Artist's proof.* . . . . . . Garavaglia *sc.*
Rest on Return from Egypt. . . . . C. Cort *sc.*
The Descent from the Cross. . . . . Villamena *sc.*
The Entombment. . . . . Egid. Sadeler *sc.*
Christ in the Garden, "Noli me tangere." . . . . R. Morghen *sc.*
Le Pardon de St. François. . . . . B. Bolswert *sc.*
St. Michelina of Pesaro in Ecstasy. . . . . . . Farjat *sc.*
The Flight of Æneas. . . . . Ag. Caracci *sc.*

SCHIDONE *pinx.*

Magdalen. *Proof.* . . . . Bettelini *sc.*
Cupid seated. Strange *sc.* *See* Portf. XXIX.
Two little School Children. Strange *sc.* *See* Portf. XXIX.

PROCACCINI *pinx.*

Rest in Egypt. *Artist's proof.* . . . . Longhi *sc.*

III. B.

Tutti gli affresco del Correggio in Parma e quattro del Parmigianino disegnati ed intagliati in rame da Paolo Toschi e dalla sua scuola. Dedicata a sua Maestà Maria Luigia Archiduchessa d'Austria, Duchessa di Parma. 1846–56. 13 numbers, all that appeared during the life of Toschi, containing 24 plates and 3 duplicates, 27 pieces.

IV. A. TITIAN, GIO. BELLINI, AND PORDENONE.

GIOVANNI BELLINI *pinx.*

Salvator Mundi. . . . . Planer *sc.*
The picture is now ascribed to Cima da Conegliano.
The same. *Artist's proof.* . . . . Planer *sc.*

TITIAN *pinx.* [Tiziano Vecellio.]

Adam and Eve. *Proof.* . . . . Giov. Folo *sc.*
The Tribute Money. *Proof.* . . . . Steinla *sc.*
The same. *Artist's proof.* . . . . Steinla *sc.*
The same. . . . . Glaser *sc.*
The same. *Artist's proof.* . . . . Glaser *sc.*
The same. *Artist's proof.* . . . . Knolle *sc.*
The Woman taken in Adultery. . . . . P. Anderloni *sc.*
The same. *Artist's proof.* . . . . P. Anderloni *sc.*
The Crowning with Thorns. . . . . Ribault *sc.*
The Entombment. . . . . Rousselet *sc.*
The same. . . . . Schiavoni *sc.*
The same. 1845. *Proof.* . . . . A. Masson *sc.*
The same subject, different composition. . . . . . P. Pontius *sc.*
"Noli me tangere," Christ as Gardener. . . . . . N. Tardieu *sc.*
The Supper at Emmaus, called La Nappe. . . . . A. Masson *sc.*
"Parce somnum rumpere." Virgin and Sleeping Child. *Proof.*
R. Morghen *sc.*
The Virgin and Child adored by Two Angels. *Proof.* . P. Anderloni *sc.*
The Virgin and Child holding Pears in his Hand. . . Picchianti *sc.*
"Mater Sapientiae," Virgin with an open Book, and Child standing on a Table. *Proof.* . . . . Bettelini *sc.*

TITIAN *pinx., continued.*

The Virgin and Child with St. John. . . . . . C. Bloemaert *sc.*

The same composition. *Proof.* . . . . G. Nardini *sc.*

The Virgin and Child, Tobias and Angels in the background. C. Visscher *sc.*

The Virgin and Child with St. John and St. Catherine. . . Matham *sc.*

"The Great Holy Family." The Virgin and Child, St. Elizabeth with the Infant St. John, St. Joseph and St. Zacharias (or St. Jerome), who points to a passage in the Scriptures, which an Angel holds up. Pieter de Jode the elder *sc.* A. Bonenfant *exc.*

The Virgin and Child with St. John the Baptist, St. Paul, St. Jerome, and St. Magdalen. . . . . Hanfstängl *sc.*

The Virgin and Child, St. Elizabeth, and the Infant St. John; the Christ Child receives the globe of empire from a kneeling Emperor (Charles V.). C. Mogalli *sc.*

The Pesaro Family in adoration before the Madonna in the presence of the Saints Peter, George, and Anthony. *Proof before letters.* . Viviani *sc.*

Holy Family, with Alfonso I. of Ferrara, his wife Lucrezia Borgia and their Boy in adoration. . . . . Hanfstängl *lith.*

The Assumption of the Virgin. *Proof, with the middle words of the inscription* "Maria in Coelum" *unshaded.* . . . . . . Schiavoni *sc.*

The same. *Artist's proof, before any letters and before the corrected coat of arms.* . . . . Schiavoni *sc.*

The Madonna with Six Saints. . . . . G. Saiter *sc.*

The Marriage of St. Catherine, composition of 7 figures. Pieter de Jode the elder *sc.*

The same subject, composition of 4 figures. . . . . . Fontana *sc.*

The Martyrdom of St. Peter the Dominican. . B. 20. Martin Rota *sc.*

The same. . . . . H. Laurent *sc.*

The same. *Proof.* . . . . Zuliani *sc.*

St. Jerome in the Desert, reading. . . . . C. Cort *sc.*

The Martyrdom of St. Lawrence. . . . . C. Cort *sc.*

St. Magdalen. . . . . Schiavoni *sc.*

The same. *Proof.* . . . . Gius. Fusinati *sc.*

La Gloria di Tiziano, or La Toussaint: All Saints before the Trinity. *Proof.* C. Cort *sc.*

The Three Stages of Life. . . . . Ravenet *sc.*

Venus Anadyomene. . . . . Saint-Aubin *sc.*

Venus of the Tribune. Strange *sc.* *See* Portf. XXIX.

Venus, and a youth playing the lute. . . . . . Hanfstängl *lith.*

Venus sleeping. . . . . Ravenet *sc.*

Venus blindfolding Cupid. Strange *sc.* *See* Portf. XXIX.

Venus urging Adonis to desist from the Chase. . Raph. Sadeler jun. *sc.*

The same. Strange *sc.* *See* Portf. XXIX.

TITIAN *pinx., continued.*

Danaë. *Proof.* . . . . Giov. Folo *sc.*
The same. Strange *sc.* *See* Portf. XXIX.
Jupiter and Antiope. . . . . B. Baron *sc.*
Diana and Callisto. . . . . C. Cort *sc.*
Perseus and Andromeda. . . . . Delignon *sc.*
The same subject, larger composition. . . . . . . C. Cort *sc.*
Flora. . . . . Joach. Sandrart *sc.*
The same. *Proof.* . . . . Rivera *sc.*
Laocoön, group of three monkeys. Woodcut. . . . Boldrini *inc.*
Sophonisba. . . . . Anker Smith *sc.*
The Four Triumphs. Four pieces after Petrarca. . . Pomarde *sc.*
P. Titian's own portrait. *Artist's proof.* . . . . . Mandel *sc.*
P. The same. . . . . L. Vorsterman jun. *sc.*
P. "Portrait of Titian," so called, in reality the portrait of some Venetian nobleman. *Proof.* . . . . François *sc.*
P. Titian and his Mistress. . . . . . . Van Dyck *sc. aq. f.*
P. Titian's Son and Nurse. (Mezzotint.) . . . John Murphy *sc.*
P. Titian's Daughter holding a Fruit Basket. *Proof.* . . . Caspar *sc.*
P. The same. *Artist's proof.* . . . . Eichens *sc.*
P. The same, the basket contains three melons. W. Hollar *sc.* *See* Portfolio XXII.
P. Titian's Daughter holding a Jewel Casket. . . . . J. Heath *sc.*
P. Titian's Mistress, in the Louvre. . . . . . . Forster *sc.*
P. "La Bella di Tiziano," in Rome. *Proof.* . . . . Perfetti *sc.*
P. Pietro Aretino. *Proof.* . . . . C. van Dalen *sc.*
P. Ariosto. . . . . N. Schenker *sc.*
P. Cardinal Beccadilli. *Proof.* . . . . Ulmer *sc.*
P. Boccaccio. . . . . C. van Dalen *sc.*
P. The Constable Bourbon. . . . . L. Vorsterman *sc.*
P. The Cornaro Family. . . . . B. Baron *sc.*
P. "Catterina Cornaro, Regina di Cipro." . . . Sam. Levi Polacco *sc.*
P. Hippolyte d'Este, Cardinal de' Medici. . . . . T. Ver Cruys *sc.*
P The same. . . . . Laugier *sc.*
P. Isabelle of Este, Wife of Duke Francesco Gonzaga II. of Mantua. Vorsterman *sc.*
P. Francis I. . . . . Moyreau *sc.*
P. Emperor Charles V. . . . . Vorsterman *sc.*
P. Another portrait of Charles V. . . . . Hess *sc.*
P. The Marquis del Guasto with his Mistress. . . . . M. Natalis *sc.*
P. Jacopo Sansovino (according to R. Weigel, *Künstlerportraits,* No. 136, the portrait of Bandinelli). . . . . Vorsterman jun. *sc.*
P. Filia Roberti Strozzi. . . . . Cunego *sc.*

TITIAN *pinx., continued.*

Portrait of a Matron in Widow's Weeds. . . . . . Basan *sc.*
Portrait of a Young Woman with a Fan in the Form of a Vane. Basan *sc.*
Portrait of a Venetian nobleman. . . . . . . Coelemans *sc.*

PORDENONE *pinx.* [Giovanni Antonio Licinio Regillo da Pordenone.]

St. Justina. . . . . C. Rahl *sc.*
P. "Catterina Cornaro Regina di Cipro." *Artist's trial proof.* Schulz *sc.*

IV. B. OTHER VENETIANS.

GIORGIONE *pinx.* [Giorgio Barbarelli.]

Jacob greeting Rachel. . . . . Hanfstängl *lith.*
The Finding of Moses. . . . . P. Aveline *sc.*
The Concert. Two Choristers, the one playing a clavecin, with a youth at his elbow, wearing a barret-cap with feathers; the other holding a violoncello. Chr. Fr. Stölzel *sc.*
Pastorale. Two young men sitting in a landscape, one playing the lute, accompanied by a young woman with a fife; a second female fetching a pitcher of water. . . . . N. Dupuis *sc.*
P. Gaston de Foix. . . . . A. Cardon *sc.*

JACOPO BASSANO *pinx.* [Jacopo da Ponte da Bassano.]

The Angel bidding Abraham quit his country. *Proof.* . C. Visscher *sc.*
The Annunciation to the Shepherds. . . . . . Egidius Sadeler *sc.*
The Adoration of the Magi. . . . . . . R. Sadeler sen. *sc.*
The Circumcision. . . . . Couché *sc.*
Christ driving the Dealers from the Temple. . . . . Kilian *sc.*
St. Christopher. . . . . Egidius Sadeler *sc.*

PALMA VECCHIO *pinx.*

Madonna and Child, with St. John and St. Catherine. . Hanfstängl *lith.*
The same picture. *Artist's proof.* . . . . Steinla *sc.*
Holy Family with the Infant St. John and St. Catherine. Hanfstängl *lith.*
Holy Family with other Figures in a landscape, the young Tobias offers a fish. J. Falck *sc.*
P. Palma's Three Daughters. . . . . Noel *lith.*

TINTORETTO *pinx.* [Jacopo Robusti.]

Jacob and Rachel at the Well. . . . . . . Claude Mellan *sc.*
Christ blessing the Children. . . . . Swanenburg *sc.*
The Great Crucifixion, on three plates. . . . Agost. Caracci *sc.*
The Entombment. *Proof.* . . . . C. Visscher *sc.*
The Miracle of St. Mark. . . . . J. Matham *sc.*
P. Tintoretto's own portrait. . . . . . A. de Marcenay *sc.*

FARINATA *pinx.*

The Martyrdom of St. Erasmus. . . . . H. David *sc.*

PAOLO VERONESE *pinx.* [Paolo Cagliari, or Caliari.]

Rebecca and Eliezer. . . . . L. Jacob *sc.*
The same subject, different composition. . . . . J. Moyreau *sc.*
The Finding of Moses. . . . . Jeaurat *sc.*
The same subject, different. . . . . Terwesten *sc.*
The same subject, different composition. . . . . Henriquez *sc.*
The Judgment of Solomon. . . . . Bartolozzi *sc.*
Susanna. . . . . Hanfstängl *lith.*
The Adoration of the Magi. . . . . Hanfstängl *lith.*
The Presentation in the Temple. . . . . . . Villamena *sc.*
The same subject, different composition. In outline. . . Honeck *sc.*
The Feast at the House of Simon, Christ as a Pilgrim sitting between a Pope and a Cardinal. In the Brera Gallery. . . . . . L. Pizzi *sc.*
The Feast at the House of Simon. Venice Gallery. . J. Saenredam *sc.*
The Marriage Feast at Cana. Dresden Gallery. . . Hanfstängl *lith.*
The Feast at the House of Simon. In the Royal Palace of Genoa. Scotto *sc.*
The Marriage Feast at Cana. The great picture in the Louvre. Vanni *sc.*
The same picture. . . . . J. G. Saiter *sc.*
The same picture. . . . . Prevost *sc.*
The Feast at the House of Simon. In the Louvre. . . Prevost *sc.*
Christ bearing the Cross. . . . . Hanfstängl *lith.*
The same picture. . . . . Preisler *sc.*
The Ascension. *Proof.* . . . . C. Visscher *sc.*
The Meeting at Emmaus. . . . . B. Audran *sc.*
The Supper at Emmaus. . . . . C. Duflos *sc.*
The Marriage of St. Catherine. . . . . . . Th. Matham *sc.*
The Vision of St. Catherine. . . . . Vendramini *sc.*
Madonna in Trono, with the little St. John, St. Francis, St. Jerome, and St. Catherine. . . . . Wagner *sc.*
St. Helena. . . . . Vorsterman *sc.*
Madonna with the Concina Family. . . . . . Hanfstängl *lith.*
The Poet conjuring up Fortune. . . . . . . Coelemans *sc.*
Wisdom leading Strength. . . . . Desplaces *sc.*
Mercury and Herse. . . . . Joullain *sc.*
Venus and Adonis. . . . . Ravenet *sc.*
The Rape of Europa. . . . . Rainaldi *sc.*
Apollo and Marsyas. . . . . Joullain *sc.*
P. Daniello Barbaro. . . . . Houbraken *sc.*
P. Paolo Veronese. . . . . Coelemans *sc.*

PALMA GIOVANE *pinx.*

St. Jerome penitent. . . . . Goltzius *sc.*

Alessandro Turchi *pinx.* [Called Orbetto.]

Venus lamenting Adonis. *Proof.* . . . . . . Beauvarlet *sc.*

V. A. BOLOGNESE SCHOOL.

Lodovico Caracci *pinx.*

Madonna col Bambino. 8vo. . . . . . R. Morghen *sc.*

Agostino Caracci *pinx.*

The Woman taken in Adultery. . . . . Bartolozzi *sc.*

Venus guiding Æneas to the Shores of Italy. *Artist's proof.* M. E. Kluge *sc.*

Landscape, with three Bathers, and a Girl in the foreground. Bartolozzi *sc.*

Annibale Caracci *pinx.*

Adoration of the Shepherds. Above, a glory, with angels making music. Lips and Forster *sc.*

Adoration of the Shepherds, one blowing a tin trumpet. . . Aliamet *sc.*

The Crucifixion. . . . . C. Bloemaert *sc.*

Pietà, the Dead Christ and his Mother, and three Holy Women. "Les cinq douleurs." . . . . Roullet *sc.*

Pietà, the Dead Christ and his Mother, with St. Magdalen, St. Francis and six Angels. . . . . P. Aquila *sc.*

Pietà, the Dead Christ and his Mother, supported by two Angels. Van den Steen *sc.*

The three Maries and Angel at the Grave. . . . . Roullet *sc.*

Head of Christ. . . . . David Weiss *sc.*

The same. . . . . Schulze *sc.*

Virgin and Child adored by two angels. . . . . Fr. Poilly *sc.*

Holy Family with a Cradle, St. John offering cherries. P. Stefanoni *sc.*

"Le Silence." The Virgin watching over the sleeping Child. Bartolozzi *sc.*

The same. *Proof.* No. 72. . . . . . . Richomme *sc.*

The Virgin in a landscape with the Child standing on her knee. Roullet *sc.*

The Assumption of the Virgin. . . . . . G. Chasteau *sc.*

St. Margaret. . . . . C. Bloemaert *sc.*

Clytie. *Proof.* . . . . Bartolozzi *sc.*

"L'Attente du Plaisir." . . . . Lempereur *sc.*

The Genius of Fame. . . . . Jardinier *sc.*

Orlando rescuing Olympia. . . . . Bartolozzi *sc.*

Alexander and Timocleia. *Proof.* . . . . . . G. F. Schmidt *sc.*

Set of 6 plates : Farnese Gallery. . . . . Volpato and Bettelini *sc.*

P. Portrait of Annibale Caracci. . . . . . C. Vermeulen *sc.*

Judah and Tamar, otherwise St. John and Magdalen, landscape with figures. Woollett *sc.* *See* Portfolio XV. A.

VANNI *pinx.*

Virgin and Child. . . . . R. Sadeler *sc.*

VILLAMENA *pinx.*

St. Francis. . . . . Villamena *sc.*

GUIDO RENI *pinx.*

The Archangel St. Michael vanquishing the Dragon. *Proof.* . . Folo *sc.*

Susannah and the Elders. *Proof before letters.* . . . C. Visscher *sc.*

The Daughter of Herodias in Oriental head-dress, holding the head of St. John on a platter. . . . . P. Fontana *sc.*

The Daughter of Herodias receiving from a page the head of St. John. J. J. Frey *sc.*

The Slaughter of the Innocents. . . . . B. Bolognoni *sc.*

The Adoration of the Shepherds. . . . . F. Poilly *sc.*

St. Joseph with the Infant Christ. 8vo. . . . . . Longhi *sc.*

Les Couseuses. *Proof before any letters.* . . . . . Beauvarlet *sc.*

La Couseuse. Begun by Nanteuil. 1*st state.* . . . . Edelinck *sc.*

The Flight into Egypt. . . . . F. Poilly *sc.*

Ecce Homo. *Proof.* . . . . A. Krüger *sc.*

The Assumption of the Virgin. *Proof.* . . . . . Bettelini *sc.*

The Assumption of the Virgin, with the Apostles below. . Fr. Bruni *sc.*

The same. *Proof.* . . Garavaglia *in.* F. Anderloni *term.*

Madonna and Child, with St. John. *Proof.* . . . . Gandolfi *sc.*

Virgin and Child in a Glory, below St. Thomas and St. Jerome. Bettelini *sc.*

The Virgin adored by the patron Saints of Bologna. . Flaminio Torre *sc.*

The Doctors of the Church. . . . . J. J. Frey *sc.*

The same. *Proof.* . . . . Sharp *sc.*

The Martyrdom of St. Andrew. . . . . Volpato *sc.*

St. Cecilia. . . . . G. Morghen *sc.*

St. Sebastian. . . . . Ferd. Gregorj *sc.*

Sibylla Persica. *Proof before any letters.* . . . . . Perfetti *sc.*

Aurora with Apollo and the Hours. . . . . . . R. Morghen *sc.*

The same. . . . . Audenaerde *sc.*

The Infant Bacchus. . . . . G. Camerata *sc.*

Cupid on the Sea-shore. . . . . P. Vitali *sc.*

The Rape of Dejanira. . . . . Bervic *sc.*

Erigone. . . . . Vermeulen *sc.*

Hope. *Proof.* . . . . Buonafede *sc.*

The Genius of Music triumphant over Love. . . . . Longhi *sc.*

The same. *Artist's proof.* . . . . Longhi *sc.*

The Union of Drawing and Color. *Artist's trial proof.* . . Schulze *sc.*

Ninus and Semiramis. . . . . Preisler *sc.*

Cleopatra. *Proof.* . . . . Rivera *sc.*

GUIDO RENI *pinx., continued.*

For the following, engraved by Strange, *see* Portf. XXIX.

The Chastity of Joseph.
Bust of the Virgin.
Angel of the Annunciation.
The Offspring of Love.
Magdalen, standing, divesting herself of her pearls.
Magdalen seated in a grotto.
Cleopatra seated.
Cleopatra standing.
Venus attired by the Graces.
Cupid sleeping.
Liberality and Modesty.
Fortune.

P. Guido Reni's portrait. . . . . Cipriani *sc.* R. Morghen *dir.*
P. Beatrice Cenci. . . . . Garavaglia *sc.*

FRANCESCO ALBANO *pinx.*

The Birth of the Virgin. . . . . . Pietro Santi Bartoli *sc.*
The Baptism of Christ. . . . . B. Audran *sc.*
La Charité humaine. . . . . J. Daullé *sc.*
Galatea. . . . . Longhi *sc.*
The same. *Artist's proof.* . . . . Longhi *sc.*
Dance of Amoretti, with the Rape of Proserpina, a square picture. Tanjé *sc.*
The same, an oval picture. *Proof.* . . . . Rosaspina *sc.*
Venus and Adonis. *Artist's proof.* . . . . Toschi *sc.*
The Four Elements, 4 plates. . . . . Baudet *sc.*

V. B. BOLOGNESE SCHOOL, *continued.*

DOMENICHINO *pinx.* [Domenico Zampieri.]

The Annunciation. . . . . Duflos *sc.*
The Mystery of the Rosary. 1*st state.* . . . . Gér. Audran *sc.*
St. John the Evangelist. 1808. . . . . Fr. Müller *sc.*
The same. 1808. . . . . Fr. Müller *sc.*
The same. 1812. . . . . Fr. Müller *sc.*
The same. 1812, newly retouched. . . . . . . Fr. Müller *sc.*
The same, copy. . . . . Fr. Müller *sc.*
The same. . . . . Bahmann *sc.*
The same. *Proof.* . . . . Bahmann *sc.*
St. John with two Angels. *Artist's proof.* . . . . . Bettelini *sc.*
The Temptation of St. Jerome. . . . . Gér. Audran *sc.*
The Communion of St. Jerome. . . . . Testa *sc.*

DOMENICHINO *pinx., continued.*

The same. . . . . Jac. Frey *sc.*
The same. . . . . P. H. Laurent *sc.*
The same. *Proof before letters.* . . . . . . Alex. Tardieu *sc.*
The same. *Proof before letters.* . . . . . . Ign. Pavon *sc.*
The Martyrdom of St. Sebastian. . . . . . Nic. Dorigny *sc.*
The same. . . . . Jac. Frey *sc.*
The Martyrdom of St. Andrew. . . . . Folo *sc.*
The Miracle of St. Nilus. . . . . Ruschweyh *sc.*
St. Agnes. Strange *sc.* *See* Portf. XXIX.
The Martyrdom of St. Agnes. . . . . Gér. Audran *sc.*
St. Cecilia. *Proof.* . . . . Sharp *sc.*
The same. Small print. 8vo. . . . . Sharp *sc.*
The same, with Basso. . . . . J. G. von Müller *sc.*
The same, with Violin. . . . . Lignon *sc.*
Sibylla Cumæa, more correctly St. Cecilia, with Bass Viol and Music Notes. Perfetti *sc.*
"La Sìbylla." *Proof before letters.* . . . . Perfetti *sc.*
Æneas saving Anchises. . . . . G. Audran *sc.*
The same. . . . . N. Outkyn *sc.*
The same. *Proof.* . . . . Delégorgue *sc.*
Diana and Callisto. *Proof.* . . . . Agricola *sc.*
The same. *First etching of the plate.* . . . . . . Agricola *sc.*
La Caccia. The Prize-shooting of Diana's Nymphs. . R. Morghen *sc.*
Circe. *Proof.* . . . . Sharp *sc.*
Glory rewarding Merit. . . . . Canale *sc.*
Lucretia. *Proof before letters.* . . . . Sharp *sc.*
P. Domenichino's own Portrait. . . . . Langlois *sc.*
P. Domenichino's Mistress. *Proof before letters.* . . . Whitfield *sc.*

GUERCINO *pinx.* [Giovanni Francesco Barbieri.]

Lot and his Daughters. *Proof.* . . . . R. Morghen *sc.*
Abraham dismissing Hagar. *Artist's proof.* . . . . . Jesi *sc.*
The same. Strange *sc.* *See* Portf. XXIX.
Jacob blessing Joseph's Children. . . . . . . Raph. Esteve *sc.*
Esther before Ahasuerus. Strange *sc.* *See* Portf. XXIX.
David with the Head of Goliath. *Artist's proof.* . . . Garavaglia *sc.*
The Circumcision. . . . . Bartolozzi *sc.*
Christ appearing to his Mother. Strange *sc.* *See* Portf. XXIX.
St. Peter raising Tabitha. . . . . C. Bloemaert *sc.*
St. Sebastian. . . . . Folo *sc.*
The Burial of St. Petronella. . . . . N. Dorigny *sc.*
The same. . . . . Jac. Frey *sc.*

GUERCINO *pinx., continued.*

Sibylla Samia. . . . . Perfetti *sc.*
The same. *Artist's proof.* . . . . Perfetti *sc.*
Aurora, followed by Tithonus. . . . . Volpato *sc.*
Day, or Dawn. . . . . Volpato *sc.*
Night. . . . . Volpato *sc.*
Cephalus and Procris. . . . . Lempereur *sc.*
Semiramis receiving the Message of Revolt. *Artist's proof.*
Catarina Piotti *sc.*
The same. *Unfinished proof.* . . . . . Catarina Piotti *sc.*
Dido on the Funeral Pile. Strange *sc.* *See* Portf. XXIX.
P. Guercino's own Portrait. . . . . . . Bartolozzi *sc.*

ANDREA SACCHI *pinx.*

"The White Friars." . . . . Jac. Frey *sc.*
Apollo rewarding Merit. Strange *sc.* *See* Portf. XXIX.
P. Andrea Sacchi's own Portrait. . . . . . . Vallet *sc.*

ELISABETTA SIRANI *pinx.*

An Infant Sleeping. . . . . Bartolozzi *sc.*

FRANCESCHINI *pinx.*

Satyr, and Children playing with a Goat. . . . . Bartolozzi *sc.*

V. B. a. DOMENICHINO.

Scenes from the Life of the Virgin, frescos in the Capella Nolfi of the Cathedral of Fano. Engraved by Dom Cunego.

16 plates. See alphabetical catalogue, under CUNEGO, p. 79.

VI. LATER ITALIAN PAINTERS: PIETRO DA CORTONA, SASSOFERRATO, CARLO DOLCE, CARLO MARATTI, AND OTHERS.

TEODORO GHISI *pinx.*

Venus and Adonis. . . . . Giorgio Ghisi *sc.*

LIVIO AGRESTI *pinx.*

The Last Supper. . . . . C. Cort *sc.*

DANIELLO CRESPI *pinx.*

Christ bearing the Cross. . . . . Felsing *sc.*

PIETRO DA CORTONA *pinx.* [Pietro Berettini da Cortona.]

Wisdom leading Youth. . . . . L. Visscher *sc.*
Two pieces: Apollo and Diana. . . . . . . C. Bloemaert *sc.*
The Finding of Romulus and Remus. Strange *sc.* *See* Portf. XXIX.
Cæsar repudiating Pompeia. Strange *sc.* *See* Portf. XXIX.

MARIO DE' FIORI *pinx.*

Concert of Birds. . . . . Earlom *sc.*

SASSOFERRATO *pinx.* [Giovanni Battista Salvi.]
Mater Amabilis. . . . . Pavon *sc.*
The same subject. *Proof.* . . . . Giov. Folo *sc.*
The same subject. *Artist's proof.* . . . . . F. Anderloni *sc.*
The same subject. . . . . G. F. Schmidt *sc.*

STEFANO DELLA BELLA *pinx.*
Pont Neuf in Paris. . . . . Stef. Della Bella *sc.*

CARLO DOLCE *pinx.*
Salvator Mundi. *Proof.* . . . . Capezzuoli *sc.*
Mater Dolorosa. *Proof.* . . . . Bartolozzi *sc.*
St. Magdalen. . . . . R. Morghen *sc.*
St. Cecilia. *Artist's proof.* . . . . Knolle *sc.*
Poesia. *Artist's proof.* . . . . R. Morghen *sc.*
P. Carlo Dolce's own Portrait. *Proof.* . . . . . Ulmer *sc.*

CARLO MARATTI *pinx.*
The Adoration of the Kings. . . . . Jac. Frey *sc.*
Dead Christ with Mourners. . . . . Audenaerde *sc.*
Madonna of the Rosaries. . . . . Audenaerde *sc.*
Infant Christ sleeping. Strange *sc.* *See* Portfolio XXIX.
St. Cecilia. Strange *sc.* *See* Portfolio XXIX.
Virgin and Child. . . . . Daullé *sc.*
The Crucifixion of St. Andrew. . . . . J. Frey *sc.*
Cleopatra. . . . . J. Frey *sc.*
Danäe. . . . . Desplaces *sc.*
P. Carlo Maratti's own Portrait. . . . . . . J. Frey *sc.*

CIGNANI *pinx.*
Joseph and Potiphar's Wife. . . . . J. Frey *sc.*

PAOLO DE MATTEIS *pinx.*
Hercules between Virtue and Vice. . . . . . . Gribelin *sc.*

CARRIERA ROSALBA *pinx.*
P. Her own Portrait. . . . . Bartolozzi *sc.*

BATONI *pinx.*
Magdalen in the Desert. Mezzotinto. . . . . . J. Pichler *sc.*

APPIANI *pinx.*
Venus and Cupid. . . . . M. Bisi *sc.*

BENVENUTO *pinx.*
Mater Dolorosa. . . . . M. Esquivel *sc.*

MAURO GANDOLFI *pinx.*
Sleeping Cupid. . . . . M. Gandolfi *sc.*

VII. A. SPANISH AND NEAPOLITAN SCHOOLS.

FRANCISCO DE RIBALTA *pinx.*

Christ bearing the Cross. . . . . Sherwin *sc.*

M. A. CARAVAGGIO *pinx.* [Michelangelo Amerighi da Caravaggio.]

Entombment. . . . . Suyderhoef *sc.*
The same subject. . . . . Audouin *sc.*
St. Francis in Ecstasy. . . . . L. Vorsterman *sc.*
The Death of the Virgin. . . . . Sim. Vallée *sc.*
The Card-players. . . . . Tanjé *sc.*

SPAGNOLETTO *pinx.* [Juseppe or Giuseppe Ribera.]

Jacob tending the Flock of Laban. . . . . Locke *sc.*
The Adoration of the Shepherds. . . . . . . Ingouf *sc.*
Christ disputing with the Doctors. . . . . . . Jos. Fisher *sc.*
St. Peter delivered from Prison. . . . . . . Pitteri *sc.*
Mater Dolorosa. *Open letters.* . . . . . Aristide Louis *sc.*
St. Gregory. . . . . Ametllér *sc.*
Diogenes with the Lantern. . . . . Daullé *sc.*
Archimedes. . . . . Balestra *sc.*

VELAZQUEZ *pinx.*

The Water-carrier of Sevilla. *Proof.* . . . . . . Ametllér *sc.*
A Shepherd. . . . . Gruner *sc.*
P. "Las Meniñas," The Maids of Honor, Velazquez painting the Infanta Margarita Maria. . . . . Audouin *sc.*
P. Infanta Margarita. *Open letters.* . . . . . Lüderitz *sc.*
P. Philip IV. *Before any letters.* . . . . . . C. Ferreri *sc.*
P. Cervantes. *Lettres grises.* . . . . Bouvier *sc.*
P. Barbarossa, the pirate. . . . . Croutelle *sc.*
P. Velazquez's own Portrait. . . . . Pannier *sc.*

ZURBARAN *pinx.*

La Pastorcita. . . . . V asquez *sc.*

MURILLO *pinx.*

Moses striking the Rock. *Proof.* . . . . . Raphael Esteve *sc.*
The Annunciation. *Proof.* . . . . Lefèvre *sc.*
St. John the Baptist. . . . . Blaschke *sc.*
The Adoration of the Shepherds. . . . . V. Green *sc.*
The Infant Christ twisting a Crown of Thorns. Strange *sc.* *See* Portf. XXIX.
La Vierge de Madrid. Conception. . . . . . Hipp. Garnier *sc.*
The Conception, in Spain. . . . . Marin Lavigne *sc.*
The Conception, the picture from Soult's collection, in the Louvre. *Proof.* L. Massard *sc.*

MURILLO *pinx.*, *continued.*

The same. *Proof.* . . . . Lefèvre *sc.*
The Conception, King Louis Philippe's picture. *Artist's proof.* Bridoux *sc.*
Madonna and Child. Dresden. . . . . Weinhold *lith.*
The same. *Artist's trial proof.* . . . . Semler *sc.*
La Vierge de Séville. Paris. . . . . Marin Lavigne *lith.*
The same. *Proof.* . . . . Herm. Eichens *sc.*
Madonna of the Rosary. Dulwich Gallery. *Proof.* . . . Rob. Graves *sc.*
Madonna and Child, in Florence. *Proof.* . . . . . . Perfetti *sc.*
Madonna and Child, in Munich. . . . . . . Hanfstängl *lith.*
Madonna and Child of the Aguado Gallery. *Proof.* . . . Lefèvre *sc.*
The Virgin in a Glory of Angels, with four Saints. *Proof.* . Nargeot *sc.*
La Vierge aux Anges. *Artist's proof.* . . . . Leroux *sc.*
Holy Family, the Christ Child standing between the Virgin and Joseph. National Gallery. *Artist's proof.* . . . . Bridoux *sc.*
Mater Dolorosa, in Seville. . . . . Weinhold *lith.*
St. Magdalen. . . . . R. Morghen *sc.*
Ste. Juste. *Proof.* No. 19. . . . . Blanchard sc.
St. Ildefonso receiving the Chasuble. . . . . Selma *sc.*
The Virgin appearing to St. Bernard. . . . . Muntaner *sc.*
The Spanish Flower-girl. *Proof.* . . . . Robinson *sc.*
P. Murillo's own Portrait. *Proof.* . . . . Blanchard *sc.*

SALVATOR ROSA *pinx.*

The Prodigal Son. . . . . S. F. Ravenet *sc.*
Diogenes in Search of an honest Man. . . . . Sharp *sc.*
Apollo and the Sibyl, landscape. . . . . John Browne *sc.*
King Laomedon refuses his tribute to Neptune and Apollo. Strange *sc.* *See* Portfolio XXIX.
Belisarius. Strange *sc.* *See* Portfolio XXIX.
Rocky landscape, with a Hermit reading. . . . . . . Wood *sc.*
P. Salvator Rosa's own Portrait. . . . . Audouin *sc.*

LUCA GIORDANO *pinx.*

The Death of Seneca. . . . . S. F. Ravenet *sc.*
Apollo and Daphne. . . . . Levasseur *sc.*

VINCENTE LOPEZ *del.*

The Holy Chalice of Valencia. . . . . Fr. Jordan *sc.*

VII. B. SALVATOR ROSA'S ETCHINGS.

The entire work of the artist, according to Bartsch, including one duplicate, together with two pieces and 7 variations not described by him. 96 plates. Specified in the Catalogue of Engravers, pp. 320 – 327.

VIII. A.

Histoire de l'Art par les Monumens, depuis sa décadence au IVe siècle jusqu'à son renouvellement au XVIe; par J. B. L. G. Seroux d'Agincourt. Paris, 1823. 6 vols. fol. with 325 plates.

VIII. B.

L'Etruria pittrice ovvero Storia della Pittura Toscana dedotta dai suoi Monumenti che si esibiscono in stampa dal secolo X. fino al presente. 2 vols. Firenze, 1791–95, fol., with 120 plates by C. Lasinio, F. Gregorj, G. Vascellini, Gaetano Cecchi, G. B. Cecchi, G. F. Ravenet, C. Colombini, B. Eredi, etc. With the portraits of the painters, and text in Italian and French, by Marco Lastri.

VIII. C.

Storia della Pittura Italiana esposta coi Monumenti, da Giovanni Rosini. Pisa, 1839–55, 4 vols. fol., and 7 vols. 8vo. with supplement. 248 plates in folio, and 245 plates in 8vo.

VIII. D. WILLIAM YOUNG OTTLEY.

A Series of plates engraved after the paintings and sculptures of the most eminent masters of the Early Florentine School. London, 1826. fol. 54 plates.

VIII. E. WILLIAM YOUNG OTTLEY.

The Italian School of Design: being a series of fac-similes of original drawings, by the most eminent painters and sculptors of Italy, etc. London, 1823. fol. 84 plates.

VIII. F. WILLIAM YOUNG OTTLEY.

Fac-simile specimens of rare & curious Engravings by Old Masters. London, 1826. 4to. 100 plates with 36 pages of introduction and 20 pages catalogue.

Also under the title: A collection of fac-similes of scarce and curious prints by the Early Masters of the Italian, German, and Flemish schools, illustrative of the history of Engraving, from the invention of the Art by Maso Finiguerra in the middle of the fifteenth century. With introductory remarks and a catalogue of the plates, 1 vol.

The 2d vol. was to carry the History of Engraving to the end of the sixteenth century. Only 29 plates for this were finished, which, in later editions, have been added to the hundred of the first volume.

VIII. G.

Original Designs of the most Celebrated Masters of the Bolognese, Roman, Florentine, and Venetian Schools in his Majesty's Collection. London, 1812. fol. With 66 plates by Bartolozzi and others. Contains under a separate title: Imitations of original designs by Leonardo da Vinci. Published by John Chamberlaine. London, 1796. 17 plates.

IX. FLEMISH, OLDEST, AND RUBENS.

JAN VAN EYCK *pinx.* Or rather ROGIER VAN DER WEYDEN the elder.
The Adoration of the Magi. *Artist's proof.* . . . . . . Hess *sc.*

HANS MEMLING *pinx.* Or rather ROGIER VAN DER WEYDEN the elder.
St. Christopher. . . . . Strixner *lith.*

JAN VAN MABUSE *pinx.* [Jan Gossaert.]
Madonna in Trono, with Two Maidens. . . . . . Strixner *lith.*

QUENTIN MATSYS *pinx.* [Sometimes METSYS. "The Smith of Antwerp."]
The Misers. . . . . R. Earlom *sc.*

PIETER PAUL RUBENS *pinx.*
St. Michael expelling the Bad Angels. The larger composition. L. Vorsterman *sc.*
The same subject. The smaller composition. . . . . J. Neeffs *sc.*
The Brazen Serpent. . . . . S. à Bolswert *sc.*
The Angel bringing Food to Elijah. . . . . . . C. Lauwers *sc.*
Judith with the Head of Holofernes. . . . . . . A. Voet *sc.*
St. Anna teaching the Virgin to read. . . . . S. à Bolswert *sc.*
The Marriage of the Virgin. . . . . S. à Bolswert *sc.*
The Nativity, with only the Virgin and Joseph. . . S. à Bolswert *sc.*
The Adoration of the Shepherds. . . . . P. Pontius *sc.*
The Adoration of the Shepherds, with the shadows on the wall. *3d state.* "S. à Bolswert" *sc.*
The same picture, same plate. *1st state.* . . . "Witdoeck *sc. et exc.*"
The Adoration of the Magi, with two torches. . . L. Vorsterman *sc.*
The Presentation in the Temple. . . . . . . P. Pontius *sc.*
The Massacre of the Innocents. (On two plates.) . . P. Pontius *sc.*
The Return from Egypt. . . . . L. Vorsterman *sc.*
The Daughter of Herodias receiving the head of St. John. S. à Bolswert *sc.*
The Feast of Herodias; Salome places the head of St. John on the table. S. à Bolswert *sc.*
The Miraculous Draught of Fishes. (On 3 plates.) . S. à Bolswert *sc.*
The Feast of Simon, with Magdalen. . . . . . R. Earlom *sc.*

PIETER PAUL RUBENS *pinx., continued.*

The same. . . . . Natalis *sc.*
The Raising of Lazarus. . . . . B. à Bolswert *sc.*
Christ bearing the Cross. . . . . P. Pontius *sc.*
The Elevation of the Cross. (On 3 plates.) . . . . Witdoeck *sc.*
Christ crucified between Two Thieves, pierced in the side. B. à Bolswert *sc.*
The Descent from the Cross. *Proof.* . . . . . . V. Green *sc.*
The same. . . . . R. Earlom *sc.*
The same. *Proof.* . . . . Claessens *sc.*
The same. *Artist's proof.* . . . . Claessens *sc.*
Dead Christ "with a Capuchin." . . . . P. Pontius *sc.*
Christ at Emmaus. . . . . Witdoeck *sc.*
Maria, Mater Dei, Regina Coeli. . . . . S. à Bolswert *sc.*
Virgin and Child. . . . . Schiavonetti *sc.*
Holy Family with a Lamb. . . . . S. à Bolswert *sc.*
Madonna and Child, Angels offering Fruit. . . . . . A. Voet *sc.*
Altar Piece of the Chapel of the Tomb of Rubens : St. George, St. Jerome, and other Saints before the Madonna. . . . . . P. Pontius *sc.*
Mater Dolorosa. . . . . Leeuw *sc.*
The Assumption of the Virgin. (Square top.) . . . S. à Bolswert *sc.*
Christ and the Apostles. 14 plates. . . . . . . Ryckeman *sc.*
The Four (Latin) Fathers of the Church, sitting, whole figures. C. Galle *sc.*
The Four (Latin) Fathers of the Church, standing in a group, three quarters length figures. . . . . Van Dalen *sc.*
St. Ambrose refusing Theodosius admission to the Church. Jac. Schmutzer *sc.*
The same. *Proof.* . . . . Jac. Schmutzer *sc.*
Conversion of St. Bavon. . . . . F. Pilsen *sc.*
St. Francis receiving the Stigmata. . . . . . L. Vorsterman *sc.*
St. Francis Xavier, standing in prayer before a crucifix. S. à Bolswert *sc.*
St. Ildefonso receiving the Chasuble. . . . . . . Witdoeck *sc.*
The Martyrdom of St. Lawrence. . . . . . L. Vorsterman *sc.*
St. Martin dividing his Cloak. . . . . Th. Chambers *sc.*
St. Roch interceding for the Plague-stricken. . . . . P. Pontius *sc.*
The Martyrdom of St. Thomas. . . . . Jac. Neeffs *sc.*
The Coronation of St. Catherine. . . . . L. Zucchi *sc.*
St. Teresa interceding for the Souls in Purgatory. . S. à Bolswert *sc.*
St. Cecilia. . . . . Witdoeck *sc.*
The Last Judgment. . . . . C. Visscher *sc.*

IX. A. a.

Châsse de Sainte Ursule, par Jean Memling. Composé & lith. par Manche & Ghémar. Bruges, 1841. fol. With 15 lithographs.

IX. B. RUBENS, SNYDERS, JORDAENS, AND OTHERS.

RUBENS *pinx.*

Diogenes and Alexander. . . . . Q. Mark *sc.*

Thomyris causing the Head of Cyrus to be immersed in blood. P. Pontius *sc.*

Decius Mus devoting himself to the Gods of Death. Andr. and Jos. Schmutzer *sc.*

Mucius Scævola before Porsenna. . . . . . Jac. Schmutzer *sc.*

The Meeting between Ferdinand II., King of Hungary, and Ferdinand, Infant of Spain, previous to the Battle of Nördlingen. . Th. van Thulden *sc.*

Mars trampling Silenus under foot, and turning his back to Venus, is crowned by Victory, in spite of Envy. . . . . Tanjé *sc.*

Neptune quelling the Storm: "Quos ego." . . . . . Daullé *sc.*

The same. *Proof.* . . . . Daullé *sc.*

The Judgment of Paris. . . . . Moitte *sc.*

The Triumph of Silenus. . . . . Giov. Folo *sc.*

Bacchus led by a Satyr and a Faun, and preceded by a Panther and two Bacchantes. . . . . Suyderhoef *sc.*

Venus detaining Adonis from the Chase. . . . . . Tassaert *sc.*

The Nuptials of Thetis and Peleus. . Fr. van den Wyngaerde *sc.*

Diana returning from the Chase, followed by three Nymphs, preceded by two Satyrs carrying fruit, and a third person. . . . . S. à Bolswert *sc.*

Meleager and Atalanta, Boar-hunt. *Proof.* . . . . Earlom *sc.*

Meleager and Atalanta with the Boar's head. . . . . Bloemaert *sc.*

Meleager and Atalanta, killing the Caledonian Boar. Theod. van Kessel *sc.*

A Lion-hunt. . . . . S. à Bolswert *sc.*

A Wolf-hunt. . . . . P. Soutman *sc.*

A Hunt of the Crocodile and Hippopotamus. . . . . P. Soutman *sc.*

A Wild Boar at Bay with three Dogs. *Proof.* . . . Lasinio figlio *sc.*

Landscape, with a Lion and two Tigers, in the background a chase after a lion. . . . . Riedinger *sc.*

A Tigress, in a rocky landscape, suckling her three cubs. Repetition of one of the figures of the preceding picture. . . . . . N. Rhein *sc.*

Lions at play. . . . . Wm. Walker *sc.*

Philemon and Baucis, great landscape. . . . . . S. à Bolswert *sc.*

Dance of Peasants, landscape. . . . . S. à Bolswert *sc.*

The Watering-place, landscape. . . . . . . J. Browne *sc.*

"Le Jardin d'Amour." . . . . Lempereur *sc.*

RUBENS *pinx., continued.*

The same. . . . . Hanfstängl *lith.*

P. Rubens, at Windsor Castle. . . . . . . P. Pontius *sc.*

P. Another Portrait of Rubens, in the Duke of Aremberg's collection. Claessens *sc.*

P. Rubens and his Wife. *Proof.* . . . . Ch. Hess *sc.*

P. Elizabeth or Isabella Brandt, Rubens's first Wife. . Stölzel *sc.*

P. Rubens and his Wife carrying Game and Fruit. *Proof.* Summerfield *sc.*

P. Helena Forman, second Wife of Rubens, wrapped in a fur pelisse. Gleditsch *sc.*

P. Two Sons of Rubens. Dresden Gallery. *Proof.* . . Daullé *sc.*

P. The same. Lichtenstein Gallery, Vienna. . . . Pichler *sc.*

P. A Son of Rubens, sitting in a baby's chair. Salvador Carmona *sc.*

P. Rubens's Son and Nurse. . . . . R. Earlom *sc.*

P. Gasp. Gusman Count Olivarez, after Velazquez. . . P. Pontius *sc.*

P. Philip IV. of Spain. . . . . P. Pontius *sc.*

P. Elizabeth of Bourbon, Queen of Philip IV. . . . P. Pontius *sc.*

P. Le Chapeau de Paille. *Proof.* . . . . . Cornillet *sc.*

P. Paracelsus. . . . . Van Sompel *sc.*

P. Les Quatre Philosophes, the portraits of Hugo Grotius, Justus Lipsius, Philip Rubens and P. P. Rubens. . . . . . . Morel *sc.*

P. Francesco de' Medici, Grand Duke of Tuscany, and Joanna of Austria, Grand Duchess of Tuscany. Edelinck *sc.* *See* Portf. XVI. D.

A "Spanish Officer." . . . . Fittler *sc.*

Portrait of a Spanish gentleman with short hair and bushy beard, wearing a full ruffle. . . . . Daullé *sc.*

FRANS SNYDERS *pinx.*

Wild Boar-hunt. . . . . Zaal *sc.*

The Game Market. . . . . Earlom *sc.*

The Fish Market. . . . . Earlom *sc.*

The Herb Market. . . . . Earlom *sc.*

The Fruit Market. . . . . Earlom *sc.*

MARTIN PEPYN *pinx.*

Susanna. . . . . P. de Balliu *sc.*

GERARD SEGHERS *pinx.* [The most correct spelling is Zegers.]

The Annunciation. . . . . S. à Bolswert *sc.*

CORNELIS SCHUT *pinx.*

Madonna and Child with St. John. . . . . . . Witdoeck *sc.*

JACOB JORDAENS *pinx.*

The Crucifixion. . . . . S. à Bolswert *sc.*

JACOB JORDAENS *pinx., continued.*

The Twelfth Night Feast, "Le roi boit." *Proof.* . E. G. Krüger *sc.*
The Family Concert. . . . . S. à Bolswert *sc.*
Fool with a Cat. . . . . Voet *sc.*
Argus watching Io and Mercury. . . . . . S. à Bolswert *sc.*

THEODORUS ROMBOUTS *pinx.*

Abraham offering up Isaac. . . . . . . S. à Bolswert *sc.*

ERASMUS QUELLINUS *pinx.*

The Beheading of St. John the Baptist. . . . Vorsterman *sc.*

IX. C. VAN DYCK.

ANTONI VAN DYCK *pinx.*

Holy Family. *Aq. fort.* . . . . Van Dyck *fec.*
Christ crowned with Thorns. . . . . . . S. à Bolswert *sc.*
Infant Christ sleeping. Strange *sc.* *See* Portfolio XXIX.
The Elevation of the Cross. . . . . S. à Bolswert *sc.*
The Crucifixion; "Christ à l'Éponge." . . . . S. à Bolswert *sc.*
Pietà. . . . . Vorsterman *sc.*
St. Jerome penitent. . . . . Beauvais *sc.*
The Virgin, with the Child standing. . . . . . . P. Pontius *sc.*
Madonna nursing the Child. . . . . Massard *sc.*
St. Rosalia crowned by the Infant Saviour. . . . . Pontius *sc.*
Charity, a woman with three children. . . . . . Caukerken *sc.*
Child playing with Love. . . . . Daullé *sc.*
Time clipping the Wings of Love. Mezzotint. . . . Mc Ardell *sc.*
P. Van Dyck. *Proof.* . . . . Mandel *sc.*
P. Van Dyck's Wife and Child as Madonna. . . . Bartolozzi *sc.*
P. Rubens and Van Dyck, on one plate. . . . . . P. Pontius *sc.*
P. Van Dyck and "Marshal Turenne," in reality Van Dyck and the Earl of Bristol. . . . . Selma *sc.*
P. P. P. Rubens. . . . . J. de Visscher *sc.*
P. P. P. Rubens, looking out of a window. . . . W. Woollett *sc.*
P. Helena Forman, Rubens's second Wife. . . . Th. Chambers *sc.*
P. "David Ryckaert" or "a Transylvanian." . . . . . Rasp *sc.*
P. Charles I., in his royal robes. Strange *sc.* *See* Portfolio XXIX.
P. Another portrait of the same with his equerry, the Marquis of Hamilton. Strange *sc.* *See* Portfolio XXIX.
P. The same. *Proof before any letters.* Strange *sc.* *See* Portfolio XXIX.
P The Children of Charles I. Strange *sc.* *See* Portfolio XXIX.
P. The Children of Charles I., with a large dog. . . . Cooper *sc.*
P. Charles I. *Artist's proof.* . . . . Mandel *sc.*
P. Charles I. and his Queen Henrietta Maria, sitting, with their children. *Artist's proof.* . . . . J. B. Massard *sc.*

ANTONI VAN DYCK *pinx.*, *continued.*

P. Charles I., three faces, for Bernini's bust. . . . . Sharp *sc.*

P. Charles I. on horseback, accompanied by his Master of the Horse. Baron *sc.*

P. Henry Danvers, Earl of Danby. . . . . . . V. Green *sc.*

P. Earl and Countess Derby. *Proof.* . . . Robinson *sc.*

P. Lord Chief Baron Wandesford. . . . . James Watson *sc.*

P. Francisco de Moncada, on horseback. . . . R. Morghen *sc.*

P. The same, bust. . . . . Suyderhoef *sc.*

P. The same, bust. Vorsterman *sc.* *See* Portfolio IX. D.

P. Francis Thomas of Savoy, Prince Carignan, three quarters length. P. Pontius *sc.*

P. Another portrait of the same, half length. P. Pontius *sc.* *See* Van Dyck's *Iconographia*, Portf. IX. D.

P. Henry Prince of Orange, Count of Nassau. . . P. Pontius *sc.*

P. Edward Sackville, Earl of Dorset. . . . . . Vertue *sc.*

P. Jacques Callot. . . . . Esme de Boulonois *sc.*

Portrait of a man in armor, with a baton in his hand, and round the other arm a scarf. Sometimes, very inappropriately, called "Cromwell." Rasp *sc.*

The same. *Proof.* . . . . Rasp *sc.*

IX. D. VAN DYCK'S ICONOGRAPHIA, PORTRAITS.

ETCHED BY VAN DYCK.

Breughel, Jan.

Breughel, Pieter.

Cornelissen, Antoni, finished by Vorsterman.

Dyck, Antoni van, finished by Neeffs.

Erasmus, Desiderius.

Franck, Frans.

Momper, Jodocus de.

Noort, Adam van.

Pontius, Paul.

Snellinx, Jan.

The same, 2d plate, finished by Pieter de Jode the younger.

Snyders, Frans, finished by Neeffs.

Suttermans, Justus.

Triest, D. Antoni, Bishop of Ghent, finished by Jode.

Vorsterman, Lucas.

Vos, Willem de, finished by Bolswert.

Vos, Paul de, finished by Bolswert.

Wael, Jan de.

VAN DYCK *pinx., continued.*

Wouwer, Jan van den, finished by Pontius.

Mirabelle, Marquis de. . . . . Blooteling *sc.*
Brouwer, Adriaan. . . . . S. à Bolswert *sc.*
Ertvelt, Andreas van. . . . . S. à Bolswert *sc.*
Lipsius, Justus. . . . . S. à Bolswert *sc.*
Pepyn, Martin. . . . . S. à Bolswert *sc.*
Lamen, Christoffel van der. . . . . . . Pieter Clouwet *sc.*
Rogiers, Theodor. . . . . Pieter Clouwet *sc.*
Scribanus, Carolus. . . . . Pieter Clouwet *sc.*
Mierevelt, Michel. . . . . W. J. Delff *sc.*
The same. 1*st state, with Martin van den Enden's address.* Hondius *sc.*
Wolfaerts, Artus. . . . . Corn. Galle the elder *sc.*
Meyssens, Jan. . . . . Corn. Galle the younger *sc.*
Taie, Chevalier Engelbert. . . . . . Corn. Galle the younger *sc.*
Opstal, Antoni van. . . . . Rob. Gaywood *sc.*
Franck, Frans, junior. . . . . W. Hondius *sc.*
Hondius, Willem. . . . . W. Hondius *sc.*
Halmal, Paul. . . . . Pieter de Jode the younger *sc.*
The same. *With Martin van den Enden's address.*
Pieter de Jode the younger *sc.*
Jordaens, Jacob. . . . . . . Pieter de Jode the younger *sc.*
Liberti, Hendrik. . . . . . . Pieter de Jode the younger *sc.*
Nole, Andreas Colyns de. . . . Pieter de Jode the younger *sc.*
Poelenburg, Cornelis. . . . . Pieter de Jode the younger *sc.*
Simons, Quintin. . . . . . . Pieter de Jode the younger *sc.*
Tulden, Diodor van. . . . . Pieter de Jode the younger *sc.*
Wallenstein. . . . . Pieter de Jode the younger *sc.*
Blancatcio, Fra J. Lelio. . . . . Nic. Lauwers *sc.*
Aremberg, Mary, Countess of. . . . . . Adriaan Lommelin *sc.*
Le Blon, Michel. . . . . Th. Matham *sc.*
Ryckaert, Martin. . . . . Neeffs *sc.*
Aremberg, Mary, Countess of. . . . . P. Pontius *sc.*
Bazan, Don Alvaro. . . . . P. Pontius *sc.*
Breuck, Jacob de. . . . . P. Pontius *sc.*
The same. 1*st state.* . . . . P. Pontius *sc.*
Carignan, Francis Thomas of Savoy, Prince of. . . . P. Pontius *sc.*
Colonna, Don Carlo. . . . . P. Pontius *sc.*
Geest, Cornelis van der. . . . . P. Pontius *sc.*
Gerbier, Balthasar. . . . . P. Pontius *sc.*

VAN DYCK *pinx.*, *continued.*

Gustavus Adolphus, King of Sweden. . . . . . P. Pontius *sc.*
Guzman, Don Diego Phelipe de, Marquis de Leganes. . P. Pontius *sc.*
Honthorst, Gerard. . . . . P. Pontius *sc.*
Huygens, Constantin. . . . . P. Pontius *sc.*
Medici, Maria de'. . . . . P. Pontius *sc.*
Miraeus, Aubertus. (Aubert Le Mire.) . . . . P. Pontius *sc.*
Mytens, Daniel. . . . . P. Pontius *sc.*
Nassau-Siegen, John, Count of. . . . . . . P. Pontius *sc.*
Palamedes, the painter Stevens, called. . . . . P. Pontius *sc.*
Pontius, or du Pont, Paulus. . . . . P. Pontius *sc.*
Ravestein, Jan van. . . . . P. Pontius *sc.*
The same. *With* "G. H." . . . . P. Pontius *sc.*
Rockox, Nicolas. 8*th state.* . . . . P. Pontius *sc.*
The same. 4*th state.* . . . . P. Pontius *sc.*
Rombouts, Theodorus. . . . . P. Pontius *sc.*
Rubens. . . . . P. Pontius *sc.*
Scaglia, Cæsar Alexander. . . . . P. Pontius *sc.*
Segers (Seghers, or Zegers), Gerard. . . . . . P. Pontius *sc.*
Steenwyck, Hendrik. . . . . P. Pontius *sc.*
Vanloon, Theodorus. . . . . P. Pontius *sc.*
The same. *With* "G. H." . . . . P. Pontius *sc.*
Vos, Simon de. . . . . P. Pontius *sc.*
Wildens, Jan. . . . . P. Pontius *sc.*
Snayers, Pieter. . . . . Stock *sc.*
Booys, Hendrik du. . . . . Corn. Vischer *sc.*
Sieveri, Helena Eleonora de, wife of H. du Booys. . Corn. Vischer *sc.*
Digby, Sir Kenelm. . . . . Robert van Voerst *sc.*
Jones, Inigo. . . . . Robert van Voerst *sc.*
Pembroke, Philip Herbert, Earl of. . . . . Robert van Voerst *sc.*
Voerst, Robert van. . . . . Robert van Voerst *sc.*
Vouet, Simon. . . . . Robert van Voerst *sc.*
Arundel, Thomas Howard, Earl of. . . . . . Vorsterman *sc.*
Bran, Hieronymus de. . . . . Vorsterman *sc.*

The plate is without Van Dyck's name. The picture is more correctly attributed to Lievens.

Callot, Jacques. . . . . Vorsterman *sc.*
Coeberger, Wenzel. . . . . Vorsterman *sc.*
Dyck, Sir Anthony van. . . . . Vorsterman *sc.*
Eynden, Hubert van den. . . . . Vorsterman *sc.*
Gentileschi, Orazio Lomi. . . . . Vorsterman *sc.*
Jode, Pieter de, the elder. . . . . Vorsterman *sc.*

VAN DYCK *pinx.*, *continued.*

Lievens, Jan. . . . . Vorsterman *sc.*
Moncada, Francisco de. . . . . Vorsterman *sc.*
Peiresc, Nicolas Claude Fabrice de. . . . . . Vorsterman *sc.*
Rockox, Nicolas. . . . . Vorsterman *sc.*
Sachtleven, Cornelis. . . . . Vorsterman *sc.*
Schut, Cornelis. . . . . Vorsterman *sc.*
Spinola, Don Ambrosio. . . . . Vorsterman *sc.*
Stevens, Pieter. . . . . Vorsterman *sc.*
Vos, Cornelis de. . . . . Vorsterman *sc.*

X. A. DUTCH, REMBRANDT AND OTHERS.

LEONARD BRAMER *pinx.*

Pyramus and Thisbe. . . . . Canot *sc.*

THEODORUS DE KEYSER *pinx.*

The Four Burgomasters of Amsterdam. . . . . Suyderhoef *sc.*
The same. *Very fine impression.* . . . . . Suyderhoef *sc.*

PALAMEDES *pinx.* [Antoni Stevens, called Palamedes.]

Le Festin Espagnol. . . . . Lempereur *sc.*

REMBRANDT *pinx.* [Harmens Rembrandt Gerritszoon, called van Ryn from the canal of the Rhine, on which was his father's mill.]

Jacob blessing the Sons of Joseph. *Proof.* . . . . Claessens *sc.*
The Sacrifice of Manoah. . . . . Houbraken *sc.*
The Feast of Ahasuerus. . . . . Hanfstängl *lith.*
The same. . . . . Riedel *sc.*
The Deposition from the Cross. Copy of Rembrandt's etching. Novelli *sc.*
The Good Samaritan. *Proof.* . . . . Longhi *sc.*
"The Night-Watch." *Proof.* . . . . Claessens *sc.*
A Firelight landscape. . . . . J. Wood *sc.*
"Rembrandt's Mill." Copy of Rembrandt's etching. . . Novelli *sc.*
The Syndics of the Halle aux Draps. . . . . . J. de Frey *sc.*
Nicol. Tulp, giving a lecture on Anatomy. . . . . J. de Frey *sc.*
P. Rembrandt, when about 56 years of age. *Proof.* . Earlom *sc.*
P. Rembrandt's Daughter. . . . . Hanfstängl *lith.*
P. "Renier Ansloo, and his Wife," more correctly his mother. Jos. Boydell *sc.*
P. The Gold-weigher. Copy of Rembrandt's etching. Wm. Baillie *sc.*
P. Coppenol, the writing-master. Copy of Rembrandt's etching. Basan *sc.*
P. Another portrait of the same. . . . . . . Fillœuil *sc.*
P. "Portrait de Rembrandt." *Open letters.* . . . . Claessens *sc.*

REMBRANDT *pinx., continued.*

A Flemish Gentleman. . . . . . . Giuseppe Canale *sc.*

An Old Man with a Cane. . . . . Tanjé *sc.*

"A Warrior," an officer with a sword of state. *Proof.* . Wm. Pether *sc.*

The Standard-bearer. *Proof.* . . . . Wm. Pether *sc.*

A Jewish Rabbi. *Proof.* . . . . Wm. Pether *sc.*

The Duke Adolphus of Guelders threatening his imprisoned Father. Berger *sc.*

The same picture. Schmidt *sc. aq. fort.* *See* Portfolio XXVIII.

A Philosopher in Contemplation. . . . . Longhi et Caronni *sc.*

A Philosopher in Meditation. . . . . . Longhi et Caronni *sc.*

JAN ASSELYN *pinx.* [Nicknamed Crabatje.]

"Le Cavalier." *Open letters.* . . . . Claessens *sc.*

FERDINAND BOL *pinx.*

Joseph presenting his Father to Pharaoh. . . . . E. G. Krüger *sc.*

Rest on the Flight to Egypt. . . . . Hanfstängl *lith.*

P. Ferdinand Bol. . . . . A. Bartsch *sc.*

ADRIAAN VAN OSTADE *pinx.*

The Smoker. *Artist's proof.* . . . . Claessens *sc.*

The Fishmonger. . . . . Claessens *sc.*

A Man with a Jug and a Pipe. . . . . . . Suyderhoef *sc.*

The Big Broom. . . . . Suyderhoef *sc.*

Jan de Moff. . . . . Suyderhoef *sc.*

The Great Knife-fight, 8 figures. . . . . . Suyderhoef *sc.*

Le Café Hollandais. . . . . Beauvarlet *sc.*

Les Patineurs. . . . . C. Visscher *sc.*

The Itinerant Musicians. . . . . C. Visscher *sc.*

The Dance in the Barn. . . . . Jan de Visscher *sc.*

Three Men smoking and drinking, and a Woman. . Jan de Visscher *sc.*

M. SORG *pinx.* [Hendrik Martens Zorg, or Sorg.]

P. Simon Episcopius. . . . . Piet. van Gunst *sc.*

GERARD DOW *pinx.* [Also spelled Dov, Dou, and Douw.]

A Hermit. . . . . Wildt *lith.*

La Femme hydropique. *Proof.* . . . . Claessens *sc.*

The Quack Doctor. *Proof.* . . . . Ch. Hess *sc.*

La Tante de Gérard Dow. . . . . Hubert *sc.*

St. John the Baptist beheaded. *Proof.* . . . . . . Longhi *sc.*
In reality painted by Gerard Honthorst.

An Old Woman eating from an iron pot on her knee. Without name of engraver, or any other inscription.

BARTHOLOMEUS VAN DER HELST *pinx.*

The Distribution of Prizes for Archery. *Artist's proof.* . . . Ulmer *sc.*

GERARD TERBURG *pinx.* [Ter Borch.]

The Trumpeter. . . . . Hanfstängl *lith.*

The Knife-fight (the smaller), 4 figures. . . . . . Suyderhoef *sc.*

The Peace of Münster. . . . . Suyderhoef *sc.*

METZU *pinx.* [Gabriel Metzu or Metsu.]

The Lace-maker. . . . . Hanfstängl *lith.*

The Game-seller. . . . . Hanfstängl *lith.*

THOMAS WYCK *pinx.*

Le Chimiste. *First impression with the inscription* "d'après le Tableau d'Eckhout." . . . . . . Hutin et Camerata *sc.*

CORNELIS (DE) VISSCHER *pinx.*

The Pancake-woman. . . . . C. Visscher *sc.*

The Rat-catcher. . . . . C. Visscher *sc.*

JAN VAN STEEN *pinx.*

Le Villageois en belle Humeur. *Open letter proof.* . . . Claessens *sc.*

CASPAR NETSCHER *pinx.*

The Quack Doctor. . . . . Folkema *sc.*

P. A gentleman with a lute accompanying a lady singing at an open window. Called Netscher and his Wife. . . . . E. G. Krüger *sc.*

PIETER DE HOOGHE *pinx.*

A Girl reading at the Window. . . . . . . Hanfstängl *lith.*

GODEFRIED SCHALKEN *pinx.*

"La Vieille inquiète," a woman with a lighted candle. . De Mautort *sc.*

EGBERT VAN HEEMSKIRK *pinx.*

A Man and Woman drinking. . . . . John Smith *sc.*

ADRIAAN VAN DER WERFF *pinx.*

Adam and Eve weeping over Abel. . . . . . . Porporati *sc.*

Dismissal of Hagar and Ishmael. . . . . Jentzen *lith.*

Bathsheba brings Abishai to David. *Proof.* . . . . Earlom *sc.*

The Judgment of Paris. *Proof.* . . . . M. Blot *sc.*

P. Lesley, Bishop of Rosse. . . . . . Piet. van Gunst *sc.*

P. Maurice, Prince of Orange. . . . . G. Valck *sc.*

P. Queen Catharine of Aragon. . . . . . Vermeulen *sc.*

P. Queen Anne Boleyn. . . . . Vermeulen *sc.*

CORNELIS DUSART *pinx.*

The Village Barber. . . . . J. Gole *sc.*

The Jocund Peasants. Woollett *sc.* *See* Portf. XV. A.

The Merry Cottagers. Woollett *sc.* *See* Portf. XV. A.

JAN VAN HUYSUM *pinx.*

A Flower Piece. *Proof.* . . . . Earlom *sc.*

JAN VAN HUYSUM *pinx., continued.*

A Fruit Piece. *Proof.* . . . . Earlom *sc.*

FRANS VAN MIERIS *pinx.*

The Trumpeter in the Guard-room. . . . . . Hanfstängl *lith.*

"De wyn is een spotter." A young Woman gone to Sleep over her Wine. Bary *sc.*

P. Mieris and his Wife in his Studio. . . . . Hanfstängl *lith.*

"A. VAN BLOMMEN" *pinx.* P. Jan van Somers, the painter. Mezzotinto. Arend van Halen ("Aquila") *sc.*

The same. The drawing in red chalk on parchment.

CORNELIS TROOST *pinx.*

Amsterdam Fair. . . . . Houbraken *sc.*

ADRIAAN DE LELIE *pinx.*

Musiciens de Village. *Open letter proof.* . . . . . Claessens *sc.*

X. A. a.

Rembrandt and his works, by John Burnet. London, 1849. Edition in folio; with 19 plates.

X. B. THE BREUGHELS, SPRANGER, GOLTZIUS, TENIERS, WOUWERMANS, BERGHEM, RUYSDAEL, AND OTHERS.

LAMBERTUS SUAVIUS *pinx.* [Lambert Susterman, or Suterman.]

St. Peter and St. John healing the Cripple. . . . . L. Suavius *sc.*

PIETER BREUGHEL [or BRUEGHEL] SEN. *pinx.*

Landscape with grotesque devilry: "Patientia est malorum — perlatio." P. Miricenus *sc.*

Fight of Peasants at Cards. . . . . Vorsterman *sc.*

DAVID PHILIPSZ. VINCKBOONS [or VINCKENBOOMS] *pinx.*

Time and Death slaying Men and Beasts. 1*st state.* B. à Bolswert *sc.*

The same. 2*d state.* . . . . B. à Bolswert *sc.*

BARTHOLOMEUS SPRANGER *pinx.*

Apotheosis of the Fine Arts. . . . . Jan Muller *sc.*

Hercules spinning. . . . . Egidius Sadeler *sc.*

P. Pieter Breughel sen. . . . . Egidius Sadeler *sc.*

pinx. et sc.

Christ teaching the Doctors.

HENDRIK STEENWYCK *pinx.*

Interior of a Church. . . . . Vandermeer *sc.*

HENDRIK GOLTZIUS *pinx.*

Mars and Venus surprised. . . . . . . H. Goltzius *sc.*
The Adoration of the Magi. . . . . . . H. Goltzius *sc.*
"Goltzius's Six Masterpieces," viz. :—
The Annunciation, in Raphael's style. . . . . . H. Goltzius *sc.*
The Visitation, in Parmegianino's style. . . . . . H. Goltzius *sc.*
The Adoration of the Shepherds, in Bassano's style. . H. Goltzius *sc.*
The Circumcision, in Dürer's style. . . . . . H. Goltzius *sc.*
The Adoration of the Magi, in Lukas van Leyden's style. H. Goltzius *sc.*
The Holy Family, in Baroccio's style. . . . . . H. Goltzius *sc.*
𝔓. H. Goltzius. . . . . H. Goltzius *sc.*
𝔓. "The Dog of Goltzius," with the Son of Dirk de Vries. H. Goltzius *sc.*

H. GOLTZIUS *del.*

The Farnese Hercules. . . . . H. Goltzius *sc.*
Emperor Commodus, as Hercules. . . . . . H. Goltzius *sc.*
Apollo Pythius. . . . . H. Goltzius *sc.*
𝔓. Coorenhert, Dirk Volckhertsz. H. Goltzius *sc.* *See* Portraits, Portfolio XVI. I.
𝔓. N. de la Faille. *Proof.* . . . . H. Goltzius *sc.*
St. Peter. Engraved by an anonymous disciple of Goltzius.
St. Paul. Engraved by an anonymous disciple of Goltzius.

PALMA GIOVANE *pinx.* St. Jerome in Penitence. H. Goltzius *sc.* *See* Portfolio IV. B.

MARTIN VAN HEEMSKIRK *pinx.* [Martin van Veen.]

𝔓. Zurenus. H. Goltzius *sc.* *See* Portfolio XVI. A.

JAN BREUGHEL *pinx.* [Brueghel.]

Adam and Eve in Paradise. *Proof.* . . . Heath and Middiman *sc.*

ABRAHAM BLOEMAERT *pinx.*

The Golden Age. . . . . Nic. de Bruyn *sc.*
The same. . . . . J. C. Visscher *sc.*
Christ appearing to St. Ignatius. . . . . . Corn. Bloemaert *sc.*

ALBERT CUYP *pinx.*

Evening. *Proof.* . . . . Ed. Goodall *sc.*

DAVID TENIERS *pinx.* [David Teniers the father, and David Teniers the son.]

The Rich Man and Lazarus. . . . . Mlle. Riollet *sc.*
The Temptation of St. Anthony. . . . . Le Bas *sc.*
Latona avenged. . . . . Le Mire *sc.*
The Alchymist. . . . . Hanfstängl *lith.*
The Quack Doctor. . . . . Tardieu *sc.*
The Village Surgeon. . . . . T. Major *sc.*
The same, similar composition. . . . . Daullé *sc.*
The Card-players. *Proof.* . . . . H. Guttenberg *sc.*

DAVID TENIERS *pinx., continued.*

Départ pour le Sabat. . . . . H. Guttenberg *sc.*
Arrivée au Sabat. . . . . J. J. Aliamet *sc.*
A Flemish Kitchen. . . . . J. B. Michel *sc.*
A Village Merry-making. . . . . Weisbrodt *sc. aq. f.*
La Fête du Hamau. . . . . F. Godefroy *sc.*
Les Amusemens de Brabant. . . . . F. Godefroy *sc.*
View near Antwerp. . . . . Le Bas *sc.*
Grand Village Festival. . . . . Major *sc.*
Dutch Pastime. *Proof.* . . . . J. Collyer *sc.*

JAN and ANDRIES BOTH *pinx.*

Banditti Prisoners, landscape. . . . . J. Browne *sc.*
Philip baptizing the Eunuch, landscape. . . . . . J. Browne *sc.*
Morning, landscape. . . . . . . W. Byrne et J. Schumann *sc.*
Evening, landscape. . . . . . . W. Byrne et Bartolozzi *sc.*

PIETER DE LAER *pinx.*

Le Coche volé. . . . . C. Visscher *sc.*
Le Coup de Pistolet. . . . . C. Visscher *sc.*
Le Four à Briques. . . . . C. Visscher *sc.*

AART VAN DER NEER *pinx.*

Vue de Boom. . . . . J. J. Aliamet *sc.*

PHILIPS WOUWERMANS *pinx.*

Le Coup de Pistolet. . . . . J. Visscher *sc.*
The Riding-Ground. . . . . W. Kobell *sc.*
Les Voitures. . . . . A. Tischler *sc.*
Retard de Chasse. . . . . A. Tischler *sc.*
Départ pour la Chasse à l'Oiseau. . . . . Moyreau *sc.*
Grande Chasse au Cerf. . . . . Moyreau *sc.*
La Fontaine de Bacchus. . . . . Moyreau *sc.*
Le Présent de Chasseur. . . . . Moyreau *sc.*
La petite Foire aux Chevaux. . . . . Moyreau *sc.*
Le Défilé d'Equipages. . . . . Moyreau *sc.*
Gardes de Cavalerie. . . . . Moyreau *sc.*
Les Marchands forains. . . . . Moyreau *sc.*
Return from Market. Strange *sc.* *See* Portfolio XXIX.

NICLAAS BERGHEM *pinx.* [Berchem; his family name was Klaasze.]

Landscape, Summer. . . . . J. Visscher *sc.*

BERGHEM *del.*

The Seamstress. . . . . J. Visscher *sc.*

BERGHEM *pinx.*

The Spinster. . . . . J. Visscher *sc.*

Berghem *pinx., continued.*

View of the Environs of Siena. *Proof.* . . . Weisbrodt *sc. aq. f.*
The same. . . . . Finished by Le Bas.
Boors' Dance in a Barn. . . . . J. Visscher *sc.*
The Ford. Landscape in the Dresden Gallery. . . J. J. Aliamet *sc.*

Paul Potter *pinx.*

"The Cowherd." The famous Young Bull. . . . Facius *sc.*

Ludolph Backhuysen *pinx.*

Vent doux. *Proof.* . . . . Canot *sc.*
Le Coup de Vent. . . . . Daudet *sc.*

Willem van de Velde *pinx.*

Vent frais. *Proof.* . . . . Canot *sc.*

Jan van der Heyden *pinx.*

Village on a Canal. . . . . Daudet *sc.*

Jacob Ruysdael *pinx.*

The Stag-hunt. . . . . Zingg *sc.*
A Waterfall. *Proof.* . . . . S. Smith *sc.*
Another Waterfall. *Proof.* . . . . Haldenwang *sc.*
View of the Coast of Scheveningen. . . . . . Le Bas *sc.*
Wood near the Hague. . . . . Weisbrodt et Le Bas *sc.*
Château de Ryswick. . . . . Bacheley *sc.*
Der Abend. . . . . Frenzel *sc.*
An old Castellated Building, on the bank of a canal. P. Vischer *sc. aq. f.*
A Watermill, with a Dwelling adjoining. . . . J. Mathieu *sc. aq. f.*

The following engravings are from pictures in the Dresden Gallery:—

The Cemetery. . . . . Primavesi *sc. aq. f.*
The same. . . . . Bruder *sc. aq. f.*
The Cloister. . . . . Bruder *sc. aq. f.*
A Waterfall, with a Rock in the foreground. . . . Rothe *sc. aq. f.*
A Cascade, with a solitary Fir in the foreground. . Bruder *sc. aq. f.*
A Bridge. . . . . Bruder *sc. aq. f.*
A Cart driven through a Swamp. . . . . . Bruder *sc. aq. f.*
A Forest, with a Road in the middle. . . . . Bruder *sc. aq. f.*

XI. GERMAN.

Lucas Cranach *pinx.* [The family name was Sunder.]

The Baptism of Christ. *Woodcut.* . . . . . . L. Cranach *sc.*
The Woman taken in Adultery. . . . . . . C. Mayer *sc.*

Albrecht Dürer *pinx.*

The Rhinoceros. *Woodcut.* . . . . A. Dürer *sc.*
The Entombment. . . . . Willem de Passe *sc.*

ALBRECHT DÜRER *pinx.*, *continued.*

P. Albrecht Dürer. *Proof.* . . . . Forster *sc.*
P. The same. *Artist's proof.* . . . . Forster *sc.*

CHRISTOPH AMBERGER *pinx.*

Herodias's Daughter with the Head of St. John. . . . Prenner *sc.*

HANS HOLBEIN (the younger) *pinx.*

The Madonna with the Meyer Family. *Proof.* . . . . Steinla *sc.*
The Virgin and Child. . . . . H. Hondius sen. *sc.*
Another Virgin and Child. . . . . Agricola *sc.*
The "Ship Great Henry." . . . . Canot *sc.*
The Virgin praying. . . . . Leybold *sc.*
P. Hans Holbein. . . . . Fried. Weber *sc.*
P. Thomas Morett, jeweller to Henry VIII. *Proof.* . Sichling *sc.*
P. The same engraved as the portrait of Duke Sforza. . Folkema *sc.*
P. Erasmus. . . . . Vorsterman *sc.*

HANS HOBLEIN *del. et inc. in lign.*

P. Erasmus with the Terminus.
The same. Copy by Chodowiecki. *See* Portfolio XXXII.

ADAM ELSHEIMER *pinx.*

The Angel and Tobit with the Fish, Landscape. . . W. Angus *sc.*
The Flight into Egypt. Marco Pitteri *sc.* *See* Portfolio XXXII.

JOHANN ROTTENHAMMER *pinx.*

The Adoration of the Shepherds. . . . . . Lucas Kilian *sc.*

THEODOR DE BRY *del.*

Pride and Folly. . . . . Th. de Bry *sc.*

JOHANN ULRICH KRAUS *del.*

The Interior of St. Peter's at the Jubilee in 1700. 1*st state or plate.* J. U. Kraus *sc.*
The same. 2*d state or plate.* . . . . . . J. U. Kraus *sc.*

PIETER DE WITTE (CANDIDO) *pinx.*

4 plates. The Four Seasons. . . . . Amling *sc.*

JOHANN DANIEL HERZ *pinx.*

The Adoration of The Shepherds. . . . . . . J. D. Herz *sc.*

ANTONIO CANALE *del.*

View of Pietra della Valle. . . . . A. Canale *sc.*

BERNARDO BELLOTTI, called CANALETTO, *pinx.*

The Bridge of Dresden. . . . . Canaletto *sc.*
View of the New Market of Dresden. . . . . . Canaletto *sc.*

DIETRICH *pinx.* [Christian Wilhelm Ernst Dietrich ; sometimes Dietrici.]

Philip baptizing the Eunuch. . . . . . . A. Bartsch *sc.*

DIETRICH *pinx.*, *continued.*

Le Mage, landscape, and

Le Mage parmi les Pasteurs, landscape. Darnstedt *sc.* *See* Portfolio XV. B.

RAPHAEL MENGS *pinx.*

The Nativity. . . . . R. Morghen *sc.*

DANIEL CHODOWIECKI *del.*

Wilhelm Tell. . . . . Chodowiecki *sc.*

FRIEDRICH HEINRICH FÜGER *pinx.*

Boy with a Palette. . . . . A. Bartsch *sc.*

JOHANN HEINRICH RAMBERG *pinx.*

The Exhibition of the Royal Academy in 1787. . . . Martini *sc.*

FRANZ SMUGLIEWICZ *del.*

The Aldobrandini Marriage, from the Antique. . . Ottaviani *sc.*

ANGELO QUAGLIO *del.*

The Cathedral of Cologne. *Artist's proof.* . . . Darnstedt *sc.*

GÜNTHER *del.*

The Cathedral of Strassburg. . . . . . . Oberthür *sc.*

XI. a.

Die Gemälde des Michael Wohlgemuth in der Frauenkirche zu Zwickau, von J. G. von Quandt. Dresden and Leipzig, 1839. 4to. With 8 lithographs.

XI. b. ALBRECHT DÜRER.

The Life of the Virgin. Woodcuts, 20 pieces.

XI. c. PETER VON CORNELIUS.

Bilder zu Goethe's Faust. Gestochen von F. Ruschweyh. Frankfurt a. M. 1816. fol. 12 plates.

XI. d. THEODOR DE BRY.

20 plates of Theodor de Bry's Virginia.

Exceedingly fine impressions of these plates may be found in a copy of Hariot's Virginia belonging to the Library of Harvard College, purchased with the bequest of the Hon. William Prescott.

XI. e. BERTEL THORWALDSEN'S BASRELIEFS.

Alexander's Entry into Babylon. Engraved by Bezzi. 18 plates.

XII. A. FRENCH SCHOOL.

SIMON VOUET *pinx.*

Holy Family. . . . . Daret *sc.*
Lucretia. . . . . C. Mellan *sc.*

LE NAIN *pinx.* [Two brothers, Louis and Mathieu, whose works are not well distinguished.]

Le Maréchal dans sa forge. *Proof.* . . Levasseur and Claessens *sc.*

NICOLAS POUSSIN *pinx.*

The Sacrifice of Noah. . . . . J. Frey *sc.*
Eliezer and Rebecca. . . . . Desnoyers *sc.*
The same. *Proof.* . . . . Desnoyers *sc.*
Moses at the Well. *Proof.* . . . . P. Anderloni *sc.*
The Rest in Egypt. *Proof.* . . . . R. Morghen *sc.*
Holy Family with Angels and Flowers. *Proof.* . . . Bartolozzi *sc.*
Holy Family at the base of a column. . . Faustino Anderloni *sc.*
Jupiter as Diana, with Callisto. . . . . Daullé *sc.*
The Judgment of Hercules. Strange *sc.* *See* Portf. XXIX.
Apollo crowning Virgil. . . . . C. Mellan *sc.*
The Dance of the Hours to the Tune of Time. . . . . R. Morghen *sc.*
Time bearing Truth above the reach of Envy and Slander. 1*st state.* Gér. Audran *sc.*
The same. 2*d state.* . . . . Gér. Audran *sc.*

FERDINAND VAN ELLE *pinx.*

P. Nicolas Poussin. . . . . Louis Ferdinand *sc.*

JACQUES STELLA *pinx.*

Madonna and Child. . . . . G. Edelinck *sc.*

LE SUEUR *pinx.*

The Four Evangelists. Nanteuil *sc.* *See* Portfolio XXXII.

CLAUDE MELLAN *pinx.*

Christ praying in the Garden. . . . . C. Mellan *sc.*
Pietà. "Factus obediens." . . . . C. Mellan *sc.*
Holy Family, or rather Rest in Egypt. . . . . . C. Mellan *sc.*
St. Francis praying. . . . . C. Mellan *sc.*
St. Alexis Romanus, dead. . . . . C. Mellan *sc.*
St. Ignatius in ecstasy. . . . . C. Mellan *sc.*
The Sudarium of St. Veronica. . . . . C. Mellan *sc.*
Perseus and Andromeda. . . . . C. Mellan *sc.*
P. Claude Mellan's portrait. *See* Portfolio XVI. C.

PHILIPPE DE CHAMPAGNE *pinx.*

Les Religieuses. . . . . Levillain *sc.*
Moses with the Tables of the Law. . . Nanteuil and Edelinck *sc.*

SIMON FRANÇOIS OF TOURS *pinx.*

The Christ Child seated on the Globe adored by Angels. . . Pitau *sc.*

LAURENT DE LA HIRE *pinx.*

Holy Family with a Lamb. . . . . W. Faithorne *sc.*

PIERRE MIGNARD *pinx.*

The Visitation. . . . . Roullet *sc.*

La Vierge au Raisin. . . . . Roullet *sc.*

The same. *Proof.* . . . . Roullet *sc.*

St. Carlo Borromeo administering the Sacrament to the Plague-stricken. Fr. de Poilly *sc.*

CARLE VANLOO *pinx.*

Ste. Geneviève. *Artist's proof.* . . . . Balechou *sc.*

Cupid standing. Strange *sc.* *See* Portfolio XXIX.

Le Coucher. . . . . Porporati *sc.*

SÉBASTIEN BOURDON *pinx.*

Rest in Egypt, the Virgin washing swaddling-clothes. E. Hainzelmann *sc.*

Holy Family. . . . . Fr. de Poilly *sc.*

CHARLES LE BRUN *pinx.*

Moses at the Well. . . . . B. Audran *sc.*

The Visitation. . . . . Fr. de Poilly *sc.*

The Presentation in the Temple. . . . . . . B. Audran *sc.*

Holy Family at Table, called "The Benedicite." . . G. Edelinck *sc.*

The Crucifixion. "Le Christ aux Anges. G. Edelinck *sc.* *See* Portfolio XIV.

The Presentation of the Virgin in the Temple. . B. Audran *sc.*

St. John in Patmos. . . . . Fr. de Poilly *sc.*

St. Mary Magdalen, portrait of Mme. de La Vallière. G. Edelinck *sc.* *See* under Edelinck's portraits, Portfolio XVI. D.

ROBERT NANTEUIL *pinx.*

The Head of the Virgin. . . . . Nanteuil *sc.*

LOUIS DE BOULLONGNE *pinx.*

The Presentation in the Temple. . . . . . P. I. Drevet *sc.*

FRANÇOIS SPIERRE *pinx.*

Christ in a Glory, blessing five Saints. . . . . F. Spierre *sc.*

JOSEPH PAROCEL *pinx.*

Fight of Cavalry. . . . . Marcenay de Ghuy *sc.*

ANTOINE COYPEL *pinx.*

Rebecca at the Well. . . . . P. I. Drevet *sc.*

JEAN ANDRAY *pinx.*

The Resurrection. . . . . P. I. Drevet *sc.*

Jean Raoux *pinx.*

Angelica and Medoro. . . . . Delaunay *sc.*

XII. A. a. PIERRE MIGNARD.

The Ceiling of the Church Val de Grace, The Felicity of the Blessed. 6 plates, joined, forming a large circle.

XII. A. b. CHARLES LE BRUN.

The Battles of Alexander.

The Passage of the Granicus. . . . . G. Audran *sc.*
The Defeat of Darius at Arbela. . . . . G. Audran *sc.*
Porus brought before Alexander. . . . . . . G. Audran *sc.*
The Triumphal Entry of Alexander into Babylon. . . G. Audran *sc.*
The Tent of Darius : the Family of Darius at the Feet of Alexander.
G. Edelinck *sc.*

XII. A. c. CHARLES LE BRUN.

The Battle of Constantine and Maxentius. . . . G. Audran *sc.*
The Triumphal Entry of Constantine into Rome. . . . G. Audran *sc.*

XII. B. FRENCH SCHOOL.

Antoine Watteau *pinx.*

La Mariée du Village. . . . . C. N. Cochin *sc.*
Les Plaisirs du Bal. . . . . Scotin *sc.*
L'Embarquement pour Cythère. . . . . . . N. Tardieu *sc.*
Fêtes Vénitiennes. . . . . L. Cars *sc.*
La Collation. . . . . Moyreau *sc.*
La Dance paysanne. . . . . B. Audran *sc.*

Jean Baptiste Oudry *pinx.*

La Surprise du Renard. . . . . Beauvarlet *sc.*

Jean Restout *pinx.*

Christ praying in the Garden. . . . . P. I. Drevet *sc.*

Pierre Subleyras *pinx.*

The Feast at the House of Simon. *Aq. fort.* . . . . Subleyras *sc.*

François Boucher *pinx.*

Diana and Endymion. . . . . Saint-Aubin *sc.*
Vertumnus and Pomona. . . . . Saint-Aubin *sc.*
Europa. . . . . Saint-Aubin *sc.*

Alexandre Roslin *pinx.* [Born in Sweden.]

P. François Boucher. . . . . Carmona *sc.*

JOSEPH MARIE VIEN *pinx.*

L'Offrande à Vénus. . . . . Beauvarlet *sc.*

La Marchande d'Amours. . . . . Beauvarlet *sc.*

JEAN BAPTISTE GREUZE *pinx.*

L'Accordée du Village. . . . . J. J. Flipart *sc.*

Le Paralytique servi par ses enfans. . . . . . J. J. Flipart *sc.*

La Mère bien aimée. . . . . J. B. Massard *sc.*

A Mother with three Children, of which the eldest blows a trumpet. *Proof.* Jardinier *sc.*

La Cruche cassée. . . . . J. B. Massard *sc.*

A Girl with a Dog. . . . . Porporati *sc.*

A Girl with a Lamb: "Innocence." *Proof.* . . . . . A. Louis *sc.*

ANTOINE PESNE *pinx.*

The Pigeon-Girl. . . . . Rasp *sc.*

HENRI DROUAIS *pinx.*

P. The two Children of Prince Turenne, as Savoyard boys, one with a marmot, the other with a hurdy-gurdy. . . . . . . Melini *sc.*

P. Charles Philippe, Count Artois, afterwards Charles X., 6 years old, and his Sister Clotilde, afterwards Queen of Sardinia, 4 years old, mounting a Goat. . . . . Beauvarlet *sc.*

ANTOINE RENOU *pinx.*

Jupiter and Io. . . . . Le Grand *sc.*

JEAN BAPTISTE LE PRINCE *pinx.*

Les Modèles. . . . . Longueil *sc.*

N. R. JOLLAIN *pinx.*

The Nymph Erigone. . . . . J. G. von Müller *sc.*

N. L. LÉPICIÉ *pinx.*

Le Repos. . . . . Bervic *sc.*

La Demande acceptée. *Proof.* . . . . Bervic *sc.*

JEAN BAPTISTE REGNAULT *pinx.*

L'Éducation d'Achille. *Proof.* . . . . Bervic *sc.*

PHILIPPE LOUIS DEBUCOURT *pinx.*

Le Juge, ou la Cruche cassée. *Proof.* . . . . . . Leveau *sc.*

FRANÇOIS MARIUS GRANET *pinx.*

Franciscans at Morning Service. . . . . W. Giller *sc.*

Ceremony of a Nun taking the Veil. . . . . . . Huffam *sc.*

LOUIS ÉDOUARD RIOULT *pinx.*

Phrosine et Mélidor. . . . . Allais *sc.*

PIERRE BOUILLON *pinx.*

A Girl with an Arrow. "Il n'est plus temps." . . . . Audouin *sc.*

A. Caraffe *inv.*

Hope supporting the Unfortunate unto the Grave. . . Desnoyers *sc.*

Jean Auguste Dominique Ingres *del.*

After the antique. L'Amour. . . . . Desnoyers *sc.*

François Gérard *pinx.*

Les Trois Ages. . . . . R. Morghen *sc.*

Bouillon *del.*

After the antique. Laocoön. . . . . Bervic *sc.*

The same. *Artist's proof.* . . . . Bervic *sc.*

XIII. A. ENGLISH SCHOOL.

Sir Peter Lely *pinx.* [Peter van der Faes, of Soest in Westphalia.]

P. Nell Gwynne, represented with a Lamb. . . . . . Valck *sc.*

Sir Godfrey Kneller *pinx.*

P. Henry Aldrich, Dean of Oxford. . . . . J. Smith *sc.*

P. François Couplet, Jesuit, Chinese Missionary. . . . J. Faber *sc.*

P. Mrs. Cross, as St. Catherine. . . . . . . J. Smith *sc.*

P. Queen Anne of England. . . . . . Peter van Gunst *sc.*

P. The Duke of Marlborough. . . . . B. Picart *sc.*

William Hogarth *pinx.*

A Midnight Modern Conversation. . . . . Hogarth *sc.*

The Harlot's Progress. 6 plates. . . . . Hogarth *sc.*

The Rake's Progress. 8 plates. . . . . Hogarth *sc.*

The Distressed Poet. . . . . Hogarth *sc.*

The Four Times of Day. 4 plates. . . . . Hogarth *sc.*

Strolling Actresses dressing in a Barn. . . . . . . Hogarth *sc.*

The Enraged Musician. . . . . Hogarth *sc.*

Marriage à la Mode. 6 plates.

G. Scotin, B. Baron, S. Ravenet, and R. F. Ravenet *sc.*

The March to Finchley. . . . . Sullivan *sc.*

Analysis of Beauty. 2 plates. . . . . Hogarth *sc.*

Election. 4 plates. . Hogarth, Grignion, Le Cave, and Aveline *sc.*

The same. 2*d state.* Hogarth, Grignion, Le Cave, and Aveline *sc.*

Caricatures. "Design'd by Wm. Hogarth."

Sigismunda. . . . . Duncarton *sc.*

The Beggar's Opera. *With the key.* . . . . Wm. Blake *sc.*

P. Bishop Benjamin Hoadly. . . . . Baron *sc.*

P. John Wilkes. . . . . Hogarth *sc.*

The Works of W. Hogarth, from the original plates, restored by James Heath, with a biography and the explanations by John Nichols, London,

William Hogarth *pinx., continued.*

Baldwin and Cradock, *s. a.*, are in the Library of Harvard College, the donation of Josiah Quincy Loring, Esq.

Sir Joshua Reynolds *pinx.*

Holy Family. . . . . W. Sharp *sc.*

The Painted Window of New College Chapel, Oxford: The Nativity, with the Shepherds, and the Cardinal Virtues, executed by Jervaise, from the original pictures of Sir Joshua Reynolds. "The painting of the Nativity was burnt at Belvoir Castle, October 6, 1816." . . . . . . Boydell *exc.*

The Infant Hercules strangling the Serpents. . . . J. Walker *sc.*

The Infant Academy. *Proof.* . . . . . . Fr. Haward *sc.*

Puck. . . . . Ch. Heath *sc.*

La Petite Rusée. Bause *sc.* See under Bause, p. 25.

Ugolino. . . . . J. Dixon *sc.*

PORTRAITS.

Sir Jeffery Amherst. . . . . J. Watson *sc.*

Lord Burghersh, a child. *Proof.* . . . . . . Bartolozzi *sc.*

Edmund Burke. . . . . J. Watson *sc.*

Master Crew, as Henry VIII. *Proof.* . . . . . . J. R. Smith *sc.*

General Eliott, Lord Heathfield. . . . . . . R. Earlom *sc.*

Thomas Erskine, Lord Erskine. . . . . J. Jones *sc.*

Charles James Fox. . . . . J. Jones *sc.*

Garrick, between Comedy and Tragedy. . . . . . Ed. Fisher *sc.*

Marquis of Granby. *Proof.* . . . . J. Watson *sc.*

Sir William Hamilton. *Proof.* . . . . H. Hudson *sc.*

Warren Hastings. . . . . Th. Watson *sc.*

John Hunter. Wm. Sharp *sc.* *See* Portfolio of Large Portraits, XVI. I.

Lord Mansfield. Bartolozzi *sc.* *See* Portfolio of Large Portraits, XVI. I.

Duke of Orleans: Égalité. . . . . J. R. Smith *sc.*

Sir Joshua Reynolds. . . . . Wm. Bond *sc.*

Richard Brinsley Sheridan. *Proof.* . . . . J. Hall *sc.*

Lord Thurlow. Bartolozzi *sc.* *See* Portfolio of Large Portraits, XVI. I.

Master Philip Yorke. *Proof.* . . . . Bartolozzi *sc.*

Duchess of Ancaster. *Artist's proof.* . . . . Houston *sc.*

Mrs. Billington, as St. Cecilia. . . . . J. Ward *sc.*

Lady Sarah Bunbury. . . . . E. Fisher *sc.*

Lady Cockburn and her three Children, as Cornelia. . C. Wilkin *sc.*

Duchess of Devonshire and her Child. . . . . . . Keating *sc.*

Lady Fenhoulet, when Anne Day. *Proof.* . . . . McArdell *sc.*

Angelica Kauffman. Morace *sc.* *See* Portfolio XIII. B, under Sir Joshua Reynolds.

Sir Joshua Reynolds *pinx., continued.*

Eliz. Montague, child of the Duke of Buccleugh. *Proof.* J. R. Smith *sc.*
Mrs. Sheridan as St. Cecilia. . . . . Dickinson *sc.*
Mrs. Siddons as Tragic Muse. . . . . Fr. Haward *sc.*
The Hon. Mrs. Stanhope. . . . . . . Caroline Watson *sc.*
The Marchioness of Tavistock at Hymen's Altar. *Artist's proof.*
E. Fisher *sc.*

XIII. B. ENGLISH SCHOOL.

Thomas Gainsborough *pinx.*

The Watering-Place, landscape. *Proof.* . . . . . W. Miller *sc.*
The Market-Cart, landscape. *Proof.* . . . . . Ed. Goodall *sc.*

Edward Penny *pinx.*

The Tailor in the Smith's Shop. . . . . Houston *sc.*

Joseph Wright *pinx.*

The Iron-Forge. . . . . R. Earlom *sc.*
The Blacksmith's Shop. . . . . R. Earlom *sc.*

John Singleton Copley *pinx.*

The Death of Chatham. . . . . Bartolozzi *sc.*
Key to the Death of Chatham.

Benjamin West *pinx.*

The Witch of Endor. . . . . Wm. Sharp *sc.*
St. Paul at Malta. . . . . Bartolozzi *sc.*
The Martyrdom of St. Stephen. *Proof.* . . . . . Dunkarton *sc.*
King Lear in the Storm. . . . . Wm. Sharp *sc.*
The same. *Etching.* . . . . Wm. Sharp *sc.*
Apotheosis of two English Princes. Strange *sc.* *See* Portfolio XXIX.
King Alfred dividing his Loaf. *Proof.* . . . . . Wm. Sharp *sc.*
The Battle of La Hogue. . . . . Woollett *sc.*
The Death of General Wolfe. *Proof.* . . . . Woollett *sc.*
William Penn treating with the Indians. . . . . . . J. Hall *sc.*

Sir Joshua Reynolds *pinx.*

𝔓. Angelica Kauffman. . . . . Morace *sc.*

Angelica Kauffman *pinx.*

"Garde à vous." Cupid. *Proof.* . . . . Porporati *sc.*
A Vestal. . . . . Schultze *sc.*
The same. *Proof.* . . . . Schultze *sc.*
Hebe. *Proof.* . . . . C. G. Krüger *sc.*
𝔓. Lady Hamilton, as Comic Muse. . . . . . . R. Morghen *sc.*
𝔓. The Family Holstein-Beck. *Proof.* . . . . R. Morghen *sc.*

Gavin Hamilton *pinx.*

La Poésie. . . . . R. Morghen *sc.*

GAVIN HAMILTON *pinx.*, *continued.*

La Peinture. . . . . R. Morghen *sc.*
𝔓. Lord Kilwarden. *Proof.* . . . . Bartolozzi *sc.*

WILLIAM HOARE *pinx.*

𝔓. William Pitt, Earl of Chatham. . . . . . . Houston *sc.*

SAMUEL WOODFORTH *pinx.*

Charles I., Interview with his Children. *Artist's proof.* . W. Sharp *sc.*

JOHN TRUMBULL *pinx.*

The Sortie from Gibraltar. *Open letter proof.* . . . . W. Sharp *sc.*
The same. *Artist's proof.* . . . . W. Sharp *sc.*
The Battle of Bunker Hill. *Proof.* . . . . J. G. von Müller *sc.*

WASHINGTON ALLSTON *pinx.*

The Witch of Endor. *Proof.* . C. E. Wagstaff and Jos. Andrews *sc.*

RICHARD RAMSAY REINAGLE *pinx.*

The Spaniel. *Proof.* . . . . . . J. Scott and J. Webb *sc.*

XIV. LARGEST PORTFOLIO.

RAPHAEL *pinx.*

The Battle of Constantine. *Engraved on 4 plates.* Passavant, II. 246.
P. Scalberge *sc.*
The same. *Proof.* . . . . Fabri *sc.*

PAOLO VERONESE *pinx.*

The Marriage Feast at Cana. In the Louvre. . . Z. Prevost *sc.*
The Feast in the House of Simon. In the Louvre. . . Z. Prevost *sc.*

BERNARDO POCCETTI *pinx.*

The Inferno, according to Dante. *On two plates.* . . . . Callot *sc.*

PIERRE MIGNARD *pinx.*

Alexander in the Tent of Darius. *On two plates.* Edelinck et P. Drevet *sc.*

CHARLES LE BRUN *pinx.*

The Crucifixion. "Le Christ aux Anges." *On two plates.* . Edelinck *sc.*

ANDREA APPIANI *pinx.*

Jacob and Rachel. *Proof.* . . . . Garavaglia *sc.*

PAUL DELAROCHE *pinx.*

𝔓. General Bonaparte crossing the Alps. . . . . A. François *sc.*

XV. LANDSCAPES. A. WOOLLETT.

37 pieces; see Catalogue of Engravers, under WOOLLETT. Battle of La Hogue, and Death of General Wolfe, *ibid.*, and Portfolio XIII. B.

XV. LANDSCAPES. B.

Nicolas Poussin *pinx.*

I Sepolcri del Pussino. . . . . Gmelin *sc.*

Gaspre Poussin *pinx.* [Gaspard or Gaspre Dughet, called Poussin.]

Il Temporale del Pussino. . . . . Gmelin *sc.*
The Hurricane. . . . . Fittler *sc.*

Claude Lorrain *pinx.* [Claude Gellée, called le Lorrain.]

Hagar directed by the Angel to the Well. . . . . John Pye sen. *sc.*
The Golden Calf. *Proof.* . . . . Lerpinière *sc.*
The Flight into Egypt. . . . . Gmelin *sc.*
The Flight into Egypt, different composition. . . . . . Vivares *sc.*
The Embarkation of St. Ursula. *Proof.* . . . . . . Fittler *sc.*
Acis and Galatea. . . . . Gmelin *sc.*
Cephalus and Procris. . . . . J. Browne *sc.*
The same, composition slightly different. *Proof.* . . . John Pye jun. *sc.*
The Landing of Æneas in Italy. . . . . J. Mason *sc.*
The Temple of Diana. . . . . Duttenhofer *sc.*
The Temple of Venus. . . . . Gmelin *sc.*
Constantine's Arch. . . . . Fittler *sc.*
"Ancient Port of Messina," Seaport with setting sun. . Le Bas *sc.*
The Musical Shepherdess. *Proof.* . . . . Wilson Lowry *sc.*
The Mill. . . . . Gmelin *sc.*
Sunrise. *Proof.* . . . . Canot *sc.*
Sunset. *Proof.* . . . . Mason *sc.*
The Ford. . . . . Vivares *sc.*
A Herdsman instructing a Shepherdess to play on the Pipe. . Vivares *sc.*
The same. . . . . Wilson *sc.*

Giovanni Francesco Grimaldi, called Bolognese, *pinx.*

Castel Gandolfi. . . . . Vivares and Chatelain *sc.*

Meindert Hobbema *pinx.*

Village in a Wood, near Antwerp. *Artist's proof.* . . . . Vivares *sc.*
The Rural Village. *Artist's proof.* . . . . J. Mason *sc.*

Filippo Lauri *pinx.*

Apollo, as herdsman to King Admetus. . . . . . Wm. Byrne *sc.*

François Millet *pinx.* [Otherwise Milet or Milé.]

Landscape with Waterfall. *Proof.* . . . . Rahl *sc.*

François Le Moine *pinx.*

Diana and Callisto. . . . . Wm. Walker *sc.*

Francesco Zuccarelli *pinx.*

The Finding of Moses. *Proof.* . . . . Sam. Smith *sc.*

Joseph Vernet *pinx.*

The Storm. . . . . Balechou *sc.*
The Calm. . . . . Balechou *sc.*
The Bathers. . . . . Balechou *sc.*
Storm by Day. . . . . J. J. Flipart *sc.*
Storm by Night. . . . . J. J. Flipart *sc.*
La Barque mise à flot. . . . . . . Marie Rosalie Bertaud *sc.*

Dietrich *pinx.*

Le Mage. . . . . Darnstedt *sc.*
Le Mage parmi les Pasteurs. . . . . Darnstedt *sc.*

Richard Wilson *pinx.*

Niobe. *Proof.* . . . . Sam. Smith *sc.*

George Smith *pinx.*

The Hop-pickers. . . . . Vivares *sc.*

Jean Pillement *pinx.*

La Chaumière Hollandaise. Winter. . . . . Canot *sc.*

Cipriani and Barrett *pinx.*

The Tempest. . . . . Middiman *sc.*
As You Like It. . . . . Middiman *sc.*

Philipp Hackert *pinx.*

St. Peter's, from Ponte Molle. . . . . Dunker *sc.*

Gmelin *pinx.*

Mare Morte, near Naples. *Proof.* . . . . Gmelin *sc.*

XVI. A. PORTRAITS, DUTCH.

Johan Sadeler *del.*

Sigismund Feyerabend. . . . . J. Sadeler *sc.*

Aldegrever *del.*

Johan van Leyden, king of the Anabaptists. . . . . Jan Muller *sc.*

Mierevelt *pinx.*

George Villiers, Duke of Buckingham. *Proof.* . . . Wm. Delff *sc.*
Hugo Grotius. . . . . Wm. Delff *sc.*

A. Bakker *pinx.*

Bartholomeus Prevost. . . . . H. Bary *sc.*

Palamedes *pinx.*

Johannes Cocceius. . . . . A. Blooteling *sc.*

A. Blooteling *pinx.*

Admiral Michiel Adriensz. Ruyter. . . . . . . A. Blooteling *sc.*
Michael-Angelus Bonarotus nobilis Florentinus. . . . A. Blooteling *sc.*

J. van Teylingen *pinx.*
Jacobus Triglandius. . . . . C. van Dalen *sc.*

David Beck *pinx.* [Otherwise, Beek.]
Christina, Queen of Sweden. . . . . Falck *sc.*

H. Goltzius *pinx.*
N. de la Faille. *Proof.* . . . . H. Goltzius *sc.*

Martin van Heemskirk *pinx.*
Zurenus. . . . . H. Goltzius *sc.*

Jacob van Campen *del.*
Laurentius Coster. . . . . C. Koning *sc.*

H. Goltzius *pinx.* ?
William I. of Orange. . . . . Sichem *sc.*

Philipp Kilian *pinx.*
Bartholomæus Kilian. . . . . Ph. Kilian *sc.*

Jan Saenredam *pinx.* [After Goltzius.]
Karel van Mander. . . . . N. Lastman *sc.*

Lievens *pinx.*
Admiral Joan van Galen. . . . . . . Michel Mouzin *sc.*
Daniel Seghers [Zegers]. . . . . P. Pontius *sc.*

Peter Isaac *pinx.*
Johan van Achen. . . . . Saenredam *sc.*

Abraham Bloemaert *pinx.*
Abraham Bloemaert. . . . . Swanenburg *sc.*

Aart van Leyden *pinx.*
Aart van Leyden. . . . . Suyderhoef *sc.*

Jan de Vos *pinx.*
Adriaan Beekerts van Thienen. . . . . . Suyderhoef *sc.*

Jan ver Spronk *pinx.*
Augustyn Bloemaert. . . . . Suyderhoef *sc.*

Jan de Vos *pinx.*
Johannes Cocceius, Theol. Prof. *Proof.* . . . . . Suyderhoef *sc.*

H. Goltzius *pinx.*
H. Goltzius. . . . . Suyderhoef *sc.*

Jan de Vos *pinx.*
Rud. Hegger. . . . . Suyderhoef *sc.*

Van Dyck *pinx.*
Francisco de Moncada. Suyderhoef *sc.* *See* under Van Dyck, Portf. IX. C.

FRANS HALS *pinx.*
Jacob de Reves, Theol. Dr. . . . . Suyderhoef *sc.*

DUBORDIEU *pinx.*
Andreas Rivet, Theol. Dr. . . . . Suyderhoef *sc.*

REMBRANDT *pinx.*
Eleazar Swalm. . . . . Suyderhoef *sc.*

FRANS HALS *pinx.*
Jac. Zaffius, Cathedr. Eccl. Harlem. Praepos. . . Van de Velde *sc.*

JOAN VAN NOORT *pinx.*
Petrus Proëlius. . . . . Jan Visscher *sc.*

JAN VISSCHER *pinx.*
Abraham vander Hulst, Vice-Admirael van Hollant en Westvrieslant.
Jan Visscher *sc.*

PALAMEDES *pinx.*
Robertus Junius. . . . . C. Visscher *sc.*

CORN. VISSCHER *pinx.*
Guilliam de Ryck, opthalmist at Amsterdam.* . . . C. Visscher *sc.*
Gellius de Bouma, Ecclesiastes Zutphaniensis.* . . . C. Visscher *sc.*

PIETER SOUTMAN *pinx.*
Petrus Scriverius, Harlemensis. . . . . C. Visscher *sc.*

FERDINAND BOL *pinx.*
Admiral Cornelis Tromp. . . . . . . Lambert Visscher *sc.*

JAN LUTMA *pinx.*
P. C. Hooft. . . . . Jan Lutma *Opus mallei.*

VAN DER WERFF *pinx.*
William I. Prince of Orange. . . . . G. Valck *sc.*

MIEREVELT *pinx.*
William I. Prince of Orange. . . . . Tanjé *sc.*
Maurice, Prince of Orange. . . . . Tanjé *sc.*
William I. Prince of Orange. *Proof.* . . . . . . Taurel *sc.*

XVI. B. PORTRAITS. HOUBRAKEN, 53 PIECES.

See the Alphabetical Catalogue of Engravers under HOUBRAKEN.

XVI. C. PORTRAITS. MELLAN, NANTEUIL, MASSON, VERMEULEN, VAN SCHUPPEN, ETC.

CLAUDE MELLAN *del.*
Claude Mellan's own Portrait. Montaiglon, p. 77. . . . . Mellan *sc.*
Cardinal Bentivoglio. . . . . M. No. 169. Mellan *sc.*
Pierre Gassendi. . . . . M. No. 189. Mellan *sc.*

* These two portraits are designated as "The Great Beards."

CLAUDE MELLAN *del., continued.*

Vincenzo Giustiniani. . . . . . . M. No. 197. Mellan *sc.*

Henri Louis Habert de Montmor. . . . M. No. 194. Mellan *sc.*

The Capuchin Father Joseph. M. No. 196. Mellan *sc.* *See* Smallest Portfolio, XXXII.

Fabri de Peyresc. . . . . M. No. 223. Mellan *sc.*

Pierre Séguier. . . . . M. No. 231. Mellan *sc.*

MIGNARD *pinx.*

Anne of Austria, Queen of Louis XIII.
Robert-Dumesnil No. 22. Nanteuil *sc.*

NANTEUIL *del.*

The same. R.-D. No. 23. Nanteuil *sc.* *See* Portfolio of Largest Portraits, XVI. I.

Cardinal Barberini. . . . . . . R.-D. No. 29. Nanteuil *sc.*

Étienne Johannot de Bartillat. . . R.-D. No. 32. Nanteuil *sc.*

Beaumanoir, Bishop of Mans. 1*st state.* . R.-D. No. 35. Nanteuil *sc.*

The same. 2*d state.* . . . . . R.-D. No. 35. Nanteuil *sc.*

LE BRUN *pinx.*

Pomponne de Bellièvre. 2*d state.* . . R.-D. No. 37. Nanteuil *sc.*

François Blondeau. . . . . . . R.-D. No. 40. Nanteuil *sc.*

Marie de Bragelogne, Veuve de Claude Le Bouthillier.
R.-D. No. 57. Nanteuil *sc.*

Charles de Lorraine. . . . . . . R.-D. No. 63. Nanteuil *sc.*

Christina of Sweden. . . . . . . R.-D. No. 67. Nauteuil *sc.*

Clermont-Tonnerre, Bishop of Noyon. 1*st state.*
R.-D. No. 68. Nanteuil *sc.*

The same. 2*d state.* . . . . . . R.-D. No. 68. Nanteuil *sc.*

Cardinal Coislin. . . . . . . R.-D. No. 69. Nanteuil *sc.*

CHAMPAGNE *pinx.*

J. B. Colbert. . . . . R.-D. No. 72. Nanteuil *sc.*

NANTEUIL *del.*

J. N. Colbert. Nanteuil *sc.* R.-D. No. 77. *See* Portfolio of Largest Portraits, XVI. I.

The same. . . . . R.-D. No. 74. Nanteuil *sc.*

Louis de Bourbon, Prince de Condé. . . R.-D. No. 79. Nanteuil *sc.*

CHAMPAGNE *pinx.*

Henri de Guénégaud. . . . . . . R.-D. No. 106. Nanteuil *sc.*

NANTEUIL *del.*

Louis Hesselin. . . . . R.-D. No. 110. Nanteuil *sc.*

Pierre Jeannin. . . . . R.-D. No. 112. Nanteuil *sc.*

Mich. La Masle. . . . . R.-D. No. 126. Nanteuil *sc.*

CHAMPAGNE *pinx.*

Michel Le Tellier. . . . . . R.-D. No. 128. Nanteuil *sc.*

NANTEUIL *del.*

The same. . . . . R.-D. No. 129. Nanteuil *sc.*

The same. . . . . R.-D. No. 135. Nanteuil *sc.*

François de la Mothe Le Vayer. . . . R.-D. No. 143. Nanteuil *sc.*

Loménie de Brienne. . . . . . R.-D. No. 148. Nanteuil *sc.*

CHAMPAGNE *pinx.*

Henri d'Orleans, Duc de Longueville. . . R.-D. No. 149. Nanteuil *sc.*

NANTEUIL *del.*

Jean Loret, poet. . . . . R.-D. No. 150. Nanteuil *sc.*

René de Longueil, Marquis de Maisons. . R.-D. No. 166. Nanteuil *sc.*

Pierre de Maridat. R.-D. No. 168. Nanteuil *sc.* 8vo. *See* Smallest Portfolio, XXXII.

Nicolas Potier de Novion. . . . . R.-D. No. 207. Nanteuil *sc.*

André Le Fèvre d'Ormesson. . . . R.-D. No. 209. Nanteuil *sc.*

Pierre Poncet. . . . . R.-D. No. 215. Nanteuil *sc.*

Claude Regnauldin. . . . . . R.-D. No. 216. Nanteuil *sc.*

Jean François Sarrasin. . . . . R.-D. No. 220. Nanteuil *sc.*

George de Scuderi. . . . . R.-D. No. 221. Nanteuil *sc.*

Pierre Seguier, de Saint-Brisson. . . . R.-D. No. 224. Nanteuil *sc.*

DUCHASTLE *pinx.*

Joh. Bapt. van Steenberghen. 1*st state.* . R.-D. No. 226. Nanteuil *sc.*

The same. 2*d state.* . . . . . R.-D. No. 226. Nanteuil *sc.*

NANTEUIL *del.*

Turenne. R. D. No. 223. Nanteuil *sc.* *See* Portfolio of Largest Portraits, XVI. I.

Nanteuil's own portrait. . . . . Eredi *sc.*

N. MIGNARD *pinx.*

Brisacier, The Gray-haired Man. 2*d state.*
Robert-Dumesnil No. 15. Masson *sc.*

The same. 4*th state.* . . . . . . R.-D. No. 15. Masson *sc.*

PIERRE MIGNARD *pinx.*

Marin Cureau de la Chambre. . . . . R.-D. No. 24. Masson *sc.*

THOS. BLANCHET *pinx.*

Gaspard Charrier. . . . . R.-D. No. 16. Masson *sc.*

N. MIGNARD *pinx.*

Pierre Dupuis. . . . . R.-D. No. 25. Masson *sc.*

The same. . . . . R.-D. No. 25. Masson *sc.*

P. MIGNARD *pinx.*

Marie de Lorraine, Duchesse de Guise. . . R.-D. No. 32. Masson *sc.*

N. Mignard *pinx., continued.*

Comte d'Harcourt. Le Cadet La Perle. R.-D. No. 34. Masson *sc.* *See* Portfolio of Largest Portraits, XVI. I.

Masson *del.* ?

Madame Helyot. 8vo. R.-D. No. 36. Masson *sc.* *See* Smallest Portfolio, XXXII.

Rouxel de Medavy. R.-D. No. 51. Masson *sc.* *See* Portfolio of Largest Portraits, XVI. I.

Masson *pinx.*

Olivier Le Fèvre d'Ormesson. . . . . . R.-D. No. 58. Masson *sc.*

Gui Patin. . . . . R.-D. No. 59. Masson *sc.*

Masson *del.*

Charles Patin. . . . . R.-D. No. 60. Masson *sc.*

Masson *pinx.*

Antoine Turgot de St. Clair. . . . . . R.-D. No. 66. Masson *sc.*

Pierre Mignard *pinx.*

P. Mignard's own Portrait. . . . . Vermeulen *sc.*

H. Rigaud *pinx.*

François de Montmorency, Duke of Luxembourg. . . Vermeulen *sc.*

Ferdinand Vouet *pinx.*

Simon Joseph Barbot de Lardeinne. . . . . Van Schuppen *sc.*

Pierre Mignard *pinx.*

G. N. de la Reynie. . . . . Van Schuppen *sc.*

C. Lefèvre *pinx.*

Alexandre Pitau (Petavius), Senator in Parliament. . . . N. Pitau *sc.*

J. Heinzelmann *del.*

J.-B. Tavernier, in Persian costume. . . . Johann Heinzelmann *sc.*

Nanteuil *del.*

Henri de Behringen. . . . . Benoît Audran *sc.*

Van Schuppen *del.*

Prince Eugene. . . . . Bernard Picart *sc.*

XVI. D. PORTRAITS. EDELINCK.

41 pieces. *See* Alphabetical Catalogue of Engravers, pp. 111 – 116.

XVI. E. a. PORTRAITS. THE DREVETS, MORIN, ROULLET, CHÉREAU, GAILLARD.

Champagne *pinx.*

Cardinal Carlo Borromeo. . . . . Morin *sc.*

JÉRÔME FRANCK *pinx.*
Jérôme Franck. . . . . Morin *sc.*

FRANÇOIS DE POILLY *del.*
François de Poilly. . . . . Roullet *sc.*

LEVIEUX *pinx.*
Pierre de St. André. . . . . Roullet *sc.*

J. COTELLE *pinx.*
Catherine Touchelle. . . . . Roullet *sc.*

BAZIN *del.*?
Madame Helyot. . . . . N. Bazin *sc.*

HYAC. RIGAUD *pinx.*
René François de Beauveau. . . . . Pierre Drevet, père, *sc.*
Jac. Nic. Colbert, Archiepiscopus. . . . Pierre Drevet, père, *sc.*
Prince de Conti. Pierre Drevet, père, *sc.* *See* Portfolio of Largest Portraits, XVI. I.

De TROY *pinx.*
Louis Auguste de Bourbon, Prince de Dombes. Pierre Drevet, père, *sc.*

LARGILLIÈRE *pinx.*
Jean Forest. . . . . Pierre Drevet, père, *sc.*

HYAC. RIGAUD *pinx.*
Louis XIV., King of France. Pierre Drevet, père, *sc.* *See* Portfolio of Largest Portraits, XVI. I.

VIVIEN *pinx.*
François Girardon. . . . . . . Pierre Drevet, père, *sc.*

HYAC. RIGAUD *pinx.*
Jean Balthasar Keller. . . . . . . Pierre Drevet, père, *sc.*

LARGILLIÈRE *pinx.*
Nicolas Lambert. . . . . Pierre Drevet, père, *sc.*
Marie de Laubespine, femme de Lambert. . Pierre Drevet, père, *sc.*

PEZEY *pinx.*
La Duchesse de Lesdiguières. . . . . Pierre Drevet, père, *sc.*

LARGILLIÈRE *pinx.*
J. M. de Mitantier. . . . . . . Pierre Drevet, père, *sc.*

HYAC. RIGAUD *pinx.*
Marie Souveraine de Neufchâtel, Duchesse de Nemours.
Pierre Drevet, père, *sc.*

G. REVEL *pinx.*
Pierre Palliot. . . . . Pierre Drevet, père, *sc.*

HYAC. RIGAUD *pinx.*
Hyacinthe Rigaud. . . . . . . Pierre Drevet, père, *sc.*

DREVET *del.*

Christine Caroline, Margrave de Brandenbourg, née Duchesse de Würtemberg. . . . . Pierre Drevet, père, *sc.*

LOUIS DE BOULLONGNE *pinx.*

Louis de Boullongne. . . . . François Chéreau *sc.*

HYAC. RIGAUD *pinx.*

Detlev à Dehn. . . . . François Chéreau *sc.*

LARGILLIÈRE *pinx.*

Math. François Geoffroy. . . . . . . François Chéreau *sc.*

HYAC. RIGAUD *pinx.*

Nicolas de Launay. . . . . François Chéreau *sc.*

TOURNIÈRE *pinx.*

Louis Pécour. . . . . François Chéreau *sc.*

HYAC. RIGAUD *pinx.*

Samuel Bernard. *See* Portfolio of Largest Portraits, XVI. I.
Pierre Imbert Drevet, fils, *sc.*

Bossuet. . . . . Pierre Imbert Drevet, fils, *sc.*

Charles Jérome de Cisternay du Fay. 8vo. Pierre Imbert Drevet, fils, *sc.* *See* Smallest Portfolio, XXXII.

Robert de Cotte. . . . . . Pierre Imbert Drevet, fils, *sc.*

TOURNIÈRE *pinx.*

Petrus Nolascus Couvay. . . . Pierre Imbert Drevet, fils, *sc.*

HYAC. RIGAUD *pinx.*

Charles Gaspard Dodun, Marquis d'Herbault. Pierre Imbert Drevet, fils, *sc.* *See* Portfolio of Largest Portraits, XVI. I.

Cardinal Dubois. . . . . . Pierre Imbert Drevet, fils, *sc.*

ADRIEN LE PRIEUR *pinx.*

Claude Le Blanc. . . . . . Pierre Imbert Drevet, fils, *sc.*

CHARLES COYPEL *pinx.*

Adrienne Le Couvreur. . . . . Pierre Imbert Drevet, fils, *sc.*

The same. 1*st state, before the correction in the inscription.*
Pierre Imbert Drevet, fils, *sc.*

HYAC. RIGAUD *pinx.*

Henri Oswald, Cardinal d'Auvergne. . . . Claude Drevet *sc.*

Philippe Louis, Comte de Sinzendorf. . . . . Claude Drevet *sc.*

JOH. RUD. HUBER *pinx.*

Christophorus Steigerus. . . . . . . Claude Drevet *sc.*

HYAC. RIGAUD *pinx.*

Charles Gaspard Guillaume de Vintimille. . . . Claude Drevet *sc.*

HYAC. RIGAUD *pinx.*
François Castanier. . . . . Robert Gaillard *sc.*

GERARD DOW *pinx.*
Galileo Galilei. . . . . Robert Gaillard *sc.*

XVI. E. b. PORTRAITS. DAULLÉ, SCHMIDT, SCHMUTZER, BERVIC, BALECHOU.

TOURNIÈRE *pinx.*
J. F. de Chastenet de Puységur. . . . . Daullé *sc.*
P. L. M. de Maupertuis. . . . . Daullé *sc.*
The same. *Proof.* . . . . Daullé *sc.*

J. L. TOCQUÉ *pinx.*
Marie, Princess of Poland, Queen of Louis XV. of France. Daullé *sc.* *See* Portfolio of Largest Portraits, XVI. I.

HYAC. RIGAUD *pinx.*
Hyacinthe Rigaud painting the Portrait of his Wife. . . . Daullé *sc.*

ANTOINE PESNE *pinx.*
Christian August, Prince of Anhalt. . . . Jacobi 66. Schmidt *sc.*

FALBE *pinx.*
Christian Friedrich Blume. . . . . . Jacobi 65. Schmidt *sc.*

SCHMIDT *del.*
Count Brühl. Jacobi 84. Schmidt *sc.* *See* Smallest Portfolio, XXXII.

ERIKSEN *pinx.*
Anton Friedrich Büsching. . . . . . Jacobi 90. Schmidt *sc.*

FONTAINE *pinx.*
Charles Gabriel de Tubières de Caylus. . . . Jacobi 40. Schmidt *sc.*

ANTOINE PESNE *pinx.*
Baron Samuel de Cocceji. . . . . . Jacobi 67. Schmidt *sc.*

J. L. TOCQUÉ *pinx.*
Nicolas Comte d'Esterhasi de Galantha. 1*st state.* Jacobi 78. Schmidt *sc.*
The same. 2*d state.* . . . . . . Jacobi 78. Schmidt *sc.*

HYAC. RIGAUD *pinx.*
Louis de Latour d'Auvergne, Comte d'Evreux. . Jacobi 42. Schmidt *sc.*

SCHMIDT *del.*
De La Mettrie. . . . . Jacobi 76. Schmidt *sc.*

MAURICE QUENTIN DE LA TOUR *ipse pinx.*
M. Quentin de La Tour. "The Laughing Painter." Jacobi 50. Schmidt *sc.*
The same person, the smaller portrait, with hat. . Jacobi 89. Schmidt *sc.*

HYAC. RIGAUD *pinx.*
Pierre Mignard. 1*st state.* . . . . . . Jacobi 59. Schmidt *sc.*
The same. 2*d state.* . . . . Jacobi 59. Schmidt *sc.*

ANTOINE PESNE *ipse pinx.*
Antoine Pesne. . . . . . . Jacobi 69. Schmidt *sc.*

SCHMIDT *del.*
François Prévost. . . . . . . Jacobi 61. Schmidt *sc.*

J. L. TOCQUÉ *pinx.*
Cyrillus Comte de Rasoumowsky. . . . Jacobi 83. Schmidt *sc.*

JACQUES ANDRÉ JOSEPH AVED *pinx.*
Jean-Baptiste Rousseau. . . . . . Jacobi 44. Schmidt *sc.*

LIOTARD *pinx.*
Const. Scarlati, Prince of Moldavia. . . . Jacobi 39. Schmidt *sc.*

HYAC. RIGAUD *pinx.*
J.-B. Silva, M. D. . . . . Jacobi 52. Schmidt *sc.*

FALBE *pinx.*
David Splittgerber. . . . . . . Jacobi 87. Schmidt *sc.*

J. L. TOCQUÉ *pinx.*
Michel, Comte de Woronzow. . . . . Jacobi 77. Schmidt *sc.*

DIETRICH *ipse pinx.*
C. W. E. Dietrich. . . . . Schmutzer *sc.*

J. STEINER *pinx.*
Prince Kaunitz, standing at a table. . . . . Schmutzer *sc.*

CALLET *pinx.*
Louis XVI. of France. Charles Clément Bervic *sc.* *See* Portfolio of Largest Portraits, XVI. I.

BERVIC *del.*
Charles Gravier, Comte de Vergennes. . Charles Clément Bervic *sc.*

LOUIS SILVESTRE *pinx.*
Count Heinrich Brühl. . . . . . . Jean Joseph Balechou *sc.*

JACQUES ANTREAU *pinx.*
Jacques Gabriel Grillot. . . . . . Jean Joseph Balechou *sc.*

FRANÇOIS DE TROY *pinx.*
Jean de Julien. . . . . Jean Joseph Balechou *sc.*

HYAC. RIGAUD *pinx.*
Auguste III., Roi de Pologne. Jean Joseph Balechou *sc.* *See* Portfolio of Largest Portraits, XVI. I.

JACQUES ANDRÉ JOSEPH AVED *pinx.*
Bertrand Claude Taschereau de Linyères. . Jean Joseph Balechou *sc.*

J. M. NATTIER *pinx.*
"La Force," portrait of the Duchess of Châteauroux.
Jean Joseph Balechou *sc.*

XVI. F. a. PORTRAITS BY BAUSE.

25 pieces, specified in the Catalogue of Engravers, pp. 25, 26, with Bause's portrait by Klauber.

XVI. F. b. PORTRAITS. GERMAN.

AMLING *del.*

Maximilian Emanuel, Duke of Bavaria, in his younger years. Amling *sc.*
Henrietta Maria Adelaide, Duchess of Bavaria. . . . Amling *sc.*

PH. ENDLICH *del.*

John Taylor, ophthalmic physician. . . . . Ph. Endlich *sc.*

J. M. BERNINGEROTH *del.*

Lebrecht Behrisch. . . . . Berningeroth *sc.*

KYMLI *pinx.*

Joseph II., "Empereur des Romains." . . . . C. G. Schulze *sc.*

A. GRAFF *pinx.*

Johan Georg Palitzsch, the Peasant Astronomer. . . C. G. Schulze *sc.*
Anton Graff. *Open letter proof.* . . . . . J. G. von Müller *sc.*
The same. *Proof before letters.* . . . . . J. G. von Müller *sc.*

DUPLESSIS *pinx.*

Louis XVI. King of France. *Proof.* J. G. von Müller *sc.* *See* Portfolio of Largest Portraits, XVI. I.

GREUZE *pinx.*

Johann Georg Wille. . . . . J. G. von Müller *sc.*

N. S. A. BELLE *pinx.*

Louis Leramberg, sculptor. . . . . . . J. G. von Müller *sc.*

J. L. TOCQUÉ *pinx.*

Louis Galloche, painter. . . . . . . J. G. von Müller *sc.*
The same. *Proof.* . . . . J. G. von Müller *sc.*

F. TISCHBEIN *pinx.*

C. T. A. M. Freyherr von Dalberg. *Proof.* . J. G. von Müller *sc.*

J. C. FRISCH *pinx.*

Moses Mendelssohn. . . . . J. G. von Müller *sc.*

P. A. WILLE *pinx.*

La Mère Brigide. . . . . J. G. von Müller *sc.*
La Petite Javotte. . . . . J. G. von Müller *sc.*

F. TISCHBEIN *pinx.*

Loder, Professor of Anatomy. *Proof.* . . . . J. G. von Müller *sc.*
Hufeland, Professor of Medicine. *Proof.* . . . . . Fr. Müller *sc.*

F. Jagemann *pinx.*
Dr. Gall. . . . . Heinrich Schmidt *sc.*

Mme. Kinson *pinx.*
Jérôme [Napoléon], Roi de Westphalie. . . J. G. et Fr. Müller *sc.*
The same. *Open letter proof.* . . . . . J. G. et Fr. Müller *sc.*
The same. *Proof before any letters.* . . . J. G. et Fr. Müller *sc.*

Friedrich Müller *pinx.*
Wilhelm Kronprinz von Würtemberg. . . . . . Fr. Müller *sc.*
Johann Peter Hebel. . . . . Fr. Müller *sc.*
The same. *Etch print.* . . . . Fr. Müller *sc.*

F. Lieder *del.*
Schleiermacher. . . . . F. Bolt *sc.*

F. Tischbein *pinx.*
August von Kotzebue. *Proof.* . . . . Bittheuser *sc.*

A. Graff *pinx.*
Goethe. *Proof.* . . . . Carl Barth *sc.*

Begas *pinx.*
Thorwaldsen. . . . . Amsler *sc.*

F. Krüger *pinx.*
Thorwaldsen. *Proof.* . . . . Gust. Lüderitz *sc.*

E. Eichens *del.*
Paolo Toschi. . . . . E. Eichens *sc.*

Robert Scheider *pinx.*
Baron von Rumohr. . . . . Aug. Semler *sc.*

H. *pinx.*
Savonarola. . . . . Carl Barth *sc.*

Kaulbach *del.*
Franz Liszt. . . . . Gonzenbach *sc.*

W. Hensel *pinx.*
Mendelssohn-Bartholdy. . . . . J. Caspar *sc.*

Doris Stork *del.*
Mozart. . . . . Mandel *sc.*

May *pinx.*
Goethe. . . . . Reyher *sc.*
Alexander von Humboldt. After a photograph. *Artist's proof.* . Trossin *sc.*

Schmidt *del.*
Dr. D. F. Strauss. . . . . Carl Mayer *sc.*

Stebbers *pinx.*
Hegel. . . . . Sichling *sc.*

XVI. F. c. PORTRAITS. FRENCH.

Éliz. Chéron *pinx.*
Louis Bourdaloue. . . . . Rocheford *sc.*

Hyac. Rigaud *pinx.*
François Girardon. . . . . Duchange *sc.*
Charles de La Fosse. . . . . Duchange *sc.*

C. de Visscher *del.*
Philip Wouwermans. . . . . N. Dupuis *sc.*

Noel Coypel *pinx.*
Noel Coypel. . . . . Jean Audran *sc.*

Vivien *pinx.*
Fénelon. . . . . Benoît Audran *sc.*

A. Pesne *pinx.*
Nicolas Vleughels. . . . . E. Jeaurat *sc.*

Le Gros *pinx.*
Claude Hallé. . . . . Nic. de Larmessin *sc.*

Antoine Coypel *pinx.*
Antoine Coypel. . . . . B. Massé *sc.*

David Kraft *pinx.*
Charles XII. of Sweden. . . . . Tanjé *sc.*

Mart. de Meytens *pinx.*
Maria Theresa, Queen of Hungary. . . . . . . Petit *sc.*

Tortebat *pinx.*
René Ant. Houasse. . . . . Ant. Trouvain *sc.*

Jouvenet *pinx.*
Jean Jouvenet. . . . . Ant. Trouvain *sc.*

Roslin *pinx.*
Hyac. Collin de Vermont. . . . . . Salvador Carmona *sc.*

Drouais *pinx.*
Edme Bouchardon. . . . . Beauvarlet *sc.*

Louis Michel Vanloo *pinx.*
Portrait of himself, as painting the portrait of his father Jean-Baptiste Vanloo. . . . . Miger *sc.*

Duplessis *pinx.*
Necker. . . . . Aug. de Saint-Aubin *sc.*

P. A. Wille fils *del.*
J. G. Wille. . . . . Ingouf *sc.*

Augustin de Saint-Aubin *del.*
Gluck. Saint-Aubin *sc.* *See* Smallest Portfolio, XXXII.

L. M. Vanloo *pinx.*
Helvetius. . . . . Aug. de Saint-Aubin *sc.*

Cochin *pinx.*
Benjamin Franklin. . . . . . . Aug. de Saint-Aubin *sc.*
Benjamin Franklin. Mezzotinto. . . . Elias Haid *sc.*

Callet *pinx.*
Charles Gravier, Comte de Vergennes. . . . . Vangelisti *sc.*

Charles de Chatillon *pinx.*
Napoleon I. . . . . P. Audouin *sc.*
Below, The Battle of Austerlitz, engraved by Duplessi-Bertaux, finished by Bovinet.

Aug. Boucher Desnoyers *del.*
Thomas Jefferson. . . . . Desnoyers *sc.*

Gérard *pinx.*
Le Roi de Rome, The infant Napoleon II. . . . Desnoyers *sc.*

Richard *pinx.*
Francis I. and his sister Marguerite of Navarre. Desnoyers *sc.* *See* Portfolio of Largest Portraits, XVI. I.

Gérard *pinx.*
Napoleon I. Desnoyers *sc.* *See* Portfolio of Largest Portraits, XVI. I.
Talleyrand. Desnoyers *sc.* *See* Portfolio of Largest Portraits, XVI. I.

Gérard *pinx.* 1803.
Napoléon. *Proof.* . . . . Richomme *sc.*

Mme. Chéradame *pinx.*
La Comtesse de Genlis. . . . . Lignon *sc.*

Gérard *pinx.*
Mademoiselle Mars. . . . . Lignon *sc.*

St. Ours *pinx.*
Saussure. . . . . Pradier *sc.*

Steuben *pinx.*
Alexander von Humboldt. . . . . Forster *sc.*

Fr. Porbus *pinx.*
Henry IV. of France. . . . . Forster *sc.*

Couder *del.*
Washington. . . . . A. Blanchard *sc.*

Biennourry *del.*
Pope Pius IX. *Proof.* . . . . A. Blanchard *sc.*

Henriquel Dupont *del.*
Mme. Pasta, as Anne Boleyn. *Proof.* . . . Henriquel Dupont *sc.*

DELAROCHE *pinx.*

Pope Gregory XVI. *Proof.* . . . . Henriquel Dupont *sc.*

H. LEHMANN *del.*

Rachel. *Proof.* . . . . Henriquel Dupont *sc.*

DELAROCHE *pinx.*

Peter the Great of Russia. *Proof.* Dupont *sc.* *See* Portfolio of Largest Portraits, XVI. I.

CALAMATTA *del.*

Masaccio. *Proof.* . . . . Calamatta *sc.*

DELAROCHE *pinx.*

Delaroche. *Proof.* . . . . Aristide Louis *sc.*

Napoleon I. *Proof.* Aristide Louis *sc.* *See* Portfolio of Largest Portraits, XVI. I.

L. MASSARD *del.*

Horace Vernet. . . . . L. Massard *sc.*

XVI. G. PORTRAITS. ITALIAN.

C. F. RUSCA *pinx.*

Count Schulenburg, Field Marshal of Venice . . Marco Pitteri *sc.*

RAPHAEL MENGS *pinx.*

Raphael Mengs. *Proof.* . . . . Cunego *sc.*

GUTTENBRUN *pinx.*

J. F. Reifenstein. . . . . G. Morghen *sc.*

Ariosto. . . . . Raphael Morghen *sc.*

Boccaccio. . . . . Raphael Morghen *sc.*

Dante. . . . . Raphael Morghen *sc.*

The same. 8vo. Raphael Morghen *sc.* *See* Smallest Portfolio, XXXII.

VAN DYCK *pinx.*

Francisco de Moncada. Raphael Morghen *sc.* *See* Portfolio of Van Dyck, X.

(After Gérard.) Napoleon I. . . . . . . Raphael Morghen *sc.*

The same. *Proof.* . . . . Raphael Morghen *sc.*

Guicciardini. . . . . Raphael Morghen *sc.*

A. BRONZINO *pinx.*

Macchiavelli. 8vo. *Proof.* Raphael Morghen *sc.* *See* Smallest Portfolio, XXXII.

The same. 8vo. *Proof.* Raphael Morghen *sc.* *See* Smallest Portfolio, XXXII.

R. MORGHEN *del.*

Michel-Angelo. Front view, bust. *Proof.* . . Raphael Morghen *sc.*

SANTARELLI *del.*

The same, in profile, head in a medallion. *Proof.* Raphael Morghen *sc.*

VASARI *pinx.*

Lorenzo de' Medici. . . . . . . Raphael Morghen *sc.*

Benvenuto Cellini. . . . . Raphael Morghen *sc.*

The same. *Proof before the square shading round the oval.* Raphael Morghen *sc.*

The same. *Artist's proof before any letters.* . . Raphael Morghen *sc.*

MIEREVELT *pinx.*

"William II. of Nassau." . . . . . . Raphael Morghen *sc.*

Petrarca. . . . . Raphael Morghen *sc.*

Torquato Tasso. . . . . Raphael Morghen *sc.*

FRANCISCO VIEIRA *pinx.*

Deodato Turchi. . . . . Raphael Morghen *sc.*

TOFANELLI *del.*

San Filippo Neri. . . . . Raphael Morghen *sc.*

ANGELICA KAUFFMAN *pinx.*

Giovanni Volpato. . . . . Raphael Morghen *sc.*

EMILIO CATENI *del.*

Gioacchino Rossini. . . . . Raphael Morghen *sc.*

RAPHAEL *pinx.*

Head of the Fornarina, engraved on silver. Raphael Morghen *sc.* *See* Smallest Portfolio, XXXII.

Portrait of a Nun, three quarters length. . . . Raphael Morghen *sc.*

FABRE *pinx.*

Vittorio Alfieri. . . . . Cipriani *sc.*

REMBRANDT *pinx.*

An Oriental Figure, whole length. "Borgomastro Olandese." . Longhi *sc.*

(In Rembrandt's style.) A Man with Book and Cane. . . Longhi *sc.*

RUBENS *pinx.*

A Negro, laughing. . . . . Longhi *sc.*

LE GROS *pinx.*

Napoleon Bonaparte at Arcole. . . . . Longhi *sc.*

The same. *Proof.* . . . . Longhi *sc.*

LONGHI *del.*

Napoleon I. as king of Italy, with a crown of laurel; bust, in profile. *Proof.* Longhi *sc.*

SCHIAVONI *pinx.*

Francis I., Emperor of Austria. . . . . Longhi *sc.*

The same. *Artist's proof.* . . . . Longhi *sc.*

LONGHI *del.*

Napoleon I., with the iron crown of Italy. *See* below, under *Vite e Ritratti di illustri Italiani.*

STUART *pinx.*

Washington. *Proof.* . . . . Longhi *sc.*

GÉRARD *pinx.*

Eugène Beauharnais, Viceroy of Italy. Longhi *sc.* *See* Portfolio of Largest Portraits, XVI. I.

M. BISI *del.*

Benjamin Franklin. . . . . Michele Bisi *sc.*

G. VASARI *pinx.*

Michel-Angelo. . . . . Giovacchino Cantini *sc.*

KÜGELGEN *pinx.*

Schiller. *Proof.* . . . . Faustino Anderloni *sc.*

FABRE *pinx.*

Vittorio Alfieri. . . . . P. Toschi et Ant. Isac *sc.*

SANTE DI TITO *pinx.*

Machiavelli. . . . . P. Toschi et Ant. Isac *sc.*

GÉRARD *pinx.*

Le Duc Decazes. . . . . P. Toschi *sc.*

The same. *Proof.* . . . . P. Toschi *sc.*

BRONZINO *pinx.*

Cosmo de' Medici. *Proof.* . . . . A. Perfetti *sc.*

Maria de' Medici. . . . . L. Martelli *sc.*

Raphael Morghen. . . . . P. Caronni *sc.*

REMBRANDT *pinx.*

Rembrandt. . . . . P. Caronni *in.*, Longhi *term.*

EMILIO CATENI *del.*

Michel-Angelo. . . . . Gioacchino Lepri *sc.*

VASARI *pinx.*

Benvenuto Cellini. . . . . Sam. Jesi *sc.*

SAMUELE JESI *del.*

Giuseppe Longhi. *Proof.* . . . . Sam. Jesi *sc.*

PORTRAITS FROM *VITE E RITRATTI DI ILLUSTRI ITALIANI.*

MARIA LONGHI *del.*

Gaetana Agnesi. . . . . Ernesta Bisi *sc.*

GIUSEPPE BOSSI *del.*

Cesare Beccaria. . . . . Gius. Benaglia *sc.*

GIUSEPPE LONGHI *del.*

Michel-Angelo Buonarroti. . . . . Longhi *sc.*
The same. *Open letter proof.* . . . . Longhi *sc.*
The same. *Proof before all letters.* . . . . . . Longhi *sc.*

MARIA LONGHI *del.*

Vittoria Colonna. . . . . Ernesta Bisi *sc.*

TEODORO MATTEINI *del.*

Enrico Dandalo. . . . . Longhi *sc.*
The same. *Proof, with merely the artists' names.* . . Longhi *sc.*
The same. *Artist's proof, only* "Longhi sc." *cut with the needle.* . Longhi *sc.*

GIUSEPPE LONGHI *del.*

Andrea Doria. . . . . Faustino Anderloni *sc.*
Gaetano Filangieri. . . . . P. Caronni *sc.*

"DOM. TINTORETTO *pinx.*, G. BOSSI *del.*"

Galileo Galilei. . . . . N. Schiavoni *sc.*

GIUSEPPE LONGHI *del.*

Giotto. . . . . C. Rampoldi *sc.*

BARTOLOZZI *del.*

Gasparo Gozzi. . . . . Bartolozzi *sc.*

GIUSEPPE LONGHI *del.*

Aldo Manuzio. . . . . Gerolamo Scotto *sc.*
Paolo Manuzio. . . . . Felice Zuliani *sc.*

PAOLO CARONNI *del.*

P. Metastasio. . . . . P. Caronni *sc.*

GIUSEPPE LONGHI *del.*

Napoleon, with the iron crown. . . . . Longhi *sc.*
The same. *Proof.* . . . . Longhi *sc.*
Andrea Palladio. . . . . P. Caronni *sc.*

GIOVITA GARAVAGLIA *del.*

Giuseppe Parini. . . . . Garavaglia *sc.*

TEODORO MATTEINI *del.*

Vettor Pisani. . . . . C. Rampoldi *sc.*
Marco Polo. . . . . Felice Zuliani *sc.*

GIUSEPPE BOSSI *del.*

Gian Battista della Porta. . . . . Beceni *sc.*, Longhi *dir.*

TEODORO MATTEINI *del.*

Fra Paolo Sarpi. . . . . Vincenzo Giaconi *sc.*

GIULIO TOMBA *del.*

Torricelli. . . . . Giulio Tomba *sc.*

Giuseppe Longhi *del.*
Amerigo Vespucci. . . . . Michele Bisi *sc.*
Alessandro Volta. "Per Nicolò Bettoni."

XVI. H. PORTRAITS. ENGLISH.

Souse *pinx.*
William Sanderson. . . . . W. Faithorne *sc.*

George Vertue *del.*
Milton, ætatis 62. . . . . Vertue *sc.*

Thomas Worlidge *del.*
John Lindsey, Earl of Crawfurd. . . . . . . Worlidge *sc.*

Federico Zuccheri *pinx.*
Mary Queen of Scots. *Proof.* . . . . . . Bartolozzi *sc.*

John Keyes Sherwin *del.*
Woollett. . . . . J. K. Sherwin *sc.*

G. F. Joseph *pinx.*
William Sharp. *Proof.* . . . . Sharp *sc.*

George Romney *pinx.*
Thomas Walker. *Proof.* . . . . Sharp *sc.*

Alexander Roslin *pinx.*
Catherine II., Empress of Russia. . . . . . Caroline Watson *sc.*

Hogarth *pinx.*
Hogarth. . . . . Samuel Ireland *fec. aq. fort.*

Sir Thomas Lawrence *pinx.*
Sir Thomas Lawrence. *Proof.* . . . . . . Samuel Cousins *sc.*
Lady Burghersh with her Infant. *Artist's proof.* . . . Longhi *sc.*

After Horatio Greenough's statue. Washington. . . . Jacopo Bernardi *sc.*

The Chandos portrait of Shakespeare, bust. *Open letters.* . Samuel Cousins *sc.*
The picture owned by Lord Ellesmere.

Shakespeare, three quarters length, near a table on which is a skull. *Proof.*
From Mr. Kingston's picture, Ashbourne, Derby. . . G. F. Storm *sc.*

Shakespeare, head; fac-simile of the picture attributed to Rich. Burbage. Published in 1851, for W. Nicol, proprietor of the Shakespeare Press Lithography.

W. H. Pickersgill *pinx.*
Cuvier. *Proof.* . . . . George T. Doo *sc.*
Hannah More. *Proof.* . . . . Worthington *sc.*

Sir Thomas Lawrence *pinx.*
Sir Walter Scott. *Proof.* . . . . J. H. Robinson *sc.*

THOMAS PHILLIPS *pinx.*
Lord Byron. *Proof.* . . . . Robert Graves *sc.*

MISS MARGARET GILLES *pinx.*
William Wordsworth. *Proof.* . . . . Edward McInnes *sc.*

STUART *pinx.*
Washington. *Proof.* . . . . . . Joseph Andrews *sc.*

HEALY *pinx.*
John Quincy Adams. *Proof.* . . . . . Joseph Andrews *sc.*
James Grahame. . . . . Joseph Andrews *sc.*

MISCELLANEOUS PORTRAITS.

JOHANN FRIEDRICH EICH *pinx.*
Pascha Weitsch. . . . . Chodowiecki *sc.*

AUGUSTIN DE SAINT-AUBIN *del.*
Carl Heinrich von Heineken. . . . . . Aug. de Saint-Aubin *sc.*

JOHANN FRIEDRICH LEYBOLD *del.*
Adam von Bartsch. . . . . J. F. Leybold *sc.*

(After a bust.) Baron von Stosch. . . . . . . Heinrich Schmidt *sc.*

JACOB MERZ *del.*
Antonio Canova. . . . . J. Merz *sc.*
Benjamin Thompson, Count Rumford. . . . . . F. Müller *sc.*
Prince Friedrich Josias of Coburg. . . . . . . F. Müller *sc.*

GRÉVEDON *del.*
Mme. Malibran-Garcia. . . . . Grévedon *lith.*

SIR THOMAS LAWRENCE *del.*
Miss Fanny Kemble. . . . . Richard J. Lane *lith.*

(After Chantrey's statue.) Washington. . . . . . J. Thomson *sc.*

LUDWIG GRIMM *del.*
"Maler" Friedrich Müller. . . . . L. Grimm *sc.*

(After Horatio Greenough's bust.) Lafayette. . . . . . D. Testi *sc.*

F. PICKERING *del.*, from a bust.
General Riego. . . . . Pickering *lith.*

WEEKES *del.*
Chantrey. . . . . Fairland *lith.*

BALLAGNY *del.*, from a bust.
Carlo Botta. . . . . Balagny *lith.*

STUART *pinx.*
Dr. Nathaniel Bowditch. . . . . G. F. Storm *sc.*

JULIUS HÜBNER *pinx.*
Friedrich Wilhelm Schadow. . . . . C. Küchler *sc.*

Welch *del.*
David B. Ogden, M. D. . . . . Brown *lith.*

Hoyt *pinx.*
Daniel Webster. . . . . H. W. Smith *sc.*

Staigg *pinx.*
The same. . . . . J. Cheney et R. W. Dodson *sc.*

XVI. I. PORTRAITS. LARGE.

Goltzius *pinx.*
Coornhert. . . . . Goltzius *sc.*
Hendrik Goltzius. . . . . Goltzius *sc.*

Beaudrun *pinx.*
Marie Thérèse of Spain, Queen of Louis XIV. . . . . N. de Poilly *sc.*

Nanteuil *pinx.*
Anne of Austria, Queen of Louis XIII. . . . . . Nanteuil *sc.*
J.-B. Colbert. . . . . Nanteuil *sc.*
Jac. Nic. Colbert, abbas Beccensis. . . . . . . Nanteuil *sc.*
Turenne. . . . . Nanteuil *sc.*

N. Mignard *pinx.*
Le Comte d'Harcourt. (Le Cadet La Perle.) . . . . Masson *sc.*

Masson *del.*
François Rouxel de Médavy. . . . . Masson *sc.*

(After Girardon's basrelief.) Édouard Colbert. . . . . . Roullet *sc.*

Hyac. Rigaud *pinx.*
Prince de Conti. . . . . P. Drevet *sc.*
Louis XIV. of France. . . . . P. Drevet *sc.*
Samuel Bernard. . . . . P. I. Drevet *sc.*
Charles Gaspard Dodun, Marquis d'Herbault. . . . . P. I. Drevet *sc.*

J. B. Piacetta *pinx.*
Goldoni. . . . . Marco Pitteri *sc.*

Tocqué *pinx.*
Mary, Princess of Poland, Queen of Louis XV. . . . . . Daullé *sc.*

Hyac. Rigaud *pinx.*
Auguste III., Roi de Pologne. . . . . Balechou *sc.*

Sir Joshua Reynolds *pinx.*
Lord Mansfield. *Proof.* . . . . Bartolozzi *sc.*
Lord Thurlow. *Proof.* . . . . Bartolozzi *sc.*

Home *pinx.*
John Hyde, Judge of Calcutta. *Proof.* . . . . W. Sharp *sc.*

Sir Joshua Reynolds *pinx.*
John Hunter. *Proof.* . . . . W. Sharp *sc.*

Benjamin West *pinx.*
Samuel Moore. *Proof.* . . . . W. Sharp *sc.*

Duplessis *pinx.*
Louis XVI. *Proof.* . . . . J. G. von Müller *sc.*

Casanova *pinx.*
Count Beloselski. *Proof.* . . . . Schulze *sc.*

L. Wolf *del.*
Frederic the Great of Prussia on Horseback. . . . . J. M. Haas *sc.*

Callet *pinx.*
Louis XVI. . . . . Bervic *sc.*

Harlow *pinx.*
Benjamin West. *Proof.* . . . . Fittler *sc.*

Thomas Phillips *pinx.*
Sir Joseph Banks. *Proof.* . . . . Schiavonetti *sc.*

Gérard *pinx.*
Eugène Beauharnais. . . . . Longhi *sc.*
The same. *Proof before border and before letters.* . . . . Longhi *sc.*

Sir Thomas Lawrence *pinx.*
The Duke of Wellington. . . . . Bromley *sc.*

Fabre *pinx.*
Guillaume Clarke, Duc de Feltre. . . . . . . R. U. Massard *sc.*

Richard *pinx.*
Francis I. and his sister Marguerite of Navarre. *Proof.* Desnoyers *sc.*

Gérard *pinx.*
Napoleon I. . . . . Desnoyers *sc.*
The same. *Proof.* . . . . Desnoyers *sc.*
Talleyrand. *Proof.* . . . . Desnoyers *sc.*

Stieler *pinx.*
Ludwig I. of Bavaria. . . . . Reindel *sc.*

Delaroche *pinx.*
Peter the Great of Russia. *Proof.* . . . . Henriquel Dupont *sc.*

W. Allston *pinx.*
S. T. Coleridge. *Proof.* . . . . Sam. Cousins *sc.*

H. Holbein *pinx.*
Calvin. . . . . Fr. Müller *sc.*

Winterhalter *pinx.*
Louis Philippe of France. *With open letters.* . . . . . Bridoux *sc.*

WINTERHALTER *pinx., continued.*

Helen of Mecklenburg, Duchess of Orleans, with the young Count of Paris in her arms. *Open letters.* . . . . A. D. Lefèvre *sc.*

SIR THOMAS LAWRENCE *pinx.*

Benjamin West. *Proof.* . . . . . . Charles Rolls *sc.*

DELAROCHE *pinx.*

Napoleon I. *Proof.* . . . . Aristide Louis *sc.*

STUART *pinx.*

Washington at Dorchester Heights. . . . . . T. Kelly *sc.*

TRUMBULL *pinx.*

Washington at Trenton. . . . . W. Warner *sc.*

STUART *pinx.*

Washington. *Proof.* . . . . Thomas Welch *sc.*

XVII. EARLIEST ITALIAN PAINTER-ENGRAVERS.

SANDRO BOTTICELLI *del.*

A Youth and a Maiden, supporting a circular shield.
Bartsch, No. 2. Ottley, No. 2. Sandro Botticelli, or Baccio Baldini, *sc.*

POLLAJUOLA *del.*

Hercules combating the Giants. . . . . B. 3. Pollajuola *sc.*

ANDREA MANTEGNA *del.*

The Entombment. . . . . B. 3. A. Mantegna *sc.*
Triumphal Procession. Roman Senators. . . B. 11. A. Mantegna *sc.*
The same. Elephants and torches. . . . B. 12. A. Mantegna *sc.*
The same. Soldiers and trophies. . . . B. 13. A. Mantegna *sc.*

ROBETTA *del.*

Adoration of the Kings. . . . . B. 6. Robetta *sc.*

RAPHAEL *del.*

Adam and Eve. . . . . . B. 1. Marc Antonio Raimondi *sc.*
The same. Copy by Crowhull.
A pen-and-ink copy of the same.
Israelites gathering Manna. . . B. 8. Agostino Veneziano *sc.*
David conquering Goliath. . . B. 10. Marc-Antonio Raimondi *sc.*
Slaughter of the Innocents, with the fir-tree.
B. 18. Marc-Antonio Raimondi *sc.*
The same. Without the fir-tree. B. 20. Marc-Antonio Raimondi *sc.*
Feast at the House of Simon. . . B. 23. Marc-Antonio Raimondi *sc.*
Descent from the Cross. . . . B. 32. Marc-Antonio Raimondi *sc.*
La Vierge au bras nu. . . . B. 34. Marc-Antonio Raimondi *sc.*
Death of Ananias. . . . . B. 42. Agostino Veneziano *sc.*
Paul at Athens. . . . . B. 44. Marc-Antonio Raimondi *sc.*

RAPHAEL *del., continued.*

La Vierge à l'escalier. . . . B. 45. Marc-Antonio Raimondi *sc.*
La Vierge sur des nues. . . . B. 47. Marc-Antonio Raimondi *sc.*

FRANCESCO FRANCIA *del.* ?

Holy Family. . . . . . B. 50. Agostino Veneziano *sc.*

RAPHAEL *del.*

La Vierge à la longue cuisse. . . B. 57. Marc-Antonio Raimondi *sc.*
Holy Family. . . . . . B. 60. Marc-Antonio Raimondi *sc.*
La Vierge au Berceau. . . . B. 63. Marc-Antonio Raimondi *sc.*

BACCIO BANDINELLI *del.*

The Martyrdom of St. Lawrence. B. 104. Marc-Antonio Raimondi *sc.*

RAPHAEL *del.*

The Five Saints. . . . B. 113. Marc-Antonio Raimondi *sc.*
St. Cecilia. . . . . . . B. 116. Marc-Antonio Raimondi *sc.*
The Martyrdom of St. Felicitas. B. 117. Marc-Antonio Raimondi *sc.*
Dido. . . . . B. 187. Marc-Antonio Raimondi *sc.*
The same. . . . . B. 187. Marc-Antonio Raimondi *sc.*
Lucretia. . . . . . . B. 192. Marc-Antonio Raimondi *sc.*
Cleopatra, or, more correctly, Ariadne.
B. 199. Marc-Antonio Raimondi *sc.*
Alexander putting Homer's Works in the Tomb of Achilles.
B. 207. Marc-Antonio Raimondi *sc.*

RAZZI [or BAZZI] *del.*

The Triumph of Titus. . . B. 213. Marc-Antonio Raimondi *sc.*

SALVIATI *del.*

Jupiter. . . . . B. 216. Marco da Ravenna *sc.*

(From the antique.) Two Fauns carrying an Infant.
B. 230. Marc-Antonio Raimondi *sc.*

RAPHAEL *del.*

The Judgment of Paris. . . B. 245. Marc-Antonio Raimondi *sc.*
Parnassus. . . . . . . B. 247. Marc-Antonio Raimondi *sc.*
A Faun accompanied by a Child. B. 296. Marc-Antonio Raimondi *sc.*
Venus wiping her left foot. . . B. 297. Marc-Antonio Raimondi *sc.*
The Vintage. . . . . . B. 306. Marc-Antonio Raimondi *sc.*

DESIGNER NOT KNOWN. Cupid and three Infants.
B. 320. Marc-Antonio Raimondi *sc.*

RAPHAEL *del.*

Venus, Juno, and Ceres. . . . B. 327. Marco da Ravenna *sc.*
Cupid and the Graces. . . B. 344. Marc-Antonio Raimondi *sc.*
Hercules and Antæus. . . . B. 347. Agostino Veneziano *sc.*

RAPHAEL *del.*, *continued.*

Galatea. . . . . . . B. 350. Marc-Antonio Raimondi *sc.*

Quos ego. . . . . . . B. 352. Marc-Antonio Raimondi *sc.*

RAPHAEL'S SCHOOL. La femme au croissant.

B. 354. Marc-Antonio Raimondi *sc.*

GIORGIONE *del.*

"Raphael's Dream." . . . B. 359. Marc-Antonio Raimondi *sc.*

RAPHAEL *del.*

Prudence. . . . . . . B. 371. Marc-Antonio Raimondi *sc.*

Two Sibyls with the Zodiac. . B. 397. Marc-Antonio Raimondi *sc.*

The Pestilence. . . . . . B. 417. Marc-Antonio Raimondi *sc.*

MICHEL-ANGELO *del.*

Les Grimpeurs. . . . . . . B. 423. Agostino Veneziano *sc.*

RAPHAEL *del.*

Lo Stregozzo. . . . . . . B. 426. Agostino Veneziano *sc.*

MICHEL-ANGELO *del.*

Two Naked Men. . . . . B. 464. Marc-Antonio Raimondi *sc.*

RAPHAEL *del.*

A Woman with a Vase. . . . . B. 474. Agostino Veneziano *sc.*

A Man with the base of a Column. . B. 477. Agostino Veneziano *sc.*

(From the antique.) A Youth extracting a Thorn from his Foot.

B. 480. Marco da Ravenna *sc.*

GIULIO CAMPAGNOLA *del.*

The Old Shepherd. . . . . . B. 7. Giulio Campagnola *sc.*

MASTER OF THE CADUCEUS *del.*

Victory. . . . . B. 23. Master of the Caduceus *sc.*

G. B. FRANCO *del.*

The Ark in the Temple of Dagon. . . . . . B. 6. Franco *sc.*

CARAVAGGIO *del.*

The Flight to Clelia. . . . . . B. 83. Giulio Bonasone *sc.*

GIULIO BONASONE *del.*

Jason and Medea. . . . . B. 98. Bonasone *sc.*

P. Michel-Angelo Buonarroti. . . . . B. 345. Bonasone *sc.*

GIORGIO GHISI *del.*

P. The same. . . . . B. 71. Giorgio Ghisi *sc.*

RAPHAEL *del.*

Holy Family with the Cradle. . . . . B. 5. Caraglio *sc.*

The Transfiguration. . . . . . . B. 6. Master of the Die *sc.*

GIULIO ROMANO *del.*

Triumph of Cybele. . . . . . . B. 18. Master of the Die *sc.*

RAPHAEL *del.*

Æneas saving Anchises. . . . . B. 72. Master of the Die *sc.*
Scipio's Victory over Syphax. . . . B. 73. Master of the Die *sc.*

MICHEL-ANGELO *del.*

The Fall of Phaëton. . . . B. 38. Beatrizet the younger *sc.*
Tityus gnawed by the Vulture. . . B. 39. Beatrizet the younger *sc.*

PERINO DEL VAGA *del.*

The Sacrifice of Iphigenia. . . . B. 43. Beatrizet the younger *sc.*

(After the antique.) The Battle of the Dacians.
B. 94. Beatrizet the younger *sc.*

RAPHAEL *del.*

The Madonna of Loretto. . . . . . . B. 5. G. Ghisi *sc.*

GIULIO ROMANO *del.*

The Birth of Memnon. . . . . . . B. 57. G. Ghisi *sc.*
The Prison. . . . . B. 66. G. Ghisi *sc.*

MICHEL-ANGELO *pinx.*

The Last Judgment. . . . . B. 28. Martin Rota *sc.*

XVIII. ITALIAN PAINTER-ENGRAVERS. THE CARACCI AND THEIR FOLLOWERS.

LODOVICO CARACCI *del.*

La Vierge aux Anges. . . . . . B. 2. Lodovico Caracci *sc.*

CORREGGIO *pinx.*

Ecce Homo. . . . . B. 20. Agostino Caracci *sc.*

PAOLO VERONESE *pinx.*

The Crucifixion. . . . . B. 21. Agostino Caracci *sc.*
Christ's Body supported by the Virgin and an Angel.
B. 102. Agostino Caracci *sc.*

FR. VANNI *pinx.*

The "great" St. Francis in Ecstasy. . B. 67. Agostino Caracci *sc.*
The "small" St. Jerome. . . . . . B. 74. Agostino Caracci *sc.*

AGOSTINO CARACCI *del.*

The "great" St. Jerome. . . . . . B. 75. Agostino Caracci *sc.*

TINTORETTO *pinx.*

St. Jerome in the Desert. . . . . . B. 76. Agostino Caracci *sc.*

PAOLO VERONESE *pinx.*

The Marriage of St. Catherine. . . . . B. 97. Agostino Caracci *sc.*

AGOSTINO CARACCI *del.*

Pan subdued by Cupid. . . . . . B. 116. Agostino Caracci *sc.*

TINTORETTO *pinx.*

Mercury and the Graces. . . .	B. 117.	Agostino Caracci *sc.*
Mars and Minerva.	B. 118.	Agostino Caracci *sc.*

ANNIBALE CARACCI *del.*

Christ crowned with Thorns. . . .	B. 3.	Annibale Caracci *sc.*
Pietà : Christ of Caprarola. . . .	B. 4.	Annibale Caracci *sc.*
The Madonna with a Porringer. . .	B. 9.	Annibale Caracci *sc.*
Holy Family of the Year 1590. . . .	B. 11.	Annibale Caracci *sc.*

GUIDO RENI *del.*

Holy Family.	B. 10.	Guido Reni *sc.*

ANNIBALE CARACCI *del.*

Holy Family and Saint Clara.	B. 50.	Guido Reni *sc.*
Madonna and Child.	B. 51.	Guido Reni *sc.*

ANNIBALE CARACCI *pinx.*

The Alms of St. Roch.	B. 53.	Guido Reni *sc.*

SIMONE CANTARINI *del.*

Holy Family, with Elizabeth and St. John.	B. 10.	Simone Cantarini *sc.*
Rest in Egypt. *Contre-épreuve.* . . .	B. 3.	Simone Cantarini *sc.*
The Rape of Europa.	B. 30.	Simone Cantarini *sc.*

ELIZABETTA SIRANI *del.*

Repose in Egypt.	B. 5.	Elizabetta Sirani *sc.*

PARMEGIANO *del.*

The Entombment.	B. 5.	Parmegiano *sc.*
The Resurrection.	B. 6.	Parmegiano *sc.*

CARLO MARATTI *del.*

Virgin and Child with St. Magdalen. . . .	B. 6.	Carlo Maratti *sc.*

RIBERA, called SPAGNOLETTO, *del.*

St. Jerome, "the smaller."	B. 4.	Spagnoletto *sc.*
The Martyrdom of St. Bartholomew. . . .	B. 6.	Spagnoletto *sc.*

PIETRO TESTA *del.*

Achilles dipped in the Water of the Styx. . .	B. 21.	Pietro Testa *sc.*

XIX. EARLIEST GERMAN PAINTER-ENGRAVERS.

LUCAS CRANACH.

The Dukes Albert and Henry of Saxony. . . . . B. 2.

THE MASTER E. S. 1466.

"Solomon adoring the Idols," or, more correctly, The Sibyl and the Emperor Augustus. . . . . B. 8.

MARTIN SCHONGAUER.

The Nativity.	B. 4.
The Flight into Egypt.	B. 7.
The Crowning with Thorns.	B. 13.
Christ before Pilate.	B. 14.
The Bearing of the Cross.	B. 16.
The Crucifixion.	B. 17.
The Entombment.	B. 18.
The Resurrection.	B. 20.
The Virgin standing, with the Child holding a Pear.	B. 28.
The Virgin crowned by Two Angels.	B. 31.
St. Anthony tormented by the Demons. *Copy.*	B. 47.
A Foolish Virgin.	B. 87.

ISRAEL VAN MECKEN.

Christ scourged.	B. 13.

GLOCKENDON.

Christ before Caiaphas.	B. 6.
Christ redeeming the First Parents and Patriarchs.	B. 13.

WENZEL VON OLMÜTZ.

St. Sebastian.	B. 30.

ALBRECHT DÜRER.

Adam and Eve.	B. 1.
The Nativity.	B. 2.
The Passion. Set of 16 plates.	B. 3–18.
Christ seized by the Jews. Duplicate from the Passion.	B. 5.
Christ Praying in the Garden.	B. 19.
The Man of Sorrows.	B. 20.
The Prodigal Son.	B. 28.
The Virgin with Long Hair and Bandlet.	B. 30.
The Virgin with Short Hair and Bandlet.	B. 33.
The Virgin nursing the Child.	B. 34.
The Virgin embracing the Child.	B. 35.
The Virgin nursing the Child.	B. 36.
The Virgin crowned by an Angel.	B. 37.
The Virgin with the Child swaddled.	B. 38.
The Virgin crowned by Two Angels.	B. 39.
The Virgin sitting by a Wall.	B. 40.
The Virgin with a Pear.	B. 41.
The Virgin with a Monkey.	B. 42.
The Virgin with a Butterfly.	B. 44.
St. Simeon.	B. 49.

ALBRECHT DÜRER, *continued.*

St. George on Horseback. . . . . B. 54.
St. Hubertus or St. Eustachius. . . . . B. 57.
St. Jerome in his Cell. . . . . B. 60.
St. Jerome in Penitence. . . . . B. 61.
St. Genevieve, or the Penance of St. Chrysostom. . . . . B. 63.
The Witch. . . . . B. 67.
The Effect of Jealousy. . . . . B. 73.
Melancholy. . . . . B. 74.
The same. . . . . B. 74.
The "great" Fortune. . . . . B. 77.
The "little" Fortune. . . . . B. 78.
Lady on Horseback. . . . . B. 82.
The same. . . . . B. 82.
The Peasant and his Wife. . . . . B. 83.
The Hostess and the Cook. . . . . B. 84.
The Oriental with his Wife and Child. . . . . B. 85.
Three Peasants in Conversation. . . . . B. 86.
The Standard-Bearer. . . . . B. 87.
Peasants at Market. . . . . B. 89.
Offers of Love. . . . . B. 93.
Gentleman and Lady walking, Death lurking behind a Tree. . . B. 94.
The Knight of Death.. . . . . B. 98.
The same. . . . . B. 98.
The same. . . . . B. 98.
The Great Cannon. . . . . B. 99.
The same, copy by Hopfer.
The Shield of Arms with a Death's-Head. . . . . . . B. 101.
The same. . . . . B. 101.
P. Archbishop Albert of Mayence. "The Little Cardinal." . . B. 102.
P. Frederic, Elector of Saxony, called the Wise. . . . . B. 105.
P. Melanchthon. . . . . B. 105.
P. Bilibald Pirkheimer. . . . . B. 106.
P. Erasmus. . . . . B. 107.

HEINRICH ALDEGREVER.

The Judgment of Solomon. . . . . B. 29.
Susanna surprised. . . . . B. 30.
The Two Elders Accused. . . . . B. 31.
The Crucifixion, after Albrecht Dürer. . . . . B. 49.
Sophonisba. . . . . B. 62.
Fortuna. . . . . B. 106.
P. Heinrich Aldegrever, when 28 years of age. . . . . B. 188.

Albrecht Altdorfer.

Christ driving the Money-changers from the Temple. . . . . B. 6.
The Virgin and Child on the Throne. . . . . B. 13.
The Virgin and Child with St. Anne. . . . . B. 14.
St. Christopher. . . . . B. 19.
The Nun, or the Widow's Mite. . . . . B. 24.

H. Brosamer.

Solomon's Idolatry. . . . . B. 2.
Bathsheba. . . . . B. 3.
A Man ridden by his Wife. . . . . B. 18.

Georg Pencz.

Abraham receiving Hagar. . . . . B. 1.
Abraham dismissing Hagar. . . . . B. 3.
Joseph sold by his Brethren. . . . . B. 11.
Thomyris with the Head of Cyrus. . . . . B. 70.
The Death of Lucretia. . . . . B. 79.
Sophonisbe. . . . . B. 82.
Artemisia. . . . . B. 83.
The Siege of Carthage, after Giulio Romano. . . . . . B. 86.
The same, copy after Pencz, by "R."
A Woman wading through a Stream, on the other side Soldiers. B. 94.
P. John Frederic, Elector of Saxony, called the Magnanimous. . B. 126.

Barthel Beham.

A Woman seated on a Cuirass. . . . . B. 20.
Apollo and Daphne. . . . . B. 25.
Cupid as Postilion. . . . . B. 32.
The Miser. . . . . B. 38.
P. Ferdinand I., Emperor of Germany. . . . . B. 61.

Hans Sebald Beham.

The Marriage-feast at Cana. . . . . B. 23.
Christ Triumphant. . . . . B. 30.
The Prodigal Son wasting his Fortune. . . . . B. 32.
St. Sebaldus. . . . . B. 65.
Dido. . . . . B. 80.
Magnanimity of Trajan. . . . . B. 82.
The same. 1*st state.* . . . . B. 82.
Patience. . . . . B. 138.
Fortune. . . . . B. 140.
Misfortune. . . . . B. 141.
Melancholy. . . . . B. 144.
A Young Woman accompanied by Death. . . . . . . B. 149.
Three Soldiers with a Dog. . . . . B. 196.

HANS SEBALD BEHAM, *continued.*

The Sentinel over the Powder-cask. . . . . B. 197.
The Ensign, with Drummer and Fifer. . . . . B. 198.
The Ensign and the Drummer. . . . . B. 199.
A Woman's Head. "Eines Weibes Havpt." . . . . . B. 220.
The Little Buffoon, with a Scroll. . . . . B. 230.

J. B. (JACOB BINK.)

Combat of eleven Naked Men. . . . . J. B. B. 21.

LAUTENSACK.

𝔓. Dr. Georgius Roggenbach. . . . . B. 9.

XX. PAINTER-ENGRAVERS. LUKAS VAN LEYDEN, JEAN DUVET.

LUKAS VAN LEYDEN.

Eve presenting the Apple to Adam. . . . . B. 10.
Cain killing Abel. . . . . B. 13.
David playing before Saul. . . . . B. 27.
The Adoration of the Magi. . . . . B. 37.
Christ bearing the Cross. . . . . B. 72.
Christ appearing to Magdalen. . . . . B. 77.
The Return of the Prodigal Son. . . . . B. 78.
The Virgin in a Glory, standing on a Crescent. . . . . . B. 82.
St. Matthew. . . . . B. 101.
St. Jerome near a Rock. . . . . B. 112.
St. Jerome in his Chamber. . . . . B. 114.
The Dance of Magdalen. . . . . B. 122.
The Monk Sergius killed by Mohammed. . . . . . . B. 126.
Virgil the Magician suspended in a Basket. . . . . . B. 136.
Ensign with a Banner. . . . . B. 140.
The Promenade. . . . . B. 144.
Gentleman and Lady. . . . . B. 145.
A Man and Woman seated, in a landscape; he is handing her a Vase. B. 148.
The Milkmaid. . . . . B. 158.
𝔓. Lukas van Leyden. . . . . B. 173.

JEAN DUVET, "the Master of the Unicorn."

A King on Horseback and Suite, fleeing from the attack of a Unicorn. B. 40. R.-D. 55.
A Unicorn led in Triumph by a King and a Queen. . B. 41. R.-D. 58.

XXI. PAINTER-ENGRAVERS. CALLOT, DELLA BELLA, QUAST, CASTIGLIONE, LE CLERC, TIEPOLO, BENIGNO BOSSI.

CALLOT *sc.*

The Inferno, according to Dante. Poccetti *inv.* Large composition engraved on two plates. Le Bl. 44; comp. Nagler, *K.-L.* XI. p. 429. *See* Portfolio XIV.

Les Batailles des Médicis, 2 plates. Roselli *inv.* No. 7, Departure of the Troops against the Turks. No. 12, The Storming of the City of Bone. Le Bl. 1217 – 1222.

CALLOT *inv. et sc.*

The Assumption of the Virgin: "Non est hic."

The Virgin receiving a Procession of Martyrs at the Gate of Heaven. Small 4to, high.

The Temptation of St. Anthony. . . H. p. 509, No. 21. Le Bl. 28.

The Martyrdom of St. Sebastian. . . H. p. 510, No. 24. Le Bl. 40.

The Crucifixion of 23 Martyrs in Japan. H. p. 510, No. 27. Le Bl. 41.

16 plates, the series of Martyrium Apostolorum. H. p. 498, No. 10. Le Bl. 162 – 177.

The Great Fair of the Madonna del Imprunetta. H. p. 515, No. 41. Le Bl. 1251.

View of Pont Neuf and Tour de Nesle. H. p. 515, No. 32. Le Bl. 1365.

View of the Louvre and Tour de Nesle. H. p. 515, No. 33. Le Bl. 1366.

La Chasse au Cerf. . . . . . H. p. 516, No. 44. Le Bl. 1162.

Les Supplices. . . . . H. p. 512, No. 7. Le Bl. 1277.

P. Louis of Lorraine. . . . . H. p. 505, No. 7. Le Bl. 1241.

Les grandes Misères de le Guerre. H. p. 500, No. 20. Le Bl. 1252–1270. 2 plates, Nos. 14 and 17 of the set of 18.

CALLOT *inv.*

Capitano di Baroni. H. p. 502, No. 29. Le Bl. 977 – 1001. 8 plates of the set of 25. They are copies.

DELLA BELLA *inv. et sc.*

Two Horsemen among a flock of Sheep near an old Tree, landscape. Jombert 79. Le Bl. 1068.

View of the Pont Neuf in Paris. Jomb. 112. Le Bl. 1047. *See* Portfolio VI.

Livre des Paysages. 13 plates. . . . Jomb. 127. Le Bl. 1082–1094.

A Polish Stable-Groom on Horseback, leading another horse through water. Le Bl. 985.

A Negro in Eastern Costume, half-size. . . Jomb. 205. Le Bl. 995.

Four Turks, half length figures. . . . . Jomb. 207. Le Bl. 993.

DELLA BELLA *inv. et sc.*

Five half length figures, — four Orientals and a Negro. Jomb. 208. Le Bl. 991.

QUAST *inv. et sc.*

4 plates, Beggars, from the series of 26.

CASTIGLIONE *inv. et sc.*

Magdalen penitent. . . . . B. 26.

SÉBASTIEN LE CLERC *inv. et sc.*

The Siege of Mons. . . . . Jomb. 246.

The Miracle of the Loaves. . . . . Jomb. 251.

Elijah taken up in a Chariot of Fire. "Above the Niagara Falls." Jomb. 293.

The young Tobit with the Angel. . . . . . . Jomb. 298.

G. B. TIEPOLO *inv. et sc.*

The Conjurer. . . . . Nagler, No. 11.

The Rider, from the *Varj Capricci* (10 plates). . . . Nagler, No. 13.

BENIGNO BOSSI *inv. et sc.*

12 plates, heads, etched.

XXII. GOUDT. WENCESLAUS HOLLAR.

GOUDT.

The Seven Plates after Abraham Elsheimer. *See* Alphabetical Catalogue.

Wenceslaus Hollar, 92 pieces. *See* Alphabetical Catalogue.

XXIII. ETCHINGS. REMBRANDT, BOL, LIEVENS, VAN DE VELDE.

REMBRANDT.

73 pieces. *See* Alphabetical Catalogue.

FERDINAND BOL.

The Officer. . . . . B. 11.

A Man with two Plumes in his Cap. . . . . B. 13.

A Woman with a Pear. . . . . B. 14.

JAN LIEVENS.

𝔓. Ephraim Bonus, a Jewish physician. . . . . B. 56. II.

𝔓. The same. . . . . B. 56. II.

𝔓. Justus van Vondel, poet. . . . . B. 57. III.

𝔓. Daniel Heinsius, Professor at Leyden. . . . . . B. 58. I.

𝔓. Jacob Gouters, Musician of Charles I. . . . . . . B. 59. I.

J. VAN DE VELDE.

The Good Samaritan. . . . . Nagler, 23.

XXIV. ETCHINGS BY BERGHEM, BOTH, CLAUDE, DUJARDIN, OSTADE, G. POUSSIN, RUYSDAEL, SWANEVELT, WATERLOO.

Berghem.

A Shepherd with his Flock, fording a Stream. . . . . . B. 9. iii.
Three Goats under a Tree. . . . . B. 50. iii.

Jan Both.

A Woman on a Mule. . . . . B. 1. v.
The Ox-cart. . . . . B. 2. v.
The Muleteer. . . . . B. 6. v.
The Ferry-boat. . . . . B. 7. v.

Claude.

Shepherds and Cattle crossing a Brook. . . . . . . R.-D. 3. i.
The Cowherd. . . . . R.-D. 8. ii.
The Dance under the Trees. . . . . R.-D. 10. iv.
The Robbers. . . . . R.-D. 12. iv.
Seaport, with a large Tower. . . . . R.-D. 13. ii.
The Wooden Bridge. . . . . R.-D. 14. ii.
The Goatherd. . . . . R.-D. 19. iii.

Karel Dujardin.

The Fountain with Water-trough. . . . . B. 1. iv.
Three Pigs lying before a Sty. . . . . B. 8. iv.
A Sheep lying before a Fence. . . . . B. 39. iv.
Savoyard Boy with dancing Dog. . . . . B. 51. iv.

Ostade.

Les Fumeurs. . . . . B. 13.
Smoker and Drinker. . . . . B. App. 24.
The Humpbacked Fiddler. . . . . B. 44.
The Fiddler and Hurdy-gurdy Boy. . . . . B. 45.

Gaspar Poussin.

Rocky Landscape, with water in the foreground, three trees, and two men. R.-D. 3.

Cornelis Bega.

Bust of an Old Woman, in oval. . . . . B. 7. i.
A Woman smoking. . . . . B. 11. i.

Jacob Ruysdael.

The Little Bridge. . . . . B. 1.
The Cottage on a Hill. . . . . B. 3.

HERMAN VAN SWANEVELT.

The Camels. . . . . B. 26.
The Fishes. . . . . B. 77.

DAVID TENIERS.

Two Monkeys smoking.

ANTONI WATERLOO.

The Great Mill. . . . . B. 119.
The Little Bridge. . . . . B. 124.
Alpheus and Arethusa. . . . . B. 125.
Apollo and Daphne. . . . . B. 126.
Mercury and Argus. . . . . B. 127.
Pan and Syrinx. . . . . B. 128.
Venus and Adonis. . . . . B. 129.
Death of Adonis. . . . . B. 130.

XXV. EVERDINGEN. ETCHINGS.

94 pieces, including 4 duplicates, namely: B. 7, B. 22, B. 41, B. 51, while 4 of the series are wanting, B. 3, B. 42, B. 81, B. 91. Specified in the Catalogue of Engravers.

XXV. a. EVERDINGEN. ETCHINGS.

Illustrations to Reinecke Fuchs, 57 pieces.

XXVI. ETCHINGS BY BOISSIEU.

65 pieces, specified in the Catalogue of Engravers.

XXVII.

Collection de vues pittoresques d'Italie, dessinées d'après nature et gravées à l'eau forte à Rome, par C. A. Dies, Ch. Reinhart, et J. Mechau. Nuremberg, chez J. Fr. Frauenholz. 1799. fol.
72 Views, without the title, each artist contributing 24. Specified in the Catalogue of Engravers under REINHART.

XXVIII. MODERN ETCHINGS.

WORLIDGE.

WORLIDGE *del.*
Style of Rembrandt. Bust of a Man, in fur cloak and head-dress.

DIETRICH.

DIETRICH *del.*
The Prodigal Son. . . . . L. 27.

DIETRICH *del.*

The Mountebank. . . . . L. 74.
Nymphs bathing near a Cave. . . . . L. 136.

G. F. SCHMIDT.

SCHMIDT *pinx.*

P. G. F. Schmidt, with the Spider. . . . . Jac. 141.
P. Mme. Schmidt, sewing. . . . . Jac. 135.
P. Dorothée Louise Viedebandt, femme de G. F. Schmidt, reading. Jac. 142.
P. Michel, Hirsch. . . . . Jac. 144.
Bust of an Oriental, with a high cap surmounted by a crescent. Jac. 114.
An Old Bearded Man, with fur cap and breastplate. . . Jac. 116.

REMBRANDT *pinx.*

Lot and his Daughters. . . . . Jac. 173.
Tobias and his Wife. . . . . Jac. 177.
The Duke Adolphus of Gueldres threatening his Imprisoned Father. Jac. 137.
A Hermit in a Grotto near a burning City. . . . . . Jac. 166.
P. Rembrandt at the age of about 60 years. . . . . . Jac. 151.
P. The same when about 28 years of age. . . . . . Jac. 150.
The Jewish Bride. . . . . Jac. 128.
P. The Princess of Orange. . . . . Jac. 147.
A Girl, with a Pug-dog in her arms. . . . . Jac. 126.
Bust of a Young Gentleman leaning his Arm on a Wall. . . Jac. 124.
The Old Persian, with a cane. . . . . Jac. 120.
Bust of a Man, face view, with bare head, a mustache and imperial; his cloak is open, showing a chain with a medallion. . . . . Jac. 127.

FLINCK *pinx.*

P. Cats instructing the young Prince William Henry of Orange. Jac. 152.
Bust of a Young Man, with curly hair, mustache, and imperial, and with two Feathers in his cap. . . . . Jac. 125.

REMBRANDT *pinx.*

P. Rembrandt's Mother reading her Bible. . . . . . Jac. 153.

VAN DYCK *pinx.*

The Virgin and Child with the Infant St. John. . . . . . Jac. 176.

OSTADE *pinx.*

Two Boors drinking and smoking. . . . . Jac. 160.

DIETRICH *pinx.*

The Presentation in the Temple. . . . . Jac. 167.

ANTOINE PESNE *pinx.*

P. Dinglinger, Jeweller in Dresden. . . . . . . Jac. 148.

C. B. RODE.

RODE *del.*

Semiramis armata. . . . . Nagler, 86.
The Resurrection of a Christian. . . . . . . Nagler, 189.

CAPTAIN W. BAILLIE.

REMBRANDT *del.*

An aged Rabbi, with large beard, represented in front view, half length.

JAN CHALON.

REMBRANDT *inv.*

An Old Woman reading.

M. A. ANGELICA KAUFFMAN.

KAUFFMAN *del.*

Juno.
Hebe.

NORBLIN.

NORBLIN *del.*

The Rat-catcher.
The Offering of the Crown of Poland to Piast.

LONGHI.

LONGHI *del.*

Bust of an Old Woman.
Bust of a Man, with feathers in his cap.
Pan and Syrinx.

J. P. DE FREY.

BREKELENKAMP *pinx.*

A Hermit in the Wilderness, reading.

F. A. M. RETZSCH.

RETZSCH *del.*

The Chess-players.
Venus and Cupid.
Three Children attempting to catch a Butterfly.

FREDERIC WILLIAM III. OF PRUSSIA *del. et sc.*

A Trooper leading a Pack-horse.

P. HESS.

P. HESS *del.*

The Painters in a Cow-house in the Alps.

REMBRANDT *inv.*

Portrait of a Young Man, with a hat.

J. A. KLEIN.

J. A. KLEIN *del.*

A Saxon Wagon.

A Spanish Pilgrim at St. Peter's in Rome.

Lazzarone: Est! Est!

J. DE CLAUSSIN.

REMBRANDT *inv.*

Head of "the Princess of Orange."

H. C. MÜCKE.

H. C. MÜCKE *inv.*

Two Friars leaning over a Parapet by a Lake.

XXIX. ENGRAVINGS BY STRANGE.

52 pieces, two portraits of Strange on one sheet. Specified in the Alphabetical Catalogue of Engravers.

XXX. ENGRAVINGS BY WILLE.

44 pieces. *See* Alphabetical Catalogue.

XXXI. ARCHITECTURAL ENGRAVINGS BY PIRANESI AND OTHERS.

PIRANESI.

PIRANESI *del.*

Maria degli Angeli: Diocletian's Baths.

Column of Antonine.

Column of Trajan.

Colosseum, exterior.

The same, interior.

Pantheon, exterior.

The same, interior.

St. Peter's, exterior.

The same, interior.

The same, back view.

San Paolo fuor dei muri, exterior.

The same, interior.

Santa Maria Maggiore, Facciata.

Quirinal Palace.

Arch of Constantine.

Acqua Felice.

Palazzo dell' Academia Francese.

G. WOUTERS.

G. WOUTERS *del.*
Piazza Navone.

F. MORELLI.

F. MORELLI *del.*
Temples of the Sibyl and of Vesta.
Castle of St. Angelo.
Tomb of Cecilia Metella.
Temple of Delle Tosse.

CRISTOFANO DELL' ACQUA.

MAGNARONI *del.*
Amphitheatre of Verona.

VOLPATO.

C. BIANCONI *del.*
Algarotti's Tomb in the Campo Santo in Pisa.

S. QUAGLIO *des. in lap.*

Palazzo Vecchio in Florence.
Duomo di Como.

LANDINI.

LANDINI *del.*
Cathedral of Milan.

STATUES.

FR. MÜLLER.

AFTER THE ANTIQUE.
Venus d'Arles. *Proof.*
The same. *Artist's proof.*

XXXII. SMALLEST PORTFOLIO.

GAULTIER *del.*
Christ sending forth his Disciples. . . . . . . Gaultier *sc.*

KAREL VAN MALLERY *del.*
The Virgin and Child. . . . . . . Karel van Mallery *sc.*

ELSTRACKE *del.*
P. Sir Richard Whittington with his Cat. . . . . . Elstracke *sc.*

CLAUDE MELLAN *del.*
P. The Capuchin Father Joseph. . . . M. 196. C. Mellan *sc.*

SIR P. LELY *pinx.*
P. Mrs. Sarah Gilly. . . . . W. Faithorne *sc.*

HOLBEIN *pinx.*
P. Froben. . . . . W. Vaillant *sc. mezzotint.*

LE SUEUR *pinx.*

The Four Evangelists. . . . . . . R.-D. 7. Nanteuil *sc.*

NANTEUIL *pinx.*

P. Pierre de Maridat. . . . . . . R.-D. 168. Nanteuil *sc.*

A. MASSON (?) *pinx.*

P. Madame Helyot. . . . . . . R.-D. 36. A. Masson *sc.*

HOLBEIN *pinx.*

P. Henry VIII. . . . . Vertue *sc.*

ELSHEIMER *pinx.*

Flight into Egypt, night piece. . . . . . . Marco Pitteri *sc.*

G. F. SCHMIDT *del.*

P. Count Brühl. . . . . Jac. 84. Schmidt *sc.*

POUGIN DE SAINT-AUBIN *del.*

P. Poullain de St. Foix. . . . . N. Le Mire *sc.*

N. LE MIRE *del.*

P. The Emperor Joseph II. . . . . N. Le Mire *sc.*

C. N. COCHIN *del.*

Apollo and Venus with the Muses and Graces. . A. de Saint-Aubin *sc.*

A. DE SAINT-AUBIN *del.*

P. Gluck. . . . . A. de Saint-Aubin *sc.*

HOLBEIN *inv.*

P. Erasmus, with the Terminus. . . . . . Chodowiecki *sc.*

P. The same. *Proof.* . . . . Chodowiecki *sc.*

CIPRIANI *del.*

Venus sailing on a Shell, surrounded by Amorini. Ticket for a Concert of Giardini. . . . . Bartolozzi *sc.*

Apollo and Daphne. Ticket for a Concert of Giardini. . Bartolozzi *sc.*

RIGAUD *pinx.*

P. Bossuet. . . . . J.-B. Grateloup *sc.*

P. Ch. J. de Cisternay du Fay. . . . . . . P. I. Drevet *sc.*

STEFANO DELLA BELLA *del.*

P. Masaniello. . . . . Duplessi-Bertaux *sc.*

FICQUET *del.*

P. Chennevière. . . . . Ficquet *sc.*

LE BRUN *pinx.*

P. Pierre Corneille. . . . . Ficquet *sc.*

AVED *pinx.*

P. J. de Crébillon. . . . . Ficquet *sc.*

FRANS HALS *pinx.*
P. René Descartes. . . . . Ficquet *sc.*

RIGAUD *pinx.*
P. Jean de La Fontaine. . . . . Ficquet *sc.*

NANTEUIL *pinx.*
P. François de la Mothe Le Vayer. . . . . . . Ficquet *sc.*

P. MIGNARD *pinx.*
P. Françoise d'Aubigné, Marquise de Maintenon. . . Ficquet *sc.*

C. COYPEL *pinx.*
P. J.-B. Poquelin de Molière. . . . . Ficquet *sc.*

DUMOUSTIER *pinx.*
P. Michel de Montaigne. . . . . Ficquet *sc.*

AVED *pinx.*
P. Jean Baptiste Rousseau. . . . . Ficquet *sc.*

LA TOUR *pinx.*
P. Jean Jacques Rousseau. . . . . Ficquet *sc.*

Æ. *pinx.*
P. Alexander Farnese. . . . . Ficquet *sc.*

G. E. PETIT *pinx.*
P. P. Bayle. . . . . Savart *sc.*

DROUAIS *pinx.*
P. Buffon. . . . . Savart *sc.*

CHAMPAGNE *pinx.*
P. J.-B. Colbert. . . . . Savart *sc.*

RIGAUD *pinx.*
P. Louis XIV. of France. . . . . Savart *sc.*

SAVART *del.*
P. Louis XVI. of France. . . . . Savart *sc.*

SANTERRE *pinx.*
P. Jean Racine. . . . . Savart *sc.*

FRANÇOIS *pinx.*
P. Stanislaus [Leczinski], King of Poland. . . . P. A. Tardieu *sc.*

LEONARDO DA VINCI *pinx.*
Head of Christ. . . . . R. Morghen *sc.*

RAPHAEL *pinx.*
Head of the Fornarina, from the Transfiguration. Engraved on silver.
R. Morghen *sc.*

AFTER AN ANTIQUE CAMEO. Head of Jupiter. . . . . R. Morghen *sc.*

TOFANELLI *del.*

P. Dante. . . . . R. Morghen *sc.*

WITHOUT NAME OF PAINTER. P. Madame Fulger. . . R. Morghen *sc.*

A. BRONZINO *pinx.*

P. Macchiavelli. . . . . R. Morghen *sc.*

The same. *Proof.* . . . . R. Morghen *sc.*

LA TOUR *pinx.*

P. Voltaire. . . . . W. Walker *sc.*

LANDSEER *pinx.*

Monkey using a Cat's Paw to get Chestnuts off a Stove. . Graves *sc.*

WITHOUT NAME OF PAINTER. P. Tasso. . . . . . . Mercurj *sc.*

L. SICHLING *del.*

P. Francis C. Gray. *Proof.* . . . . L. Sichling *sc.*

AFTER A MEDAL. P. Goethe. (Relief.) . . . . Achille Collas *sc.*

XXXIII. PORTFOLIO OF MISCELLANEOUS MODERN ARTISTS.

SIR THOMAS LAWRENCE *pinx.*

P. Miss McDonald. *Proof.* . . . . S. Cousins *sc.*

P. Master Lambton. *Proof.* . . . . S. Cousins *sc.*

P. Pope Pius VII. *Proof.* . . . . S. Cousins *sc.*

P. The Duchess of Sutherland. *Proof.* . . . . . S. Cousins *sc.*

P. Mrs. Wolff. *Proof.* . . . . John Bromley *sc.*

P. The Right Hon. Lady Nugent. . . . . . Richard Lane *lith.*

TURNER *pinx.*

Venice. *Proof before letters, India paper.* . . . . William Miller *sc.*

Oberwesel. *Proof.* . . . . J. T. Willmore *sc.*

WILKIE *pinx.*

The Reading of the Will. . . . . John Burnet *sc.*

Distraining for Rent. . . . . Abr. Raimbach *sc.*

STOTHARD *pinx.*

The Procession of the Flitch of Bacon. *Proof before letters.* J. H. Watt *sc.*

C. R. LESLIE *pinx*

Uncle Toby and the Widow Wadman in the Sentry-box. *Open letter proof.* M. J. Danforth *sc.*

The Manuscript. *Open letter proof.* . . . . . . W. H. Watt *sc.*

Sancho Panza and the Duchess. *Proof.* . . . . . Humphrys *sc.*

Griselda. *Proof.* . . . . Posselwhite *sc.*

The Sisters of Bethany. . . . . M. J. Danforth *sc.*

NEWTON *pinx.*

The Bride. *Proof.* . . . . G. T. Doo *sc.*

NEWTON *pinx., continued.*

Dutch Girl. *Proof.* . . . . G. T. Doo *sc.*

Bassanio and Portia. *Proof.* . . . . G. T. Doo *sc.*

Shylock and Jessica. *Proof.* . . . . G. T. Doo *sc.*

Yorick and the Grisette. *Proof.* . . . . G. T. Doo *sc.*

The Vicar of Wakefield. . . . . John Burnet *sc.*

The same. *Artist's proof.* . . . . John Burnet *sc.*

EDWIN LANDSEER *pinx.*

Odin. Head of a Dog. . . . . Thomas Landseer *sc.*

Favorite Pony and Spaniels. . . . . . Thomas Landseer *sc.*

Sleeping Bloodhound. . . . . Thomas Landseer *sc.*

Favorites, Horse and Dog. . . . . W. Giller *sc.*

Return from Hawking. *Proof.* . . . . S. Cousins *sc.*

Bolton Abbey in the Olden Time. *Proof.* . . . . S. Cousins *sc.*

Highland Drovers departing for the South. *Proof.* . . . J. H. Watt *sc.*

"Suspense." *Proof.* . . . . B. P. Gibbon *sc.*

The Shepherd's Chief Mourner. *Proof.* . . . . B. P. Gibbon *sc.*

The Shepherd's Grave. *Proof.* . . . . B. P. Gibbon *sc.*

The Lassie herding Sheep. *Proof.* . . . . . John Burnet *sc.*

P. Sutherland Children with a Fawn. *Proof.* . . . . S. Cousins *sc.*

P. Maria. Twelfth Night. Marchioness of Abercorn. *Artist's proof on India paper.* . . . . J. H. Robinson *sc.*

Little Red Ridinghood. *Proof.* . . . . J. H. Robinson *sc.*

EASTLAKE *pinx.*

Pilgrims coming in sight of Rome. *Proof.* . . . . . G. T. Doo *sc.*

MIDDLETON *pinx.*

P. Lady Cust. *Proof before letters.* . . . . . Henry Cousins *sc.*

JACOB THOMPSON *pinx.*

The Ferry. *Proof.* . . . . J. T. Willmore *sc.*

JAMES E. DOYLE *pinx.*

P. A Literary Party at Sir Joshua Reynolds's. *Proof.* Wm. Walker *sc.*

CANOVA *sculp. in marm.*

P. Statue of Napoleon represented as Jupiter. *Proof.* . Ricciani *sc.*

GÉRARD *pinx.*

P. The Entry of Henry IV. into Paris. *Proof.* With key. Toschi *sc.*

The Battle of Austerlitz. *Proof.* . . . . . Jean Godefroy *sc.*

HORACE VERNET *pinx.*

P. Vittoria of Albano. *Artist's proof, on India paper.* . . H. Cousins *sc.*

LÉOPOLD ROBERT *pinx.*

Les Moissonneurs. *Proof on India paper.* . Denzler and Hesslöhl *sc.*

The same. *Proof on India paper.* . . . . . . Z. Prévost *sc.*

LÉOPOLD ROBERT *pinx., continued.*

Les Moissonneurs. *Proof on India paper.* . . . P. Mercurj *sc.*
The same. *Proof on India paper.* . . . . Desclaux *sc.*
Les Pêcheurs de l'Adriatique. *Proof.* . . . . . Z. Prévost *sc.*
The same. *Proof on India paper.* . . . . . . Desclaux *sc.*
Fête à la Madonne de l'Arc. *Proof on India paper.* . . Z. Prévost *sc.*
La Vedova. *Proof on India paper.* . . . . Eduard Mandel *sc.*

ARY SCHEFFER *pinx.*

Christus Consolator. *Impression before the retouch.* Henriquel Dupont *sc.*

ARY SCHEFFER *pinx.*

Christus Remunerator. *Proof on India paper.* . . . A. Blanchard *sc.*
St. Cecilia. *Artist's proof No.* 39, *on India paper.* . . J. Bernardi *sc.*
L'Enfant charitable. *Proof.* . . . . Thevenin *sc.*
Mignon regrettant la Patrie. *Proof No.* 44. . . . . A. Louis *sc.*
Mignon aspirant au Ciel. *Proof No.* 44. . . . . . A. Louis *sc.*
Francesca da Rimini. . . . . Calamatta *sc.*

DELAROCHE *pinx.*

La Vierge à la Vigne. *Open letters.* . . . . Jesi *sc.*
Mary in the Desert. *Proof before letters.* . . . Ach. Martinet *sc.*
St. Cecilia. *Proof.* . . . . F. Forster *sc.*
St. Amélie. *Artist's proof.* . . . . P. Mercurj *sc.*
Les Pélerins. *Proof before letters.* . . . . . Jules François *sc.*
Mother and Child. *Proof before letters.* . . . A. François *sc.*
Lord Strafford on his Way to Execution, receiving the Blessing of Archbishop Laud. *Open letters.* . . . . Henriquel Dupont *sc.*
Charles I. in the Guard-room. *Proof before letters.* . Ach. Martinet *sc.*

L. GALLAIT *pinx.*

The Last Moments of Count Egmont in Prison. *Proof before letters.* Ach. Martinet *sc.*

PAOLO MERCURJ *del.*

P. Columbus. *Proof before letters.* . . . . . . P. Mercurj *sc.*

AUGUSTE GENDRON *pinx.*

The Willis. . . . . Fanoli *lith.*

OVERBECK *pinx.*

Hagar in the Desert. *Proof before letters, on India paper.* L. Gruner *sc.*
Moses at the Well. . . . . L. Gruner *sc.*
Madonna and Child, with St. Elizabeth and St. John, and a Lamb. *Artist's proof, on India paper.* . . . . Felsing *sc.*
Dead Christ and Virgin. *Proof before letters, on India paper.* L. Gruner *sc.*
Christ as the Good Shepherd. *Proof before letters.* . . . L. Gruner *sc.*
The Triumph of Religion in the Arts. . . . . . . Amsler *sc.*

OVERBECK *pinx., continued.*

Sofronia and Olindo. *Proof before letters, on India paper.* A. Krüger *sc.*

VEIT *pinx.*

The Years of Plenty. *Open letters. On India paper.* . . C. Müller *sc.*

Introduction of the Fine Arts into Germany through Christianity. Eduard Schäffer *sc.*

The Two Marys at the Grave. . . . . Hahn *lith.*

BEGAS *pinx.*

Die Lurlei. *Open letters.* . . . . Eduard Mandel *sc.*

JULIUS SCHNORR *pinx.*

Siegfried's Body carried to Worms. From the Nibelungen frescos in Munich. Langer *sc.*

Chriemhilde exciting the Huns to Vengeance. From the same. Langer *sc.*

H. M. HESS *pinx.*

Christ blessing the Little Children. *Open letters.* . A. Reindel *sc.*

The Adoration of the Magi and Shepherds. . . . Schreiner *lith.*

The Virgin enthroned. . . . . Schreiner *lith.*

AUGUST RIEDEL *pinx.*

Judith. *Artist's proof.* . . . . Lutz *sc.*

STEINBRÜCK *pinx.*

St. Genoveva of Brabant with her Child. *Artist's proof.* . Felsing *sc.*

WINTERHALTER *pinx.*

A Little Girl (a portrait) leaning on a Dog, in a landscape. *Proof before letters.* Alphonse Martinet *sc.*

HILDEBRAND *pinx.*

The Warrior and his Child. *Proof.* . . . . Eduard Mandel *sc.*

KAULBACH *pinx.*

Die Hunnenschlacht. *Unfinished proof.* . . . . . J. C. Thäter *sc.*

PH. FOLTZ *pinx.*

Des Sängers Fluch. . . . . Hanfstängl *sc.*

MÜCKE *pinx.*

St. Catherine's Body borne by Angels. *Artist's proof, on India paper.* Felsing *sc.*

JULIUS HÜBNER *pinx.*

Roland delivering the Princess of Galicia from the Robbers' Cave. J. Keller *sc.*

A. DRÄGER *pinx.*

A Girl playing the Mandoline. . . . . . . J. Felsing *sc.*

POLLACK *pinx.*

Italian Shepherd Boy. *Proof on India paper.* . Eduard Mandel *sc.*

L. Blanc *pinx.*

Die Kirchgängerin. . . . . Hoffmann *sc.*
The same. . . . . Beck *lith.*

Lessing *pinx.*

Landscape. The Smugglers. . . . . Mützel *lith.*
A Congregation of Hussites. *Proof.* . . . . . Hoffmann *sc.*

Bendemann *pinx.*

Jeremiah sitting amidst the Ruins of Jerusalem. *Open letters.* Felsing *sc.*
Captive Jews weeping at the Waters of Babylon. . . . Ruschweyh *sc.*
The same. . . . . Wildt *lith.*
Maidens at the Fountain. *Proof.* . . . . Felsing *sc.*

Köhler *pinx.*

Poesia. *Proof.* . . . . Felsing *sc.*

Deger *pinx.*

Himmelskönigin. *Proof.* . . . . Keller *sc.*
Regina Coeli. . . . . Keller *sc.*

THE END.

Cambridge: Electrotyped and Printed by Welch, Bigelow, & Co.

www.ingramcontent.com/pod-product-compliance
Lightning Source LLC
LaVergne TN
LVHW021229110826
845150LV00002B/277

9781425563257